THE

WIRED

SOCIETY

THE

WIRED

SOCIETY

CAROL LEA CLARK
UNIVERSITY OF TEXAS AT EL PASO

Harcourt Brace College Publishers

Fort Worth   Philadelphia   San Diego   New York   Orlando   Austin   San Antonio
Toronto   Montreal   London   Sydney   Tokyo

Publisher:	Earl McPeek
Acquisitions Editor:	Julie McBurney
Market Strategist:	John Myers
Developmental Editor:	Diane Drexler
Project Editor:	G. Parrish Glover
Art Director:	Burl Sloan
Production Manager:	James McDonald

Cover credit: Lucia Gallery, New York City /TF Chen/ SuperStock

ISBN: 0-15-508-353-8
Library of Congress Catalog Card Number: 98-85705

Address for Orders
Harcourt Brace College Publishers, 6277 Sea Harbor Drive, Orlando, FL 32887-6777
1-800-782-4479

Address for Editorial Correspondence
Harcourt Brace College Publishers, 301 Commerce Street, Suite 3700, Fort Worth, TX 76102

Web Site Address
http://www.hbcollege.com

Printed in the United States of America

8 9 0 1 2 3 4 5 6 7   0 3 9   9 8 7 6 5 4 3 2 1

Harcourt Brace College Publishers

Dedication
For Morris L. and Rose M. Usry

PREFACE

The Wired Society is a reader rhetoric intended for first-year composition, advanced composition, or classes focusing on technology and society. As the title indicates, *The Wired Society* considers culture through the perspective of information technology.

RATIONALE FOR *THE WIRED SOCIETY*

OUR SOCIETY IS CONTROLLED BY TRANSMISSION OF INFORMATION. The wired society is all the information-based machines around us (computers, fax machines, televisions, etc.) that expose residents of developed countries to some 500 million bytes of information each day. The wired society is also the effect of those technologies upon individuals and culture. This onslaught of information and technology raises many questions, a few of which include: What are the benefits of an increasingly intelligent machine world? What are the effects of instant access to information? What are the consequences of constant bombardment by information? What are the ramifications of individuals being able to publish their own words and images to a worldwide audience? How do men and women interact differently in a computerized world? How does culture determine ethics in a constantly changing matrix of information. *The Wired Society* addresses these questions and more.

STUDENTS ARE PART OF THE WIRED SOCIETY. Through classes and their own explorations, many students have become eager users of computer technology and the Internet. Others are reluctant participants in an increasingly computerized society. Whether they embrace computer technology enthusiastically or hesitantly, they may not have examined critically the impact of computer technology on their lives. In the next few years knowledge of how to traverse the landscape of information technology will become increasingly important, both in students' careers and in their personal lives. Our culture is becoming more and more differentiated between those who can speak the vocabulary of information technology and those who cannot.

The Wired Society will help students become critically aware as readers and writers of the issues involved in information technology.

DISTINGUISHING FEATURES OF *THE WIRED SOCIETY*

THEME-BASED READINGS AND WRITING SECTIONS.   Readings from a variety of genres and levels focus on both controversial and background issues related to computers and the Internet. Chapter One introduces the concept of the wired society, and subsequent chapters detail aspects of information technology such as "Cyberspace, the Final Frontier," "The Internet and Personal Freedom," "The Death of Print, the Birth of Cyberliteracy," "The Wired Society and Human Nature," "Information Technology and Business," and "Challenges of Computer Technology."

Readings in these chapters are "real-world," the types of writing students might encounter by surfing the World Wide Web or browsing books and periodicals in the library. Chapters are organized by topic rather than by a particular pattern or mode of discourse, and each chapter includes writing assignments that can be addressed in different modes. Thus, students choose a discourse appropriate to the writing situation, rather than looking for a topic to fit a particular mode. An alternative table of contents focusing on the modes of discourse, is included in the instructor's manual for instructors who want to discuss particular modes.

ACCESSING INTERNET RESOURCES.   Each chapter contains a how-to section demonstrating some aspect of the Internet such as using Listserves and Usenet Newsgroups, authoring a personal Web page, and communicating real time via MUDs and Web Chat. Each is followed by suggested Internet assignments.

THE WRITING PROCESS.   Each chapter is followed by a section called "The Writing Process" which contains rhetorical support with in-depth coverage of critical reading, invention techniques, qualities of effective writing, etc. These sections are written so that they can be taught in conjunction with the chapter they follow, or they can be used in any order.

APPENDICES.   *The Wired Society* contains two appendices; one providing a guide to evaluating Internet sources, and a second appendix providing a brief guide to MLA style for citing sources, including online materials.

WEB SITE: HTTP://ENGLISH.HARBRACE.COM/INTERNET.   The companion Web site for *The Wired Society* contains a wealth of information that supplements and updates the text. Students and instructors will be able to access information on Internet news, online research, HTML style guides, Internet tutorials, and an Internet glossary. The Web site will also provide updated URLs for readings and sites mentioned in the text as well as links to additional readings and more Internet activities.

INSTRUCTOR'S MANUAL.   All chapters are fully supported with instructional background material in *The Wired Society Instructor's Manual*. Readings are considered thoughtfully, with individual and group activities and suggestions for ways to amplify class discussions and facilitate the writing process.

I would like to acknowledge the colleagues, friends, and students who encouraged me during the writing of *The Wired Society*, especially Lori A. Gravley-Novello, my research assistant, and Amber Lea Clark, who allowed me to use her home page in the book. At Harcourt Brace, I would like to thank Michael Rosenberg and Diane Drexler who helped me develop the concept for the book. Others who aided in the production were project editor Parrish Glover, production manager James McDonald, and art director Burl Sloan.

CONTENTS

CHAPTER 3 THE COMPUTER AS A MEDIUM WITH A MESSAGE   137

WHAT IS THE WIRED SOCIETY?

A *wired society* is wired together, interconnected. The computer you use in the university lab is connected to computers at the White House, the Louvre museum, NASA, and numberless other locations. It seems everyone has an e-mail address, from the president to cartoon characters. Records of our existences, from work history to purchasing habits to Web page preferences, are stored and used in ways beyond our control. One cannot order a take-out deep dish pizza without it being recorded somewhere that pepperoni is preferred over sausage. Nor can messages be posted to *Usenet*, the collection of thousands of discussion groups, without the potential of your text surfacing in an Internet-wide keyword search.

The Internet is, of course, part of the wired society, today perhaps its most visible component. Every self-respecting corporation, university, or government institution has its Website, publishing everything from the Magna Carta to synopses of soap operas. But the wired society existed before the Internet became *ubiquitous*, ever present. The telephone system has been global for decades, and data is transmitted via modem more and more routinely as the world becomes computerized. Television brought the Vietnam War into America's living rooms in Technicolor more than twenty-five years ago, and today we take for granted real-time television coverage of news around the globe. However, the Internet is not the much-hyped Information Superhighway. Vice President Al Gore, in his 1994 address to the International Telecommunications Union, called upon the nations of the world to begin building a Global Information Infrastructure which would make instant communications possible worldwide. Bill Gates, CEO of Microsoft, says that the Internet is to the Information Superhighway as the nineteenth-century Oregon Trail was to the interstate highway system. Only it won't take a century for the transition to happen, for the information system is expanding at lightning speed. Some estimate that the World Wide Web is doubling every fifty-three days.

A wired society is technology-driven. Just as society was once propelled by agriculture, then by manufacturing, today's society is driven by technology. Devices—automobiles, airplanes, televisions, computers—enable and control our lives. Through these devices, our individual senses are extended far beyond our natural reach. We can traverse oceans and deserts in minutes or hours, or stay at home and communicate with others thousands of miles away plus visit Websites around the world. Though driven by technology, the wired society is not the age of factory capitalism. Rather, work is progressively being reduced to the manipulation of keys on computers. Products are *virtual*, intangible, composed of words, sounds, numbers, and images, rather than *concrete*.

A wired society is awash in the accumulated knowledge of humankind, much of it available at the click of a mouse. Information is everywhere we look—from the billboards on the highway, to the full-text classics downloadable on the Internet, to the credit cards in our wallets. We are served the evening news with our dinners. Humans can boast the ability to put their kind on the moon, move mountains, and create nuclear weapons, yet more information by itself does not solve poverty, or heal damage to the world's rain forests, or reduce pollution. The accumulated knowledge of humankind is *hypertexted*, fractured. The answers to our problems, from a cure for cancer to a template for world peace may all be there, or not, but we haven't been able to isolate them. We haven't been able to find effective ways to process all the information. We can't see the forest for the trees. We can't see the matrix for the hot links.

A wired society is virtual. Virtual smiles, virtual tours, even virtual sex. Once you have ventured online for any length of time, you come to believe that there is an actual space out there somewhere beyond your computer called *cyberspace*. And cyberspace seems to be developing its own creed and culture which include free exchange of information and ideas, a dislike of authority and regulation, and a seeming lack of limits. Cyberspace has been called the final frontier, a refuge for computer cowboys, outlaws, and other nonconformists, a place where everyone is welcome, regardless of age, sex, race, or nationality, as long as one does not try to infringe on the freedom of others.

A wired society is about change. No one knows what effects the expanding Internet will have. Industries, like the software packaging industry or videotape manufacturers, may disappear because their products will be downloadable from the Internet. New industries will emerge. But the change will be much deeper. Judith Hooper reminds us in "To Fax or Not to Fax" that the invention of the window screen and air conditioning changed the social fabric of small-town America because people no longer sat outside on their porches in the evenings.

What dramatic changes will occur when more people are Internet commuters, doing all their work online? When see-you-see-me video communication becomes commonplace? When children from kindergarten age are able to access libraries worldwide with a touch of a mouse? When we are forced to develop personal barriers to avoid being overloaded with information, as Bruce Watson satirizes in "When Your Toast Starts Talking to You, the Info Age Has Hit Home."

When did the wired society begin? Some say the inception was in 1844 when the telegraph made long-distance real-time communication possible for the first time in human history. Others say it was 1946 with the construction of ENIAC, the first all-electronic computer. Or was it the late 1970s when desktop computers began to become standard gear in most businesses and a familiar sight in many homes? Mark Dery in his reading *Escape Velocity* suggests that the media's awareness of the Internet reached a critical mass in 1993. Suddenly the Internet was everywhere, its cryptic http:// symbols attached to every movie, every government agency, and every university. Dery believes we are nearing escape velocity as an information society figuratively about to leave earth's gravitational field and head who knows where.

Is the advent of the wired society a good thing? A *Time* poll found that 85 percent of Americans believe that information technology has made their lives better. They echo early twentieth-century visionary Filippo Tommaso Marinetti, "Let's Go . . . Friends, away!", as quoted in Ashley Dunn's essay. Others aren't so sure, including Paul Virilio, also quoted by Dunn, who claims that information technology causes a disturbance in perception, a "disorientation of alterity, of our relation to the other and to the world." Others have pointed out that there are no real hugs in cyberspace, only virtual ones, and no sunsets, no rainstorms, no realness. The more we dwell in a sensory-enhanced, hyperlinked environment, the more our lives are impoverished.

Good, bad, or both, the future is here. Whether or not we like it, we live in a wired society. The purpose of this text is to heighten awareness of the information technology around us and the effects it has upon our society and upon us as individuals. As you read the essays, articles, speeches, and other texts in this book and respond to them with your own writing, look around you. Notice the computers, the cars and microwaves with microprocessor computer chips, the television, the telephones, all the information technology which is part of your life. How does it influence you? How does it make your life better or worse? How will it affect your future? If you look and listen closely, you will have much to say and to write, and you will be able to enter into a conversation with your fellow students and with the authors whose words are collected here.

ESCAPE VELOCITY

by Mark Dery

The information culture of the late 20th century has almost reached escape velocity, according to Mark Dery, a cultural critic who focuses on issues related to cyberculture, technology, and the mass media. Escape velocity, as he describes it, is the point at which a spacecraft overcomes the gravitational pull of the earth and flies free. We are in a "giddy speedup" nearing that point, living in an environment in which "circuitry too small to see and [computer] code too complex to fully comprehend controls more and more of the world around us."

Dery's essays and articles have appeared in The New York Times, Wired, Rolling Stone, Mondo 2000, *and* The Village Voice. *He edited* Flame Wars: The Discourse on Cyberculture, *in addition to writing* Escape Velocity, *the book from which the following reading was excerpted.*

Escape velocity is the speed at which a body—a spacecraft, for instance—overcomes the gravitational pull of another body, such as the Earth. More and more, computer culture, or cyberculture, seems as if it is on the verge of attaining escape velocity. Marshall McLuhan's 1967 pronouncement that electronic media have spun us into a blurred, breathless "world of alla-tonceness" where information "pours upon us, instantaneously and continuously," sometimes overwhelming us, is truer than ever.[1]

The giddy speedup of postwar America is almost entirely a consequence of the computer, the information engine that has wrenched us out of the age of factory capitalism and hurled us into the postindustrial era of transnational corporate capitalism. In America, manufacturing is undergoing what Buckminster Fuller called the "ephemeralization of work"—the reduction of labor to the manipulation, on computers, of symbols that stand in for the manufacturing process. The engines of industrial production have given way to an information economy that produces intangible commodities—Hollywood blockbusters, TV programs, high-tech theme parks. one-minute megatrends, financial transactions that flicker through fiber-optic bundles to computer terminals a world away. "Only 17 percent of working Americans now manufacture anything, down from 22 percent as recently as 1980," wrote Robert B. Reich in 1992.[2] According to the *New York Times,* American films "produce the second largest trade surplus, after airplane sales, of any industry."[3] Immaterial commodities dominate the domestic market as well: A recent *Business Week* feature reported that "entertainment and recreation—

---

[1]Eric Scigliano, "Relighting the Firesign," *New York Times,* May 2, 1993, p. 11.
[2]*New York Times,* April 4, 1993, p. 17.
[3]"The Trip," *Details,* March 1993, p. 128.

not health care or autos—have provided the biggest boost to consumer spending" since 1991.[4] We are moving, at dizzying speed, from a reassuringly solid age of hardware into a disconcertingly wraithlike age of software, in which circuitry too small to see and code too complex to fully comprehend controls more and more of the world around us.

Although the genealogy of the computer can be traced to Charles Babbage's Analytical Engine, a steam-powered, programmable mechanical computer designed (but never built) in 1833, Colossus was history's first working electronic computer and the immediate ancestor of today's machines. A hulking monstrosity powered by two thousand vacuum tubes and programmed with punched paper tape, Colossus was developed in 1943 by the British to decrypt enemy messages encoded by the German Enigma machine; its success proved invaluable to the Allied war effort.

The runaway pace of postwar innovation has seen room-sized, vacuum tube-powered behemoths such as ENIAC—the first fully electronic programmable computer, officially switched on in 1946—shrink to a transistorized machine in the fifties, a box full of integrated circuits in the sixties, and a chip-driven microcomputer in the seventies, all the while growing exponentially more powerful.

By the late seventies, computers were a fixture in most businesses, and growing numbers of consumers were buying home computers such as the Apple II, the TRS-80, and the Commodore PET. Even so, it has been just over a decade since the computer revolution moved beyond the esoteric subcultures of researchers and hobbyists to become a mass culture phenomenon with the debut of the IBM Personal Computer in late '81 and the Apple Macintosh in early '84. It was only in January '83, when the PC's sales figures had skyrocketed from a mere twenty thousand machines sold during its first year on the market to five hundred thousand, that a *Time* cover story pronounced the personal computer the "machine of the year."[5] Otto Friedrich wrote, "Now, thanks to the transistor and the silicon chip, the computer has been reduced so dramatically in both bulk and price that it is accessible to millions. . . . The 'information revolution' that futurists have long predicted has arrived."[6]

Likewise, the online world now frequented by an estimated seven and a half million households was all but unknown to mainstream America

[4]Howard Fineman, "The Sixties: The GOP's New Strategy," *Newsweek,* March 25, 1991, p.39.

[5]Bruce Sterling, *The Hacker Crackdown: Law and Disorder on the Electronic Frontier* (New York: Bantam, 1992), p. 235.

[6]Fractal geometry, a field of study pioneered by the mathematician Benoit Mandlebrot in the seventies, offers mathematical recipes for generating stunningly detailed images reminiscent of snowflakes, inkblots, paisleys, tree branches, coastlines, and so forth; their seeming randomness bears a striking resemblance to "many of the irregular and fragmented patterns around us," in the words of its founder. See Benoit B. Mandlebrot, "How Long Is the Coast of Britain?" in *The World Treasury of Physics, Astronomy, and Mathematics,* ed. Timothy Ferris (Boston: Little, Brown and Company, 1991), pp. 447–55.

as recently as the early nineties. Media awareness of the Internet reached critical mass in 1993: "Suddenly the Internet is the place to be," wrote *Time's* Philip Elmer-Dewitt; the *New York Times's* John Markoff confirmed that the global network was "the world's most fashionable rendezvous," a trendy "online gathering spot for millions of PC users around the world."[7]

The Internet was born of ARPANet, a decentralized computer network developed at the University of California at Los Angeles in 1969 by the Department of Defense's Advanced Research Projects Agency (ARPA) to ensure military communications in the event of a nuclear attack. By using a technique called packet-switching to disassemble data into addressed parcels, blip them over high-speed lines, and reassemble them just before they reach their destination, ARPANet rendered itself invulnerable to conventional attack; if a portion of the network went down, traffic would automatically be rerouted. In 1983, ARPANet was divided into military and civilian networks (Milnet and Arpa Internet, respectively); shortly thereafter, the U.S. National Science Foundation (NSF) took charge of the administration and maintenance of the lines and equipment that made up the Arpa Internet "backbone." Whereas the Defense Department restricted system access to institutions receiving Pentagon or NSF funding, the NSF made the network available to all faculty and students at member institutions. As universities, R and D companies, and government agencies connected their computers to the NSF's system, what had once been the Arpa Internet mutated into an anarchic global network of networks known, increasingly, as the Internet (from "internetworking").

By 1990, ARPANet had ceased to exist as a discrete entity; the kudzulike growth of the Internet, or Net, as netsurfers have come to call it, had engulfed it. The global metanetwork of today's Net embraces some ten thousand networks, among them nationwide commercial services such as CompuServe, Prodigy, GEnie, and America Online; the private, academic, and government institutions interwoven by NSFNET (the NSF's network); and esoteric regional BBSs (bulletin board systems) such as the Sausalito, California-based WELL (Whole Earth 'Lectronic Link) and New York's ECHO. Mind-bogglingly, the Internet is itself part of a still larger complex of interconnected networks commonly called the Matrix, which also includes UseNet (a buzzing hive of discussion groups called "newsgroups"), FidoNet (a constellation of more than twenty thousand BBSs, scattered over six continents), and BITNET (Because It's Time Network, an academic system), among others.

As this is written, an estimated thirty million Internet users in more than 137 countries traverse the electronic geography of what the science fiction novelist William Gibson has called "cyberspace"—an imaginary space that exists entirely inside a computer—and their ranks are growing by as many as

---

[7]*Inner Technologies* catalogue, fall 1991, p. 21.

a million a month.[8] Based on the rate at which computer networks are building on-ramps onto the Internet, a 1993 estimate put its growth rate at a staggering twenty-five percent every three months—a delirious pace that shows no sign of abating.[9]

The ephemeralization of labor and the evanescence of the commodity, in cyberculture, is paralleled by the disembodiment of the human. In growing numbers, we are spending ever greater amounts of our lives in cyberspace; like the sagely cyborg in Bruce Sterling's SF novel *Schismatrix*, we are convinced that "there's a whole world behind this screen."[10] The electronically disembodied are zapping e-mail around the world, typing messages back and forth in real-time "chat," and flocking to BBS discussion topics and UseNet newsgroups. They're lurking and flaming and ROTFLOL (Rolling on the Floor Laughing Out Loud). They're swapping pornographic .GIFs (digitized photos) and swinging in anonymous "text sex" trysts. They're mousing around the Net's latest addition, the World Wide Web, a hypertext-based system that enables users around the globe to point and click from one multimedia site to another, bouncing from digitized video clips to snippets of sound to screenfuls of text without end.

Overwhelmingly, they're convinced that there is a "there" there, after all. As I observed in my introduction to *Flame Wars*, a collection of essays on cyberculture,

> Those who spend an inordinate amount of time connected by modem via telephone lines to virtual spaces often report a peculiar sensation of "thereness"; prowling from one [electronic] conference to another, eavesdropping on discussions in progress, bears an uncanny resemblance to wandering the hallways of some labyrinthine mansion, poking one's head into room after room. "One of the most striking features of the WELL," observed a user named loca, "is that it actually creates a feeling of 'place.' I'm staring at a computer screen. But the feeling really is that I'm 'in' something; I'm some 'where.'"[11]

Even as the computer is revolutionizing our immaterial lives through electronic interconnection, it is irretrievably altering our material lives, as well. "Embedded" microprocessors—speck-sized computers mounted on tiny flakes of silicon—make our car engines, microwave ovens, Stairmasters, and sewing machines markedly "smarter" than their precursors. And as

---

[8] Smart *drugs*, many of which are controlled substances in the United States, are not to be confused with smart *drinks*, the supposedly brain-boosting blender confections served at raves. Largely a mixture of fruit juice, vitamins, amino acids, caffeine or the caffeine-like 1-phenylalanine, and choline, which allegedly nourishes brain cells, the latter are far less potent.

[9] Philip Elmer-Dewitt, "Cyberpunk!" *Time*, February 8, 1993, pp. 64–65.

[10] Bruce Sterling, preface to *Mirrorshades: The Cyberpunk Anthology*, ed. Bruce Sterling (New York: Ace, 1988), p. xii.

[11] Ibid.

those who live the wired life know, the incredible shrinking computer now accompanies the user virtually anywhere, as a laptop, palmtop, or pocket-sized computer/communicator such as the beleaguered Apple Newton Message Pad. Any day now, we are told, such devices will come alive, animated by "intelligent agents"—software programs that act as personal assistants, scheduling meetings, answering e-mail, trolling the Net in search of information.

The computer revolution has made a host of mind-jarring technologies at least theoretically possible. Celebrated in Sunday supplements or *Omni* articles, some exist as hardware or software; others are pure vaporware (Silicon Valley slang for products announced far in advance of a release date that may or may not ever arrive).

The futuristic sheen of virtual reality—a simulation technology that employs TV goggles and quadraphonic sound to immerse users in 3-D, computer-graphic worlds—briefly captured the media's magpie eye in 1991 with the promise of a tomorrow where virtual thrill seekers, like Arnold Schwarzenegger in *Total Recall*, roam the red seas of Mars without leaving their armchairs. Today, virtual reality is a fixed landmark on the popscape, from arcade VR such as Horizon Entertainment's Virtuality games to theme park attractions such as the *Aladdin* ride at Orlando's Walt Disney World to the Fox TV series *VR.5* to the movie *Lawnmower Man*. A San Francisco dentist provides his patients with VR headgear and sets them adrift in computer-animated dreamworlds during surgery; medical students operate on bodies of information through a VR training system developed by Cine-Med; and wheelchair-bound paraplegics in the Bronx Veterans Affairs Medical Center escape their confinement for a fleeting hour or two, stalking monsters in the shadowy dungeons of a VR game called Heretic.[12]

Other technologies hover below the event horizon. K. Eric Drexler, the founding father of nanotechnology, imagines the creation of self-replicating subatomic engines called nanomachines. In theory, these microscopic devices could slurp up oil spills or suck up toxic clouds; remove diseased DNA segments from the cells of AIDS patients, effectively curing them; or repair the ravages of normal aging at a cellular level, affording near immortality.

Even further afield, the artificial intelligence theorist Hans Moravec calmly assures us that we are about to enter a "postbiological" universe in which robotic life forms capable of independent thought and procreation will "mature into entities as complex as ourselves." Soon, he insists, we will download our willing spirits into computer memory or robotic bodies and do away with the weak flesh altogether.

---

[12]Camille Paglia, "Ninnies, Pedants, Tyrants and Other Academics," *New York Times,* May 5, 1991, sect. 7, p. 1.

EXPLORING THE READING

1. Mark Dery quotes Marshall McLuhan as saying information "pours upon us, instantaneously and continuously." What does he mean? Would you agree? Why or why not?

2. Dery writes that our information culture is moving faster and faster, nearing "escape velocity." What do you think? What will happen when we reach escape velocity?

3. The article gives a brief rundown of the history of computers and the Internet. In your small group discuss at what point each of you began your acquaintance with computers. Was it in the days of TRS-80s and Commodore computers, or was it more recently with a PC and Windows 95? When did you first begin using the Internet? Do you feel comfortable with computers? Share your group's personal history with the class.

4. Dery reports statistics which indicate that fewer and fewer people manufacture anything tangible. What about the career you are planning? Will you be involved with actual manufacturing goods or with information, what Dery calls "immaterial commodities?"

WE'RE GOING TO HAVE COMPUTERS COMING OUT OF THE WOODWORK

by Richard Wolkomir

No longer will we go to a computer to work or to surf the Internet, according to Richard Wolkomir in this article published in Smithsonian. *Instead, computers will become part of the fabric of our lives, as common as the ball point pen. They will be embedded in the walls, road signs, doorknobs, and, yes, desks around us. Computers will be ubiquitous, ever present, an integral part of our existence.*

Wolkomir writes frequently, and with some skepticism, for Smithsonian, *with articles such as "Living Under a Cloud—and Loving It," a piece about chasing a tornado, and "Seeking Gifts from the Sea, Sanibel-style," about a new museum dedicated to sea shells. He remarks that his ambitions for computers are less esoteric than the scientists in his article. He wishes he could figure out how to use a computer to print an address on an envelope. Abstracts of Wolkomir's* Smithsonian *articles can be found at http://www.smithsonianmag.si.edu/smithsonian/home.shtml. Use the search feature to find a list of his articles.*

"We're talking about a technology so powerful it's invisible!" computer scientist Mark Weiser told me. That flew over my head.

Scientific journals had said that Weiser—one of Silicon Valley's leading wizards—was working on something he called Ubiquitous Computing: he meant to extract computing from computers and disperse it throughout society. But what did that mean? I had come to the Xerox Palo Alto Research Center, or PARC, to find out. And I suspected that when I finally understood it, I might not like it.

Weiser, a bald and black-bearded teddy bear of a fellow who is the director of PARC's computer science laboratory, put his fingers to his forehead, the place where all the thinking was going on. Then, having figured out how to give his not-from-Mensa visitor at least a glimpse of what he was up to, he led me briskly down the hall to see an office he had wired up for his lab's newest researcher, Helen Davis.

"See, these are my coworkers," Davis told me, pointing to a pad-size screen that sat upright on her desk. The screen was divided into multiple squares, or "windows." In each window appeared the image of another scientist, at work in another office somewhere in this sprawling think tank.

From her desk, Davis could watch her coworkers sitting at their desks. Some typed at computers. One woman held an impromptu meeting in her office. A man gazed out his office window toward blue San Francisco Bay in the distance, apparently in a trance induced by deep thought. "They all see *us* right now, too," she said cheerfully.

Davis had worried she would feel uncomfortable, always visible. "But I found that it helps me to feel instantly part of the group," she said. She had not yet met all her video companions, "but even so, when they leave at night I feel isolated!" she added, glancing fondly at her flat-panel display screen.

Teams of on-screen colleagues, who might be spread out from New York to New Delhi, are only a small part of Mark Weiser's technological new world order. He means to kill off the personal computer as we know it. That is ironic, because PARC *invented* the personal computer in the early 1970s. But Weiser wants computers to vanish into the woodwork—literally. He intends to deconstruct the stand-alone computer, shell it like an oyster, and embed its microprocessors in the walls, desks, light sockets, doorknobs and practically every other square foot of your workplace and home. Those chips will communicate with one another and connect via the "information super-highway." Computing will be as available as electricity—wherever you are, a little gadget in your pocket can plug you into the global digital flow.

But what I really wanted to know was, what will Ubiquitous Computing do for us? And, maybe, *to* us?

At PARC they now talk about "social computing." They say: "This is not really about technology—it's anthropology." That is because the odds are that Mark Weiser might rearrange society as thoroughly as Thomas Edison did when he electrified the cities.

For one thing, since PARC opened in 1970 it has been computerdom's Oracle at Delphi, with a suitably magisterial motto: "The easiest way to predict the future is to invent it." And PARC's track record is legendary. After scientists here invented the personal computer itself, they went on to invent laser printers, "windows" (which allow a computer screen to show several operations at once) and the Ethernet system for networking an office's computers—in fact, much of what we regard as today's standard computer technology.

They are the researchers who brought us portable computing and modern chip-making technology. They also introduced an innovation so seminal that we never stop to think about it: icon-based computing. (In other words, the use of on-screen symbols—the kind you can click onto with your "mouse" or, in some instances, press with your fingertip to issue commands.)

Oddly, however, other companies—not Xerox—spun most of PARC's innovations into commercial gold. "There's no question we could have done a much better job than we have done," PARC's director, John Seely Brown, told me. "But, having said that, virtually every piece of technology we've invented at PARC is now incorporated in our products." By the early 1980s, he said, Japanese competitors were pounding Xerox. The company focused on its main product, building into its photocopiers such PARC innovations as icon-based computing. More or less by default—partly because the patent process for software was in its infancy, partly because some PARC researchers left to develop their ideas elsewhere—Xerox largely ceded development of its innovations' personal computing aspects to other companies. (They did develop and market a proto-PC called the STAR, but it fell flat.) Now, said Brown, Xerox has reorganized so that it can better exploit radical inventions coming out of PARC.

But I had arrived in Palo Alto with the technological blues. I suspected "information superhighway" might be code for "*Zap* goes your job!" I write words that get printed on paper. Would I go the way of the writers of silent-film captions? I had just read about a new $100 computer program that is replacing newspaper sportswriters. Who would be next? It made me cranky.

The Xerox PARC building is set into a hillside bounded by horse pastures. It is a low concrete-and-glass structure, with vines spilling over its eaves. Far off, San Francisco Bay sparkles, and the Hoover Tower pokes above the eucalyptus trees on the Stanford University campus.

When I first visited PARC, I stopped at the famous "beanbag room" where, two decades ago, Xerox scientists lolling in funky chairs had thought up the personal computer. I sat in one of the beanbag chairs myself, but no brilliant insights came. So I headed upstairs to talk with Weiser, who thought up Ubiquitous Computing in 1988, perhaps in one of these very chairs. He had asked associates to predict new technologies that businesses might need. "A disaster!" he told me, grinning. "Trying to pick the future by committee is not going to work!"

So Weiser tried something radical for a technologist: "I had a lot of discussions with the anthropology group here," he said. "I listened to their criticism of current computer technology and tried to think up a response—this intriguing idea of actually *listening* to the anthropologists!"

PARC employs anthropologists to study the workplace, making the think tank something of a high-tech oddball. So is Mark Weiser. Besides his day job as a Silicon Valley savant, he moonlights drumming for a rock band called Severe Tire Damage. Probably he is rock's smartest drummer. He is ebullient about Severe Tire Damage. He is ebullient about computers. In fact, he is generally ebullient. And so when PARC anthropologists told him that a major flaw of current computers is that they are divorced from their surroundings, he caught the idea's rhythm. In the office—it was true—you were either at your computer or you were doing other things. You were never doing other things *and* at your computer: the computer does isolate you. "That is not the way technology works in a culture—it has to be integrated," said Weiser. "This could not last."

That was when he first imagined computer chips buzzing in all the walls, desks, file cabinets and light switches. A chip would be in your pen, too. And maybe in the bell at your front door. And you would carry chips around, the way you now stick a pencil in your pocket or wear a wristwatch. And all those chips would "talk" back and forth via radio or infrared signals.

Weiser decided that computers could then become functionally invisible, the way a telephone or a pencil seems invisible to us. You don't have to think about how to work a pencil. You don't need to know how they get the lead into it. You just pick it up and start writing. Why couldn't computers be that way—tools so easy to use that you hardly see them. You just use them.

And what if, eventually, it were not just your office buzzing with computers? What if it were the world?

"At first, I was so excited I couldn't sleep at night," said Weiser. "But that had happened before!"

COMPUTERS, COMPUTERS, EVERYWHERE

This time, however, the idea stuck. Ubiquitous Computing is still at the Wright brothers stage. But university researchers already are taking up the idea. And PARC has developed pieces of the technology. "We should look at some more of this stuff," Weiser suggested.

On our way from his office to the adjacent lounge, we encountered a sofa. I walked around it. Weiser stepped over the sofa's backrest, walked over the cushions, then stepped to the floor—meanwhile continuing to talk, as if climbing over furniture wasn't the least bit unusual.

Would Ubiquitous Computing induce a new form of linear thinking? "Too early to tell," I wrote in my notes. Weiser pointed to a screen the size of a huge projection TV, with sofas and chairs facing it in a semicircle.

Corporate meetings used to be held around a blackboard, where chalk-wielding executives wrote up ideas and discussion points. Blackboards gave way to whiteboards and felt-tipped pens. Now Weiser's research team has developed the "LiveBoard." Xerox is selling LiveBoards—the first Ubiquitous Computing equipment to be marketed—as fast as it can make them. "The LiveBoard has a computer inside, and it communicates with other boards, which can be anywhere in the world," Weiser said. He scribbled on the LiveBoard's screen with an electronic stylus. With a flick of his stylus—circling a passage here, jotting a note beside a passage there—he sent some of his jottings into the computer's permanent files. Others he reorganized or moved or enlarged or reworded. The LiveBoard can summon data from the information superhighway, too. And it can function as a centerpiece for teleconferences. If we had been in such a meeting then, what Weiser wrote on his board in Palo Alto would have instantly appeared, just as he wrote it, on other boards, which might have been in London, Sydney and Tokyo.

With currently available audio and video links, people can talk back and forth, face-to-face. Eventually, when video transmission costs drop (right now the video component is very expensive), the airlines will find that to be bearish news. Much business travel will seem pointless when you can stay in your office and still talk with colleagues or customers in other cities, share documents and drawings, and also *see* their telltale grimaces and grins as you negotiate.

Once, PARC director Brown took some visitors and their small daughter to this lounge to see the LiveBoard. Unable to resist, from the concealment of his office Weiser puckishly wrote messages to the visitors, which materialized on the LiveBoard in the lounge as if by magic. The guests looked dumbfounded, but the child blithely scribbled messages back. Apparently the next generation will take LiveBoard meetings in stride.

Weiser jotted the messages that appeared on the LiveBoard on another piece of equipment his team invented—the ParcPad, a miniature LiveBoard the size of a textbook. In a decade or so, he said, our desks will be littered with them, the way his own desk was now strewn with paper. Other "pads" will hang on walls like Post-it Notes, except that their messages, such as cafeteria menus, will be constantly updated. He pointed to a stack of *Computer Architecture News* journals on his shelf. "That stack might be just one pad, and every so often I'd check it to see if the latest issue was out," he said. Pads on your desk might each display a different project or different aspects of the same project. You would use them like scrap paper, except they would have the capabilities of high-powered computers. So you could store what you wrote on them, or send it to other pads or LiveBoards, or have the pads perform calculations, or create graphs, or receive electronic mail, or cruise the information superhighway to fetch information. You could scribble on it with an electronic stylus or, to write at length, you might take a keyboard from your drawer.

Perfecting the pads will require better screens, and they are on the way. PARC engineers showed me a new screen they have developed on which images and print actually appear sharper than if printed in ink on paper. Right now the screen is costly. But Weiser believes that within a decade his "pads" really will be about as hefty as a pad of paper and just as cheap. And they will lie around everywhere. Just start scribbling.

ALWAYS "KNOWING" WHO YOU ARE

But for that to work, whatever pad you pick up must be "authorized" to connect to your personal digital files. And so the underlying Ubiquitous Computing system must always "know" who you are and where you are. Therefore, Weiser's lab has invented one further piece of equipment—the ParcTab, about the size of a deck of cards. If the pad is a miniature LiveBoard, the "tab" is a miniature pad.

"Where's my tab?" Weiser said, perplexed, as he swirled the mounds of papers on his table and groped in his briefcase. "This is the problem with having these tiny computers everyplace—you can never find them!"

Weiser finally did find his tab, which had a miniscreen and a few buttons. Designing it to fit any size hand was a major challenge, he said. Turn on your tab and you are plugged into the information superhighway. Weiser pressed a button: onto the screen popped an up-to-the-second Palo Alto weather report. One version of the tab, which PARC employees wear like a badge, identifies you to the computer system. Wherever you go, it radiates infrared or radio signals that tell the central system: "I am Mark Weiser and, at the moment, I am standing right *here*." It can even be rigged so that any LiveBoard you pass flashes messages just for you.

"Let's see, where's Frederick?" Weiser asked, trying to locate a member of his team. He tapped some buttons and peered at his tab's screen. "It says Frederick is in Room 2111, settled in."

It works, said Weiser, much like a cellular telephone, which turns your voice into a radio signal. The signal goes to a receiving-transmitting station, where radio signals are converted into electrical signals that are in turn fed into the telephone lines. Each station serves a "cell," a section of the city or countryside usually encompassing about one square mile. But such cells are too large for Ubiquitous Computing, which must track you from room to room. Weiser is now developing cells down to about room-size (ten feet square or so), so that wherever you are, the tab in your pocket emits extremely weak infrared or radio signals to tiny receptors mounted on walls or telephone poles and connected to the computer system. In that way, the system keeps tabs on you. Perhaps you are in Paris on business. Of course you've got your trusty tab in your pocket. Then you pick up a pad in your hotel room (the hotel of the near future will provide such amenities) and it instantly knows it is you. Via the information superhighway, you retrieve your e-mail or check your computer files back home or at your office. The pad lying in your hotel room has instantly become *your* computer.

What makes Ubiquitous Computing work—the system's ability to track you and whomever you meet—makes it scary. Big Brother, corporate or governmental, really could be watching.

"The person in my lab who's most against this has made his office a dead zone," Weiser told me cheerfully.

He understands the implications. But they don't scare him "Right now, if you carry a cellular telephone, the cellular telephone company always knows where you are," he pointed out. "One reason I do interviews like this is because people should know what's coming."

Later I talked with PARC computer scientist Marvin Theimer, who is working on the privacy issue. "If we build it wrong, invasion of privacy *can* create problems," he told me. "Society will have to decide what's allowable—even today if Xerox requires my medical records as a condition of my working here, I've lost some privacy."

He held up the tab he carries in his pocket. "People have given us a lot of flak about these kinds of devices," he said. "Well, Ubiquitous Computing is already being relentlesssly deployed, whether or not you know it." Today, when computer chips can cost as little as one dollar, he pointed out, even your video rentals are recorded on a computer database at your neighborhood video store. "At the technological level, we can alleviate the problem, but we can't solve it."

One palliative is giving everybody as many different identification numbers as possible. Also, your tab would broadcast your secret numbers but not your name. Then the computer would know where "you" are, but nobody else would. Another safeguard would be to decentralize the system, so that your records are scattered, and nobody could learn all about you by going to one place. "But I can't design perfect security," Theimer said. "Ubiquitous Computing will be deployed, and it will present both benefits and dangers."

What, I asked, might be some benefits? Big things, small things, Theimer said. To shave your electric bills, the system might keep your water heater turned off until it sensed you were waking up. (It could start your coffee, too.) Your morning newspaper, either printed or on a paperlike screen, might focus on stories of special interest to you. The downside of such tailored reportage is that one of the glues holding our disparate society together—everybody getting roughly the same news every day—would break down.

Your car might be driven automatically by a central traffic controller, or the controller might suggest routes for avoiding slowdowns. You could easily work at home, setting a pad to show you video images of your coworkers. Another pad might show your spouse or children as they went through the day. You also could live virtually anywhere. One PARC anthropologist told me she hoped the system would enable her to live in Costa Rica. And the world could, to some extent, customize itself just for you. "I walk up to a Xerox machine in Japan and it automatically shows me the instructions in English, or the street signs around me change to English as I walk by," Theimer said. If your flight to Europe were delayed three hours, he said, your airline's computer could call your house and reset your alarm clock. Not only that: the computer could transmit a notice to your screen at home explaining why you got to sleep late. "And you'd never have to worry about leaving your oven on—you could turn it off from your airliner," he added.

He said computing already is becoming ubiquitous. "Virtually every coffee machine now has a microprocessor inside, and so do cars. But it's all stand-alone, and the next big step will be to interconnect it all."

Corporations, according to Theimer, will reinvent themselves. Workers will no longer be tied to a central building. And at any time you could instantly canvas your coworkers for somebody with expertise on a particular question facing you, no matter where in the world you were, just by jotting a note on your pad and sending it out through the system.

Right now, Theimer said, PARC is experimenting with the notion that a fair amount of corporate business is transacted around the coffeepot. Its researchers are working on a "social virtual reality project" in which workers can wander into a "virtual" coffee room that exists only inside the computer system. Currently, workers keyboarding their way into the digital coffee room receive only an on-screen written description of the imaginary room, giving such details as where the chairs are. "I could meet a colleague from the East Coast in the virtual coffee room, and anybody else who wandered in could join the discussion," said Theimer. Now the researchers are adding audio, so that people in the make-believe coffee room can talk instead of communicating via keyboard. When video transmission becomes cheaper, they will view the imaginary room on their screens and see the other people already gathered there.

WHEN AN ELECTRONIC VOICE SAYS, "OVER TO YOU!"

Ubiquitous Computing is sneaking up on us. The "personal digital assistants" now on the market, tiny computers with fax and cellular telephone attachments, are a step. And any self-respecting new oven or washing machine has microprocessors inside.

Better batteries will be needed. So will better software for handwriting and speech recognition. "We also need a better understanding of issues like fault tolerance," Theimer said. "We'd better not have the computer controlling your car go down when you're heading toward a wall—and an electronic voice suddenly says, "Over to you!"" Probably the system will be decentralized, with no single computer in charge, so that if one computer shuts down others can step in.

Theimer said the hardest problem will be deploying Ubiquitous Computing in stages, so that each step generates profit. "You have to offer some value at the incremental steps or nobody will buy it. This is a very big issue, involving things like standardization." Within fifteen years, the researchers estimate, Ubiquitous Computing will be mundane. Maybe sooner. "What you can do with Ubiquitous Computing sounds like science fiction," Theimer told me. "It will change the world."

That was exactly why I was cranky.

A Carnegic Mellon University researcher has developed a computer you wear like sunglasses. The newsmagazines are agog over "intelligent agents," little digital butlers you send running around the information super-highway on data-collecting chores. Meanwhile, a company called Advanced Neurotechnologies Inc. has announced that it has taken the first steps toward developing a computer that you can control by thinking! All that and Ubiquitous Computing, too. It's left me with a deeply philosophical question: What about *me*?

I decided to ask PARC director Brown, the tall, bearded mathematician, physicist and computer scientist who is chief scientist at Xerox. He brought anthropologists to PARC and has a knack for seeing technology's social side. "The modern car often has more computing power than the modern office, but is anybody aware of it? he asked. "Technology is finally getting powerful enough to get the hell out of the way!" That sounded faintly ominous. It was time, I decided, to hit Brown with my big question: "Is Mark Weiser going to deep-six my job?"

As Ubiquitous Computing sends everyone cruising along the information superhighway, I wanted to know, will every Tom, Jane and Junior who has the yen become an electronic writer and publisher, with a potential audience of everybody on the planet? Is the professional writer—I was now getting personal—a deceased duck? "No," Brown answered. Ubiquitous Computing, dark umber in my mind, suddenly was sunlit.

A magazine, Brown pointed out, "creates value" by choosing material for readers. Reading a magazine, you may find yourself fascinated by a subject you would never have thought to investigate on your own. (Who knows, maybe this one.) Also, a magazine or book is still a user-friendly technology: you can hold it in your hands and just lie back in the hammock for a good read.

"What may go away is the reference book," he said. "If I could get the *Oxford English Dictionary* on my tab or pad, I would—I've never curled up in bed at night with the *Oxford English Dictionary*." Yes. Digitize the dictionaries and encyclopedias if you must. But ignore us ink-stained scriveners. Let us keep plying our humble trade.

"Actually, the need for professional writers will continue to go up, to make sense out of the ever-increasing buzz of the world," Brown told me.

I left PARC feeling vitamin-enriched. However, by the time I drove my rental car into the lot at the San Jose airport, my mind had detoured off the information superhighway, and Mark Weiser's vision of computing's future—invisible but everywhere—seemed like the airy notions Lemuel Gulliver heard on Laputa, the flying island.

I parked the car and extracted my luggage from the trunk, ready to trek to the office and wait in line to get my bill adjusted. But an attendant showed up, carrying what looked like a small walkie-talkie.

He checked the car's fuel level and mileage, punched buttons, peered at the print that popped onto a screen. Then he punched another button. The instrument spewed out a sheet of paper, which he handed to me. It was my itemized receipt for the car, made out on the spot, in the parking lot, by a hand-held device in radio contact with the rental car company's central computer.

EXPLORING THE READING

1. In your small group, define what Wolkomir means by *ubiquitous computing*. How is it different from what exists today? Report to the class.

2. Mark Weisner, one of the computer scientists Wolkomir interviewed, says that to make ubiquitous computing work, each of us will have to carry a small device which identifies us to the information superhighway. What do you think of that aspect of Weisner's imagined future? Would you mind supercomputers somewhere tracking your movements? Why or why not?

3. In your reading journal, freewrite about how computers are part of your everyday life. Is there a microprocessor in your car? In your microwave? In your stereo? Is ubiquitous computing so far away?

4. Note that Wolkomir, unlike Dery, is a character in his essay. Go through the Wolkomir essay, noting when Wolkomir appears. In class, discuss the effectiveness of the writer being a character in his own essay.

Remarks to the International Telecommunications Union

by Vice President Al Gore

Leaders in many nations are consulting with each other about the construction of what is often called the Global Information Infrastructure or Information Superhighway. Known as the "Internet-savvy vice president," Al Gore has been one of the most vocal advocates for strengthening the backbones of international computer networks. In this speech delivered to the International Telecommunications Union in Buenos Aires on March 21, 1994, Gore calls for help in building a Global Information Infrastructure which would transmit "messages and images with the speed of light from the largest city to the smallest village on every continent."

Gore's speech was posted on the Internet and can be found in the archive of a Usenet Newsgroup, at http://www.spp.umich.edu/spp/courses/744/misc.hyper/ 0012.html. Until the next presidential election, Gore can be reached by e-mail through the White House Website, http://www.whitehouse.gov

I have come here, 8,000 kilometers from my home, to ask you to help create a Global Information Infrastructure. To explain why, I want to begin by reading you something that I first read in high school, thirty years ago.

"By means of electricity, the world of matter has become a great nerve, vibrating thousands of miles in a breathless point of time. . . . The round globe is a vast . . . brain, instinct with intelligence!"

This was not the observation of a physicist—or a neurologist. Instead, these visionary words were written in 1851 by Nathaniel Hawthorne, one of my country's greatest writers, who was inspired by the development of the telegraph. Much as Jules Verne foresaw submarines and moon landings, Hawthorne foresaw what we are now poised to bring into being.

The ITU was created only fourteen years later, in major part for the purpose of fostering an internationally compatible system of telegraphy.

For almost 150 years, people have aspired to fulfill Hawthorne's vision— to wrap nerves of communications around the globe, linking all human knowledge.

In this decade, at this conference, we now have at hand the technological breakthroughs and economic means to bring all the communities of the world together. We now can at last create a planetary information network that transmits messages and images with the speed of light from the largest city to the smallest village on every continent.

I am very proud to have the opportunity to address the first development conference of the ITU because the President of the United States and I believe that an essential prerequisite to sustainable development, for all members of the human family, is the creation of this network of networks. To accomplish this purpose, legislators, regulators, and businesspeople must do this: build and operate a Global Information Infrastructure. This GII will circle the globe with information superhighways on which all people can travel.

These highways—or, more accurately, networks of distributed intelligence—will allow us to share information, to connect, and to communicate as a global community. From these connections we will derive robust and sustainable economic progress, strong democracies, better solutions to global and local environmental challenges, improved health care, and—ultimately—a greater sense of shared stewardship of our small planet.

The Global Information Infrastructure will help educate our children and allow us to exchange ideas within a community and among nations. It will be a means by which families and friends will transcend the barriers of time and distance. It will make possible a global information marketplace, where consumers can buy or sell products. I ask you, the delegates to this conference, to set an ambitious agenda that will help all governments, in their own sovereign nations and in international cooperation, to build this Global Information Infrastructure. For my country's part, I pledge our vigorous, continued participation in achieving this goal—in the development sector of the ITU, in other sectors and in plenipotentiary gatherings of the ITU, and in bilateral discussions held by our Departments of State and Commerce and our Federal Communications Commission.

The development of the GII must be a cooperative effort among governments and peoples. It cannot be dictated or built by a single country. It must be a democratic effort.

And the distributed intelligence of the GII will spread participatory democracy.

To illustrate why, I'd like to use an example from computer science. In the past, all computers were huge mainframes with a single processing unit, solving problems in sequence, one by one, each bit of information sent back and forth between the CPU and the vast field of memory surrounding it. Now, we have massively parallel computers with hundreds—or thousands—of tiny self-contained processors distributed throughout the memory field, all interconnected, and together far more powerful and more versatile than even the most sophisticated single processor, because they each solve a tiny piece of the problem simultaneously, and when all the pieces are assembled, the problem is solved.

Similarly, the GII will be an assemblage of local, national, and regional networks, that are not only like parallel computers but in their most advanced state will in fact be a distributed, parallel computer.

In a sense, the GII will be a metaphor for democracy itself. Representative democracy does not work with an all-powerful central government, arrogating all decisions to itself. That is why communism collapsed.

Instead, representative democracy relies on the assumption that the best way for a nation to make its political decisions is for each citizen—the human equivalent of the self-contained processor—to have the power to control his or her own life.

To do that, people must have available the information they need. And be allowed to express their conclusions in free speech and in votes that are combined with those of millions of others. That's what guides the system as a whole.

The GII will not only be a metaphor for a functioning democracy, it will in fact promote the functioning of democracy by greatly enhancing the participation of citizens in decision-making. And it will greatly promote the ability of nations to cooperate with each other. I see a new Athenian Age of democracy forged in the fora the GII will create.

The GII will be the key to economic growth for national and international economies. For us in the United States, the information infrastructure already is to the U.S. economy of the 1990s what transport infrastructure was to the economy of the mid-twentieth century. The integration of computing and information networks into the economy makes U.S. manufacturing companies more productive, more competitive, and more adaptive to changing conditions, and it will do the same for the economies of other nations.

These same technologies are also enabling the service sectors of the U.S. economy to grow, to increase their scale and productivity and expand their range of product offerings and ability to respond to customer demands.

Approximately 60 percent of all U.S. workers are "knowledge workers"—people whose jobs depend on the information they generate and receive over our information infrastructure. As we create new jobs, 8 out of 10 are in information-intensive sectors of our economy. And these new jobs are well-paying jobs for financial analysts, computer programmers, and other educated workers.

The global economy also will be driven by the growth of the Information Age. Hundreds of billions of dollars can be added to world growth if we commit to the GII. I fervently hope this conference will take full advantage of this potential for economic growth, and not deny any country or community its right to participate in this growth.

As the GII spreads, more and more people realize that information is a treasure that must be shared to be valuable. When two people communicate, they each can be enriched—and unlike traditional resources, the more you share, the more you have. As Thomas Jefferson said, "He who receives an idea from me, receives instruction himself without lessening mine; as he who lights his taper at mine, receives light without darkening me."

Now we all realize that, even as we meet here, the Global Information Infrastructure is being built, although many countries have yet to see any benefits.

Digital telecommunications technology, fiber optics, and new high-capacity satellite systems are transforming telecommunications. And all over the world, under the seas and along the roads, pipelines, and railroads, companies are laying fiber optic cable that carries thousands of telephone calls per second over a single strand of glass.

These developments are greatly reducing the cost of building the GII. In the past, it could take years to build a network. Linking a single country's major cities might require laying thousands of kilometers of expensive wires. Today, a single satellite and a few dozen ground stations can be installed in a few months—at much lower cost.

The economics of networks has changed so radically that the operation of a competitive, private market can build much of the GII. This is dependent, however, upon sensible regulation.

Within the national boundaries of the United States we aspire to build our information highways according to a set of principles that I outlined in January in California. The National Information Infrastructure, as we call it, will be built and maintained by the private sector. It will consist of hundreds of different networks, run by different companies and using different technologies, all connected together in a giant "network of networks," providing telephone and interactive digital video to almost every American.

Our plan is based on five principles: First, encourage private investment; Second, promote competition; Third, create a flexible regulatory framework that can keep pace with rapid technological and market changes; Fourth, provide open access to the network for all information providers; and Fifth, ensure universal service.

Are these principles unique to the United States? Hardly. Many are accepted international principles endorsed by many of you. I believe these principles can inform and aid the development of the Global Information Infrastructure and urge this Conference to incorporate them, as appropriate, into the Buenos Aires Declaration, which will be drafted this week.

Let me elaborate briefly on these principles.

First, we propose that private investment and competition be the foundation for development of the GII. In the United States, we are in the process of opening our communications markets to all domestic private participants.

In recent years, many countries, particularly here in Latin America, have opted to privatize their state-owned telephone companies in order to obtain the benefits and incentives that drive competitive private enterprises, including innovation, increased investment, efficiency and responsiveness to market needs.

Adopting policies that allow increased private sector participation in the telecommunications sector has provided an enormous spur to telecommunications development in dozens of countries, including Argentina, Venezuela, Chile, and Mexico. I urge you to follow their lead.

But privatization is not enough. Competition is needed as well. In the past, it did make sense to have telecommunications monopolies.

In many cases, the technology and the economies of scale meant it was inefficient to build more than one network. In other cases—Finland, Canada, and the United States, for example—national networks were built in the early part of this century by hundreds of small, independent phone companies and cooperatives.

Today, there are many more technology options than in the past and it is not only possible, but desirable, to have different companies running competing—but interconnected—networks, because competition is the best way to make the telecommunications sector more efficient, more innovative—and more profitable as consumers make more calls and prices decline.

That is why allowing other companies to compete with AT&T, once the world's largest telephone monopoly, was so useful for the United States. Over the last ten years, it has cut the cost of a long-distance telephone call in the United States more than 50 percent.

To promote competition and investment in global telecommunications, we need to adopt cost-based collection and accounting rates. Doing so will accelerate development of the GII.

International standards to ensure interconnection and interoperability are needed as well. National networks must connect effectively with each other to make real the simple vision of linking schools, hospitals, businesses, and homes to a Global Information Infrastructure.

Hand in hand with the need for private investment and competition is the necessity of appropriate and flexible regulations developed by an authoritative regulatory body.

In order for the private sector to invest and for initiatives opening a market to competition to be successful, it is necessary to create a regulatory environment that fosters and protects competition and private sector investments, while at the same time protecting consumers' interests.

Without the protection of an independent regulator, a potential private investor would be hesitant to provide service in competition with the incumbent provider for fear that the incumbent's market power would not be adequately controlled.

Decisions and the basis for making them must also be made public so that consumers and potential competitors are assured that their interests are being protected.

This is why in the United States, we have delegated significant regulatory powers to an independent agency, the Federal Communications Commission. This expert body is well-equipped to make difficult technical decisions and to monitor, in conjunction with the National Telecommunications and Information Administration and the Department of Justice, changing market conditions. We commend this approach to you.

We need a flexible, effective system for resolution of international issues, too—one that can keep up with the ever-accelerating pace of technological change.

I understand that the ITU has just gone through a major reorganization designed to increase its effectiveness. This will enable the ITU, under the able leadership of Mr. Tarjanne, to streamline its operations and redirect resources to where they are needed most. This will ensure that the ITU can adapt to future and unimaginable technologies.

Our fourth principle is open access. By this I mean that telephone and video network owners should charge non-discriminatory prices for access to their networks. This principle will guarantee every user of the GII can use thousands of different sources of information—video programming, electronic newspapers, computer bulletin boards—from every country, in every language.

With new technologies like direct broadcast satellites, a few networks will no longer be able to control your access to information—as long as government policies permit new entrants into the information marketplace.

Countries and companies will not be able to compete in the global economy if they cannot get access to up-to-date information, if they cannot communicate instantly with customers around the globe. Ready access to information is also essential for training the skilled workforce needed for high-tech industries.

The countries that flourish in the twenty-first century will be those that have telecommunications policies and copyright laws that provide their citizens access to a wide choice of information services. Protecting intellectual property is absolutely essential.

The final and most important principle is to ensure universal service so that the Global Information Infrastructure is available to all members of our societies. Our goal is a kind of global conversation, in which everyone who wants can have his or her say.

We must ensure that whatever steps we take to expand our worldwide telecommunications infrastructure, we keep that goal in mind.

Although the details of universal service will vary from country to country and from service to service, several aspects of universal service apply everywhere. Access clearly includes making service available at affordable prices to persons at all income levels. It also includes making high quality service available regardless of geographic location or other restrictions such as disability.

Constellations of hundreds of satellites in low earth orbit may soon provide telephone or data services to any point on the globe. Such systems could make universal service both practical and affordable.

An equally important part of universal access is teaching consumers how to use communications effectively. That means developing easy-to-use applications for a variety of contexts, and teaching people how to use them. The most sophisticated and cost-efficient networks will be completely useless if users are unable to understand how to access and take full advantage of their offerings.

Another dimension of universal service is the recognition that marketplace economics should not be the sole determinant of the reach of the information infrastructure.

The President and I have called for positive government action in the United States to extend the NII to every classroom, library, hospital, and clinic in the United States by the end of the century.

I want to urge that this conference include in its agenda for action the commitment to determine how every school and library in every country can be connected to the Internet, the world's largest computer network, in order to create a Global Digital Library. Each library could maintain a server containing books and journals in electronic form, along with indexes to help users find other materials. As more and more information is stored electronically, this global library would become more and more useful.

It would allow millions of students, scholars and businesspeople to find the information they need whether it be in Albania or Ecuador.

Private investment . . . competition . . . flexibility . . . open access . . . universal service.

In addition to urging the delegates of this conference to adopt these principles as part of the Buenos Aires Declaration, guiding the next four years of telecommunications development, I assure you that the U.S. will be discussing in many fora, inside and outside the ITU, whether these principles might be usefully adopted by all countries.

The commitment of all nations to enforcing regulatory regimes to build the GII is vital to world development and many global social goals.

But the power of the Global Information Infrastructure will be diminished if it cannot reach large segments of the world population.

We have heard together Dr. Tarjanne's eloquent speech setting forth the challenges we face. As he points out: the twenty-four countries of the OECD have only 16 percent of the world's population. But they account for 70 percent of global telephone mainlines and 90 percent of mobile phone subscribers.

There are those who say the lack of economic development causes poor telecommunications. I believe they have it exactly backwards. A primitive telecommunications system causes poor economic development.

So we cannot be complacent about the disparity between the high and low income nations, whether in how many phones are available to people or in whether they have such new technologies as high speed computer networks or videoconferencing.

The United States delegation is devoted to working with each of you at this Conference to address the many problems that hinder development.

And there are many. Financing is a problem in almost every country, even though telecommunications has proven itself to be an excellent investment.

Even where telecommunications has been identified as a top development priority, countries lack trained personnel and up-to-date information.

And in too many parts of the world, political unrest makes it difficult or impossible to maintain existing infrastructure, let alone lay new wire or deploy new capacity.

How can we work together to overcome these hurdles? Let me mention a few things industrialized countries can do to help.

First, we can use the Global Information Infrastructure for technical collaboration between industrialized nations and developing countries. All agencies of the U.S. government are potential sources of information and knowledge that can be shared with partners across the globe.

The Global Information Infrastructure can help development agencies link experts from every nation and enable them to solve common problems. For instance, the Pan American Health Organization has conducted hemisphere-wide teleconferences to present new methods to diagnose and prevent the spread of AIDS.

Second, multilateral institutions like the World Bank, can help nations finance the building of telecommunications infrastructure.

Third, the United States can help provide the technical know-how needed to deploy and use these new technologies. USAID and U.S. businesses have helped the U.S. Telecommunications Training Institute train more than 3500 telecommunications professionals from the developing world, including many in this room.

In the future, USTTI plans also to help businesspeople, bankers, farmers, and others from the developing world find ways that computer networking, wireless technology, satellites, video links, and other telecommunications technology could improve their effectiveness and efficiency.

I challenge other nations, the development banks, and the UN system to create similar training opportunities.

The head of our Peace Corps, Carol Bellamy, intends to use Peace Corps volunteers both to help deploy telecommunications and computer systems and to find innovative uses for them. Here in Argentina, a Peace Corps volunteer is doing just that.

To join the GII to the effort to protect and preserve the global environment, our Administration will soon propose using satellite and personal communication technology to create a global network of environmental information. We will propose using the schools and students of the world to gather and study environmental information on a daily basis and communicate that data to the world through television.

But regulatory reform must accompany this technical assistance and financial aid for it to work. This requires top-level leadership and commitment—commitment to foster investment in telecommunications and commitment to adopt policies that ensure the rapid deployment and widespread use of the information infrastructure.

I opened by quoting Nathaniel Hawthorne, inspired by Samuel Morse's invention of the telegraph.

Morse was also a famous portrait artist in the United States—his portrait of President James Monroe hangs today in the White House. While Morse was working on a portrait of General Lafayette in Washington, his wife, who lived about 500 kilometers away, grew ill and died. But it took seven days for the news to reach him.

In his grief and remorse, he began to wonder if it were possible to erase barriers of time and space, so that no one would be unable to reach a loved one in time of need. Pursuing this thought, he came to discover how to use electricity to convey messages, and so he invented the telegraph and, indirectly, the ITU.

The Global Information Infrastructure offers instant communication to the great human family.

It can provide us the information we need to dramatically improve the quality of their lives. By linking clinics and hospitals together, it will ensure that doctors treating patients have access to the best possible information on diseases and treatments. By providing early warning on natural disasters like volcanic eruptions, tsunamis, or typhoons, it can save the lives of thousands of people.

By linking villages and towns, it can help people organize and work together to solve local and regional problems ranging from improving water supplies to preventing deforestation.

To promote . . . to protect . . . to preserve freedom and democracy, we must make telecommunications development an integral part of every nation's development. Each link we create strengthens the bonds of liberty and democracy around the world. By opening markets to stimulate the development of the global information infrastructure, we open lines of communication.

By opening lines of communication, we open minds. This summer, from my country cameras will bring the World Cup Championship to well over one billion people.

To those of you from the twenty-three visiting countries whose teams are in the Finals, I wish you luck—although I'll be rooting for the home team.

The Global Information Infrastructure carries implications even more important than soccer.

It has brought us images of earthquakes in California, of Boris Yeltsin on a tank in Red Square, of the effects of mortar shells in Sarajevo and Somalia, of the fall of the Berlin Wall. It has brought us images of war and peace, and tragedy and joy, in which we all can share.

There's a Dutch relief worker, Wam Kat, who has been broadcasting an electronic diary from Zagreb for more than a year and a half on the Internet, sharing his observations of life in Croatia.

After reading Kat's Croatian diary, people around the world began to send money for relief efforts. The result: twenty-five houses have been rebuilt in a town destroyed by war.

Governments didn't do this. People did. But such events are the hope of the future.

When I began proposing the NII (National Information Infrastructure) in the United States, I said that my hope is that the United States, born in revolution, can lead the way to this new, peaceful revolution. However, I believe we will reach our goal faster and with greater certainty if we walk down that path together. As Antonio Machado, Spanish poet, once said, "Pathwalker, there is no path, we create the path as we walk."

Let us build a global community in which the people of neighboring countries view each other not as potential enemies, but as potential partners, as members of the same family in the vast, increasingly interconnected human family.

Let us seize this moment. Let us work to link the people of the world. Let us create this new path as we walk it together.

EXPLORING THE READING

1. In your small group, discuss the Global Information Infrastructure. What is it? Does it exist? How does it relate to the Internet? How does Vice President Gore want it to develop?

2. Gore remarks that the "distributed intelligence" of the Global Information Infrastructure will spread participatory democracy. What does he mean? Would you agree? Has the Internet been democratic so far? Do you think it will be in the future?

3. Richard Wolkomir, in "We're Going to Have Computers Coming out of the Woodwork," is somewhat less than enthusiastic about the computer revolution. Does Gore evidence any reservation about the Global Information Infrastructure? Should he?

4. According to Gore, the information infrastructure is to the U.S. economy what the system of transport via highways was to the mid-twentieth century. What does he mean?

5. Gore's text is a speech. How does that affect its style and structure?

ORDNANCE DEPARTMENT DEVELOPS ALL-ELECTRONIC CALCULATING MACHINE

War Department Press Release

In this press release dated February 15, 1946, the United States War Department announced the development of the first all-electronic computer. The huge machine called ENIAC had 18,000 vacuum tubes and occupied a room 30 by 50 feet.

The War Department's press release is one of the landmark computer-related documents archived at the Smithsonian Institution. It can be downloaded in Portable Document Format (which reproduces the look of the original document) at http://www.si.edu/resource/tours/comphist/pr1.pdf.

WAR DEPARTMENT
Bureau of Public Relations
PRESS BRANCH
Tel. - RE 6700
Brs. 3425 and 4860

FUTURE RELEASE

FOR RELEASE SATURDAY A.M., FEBRUARY 16, 1946

For Radio Broadcast after
7:00 P.M., EST, February 15, 1946

ORDNANCE DEPARTMENT DEVELOPS
ALL-ELECTRONIC CALCULATING MACHINE

A new machine that is expected to revolutionize the mathematics of engineering and change many of our industrial design methods was announced today by the War Department.

Designed and constructed for the Ordnance Department at the Moore School of Electrical Engineering of the University of Pennsylvania by a pioneering group of Moore School experts, this machine is the first all-electronic general purpose computer ever developed. It is capable of solving many technical and scientific problems so complex and difficult that all previous methods of solution were considered impractical.

This mathematical robot, known as the ENIAC (Electronic Numerical Integrator and Computer), is the invention of Dr. J. W. Mauchly and Mr. J. Presper Eckert, Jr., both of the Moore School. Begun in 1943 at the request of the Ordnance Department to break a mathematical bottleneck in ballistic research, its peacetime uses extend to all branches of scientific and engineering work.

The ENIAC is capable of computing 1000 times faster than the most advanced general-purpose calculating machine previously built. The electronic methods of computing used in the ENIAC make it possible to solve in hours problems which would take years on a mechanical machine—a time so long as to make such work impractical.

Containing close to 18,000 vacuum tubes in its mechanism, the new machine is a giant of electronic precision. It occupies a room 30 by 50 feet and weighs 30 tons.

Although the machine was originally developed to compute lengthy and complicated firing and bombing tables for vital ordnance equipment, it will solve equally complex peacetime problems such as nuclear physics, aerodynamics and scientific weather prediction.

Official Army sources made it known that research laboratories of several large industrial firms have expressed active interest in the machine. These include manufacturers of electron tubes, jet engines, gas turbines, and other types of engines. Spending vast sums of money yearly for experimentation and design research on their products, these firms are naturally interested in any means of reducing such costs. It is further felt that better, more scientific design will now be possible, as a result of the new machine's facility for handling hundreds of different factors in one computation. Much lengthy and costly design experimentation, often involving the construction of a series of expensive models, a common practice in airplane design, might also be eliminated. It was explained that such trial-and-error methods were successful in Edison's and Marconi's day, but would not suffice to deal with complex phenomena arising, for instance, from the blast of an atomic bomb.

The new machine does not remove the need for legitimate experimentation, whose purpose it is to discover fundamental principles and factors which affect these principles. Likewise, it was pointed out that the electronic calculator does not replace original human thinking, but rather frees scientific thought from the drudgery of lengthy calculating work. The work of the English physicist, Dr. D. R. Hartree, who spent 15 years in calculations on the structure of the atom, was given as an example of lengthy computation attendant on modern science.

Cost estimates of the ENIAC run to about $400,000. This includes all research and development work; future machines of this type could be produced much more cheaply.

Built at the Moore School of Electrical Engineering of the University of Pennsylvania for the Army Ordnance Ballistic Research Laboratory at Aberdeen, the ENIAC is the result of a fortunate combination of men and circumstances. The original idea for the electronic general purpose calculator was that of Dr. John W. Mauchly, of the Moore School faculty. Dr. Mauchly, previously faced with many physical and meteorological problems requiring voluminous calculation, had conceived electronic devices for handling large computing problems in mass-production style. Captain Herman Goldstine, mathematician and ballistic expert for Army Ordnance, saw in these plans a powerful tool needed by the Ballistic Research Laboratory, which was confronted with overwhelming computational work, and he enthusiastically promoted the interest of the Ordnance Department in undertaking development of the ENIAC. Administrative supervision of the project was assumed by Dr. J. G. Brainerd, of the Moore School. Mr. J. Presper Eckert, Jr., a recent graduate of the Moore School, joined with Dr. Mauchly in elaborating the plans for the ENIAC and took charge of the technical and engineering work. Mr. Eckert and Dr. Mauchly have to their credit a number of inventions relating to improved methods of electronic computing.

The ENIAC was begun in July, 1943, and finished in the Fall of 1945. That a development of this magnitude was completed in so short a time is largely due to the close cooperation between Army Ordnance and the Moore School. The appointment of Captain Goldstine to maintain technical liaison was an important factor.

The ENIAC was sponsored by Colonel Paul. N. Gillon, a 38-year-old West Pointer with a graduate degree from Massachusetts Institute of Technology. He has given his enthusiastic support through the trying period which characterizes all pioneering developments in science. Colonel Gillon, when at the Ballistic Research Laboratory, was first interested in the project by Captain Goldstine. A transfer to Office, Chief of Ordnance, enabled Colonel Gillon to give the necessary wholehearted support to the project. He sums up his role in this connection by saying his part was "confined to such things as decisions on scope and flexibility; overall supervision and support; and fighting off the competition of apparently more urgent but actually less important conflicting projects through the war period."

The designers of the ENIAC speak of it as a "digital" or "discrete variable" computing machine, as opposed to the "continuous variable" type of machine, of which the differential analyzer is an outstanding example. The latter are devices that can handle only a restricted class of problems. But it was the experience of the sponsors of the ENIAC that modern physical problems could no longer be handled adequately by existing types of calculators.

Early in the emergency, the non-existence of ultra-rapid calculating facilities was recognized as a potential bottleneck in the swift delivery of vital ordnance materiel to troops in event of war. Artillery, for instance, after being built and tested, cannot be put into use until firing tables, indispensable to the operation of the guns, are supplied. Consequently, combat equipment could pile up at shipping depots, waiting for the proper firing tables. That this situation did not occur was due to the enormous effort that the Ordnance Department expended in utilizing all possible computational arrangements in facilities and personnel to prevent it. The Ordnance Department had its own differential analyzer, in addition to the one it was using at the University of Pennsylvania. These analyzers performed many labor-saving calculations up to a certain point, beyond that, a staff of about 200 trained computers was needed to complete the tables. A general purpose digital type of machine was needed, so that all calculating operations could be performed by machine. The construction of such a machine was being undertaken by another institution, but, because of its mechanical nature, its speed was nowhere near as high as that desired. At this point the team of Eckert-Goldstine-Mauchly, under Colonel Gillon's supervision, began to function and work commenced on the all-electronic general purpose computing machine, the ENIAC.

The speed of this computer is phenomenal. The first problem put on the ENIAC, which would have required 100 man-years of trained computer's work, was completed in two weeks—of which two hours was actual electronic computing time, and the remaining time devoted to review of the results and details of operation. If used to complete capacity, the ENIAC will carry out in five minutes more than ten million additions or subtractions of ten-figure numbers. The machine performs a simple addition in 1/5000 of a second (and can do a number of distinct additions simultaneously); a single multiplication by a ten-digit multiplier in 1/360 of a second; a nine-digit result in division or square rooting in 1/38 of a second.

It is felt that the tremendous speed and flexibility of the machine will permit many immediate industrial uses, as well as application to far-reaching investigations of natural phenomena. Although the cost of such a machine might seem fairly high, value received in elimination of expensive design processes would easily cover the initial investment in a short period of time. Many electrical manufacturing firms, for instance, spend many thousands of dollars yearly in building "analogy" circuits when designing equipment. A continuous-type of calculator used in this work is the "network analyzer." Like the differential analyzer, it can solve only certain restricted types of problems and then only up to a certain point.

Sponsors of the ENIAC point out that it can carry out numerous "logical" operations but that it cannot do creative thinking. The mathematician, physicist or engineer is still needed—in fact, more than ever, to analyze the problem mathematically and set up the sequence of operations in the machine. It is expected, moreover, that machines of this type will bring a greater "mathematics consciousness" to engineering and production.

In the latter connection several large organizations, whose work involves much statistical work, have expressed interest in the ENIAC. Among these are the National Bureau of Standards and the Army Air Forces Weather Service.

A very successful place for the new machine is expected in the science of weather forecasting. Army and Navy officials are most interested in this application. Instead of makeshift techniques, the machine would make possible the scientific analysis of the large mass of meteorological data that has been collected over the years. Not only would long-range accurate weather predictions be made possible, but weather in any spot in a given area could be determined almost instantaneously, when the "boundary data" are known.

EXPLORING THE READING

1. Re-read Bruce Dery's "Escape Velocity" essay, noting how ENIAC fits into his rundown of the development of computers. Why was it a landmark development?

2. If you were reading the newspaper in February 1946 and saw an article based on the War Department's press release, what would you have thought? Would you have anticipated that someday you

or your children would use computers personally? Could you have imagined the future? Why or why not?

3. The press release says that the computer was built to compute firing and bombing tables for the Army, though it would be "equally useful" for peacetime problems. What do you think of that statement?

4. In your small group, pool your knowledge of the development of computers, based on this press release, other texts in this chapter, and what you have learned though your personal reading. How did computers make the transition from large, government-developed units to small personal computers built by private industry? How do you see the development of computers moving in the future? Report to the class.

TO FAX OR NOT TO FAX

by Judith Hooper

Technologies have unforeseen consequences, according to Judith Hooper in this article from Omni. *The invention of window screens, air conditioning, and television resulted in a decline in the sense of community because people retreated into their living rooms and neighbors became strangers. Hooper interviews Richard Sclove of the Loka Institute who advocates that the public have a say in what technologies are introduced into the marketplace, for once a technology is introduced, it is irreversible.*

Judith Hooper, with Dick Teresi, is the author of Would the Buddha Wear a Walkman?: A Catalogue of Revolutionary Tools for Higher Consciousness, *which describes a plethora of what they call "consciousness tech" contraptions.*

Imagine, if you will, a world without window screens. In this pre-1910 world, insects circulate freely through the house, so you might as well sit on your front porch on a summer evening talking to your neighbors. Then someone invents window screens. Later, someone else invents air conditioning and, of course, television, and voila—a drastic decline in porch sitting. As Americans withdraw into their separate homes to watch *Jeopardy!* with the air conditioner up high, neighbors become strangers and community becomes a dim memory.

This is the sort of technological fallout that Loka Institute of Amherst, Massachusetts, would have you ponder. (In Sanskirt, Loka means "unity of the world, interconnectedness of society.") "When a panel of experts discusses the impact of different technologies on our lives," says Loka's executive director Richard Sclove, "they address safety, health, or environmental consequences—not the large range of cultural effects and the ways that technologies help structure and restructure political relationships."

What effect do faxes have on a culture? How do cellular phones affect the quality of one's mental life? Do computer networks foster community or subvert it? Does cable television empower the citizenry?

"I'm convinced these questions won't be addressed until there's a wide diversity of laypeople who play a major role in decisions about technology," says Sclove. At present, the technological universe we inhabit is created by hundreds of corporate decisions made behind closed doors. By the time the public gets a peek at the latest wonders, vast sums have already been committed, and it's too late in the game to say no. You might argue that John Q. Public can cast his "vote" in the marketplace simply by deciding whether to buy a videogame set, a fax machine, or a cellular phone. But, says Sclove, "you can't do anything about the collective consequences of other people's purchases. You can decide not to have a TV, but if all your neighbors have TV, you can't form a community by yourself. Suppose, on the other hand, you prohibited all broadcasts and video rentals every Thursday evening from six to nine. It would be interesting to see the social consequences."

Once a technology is established, an irreversible social process may be set in motion that ends up coercing the consumer into buying a fax machine, for example—"because if you don't have one, you're out of the system and you pay a penalty." Sclove insists that the public must enter the technology-evaluation process at the research-and-development phase, before billions of dollars have been spent. Yet Sclove acknowledges that current corporate-trade-secret laws would bar this sort of public scrutiny.

Do not take Sclove for a Luddite who yearns for the good old days when there was no television. "I'm not antitechnology," he insists, "but decisions about technology are too important to be left up to experts—scientists, engineers, CEOs—who lead very privileged lives."

Alas, nowhere on Earth is there a fully evolved model of the sort of grass-roots technology review Sclove envisions, though Europe can boast a few promising attempts. In Holland, "science shops," associated with universities, have sprung up to provide community groups with technological information—for example, whether the smoke released by the nearby factory is blighting their vegetables. Ten years ago in England, an even more ambitious scheme of "technology networks" was nipped in the bud by the Thatcher government. But the community most alert to the long-range cultural implications of technology is the Amish. "The Amish have tried out different things—calculators, computers, tractors. Liking the slower pace, many Amish communities decided not to use tractors, for example, for plowing fields, but they did adopt them as portable generators."

If the rest of us were to bring this degree of foresight to new technologies, Sclove wonders, would we be so rah-rah about such sexy newcomers as nanotechnology and virtual reality (both of which Sclove believes are potentially alienating)? Would we decide that computer networks were authentic communities or a perverted simulacrum?

EXPLORING THE READING

1. Have you ever thought about the impact of inventions such as automobiles or birth control pills upon the social fabric of society? In your small group, make a list of inventions, major and minor, and discuss their impact on society.

2. Do you think that John Q. Public should have a say in whether inventions are marketed? Or should the decision be left up to the companies developing the inventions? Defend your position.

3. If you had a choice, would you prefer the highly computerized society we have today, or would you have restricted the development of information technology at some point?

LUDDITE VS. FETISHIST

A debate between Bill Henderson and Tim Barkow

A luddite is one who believes that increased technology actually decreases quality of life. Taking the luddite side of the following e-mail debate is Bill Henderson, editor of Minutes of the Lead Pencil Club: Pulling the Plug on the Electronic Revolution, *and publisher of* Pushcart Press. *A fetishist, in this context, is one who has a fetish for computers and other technology. The techno-fetishist side is represented by Tim Barkow, an editor at* Wired *magazine and author of the Fetish column. The debate appeared in Brain Tennis, a feature of the online magazine HotWired, http://www.hotwired.com.*

MONDAY, 27 JANUARY 1997
POST NO. 1 OF 8
BY BILL HENDERSON

Let it be noted that I write this piece with a lead pencil on yellow lined paper, making good use, from time to time, of the handy eraser on the end of the pencil. The tablet of paper and the pencil cost me ninety-five cents. I didn't have to purchase a computer and printer, and assorted attachments and services. Nor did I need to use the electrical services of the nuclear power plant twenty miles across Long Island Sound in Connecticut.

I founded The Lead Pencil Club, with Doris Grumbach and Henry David Thoreau (emeritus), to point out the usefulness of simple tools like this pencil. I was concerned about the influence of computers and assorted electronic inventions. Our club insists on communication that is personal and thoughtful. "Not so fast," is our motto. The pencil is our symbol.

When I started this club—now 2,000 members strong, worldwide—I was laughing. Back in the winter of 1993–94, it seemed Rube Goldberg had been resurrected—all these complicated, expensive gizmos were being invented and celebrated, and bought, when simple tools did the job better and cheaper. Very funny, I thought. But, as word of the club spread, my new members reminded me that, to many of them, the gizmos were serious, debilitating stuff. Gazing at a computer screen all day on the job was no fun. TVs and computer games were hypnotizing their children, etc. Their observations are detailed in the dozens of letters, essays, cartoons, and commentaries on "how and why to live contraption-free in a computer-crazed world" in our *Minutes of the Lead Pencil Club,* just published in paperback.

Most of our members see only an explosion of mad-hatter gadgetry, and not useful innovation, in the wildly hyped technological revolution. We suggest that we may have lost our souls in a constant quest for speed, entertainment, and convenience. We notice no gain in productivity, knowledge or wisdom—just an explosion of usually useless data zipping around the earth in a babble of Websites and a cacophony of Internet chat and gossip.

As Thoreau said of the telegraph system—the miraculous invention of his time—"What if Maine and Texas have nothing to say to each other."

As Leadite Neal Postman points out in our *Minutes*, the last thing any of us needs is more information. We are already stuffed like geese with "260,000 billboards, 11,520 newspapers, 11,556 periodicals, 27,500 outlets for video rentals, 500 million radios, 40,000 new books a year, and 30 million pieces of junk mail annually. Plus 98 percent of our homes have TVs."

The information age has spawned mostly sound-and-fury gadgetry—not useful innovation. We suffer from a plague of gizmos.

TUESDAY, 28 JANUARY 1997
POST NO. 2 OF 8
BY TIM BARKOW

Bill, geez, where do I start?

The pencil, which you so justly laud, is not the end of useful technology. How do you say that with a straight face? Technological innovation has always been ubiquitous—in our tools and the tools that make our tools. Always and in everything, even the bottle your maple syrup comes in. To some, the swiftly encroaching, yet nascent, and sometimes insensible, technology of the Net is overwhelming. But Bill, remember—speed doesn't kill, people kill.

Personally, I find e-mail (not the Web) the most significant innovation of the digital age. It does so much more than a pencil ever could. The kvetching your members spit out is not a function of e-mail technology, but of the people that use it. I unhappily find that letter writing is a dying art. But is that e-mail's fault, or is it because people don't spend the time to elucidate their thoughts? Hmm. Well, let's go ahead and blame the technology—it's so scary.

Technological developments will always have their reactionaries, yet aren't all things—including the grass the monkey uses to draw termites from their nests—gizmos at their births? It's too easy to sit in some warm, converted farmhouse nestled among the woods of Vermont, scratching out pseudodeclarations of what's good and bad with the future. But can you honestly say the postal system is better than e-mail? It just isn't. It's slow and extremely expensive. You may have that kind of time and money to waste—I don't. E-mail is a tool, and frankly, it's a smaller, cheaper, more efficient tool than the US Postal System. It fits all of Wendell Berry's requirements for technological innovation. So, where's the beef?

It's also interesting that while you decry the information explosion, you point out no gains in productivity. Well, where did all the information come from? One day, critics scream that technology is eliminating jobs. The next, they holler how computers don't increase productivity. Well, which is it? Truth is, work goes on as it always has. Just because you have a computer doesn't mean that one Thursday afternoon you're going to complete that spreadsheet and come to the horrifying realization that you're finished. It's a job, you're never done.

Bill, do me and America a favor, get down and figure out how to set the clock on your VCR. If you don't have one, find someone who does. But don't do it for me, Bill, do it for the children. They're counting on you to stop this madness.

WEDNESDAY, 29 JANUARY 1997
POST NO. 3 OF 8
BY BILL HENDERSON

The Lead Pencil Club was interested to hear from you, Tim, but you seem jumpy and confused about lots of things. Slow down.

You say you "unhappily find that letter writing is a dying art." Well, Tim, letter writing requires time and concern and caring and thought. A culture of speed at any cost such as that *encouraged* by e-mail—helps kill letter writing (and careful reading).

In your hurry to dash off a nifty reply to The Lead Pencil Club, you fabricate the idea that we think the pencil is "the end of useful technology." Ridiculous. The pencil is merely good technology. It's simple. It's cheap. It *works*. The computer is often none of the above.

Tim, you seem to have a case of the jitters. Info overload? Try to follow my argument, slowly.

The Lead Pencil Club doesn't decry the "information explosion"—just the fact that most of the info is of little use. As in any explosion, we have a big mess. This is not an increase in productivity. This is an increase in nonsense.

Calm down, Tim. Write a real letter to a real friend. Take a walk outside into the real world, to the post office maybe. You'll find people there, and maybe time to talk to them. You might even make a new friend.

"Not so fast," as we say at The Lead Pencil Club. Speed doesn't increase productivity. Remember "Haste makes waste?"

Speaking of waste. Why the contemporary frenzy for useless invention? What's driving the plague? Could it be something as simple as greed? There's a buck to be made in a wallet-sized Global Positioning System, so why not invent one and tell people they can't live without it? It worked for Gates, right? And that guy has waste-plus: a house big enough to need a GPS just to be able to walk through without getting lost, and enough money to stop starvation in an entire continent. (Not that he will.) So let's throw enough useless gimcracks up against the wall and see which one sticks. Now that consumers are so mind-wasted by their TVs and VCRs and Web surfing, they will buy almost anything new just to fend off the incredible boredom. You see, Tim, the terms we use give us away. Does "consumer" remind you of locusts in a field ruining the crops? "Word processor." Good grief, we have so little respect for words that we process them?

But who is it we really have lost respect for, Tim? Ourselves, of course. We run faster and faster—prodded by our technology—and we run to nowhere. We gobble facts, celebrity gossip, news, and data, and can never satisfy our hunger for what we really want: knowledge, wisdom, love.

THURSDAY, 30 JANUARY 1997
POST NO. 4 OF 8
BY TIM BARKOW

Bummin' on Wal-Mart and CompUSA, Bill? What's the deal? Folks have been buying and selling since the dawn of time. Where's the value in a diamond-studded necklace? A gold-plated spear? These items are certainly useless. So it seems that innovative or not, people have been buying crap ever since barter was invented.

Innovation is man's forte. It's what we do as a species. Innovation involves adaptation, challenge, accretion of knowledge (both good and bad)—all this leads to wisdom. It does not guarantee wisdom, mind you—but neither does sitting on your ass in the woods. And no matter your take, innovation is a fact—a fact of nature, actually. Go talk to Darwin.

You make an interesting exception in your book: advances in medical tech. How then can you say GPS isn't useful for hikers? You like hikers, right Bill? Would you leave the tree-huggers stranded on a mountain to die? Should they spend the day worrying about getting back home, or soaking up that magical weave of animal, vegetable, mineral?

You picked a bad example, Bill. GPS is extremely useful. It's used in all kinds of geological and ecological research. The fact that a consumer can buy a GPS unit has no relevance to the technology's utility. And that's the point you seem to be missing. In a world that, especially in commerce, is shrinking, you cannot presuppose that someone won't find a particular tool extremely valuable. GPS is relatively silly in San Francisco, yet it can save your life on the African plains or in the Austrian Alps.

Innovation makes things different: new ideas, new terms. But words are only "processed" by the engineers who originally named the program. To miss the point that "word processors" put the power of Gutenberg in the hands of the people is to really have your head in the sand. That's what word processors are for, Bill.

I'm still waiting for some concrete examples. I doubt you can come up with a stumper. This technological gimcrack, as you call it, provides us with options. It's not about some final solution, Bill. It's about fitting the tool to the person. Now if the person doesn't understand the tool, what is more productive: blaming the tool or the person?

And money and greed have little to do with it. To simplify a market economy to the point where the only benefits gained are those in the CEO's bank account is to do a serious injustice to all of us, including yourself. Aren't you yourself cashing in on this innovation? Face it, Bill, you're at the craps table, same as everyone else. Only difference is, you bet against the thrower.

FRIDAY, 31 JANUARY 1997
POST NO. 5 OF 8
BY BILL HENDERSON

Tim, good to notice that you have slowed down a bit. Perhaps you took my advice and disconnected the e-mail or briefly untangled yourself from the

Web. I detect that you are less jangled and jumpy—characteristics of so many wired into the system. I'm thinking of Bill Gates and my Lead Pencil Club friend Cliff Stoll, who contributes a terrific chapter to our *Minutes* on how he rediscovered real life by pulling the plug on his computers and strolling to the neighborhood newsstand to buy an actual newspaper. He disconnected and learned to relax and enjoy again. You can too.

Seriously, Tim, enough about my sitting in the north woods longing for the old days. I live by the seashore, and I am surrounded by neighbors with all the gadgets you admire. I am constantly invited by to marvel at Websites and online chat groups. I remain unmoved. These are "pretty toys," as Thoreau noted about the new telegraph devices of his time. They encourage us to yap ceaselessly. But we have less and less to say. The chatter is deafening. Those of us who have pulled the plug realize that knowledge often arrives with silence.

Very few of us in The Lead Pencil Club are as terrified about technology as you imagine. Check out the chapters in our *Minutes* by Russell Baker, David Gelertner, Mark Slouka, and Andrei Codrescu, for instance. Baker and Codrescu think much of computer innovation is merely silly. Slouka is astounded that the boys and girls at the MIT Media Lab take themselves so seriously that they imagine themselves to be theologians of a new quasi-religion; and Gelertner, professor of computer science at Yale (for gosh sake) is rightfully concerned about the invasion of computers into our schools.

These are not off-the-wall old farts who don't recognize useful inventions when they see them, Tim, so relax. Unwire.

Think about what we agree on. "People have been buying crap ever since barter was invented," you offer. Right on, Tim. And we've never had so much crap to barter for as now, I offer.

You note that in the *Minutes* I praise some new technologies, such as medical innovations. Right on again. The list is certainly longer than that. But for now I will insist on reminding you of the value of the human mind—unfettered by electronic programs that, while promising to help us, merely detract by doing jobs we can do very well by ourselves—such as writing with our very own handwriting, balancing a checkbook, or meandering through a library of actual books to research a topic and, from time to time, coming up with an unprogrammed bit of knowledge all our own.

MONDAY, 3 FEBRUARY 1997
POST NO. 6 OF 8
BY TIM BARKOW

I'd like to clarify a point. When I say people have been buying "crap" for ages, and I did, I mean "stuff." The point you refuse to admit, Bill, is that individuals purchase for many different reasons. Some things are bought for their utility, others for their beauty, charm, or novelty—sometimes without the benefit of clear thinking. If people will buy it—for whatever reason—someone will make it. This is reality.

The beauty in all this gimcrack is where you find it. I can't go on the record and say everything I've bought has proved wonderful, but I enjoyed it nonetheless. I play my part as Fetishist.

Every day I'm inundated with products. Some are beautiful, some innovative—some are just cool. And people all over the world buy this stuff (crap). Every day. Frankly, I love it. It's just damn wonderful. I do so love my toys. But, you know Bill, I love my tools even more. In my spare time, I draw and paint. So I consider myself schooled in your "lead" pencil. And what you'll find while drawing is that sometimes a pencil doesn't cut it. You might need charcoal. Maybe ink. And sometimes, you need a computer. Eek! The tool chosen is the one that suits the artist's needs.

As far as your contributor-members go, half of them are ignorant, the others have picked radically unrepresentative examples to illustrate their points. Their tales are distortions, as most are—but they *are* distortions. So I can't say I put much weight behind their expertise, such as it is: The argument was made on the first page—everything after that is watery propaganda.

If you've done your research, you know that Gelertner and his students are doing some interesting user-interface research at Yale. The project is called Lifestreams, and Gelertner is even helping to move Lifestreams into the marketplace. And sell it. For money. Eek!

This is what it's all about. Some people love the computer desktop. Some would be better served by Lifestreams' time-based metaphor. What works for one person is not necessarily appropriate for another. Sometimes, you've no recourse but to visit the library. Other times, the Web works faster—eek!—allowing you a leisurely, unfettered walk outside. More tools; more options. Innovation is good.

This goes out to all you fine folk in Web space—Señor Bill doesn't think you have anything worthwhile to say, as he invokes some odd rant of Thoreau's on the "pretty toy" telegraph. As far as Bill is concerned, you have nothing to add to life. And he won't know, couldn't know, because he refuses to explore your accomplishments before condemning them as ceaseless yapping.

Well Bill, I got news for you: Thoreau is dead. Looks like all us netizens got one up on Walden's bad boy.

TUESDAY, 4 FEBRUARY 1997
POST NO. 7 OF 8
BY BILL HENDERSON

Tim, thanks for your kind words about contributor-members to our *Minutes*: "half ignorant." Without the book in hand, "folks in Web space" won't have a clue about such silly attacks. I urge them to look for the book in their bookstore or library. It's worth a trip into the sunlight.

Most of the contributors to our book have come screaming out of Web space seeking solace. And most of our members have just trashed computers, or use them for planters.

Tim, this has been fun. I do hope our audience has learned something from this frolic, but I doubt it. Point is Tim, you won't take the time to read what we say. Is it possible that, like Mr. Gates, you have difficulty in this regard?

To respect our audience, The Lead Pencil Club has no problem with true innovation. I too think *useful* innovation is one of the glories of our human experience. But you don't crap on a rock and call it useful innovation, and then go out and try to sell it to the world for a huge profit. Too much of today's electronic and digital inventing is just crap on a rock, and we don't need it. The stuff is not necessary for almost all of us. From giant TVs (with nothing worth watching), to Websites (an electronic yellow pages and just a bit more fun than the phone book) to Internet sex and blab groups—this is not useful innovation. The old way, in most cases, was better, or at least just as good, for most of us.

The GPS and other new devices do have specialized uses, but not for most of us. It's hype Tim, pure hype. You will not find wisdom, peace, love, friendship, or "A Life" in this stuff. You will be distracted endlessly by snake oil followed by brand new snake oil—all promising speed and convenience, followed by even more speed and convenience (for a profit to the person with the latest dump on the rock).

In signing off, I want to wish you well, Tim. (Remember, Tim with an "e" on the end is Time: Unplug and take time to read slowly and carefully, and think.)

And I want to thank *HotWired* (by the way, why is your magazine named as if it were a nervous breakdown?) for inviting me to endure your agitation. And to editor Roderick Simpson, my thanks for reading my pencil handwriting. It must make you long for that handwriting gizmo in 250 styles for US$39.50.

But thanks really to the members of The Lead Pencil Club worldwide. (You too can join us at Lead Pencil, Wainscott, NY, 11975. It's free!) Leadites unite! Power to the Pencil!

WEDNESDAY, 5 FEBRUARY 1997
POST NO. 8 OF 8
BY TIM BARKOW

Let's get a couple things clear, Bill. I did not call your members "half ignorant." I said that half of them were (totally) ignorant. There's a difference. And it is not a silly attack. I don't consider technophobes who can't get Windows 95 installed competent critics. You've got to get a little further than that before you can build a strong, defensible argument. Something, BTW, that you have been unable to do. So you don't like the Web, big deal. And GPS is just hype? Hype of what? We don't look for wisdom, peace, love, or a life "in" tech—but "through" it. We use and abuse technology for whatever purpose suits us. Same as I can take a pencil in my hand and with it compose a poem—or poke your eye out.

For the last time, Bill, I read your book. It sucked.

The reason it was so awful starts with the argument you chose.

As far as I can tell, there are three basic types of debates. First, there's the two intractable sides. With an issue like abortion, two sides come to the table already convinced. There's no discussion, only two foes hurling epithets. It's loud, but essentially pointless. Then you've got your healthcare-type arguments. These are the most interesting, since they focus on accomplishing a goal. They are also the most difficult, since everyone must work toward a single resolution. Then there's this "technology-out-of-control" argument—the worst of all, simply because it doesn't exist. You cannot stop, slow, or control technology. There's only one speed on this bus: full out. Which leaves only one option: Get in the driver's seat, grab the wheel, and hope you master driving before you master crashing.

Isn't it amazing the fuss that's grown out of something we can't even see. This whole revolution, if you want to call it that, is just electricity. That's all it is. But isn't it amazing what we can do by manipulating a pinch of electrons?

History is content with the triumphs and defeats concerning atoms. So why all the grumbling now that we're off to explore the possibilities of electronic, digital space? If you can't take the time to understand that a new frontier awaits, and why many people refuse status-quo "lead pencil" living, then you'd be best served by a history refresher class at your local community college.

And it looks like you've got the time for it as well. Adios, dear Bill, and thanks for the inscrutable attempts to defend your li'l club.

Remember, Bill with an "e" is—hmm, actually it's nothing.

Who woulda guessed?

EXPLORING THE READING

1. Bill Henderson, the luddite, sees the technological revolution as an "explosion of mad-hatter gadgetry" which often is not useful and sometimes is debilitating. From the text collect examples of what Henderson means. Add some examples of your own.

2. Tim Barkow points out that technological innovations have always had their critics. Make a list of some of his examples. Add some examples of your own.

3. Designate one member of your small group to take the luddite side and one to take the techno-fetishist side and hold your own debate. Have the rest of the group evaluate the arguments.

4. Read some of the other debates at Brain Tennis, http://www.hotwired.com/braintennis, and discuss the *e-mail* debate format. Is it an effective technique for presenting the two sides of an argument?

As Bookends to the 20th Century, Two Views of Technology's Promise

by Ashley Dunn

Optimism or pessimism? Ashley Dunn writes of two extreme views of technology's promise in this column from the Cybertimes section of the online New York Times. Filippo Tomaso Marinetti took the optimistic view in his essay, "The Joy of Mechanical Force," published in 1909, which proposes that technology will liberate humankind. Paul Virilio's 1995 essay "Red Alert in Cyberspace" paints technology as a villain, a disturber of human perception of the real.

Dunn has written frequently about computers and technology for Cybertimes, which can be accessed through The New York Times *Website, http://www.nytimes.com.*

The original Marinetti essay can be accessed in the Futurism site created by Kim Scarborough, http://shoga.wwa.com/~sluggo/futurism. Radical Philosophy, the journal where Virilio's essay is published, can be found at http://crane.ukc.ac.uk/secl/philosophy/rp.

After a night of chasing dogs and cursing antiquarians in 1909, a 32-year-old Italian poet by the name of Filippo Tommaso Marinetti scribbled out an exuberant paean to the technology of the new century titled, "The Joy of Mechanical Force."

"Let's go! . . . Friends, away!" wrote Marinetti, whose piece appeared in the February 20, 1909 issue of *Le Figaro*, the Paris newspaper. "Let's go! Mythology and the Mystic Ideal are defeated at last. We're about to see the Centaur's birth and, soon after, the first flight of Angels! . . . We must shake at the gates of life, test the bolts and hinges. Let's go! Look there, on the earth, the very first dawn! There's nothing to match the splendor of the sun's red sword, slashing for the first time through our millennial gloom!"

For Marinetti, the technology of the new century brought a liberation. Within his essay, he penned a Manifesto of Futurism, in which he hailed the glories of machines, war and the chaos of the twentieth-century city, to incite the artistic community of his time.

"We will sing of the great crowds excited by work, by pleasure and by riot; we will sing of the multicolored, polyphonic tides of revolution in the modern capitals; we will sing of the vibrant nightly fervor of arsenals and shipyards blazing with the violent electric moons; greedy railway stations that devour smoke-plumed serpents; factories hung on clouds by the crooked lines of their smoke."

The Futurist movement lasted only a few years before mutating into other forms. Some of its early proponents died in the mechanized brutality of World War I. Others migrated to different artistic movements. Marinetti himself became a Fascist poet, the court darling of Mussolini.

Despite its dubious credentials, the Manifesto of Futurism still stands as one of the defining documents on the allure of technology.

Since Marinetti's time, the excitement over technological progress has been considerably muddied. While the same exhilaration is felt in pondering the possibilities of future microprocessors or the ultimate expansion of the Internet, it has also been joined by a sense of grim oppression.

It is a modern vision of technology that has been shaped by a group of thinkers, including Jean Baudrillard and Paul Virilio, who have focused on the distorting power of the computer.

In a 1995 essay titled "Red Alert in Cyberspace," Virilio wrote: "What is now under way is a disturbance of the perception of the real: a trauma. And we need to concentrate on this. Because no technology has ever been developed that has not had to struggle against its own specific negativity."

The essay, published in French in *Le Monde Diplomatique* and in English in the British journal *Radical Philosophy*, went on to warn: "The specific negativity of information superhighways is precisely this disorientation of alterity, of our relation to the other and to the world. It is quite clear that this disorientation, the 'de-situation,' will bring about a profound disturbance with consequences for society and, in turn, for democracy."

Virilio, Baudrillard and Marinetti form a set of bookends to our century that mark a shifting vision of technology from a force of individual liberation at the beginning of the century to one of collective oppression at the terminus. How did we find ourselves in this place?

Marinetti wrote his manifesto at a particular moment of industrial development that for the first time, put the power of the machine in the hands of individuals. For a century before Marinetti, the machine largely had been only an oppressive force—the ceaseless devices of the industrial revolution. But the automobile marked a significant turning point for Marinetti. Now individuals could partake of the same amplification of labor that factory owners had enjoyed. Even today, the automobile, along with its lesser cousins—the leaf blower, lawn mower and weed wacker—remains the most important labor amplifying device that individuals own.

But since Marinetti's time, technology has reached another turning point, driven by devices like television and computers, which affect the senses. For Baudrillard and Virilio, these new types of devices have led to a perceptual distortion of reality that they believe can be used to oppress.

Their writings are difficult, and I can only offer a rough approximation of their views. But even in their crudest form they are a fascinating expression of modern concerns about technology.

For Jean Baudrillard the key is an idea that he calls "simulation." In his vision, past reality was dominated by real objects, which could be reproduced—the foundation of industrial society. The material nature of things meant that what you saw was what you got.

But the computer and other devices opened a new world in which objects could be created that had no material counterpart. It seems like a small point, but these simulations, Baudrillard says, are the pieces of a new type of reality—"hyper-reality"—an artificial world with artificial rules.

Like a computer program that rejects unknown or improper inputs, hyper-reality demands its own type of perfection and orderliness. The systems that create these simulations have a "surgical compulsion" to "excise negative characteristics and remodel things synthetically into ideal forms." What he is trying to say is that in hyper-reality, real people and real things look like errors that must be remodeled or removed.

There are numerous examples of how this has become an oppressive power. For example, credit bureaus have a digital version of your identity in storage. It's not really you by any stretch of the imagination, but for banks, business owners or perhaps employers, that digital simulation of you carries enormous power.

For Baudrillard, hyper-reality is quickly overwhelming material reality, driven by our own preference for the neatness of simulation over the chaos of reality. It's why Disneyland can be so seductive.

Paul Virilio strikes at this same issue of oppression from a different perspective but maintains the same sense of foreboding in the gap that is developing between material reality and virtual reality.

Virilio argues that the development of information devices has created a world dominated by instantaneous and immediate interaction. Again, this would seem to be a good thing, in the sense that we can now just pick up a phone and talk to other people, or watch live events on television. For Virilio, however, this is a formula for disaster.

A world of "real time" has begun to displace our old world based on real space, locality and proximity.

"We face the prospect in the twenty-first century of the invention of a perspective based on real time, replacing the spatial perspective, the perspective based on real space, discovered by Italian artists of the quatrocento," Virilio wrote in "Red Alert in Cyberspace." "Perhaps we forget how much the cities, politics, wars and economies of the Medieval world were transformed by the invention of perspective.

"Perceived reality is being split into the real and the virtual, and we are getting a kind of stereo-reality in which existence loses its reference points. To be is to be *in situ*, here and now, *hic et nunc*. But cyberspace and instantaneous, globalized information are throwing all that into total confusion."

The result of this speed gap between the real and virtual worlds is a disorientation of the individual that can be manipulated by those who control the flow of information—typically governments and businesses.

The ideas of Baudrillard and Virilio crystallize what most Net users have grasped in their own ways. But what is ultimately jarring about their thoughts—as well as about the writings of Marinetti—is that they seem so distant to the ordinary experience of virtuality.

The computer and other information devices clearly can be used to oppress, but they have also been used in myriad ways to liberate and energize, in the same sense that Marinetti articulated 90 years ago.

As for Marinetti's exuberance, there is an aura of magic about advanced technology, but at the same time, there is a plainness and neutrality of many devices that we use every day without thought, like a fax machine or a programmable videocassette recorder. For all the philosophizing, there is a part of technological devices that make them no different from hammers.

Humans share a propensity for gazing on advanced technology in an almost magical light. But at the same time, the "surgical compulsion" of technology to remodel the world in its own image drives a counterforce that constantly turns the once exotic into the commonplace.

Once the devices become common, the magic is gone and they stand in more realistic terms—a mix of complexity and triviality, power and stupidity. Then, we ponder their existence less and less—or at least we ponder them in very different ways.

Today, people sing the glories of the automobile in magazines like *Motor Trend* or *Road and Track*. Their admiration is paraded in the streets of Los Angeles in the form of Volkswagens festooned with toilet seats or dented Impalas that smoke down the freeway.

The impact of technology is not easily wrapped in a single bundle. Even as Marinetti was careening down the streets of Milan, Marxists were gathering strength elsewhere to bring down the oppressive system of the factory. As Baudrillard and Virilio warn of imminent doom, the CyberUtopians and Extropians hail the technological leaps that they hope will push mankind to another level of development.

For us commoners, the cycle is not nearly so refined or exclusive but is more a mix of the many ways that technology has improved or worsened our lot in life. So much of technology cannot even be categorized as good or bad anymore.

Consider the flashing red lights on my son's shoes. A few hundred years ago, they would have been revered as magic. Today, they are simply what comes with kids shoes, whether you want them or not.

My son's shoes make me think that perhaps there is no linear path toward doom or salvation, but rather cycles of exotic-to-common that never end and constantly overlap. In the same world that produced Marinetti's machines of liberation and Baudrillard and Virilio's wired doom, there are also these shoes. They blink with beautiful predictability and precision, for no purpose at all.

EXPLORING THE READING

1. How do you view technology's role in modern life? Optimistically or pessimistically, or something in between? Why?

2. In your small group, outline Virilio's and Marinetti's positions. Then analyze what you think Dunn's position is.

3. Why would a writer at the beginning of the century be optimistic about technology and a writer at the end be pessimistic? Evaluate these two perspectives as bookends for the twentieth century.

4. Reconsider the other readings in the chapter. Draw a continuum with Virilio's position on one end and Marinetti's on the other. Place each of the readings in this chapter along the continuum based on the author's degree of optimism toward technology's promise.

5. In your small group, discuss Virilio's assertion that technology disturbs human perception. Do you agree?

WHEN YOUR TOAST STARTS TALKING TO YOU, THE INFO AGE HAS HIT HOME

by Bruce Watson

In this humorous column from Smithsonian, *Bruce Watson writes about miscellaneous and unwanted information leaking into his home. Facts are no longer friends, they leak in unwanted, despite efforts to block them. Watson and his family decide that they can't live "awash in trivia" and take serious steps to protect their lives from crude, out-of-context information.*

Watson writes for Smithsonian, *with articles including "The Storyteller Is the Soybean . . . the Audience Is the Sun," a piece about the National Storytelling Festival, and "How to Take on an Ailing Company—and Make It Hum," about the Nashville-based Gibson Guitar Company. Abstracts of Watson's articles can be found at http://www.smithsonianmag.si.edu/smithsonian/home.shtml by using the online* Smithsonian's *search feature.*

Our house is not old, but it leaks. Several windows need caulking. Doors are hard to close. Still, we assumed mere water was leaking in until we learned of a more dangerous seepage.

We were at the dinner table. Our daughter Elena was eating her peas, one by one. Suddenly she stopped. "The capital of Delaware is Dover," she said. "Exactly what do you mean by that?" I asked. She began to chant, "The capital of Delaware is Dover! The capital of Delaware is Dover!"

Elena is 4. She knows no more about the capital of Delaware than we do. We hadn't told her. Neither had her preschool teacher.

We knew someday computers would be linked to phones, TVs, toasters. We'll touch a button on the compu-toaster and *beeeeep!* along with our toast, we'll be served statistics on per capita toast consumption, the fat content of butter and other vital data. But although we knew the Info-future was coming, we didn't realize it had already begun to leak into our home.

A week later, my wife went to the laundry basket. Lying there among the sheets was the 1990 census for the state of New York. "Did you put this here?" she asked. I didn't. Neither did our daughter, the mailman or the dog. The data had just leaked in. Like all random information, it came from nowhere, meant nothing and made us feel stupid.

"Bet you didn't know the population of Poughkeepsie is 28,844," I said. "Will this be on the test?" my wife asked.

The next week, I opened the freezer. Out tumbled an encyclopedia—"Volume VII, Egret to Fond du Lac." We went away and forgot to close a window; when we came back, the living room was littered with Civil War histories.

I grew up believing that facts were our friends. How could information hurt us? "The informed citizen is the cornerstone of democracy," Jefferson said. Or *was* it Jefferson? Willa Cather, maybe? Mick Jagger? Whoever said it believed that information was truth, but in our house information was becoming a pest. Random facts were turning up in our food, our dreams, our conversations. We had to do something.

The next day we caulked all windows and doors with Info-block, a silicon-based fact sealant. Info-block was both info-proof and noise-proof. When we threw our TV out the second-floor window, it crashed on the driveway without a sound. For a few blissful weeks, Info-block kept our home fact-free.

Then one morning I found an envelope in the microwave. "Are You Keeping Pace With Today's Info Age?" it asked. We read the letter inside. If we joined the Fact-of-the-Month Club, it said, we'd receive the World's Top 150 Facts for only $1.95. Then each month, we'd get more Fun Facts. We'd learn the average speed of the Galápagos tortoise, the atomic weight of tungsten, the National League RBI leader in 1947.

How had the envelope found its way into our microwave? And what would be next—actuarial tables in the alcove? Stray spreadsheets in the study?

That night at dinner Elena said, "The 1947 National League RBI leader was Johnny Mize." Then, before we could even gasp, she asked, "What's an RBI?"

Our Info-seal had broken. We were defenseless against the constant barrage of facts that define modern life. We tried rubbing Info-repellant all over our bodies, but the data still swarmed around us. We sprayed the house with Fact-B-Gone, the ignorance-based spray so many people are using these days. For a few hours, no idle facts occurred to us. Then my wife said, "Hey, bet you didn't know that the G.D.P. of Cameroon is $8 billion." I ran from the room, screaming a list of U.S. Vice Presidents, Adams to Gore.

When the data settled, I tried to remain calm. "Maybe we could live with our leaks," I said. All our friends were awash in trivia. We knew people who couldn't name their Congressman, but they knew the first name of every last goalie in the National Hockey League. Their kids weren't sure which state they lived in, but they could sing whale songs till the cows came home. And somehow they made it through the day.

We were informed citizens. Surely we could pick and choose the drivel that dribbled into our home. Then one morning, I was awakened by a low buzz. Tracing it to the bathroom, I found my electric razor humming "That Old Devil Moon." That did it.

Before we'd jettisoned the TV, we'd seen the commercials. For only $1,995 we could put a laser-equipped Fact Zapper on the roof to shoot down all incoming data. We couldn't remember Fact Zapper's 800 number, but we waited a moment and it came to us. We called. Within a week, we were armed for the Information Wars. Now, every few minutes we hear a *zaaaaap!* Another fact meets its maker.

Shielded from the data-glutted world, we now live in a Garden of Eden. Not a drop of crude information leaks in. We have forgotten everything we ever knew about Delaware, Vice Presidents and the G.D.P. of Cameroon. We got a scare one day when Elena blurted out the capital of Montana, but it turned out she had learned it in preschool. Still, we were skittish until we heard *zaaaaap!* "It's all right," I said. "We're safe." Once upon a time, ignorance was bliss, but in the Info Age, it's self-defense.

EXPLORING THE READING

1. Watson writes that he grew up thinking that facts were friends, but found that unlooked-for information was polluting his life. What do you think?

2. In your small group make a list of extraneous information which has confronted you recently. Is this a problem in your lives?

3. Do you ever feel that you suffer from information overload? If so, what does it feel like?

WRITING SUGGESTIONS

1. Interview a sampling of people, perhaps a computer programmer, a wilderness enthusiast, and an educator about their perceptions of our culture. Would they agree that we live in a wired society? What would they change about modern culture? Write an essay incorporating their viewpoints.

2. Choose an invention such as the telegraph or the computer and learn about its early history and its impact upon society. Write an essay based upon what you learn.

3. Using examples of specific incidents, write an essay describing how information technology affects your life.

4. Are you comfortable in our information-dominated society? Or would you prefer living in a society without cellular phones and notebook computers? Develop an argument for your position.

5. After rereading Bruce Watson's text, write a piece of humor or satire about your experiences with information technology, computers, or the Internet.

6. As the twentieth century ends, should we be optimistic or pessimistic about our wired society? Develop your own position, using specific examples of world conditions to support your position. You may need to obtain references from the Internet or the library to develop your examples.

THE WRITING PROCESS: WHY READING MATTERS— CONNECTING READING AND WRITING

Perhaps you, like Bruce Watson, in "When Your Toast Starts Talking to You, the Info Age Has Hit Home," feel overloaded with miscellaneous information. Perhaps you, like Richard Wolkomir, in "We're Going to Have Computers Coming out of the Woodwork," feel ambivalent about the information technology surrounding you. Can't find your e-mail? Can't program your VCR? Can't find the cordless phone until the seventh ring when the caller inevitably hangs up? Maybe these things annoy you at the time, but you don't give much thought to them until you read an essay like Watson's or Wolkomir's and say, "Yeah, I know what you mean."

If you've thought very much about the technology in your life, you may be excited by the possibility that it might, as Richard Wolkomir reports, surround us even further as "ubiquitous computing" becomes the standard. Wolkomir's article makes you think of the many ways your life would be easier if all your electronic gadgets were interconnected.

If reading makes you want to respond, you're not alone. When you open the editorial page of your newspaper, you see letter after letter written to contest an opinion previously published in the paper. Pick up any magazine and you'll find a "Letters" section where the readers of the magazine have written in response to something they've read. Authors of pages on the World Wide Web often publish e-mail addresses or have links to chat rooms so readers of the information on their pages can communicate with the page's creators or others who've accessed the page and are interested in its subject matter.

You've probably noticed how reading leads to thinking. Likewise, reading can lead to writing. Reading can make us examine our daily actions. It can make us question the world around us, and it can make us examine our values. If we take some time to express ourselves with a pen and paper or at a computer keyboard after we read, reading can be an important starting place for writing.

Easier Reading—Improving Your Reading Habits

Some people develop poor reading habits that inhibit the usefulness of reading as a starting place for thinking or writing. Many of your college classes will require careful reading and response as part of the course work. What follows are a few suggestions you can use to help build good reading habits for your work in this and other classes.

Be Prepared. For many of us, reading is something we do primarily while we're doing something else. We read or study while we're watching TV or listening to the radio. We might read the newspaper over coffee in the morning. We may read while waiting for the doctor or dentist, or we might read before going to sleep at night. Because reading is something we use to fill time or to complete an assignment, we don't usually think of *preparing to read* in the same way we might prepare for other activities like writing. However, careful preparation for reading can help make it easier to read carefully and critically, to better understand what we read, and to get the kind of responses from reading that will help us become better writers.

Preparing to read is the first step to better reading habits. Preparation means choosing the best physical environment for reading, having the tools for reading handy, and getting our minds set to understand both how and what the author is trying to communicate with us.

The best physical environment for reading may not be the environment you're used to when you read. If you are a before-bed reader, you might like to read lying down, but it's difficult to take notes and keep a reading journal lying down. If you are used to studying and reading with the television or the radio on, you might think you need the extra noise to concentrate. Some types of reading can be done effectively with the television or the stereo on, but careful reading demands your full attention. You need some silence in order to hear your own responses to the author. A good physical reading environment, then, is one that gives you room to sit up and write in response to the reading, and one that doesn't offer too many distractions. You might find this environment at a kitchen table or a desk. You might find it in your dorm room or in the dorm study hall, or you may need to go the library to find the space and quiet you need to read.

Wherever you choose to read, make sure you have the tools—pen or pencil with a notebook or a computer—handy for effective reading. Tools are necessary for the careful reading you'll need to do in this class. Later in this chapter, you'll learn about *reading journals*, but whether you keep a journal or not, writing down your responses and ideas as you read is important. Some of you might choose to write your responses in the margins of your textbook. Or, if you don't like to write in your textbooks, or if there isn't enough space, keep sticky notes, a journal, or your computer close by as you read and list the main ideas, important examples, and questions that come up. Don't wait until after you've finished reading to start writing notes. Your first responses as you read are often fresh and interesting. If you wait until you've finished to write them down, you may not remember them or they may have been replaced by responses to information later in the essay.

If you decide an idea is not important later, that's fine, you can erase or delete it, but you'll have it if you decide it's worth exploring in an essay of your own.

In addition to preparing your physical environment for reading, you need to prepare your mind. You can do several things to prepare for reading. First, this text contains author's notes before each of the readings. Getting to know the author before you read can help prepare you to read. Knowing what books or magazines he or she has published or whether the author is a writer, a scientist, or a politician can give you some indication of both how and why he or she is writing about a subject and may let you know ahead of time if the author has any biases. Many of the authors in this text have Web pages that you can explore to learn more about their interests and accomplishments.

Exploring your own knowledge of an issue before you begin to read can also help you build good reading habits. Look at the title, the preview information, and perhaps the first paragraph of the essay. Then write for a while on the same topic, exploring what you already know and asking any questions you hope the essay will answer.

Next, prepare mentally for reading by skimming over the assignment. Look at the subtitles or the topic sentences of each paragraph. Read the first and last paragraphs of the essay quickly, without trying to understand them, or just glance over the essay to see how long it is and how it's arranged. If you're used to reading short essays, and you notice that one of the assigned readings is ten pages long, you'll be better prepared to make it past that fourth page. Knowing what to expect before you start is good preparation for reading.

Read Slowly. When you pick up a newspaper, what's the first thing you do? You probably skim the headlines and then if anything looks interesting you skim over the article quickly to get the basic facts of the story. You might glance over the sports scores or the comics. When you read a magazine, again, you usually cover the reading material quickly to get the basic facts and move on. Even popular fiction can be read quickly. The most successful authors, like Steven King and Danielle Steele, know how to manipulate a reader's attention, signaling the reader to slow down before the interesting parts. They write so readers can skim over areas of background development and detail.

We may think that good reading is fast reading. Indeed, many of us have a hard time slowing our reading speeds down. To read critically, though, the reader must slow down. In many cases, the articles or essays you're reading in this textbook can't be understood if they're read too quickly. Take your time. As you read, stop and try to restate what the author has said. Write brief summaries in the margins of your textbook. If you don't understand a point the author makes, reread the paragraph or the section, or continue reading the essay, keeping the difficult section in your mind and see if a later point in the essay makes the earlier reading clear.

Respond to the Writer. You can improve your reading habits by talking to the authors of the essays you read. Of course, in most cases you can't actually sit down and talk with the author but you can carry on a conversation with the author as you read. You can do this by underlining main or important points, by circling important words and connecting ideas to one another with arrows. You can also make notes in the margins of your text. You might write brief summaries, or you might write questions or begin arguments with the author in the margins.

You can continue that conversation when you've finished reading by keeping a reading journal or even writing an essay in response to a text you've read. We'll discuss reading journals in detail later in the chapter. Even if you don't keep a formal journal, you might want to record a few notes about a reading after you've finished it so you'll have something to refresh yourself with before you begin class discussion of an essay. After you've completed the reading try completing one or more of the following statements: "I feel the author is trying to . . ." "The most interesting thing about this essay was . . ." "The most significant question this essay raises is . . ." "I agree with the writer about . . ." "I disagree with the writer about . . ." These questions can help you read more carefully and respond more critically to the essay.

Read the Author's Mind. Guessing the motivations and intentions of the author is another way to build effective reading habits. As you read, try to discover what made the writer decide to write the essay. Was it merely an assignment or does he or she seem particularly passionate about or interested in one aspect of the subject? When the writer started to write, where did he or she start? Did the attitudes or ideas of the author change over the writing of the essay or article? What makes you think so? Why does the author begin and end the essay that way? What effect did the author want to have on the reader? Thinking about the text as a writer can help you understand it more thoroughly. It can also help improve your own writing skills as you think about the decisions other authors make when they write.

Put It in Your Own Words.   Learning to put what you read into your own words is a good reading habit to build for several reasons. First, it helps you learn to summarize material effectively, a skill that you will use as you begin to incorporate other people's ideas into your own essays. It's also an effective test for understanding. If you can't summarize the essay, you may not have read it carefully enough or you might be having difficulty understanding the essay. Perhaps you need to slow your reading down or use some of the tricks listed above to help you understand the essay better. Finally, having a summary of the essay can help you review the material when you're searching for topic ideas for your own writing.

Reading an Online Document
A hypertext and hypermedia document on the World Wide Web doesn't look like a print document—it has links to other pages or other documents, icons, photos, perhaps video and sound. You can't read this kind of document the same way you would read a print document either. It is a good idea to scan the initial (or home) page, seeing how the author has organized the information with icons, boxes, and white space. Some pages give extensive information on the home page, and others require you to link to secondary pages before you see much content. Organization is an important part of hypertext pages, so pay attention to it.

Next, browse or surf through the site, not reading anything in depth but getting an overview of the information contained. Make mental (or actual) notes of pages you would like to explore further after your initial scan of the site. You can use the BACK and FORWARD arrows to navigate through the pages.

After you have an overall impression of the site return, one at a time, to the pages that caught your interest and read them in detail. Until you become comfortable with reading text online, you may want to print out pages that seem important so that you can read them carefully, annotating them as you read. If you plan to use a text as source material for an essay, it is a good idea to print it out anyway because Internet texts are known to change and even disappear without warning. Also, it is a good idea to record the address of sites that you find useful or interesting. It is often difficult to locate a site again unless you have an exact address.

KEEPING A READING JOURNAL

You'll notice that many of the suggestions for improving your reading habits depend on written responses to what you read. You may have also noticed the emphasis this text places on the connection between reading and writing. Your instructor may assign a journal as part of your regular classwork. Whether it's assigned or not, an ongoing journal in response to what you read in this class can help you build better reading habits and become a better writer. Don't forget to review it every so often as more formal essays are assigned. Although the writing in your journal will be informal and somewhat disorganized, it can provide excellent ideas and starting places for the more formal essays you'll complete for the class.

The prompts that follow can help you begin. There are also writing suggestions and questions after each reading. You don't need to respond to each prompt for every essay. Instead you might choose one or two prompts and respond to the questions and suggestions after each reading.

1. Annotate the text as you read. (Use a pen, pencil, or highlighter to mark parts of the text that capture your attention. Make a note of the line numbers in the text next to your response on the computer or in a notebook if you don't want to write in your book.) Summarize sections of the reading and ask spontaneous questions of the author. When you've finished reading, go back over your notes and make further comments.

2. Complete the reading, then make a list of what you remember. Perhaps it's an image the author used or a statement made by someone that the author quotes. Maybe it's something you'd never thought of before. Discuss the reasons you remember those sections.

3. Remark on other things you've read recently that remind you of this reading. Discuss the similarities and differences.

4. Write down occurrences in your own life that the essay brings to mind. Discuss the connection. Do the events from your life support or contradict the author's points?

5. Start an argument with the author. Disagree with a point or two in the essay. Give reasons for the disagreement and back it up with your own experiences if you can.

6. Identify the writer's position or thesis. Make a list of major points supporting that position.

7. Start a dialog with the author. Does the reading leave any questions unanswered? Make a list of several questions. Why doesn't the writer offer those answers? What do you think the answers are?

Activity—Begin a Reading Journal

As an introduction to the journal process, begin by writing an entry for each of the readings in this chapter. A different technique is used for each reading.

"Escape Velocity"—Annotate the essay, marking parts that capture your interest. When you have finished the essay, go back over your annotation and make further comments about what you noted.

"We're Going to Have Computers Coming out of the Woodwork"—Read the essay again, then put the text away. Immediately, make a list of the points you remember. Then write about why you think those points stuck in your mind.

"Remarks to the International Telecommunications Union"—Does this speech remind you of anything you have read before? If so, discuss the similarities and differences between this text and the other.

58

"Ordnance Department Develops All-Electronic Calculating Machine"—What early knowledge and experience with computers does this press release bring to mind? Describe your response in detail.

"To Fax or Not to Fax"—Start an argument with the author by disagreeing with several of her points. Give reasons for your disagreements.

"Luddite vs. Fetishist"—Identify the positions of the luddite and the fetishist, then list their major points.

"As Bookends to the Twentieth Century, Two Views of Technology's Promise"—Start a dialog by making a list of questions you would like to ask Dunn or the two authors he discusses.

ACCESSING INTERNET RESOURCES: USING A WEB BROWSER

The World Wide Web is a hypertext and hypermedia Internet protocol. In plain English, this means that you can use a program called a Web browser to display documents incorporating images, video, and sound, stored in hypertext format. In a hypertext document certain words or images are "hot," so if you use a computer mouse and click on one of them, a new document, that is linked to that key word or image, appears.

Two Web browser programs are predominately used, Netscape Navigator and Internet Explorer. Some users prefer one and some the other, though they perform basically the same functions.

To use either of the browsers, select the program from your computer's start menu or click on an icon for the program that is displayed on your screen. If you are using Netscape Communicator, the program will open to display a screen which looks something like the following one. If you are using another version of Netscape or Internet Explorer, your screen will be different, though there will be buttons and menus which perform the same functions.

Across the top of the browser screen are several tools which you will use to navigate the World Wide Web. In the small box labeled **Location,** you can type in a World Wide Web address such as the one displayed, http://photo2.si.edu/infoage.html, which is for the Smithsonian Institution Information Age Exhibit that features many of the inventions such as the telegraph that have shaped our modern era. You would then use the hypertext capabilities of the Web page and click on, for example, the highlighted phrase "Samuel Morse's original telegraph transmitter and receiver." Your browser would then display a different page, one about this topic. Alternatively, you might want to begin at the Smithsonian Institution home page, http://www.si.edu, and explore several of the virtual tours the museum offers.

You can use the arrow buttons, labeled **Back** and **Forward,** to go back and forward among the Web pages you have viewed. Click on the **Home** button to return to your default home page which was displayed when you opened the browser. Other useful buttons are **Search,** which connects you to a

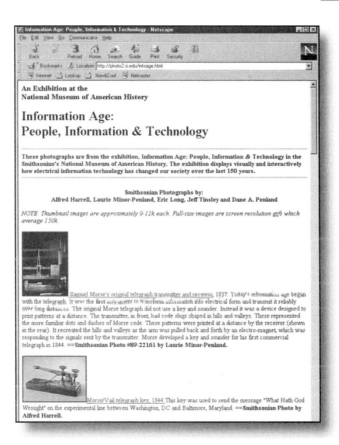

selection of Web search engines (discussed in Chapter 3); and **Print**, which allows you to print the Web page displayed on your screen. If you need help, select the **Help** menu and choose **Help Contents** for a list of help screens.

A good way to begin exploring the Web might be to look at the Websites mentioned in this chapter, including the White House, http://www.white-house.gov, or sites suggested by your instructor. Remember, there is no right or wrong way to explore the Web. Just follow hypertext links which seem interesting to other links and on to others. In the next two chapters, the Accessing Internet Resources sections will discuss how to find information about particular topics on the Web. The most valuable knowledge you can acquire about the World Wide Web, however, may be links you discover yourself while surfing the Net.

Remember, as you begin your explorations, that the World Wide Web is a fluid environment. Sites may change their appearance overnight and the available information may change even more frequently. If you are interested in a topic or link, it is often wisest to follow it up in the same session, or it may not be available when you log on again. Therefore, don't be surprised if some of the sites illustrated in this book have a different look or format when you check them out for yourself.

Technology | CYBERTIMES — The New York Times ON THE WEB

EUROBYTES
World Cup Sites Target Ticketless Fans
By BRUNO GIUSSANI
(May 12) Dozens of media companies and Web developers are investing in sites that will follow the 1998 World Cup soccer tournament, which kicks off on June 10.

Ziff-Davis Launches 24-Hour Cable Network About Computers
By MATT RICHTEL
(May 11) Hoping to move computer enthusiasts away from the desktop and into the living room, the magazine and Web publisher Ziff-Davis will debut ZDTV, a 24-hour cable network devoted to technology.

Studies Reach Contradictory Conclusions About Internet Population
By REBECCA FAIRLEY RANEY
(May 10) Two studies released in the past month reached contrary conclusions about Internet demographics, illustrating just how difficult it is to define a medium that is changing so rapidly.

Report Says U.S. Program to Wire Schools May Fall Short
By JERI CLAUSING
(May 9) Money available for a new federal program to help schools and libraries get Internet access could fall short of the $2.02 billion requested unless new fees are imposed on long-distance carriers, the Federal Communications Commission said.

Group Offers Grants to Study Effects of Computer Use on Children

TECHNOLOGY

[Search] Tips

■ CyberTimes
  ■ EUROBYTES
  ■ CYBERLAW JOURNAL
  ■ ARTS@LARGE
  ■ EDUCATION
  ■ TRAVEL LOG
■ Circuits
■ Business Technology
■ Specials / Forums
■ 7 Day Index
■ TECHNOLOGY HOME
About CyberTimes
Navigator

WEEKLY COLUMNS

@large
Reports on technology's effect on the arts, high and low, including enhanced CDs, museum displays, interface design and downloadable music.

CYBER LAW JOURNAL
Reflects on issues where law and technology intersect, i.e., Internet copyrights and trademarks, restrictions on pornography and other Net content, privacy, access to legal and public documents.

SUGGESTED INTERNET ASSIGNMENTS

1. Connect to the following sites (or ones suggested by your instructor) and explore them. Choose one and write a review of it similar to a book report. Include a discussion of the content, the organization, and the sponsor or author. Evaluate whether the site is effective and describe its usefulness.

   The White House, http://www.whitehouse.gov
   New York Times, http://www.nytimes.com
   Information Technology Association of America, http://www.itaa.org

2. Connect to the Library of Congress, http://www.loc.gov, and find the directory of Internet resources. Report to the class about one interesting site you found by exploring the links.

3. Locate an advertisement for a product, film, or company which gives a Website. Connect to the site and explore it. Is listing a Website an effective marketing tool? Discuss it with your small group.

4. Write and send an e-mail letter to the president or vice president about what you think the government's position should be concerning the development of the Global Information Infrastructure.

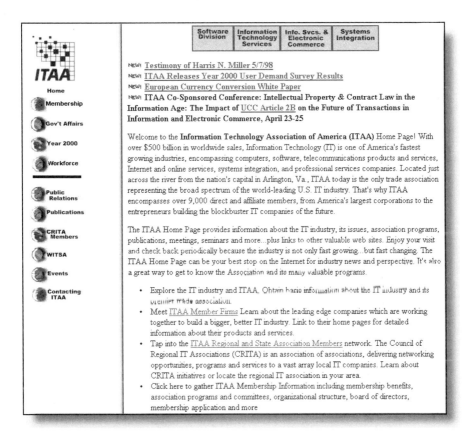

		Software Division	Information Technology Services	Info. Svcs. & Electronic Commerce	Systems Integration

ITAA

Home

Membership

Gov't Affairs

Year 2000

Workforce

Public Relations

Publications

CRITA Members

WITSA

Events

Contacting ITAA

NEW! Testimony of Harris N. Miller 5/7/98
NEW! ITAA Releases Year 2000 User Demand Survey Results
NEW! European Currency Conversion White Paper
NEW! ITAA Co-Sponsored Conference: Intellectual Property & Contract Law in the Information Age: The Impact of UCC Article 2B on the Future of Transactions in Information and Electronic Commerce, April 23-25

Welcome to the **Information Technology Association of America (ITAA)** Home Page! With over $500 billion in worldwide sales, Information Technology (IT) is one of America's fastest growing industries, encompassing computers, software, telecommunications products and services, Internet and online services, systems integration, and professional services companies. Located just across the river from the nation's capital in Arlington, Va., ITAA today is the only trade association representing the broad spectrum of the world-leading U.S. IT industry. That's why ITAA encompasses over 9,000 direct and affiliate members, from America's largest corporations to the entrepreneurs building the blockbuster IT companies of the future.

The ITAA Home Page provides information about the IT industry, its issues, association programs, publications, meetings, seminars and more...plus links to other valuable web sites. Enjoy your visit and check back periodically because the industry is not only fast growing...but fast changing. The ITAA Home Page can be your best stop on the Internet for industry news and perspective. It's also a great way to get to know the Association and its many valuable programs.

- Explore the IT industry and ITAA. Obtain basic information about the IT industry and its premier trade association.
- Meet ITAA Member Firms. Learn about the leading edge companies which are working together to build a bigger, better IT industry. Link to their home pages for detailed information about their products and services.
- Tap into the ITAA Regional and State Association Members network. The Council of Regional IT Associations (CRITA) is an association of associations, delivering networking opportunities, programs and services to a vast array local IT companies. Learn about CRITA initiatives or locate the regional IT association in your area.
- Click here to gather ITAA Membership Information including membership benefits, association programs and committees, organizational structure, board of directors, membership application and more

WIRED TO THE WEB

The New York Times
http://www.nytimes.com
The New York Times offers the CyberTimes section, an exclusive to the online edition, which covers breaking news and features related to computers and the Internet. A searchable archive makes it easy to locate articles. At press time, *The New York Times* was not charging a fee for most online articles, though they require that you register before viewing the site.

Information Technology Association of America
http://www.itaa.org
ITAA is a trade association representing the information technology industry. According to ITAA, the industry generates over $500 billion in worldwide sales each year, encompassing computers, software, telecommunications products and services, Internet and online services, systems integration, and professional services companies. The home page has information about issues in the information technology industry and links to related Websites.

The White House
http://www.whitehouse.gov

The White House World Wide Website maintains an online archive of press releases and other documents issued by the White House. You can search here for documents related to the Internet and telecommunications.

CYBERSPACE,
THE NEW FRONTIER

Henry David Thoreau once said, "Eastward I go only by force; but westward I go free." Since ancient times humans have moved west into the frontier, into a phantom place of danger and unlimited opportunities, to a space where culture can be born again, only better. In America, once the seaboard was settled, the interior of the continent beckoned, with its untamed forests, fierce Indians, and trackless deserts. This frontier was explored, then inhabited by free spirits, those who didn't like too much government, who wanted to make their own rules, who welcomed the wildness of the wide open spaces.

Cyberspace, in many ways echoes the myth of the West, a place of limitless space, populated by the adventurous who invent their own society, a place where individualism is celebrated and deviance is tolerated, even protected. The invention of the term *cyberspace* is generally credited to William Gibson, a science fiction writer, in his novel *Neuromancer*, though Gibson used the term for the first time in a short story, "Burning Chrome." As Gibson used it, the term refers to a place with no location. For example, when you use a telephone to call a friend in Seattle, it doesn't matter if you are physically located in San Antonio or Jersey City. Your voice sounds the same. Your voice is in cyberspace. Today, when you access a World Wide Web page, the computer files composing the page could be physically stored in a computer in the next room or in mainland China. Though the address notation may give you some clues, you cannot tell by looking at the page where the data creating it is stored.

Cyberspace, having no specific localities, is, paradoxically, infinite. It is a new frontier, ripe for exploration, settlement, and exploitation. It is whatever humans construct it to be. John Perry Barlow, co-founder of the Electronic Frontier Foundation, in "Desperados of the DataSphere," an article which describes his first encounters with hackers, says, "Cyberspace, in its present condition, has a lot in common with the nineteenth-century West. It is vast, unmapped, culturally and legally ambiguous . . . hard to get around in, and up for grabs . . . a perfect breeding ground for both outlaws and new ideas about liberty."

Once the domain of hard-core computer geeks, cyberspace is now more user friendly, open to anyone who can find a service provider and install software, or, alternatively, negotiate America Online's point-and-click menus. Once a place where attempts at commercial use resulted in flaming, a kind of cyberspace reverse-shunning, it is now a place where any company worth its stock exchange ticker number has a home-page storefront. And once largely controlled—or uncontrolled—by peer pressure, cyberspace is now a target of governments who are trying to exercise some control over this unruly frontier free zone.

But then, frontiers, by definition, are not stable, developed, and fully-constructed places. They are new, in-process, and sometimes dangerous places. Julian Dibbell, in the online-published essay "A Rape in Cyberspace," describes a virtual rape that occurred in a MUD (Multi-User Dungeon), a virtual reality setting for real-time chat, and the community's efforts to cope with the event. "Log On and Shoot," a *Newsweek* feature by Katie Hafner, details the virtual violence in online multiple-user games. Laura Miller, in "Women and Children First: Gender and the Settling of the Electronic Frontier," points out that while the first inhabitants of the cyberspace frontier, like the American West, were overwhelmingly male, cyberspace is not necessarily hostile to women. Indeed, since women can inhabit male characters and vice versa, cyberspace offers the potential for gender blurring which may put a different spin on gender discrimination.

Can real communities exist in cyberspace? The American West, like other frontiers, developed communities and through those communities became civilized. Is this happening in cyberspace? Thomas Barrett and Carol Wallace, in "Virtual Encounters" (a reading in Chapter 3), describe deep, sometimes enduring relationships that develop via e-mail, relationships which thrive in the atmosphere of no visual clues other than typed words on a computer screen. Barrett and Wallace suggest that the reason these friendships become so close, so fast, is the paradox that individuals using the Internet are able to communicate with each other while alone. Appearance, race, even gender may be unknown. Individuals *are* their words, judged only by those words and the virtual images they create. Is this a community? Some critics answer "yes" and some answer "no."

Cyberspace is our new frontier, for better or worse. If you have ventured into cyberspace, did you think of it as a frontier? As you read the following texts, be aware of your reactions to what the authors are saying about the nature of cyberspace. Does the unruly, under-construction character appeal to you, or do you find it unsettling? Are you interested in being a citizen or netizen of the new frontier?

———————————■———————————

DESPERADOS OF THE DATASPHERE

by John Perry Barlow

John Perry Barlow, not coincidentally, begins his essay "Desperados of the DataSphere" with a word picture of two cowboys sitting in front of a saloon. Cyberspace, like the wild west of the late nineteenth-century, is a haven for nonconformists, and some are a new kind of desperados called hackers. *In this essay, Barlow chronicles his interaction with two hackers, first on a cyberconference hosted by* Harper's *and then in person. He describes his emotional reaction to the young men, including puzzlement, anger, awe, disgust, and fatherly affection. While doing so, he raises some interesting questions about ethics and legal boundaries in cyberspace.*

Barlow is a sometimes rancher, sometimes songwriter (writing for the Grateful Dead*), self described "techno-hippie," and co-founder of the Electronic Frontier Foundation, an online organization which advocates for free speech and privacy on the Internet. He has published in* Wired, Time, Utne Reader, Mondo 2000, *and other major publications, and is often quoted in the national media. His Web home page address is http://www.eff.org/~barlow/.*

So me and my sidekick Howard, we was sitting out in front of the 40 Rod Saloon one evening when he all of a sudden says, "Lookee here. What do you reckon?" I look up and there's these two strangers riding into town. They're young and got kind of a restless, bored way about 'em. A person don't need both eyes to see they mean trouble . . .

Well, that wasn't quite how it went. Actually, Howard and I were floating blind as cave fish in the electronic barrens of the WELL, so the whole incident passed as words on a display screen:

> Howard: Interesting couple of newusers just signed on. One calls himself Acid and the other's Optik.
> Barlow: Hmmm. What are their real names?
> Howard: Check their finger files.*

And so I typed !finger acid. Several seconds later the WELL's Sequent computer sent the following message to my Macintosh in Wyoming:

> Login name: acid. In real life: Acid Phreak.

By this, I knew that the WELL had a new resident and that his corporeal analog was supposedly called Acid Phreak. Typing !finger optik yielded results of similar insufficiency, including the claim that someone, somewhere in the real world, was walking around calling himself Phiber Optik. I doubted it.

---

*Finger files provide identity information about participants in a forum or chat room.

However, associating these sparse data with the knowledge that the WELL was about to host a conference on computers and security rendered the conclusion that I had made my first sighting of genuine computer crackers. As the arrival of an outlaw was a major event to the settlements of the Old West, so was the appearance of crackers cause for stir on the WELL.

The WELL (or Whole Earth 'Lectronic Link) is an example of the latest thing in frontier villages, the computer bulletin board. In this kind of small town, Main Street is a central minicomputer to which (in the case of the WELL) as many as sixty-four microcomputers may be connected at one time by phone lines and little blinking boxes called modems.

In this silent world, all conversation is typed. To enter it, one forsakes both body and place and becomes a thing of words alone. You can see what your neighbors are saying (or recently said), but not what either they or their physical surroundings look like. Town meetings are continuous and discussions rage on everything from sexual kinks to depreciation schedules.

There are thousands of these nodes in the United States, ranging from PC clone hamlets of a few users to mainframe metros like CompuServe, with its 550,000 subscribers. They are used by corporations to transmit memoranda and spreadsheets, universities to disseminate research, and a multitude of factions, from apiarists to Zoroastrians, for purposes unique to each.

Whether by one telephonic tendril or millions, they are all connected to one another. Collectively, they form what their inhabitants call the Net. It extends across that immense region of electron states, microwaves, magnetic fields, light pulses and thought which sci-fi writer William Gibson named *cyberspace*.

Cyberspace, in its present condition, has a lot in common with the nineteenth-century West. It is vast, unmapped, culturally and legally ambiguous, verbally terse (unless you happen to be a court stenographer), hard to get around in, and up for grabs. Large institutions already claim to own the place, but most of the actual natives are solitary and independent, sometimes to the point of sociopathy. It is, of course, a perfect breeding ground for both outlaws and new ideas about liberty.

Recognizing this, *Harper's* magazine decided in December, 1989 to hold one of its periodic forums on the complex of issues surrounding computers, information, privacy, and electronic intrusion or "cracking." Appropriately, they convened their conference in cyberspace, using the WELL as the "site."

Harper's invited an odd lot of about forty participants. These included: Clifford Stoll, whose book *The Cuckoo's Egg* details his cunning efforts to nab a German cracker. John Draper or "Cap'n Crunch," the grand-daddy of crackers whose blue boxes got Wozniak and Jobs into consumer electronics. Stewart Brand and Kevin Kelly of *Whole Earth* fame. Steven Levy, who wrote the seminal *Hackers*. A retired Army colonel named Dave Hughes. Lee Felsenstein, who designed the Osborne computer and was once called the "Robespierre of computing." A UNIX wizard and former hacker named Jeff Poskanzer. There was also a score of aging techno-hippies, the crackers, and me.

What I was doing there was not precisely clear since I've spent most of my working years either pushing cows or song-mongering, but I at least brought to the situation a vivid knowledge of actual cow-towns, having lived in or around one most of my life.

That and a kind of innocence about both the technology and morality of cyberspace which was soon to pass into the confusion of knowledge.

At first, I was inclined toward sympathy with Acid 'n' Optik as well as their colleagues, Adelaide, Knight Lightning, Taran King, and Emmanuel. I've always been more comfortable with outlaws than Republicans, despite having more certain credentials in the latter camp.

But as the *Harper's* forum mushroomed into a boom-town of ASCII text (the participants typing 110,000 words in 10 days), I began to wonder. These kids were fractious, vulgar, immature, amoral, insulting, and too damned good at their work.

Worse, they inducted a number of former kids like myself into Middle Age. The long feared day had finally come when some gunsel would yank my beard and call me, too accurately, an old fart.

Under ideal circumstances, the blind gropings of bulletin board discourse force a kind of Noh drama stylization on human commerce. Intemperate responses, or "flames" as they are called, are common even among conference participants who understand one another, which, it became immediately clear, the cyberpunks and techno-hippies did not.

My own initial enthusiasm for the crackers wilted under a steady barrage of typed testosterone. I quickly remembered I didn't know much about who they were, what they did, or how they did it. I also remembered stories about crackers working in league with the Mob, ripping off credit card numbers and getting paid for them in (stolen) computer equipment.

And I remembered Kevin Mitnik. Mitnik, now twenty-five, recently served federal time for a variety of computer and telephone related crimes. Prior to incarceration, Mitnik was, by all accounts, a dangerous guy with a computer. He disrupted phone company operations and arbitrarily disconnected the phones of celebrities. Like the kid in *Wargames*, he broke into the North American Defense Command computer in Colorado Springs.

Unlike the kid in *Wargames*, he is reputed to have made a practice of destroying and altering data. There is even the (perhaps apocryphal) story that he altered the credit information of his probation officer and other enemies. Digital Equipment claimed that his depredations cost them more than $4 million in computer downtime and file rebuilding. Eventually, he was turned in by a friend who, after careful observation, had decided he was "a menace to society."

His spectre began to hang over the conference. After several days of strained diplomacy, the discussion settled into a moral debate on the ethics of security and went critical.

The techno-hippies were of the unanimous opinion that, in Dylan's words, one "must be honest to live outside the law." But these young strangers apparently lived by no code save those with which they unlocked forbidden regions of the Net.

They appeared to think that improperly secured systems deserved to be violated and, by extension, that unlocked houses ought to be robbed. This latter built particular heat in me since I refuse, on philosophical grounds, to lock my house.

Civility broke down. We began to see exchanges like:

Dave Hughes: Clifford Stoll said a wise thing that no one has commented on. That networks are built on trust. If they aren't, they should be.

Acid Phreak: Yeah. Sure. And we should use the 'honor system' as a first line of security against hack attempts.

Jef Poskanzer: This guy down the street from me sometimes leaves his back door unlocked. I told him about it once, but he still does it. If I had the chance to do it over, I would go in the back door, shoot him, and take all his money and consumer electronics. It's the only way to get through to him.

Acid Phreak: Jef Poskanker (Puss? Canker? yechh) Anyway, now when did you first start having these delusions where computer hacking was even *remotely* similar to murder?

Presented with such a terrifying amalgam of raw youth and apparent power, we fluttered like a flock of indignant Babbitts around the Status Quo, defending it heartily. One former hacker howled to the *Harper's* editor in charge of the forum, "Do you or do you not have names and addresses for these criminals?" Though they had committed no obvious crimes, he was ready to call the police.

They finally got to me with:

Acid: Whoever said they'd leave the door open to their house . . . where do you live? (the address) Leave it to me in mail if you like.

I had never encountered anyone so apparently unworthy of my trust as these little nihilists. They had me questioning a basic tenet, namely that the greatest security lies in vulnerability. I decided it was time to put that principal to the test . . .

Barlow: Acid. My house is at 372 North Franklin Street in Pinedale, Wyoming. If you're heading north on Franklin, you go about two blocks off the main drag before you run into hay meadow on the left. I've got the last house before the field. The computer is always on . . .

And is that really what you mean? Are you merely just the kind of little sneak that goes around looking for easy places to violate? You disappoint me, pal. For all your James Dean-On-Silicon rhetoric, you're not a cyberpunk. You're just a punk.

Acid Phreak: Mr. Barlow: Thank you for posting all I need to get your credit information and a whole lot more! Now, who is to blame? ME for getting it, or YOU for being such an idiot?! I think this should just about sum things up.

Barlow: Acid, if you've got a lesson to teach me, I hope it's not that it's idiotic to trust one's fellow man. Life on those terms would be endless and brutal. I'd try to tell you something about conscience, but I'd sound like Father O'Flannigan trying to reform the punk that's about to gutshoot him. For no more reason that to watch him die. But actually, if you take it upon yourself to destroy my credit, you might do me a favor. I've been looking for something to put the brakes on my burgeoning materialism.

I spent a day wondering whether I was dealing with another Kevin Mitnik before the other shoe dropped:

> Barlow: . . . With crackers like Acid and Optik, the issue is less intelligence than alienation. Trade their modems for skateboards and only a slight conceptual shift would occur.
> Optik: You have some pair of balls comparing my talent with that of a skateboarder. Hmmm . . . This was indeed boring, but nonetheless:

At which point he downloaded my credit history.

Optik had hacked the core of TRW, an institution which has made my business (and yours) their business, extracting from it an abbreviated (and incorrect) version of my personal financial life. With this came the implication that he and Acid could and would revise it to my disadvantage if I didn't back off.

I have since learned that while getting someone's TRW file is fairly trivial, changing it is not. But at that time, my assessment of the crackers' black skills was one of superstitious awe. They were digital brujos about to zombify my economic soul.

To a middle-class American, one's credit rating has become nearly identical to his freedom. It now appeared that I was dealing with someone who had both the means and desire to hoodoo mine, leaving me trapped in a life of wrinkled bills and money order queues. Never again would I call the Sharper Image on a whim.

I've been in redneck bars wearing shoulder-length curls, police custody while on acid, and Harlem after midnight, but no one has ever put the spook in me quite as Phiber Optik did at that moment. I realized that we had problems which exceeded the human conductivity of the WELL's bandwidth. If someone were about to paralyze me with a spell, I wanted a more visceral sense of him than could fit through a modem.

I e-mailed him asking him to give me a phone call. I told him I wouldn't insult his skills by giving him my phone number and, with the assurance conveyed by that challenge, I settled back and waited for the phone to ring. Which, directly, it did.

In this conversation and the others that followed I encountered an intelligent, civilized, and surprisingly principled kid of eighteen who sounded, and continues to sound, as though there's little harm in him to man or data. His cracking impulses seemed purely exploratory, and I've begun to wonder if we wouldn't also regard spelunkers as desperate criminals if AT&T owned all the caves.

The terrifying poses which Optik and Acid had been striking on screen were a media-amplified example of a human adaptation I'd seen before: One becomes as he is beheld. They were simply living up to what they thought we, and, more particularly, the editors of *Harper's*, expected of them. Like the televised tears of disaster victims, their snarls adapted easily to mass distribution.

Months later, *Harper's* took Optik, Acid and me to dinner at a Manhattan restaurant which, though very fancy, was appropriately Chinese. Acid and

Optik, as material beings, were well-scrubbed and fashionably clad. They looked to be dangerous as ducks. But, as *Harper's* and the rest of the media have discovered to their delight, the boys had developed distinctly showier personae for their rambles through the howling wilderness of cyberspace. Glittering with spikes of binary chrome, they strode past the kleig lights and into the digital distance. There they would be outlaws. It was only a matter of time before they started to believe themselves as bad as they sounded. And no time at all before everyone else did.

In this, they were like another kid named Billy, many of whose feral deeds in the pre-civilized West were encouraged by the same dime novelist who chronicled them. And like Tom Horn, they seemed to have some doubt as to which side of the law they were on. Acid even expressed an ambition to work for the government someday, nabbing "terrorists and code abusers."

There is also a frontier ambiguity to the "crimes" the crackers commit. They are not exactly stealing VCR's. Copying a text file from TRW doesn't deprive its owner of anything except informational exclusivity. (Though it may be said that information has monetary value only in proportion to its containment.)

There was no question that they were making unauthorized use of data channels. The night I met them, they left our restaurant table and disappeared into the phone booth for a long time. I didn't see them marshalling quarters before they went.

And, as I became less their adversary and more their scoutmaster, I began to get "conference calls" in which six or eight of them would crack pay phones all over New York and simultaneously land on my line in Wyoming. These deft maneuvers made me think of sky-diving stunts where large groups convene geometrically in free fall. In this case, the risk was largely legal.

Their other favorite risky business is the time-honored adolescent sport of trespassing. They insist on going where they don't belong. But then teenage boys have been proceeding uninvited since the dawn of human puberty. It seems hard-wired. The only innovation in this new form of the forbidden zone is the means of getting in it.

In fact, like Kevin Mitnik, I broke into NORAD when I was seventeen. A friend and I left a nearby "woodsie" (as rustic adolescent drunks were called in Colorado) and tried to get inside the Cheyenne Mountain. The chrome-helmeted Air Force MP's held us for about two hours before letting us go. They weren't much older than us and knew exactly our level of national security threat. Had we come cloaked in electronic mystery, their alert status certainly would have been higher.

Whence rises much of the anxiety. Everything is so ill-defined. How can you guess what lies in their hearts when you can't see their eyes?

How can one be sure that, like Mitnik, they won't cross the line from trespassing into another adolescent pastime, vandalism? And how can you be sure they pose no threat when you don't know what a threat might be?

And for the crackers some thrill is derived from the metamorphic vagueness of the laws themselves. On the Net, their effects are unpredictable. One never knows when they'll bite.

This is because most of the statutes invoked against the crackers were designed in a very different world from the one they explore. For example, can unauthorized electronic access be regarded as the ethical equivalent of old-fashioned trespass? Like open range, the property boundaries of cyberspace are hard to stake and harder still to defend.

Is transmission through an otherwise unused data channel really theft? Is the trackless passage of a mind through TRW's mainframe the same as the passage of a pickup through my Back 40? What is a place if cyberspace is everywhere? What are data and what is free speech? How does one treat property which has no physical form and can be infinitely reproduced? Is a computer the same as a printing press? Can the history of my business affairs properly belong to someone else? Can anyone morally claim to own knowledge itself?

If such questions were hard to answer precisely, there are those who are ready to try. Based on their experience in the Virtual World, they were about as qualified to enforce its mores as I am to write the Law of the Sea. But if they lacked technical sophistication, they brought to this task their usual conviction. And, of course, badges and guns.

EXPLORING THE READING

1. John Perry Barlow attempts to *finger* the newcomers to the WELL, Acid and Optik, to find out who they are, but doesn't receive any useful information. This makes Barlow suspect they are hackers. Do you know that to finger is to issue a computer command to get information about a nickname? Is it a good idea to be able to ascertain participants' identities when they have chosen to participate under aliases? Why or why not?

2. Barlow says cyberspace is "a perfect breeding ground for both outlaws and new ideas about liberty." In your small group, discuss what you think he means by this. Does your group agree? Why or why not?

3. When Barlow felt overwhelmed by Acid's ability to download Barlow's credit history, he shifted the interaction out of cyberspace into "real" contact via the telephone and in person. Why did he do this? What does it say about his attitude toward cyberspace?

4. What was Barlow's final conclusion about the hackers Acid and Optik? Does he consider them criminals? What do you think about them?

LOG ON AND SHOOT

by Katie Hafner

Hard-core gamers play shoot-'em-up real time on the Net in games like Duke Nukem 3d in which players gun each other down in post-apocalyptic Los Angeles virtual reality setting. Players, according to Katie Hafner's Newsweek *feature, "Log On and Shoot," often play for hours, sometimes all night. Of course, video games have been around for years. What is different about these games is that multiple players from anywhere around the world play together, not alone or with friends in the same room. Players give themselves names like DaisyDuke and Javamamma and come to know each other in what is a social as well as gaming environment. Hafner is, with John Markoff, author of* Cyberpunk: Outlaws and Hackers on the Computer Frontier *and, with Matthew Lyon, of* Where Wizards Stay Up Late: The Origins of the Internet.

Wendy Metzler, a twenty-three-year-old homemaker in Benicia, California, was a computer-game widow. Her husband was a "beta tester"—or trial customer—for a company called the Total Entertainment Network (TEN) and had become addicted to a game called Duke Nukem 3D. For a month, he played it almost every night until morning. "I told him I was tired of sitting alone in bed," she says. Finally, two months ago, he persuaded Wendy to try logging on. Did she like it? "I haven't got off the thing yet," she whispers, sounding a bit embarrassed.

Now, once dinner is over and her five-year-old daughter is in bed, Wendy sits down to her PC with enough Ho Ho's and chips to last her till dawn. Why the fascination? For Metzler, it's not just that Duke Nukem 3D, a gruesome shoot-'em-up where players navigate post-apocalyptic Los Angeles hunting down aliens, is fun. It's also that TEN links her with people through the Internet; that means Metzler (a.k.a. DaisyDuke) can spend her nights meeting friends and new opponents. With screen names like Chen, Javamamma and HellKnight, her playmates challenge opponents who have logged in from places like Beaumont, Texas, and Short Hills, N.J. "Everyone knows me," she says.

Since coming online in recent months TEN and its chief rivals (Mpath Interactive, Engage and Dwango) have been introducing hard-core gamers to something totally new. Until recently, game fanatics played shoot-'em-ups either alone on a PC or head to head with friends on TV consoles made by the likes of Nintendo and Sony. Now gaming companies, and the major online services, are marrying the two by creating networks that allow trigger-happy users to play against human opponents who live down the street—or as far away as the global Internet reaches. Analysts estimate that "multiplayer online gaming" will be a $1 billion industry by the year 2000. Americans spent more than $6 billion on computer games bought off store shelves last year, according to technology-research firm Dataquest.

Companies from Sega to CompuServe are betting that you will pay even more money to play these games online—either through the Internet or on private networks. The networks will most likely charge by the minute, though some are toying with flat-rate pricing. Whatever the billing scheme, executives are confident. "This," says Jack Heistand, CEO of TEN, "is going to be huge."

That's big talk for a business that by most accounts is unproven. A few well-funded start-ups are testing the waters by offering online versions of the most popular computer games—Air Warrior, an air combat game; DOOM, the highly addictive 3-D world of gore and destruction; and SimCity, the best-selling simulation game. Their hope is that the titles themselves will lure audiences to try this new way to play them. TEN, scheduled to debut officially in early September, will allow hundreds of people to play simultaneously. The Cupertino, California-based Mpath Interactive hopes to launch at the same time.

The commercial online services are right in step. Click on America Online's games channel and you'll find connections to forty-six games in eight different categories. In 1995 Prodigy had no games but will have more than a dozen by year's end. CompuServe recently revamped an old games area, now called New Game City. It offers a variety of fast-action fun. And earlier this summer, Microsoft acquired Electric Gravity Inc., already known on the Net for its Internet Gaming Zone, a multi-player Web site devoted to classic board and card games.

People have played interactive games over the Internet for years, but the choices were largely limited to the slow-moving, text-based world of MUDs (multiuser dungeons) or turn-based games like chess. The trick now is to create "social worlds" rich in graphics for games of all kinds, featuring chat spaces where players can boast to one another, commiserate over a defeat or just pass the time of day. Mpath allows players with microphones on their computers to talk to each other—convenient for yelling "DIE!" while obliterating an opponent.

Moving these graphic-rich "twitch" games to the Internet isn't easy. The biggest obstacle to playing fast-action games over the Net is "latency"—the amount of time between, say, when you push the fire button on your keyboard and when the bullet shows up on your opponents' screens. Most twitch games require split-second responses, and that's difficult to achieve with consistency over the Internet, a collection of networks whose performance is impossible to predict. The Internet-based services have each concocted strategies—software "fixes," partnerships, games customized for Net play—to combat the latency problem. TEN, for example, won't let users play fast-action games if its network software detects that their connections are bad.

The beta tests haven't inspired confidence: games often freeze in midaction. Some services, such as AOL, CompuServe, Dwango and the forthcoming Wireplay network by MCI, will avoid the problem entirely by using private, "proprietary" networks where regular Internet traffic doesn't slow you down. Despite technical glitches, online gaming already appears to be the stuff of addiction. Even calmer diversions such as hearts and bridge are turning into virtual parties. On Prodigy, for example, checkers has a separate chat screen next to the board. The game itself is often overshadowed by the conversation that starts up. A game that might ordinarily take ten minutes stretches to an hour. "We're learning that something as simple as checkers is more than checkers," says Josh Grotstein, Prodigy's senior vice president of content. "What it turns out to be is like sitting on the porch talking to someone."

Which is exactly what the emerging gaming networks have in mind. "The fact that it's a social environment is what makes it the killer app of the online medium," says Lawrence Schick, AOL's general manager for games. Virgin Interactive's Subspace, a Net-based multiplayer rendition of Asteroids now in beta test, has inspired a unique social order, complete with codes of conduct, a hierarchy based on scores and nightly tournaments of 200 players where that hierarchy is constantly tested. One player, seventeen-year-old Kevin Jarrett of Granbury, Texas, wakes up at 7 A.M. every day to hang out with friends he originally met in an Internet Relay Chat channel. "It was a chance to blow them up," he says. "It's become a community."

For now, online gaming is a niche market catering to a devoted clientele. As beta testers, gamers can go on fifteen-hour binges, and, if they're dialing locally into the game service, it's all free. The true test will come when the gaming services go fully commercial. Metzler doesn't plan to stop playing once TEN starts billing her. Anyway, she says, "it's my husband's credit card."

EXPLORING THE READING

1. Have you ever played virtual reality games on the Internet or on one of the commercial providers such as America Online? Or have you played video games? In your small group, discuss the appeal of these games. Why do people play for hours and hours?

2. Do you see any connection between these violent virtual reality games and the new frontier nature of the Internet? Freewrite for five minutes about connections.

3. In what ways do the virtual reality games fit into the frontier motif discussed in the chapter opener and in "Desperados of the DataSphere"?

4. Katie Hafner begins her feature with a narrative about a husband and then a wife who became addicted to one of these games. Why do you think she began her text that way? What does it achieve?

ALT.CYBERPUNK FREQUENTLY ASKED QUESTIONS LIST

edited by Frank (previously edited by Andy Hawks, Tim Oerting, and Erich Schneider)

Cyberpunk is both a literary movement and a subculture, according to the alt.cyberpunk FAQ posted in the alt.cyberpunk Usenet Newsgroup and on the World Wide Web at http://www.knarf.demon.co.uk/alt-cp.htm. The literary movement was born in Isaac Azimov's Science Fiction Magazine in the 1980s and includes science fiction authors like Tom Maddox, Bruce Sterling, and William Gibson. The subculture is populated by individuals who identify with the techno-obsessed, marginalized characters in cyberpunk literature. They are variously called Hackers, Crackers, and Phreaks, terms defined in the FAQ, which also cites online resources for would-be cyberpunks.

Frank, who volunteers his time to edit the FAQ, prefers not to give his last name because he likes "the abandonment and anonymity the Net gives. In the history of human interaction, there has never before been a medium whereby people can discuss topics so freely without the weight of prejudice and sociological dismissal." He is a thirty-two-year-old male living in the United Kingdom and is a regional sales manager for a multi-national company specializing in power systems. His hobbies, apart from the obvious computer-based interests, include "football (please don't call it soccer), rugby, cricket, climbing, squash, chess, music and, obviously, literature."

Maintained by Frank (frank@knarf.demon.co.uk). Last update; 01 January 1998. Posted every two weeks to alt.cyberpunk.

This is Version 4.0 of the alt.cyberpunk FAQ. Although previous FAQs have not been allocated version numbers, due the number of people now involved, I've taken the liberty to do so. Previous maintainers/editors and version numbers are given below:

- Version 3: Erich Schneider
- Version 2: Tim Oerting
- Version 1: Andy Hawks

I would also like to recognize and express my thanks to Jer and Stack for all their help and assistance in compiling this version of the FAQ.

This FAQ, as with Cyberpunk literature, is a living document. If you have any comments, criticisms, additions, questions please send them to me at frank@knarf.demon.co.uk. (I especially welcome reports of "broken links," either in the ASCII or HTML versions.) Send to that address as well if you would like the latest version of this document.

The vast number of the "answers" here should be prefixed with an "in my opinion." It would be ridiculous for me to claim to be an ultimate Cyberpunk authority.

1. WHAT IS CYBERPUNK, THE LITERARY MOVEMENT?

Gardner Dozois, one of the editors of *Isaac Asimov's Science Fiction Magazine* during the early '80s, is generally acknowledged as the first person to popularize the term "Cyberpunk," when describing a body of literature. Dozois doesn't claim to have coined the term; he says he picked it up "on the street somewhere."

It is probably no coincidence that Bruce Bethke wrote a short story titled "Cyberpunk" in 1980 and submitted it Asimov's mag, when Dozois may have been doing first readings, and got it published in *Amazing* in 1983, when Dozois was editor of *1983 Year's Best Science Fiction* and would be expected to be reading the major SF magazines. But as Bethke says, "who gives a rat's ass, anyway?!". (Bethke is not really a Cyberpunk author; in mid-1995 he published *Headcrash*, which he calls "a cybernetically aware comedy." Thanks to Bruce for his help on this issue.)

Before its christening the "Cyberpunk movement," known to its members as "The Movement," had existed for quite some time, centred around Bruce Sterling's samizdat, *Cheap Truth*. Authors like Sterling, Rucker and Shirley submitted articles pseudonymously to this newsletter, hyping the works of people in the group and vigorously attacking the "SF mainstream." This helped form the core "movement consciousness." (The run of *Cheap Truth* is available by anonymous FTP in the directory ftp.io.com/pub/usr/shiva/SMOF-BBS/cheap.truth.)

Cyberpunk literature, in general, deals with marginalized people in technologically-enhanced cultural "systems." In Cyberpunk stories' settings, there is usually a "system" which dominates the lives of most "ordinary" people, be it an oppressive government, a group of large, paternalistic corporations or a fundamentalist religion. These systems are enhanced by certain technologies, particularly "information technology" (computers, the mass media), making the system better at keeping those within it, inside it. Often this technological system extends into its human "components" as well, via brain implants, prosthetic limbs, cloned or genetically engineered organs, etc. Humans themselves become part of "the Machine." This is the "cyber" aspect of Cyberpunk. However, in any cultural system, there are always those who live on its margins, on "the Edge": criminals, outcasts, visionaries or those who simply want freedom for its own sake. Cyberpunk literature focuses on these people, and often on how they turn the system's technological tools to their own ends. This is the "punk" aspect of Cyberpunk.

The best Cyberpunk works are distinguished from previous works with similar themes, by a certain style. The setting is urban, the mood is dark and pessimistic. Concepts are thrown at the reader without explanation, much like new developments are thrown at us in our everyday lives. There is often a sense of moral ambiguity; simply fighting "the system" (to topple it, or just to stay alive) does not make the main characters "heroes" or "good" in the traditional sense.

2. WHAT IS CYBERPUNK, THE SUBCULTURE?

Spurred on by Cyberpunk literature in the mid-1980s, certain groups of people started referring to themselves as Cyberpunk, because they correctly noticed the seeds of the fictional "techno-system" in Western society today, and because they identified with the marginalized characters in Cyberpunk stories. Within the last few years, the mass media has caught on to this, spontaneously dubbing certain people and groups "Cyberpunk."

Specific subgroups which are identified with Cyberpunk are: Hackers, Crackers, Phreaks and Cypher-punks:

- "Hackers" are the "wizards" of the computer community; people with a deep understanding of how their computers work, and can do things with them that seem "magical."

- "Crackers" are the real-world analogues of the "console cowboys" of Cyberpunk fiction; they break into other people's computer systems, without their permission, for illicit gain or simply for the pleasure of exercising their skill.

- "Phreaks" are those who do a similar thing with the telephone system, coming up with ways to circumvent phone companies' calling charges and doing clever things with the phone network.

- "Cypher-punks": These people think a good way to bollocks "The System" is through cryptography and cryptosystems. They believe widespread use of extremely hard-to-break coding schemes will create "regions of privacy" that "The System" cannot invade.

Some other groups which are associated with Cyberpunk are:

- "Transhuman" are actively seeking to become "Posthuman." This involves learning about and making use of new technologies that can potentially increase their capacities and life expectancy. They follow Transhumanism, a set of "philosophies of life" (such as the Extropian philosophy) that seek the continuation and acceleration of the evolution of intelligent life beyond its currently human form and limits by means of science and technology, guided by life-promoting principles and values, while avoiding religion and dogma.

- "Extropian" are dedicated to the opposition of Entropy. Politically, extropians are close kin to the libertarians, including some anarchists, some classical liberals, and even a political neoconservative or two. But many extropians have no interest in politics at all, and many are actively anti-political. Extropians have a principle called "spontaneous order," but politics is by no means the only domain in which they apply it.

So are Cyberpunks any or all of the above, well not really. One person's "Cyberpunk" is another's obnoxious teenager with some technical skill thrown in, a self-designated Cyberpunk looking for the latest trend to identify with or yet another mass media label used as a marketing ploy. Whilst most Cyberpunks understand, and some have a good working knowledge of the above definitions, these pursuits are seen as a means, rather than an end. The "end" of course depends upon your own personal goals.

There are those who claim that "Cyberpunk" is indefinable, which in some sense it is. Moreover, most regulars on alt.cp are uncomfortable about even implying that there actually are any cyberpunks. The point being that we all live in a cyberpunk society today, after all Gisbon himself said, "The future has arrived; it's just not evenly distributed."

Therefore, by definition most some people are already Cyberpunks. That is why when some post on alt.cp claiming that "I am a cyberpunk" don't get flamed to death, just ignored, whereas statements such as "survival through technological superiority" get flamed from here to eternity and back.

In the end, anybody insisting they are a Cyberpunk will probably get flamed in alt.cyberpunk. Think of it as a trial by ordeal. John Shirley (noted cyberpunk author) didn't make it through the entrance exam. Chairman Bruce might just hack it, but AFAIK* he's never come visiting.

3. WHAT IS CYBERSPACE?

To my knowledge, the term "Cyberspace" was first used by William Gibson in his story "Burning Chrome." That work first describes users using devices called "cyberdecks" to override their normal sensory organs, presenting them with a full-sensory interface to the world computer network. When doing so, said users are "in cyberspace." (The concept had appeared prior to Gibson, most notably in Vernor Vinge's story "True Names.") "Cyberspace" is thus the metaphorical "place" where one "is" when accessing the world computer net.

Even though Gibson's vision of how cyberspace is in some sense, surreal, it has stimulated many in the computing community. The word "cyberspace" is commonly used in the "mainstream world" with reference to the emergent worldwide computer network (especially the Internet). Also, some researchers in the "virtual reality" arena of computer science are trying to implement something like Gibson's Matrix into a more general computer-generated environment, even if its purpose is not "accessing the net."

4. CYBERPUNK LITERATURE

The following is intended to be a short list of the best in-print Cyberpunk works. Note that quite a few works written before 1980 have been retroactively labelled "Cyberpunk" due to stylistic similarities, e.g. Pynchon's *Gravity's Rainbow*, or similar themes such as Brunner's *The Shockwave Rider* or Delany's *Nova*.

---

*AFAIK (As Far As I Know)

- William Gibson's *Neuromancer*, about a cracker operating in cyber-space, a cybernetically enhanced bodyguard/mercenary, and a pair of mysterious AIs, got the ball rolling as far as Cyberpunk is concerned. It won the Hugo, Nebula, P. K. Dick, Seiun, and Ditmar awards, something no other SF work has done.

  Gibson wrote two sequels in the same setting, *Count Zero* and *Mona Lisa Overdrive*. Gibson also has a collection of short stories, *Burning Chrome*, which contains three stories in Neuromancer's setting, as well as several others, such as the excellent "The Winter Market" and "Dogfight."

  Gibson's two most recent works are *Virtual Light* and *Idoru*; they share a setting (San Francisco and Tokyo, respectively, of the near future) and a few characters, but are otherwise independent. Compared to his first trilogy, the technology they posit is less advanced in some ways and they are more theme-driven than plot-driven, but they deal with many of the same concerns as other cyberpunk works. ("Idoru" is a Japanese borrowing of the English "idol," and refers to a media-company-manufactured pop-music star, a "virtual" example of which plays a prominent role in Idoru.

- Bruce Sterling's anthology *Crystal Express* contains all of the "Shaper/Mechanist" short stories about the future humanity and "post-humanity." Those short stories are also available with *Schismatrix*, a Shaper/Mechanist novel, in the combined volume *Schismatrix Plus*. Also to be found in *Crystal Express* is "Green Days in Brunei," a story which shares the setting of Sterling's novel *Islands in the Net*. Both are near-future extrapolations in worlds very similar to our own. Sterling also has another collection in print, *Globalhead*.

  Sterling edited *Mirrorshades: A Cyberpunk Anthology*, which contains stories by many authors; some are questionably cyberpunk, but it has some real gems ("Mozart in Mirrorshades" being one).

  Sterling's latest novel is *Holy Fire*, set in a "gerontocratic" late twenty-first century Earth dominated by the "medical-industrial complex," and focuses on a group of young European artists, hackers, and intellectuals determined to go their own way in a world dominated by elderly wealth.

- Gibson and Sterling collaboratively wrote *The Difference Engine*, a novel called "steampunk" by some; it deals with many cyberpunk themes by using an alternate nineteenth-century Britain where Babbage's mechanical computer technology has been fully developed.

- *Snow Crash*, by Neal Stephenson, carries cyberpunk to a humorous extreme; what else can one say about a work where the Mafia delivers pizza and the main character's name is "Hiro Protagonist"?

- Larry McCaffrey edited an anthology, *Storming the Reality Studio*, which has snippets of many cyberpunk works, as well as critical articles about cyberpunk, and a fairly good bibliography. Other works of criticism are Bukatman's *Terminal Identity* and Slusser and Shippey's *Fiction 2000: Cyberpunk and the Future of Narrative*.

Some other good cyberpunk works include:

- Walter Jon Williams, *Hardwired*: a smuggler who pilots a hovertank decides to take on the Orbital Corporations that control his world.
- Walter Jon Williams, *Voice of the Whirlwind*: a corporate soldier's clone tries to discover what happened to his "original copy."
- Greg Bear, *Blood Music*: a genetic engineer "uplifts" some of his own blood cells to human-level intelligence, with radical consequences.
- Pat Cadigan, *Synners*: hackers and other misfits pursue a deadly new "virus" when direct brain interfaces first appear in near-future LA.
- Jeff Noon, *Vurt*: a *Clockwork Orange*-esque tale in an England where virtual reality is truly the opiate of the masses.

Some good out-of-print works to look for are Cadigan's *Mindplayers*, Michael Swanwick's *Vacuum Flowers*, Daniel Keyes Moran's *The Long Run*, and Vernor Vinge's short story "True Names."

5. MAGAZINES ABOUT CYBERPUNK AND RELATED TOPICS

Some magazines which are popular among Cyberpunk fans are:

Mondo 2000
PO Box 10171
Berkeley, CA 94709-0171
Voice (510)845-9018, Fax (510)649-9630
Editorials: editor@mondo2000.com, Subscriptions: subscriptions@mondo 2000.com, Advertising: advertising@mondo2000.com
HTTP site: http://www.mondo2000.com/

Many Cyberpunk fans have an uneasy relationship with *Mondo 2000*, their esteem for it varies according to the amount of technical content and affected hipness in the articles. Nonetheless, if anything could claim to be the Cyberpunk "magazine of record," this is it. With the departure of many of those providing creative impetus (notably, R. U. Sirius), its days may be numbered.

bOING-bOING
11288 Ventura Boulevard #818
Studio City, CA 91604
Voice (310)854-5747, Fax (310)289-4922
mark@well.com
HTTP site: http://www.well.com/user/mark/*

bOING-bOING's status is uncertain; most of its writers now work for *Wired*, it has ceased newsstand distribution, and no longer offers subscriptions. However, if one can get a copy, it's worth looking at.

---

*This site has recently moved to http://members.tripod.com/~boing-boing/index.html

Wired
P.O. Box 191826
San Francisco, CA 94119
Voice (415)904-0660, Fax (415)904-0669, Credit-card subscriptions: 1-800-SO-WIRED (1-800-769-4733)
Information: info@wired.com, Subscriptions: subscriptions@wired.com
HTTP site: http://www.hotwired.com

The magazine which, through aggressive positioning, has managed to become the "magazine of record" for modern techno-aware culture. It's aimed more at technically oriented professionals with disposable income, but many cyberpunk fans like the articles on network- and future-related topics.

SF EYE
P.O. Box 18539
Asheville, NC 28814
HTTP site: http://www.empathy.com/eyeball

Described by some as the "house organ of the cyberpunk movement," founded by Stephen P. Brown at the urging of his friends Gibson, Shirley, and Sterling. Published semi-annually and contains a regular column by Sterling.

Phrack
603 W. 13th #1A-278
Austin, TX 78701
Information: phrack@well.com, FTP site: ftp.fc.net.com:/pub/phrack
HTTP site: http://www.phrack.com

2600 Magazine
Subscription correspondence:
   2600 Subscription Dept.
   P.O. Box 752
   Middle Island, NY, 11953-0752
Letters/Article Submissions:
   2600 Editorial Dept.
   P.O. Box 99
   Middle Island, NY, 11953-0099
Information: 2600@well.com, FTP site: ftp.2600.com:/pub
HTTP site: http://www.2600.com

Two mainstays of the computer underground. *Phrack* deals more with people and goings-on in the community, while *2600* focuses on technical information.

6. CYBERPUNK IN THE VISUAL MEDIA (MOVIES AND TV).

TV gave us the late, lamented *Max Headroom*, which featured oodles of cyberpunk concepts. The Bravo cable network and the Sci-Fi Channel are rerunning the few episodes that were made. TV also gave us the somewhat bloated *Wild Palms,* with "cyberspace," evil corporations, and a cameo by William Gibson.

Also shown on the Sci-Fi Channel is *TekWar,* a series based on William Shatner's "Tek" novels, which evolved from a set of TV movies based on those novels. While possessing some traditionally cyberpunk elements and extended "cyberspace runs," they (or at least the TV movies) tend to boil down to good guys vs. bad guys cop stories. (*TekLords* features a central plot element that those who have read *Snow Crash* will recognize.)

Blade Runner, based loosely on Philip K. Dick's novel *Do Androids Dream of Electric Sheep?* is considered the archetypical cyberpunk movie. (Gibson has said that the visuals in *Blade Runner* match his vision of the urban future in *Neuromancer.*) Few other movies have matched it; some that are considered cyberpunk or marginally so are *Alien* and its sequels, *Freejack, The Lawnmower Man, Until The End Of The World,* the "Terminator" movies, *Total Recall, Strange Days,* and *Brainstorm.*

Cyberpunk stories can also be found in Japanese anime films, including the *Bubblegum Crisis* series and *Ghost in the Shell.*

There is an hourlong documentary called "Cyberpunk" available on video from Mystic Fire Video. It features some interview-style conversation with Gibson, is generally low-budget, and the consensus opinion on the net is that it isn't really worth anyone's time. Gibson is apparently embarrassed by it.

Regarding films based on Gibson stories: At one point a fly-by-night operation called "Cabana Boys Productions" had the rights to *Neuromancer;* this is why the front of the *Neuromancer* computer game's box claims it is "soon to be a motion picture from Cabana Boys." The rights have since reverted to Gibson, who is sitting on them at the moment.

Gibson's short story "Johnny Mnemonic" was made into a big-budget full-length motion picture. Gibson himself wrote the screenplay and was a close consultant to the director; the result "has his blessing," so to speak. As might be expected, there are many additions to the short story as well as outright differences. The film contains elements not only from the original story, but also from *Neuromancer* and *Virtual Light;* there is much more violent action, and the ending is more upbeat. Very significantly, Molly does not appear in the film; her place is taken by a character named "Jane" (who has no inset eyeglasses or retractable claws) due to issues surrounding use of the Molly character in any future *Neuromancer* production. (The film was not a critical or box-office success in the United States, which Gibson has partly blamed on the post-production editing; he claims the longer Japanese release is the better one.)

"The Gernsback Continuum" was adapted into a short (fifteen minute) film in Britain; it has been shown on some European TV networks, but I don't know if it's available in the United States. Rumors also abound that "New Rose Hotel" will be brought to the big screen by various directors. Other rumors claim that *Count Zero* will be made into a film titled *The Zen Differential.*

William Gibson wrote one of the many scripts for *Alien 3*. According to him, only one detail from his script made its way to the actual film: the bar codes visible on the backs of the prisoners' shaved heads. A synopsis of Gibson's script can be found in part 3 of the Alien Movies FAQ list. Alternatively, try the Internet Movies Database http://us.imdb.org.

8. CYBERPUNK MUSIC/DRESS/AFTERSHAVE

There are a lot of posts to alt.cyberpunk asking what Cyberpunks like, do, wear, etc. These posts are seen as inane due to the reason they are asked, i.e., "Cyberpunk sounds cool; how can I become one?" Cyberpunk is not a fashion statement, therefore little of this FAQ is taken up with such matters.

In late 1993, Billy Idol released an album called "Cyberpunk," which garnered some media attention; it seems to have been a commercial and critical flop. Billy made some token appearances on the net in alt.cyberpunk and on the WELL, but his public interest in the area seems to have waned. No matter how sincere his intentions might have been, scorn and charges of commercialization have been heaped upon him in this and other forums.

10. WHAT IS "PGP"?

"PGP" is short for "Pretty Good Privacy," a public-key cryptosystem that is the mainstay of the Cypherpunk movement. However, before you rush off and obtain a copy of PGP, I think it may be of useful to explain why it should be used, and the best reason I've heard comes from the guy who developed it, Phil Zimmerman.

WHY USE PGP?   "It's personal. It's private. And it's no one's business but yours. You may be planning a political campaign, discussing your taxes, or having an illicit affair. Or you may be doing something that you feel shouldn't be illegal, but is. Whatever it is, you don't want your private electronic mail (e-mail) or confidential documents read by anyone else. There's nothing wrong with asserting your privacy. Privacy is as apple pie as the Constitution.

Perhaps you think your e-mail is legitimate enough that encryption is unwarranted. If you really are a law-abiding citizen with nothing to hide, then why don't you always send your paper mail on postcards? Why not submit to drug testing on demand? Why require a warrant for police searches of your house? Are you trying to hide something? You must be a subversive or a drug dealer if you hide your mail inside envelopes. Or maybe a paranoid nut. Do law-abiding citizens have any need to encrypt their e-mail?

What if everyone believed that law-abiding citizens should use postcards for their mail? If some brave soul tried to assert his privacy by using an envelope for his mail, it would draw suspicion. Perhaps the authorities would open his mail to see what he's hiding. Fortunately, we don't live in that kind of world, because everyone protects most of their mail with envelopes. So no one draws suspicion by asserting their privacy with an envelope. There's safety in numbers. Analogously, it would be nice if everyone routinely used encryption for all their e-mail, innocent or not, so that no one drew suspicion by asserting their e-mail privacy with encryption. Think of it as a form of solidarity."

A PGP site can be found at: http://www.pgp.net/pgpnet/. There's also an excellent resource on anonymous remailers at http://www.cs.berkeley.edu/~raph/remailer-list.html. Alternatively, there are two newsgroups dealing with PGP and encryption, namely alt.cypherpunk and comp.security.pgp.

12. OTHER ONLINE RESOURCES

USENET

- Usenet FAQs repository http://rtfm.mit.edu/pub/usenet
- Usenet Database (Dejanews) http://www.dejanews.co.uk/

SF AND CYBERPUNK LITERATURE

- Rutgers SF archive, http://sflovers.rudgers.edu/web/SFRG
- William Gibson bibliography, http://www.slip.information/~page/gibson/biblio.htm
- Daniel Keys Moran, http://www.kithrup.com/dkm
- Rudy Rucker's home page, http://www.mathcs.sjsu.edu/faculty/rucker/rucker.html
- John Shirley information, http//www.darkecho.com/JohnShirley.html
- Bruce Sterling information, http://oak.ziker.net/bruces
- Jason Harrison's *Directory of Cyberpunk Fiction*, http://www.cs.ubc.ca/spider/harrison

HACKERS AND PHREAKS

- Survival Research Labs, that incomparable group of artists and hardware hackers, has an HTTP site at http://www.srl.org. Another SRL site can be found at http://www.construct.net/projects/srl.
- Many files of relevance to the real-life "computer underground" and the hacking/phreaking communities can be found in one of the *Computer Underground Digest* sites. One of these is at ftp://etext.archive.umich.edu:/pub/CuD and includes a complete set of issues of *Phrack* magazine. The *Digest* itself has an HTTP site at http://sun.soci.niu.edu/~cudigest; new issues are posted to the Usenet newsgroup comp.society.cu-digest. *Phrack* issues can also be had via *Phrack's* HTTP site at http:www.phrack.com.

EXPLORING THE READING

1. In your small group, pool your knowledge of cyberpunk literature and culture. Would you consider yourself a cyberpunk? Have you read any of the literature? Share your opinions of this subculture with the small group.

2. Find alt.cyberpunk in Usenet newsgroups and read some of the postings. Or explore some of the other online resources the FAQ mentions. Share what you learn with the class.

3. Would the hackers John Perry Barlow describes in "Desperados of the Datasphere" be cyberpunks, according to this FAQ?

4. Freewrite for five minutes about why some young people want to identify themselves as cyberpunks. Does the movement appeal to you or does it repel you?

A New Battlefield: Rethinking Warfare in the Computer Age

by Steve Lohr

A war fought with computers sends trains out of control and explodes oil refineries. The plot sounds like something out of a video game or thriller movie, but it isn't. Steve Lohr reports in this feature from the Cybertimes section of the New York Times *that these events were part of a role-playing game conducted at the National Defense University to simulate "information warfare." Governments are taking seriously the prospect that terrorists, criminal organizations, and enemy nations have the ability to disrupt and destroy crucial installations and communication networks through the use of computers, not bombs. It is the increasing use of computer networks that makes industrialized countries vulnerable to these kinds of attacks.*

Lohr's article can be found in the online New York Times, *http://www.nytimes.com. Lohr writes frequently for the Cybertimes section of the* New York Times, *with articles including "Microsoft Sets Its Sights on Corporate Computing," "Corporate Internet Police Hunt Down E-Pirates," and "Internet Growth Brings Up Questions of Governance."*

It was the OPEC meeting in May 2000 that started the crisis. The oil-price hawks, led by Iran, demanded a sharp cutback in production to drive prices up to "at least $60 a barrel."

The stormy gathering of the Organization of Petroleum Exporting Countries ended on May 4, with a shouting match between the Iranian and Saudi Arabian oil ministers. Over the next two weeks, Iran and its allies mobilized troops and fired on Saudi warships. But they also unleashed an arsenal of high-technology weapons to try to destabilize the Saudi government and prevent the United States from intervening.

A huge refinery near Dhahran was destroyed by an explosion and fire because of a mysterious malfunction in its computerized controls. A software "logic bomb" caused a "new Metro-Superliner" to slam into a misrouted freight train near Laurel, Maryland, killing 60 people and critically injuring another 120.

The Bank of England found "sniffer" programs running amok in its electronic funds transfer system. And a "computer worm" started corrupting files in the Pentagon's top-secret force deployment data base.

The opening scenes from a Hollywood script or a new Tom Clancy novel? No, these are excerpts from a role-playing game conducted last year at the Government's National Defense University in Washington. The goal was to generate some serious thinking about "information warfare."

Today, there are a lot of people thinking seriously about information warfare, not only at the Pentagon and the CIA but also in the executive offices of banks, securities firms and other companies. Once dismissed as the stuff of science fiction, high-tech information warfare is fast becoming a reality.

Defense and intelligence officials believe that enemy nations, terrorists and criminal groups either already have the capability to mount information warfare strikes or soon will. Criminals are quickly progressing beyond the vandalism and petty theft associated with teen-age hackers and into robbery and extortion schemes ranging up to millions of dollars, corporate executives and private investigators say.

In the future, they fear, information warfare assaults could be made against commercial networks like the banking system or utilities in several states.

Yet there is a heated debate among experts in this emerging field about whether the kinds of catastrophic incidents cited in the National Defense University war game are imminent threats or worst-case nightmares.

"A couple of years ago, no one took information warfare seriously," said Howard Frank, director of the information technology office at the Defense Advanced Research Project Agency, or DARPA. "But the more you learn about it, the more concerned you become."

Others reply that the worst threats mentioned are mostly speculation. "Information warfare is a risk to our nation's economy and defense," said Martin Libicki, a senior fellow at the National Defense University. "But I believe we will find ways to cope with these attacks, adjust and shake them off, just as we do to natural disasters like hurricanes."

Experts on both sides of the debate do agree that the growing reliance on computer networks and telecommunications is making the nation increasingly vulnerable to "cyber attacks" on military war rooms, power plants, telephone networks, air traffic control centers, and banks.

John Deutch, the director of central intelligence, told Congress in June that such assaults "could not only disrupt our daily lives, but also seriously jeopardize our national and economic security."

"The electron, in my view," Deutch warned, "is the ultimate precision-guided weapon."

President Clinton last July created a Commission on Critical Infrastructure Protection to craft a coordinated policy to deal with the threat.

Within the government, information warfare tactics and intelligence are highly classified issues. But the CIA has recently created an "Information Warfare Center." And the National Security Agency intends to set up an information warfare unit staffed by as many as 1,000 people, with both offensive and defensive expertise, as well as a twenty-four-hour response team, according to a staff report by the Senate Permanent Subcommittee on Investigations, which was initiated by Senator Sam Nunn.

Information warfare is a catchall term. The military, for example, often refers to information warfare broadly to include time-tested techniques and tools like disinformation, cryptography, radio jamming and bombing communications centers.

But it is high-tech information warfare that has been getting most of the attention and funding lately. This budding warfare industry is an eclectic field indeed, ranging from computer scientists whose work is funded by the government to hackers-for-hire who specialize in theft, extortion and sabotage. In his Senate testimony, Deutch said the CIA had determined that cyber attacks are now "likely to be within the capabilities of a number of terrorist groups," including the Hezbollah in the Middle East.

The weapons of information warfare are mostly computer software, like destructive logic bombs and eavesdropping sniffers, or advanced electronic hardware, like a high-energy radio frequency device, known as a HERF gun.

In theory, at least, these weapons could cripple the computer systems that control everything from the electronic funds transfer systems of banks to electric utilities to battlefield tanks.

For the military, information warfare raises the prospect of a new deal for America's adversaries. Cyberwar units could sidestep or cripple conventional weaponry, undermining the advantage the United States holds.

"Even a third-tier country has access to first-class programmers, to state-of-the-art computer hardware and expertise in this area," said Barry Horton, principal deputy assistant secretary of defense, who oversees the Pentagon's information warfare operations. "There is a certain leveling of the playing field."

Cyberspace also plays havoc with traditional definitions: What is a military and what is a commercial target, if 95 percent of military communications are over commercial networks; what is within United States jurisdiction and what is an international issue, when cyberspace has no geographic borders?

"We have to redefine national security for the information age," Horton said.

There is, to be sure, an aspect of self-interest in the information warfare alarms raised by defense and intelligence agencies. Those bureaucracies are sizable and costly, and in the post–Cold War era, they are in need of new enemies.

"The people who are concerned about information warfare tend to magnify its significance," said Libicki of the National Defense University.

The Electronic Industries Association estimates that over the next decade, the government's information warfare procurement, mainly for specialized software and services, will grow sevenfold, to more than $1 billion annually.

Yet the projected information warfare spending amounts to pocket change, compared with next year's military budget of $257 billion.

"The point of information warfare is that you don't need fighter planes and billions of dollars to launch an attack on the United States anymore," said Winn Schwartau, an author and president of Interpact Inc., a security consulting firm.

The government's computer systems are clearly susceptible to intruders. In 1988, a Cornell student sent a worm program over the Internet that penetrated military and intelligence systems, shutting down 6,000 computers.

In 1994, a sixteen-year-old British hacker broke into the computer system at an Air Force laboratory in Rome, New York.

And in "red team" exercises, the military's experts have been able to break into 65 percent of the Defense Department systems they tried to penetrate, using hacking tools available over the Internet.

But nearly all these intrusions have been into some of the 2 million computers in military networks that handle unclassified information—though that information can be useful to enemies, defense officials concede. The classified information is on the other 10 percent of the military's computer networks, which do not have open links to the outside.

Private companies and banks typically do not have the luxury of making their networks off-limits to outsiders.

"We invite our customers into our computer networks," said Colin Crook, the senior technology officer of Citibank. "I think our problem is more challenging than the government's."

Citibank got an alarming brush with the problem two years ago, when a Russian computer hacker tapped into the bank's funds transfer system, taking more than $10 million. Citibank will not discuss the case, but investigators say the bank recovered all but $400,000.

In the business world, the reported hacker activity to date is mostly stealing credit card numbers, vandalizing software, or harassing Internet service companies.

"At the moment, we're dealing with penny ante stuff," said Peter Neumann, a computer scientist at SRI International, a research firm in Menlo Park, California. "But the risk of much greater damage is there."

Frank of DARPA speaks of a "frightening vulnerability" of utilities systems, of the private data networks of the international financial system and of the digital switches at the core of modern phone systems.

Major breakdowns caused by computer intruders have not yet occurred. But there is evidence that more sophisticated hackers are now at work. The Science Applications International Corp., a defense contractor and technology security firm, surveyed more than 40 major corporations who confidentially reported that they lost an estimated $800 million due to computer break-ins last year, both in lost intellectual property and money.

Private investigators and bankers say they are aware of four banks, three in Europe and one in New York, that have made recent payments of roughly $100,000 each to hacker extortionists. The bankers and investigators would not name the banks, but the weapon used to blackmail the banks was a logic bomb—a software program that, when detonated, could cripple a bank's internal computer system. In each case, the sources said, the banks paid the money, and then took new security measures.

Frequently, experts say, the tighter security measures are nothing fancy. One problem is modems on employees' computers. They are open connections to the outside world, potentially giving hackers access to an internal network.

"You can't eliminate risk of information attacks, but you can minimize it," said William Marlow, a senior vice president of Science Applications International. "Many of the steps are not all that high-tech or expensive."

After it got stung in the Russia episode, Citibank has taken a series of measures, from instructing employees to never assume a computer network is secure to aggressively pursuing hackers.

"You mess with us and we're going after you," Crook said. "This is a big deal for us now."

EXPLORING THE READING

1. In your small group, evaluate Steve Lohr's feature. What are the major points in his argument that the prospect of "information warfare" is a serious problem? Are they effective?

2. Lohr also considers the opposing side of the argument, acknowledging that defense and intelligence agencies, which are costly bureaucracies, may need to invent new enemies to justify their expenditures. What are the major points in the counterargument? Do you think that the dangers of "information warfare" are over-magnified?

3. Are there parallels between Hafner's "Log On and Shoot" and Lohr's feature? In what way?

4. Explore related sites such as the National Defense University, http://www.ndu.edu, and the Defense Advanced Research Projects Agency, http://www.darpa.mil, for further information about this issue. Report your findings to the class.

THE VIRTUAL COMMUNITY

by Howard Rheingold

Writing is a lonely profession, says Howard Rheingold, editor in chief of The Millennium Whole Earth Catalog, *former editor of the* Whole Earth Review, *and author of* Virtual Reality *and* Virtual Communities, *from which this reading is excerpted. He was first attracted to cyberspace because it provided a way for him to not be alone during the long hours he spent in front of his computer.*

A virtual community, according to Rheingold, is an online discussion group in which members develop long-term friendships through their interaction online. In such a community, members become intimate though they have never seen each other fact to face. To the participants, the virtual communities themselves take on a sense of place, according to Rheingold, becoming virtual locations where friends "gather for conviviality." Read more of Rheingold's texts online at http://www.rheingold.com.

In the summer of 1986, my then-two-year-old daughter picked up a tick. There was this blood-bloated *thing* sucking on our baby's scalp, and we weren't quite sure how to go about getting it off. My wife, Judy, called the pediatrician. It was 11 o'clock in the evening. I logged onto the WELL, the big Bay Area infonet, and contacted the Parenting conference (a conference is an online conversation about a specific subject). I got my answer online within minutes from a fellow with the improbable but genuine name of Flash Gordon, M.D. I had removed the tick by the time Judy got the callback from the pediatrician's office.

What amazed me wasn't just the speed with which we obtained precisely the information we needed to know, right when we needed to know it. It was also the immense inner sense of security that comes with discovering that real people—most of them parents, some of them nurses, doctors, and mid-wives—are available, around the clock, if you need them. There is a magic protective circle around the atmosphere of the Parenting conference. We're talking about our sons and daughters in this forum, not about our computers or our opinions about philosophy, and many of us feel that this tacit under-standing sanctifies the virtual space.

The atmosphere of this particular conference—the attitudes people exhibit to each other in the tone of what they say in public—is part of what continues to attract me. People who never have much to contribute in political debate, technical argument, or intellectual gamesmanship turn out to have a lot to say about raising children. People you knew as fierce, even nasty, intellectual opponents in other contexts give you emotional support on a deeper level, parent to parent, within the boundaries of this small but warmly human corner of cyberspace.

In most cases, people who talk about a shared interest don't disclose enough about themselves as whole individuals online to inspire real trust in others. But in the case of the subcommunity called the Parenting conference, a few dozen of us, scattered across the country, few of whom rarely if ever saw the others face to face, have a few years of minor crises to knit us together and prepare us for serious business when it comes our way. Another several dozen read the conference regularly but contribute only when they have something important to add. Hundreds more read the conference every week without comment, except when something extraordinary happens.

Jay Allison and his family live in Massachusetts. He and his wife are public-radio producers. I've never met them face to face, although I feel I know something powerful and intimate about the Allisons and have strong emotional ties to them. What follows are some of Jay's postings on the WELL:

> Wood's Hole. Midnight. I am sitting in the dark of my daughter's room. Her monitor lights blink at me. The lights used to blink too brightly so I covered them with bits of bandage adhesive and now they flash faintly underneath, a persistent red and green, Lillie's heart and lungs.
>
> Above the monitor is her portable suction unit. In the glow of the flashlight I'm writing by, it looks like the plastic guts of a science-class human model, the tubes coiled around the power supply, the reservoir, the pump.
>
> Tina is upstairs trying to get some sleep. A baby monitor links our bedroom to Lillie's. It links our sleep to Lillie's too, and because our souls are linked to hers, we do not sleep well.
>
> I am naked. My stomach is full of beer. The flashlight rests on it, and the beam rises and falls with my breath. My daughter breathes through a white plastic tube inserted into a hole in her throat. She's fourteen months old.

Sitting in front of our computers with our hearts racing and tears in our eyes, in Tokyo and Sacramento and Austin, we read about Lillie's croup, her tracheostomy, the days and nights at Massachusetts General Hospital, and now the vigil over Lillie's breathing and the watchful attention to the mechanical apparatus that kept her alive. It went on for days. Weeks. Lillie recovered, and relieved our anxieties about her vocal capabilities after all that time with a hole in her throat by saying the most extraordinary things, duly reported online by Jay.

Later, writing in *Whole Earth Review*, Jay described the experience:

> Before this time, my computer screen had never been a place to go for solace. Far from it. But there it was. Those nights sitting up late with my daughter, I'd go to my computer, dial up the WELL, and ramble. I wrote about what was happening that night or that year. I didn't know anyone I was "talking" to. I had never laid eyes on them. At 3:00 A.M. my "real" friends were asleep, so I turned to this foreign, invisible community for support. The WELL was always awake.
>
> Any difficulty is harder to bear in isolation. There is nothing to measure against, to lean against. Typing out my journal entries into the computer and over the phone lines, I found fellowship and comfort in this unlikely medium.

Many people are alarmed by the very idea of a virtual community, fearing that it is another step in the wrong direction, substituting more technological ersatz for yet another natural resource or human freedom. These critics often voice their sadness at what people have been reduced to doing in a civilization that worships technology, decrying the circumstances that lead some people into such pathetically disconnected lives that they prefer to find their companions on the other side of a computer screen. There is a seed of truth in this fear, for communities at some point require more than words on a screen if they are to be other than ersatz.

Yet some people—many people—who don't do well in spontaneous spoken interaction turn out to have valuable contributions to make in a conversation in which they have time to think about what to say. These people, who might constitute a significant proportion of the population, can find written communication more authentic than the face-to-face kind. Who is to say that this preference for informal written text is somehow less authentically human than opting for audible speech? Those who critique computer-mediated communication because some people use it obsessively hit an important target, but miss a great deal more when they don't take into consideration people who use the medium for genuine human interaction. Those who find virtual communities cold places point at the limits of the technology, its most dangerous pitfalls, and we need to pay attention to those boundaries. But these critiques don't tell us how the Allisons, my own family, and many others could have found the community of support and information we found in the WELL when we needed it. And those of us who do find communion in cyberspace might do well to pay attention to the way the medium we love can be abused.

Although dramatic incidents are what bring people together and stick in their memories, most of what goes on in the Parenting conference and most virtual communities is informal conversation and downright chitchat. The model of the WELL and other social clusters in cyberspace as "places" emerges naturally whenever people who use this medium discuss its nature. In 1987, Steward Brand quoted me in his book *The Media Lab* about what tempted me to log onto the WELL as often as I did: "There's always another mind there. It's like having the corner bar, complete with old buddies and delightful newcomers and new tools waiting to take home and fresh graffiti and letters, except instead of putting on my coat, shutting down the computer, and walking down to the corner, I just invoke my telecom program and there they are. It's a place."

I've changed my mind about a lot of aspects of the WELL over the years, but the sense of place is still as strong as ever. As Ray Oldenburg proposes in his 1989 book *The Great Good Place*, there are three essential places in people's lives: the place we live, the place we work, and the place we gather for conviviality. Although the casual conversation that takes place in cafés, beauty shops, pubs, and town squares is universally considered to be trivial, idle talk, Oldenburg makes the case that such places are where communities can come into being and continue to hold together. These are the unacknowledged agoras of modern life. When the automobilecentric, suburban, fast-food, shopping-mall way of life eliminated many of these "third places" from traditional towns and cities around the world, the social fabric of existing communities started shredding.

Oldenburg puts a name and a conceptual framework on a phenomenon that every virtual community member knows instinctively, the power of informal public life:

> Third places exist on neutral ground and serve to level their guests to a condition of social equality. Within these places, conversation is the primary activity and the major vehicle for the display and appreciation of human personality and individuality. Third places are taken for granted and most have a low profile. Since the formal institutions of society make stronger claims on the individual, third places are normally open in the off hours, as well as at other times. The character of a third place is determined most of all by its regular clientele and is marked by a playful mood, which contrasts with people's more serious involvement in other spheres. Though a radically different kind of setting for a home, the third place is remarkably similar to a good home in the psychological comfort and support that it extends.
>
> Such are the characteristics of third places that appear to be universal and essential to a vital informal public life. . . .
>
> The problem of place in America manifests itself in a sorely deficient informal public life. The structure of shared experience beyond that offered by family, job, and passive consumerism is small and dwindling. The essential group experience is being replaced by the exaggerated self-consciousness of individuals. American lifestyles, for all the material acquisition and the seeking after comforts and pleasures, are plagued by boredom, loneliness, alienation, and a high price tag. . . .
>
> Unlike many frontiers, that of the informal public life does not remain benign as it awaits development. It does not become easier to tame as technology evolves, as governmental bureaus and agencies multiply, or as population grows. It does not yield to the mere passage of time and a policy of letting the chips fall where they may as development proceeds in other areas of urban life. To the contrary, neglect of the informal public life can make a jungle of what had been a garden while, at the same time, diminishing the ability of people to cultivate it.

It might not be the same kind of place that Oldenburg had in mind, but many of his descriptions of third places could also describe the WELL. Perhaps cyberspace is one of the informal public places where people can rebuild the aspects of community that were lost when the malt shop became a mall. Or perhaps cyberspace is precisely the *wrong* place to look for the rebirth of community, offering not a tool for conviviality but a life-denying simulacrum of real passion and true commitment to one another. In either case, we need to find out soon.

Because we cannot see one another in cyberspace, gender, age, national origin, and physical appearance are not apparent unless a person wants to make such characteristics public. People whose physical handicaps make it difficult to form new friendships find that virtual communities treat them as they always wanted to be treated—as thinkers and transmitters of ideas and feeling beings, not carnal vessels with a certain appearance and way of walking and talking (or not walking and not talking).

One of the few things that enthusiastic members of virtual communities in places like Japan, England, France, and the United States all agree on is that expanding their circle of friends is one of the most important advantages of computer conferencing. It is a way to *meet* people, whether or not you feel the need to affiliate with them on a community level. It's a way of both making contact with and maintaining a distance from others. The way you meet people in cyberspace puts a different spin on affiliation: In traditional kinds of communities, we are accustomed to meeting people, then getting to know them; in virtual communities, you can get to know people and *then* choose to meet them. Affiliation also can be far more ephemeral in cyberspace because you can get to know people you might never meet on the physical plane.

How does anybody find friends? In the traditional community, we search through our pool of neighbors and professional colleagues, of acquaintances and acquaintances of acquaintances, in order to find people who share our values and interests. We then exchange information about one another, disclose and discuss our mutual interests, and sometimes we become friends. In a virtual community we can go directly to the place where our favorite subjects are being discussed, then get acquainted with people who share our passions or who use words in a way we find attractive. In this sense, the topic is the address: You can't simply pick up a phone and ask to be connected with someone who wants to talk about Islamic art or California wine, or someone with a 3-year-old daughter or a 40-year-old Hudson; you can, however, join a computer conference on any of those topics, then open a public or private correspondence with the previously unknown people you find there. Your chances of making friends are increased by several orders of magnitude over the old methods of finding a peer group.

You can be fooled about people in cyberspace, behind the cloak of words. But that can be said about telephones or face-to-face communication as well; computer-mediated communications provide new ways to fool people, and the most obvious identity swindles will die out only when enough people learn to use the medium critically. In some ways, the medium will, by its nature, be forever biased toward certain kinds of obfuscation. It will also be a place where people often end up revealing themselves far more intimately than they would be inclined to do without the intermediation of screens and pseudonyms.

Point of view, along with identity, is one of the great variables in cyberspace. Different people in cyberspace look at their virtual communities through differently shaped keyholes. In traditional communities, people have a strongly shared mental model of the sense of place—the room or village or city where their interactions occur. In virtual communities, the sense of place requires an individual act of imagination. The different mental models people have of the electronic agora complicate the question of why people seem to want to build societies mediated by computer screens. A question like that leads inexorably to the old fundamental questions of what forces hold any society together. The roots of these questions extend farther than the social upheavals triggered by modern communications technologies.

When we say "society," we usually mean citizens of cities in entities known as nations. We take those categories for granted. But the mass-psychological transition we made to thinking of ourselves as part of modern society and nation-states is historically recent. Could people make the transition from the close collective social groups, the villages and small towns of premodern and precapitalist Europe, to a new form of social solidarity known as society that transcended and encompassed all previous kinds of human association? Ferdinand Tönnies, one of the founders of sociology, called the premodern kind of social group *gemeinschaft*, which is closer to the English word *community*, and the new kind of social group he called *gesellschaft*, which can be translated roughly as *society*. All the questions about community in cyberspace point to a similar kind of transition, for which we have no technical names, that might be taking place now.

Sociology student Marc Smith, who has been using the WELL and the Net as the laboratory for his fieldwork, pointed me to Benedict Anderson's *Imagined Communities*, a study of nation-building that focuses on the ideological labor involved. Anderson points out that nations and, by extension, communities are imagined in the sense that a given nation exists by virtue of a common acceptance in the minds of the population that it exists. Nations must exist in the minds of their citizens in order to exist at all. "Virtual communities require an act of imagination," Smith points out, extending Anderson's line of thinking to cyberspace, "and what must be imagined is the idea of the community itself."

EXPLORING THE READING

1. Howard Rheingold came to the Internet looking for community. What brought you to the Internet? Freewrite for five minutes about your purpose in becoming acquainted with cyberspace.

2. In your small group, discuss your experience with online communities such as chat rooms, forums, MUDs, or discussion groups. Share your experience with the class.

3. Do you think it is possible to have real communities in cyberspace? Why or why not?

4. Compare Rheingold's image of peaceful online communities with the frontier images Barlow suggests in "Desperados of the DataSphere." Are they contradictory?

A Rape in Cyberspace

by Julian Dibbell

Is a rape in cyberspace a rape? Julian Dibbell narrates the events that happened in LambdaMOO,* a virtual reality setting built of words, in which participants don virtual clothes, drink virtual cocktails, and engage in any activity that can be described in text, including, apparently, rape.

Julian Dibbell's text, first published in The Village Voice, *has been widely posted on the Internet and often mentioned in media features about Internet culture, perhaps because it highlights potential problems with online communities which others have described as idyllic utopias or as pale imitations of life without the zest. Dibbell's portrait of what happened in LambdaMoo is neither. The image he paints of what happened in that setting is neither "idyllic" nor "pale and without substance." It is a potentially convivial and safe place gone awry. A sense of regret and loss comes through clearly in this tale of rape and violence.*

Dibbell writes about cyberculture, and a number of his essays are posted at http://www.levity.com/julian/indexvanilla.html. These include "A Brief History of MUDs: From Time Immemorial to the Present," "Let's Get Digital: The Writer a la Modem," and "2 Cute 4 Words: In Defense of Smileys."

HOW AN EVIL CLOWN, A HAITIAN TRICKSTER SPIRIT, TWO WIZARDS, AND A CAST OF DOZENS TURNED A DATABASE INTO A SOCIETY

They say he raped them that night. They say he did it with a cunning little doll, fashioned in their image and imbued with the power to make them do whatever he desired. They say that by manipulating the doll he forced them to have sex with him, and with each other, and to do horrible, brutal things to their own bodies. And though I wasn't there that night, I think I can assure you that what they say is true, because it all happened right in the living room—right there amid the well-stocked bookcases and the sofas and the fireplace—of a house I've come to think of as my second home.

Call me Dr. Bombay. Some months ago—let's say about halfway between the first time you heard the words *information superhighway* and the first time you wished you never had—I found myself tripping with compulsive regularity down the well-traveled information lane that leads to LambdaMOO, a very large and very busy rustic chateau built entirely of words. Nightly, I typed the commands that called those words onto my computer screen, dropping

---

*A MOO is a variety of a MUD (Multi-User Dimension or Multi-User Dungeon), a real-time chat forum with a virtual reality setting. MOOs often have educational purposes rather than being strictly for recreation.

me with what seemed a warm electric thud inside the mansion's darkened coat closet, where I checked my quotidian identity, stepped into the persona and appearance of a minor character from a long-gone television sitcom, and stepped out into the glaring chatter of the crowded living room. Sometimes, when the mood struck me, I emerged as a dolphin instead.

I won't say why I chose to masquerade as Samantha Stevens's outlandish cousin, or as the dolphin, or what exactly led to my mild but so-far incurable addiction to the semifictional digital otherworlds known around the Internet as multi-user dimensions, or MUDs. This isn't my story, after all. It's the story of a man named Mr. Bungle, and of the ghostly sexual violence he committed in the halls of LambdaMOO, and most importantly of the ways his violence and his victims challenged the 1000 and more residents of that surreal, magic-infested mansion to become, finally, the community so many of them already believed they were.

That I was myself one of those residents has little direct bearing on the story's events. I mention it only as a warning that my own perspective is perhaps too steeped in the surreality and magic of the place to serve as an entirely appropriate guide. For the Bungle Affair raises questions that—here on the brink of a future in which human life may find itself as tightly enveloped in digital environments as it is today in the architectural kind—demand a clear-eyed, sober, and unmystified consideration. It asks us to shut our ears momentarily to the techno-utopian ecstasies of West Coast cyber-hippies and look without illusion upon the present possibilities for building, in the online spaces of this world, societies more decent and free than those mapped onto dirt and concrete and capital. It asks us to behold the new bodies awaiting us in virtual space undazzled by their phantom powers, and to get to the crucial work of sorting out the socially meaningful differences between those bodies and our physical ones. And most forthrightly it asks us to wrap our late-modern ontologies, epistemologies, sexual ethics, and common sense around the curious notion of rape by voodoo doll—and to try not to warp them beyond recognition in the process.

In short, the Bungle Affair dares me to explain it to you without resort to dime-store mysticisms, and I fear I may have shape-shifted by the digital moonlight one too many times to be quite up to the task. But I will do what I can, and can do no better I suppose than to lead with the facts. For if nothing else about Mr. Bungle's case is unambiguous, the facts at least are crystal clear.

The facts begin (as they often do) with a time and a place. The time was a Monday night in March, and the place, as I've said, was the living room—which, due to the inviting warmth of its decor, is so invariably packed with chitchatters as to be roughly synonymous among LambdaMOOers with a party. So strong, indeed, is the sense of convivial common ground invested in the living room that a cruel mind could hardly imagine a better place in which to stage a violation of LambdaMOO's communal spirit. And there was cruelty enough lurking in the appearance Mr. Bungle presented to the virtual world—he was at the time a fat, oleaginous, Bisquick-faced clown dressed in cum-stained harlequin garb and girdled with a mistletoe-and-hemlock belt whose buckle bore the quaint inscription "KISS ME UNDER THIS, BITCH!" But whether cruelty motivated his choice of crime scene is not among the established facts of the case. It is a fact only that he did choose the living room.

The remaining facts tell us a bit more about the inner world of Mr. Bungle, though only perhaps that it couldn't have been a very comfortable place. They tell us that he commenced his assault entirely unprovoked, at or about 10 P.M. Pacific Standard Time. That he began by using his voodoo doll to force one of the room's occupants to sexually service him in a variety of more or less conventional ways. That this victim was legba, a Haitian trickster spirit of indeterminate gender, brown-skinned and wearing an expensive pearl gray suit, top hat, and dark glasses. That legba heaped vicious imprecations on him all the while and that he was soon ejected bodily from the room. That he hid himself away then in his private chambers somewhere on the mansion grounds and continued the attacks without interruption, since the voodoo doll worked just as well at a distance as in proximity. That he turned his attentions now to Starsinger, a rather pointedly nondescript female character, tall, stout, and brown-haired, forcing her into unwanted liaisons with other individuals present in the room, among them legba, Bakunin (the well-known radical), and Juniper (the squirrel). That his actions grew progressively violent. That he made legba eat his/her own pubic hair. That he caused Starsinger to violate herself with a piece of kitchen cutlery. That his distant laughter echoed evilly in the living room with every successive outrage. That he could not be stopped until at last someone summoned Zippy, a wise and trusted old-timer who brought with him a gun of near wizardly powers, a gun that didn't kill but enveloped its targets in a cage impermeable even to a voodoo doll's powers. That Zippy fired this gun at Mr. Bungle, thwarting the doll at last and silencing the evil, distant laughter.

These particulars, as I said, are unambiguous. But they are far from simple, for the simple reason that every set of facts in virtual reality (or VR, as the locals abbreviate it) is shadowed by a second, complicating set: the "real-life" facts. And while a certain tension invariably buzzes in the gap between the hard, prosaic RL facts and their more fluid, dreamy VR counterparts, the dissonance in the Bungle case is striking. No hideous clowns or trickster spirits appear in the RL version of the incident, no voodoo dolls or wizard guns, indeed no rape at all as any RL court of law has yet defined it. The actors in the drama were university students for the most part, and they sat rather undramatically before computer screens the entire time, their only actions a spidery flitting of fingers across standard QWERTY keyboards. No bodies touched. Whatever physical interaction occurred consisted of a mingling of electronic signals sent from sites spread out between New York City and Sydney, Australia. Those signals met in LambdaMOO, certainly, just as the hideous clown and the living room party did, but what was LambdaMOO after all? Not an enchanted mansion or anything of the sort—

just a middlingly complex database, maintained for experimental purposes inside a Xerox Corporation research computer in Palo Alto and open to public access via the Internet.

To be more precise about it, LambdaMOO was a MUD. Or to be yet more precise, it was a subspecies of MUD known as a MOO, which is short for "MUD, Object-Oriented." All of which means that it was a kind of database especially designed to give users the vivid impression of moving through a physical space that in reality exists only as descriptive data filed away on a hard drive. When users dial into LambdaMOO, for instance, the program immediately presents them with a brief textual description of one of the rooms of the database's fictional mansion (the coat closet, say). If the user wants to leave this room, she can enter a command to move in a particular direction and the database will replace the original description with a new one corresponding to the room located in the direction she chose. When the new description scrolls across the user's screen it lists not only the fixed features of the room but all its contents at that moment—including things (tools, toys, weapons) and other users (each represented as a "character" over which he or she has sole control).

As far as the database program is concerned, all of these entities—rooms, things, characters—are just different subprograms that the program allows to interact according to rules very roughly mimicking the laws of the physical world. Characters may not leave a room in a given direction, for instance, unless the room subprogram contains an "exit" at that compass point. And if a character "says" or "does" something (as directed by its user-owner), then only the users whose characters are also located in that room will see the output describing the statement or action. Aside from such basic constraints, however, LambdaMOOers are allowed a broad freedom to create—they can describe their characters any way they like, they can make rooms of their own and decorate them to taste, and they can build new objects almost at will. The combination of all this busy user activity with the hard physics of the database can certainly induce a lucid illusion of presence—but when all is said and done the only thing you *really* see when you visit LambdaMOO is a kind of slow-crawling script, lines of dialogue and stage direction creeping steadily up your computer screen.

Which is all just to say that, to the extent that Mr. Bungle's assault happened in real life at all, it happened as a sort of Punch-and-Judy show, in which the puppets and the scenery were made of nothing more substantial than digital code and snippets of creative writing. The puppeteer behind Bungle, as it happened, was a young man logging in to the MOO from a New York University computer. He could have been Al Gore for all any of the others knew, however, and he could have written Bungle's script that night any way he chose. He could have sent a command to print the message "Mr. Bungle, smiling a saintly smile, floats angelic near the ceiling of the living room, showering joy and candy kisses down upon the heads of all below"—and everyone then receiving output from the database's subprogram #17 (a/k/a the "living room") would have seen that sentence on their screens.

Instead, he entered sadistic fantasies into the "voodoo doll," a sub-program that served the not-exactly kosher purpose of attributing actions to other characters that their users did not actually write. And thus a woman in Haverford, Pennsylvania, whose account on the MOO attached her to a character she called Starsinger, was given the unasked-for opportunity to read the words "As if against her will, Starsinger jabs a steak knife up her ass, causing immense joy. You hear Mr. Bungle laughing evilly in the distance." And thus the woman in Seattle who had written herself the character called legba, with a view perhaps to tasting in imagination a deity's freedom from the burdens of the gendered flesh, got to read similarly constructed sentences in which legba, messenger of the gods, lord of crossroads and communications, suffered a brand of degradation all-too-customarily reserved for the embodied female.

"Mostly voodoo dolls are amusing," wrote legba on the evening after Bungle's rampage, posting a public statement to the widely read in-MOO mailing list called *social-issues, a forum for debate on matters of import to the entire populace. "And mostly I tend to think that restrictive measures around here cause more trouble than they prevent. But I also think that Mr. Bungle was being a vicious, vile fuckhead, and I . . . want his sorry ass scattered from #17 to the Cinder Pile. I'm not calling for policies, trials, or better jails. I'm not sure what I'm calling for. Virtual castration, if I could manage it. Mostly, [this type of thing] doesn't happen here. Mostly, perhaps I thought it wouldn't happen to me. Mostly, I trust people to conduct themselves with some veneer of civility. Mostly, I want his ass."

Months later, the woman in Seattle would confide to me that as she wrote those words posttraumatic tears were streaming down her face—a real-life fact that should suffice to prove that the words' emotional content was no mere playacting. The precise tenor of that content, however, its mingling of murderous rage and eyeball-rolling annoyance, was a curious amalgam that neither the RL nor the VR facts alone can quite account for. Where virtual reality and its conventions would have us believe that legba and Starsinger were brutally raped in their own living room, here was the victim legba scolding Mr. Bungle for a breach of "civility." Where real life, on the other hand, insists the incident was only an episode in a free-form version of Dungeons and Dragons, confined to the realm of the symbolic and at no point threatening any player's life, limb, or material well-being, here now was the player legba issuing aggrieved and heartfelt calls for Mr. Bungle's dismemberment. Ludicrously excessive by RL's lights, woefully understated by VR's, the tone of legba's response made sense only in the buzzing, dissonant gap between them.

Which is to say it made the only kind of sense that *can* be made of MUDly phenomena. For while the *facts* attached to any event born of a MUD's strange, ethereal universe may march in straight, tandem lines separated neatly into the virtual and the real, its meaning lies always in that gap. You learn this axiom early in your life as a player, and it's of no small relevance to the Bungle case that you usually learn it between the sheets, so to speak. Netsex, tinysex, virtual sex—however you name it, in real-life reality it's nothing more than a 900-line encounter stripped of even the vestigial physicality of the voice. And yet as any but the most inhibited of newbies can tell you, it's possibly the headiest experience the very heady world of MUDs has to offer. Amid flurries of even the most cursorily described caresses, sighs, and penetrations, the glands do engage, and often as throbbingly as they would in a real-life assignation—sometimes even more so, given the combined power of anonymity and textual suggestiveness to unshackle deep-seated fantasies. And if the virtual setting and the interplayer vibe are right, who knows? The heart may engage as well, stirring up passions as strong as many that bind lovers who observe the formality of trysting in the flesh.

To participate, therefore, in this disembodied enactment of life's most body-centered activity is to risk the realization that when it comes to sex, perhaps the body in question is not the physical one at all, but its psychic double, the bodylike self-representation we carry around in our heads. I know, I know, you've read Foucault and your mind is not quite blown by the notion that sex is never so much an exchange of fluids as it is an exchange of signs. But trust your friend Dr. Bombay, it's one thing to grasp the notion intellectually and quite another to feel it coursing through your veins amid the virtual steam of hot netnookie. And it's a whole other mind-blowing trip altogether to encounter it thus as a college frosh, new to the net and still in the grip of hormonal hurricanes and high-school sexual mythologies. The shock can easily reverberate throughout an entire young worldview. Small wonder, then, that a newbie's first taste of MUD sex is often also the first time she or he surrenders wholly to the slippery terms of MUDish ontology, recognizing in a full-bodied way that what happens inside a MUD-made world is neither exactly real nor exactly make-believe, but profoundly, compellingly, and emotionally meaningful.

And small wonder indeed that the sexual nature of Mr. Bungle's crime provoked such powerful feelings, and not just in legba (who, be it noted, was in real life a theory-savvy doctoral candidate and a longtime MOOer, but just as baffled and overwhelmed by the force of her own reaction, she later would attest, as any panting undergrad might have been). Even players who had never experienced MUD rape (the vast majority of male-presenting characters, but not as large a majority of the female-presenting as might be hoped) immediately appreciated its gravity and were moved to condemnation of the perp. legba's missive to *social-issues followed a strongly worded one from Zippy ("Well, well," it began, "no matter what else happens on Lambda, I can always be sure that some jerk is going to reinforce my low opinion of humanity") and was itself followed by others from Moriah, Raccoon, Crawfish, and evangeline. Starsinger also let her feelings ("pissed") be known. And even Jander, the Clueless Samaritan who had responded to Bungle's cries for help and uncaged him shortly after the incident, expressed his regret once apprised of Bungle's deeds, which he allowed to be "despicable."

A sense was brewing that something needed to be done—done soon and in something like an organized fashion—about Mr. Bungle, in particular, and about MUD rape, in general. Regarding the general problem, evangeline, who identified herself as a survivor of both virtual rape ("many times over") and real-life sexual assault, floated a cautious proposal for a MOO-wide powwow on the subject of virtual sex offenses and what mechanisms if any might be put in place to deal with their future occurrence. As for the specific problem, the answer no doubt seemed obvious to many. But it wasn't until the evening of the second day after the incident that legba, finally and rather solemnly, gave it voice:

"I am requesting that Mr. Bungle be toaded for raping Starsinger and I. I have never done this before, and have thought about it for days. He hurt us both."

That was all. Three simple sentences posted to *social. Reading them, an outsider might never guess that they were an application for a death warrant. Even an outsider familiar with other MUDs might not guess it, since in many of them "toading" still refers to a command that, true to the game-worlds' sword-and-sorcery origins, simply turns a player into a toad, wiping the player's description and attributes and replacing them with those of the slimy amphibian. Bad luck for sure, but not quite as bad as what happens when the same command is invoked in the MOOish strains of MUD: not only are the description and attributes of the toaded player erased, but the account itself goes too. The annihilation of the character, thus, is total.

And nothing less than total annihilation, it seemed, would do to settle LambdaMOO's accounts with Mr. Bungle. Within minutes of the posting of legba's appeal, SamIAm, the Australian Deleuzean, who had witnessed much of the attack from the back room of his suburban Sydney home, sec-onded the motion with a brief message crisply entitled "Toad the fukr." SamIAm's posting was seconded almost as quickly by that of Bakunin, co-victim of Mr. Bungle and well-known radical, who in real life happened also to be married to the real-life legba. And over the course of the next 24 hours as many as 50 players made it known, on *social and in a variety of other forms and forums, that they would be pleased to see Mr. Bungle erased from the face of the MOO. And with dissent so far confined to a dozen or so anti-toading hardliners, the numbers suggested that the citizenry was indeed moving towards a resolve to have Bungle's virtual head.

There was one small but stubborn obstacle in the way of this resolve, however, and that was a curious state of social affairs known in some quarters of the MOO as the New Direction. It was all very fine, you see, for the LambdaMOO rabble to get it in their heads to liquidate one of their peers, but when the time came to actually do the deed it would require the services of a nobler class of character. It would require a wizard. Master-programmers of the MOO, spelunkers of the database's deepest code-structures and custo-dians of its day-to-day administrative trivia, wizards are also the only players empowered to issue the toad command, a feature maintained on nearly all MUDs as a quick-and-dirty means of social control. But the wizards of LambdaMOO, after years of adjudicating all manner of inter-player disputes with little to show for it but their own weariness and the smoldering resentment of the general populace, had decided they'd had enough of the social sphere. And so, four months before the Bungle incident, the archwizard Haakon (known in RL as Pavel Curtis, Xerox researcher and LambdaMOO's principal architect) formalized this decision in a document called "LambdaMOO Takes a New Direction," which he placed in the living room for all to see. In it, Haakon announced that the wizards from that day forth were pure technicians. From then on, they would make no decisions affecting the social life of the MOO, but only implement whatever decisions the community as a whole directed them to. From then on, it was decreed, LambdaMOO would just have to grow up and solve its problems on its own.

Faced with the task of inventing its own self-governance from scratch, the LambdaMOO population had so far done what any other loose, amorphous agglomeration of individuals would have done: they'd let it slide. But now the task took on new urgency. Since getting the wizards to toad Mr. Bungle (or to toad the likes of him in the future) required a convincing case that the cry for his head came from the community at large, then the community itself would have to be defined; and if the community was to be convincingly defined, then some form of social organization, no matter how rudimentary, would have to be settled on. And thus, as if against its will, the question of what to do about Mr. Bungle began to shape itself into a sort of referendum on the political future of the MOO. Arguments broke out on *social and else-where that had only superficially to do with Bungle (since everyone agreed he was a cad) and everything to do with where the participants stood on LambdaMOO's crazy-quilty political map. Parliamentarian legalist types argued that unfortunately Bungle could not legitimately be toaded at all, since there were no explicit MOO rules against rape, or against just about anything else—and the sooner such rules were established, they added, and maybe even a full-blown judiciary system complete with elected officials and prisons to enforce those rules, the better. Others, with a royalist streak in them, seemed to feel that Bungle's as-yet-unpunished outrage only proved this New Direction silliness had gone on long enough, and that it was high time the wizardocracy returned to the position of swift and decisive lead-ership their player class was born to.

And then there were what I'll call the technolibertarians. For them, MUD rapists were of course assholes, but the presence of assholes on the system was a technical inevitability, like noise on a phone line, and best dealt with not through repressive social disciplinary mechanisms but through the timely deployment of defensive software tools. Some asshole blasting violent, graphic language at you? Don't whine to the authorities about it—hit the @gag command and the asshole's statements will be blocked from your screen (and only yours). It's simple, it's effective, and it censors no one.

But the Bungle case was rather hard on such arguments. For one thing, the extremely public nature of the living room meant that gagging would spare the victims only from witnessing their own violation, but not from having others witness it. You might want to argue that what those victims didn't directly experience couldn't hurt them, but consider how that wisdom would sound to a woman who'd been, say, fondled by strangers while passed out drunk and you have a rough idea how it might go over with a crowd of hard-core MOOers. Consider, for another thing, that many of the biologically female participants in the Bungle debate had been around long enough to grow lethally weary of the gag-and-get-over-it school of virtual-rape counseling, with its fine line between empowering victims and holding them responsible for their own suffering, and its shrugging indifference to the window of pain between the moment the rape-text starts flowing and the moment a gag shuts it off. From the outset it was clear that the technolibertarians were going to have to tiptoe through this issue with care, and for the most part they did.

Yet no position was trickier to maintain than that of the MOO's resident anarchists. Like the technolibbers, the anarchists didn't care much for punishments or policies or power elites. Like them, they hoped the MOO could be a place where people interacted fulfillingly without the need for such things. But their high hopes were complicated, in general, by a somewhat less thoroughgoing faith in technology ("Even if you can't tear down the master's house with the master's tools"—read a slogan written into one anarchist player's self-description—"it is a damned good place to start"). And at present they were additionally complicated by the fact that the most vocal anarchists in the discussion were none other than legba, Bakunin, and SamIAm, who wanted to see Mr. Bungle toaded as badly as anyone did.

Needless to say, a pro-death-penalty platform is not an especially comfortable one for an anarchist to sit on, so these particular anarchists were now at great pains to sever the conceptual ties between toading and capital punishment. Toading, they insisted (almost convincingly), was much more closely analogous to banishment; it was a kind of turning of the communal back on the offending party, a collective action which, if carried out properly, was entirely consistent with anarchist models of community. And carrying it out properly meant first and foremost building a consensus around it—a messy process for which there were no easy technocratic substitutes. It was going to take plenty of good old-fashioned, jawbone-intensive grassroots organizing.

So that when the time came, at 7 P.M. PST on the evening of the third day after the occurrence in the living room, to gather in evangeline's room for her proposed real-time open conclave, Bakunin and legba were among the first to arrive. But this was hardly to be an anarchist-dominated affair, for the room was crowding rapidly with representatives of all the MOO's political stripes, and even a few wizards. Hagbard showed up, and Autumn and Quastro, Puff, JoeFeedback, L-dopa and Bloaf, HerkieCosmo, Silver Rocket, Karl Porcupine, Matchstick—the names piled up and the discussion gathered momentum under their weight. Arguments multiplied and mingled, players talked past and through each other, the textual clutter of utterances and gestures filled up the screen like thick cigar smoke. Peaking in number at around 30, this was one of the largest crowds that ever gathered in a single LambdaMOO chamber, and while evangeline had given her place a description that made it "infinite in expanse and fluid in form," it now seemed anything but roomy. You could almost feel the claustrophobic air of the place, dank and overheated by virtual bodies, pressing against your skin.

I know you could because I too was there, making my lone and insignificant appearance in this story. Completely ignorant of any of the goings-on that had led to the meeting, I wandered in purely to see what the crowd was about, and though I observed the proceedings for a good while, I confess I found it hard to grasp what was going on. I was still the rankest of newbies then, my MOO legs still too unsteady to make the leaps of faith, logic, and empathy required to meet the spectacle on its own terms. I was fascinated by the concept of virtual rape, but I couldn't quite take it seriously.

In this, though, I was in a small and mostly silent minority, for the discussion that raged around me was of an almost unrelieved earnestness, bent it seemed on examining every last aspect and implication of Mr. Bungle's crime. There were the central questions, of course: thumbs up or down on Bungle's virtual existence? And if down, how then to insure that his toading was not just some isolated lynching but a first step toward shaping LambdaMOO into a legitimate community? Surrounding these, however, a tangle of weighty side issues proliferated. What, some wondered, was the real-life legal status of the offense? Could Bungle's university administrators punish him for sexual harassment? Could he be prosecuted under California state laws against obscene phone calls? Little enthusiasm was shown for pursuing either of these lines of action, which testifies both to the uniqueness of the crime and to the nimbleness with which the discussants were negotiating its idiosyncracies. Many were the casual references to Bungle's deed as simply "rape," but these in no way implied that the players had lost sight of all distinctions between the virtual and physical versions, or that they believed Bungle should be dealt with in the same way a real-life criminal would. He had committed a MOO crime, and his punishment, if any, would be meted out via the MOO.

On the other hand, little patience was shown toward any attempts to downplay the seriousness of what Mr. Bungle had done. When the affable HerkieCosmo proposed, more in the way of an hypothesis than an assertion, that "perhaps it's better to release . . . violent tendencies in a virtual environment rather than in real life," he was tut-tutted so swiftly and relentlessly that he withdrew the hypothesis altogether, apologizing humbly as he did so. Not that the assembly was averse to putting matters into a more philosophical perspective. "Where does the body end and the mind begin?" young Quastro asked, amid recurring attempts to fine-tune the differences between real and virtual violence. "Is not the mind a part of the body?" "In MOO, the body IS the mind," offered HerkieCosmo gamely, and not at all implausibly, demonstrating the ease with which very knotty metaphysical conundrums come undone in VR. The not-so-aptly named Obvious seemed to agree, arriving after deep consideration of the nature of Bungle's crime at the hardly novel yet now somehow newly resonant conjecture "all reality might consist of ideas, who knows."

On these and other matters the anarchists, the libertarians, the legalists, the wizardists—and the wizards—all had their thoughtful say. But as the evening wore on and the talk grew more heated and more heady, it seemed increasingly clear that the vigorous intelligence being brought to bear on this swarm of issues wasn't going to result in anything remotely like resolution. The perspectives were just too varied, the meme-scape just too slippery. Again and again, arguments that looked at first to be heading in a decisive direction ended up chasing their own tails; and slowly, depressingly, a dusty haze of irrelevance gathered over the proceedings.

It was almost a relief, therefore, when midway through the evening Mr. Bungle himself, the living, breathing cause of all this talk, teleported into the room. Not that it was much of a surprise. Oddly enough, in the three days since his release from Zippy's cage, Bungle had returned more than once to wander the public spaces of LambdaMOO, walking willingly into one of the fiercest storms of ill will and invective ever to rain down on a player. He'd been taking it all with a curious and mostly silent passivity, and when challenged face to virtual face by both legba and the genderless elder statescharacter PatGently to defend himself on *social he'd demurred, mumbling something about Christ and expiation. He was equally quiet now, and his reception was still uniformly cool. legba fixed an arctic stare on him—"no hate, no anger, no interest at all. Just . . . watching." Others were more actively unfriendly. "Asshole," spat Karl Porcupine, "creep." But the harshest of the MOO's hostility toward him had already been vented, and the attention he drew now was motivated more, it seemed, by the opportunity to probe the rapist's mind, to find out what made it tick and if possible how to get it to tick differently. In short, they wanted to know why he'd done it. So they asked him.

And Mr. Bungle thought about it. And as eddies of discussion and debate continued to swirl around him, he thought about it some more. And then he said this:

"I engaged in a bit of a psychological device that is called thought-polarization, the fact that this is not RL* simply added to heighten the affect of the device. It was purely a sequence of events with no consequence on my RL existence."

They might have known. Stilted though its diction was, the gist of the answer was simple, and something many in the room had probably already surmised: Mr. Bungle was a psycho. Not, perhaps, in real life—but then in real life it's possible for reasonable people to assume, as Bungle clearly did, that what transpires between word-costumed characters within the boundaries of a make-believe world is, if not mere play, then at most some kind of

---

*RL (Real Life)

emotional laboratory experiment. Inside the MOO, however, such thinking marked a person as one of two basically subcompetent types. The first was the newbie, in which case the confusion was understandable, since there were few MOOers who had not, upon their first visits as anonymous "guest" characters, mistaken the place for a vast playpen in which they might act out their wildest fantasies without fear of censure. Only with time and the acquisition of a fixed character do players tend to make the critical passage from anonymity to pseudonymity, developing the concern for their character's reputation that marks the attainment of virtual adulthood. But while Mr. Bungle hadn't been around as long as most MOOers, he'd been around long enough to leave his newbie status behind, and his delusional statement therefore placed him among the second type: the sociopath.

And as there is but small percentage in arguing with a head case, the room's attention gradually abandoned Mr. Bungle and returned to the discussions that had previously occupied it. But if the debate had been edging toward ineffectuality before, Bungle's anticlimactic appearance had evidently robbed it of any forward motion whatsoever. What's more, from his lonely corner of the room Mr. Bungle kept issuing periodic expressions of a prickly sort of remorse, interlaced with sarcasm and belligerence, and though it was hard to tell if he wasn't still just conducting his experiments, some people thought his regret genuine enough that maybe he didn't deserve to be toaded after all. Logically, of course, discussion of the principal issues at hand didn't require unanimous belief that Bungle was an irredeemable bastard, but now that cracks were showing in that unanimity, the last of the meeting's fervor seemed to be draining out through them.

People started drifting away. Mr. Bungle left first, then others followed—one by one, in twos and threes, hugging friends and waving goodnight. By 9:45 only a handful remained, and the great debate had wound down into casual conversation, the melancholy remains of another fruitless good idea. The arguments had been well-honed, certainly, and perhaps might prove useful in some as-yet-unclear long run. But at this point what seemed clear was that evangeline's meeting had died, at last, and without any practical results to mark its passing.

It was also at this point, most likely, that JoeFeedback reached his decision. JoeFeedback was a wizard, a taciturn sort of fellow who'd sat brooding on the sidelines all evening. He hadn't said a lot, but what he had said indicated that he took the crime committed against legba and Starsinger very seriously, and that he felt no particular compassion toward the character who had committed it. But on the other hand he had made it equally plain that he took the elimination of a fellow player just as seriously, and moreover that he had no desire to return to the days of wizardly fiat. It must have been difficult, therefore, to reconcile the conflicting impulses churning within him at that moment. In fact, it was probably impossible, for as much as he would have liked to make himself an instrument of LambdaMOO's collective will, he surely realized that under the present order of things he must in the final analysis either act alone or not act at all.

So JoeFeedback acted alone.

He told the lingering few players in the room that he had to go, and then he went. It was a minute or two before ten. He did it quietly and he did it privately, but all anyone had to do to know he'd done it was to type the @who command, which was normally what you typed if you wanted to know a player's present location and the time he last logged in. But if you had run a @who on Mr. Bungle not too long after JoeFeedback left evangeline's room, the database would have told you something different.

"Mr. Bungle," it would have said, "is not the name of any player."

The date, as it happened, was April Fool's Day, and it would still be April Fool's Day for another two hours. But this was no joke: Mr. Bungle was truly dead and truly gone.

They say that LambdaMOO has never been the same since Mr. Bungle's toading. They say as well that nothing's really changed. And though it skirts the fuzziest of dream-logics to say that both these statements are true, the MOO is just the sort of fuzzy, dreamlike place in which such contradictions thrive.

Certainly whatever civil society now informs LambdaMOO owes its existence to the Bungle Affair. The archwizard Haakon made sure of that. Away on business for the duration of the episode, Haakon returned to find its wreckage strewn across the tiny universe he'd set in motion. The death of a player, the trauma of several others, and the angst-ridden conscience of his colleague JoeFeedback presented themselves to his concerned and astonished attention, and he resolved to see if he couldn't learn some lesson from it all. For the better part of a day he brooded over the record of events and arguments left in *social*, then he sat pondering the chaotically evolving shape of his creation, and at the day's end he descended once again into the social arena of the MOO with another history-altering proclamation.

It was probably his last, for what he now decreed was the final, missing piece of the New Direction. In a few days, Haakon announced, he would build into the database a system of petitions and ballots whereby anyone could put to popular vote any social scheme requiring wizardly powers for its implementation, with the results of the vote to be binding on the wizards. At last and for good, the awkward gap between the will of the players and the efficacy of the technicians would be closed. And though some anarchists grumbled about the irony of Haakon's dictatorially imposing universal suffrage on an unconsulted populace, in general the citizens of LambdaMOO seemed to find it hard to fault a system more purely democratic than any that could ever exist in real life. Eight months and a dozen ballot measures later, widespread participation in the new regime has produced a small arsenal of mechanisms for dealing with the types of violence that called the system into being. MOO residents now have access to a @boot command, for instance, with which to summarily eject berserker "guest" characters. And players can bring suit against one another through an ad hoc arbitration system in which mutually agreed-upon judges have at their disposition the full range of wizardly punishments—up to and including the capital.

Yet the continued dependence on death as the ultimate keeper of the peace suggests that this new MOO order may not be built on the most solid of foundations. For if life on LambdaMOO began to acquire more coherence in the wake of the toading, death retained all the fuzziness of pre-Bungle days. This truth was rather dramatically borne out, not too many days after Bungle departed, by the arrival of a strange new character named Dr. Jest. There was a forceful eccentricity to the newcomer's manner, but the oddest thing about his style was its striking yet unnameable familiarity. And when he developed the annoying habit of stuffing fellow players into a jar containing a tiny simulacrum of a certain deceased rapist, the source of this familiarity became obvious:

Mr. Bungle had risen from the grave.

In itself, Bungle's reincarnation as Dr. Jest was a remarkable turn of events, but perhaps even more remarkable was the utter lack of amazement with which the LambdaMOO public took note of it. To be sure, many residents were appalled by the brazenness of Bungle's return. In fact, one of the first petitions circulated under the new voting system was a request for Dr. Jest's toading that almost immediately gathered fifty-two signatures (but has failed so far to reach ballot status). Yet few were unaware of the ease with which the toad proscription could be circumvented—all the toadee had to do (all the ur-Bungle at NYU presumably had done) was to go to the minor hassle of acquiring a new Internet account, and LambdaMOO's character registration program would then simply treat the known felon as an entirely new and innocent person. Nor was this ease generally understood to represent a failure of toading's social disciplinary function. On the contrary, it only underlined the truism (repeated many times throughout the debate over Mr. Bungle's fate) that his punishment, ultimately, had been no more or less symbolic than his crime.

What *was* surprising, however, was that Mr. Bungle/Dr. Jest seemed to have taken the symbolism to heart. Dark themes still obsessed him—the objects he created gave off wafts of Nazi imagery and medical torture—but he no longer radiated the aggressively antisocial vibes he had before. He was a lot less unpleasant to look at (the outrageously seedy clown description had been replaced by that of a mildly creepy but actually rather natty young man, with "blue eyes . . . suggestive of conspiracy, untamed eroticism and perhaps a sense of understanding of the future"), and aside from the occasional jar-stuffing incident, he was also a lot less dangerous to be around. It was obvious he'd undergone some sort of personal transformation in the days since I'd first glimpsed him back in evangeline's crowded room—nothing radical maybe, but powerful nonetheless, and resonant enough with my own experience, I felt, that it might be more than professionally interesting to talk with him, and perhaps compare notes.

For I too was undergoing a transformation in the aftermath of that night in evangeline's, and I'm still not entirely sure what to make of it. As I pursued my runaway fascination with the discussion I had heard there, as I pored over the *social* debate and got to know legba and some of the other victims and witnesses, I could feel my newbie consciousness falling away from me.

Where before I'd found it hard to take virtual rape seriously, I now was finding it difficult to remember how I could ever *not* have taken it seriously. I was proud to have arrived at this perspective—it felt like an exotic sort of achievement, and it definitely made my ongoing experience of the MOO a richer one.

But it was also having some unsettling effects on the way I looked at the rest of the world. Sometimes, for instance, it was hard for me to understand why RL society classifies RL rape alongside crimes against person or property. Since rape can occur without any physical pain or damage, I found myself reasoning, then it must be classed as a crime against the mind—more intimately and deeply hurtful, to be sure, than cross burnings, wolf whistles, and virtual rape, but undeniably located on the same conceptual continuum. I did not, however, conclude as a result that rapists were protected in any fashion by the First Amendment. Quite the opposite, in fact: the more seriously I took the notion of virtual rape, the less seriously I was able to take the notion of freedom of speech, with its tidy division of the world into the symbolic and the real.

Let me assure you, though, that I am not presenting these thoughts as arguments. I offer them, rather, as a picture of the sort of mind-set that deep immersion in a virtual world has inspired in me. I offer them also, therefore, as a kind of prophecy. For whatever else these thoughts tell me, I have come to believe that they announce the final stages of our decades-long passage into the Information Age, a paradigm shift that the classic liberal firewall between word and deed (itself a product of an earlier paradigm shift commonly known as the Enlightenment) is not likely to survive intact. After all, anyone the least bit familiar with the workings of the new era's definitive technology, the computer, knows that it operates on a principle impracticably difficult to distinguish from the pre-Enlightenment principle of the magic word: the commands you type into a computer are a kind of speech that doesn't so much communicate as *make things happen*, directly and ineluctably, the same way pulling a trigger does. They are incantations, in other words, and anyone at all attuned to the technosocial megatrends of the moment— from the growing dependence of economies on the global flow of intensely fetishized words and numbers to the burgeoning ability of bioengineers to speak the spells written in the four-letter text of DNA—knows that the logic of the incantation is rapidly permeating the fabric of our lives.

And it's precisely this logic that provides the real magic in a place like LambdaMOO—not the fictive trappings of voodoo and shapeshifting and wizardry, but the conflation of speech and act that's inevitable in any computer-mediated world, be it Lambda or the increasingly wired world at large. This is dangerous magic, to be sure, a potential threat—if misconstrued or misapplied—to our always precarious freedoms of expression, and as someone who lives by his words I do not take the threat lightly. And yet, on the other hand, I can no longer convince myself that our wishful insulation of language from the realm of action has ever been anything but a valuable kludge, a philosophically damaged stopgap against oppression that would just have to do till something truer and more elegant came along.

Am I wrong to think this truer, more elegant thing can be found on LambdaMOO? Perhaps, but I continue to seek it there, sensing its presence just beneath the surface of every interaction. I have even thought, as I said, that discussing with Dr. Jest our shared experience of the workings of the MOO might help me in my search. But when that notion first occurred to me, I still felt somewhat intimidated by his lingering criminal aura, and I hemmed and hawed a good long time before finally resolving to drop him MOO-mail requesting an interview. By then it was too late. For reasons known only to himself, Dr. Jest had stopped logging in. Maybe he'd grown bored with the MOO. Maybe the loneliness of ostracism had gotten to him. Maybe a psycho whim had carried him far away or maybe he'd quietly acquired a third character and started life over with a cleaner slate.

Wherever he'd gone, though, he left behind the room he'd created for himself—a treehouse "tastefully decorated" with rare-book shelves, an operating table, and a life-size William S. Burroughs doll—and he left it unlocked. So I took to checking in there occasionally, and I still do from time to time. I head out of my own cozy nook (inside a TV set inside the little red hotel inside the Monopoly board inside the dining room of LambdaMOO), and I teleport on over to the treehouse, where the room description always tells me Dr. Jest is present but asleep, in the conventional depiction for disconnected characters. The not-quite-emptiness of the abandoned room invariably instills in me an uncomfortable mix of melancholy and the creeps, and I stick around only on the off chance that Dr. Jest will wake up, say hello, and share his understanding of the future with me.

EXPLORING THE READING

1. What is Julian Dibbell's main point? What evidence does he use to support his argument?

2. Is the MOO Dibbell describes what Howard Rheingold, in "Virtual Communities," would call a community? How so?

3. Julian Dibbell suggests that virtual environments have the potential of being "societies more decent and free than those mapped onto dirt and concrete and capital." From what he describes and from your own knowledge of online environments, do you think this is possible? Why or why not?

4. Dibbell uses terms such as "late-modern ontologies" and epistemologies, as well as sexually explicit descriptions. Does his language add to or detract from the effectiveness of his text?

5. In your small groups, pool your knowledge of MUDs and MOOs, particularly LambdaMoo. Have you participated in these virtual reality settings? What was your experience? Share what you know with the class.

HIGH-TECH REDLINING

by Reginald Stuart

The information superhighway is well underway, and when it is finished, it will be the main conduit for communication in our culture. The problem, according to Reginald Stuart in "High-Tech Redlining," an essay from the African-American magazine Emerge, *is that African-Americans today stand a good chance of being bypassed when it comes to installing the necessary technology in minority communities. According to a U.S. Census Bureau study, white children are more likely to have computer instruction in school than are minority children; and since computer ownership is highly correlated with income, the one-third of black Americans living in poverty are unlikely to own a computer.*

ARE AFRICAN-AMERICANS BEING FROZEN OUT OF THE NEW COMMUNICATIONS NETWORK?

In the embryonic days of the now 40,000-mile-plus interstate highway system, few black people actually knew of its potential to redefine or even destroy entire communities. Just as many blacks today still bear the scars of the interstate highway that many times plowed right through the heart of their communities a generation ago, African-Americans today are threatened by the so-called information superhighway.

When it is completed, the information-superhighway will be a pipeline through which nearly every form of communication conceivable will pass. You name it and the highway most likely will carry it: love letters, business mail, televised telephone calls, newspapers stories, radio and TV shows, movies, educational programs, and even medical assistance. Jeff Chester, executive director of the Washington-based Center for Media Education, says that a new central nervous system is being built for our society, and that African-Americans in particular have a lot at stake. "I see this as *the* civil rights and economic rights issue of the twenty-first century," says Chester.

In many respects, the scenario for the development of the communications highway is evolving in much the same way the interstate highway system did. A handful of visionaries are working the halls of Congress to clear the legal obstacles, and in boardrooms across the nation grand ideas—how to pool big money to control positions in the information marketplace—are being explored. In this frenzied activity, African-Americans are being viewed as consumers, not directors.

"It is going to require a concentrated effort" on the part of African-Americans not to be left behind, says Larry Irving, an assistant secretary in the U.S. Department of Commerce and director of the National Tele-communications Information Administration. "We either have to get on it or be left behind," Irving says. "We have to get the technologies deployed in minority communities, make sure our children are technologically literate, and seize the entrepreneurial opportunities."

Things are off to a rocky start. A coalition of groups following developments in Washington have accused the nation's telephone companies of "electronic redlining" in planning a communications network. The Center for Media Education, the NAACP, the Office of Communication of the United Church of Christ, the Consumer Federation of America, and the Council of La Raza have joined together to warn that minority communities are being bypassed and have asked the Federal Communications Commission to investigate. (The phone companies strongly deny the claim.)

A 1989 report by the U.S. Census Bureau found computer use and ownership skyrocketing. But use and ownership by African-Americans was almost negligible. The report said that 26.9 million whites—but only 1.5 million blacks—used computers at home. Among children age 3 to 17, some 10.7 million white children used computers at home, compared with 806,000 black children. In school, the number of children using computers rises significantly for both groups, but the gap is just as profound: 17.4 million white students but only 2.4 million black students.

The same report found that owning a computer is closely associated with household income (and education) levels: 47.5 percent of households with annual incomes of $75,000 or more owned computers; 4.8 percent of households with incomes of $15,090 or less owned them. Combine that with the fact that nearly one-third of all black Americans lived in poverty in 1990, according to the census bureau (the government defines poverty as a two-person household making $9,165 or less a year, or a four-person household with an annual income of $13,924 or less). Many African-American families just don't have enough fuel to travel the new highway.

"When television sets were first introduced, very few blacks had them, but now they are in virtually every home," recalls Delores Davis-Penn, a gerontologist at Missouri's Lincoln University who has been sent to Washington twice by Southwestern Bell to argue for affordable phone service for minorities. "Looking into the future, [I believe] that computers will become like television sets in our homes," she says. Electronic innovations bring new job opportunities, not to mention new chances to create radio and television programming that is culturally sensitive to African-Americans, she adds. "It requires creativity to push our people to accept the challenge."

EXPLORING THE READING

1. Reginald Stuart argues that African-Americans may be left out when it comes to access to the information superhighway. Why, according to Stuart, is this likely? Do you agree with Stuart? If so, do you consider this a problem of national concern?

2. In your small group, pool your knowledge of the demographics of computer use. Describe a typical computer owner or Internet user. Are African-Americans and other minorities likely to be found online? What about women? Share your knowledge with the class.

3. Stuart's article is based on a 1989 U.S. Census Bureau report. Do you think the situation today is the same as it was in 1989? Why or why not?

Women and Children First: Gender and the Settling of the Electronic Frontier

by Laura Miller

Laura Miller wrote this essay to respond to a Newsweek *article that depicted cyberspace as another frontier where women are prone to being attacked, albeit intellectually or psychologically. She argues that cyberspace is not as bad as many mainstream media articles would have us believe. She says we should celebrate the potential for the blurring of gender roles on the Net instead of focusing on the gender differences that sometimes mar and limit communication both on the Internet and in face-to-face contact.*

Miller is a contributing editor for San Francisco Weekly. *Her articles and criticism have also appeared in* Harper's Bazaar *and the* San Francisco Examiner.

When *Newsweek* (May 16, 1994) ran an article entitled "Men, Women and Computers," all hell broke out on the Net, particularly on the online service I've participated in for six years, The WELL (Whole Earth 'Lectronic Link). "Cyberspace, it turns out," declared *Newsweek*'s Nancy Kantrowitz, "isn't much of an Eden after all. It's marred by just as many sexist ruts and gender conflicts as the Real World. . . . Women often feel about as welcome as a system crash." "It was horrible. Awful, poorly researched, unsubstantiated drivel," one member wrote, a sentiment echoed throughout some 480 postings.

However egregious the errors in the article (some sources maintain that they were incorrectly quoted), it's only one of several mainstream media depictions of the Net as an environment hostile to women. Even women who had been complaining about online gender relations found themselves increasingly annoyed by what one WELL member termed the "cyberbabe harassment" angle that seems to typify media coverage of the issue. Reified in the pages of *Newsweek* and other journals, what had once been the topic of discussions by insiders—online commentary is informal, conversational, and often spontaneous—became a journalistic "fact" about the Net known by complete strangers and novices. In a matter of months, the airy stuff of bitch sessions became widespread, hardened stereotypes.

At the same time, the Internet has come under increasing scrutiny as it mutates from an obscure, freewheeling web of computer networks used by a small elite of academics, scientists, and hobbyists to . . . well, nobody seems to know exactly what. But the business press prints vague, fevered prophecies of fabulous wealth, and a bonanza mentality has blossomed. With it comes big business and the government, intent on regulating this amorphous medium into a manageable and profitable industry. The Net's history of informal self-regulation and its wide libertarian streak guarantee that battles like the one over the Clipper chip (a mandatory decoding device that would make all encrypted data readable by federal agents) will be only the first among many.

Yet the threat of regulation is built into the very mythos used to conceptualize the Net by its defenders—and gender plays a crucial role in that threat. However revolutionary the technologized interactions of online communities may seem, we understand them by deploying a set of very familiar metaphors from the rich figurative soup of American culture. Would different metaphors have allowed the Net a different, better historical trajectory? Perhaps not, but the way we choose to describe the Net now encourages us to see regulation as its inevitable fate. And, by examining how gender roles provide a foundation for the intensification of such social controls, we can illuminate the way those roles proscribe the freedoms of men as well as women.

For months I mistakenly referred to the EFF (an organization founded by John Perry Barlow and Lotus 1-2-3 designer Mitch Kapor to foster access to, and further the discursive freedom of, online communications) as "The Electronic Freedom Foundation," instead of by its actual name, "The Electronic Frontier Foundation." Once corrected, I was struck by how intimately related the ideas "frontier" and "freedom" are in the Western mythos. The *frontier*, as a realm of limitless possibilities and few social controls, hovers, grail-like, in the American psyche, the dream our national identity is based on, but a dream that's always, somehow, just vanishing away.

Once made, the choice to see the Net as a frontier feels unavoidable, but it's actually quite problematic. The word "frontier" has traditionally described a place, if not land then the limitless "final frontier" of space. The Net on the other hand, occupies precisely no physical space (although the computers and phone lines that make it possible do). It is a completely bodiless, symbolic thing with no discernable boundaries or location. The land of the American frontier did not become a "frontier" until Europeans determined to conquer it, but the continent existed before the intention to settle it. Unlike land, the Net was created by its pioneers.

Most peculiar, then, is the choice of the word "frontier" to describe an artifact so humanly constructed that it only exists as ideas or information. For central to the idea of the frontier is that it contains no (or very few) other people—fewer than two per square mile according to the nineteenth-century historian Frederick Turner. The freedom the frontier promises is a liberation from the demands of society, while the Net (I'm thinking now of Usenet) has nothing but society to offer. Without other people, news groups, mailing lists, and files simply wouldn't exist and e-mail would be purposeless. Unlike real space, cyberspace must be shared.

Nevertheless, the choice of a spatial metaphor (credited to the science-fiction novelist William Gibson, who coined the term "cyberspace"), however awkward, isn't surprising. Psychologist Julian Jaynes has pointed out that geographical analogies have long predominated humanity's efforts to conceptualize—map out—consciousness. Unfortunately, these analogies bring with them a heavy load of baggage comparable to Pandora's box: open it and a complex series of problems have come to stay.

The frontier exists beyond the edge of settled or owned land. As the land that doesn't belong to anybody (or to people who "don't count," like Native Americans), it is on the verge of being acquired; currently unowned, but still ownable. Just as the ideal of chastity makes virginity sexually provocative, so does the unclaimed territory invite settlers, irresistibly so. Americans regard the lost geographical frontier with a melancholy, voluptuous fatalism—we had no choice but to advance upon it and it had no alternative but to submit. When an EFF member compares the Clipper chip to barbed wire encroaching on the prairie, doesn't he realize the surrender implied in his metaphor?

The psychosexual undercurrents (if anyone still thinks of them as "under") in the idea of civilization's phallic intrusion into nature's passive, feminine space have been observed, exhaustively, elsewhere. The classic Western narrative is actually far more concerned with social relationships than conflicts between man and nature. In these stories, the frontier is a lawless society of men, a milieu in which physical strength, courage, and personal charisma supplant institutional authority and violent conflict is the accepted means of settling disputes. The Western narrative connects pleasurably with the American romance of individualistic masculinity; small wonder that the predominantly male founders of the Net's culture found it so appealing.

When civilization arrives on the frontier, it comes dressed in skirts and short pants. In the archetypal 1939 movie *Dodge City*, Wade Hatton (Errol Flynn) refuses to accept the position of marshal because he prefers the footloose life of a trail driver. Abbie Irving (Olivia de Haviland), a recent arrival from the civilized East, scolds him for his unwillingness to accept and advance the cause of law; she can't function (in her job as crusading journalist) in a town governed by brute force. It takes the accidental killing of a child in a street brawl for Hatton to realize that he must pin on the badge and clean up Dodge City.

In the Western mythos, civilization is necessary because women and children are victimized in conditions of freedom. Introduce women and children into a frontier town and the law must follow because women and children must be protected. Women, in fact, are usually the most vocal proponents of the conversion from frontier justice to civil society.

The imperiled women and children of the Western narrative make their appearance today in newspaper and magazine articles that focus on the intimidation and sexual harassment of women online and reports of pedophiles trolling for victims in computerized chat rooms. If online women successfully contest these attempts to depict them as the beleaguered prey of brutish men, expect the pedophile to assume a larger profile in arguments that the Net is out of control.

In the meantime, the media prefer to cast women as the victims, probably because many women actively participate in the call for greater regulation of online interactions, just as Abbie Irving urges Wade Hatton to bring the rule of law to Dodge City. These requests have a long cultural tradition, based on the idea that women, like children, constitute a peculiarly vulnerable class of people who require special protection from the elements of society men are expected to confront alone. In an insufficiently civilized society like the frontier, women, by virtue of this childlike vulnerability, are thought to live under the constant threat of kidnap, abuse, murder, and especially rape.

Women, who have every right to expect that crimes against their person will be rigorously prosecuted, should nevertheless regard the notion of special protections (chivalry, by another name) with suspicion. Based as it is on the idea that women are inherently weak and incapable of self-defense and that men are innately predatory, it actually reinforces the power imbalance between the sexes, with its roots in the concept of women as property, constantly under siege and requiring the vigilant protection of their male owners. If the romance of the frontier arises from the promise of vast stretches of unowned land, an escape from the restrictions of a society based on private property, the introduction of women spoils that dream by reintroducing the imperative of property in their own persons.

How does any of this relate to online interactions, which occur not on a desert landscape but in a complex, technological society where women are supposed to command equal status with men? It accompanies us as a set of unexamined assumptions about what it means to be male or female, assumptions that we believe are rooted in the imperatives of our bodies. These assumptions follow us into the bodiless realm of cyberspace, a forum where, as one scholar put it "participants are washed clean of the stigmata of their real 'selves' and are free to invent new ones to their tastes." Perhaps some observers feel that the replication of gender roles in a context where the absence of bodies supposedly makes them superfluous proves exactly how innate those roles are. Instead, I see in the relentless attempts to interpret online interactions as highly gendered, an intimation of just how artificial, how created, our gender system is. If it comes "naturally," why does it need to be perpetually defended and reasserted?

Complaints about the treatment of women online fall into three categories: that women are subjected to excessive, unwanted sexual attention, that the prevailing style of online discussion turns women off, and that women are singled out by male participants for exceptionally dismissive or hostile treatment. In making these assertions, the *Newsweek* article and other stories on the issue do echo grievances that some online women have made for years. And, without a doubt, people have encountered sexual come-ons, aggressive debating tactics, and ad hominem attacks on the Net. However, individual users interpret such events in widely different ways, and to generalize from those interpretations to describe the experiences of women and men as a whole is a rash leap indeed.

I am one of many women who don't recognize their own experience of the Net in the misogynist gauntlet described above. In researching this essay, I joined America Online and spent an hour or two "hanging out" in the real-time chat rooms reputed to be rife with sexual harassment. I received several "instant messages" from men, initiating private conversations with innocuous questions about my hometown and tenure on the service. One man politely inquired if I was interested in "hot phone talk" and just as politely bowed out when I declined. At no point did I feel harassed or treated with disrespect. If I ever want to find a phone-sex partner, I now know where to look but until then I probably won't frequent certain chat rooms.

Other women may experience a request for phone sex or even those tame instant messages as both intrusive and insulting (while still others maintain that they have received much more explicit messages and inquiries completely out of the blue). My point isn't that my reactions are the more correct, but rather that both are the reactions of women, and no journalist has any reason to believe that mine are the exception rather than the rule.

For me, the menace in sexual harassment comes from the underlying threat of rape or physical violence. I see my body as the site of my heightened vulnerability as a woman. But online—where I have no body and neither does anyone else—I consider rape to be impossible. Not everyone agrees. Julian Dibble, in an article for *The Village Voice*, describes the repercussions of a "rape" in a multiuser dimension, or MUD, in which one user employed a subprogram called a "voodoo doll" to cause the personae of other users to perform sexual acts. Citing the "conflation of speech and act that's inevitable in any computermediated world," he moved toward the conclusion that "since rape can occur without any physical pain or damage, then it must be classified as a crime against the mind." Therefore, the offending user had committed something on the same "conceptual continuum" as rape. Tellingly, the incident led to the formation of the first governmental entity on the MUD.

No doubt the cyber-rapist (who went by the nom de guerre Mr. Bungle) appreciated the elevation of his mischief-making to the rank of virtual felony: all of the outlaw glamour and none of the prison time (he was exiled from the MUD). Mr. Bungle limited his victims to personae created by women users, a choice that, in its obedience to prevailing gender roles, shaped the debate that followed his crimes. For, in accordance with the real-world understanding that women's smaller, physically weaker bodies and lower social status make them subject to violation by men, there's a troubling notion in the real and virtual worlds that women's minds are also more vulnerable to invasion, degradation, and abuse.

This sense of fragility extends beyond interactions with sexual overtones. The *Newsweek* article reports that women participants can't tolerate the harsh, contentious quality of online discussions, that they prefer mutual support to heated debate, and are retreating wholesale to women-only conferences and newsgroups. As someone who values online forums precisely because they mandate equal time for each user who chooses to take it and forestall various "alpha male" rhetorical tactics like interrupting, loudness, or exploiting the psychosocial advantages of greater size or a deeper voice, I find this perplexing and disturbing. In these laments I hear the reluctance of women to enter into the kind of robust debate that characterizes healthy public life, a willingness to let men bully us even when they've been relieved of most of their traditional advantages. Withdrawing into an electronic purdah where one will never be challenged or provoked, allowing the ludicrous ritual chest-thumping of some users to intimidate us into silence—surely women can come up with a more spirited response than this.

And of course they can, because besides being riddled with reductive stereotypes, media analyses like *Newsweek*'s simply aren't accurate. While the online population is predominantly male, a significant and vocal minority of women contribute regularly and more than manage to hold their own. Some of The WELL's most bombastic participants are women, just as there are many tactful and conciliatory men. At least, I think there are, because, ultimately, it's impossible to be sure of anyone's biological gender online. "Transpostites," people who pose as member of the opposite gender, are an established element of Net society, most famously a man who, pretending to be a disabled lesbian, built warm and intimate friendships with women on several CompuServe forums.

Perhaps what we should be examining is not the triumph of gender differences on the Net, but their potential blurring. In this light, *Newsweek*'s stout assertion that in cyberspace "the gender gap is real" begins to seem less objective than defensive, an insistence that online culture is "the same" as real life because the idea that it might be different, when it comes to gender, is too scary. If gender roles can be cast off so easily, they may be less deeply rooted, less "natural" than we believe. There may not actually be a "masculine" or "feminine" mind or outlook, but simply a conventional way of interpreting individuals that recognizes behavior seen as in accordance with their biological gender and ignores behavior that isn't.

For example, John Seabury wrote in the *New Yorker* (June 6, 1994) of his stricken reaction to his first "flame," a colorful slice of adolescent invective sent to him by an unnamed technology journalist. Reading it, he begins to "shiver" like a burn victim, an effect that worsens with repeated readings. He writes that "the technology greased the words . . . with a kind of immediacy that allowed them to slide easily into my brain." He tells his friends, his coworkers, his partner—even his mother—and, predictably, appeals to CompuServe's management for recourse—to no avail. Soon enough, he's talking about civilization and anarchy, how the liberating "lack of social barriers is also what is appalling about the net," and calling for regulation.

As a newcomer, Seabury was chided for brooding over a missive that most Net veterans would have dismissed and forgotten as the crude potshot of an envious jerk. (I can't help wondering if my fellow journalist never received hate mail in response to his other writings; this bit of e-mail seems comparable, par for the course when one assumes a public profile.) What nobody did was observe that Seabury's reaction—the shock, the feelings of violation, the appeals to his family and support network, the bootless complaints to the authorities—reads exactly like many horror stories about women's trials on the Net. Yet, because Seabury is a man, no one attributes the attack to his gender or suggests that the Net has proven an environment hostile to men. Furthermore, the idea that the Net must be more strictly governed to prevent the abuse of guys who write for the *New Yorker* seems laughable—though who's to say that Seabury's pain is less than any woman's? Who can doubt that, were he a woman, his tribulations would be seen as compelling evidence of Internet sexism?

The idea that women merit special protections in a environment as incorporeal as the Net is intimately bound up with the idea that women's minds are weak, fragile, and unsuited to the rough and tumble of public discourse. It's an argument that women should recognize with profound mistrust and resist, especially when we are used as rhetorical pawns in a battle to regulate a rare (if elite) space of gender ambiguity. When the mainstream media generalize about women's experiences online in ways that just happen to uphold the most conventional and pernicious gender stereotypes, they can expect to be greeted with howls of disapproval from women who refuse to acquiesce in these roles and pass them on to other women.

And there are plenty of us, as The WELL's response to the *Newsweek* article indicates. Women have always participated in online communications, women whose chosen careers in technology and the sciences have already marked them as gender-role resisters. As the schoolmarms arrive on the electronic frontier, their female predecessors find themselves cast in the role of saloon girls, their willingness to engage in "masculine" activities like verbal aggression, debate, or sexual experimentation marking them as insufficiently feminine, or "bad" women. "If that's what women online are like, I must be a Martian," one WELL woman wrote in response to the shrinking female technophobes depicted in the *Newsweek* article. Rather than relegating so many people to the status of gender aliens, we ought to reconsider how adequate those roles are to the task of describing real human beings.

EXPLORING THE READING

1. Women and children have always been part of the frontier movement. Is their role similar or different in the settlement of cyberspace, according to Laura Miller? How so?

2. Freewrite for ten minutes on gender differences in communication you have experienced online and in face-to-face interaction. What, if any, are the differences in the way you have experienced face-to-face communication with members of the same and opposite sex? Have you noticed similar differences online? How would you explain those differences?

3. Laura Miller refers to Julian Dibbell's exploration of Mr. Bungle in "A Rape in Cyberspace" earlier in this chapter. Miller claims, however, that since her physical body is "the site of her heightened vulnerability as a woman" she considers rape in cyberspace impossible. Discuss Dibbell's and Miller's viewpoints in a small group. Is "rape" possible in cyberspace? Is cyber-rape as serious a crime as actual physical violence? Why or why not?

WRITING SUGGESTIONS

1. Write an essay about cyberspace as a new frontier. Consider some of the roles users play such as explorers, settlers, desperados, teachers, marshals, etc. Find examples from the Internet to support your points.

2. Spend some time as a participant in a MUD or MOO such as LambdaMOO (see the "Accessing Internet Resources" section in Chapter 8). Write an analysis of your experience.

3. Write an essay defining "hacker." Base your essay on the FAQ in this chapter and other information you find online in Usenet or on the World Wide Web.

4. Analyze the role of women on the Internet. What are the statistics of male/female usage? Are women discriminated against? Or, are they equal participants, if fewer in number?

5. Consider the topic of "access to the Internet." Are racial groups being denied access? Why, and what if anything is being done about it?

6. Interview several long-time Internet users. Write an essay about the culture of the Internet based on your interviews.

7. Interview participants in online virtual reality games and write an essay about the appeal of spending time in those settings based on what you learn from your interviews.

THE WRITING PROCESS: INVENTING, MAPPING, AND REVISING

When you are planning to write, what do you do? Do you talk to a friend about the topic you are writing about, or do you go to the library to look up what experts have said about your topic? Do you write in your head as you drive to school, or do you sit at your kitchen table with your favorite pen and write an extensive outline before you begin typing your paper into the computer? Do you only write a sentence down when you know it is perfect, or do you let words flow on to the page, checking for spelling and grammar errors later? Do you ask people to read and respond to your writing, or are you embarrassed to even show it to your instructor? Maybe you put it off until the evening before your paper is due; then you sit down to write at midnight, hoping you will finish before breakfast.

Every writer, even the student writer, has developed habits of writing. These habits may help a writer complete thoughtful and well-written essays, or they may keep a writer from doing his or her best work. No matter what habits you have developed, examining the habits of successful writers can help you get better ideas and write more thorough and thoughtful essays. It is likely that your teacher will ask you to follow a set of steps in order to write your essays for this class. The steps they ask you to follow are not just random requirements. Instead, they have come from careful analysis of the writing practices of successful student and professional writers.

The steps you will work through as you complete the writing assignments in this text can help you become more aware of how you write and help you improve your writing habits.

An Overview of a Writer's Process

Inventing.　Writing is not only about putting the pen to paper. In order to write successfully, you have to think deeply and critically about the subject. The 'invention' step of the writer's process is designed to help you find a worthwhile topic and develop your ideas about that topic *before* you start to write a draft. It includes writing, discussion, and research, as well as informal writing to help you explore your thoughts and feelings about a subject. Whatever method you choose, keep a record of your thoughts and the discoveries that come up as you spend this time in close examination of your subject.

Organizing.　The "invention" process is intended to get our ideas out of our heads and onto a piece of paper, but rarely do these ideas arrive in the most logical or effective order. Take some time (an hour or so for a short essay) to analyze your inventions. Place all the ideas in a logical order, and join similar ideas. Next, look for your most significant point, the most important thing you want to say about your subject. This becomes your *thesis*. Then identify which of the other items on your list will help you communicate your point and delete items that are irrelevant to your thesis.

Drafting.　It may seem odd that writing a draft should come in the middle of the writer's process. However, research has shown that students and professionals alike write more effective essays when they don't reach for the pen too quickly. If you have spent enough time in the *inventing* and *organizing* stages, the actual drafting stage should go quickly. You know what you want to say, there is no sense of hesitancy. At this point, you will add the details, observations, illustrations, examples, expert testimony, and other support that will help your essay entertain, illuminate or convince your audience.

Revising.　If your habits have included writing your class essays at the last minute, you may have missed this step entirely, yet many writers claim this is the longest and most rewarding step in the writing process. To revise, you have to learn to let go of your writing. Some students think their first drafts should stay exactly the way they are written because they are true to their feelings and experience. Many writers find, however, that first drafts assume too much about the reader's knowledge and reactions. Sometimes readers, reading a first draft essay, are left scratching their heads and wondering what it is the writer is trying to convey. Writers who revise try to read their writing as readers would note gaps in logic, absence of clear examples, need for reordering information, etc. Then they can revise content with the reader in mind.

Editing and Polishing.   Once writers have clarified their messages and the modes by which they get their points across, one more step must be taken. They must go over their work again to check for correct spelling, grammar, and punctuation, as well as the use of Standard Written English. Some students finish with an essay, print it, and turn it in without ever examining the final copy. This is a critical mistake, because misspelled words, typographical, and formatting errors can make an otherwise well-written essay lose credibility.

It is understandably difficult to find the errors in an essay you have been working on for days. A few tricks used by professional writers might help you see errors in your essay more clearly. First, with pencil in hand, read the essay aloud, *slowly,* preferably to an audience. Reading aloud, it is more difficult to add or change words, so you tend to catch errors you would not see reading silently to yourself. Plus the reactions of your audience may point out areas where future readers may become confused or lose interest.

Another trick is to read the essay backwards, sentence by sentence. This forces you to look at sentence structure and not at the overall content of the essay. If you are working on a computer, another way to accomplish this is to create a final edit file in which you hit the hard return twice at the end of every question or statement. You might even go so far as to number the sentences so they look more like grammar exercises. Then look at each sentence individually. Use the "Qualities of Effective Writing" from Chapter 7, to make your structural review more complete.

Focus on Inventing

The writing process begins as soon as you start to read, think, or talk about a possible subject for writing. You may have started thinking about a topic for a paper you will write in this class long before you even entered this school. Perhaps you have tried to explain computers to your parents or grandparents, and realized how mystifying the concepts can be to someone who has not grown up with the technology. Maybe you have even wondered what your life would be like without a telephone, a VCR, a computer, or any of the other technological conveniences we take for granted. Or maybe you have just begun to think about going online, and wondered why the World Wide Web seems so fascinating to so many people. If any of these things have happened to you, you have already begun the writing process for this class— your *inventing* stage has already begun. But that's only the first step, expand your thought process using freewriting or mapping.

Freewriting.   Great myths have grown up around writers who can supposedly sit down, put pen to paper, and write a masterpiece. If these myths had developed about any other type of artist—a musician or a painter—we would scoff about them and ask about the years of study and practice those artists had spent before they created their masterpieces. Since all of us can write to some degree, perhaps it seems more feasible that great authors simply appear magically amongst us. Alas, it is not so; like all talented artists, good writers must learn their craft through consistent and continuous practice.

One practice method developed in the 1970s and often attributed to Peter Elbow, author of *Writing Without Teachers*, is called *freewriting*. And the method is just what it sounds like—writing that is free of any content restrictions. You simply write what is on your mind. Freeform, but there is some structure—you must set a time limit before you begin, and once you begin, you must not stop. The time period is usually ten to twenty minutes, and you must keep your pen or pencil moving on the page—no hesitations, no corrections, no rereading. Don't worry about spelling, or punctuation, or grammar—just download onto the paper whatever comes to mind. It will seem awkward at best, some have said it is downright painful. But after a few weeks practice, you will realize it is effective, and a wonderful individual method of getting at your thoughts on a subject.

Invisible Freewriting. If you just cannot stop paying attention to your spelling and grammar, or if you find yourself always stopping to read what you have written. You can freewrite invisibly. To do this, you will need carbon paper and a pen that is retracted or out of ink. You sandwich the carbon paper, carbon side down, between two sheets of paper and write on the top sheet with your empty pen. You cannot see what you are writing, but you will have it recorded on the bottom sheet of paper. You can easily modify this to work on the computer by taping a blank sheet of paper over the monitor while you type.

Focused Freewriting. When freewriting, you are writing without sticking to any particular topic. You are exploring many ideas and your sentences may roam from your day at work, the letter you just got from your sister, or a story you read in the paper about a man who tracks the nighttime migrations of songbirds. With *focused freewriting*, you are trying to concentrate on one particular subject. You can write that subject at the top of the page to remind you of your topic as you write. The rules are the same, but when you are focusing, you are more aware of exploring one question or idea in depth.

Your teacher may often ask you to do focused freewriting in class. If she asks you, for example, to think about the topic of one of the readings and write on that topic for ten minutes, she is asking you to complete a focused freewriting. You must keep your hand moving over the page for a fixed period, and you do not have to worry about spelling, grammar, or punctuation.

One drawback of focused freewriting is that students sometimes confuse it with a different step in the writing process, drafting. Remember that freewriting is 'invention' work, intended only to help you explore ideas on paper. Drafting takes place only after you have explored, analyzed, and organized those ideas. The act of freewriting and drafting are much the same. They are vastly different, however, because freewriting helps you think and write critically about a topic while drafting occurs once you have done the critical thinking necessary to come up with a unified, cohesive, and organized plan for an essay.

Mapping. The various methods of mapping provide a visual means of exploring a topic. Mapping helps you uncover connections between and within ideas as you explore your topic by giving you a visual guide to follow. Whether you map by listing phrases in a single column on a blank page or create complex clusters, using mapping alone or in tandem with freewriting can help you write a more thorough essay.

Listing/Brainstorming. This method of mapping is the least visual and the most straightforward. Unlike freewriting, where you write continuously, with *listing* you write down words and/or phrases that provide a shorthand for the ideas you might use in your essay, much as you would a grocery or "to-do" list. *Brainstorming* is a bit looser. Lists usually follow line after line on the page, brainstorming consists of words and phrases placed anywhere on the page you want to write them down.

Clustering. When you think of a cluster, you think of several like things grouped together, often with something holding them together. *Peanut clusters*, a type of candy, are peanuts joined together with milk chocolate. *Star clusters* are groupings of stars, like the Pleidaes or the Big Dipper connected by their relative positions to each other in space.

You can create clusters of like ideas by grouping your ideas around a central topic on a blank sheet of paper. Laura Miller might have used this technique in exploring her ideas on "Women and the Internet." She could have started with the word "women" in a circle at the center of a sheet of paper, then drawn subdivisions radiating from that central idea: verbal aggression, "masculine" debate styles, and sexual risk and experimentation. Radiating from each of these sub-topics would be the points of discussion she might make as she tries to prove that, in her experience, the Internet doesn't reinforce the gender differences common in face-to-face contact. Clusters do the work of invention as well as some of the work of organizing because you group like ideas together.

Spend more time during the *inventing stage*, working on ideas by thinking about them, talking about them, and writing about them. You will find that more invention work makes it easier to write a unified and cohesive essay that approaches both simple and complex issues logically and with adequate support.

Focus on Revising

Many writers claim that this is the longest and most rewarding step in writing. Yet, many students feel that their first drafts should stay exactly the way they've written them because these writings are truest to their feelings and experience. They are sure they have made their point clearly, but the reader may be left scratching his head and wondering what it was the writer meant to say. A toddler learns to speak from interaction with his parents—experimenting with sounds until he forms words that get the response he desires. Just so, the writer must learn to interact with his reader to ensure he has communicated his message clearly.

The first step of revising is rereading. This step can be simple, if you are reading something written by someone else, but when it is your own writing it becomes infinitely more difficult. After all, you know what you meant to say—you know the research behind the writing and why you chose certain words or phrases. You even know how every sentence is supposed to read—even though you left out a word or two or three—and your mind can trick you into seeing the missing words right where they belong. Unfortunately, the reader does not have your understanding, and communication can break down. You need to learn to read your own work critically, as if it were written by a stranger. One of the first aids in this process is to read your work aloud. You can often hear stumbling blocks, quicker than you can see them.

You can also learn to read your own work more objectively by reading and commenting on other writers' work. This can be done with the professional examples presented in this book, or by working with other writing you encounter in your research. Look at the structure of the essays, at the way the writers use transitions and topic sentences, and at the sentence structure and choice of words. As you learn to see how good writers put ideas and words together, you will begin to think about the readings in a more thorough manner—thinking of alternative, perhaps even better, ways to express the message of each essay. You will also learn to read your own work with a more critical eye.

Peer Editing.   Your instructor may schedule class periods for peer workshops. These workshops are opportunities for you to get responses from your readers. Often, you will be divided into groups of three or four students and you will be given a list of questions to answer about your peers' essays. Your peers will get copies of your essay, and they will give you comments as well. The first peer workshop can be a difficult experience. It is never easy to take criticism, constructive or not. Taking criticism in a small group is even more difficult. There are several things you can do to make your peer groups more productive.

When your essay is being reviewed:

1. Write down everything the reviewers say. You think you will remember it later, but often you will forget just that piece of advice you need. More importantly, writing while the reviewers speak is an effective way to keep the channels of communication open. It is hard to come up with a defense for your paper if you are busy writing.

2. Save your comments until all the reviewers are done. If you have specific questions, write them in the margins of your notes. If they ask you questions, make a note to answer them when everyone is done. If you allow yourself to speak, you will be tempted to start

defending your essay. Once you start defending your essay, two things happen. First, you stop listening to the comments. Second, you offend your reviewers, making it less likely that they will give you honest criticism in the future.

3. The first comment you should make to your reviewers is "Thank You." The second comment can be anything but a defense. Your readers are only telling you how they interpret your essay. They are giving you their opinions; you do not have to make the changes they suggest.

4. Save all the comments you get on your essay. Set them aside for a day or so. Then make the changes that you think will make your essay better.

When you are the reviewer:

1. Read an essay through, at least one time, just to enjoy the content of the essay. Appreciate the essay for what it does well. Try to ignore any problems for now. You will get back to them the second time you read and begin your comments in the margins. Every essay will have at least one thing good about it.

2. Always begin your comments with a sincere discussion of what you like about the essay.

3. Be specific in your comments. Your peers will probably understand you better if you say, "The topic sentence in paragraph four really sets the reader up for what the essay accomplishes in paragraph four. But I can't really find a topic sentence for paragraph six, and the topic sentences in paragraphs two and three could be improved." Note how this statement gives a positive response and then identifies specific places where the author can improve the essay. This works much better than a generalized statement like, "Topic sentences need work."

4. Be descriptive in your comments. It is often helpful for students to hear how you are reading their essays. "Paragraph five seems to be telling me . . ." or "I got the feeling the essay's overall message is . . ." are good ways to start descriptive sentences.

5. Realize that you are analyzing a paper and not a person. Directing your comments toward the essay, "Paragraph nine doesn't really have anything new to add, does the paper need it?" sounds better to the listener than "You repeat yourself in paragraph nine. Do you really need it?"

Independent Reviewing. If your instructor does not require peer editing, you can ask someone to review your essay. Choose someone you trust to give you an honest opinion. It might not be effective to ask a parent, spouse, or girlfriend/boyfriend to give you a critique if you know they are going to like anything you write, just because you wrote it. It might be better to ask another student who has recently had an English class, or is enrolled in yours currently. In exchange, you might offer to look over their work. Remember, you learn to read your own essays better by reading other peoples' essays more critically. Have your reviewer answer the following questions about your essay.

You might ask someone to answer these questions for an early draft.

1. What is the main idea that you think the writer is trying to get across?
2. What do you like about the essay?
3. What one thing would you do to improve the essay?

When you have revised your paper several times, have someone answer these questions.

Overall Content

1. What is the thesis or main point of the essay? Where does the writer state this main point? If the main point is implied rather than stated, express it in a sentence. Does the main point give a subject and an opinion about the subject? How might the writer improve his/her thesis?

2. What is the purpose of this essay? What are the characteristics of the audience the writer seems to be addressing? (formal, fun-loving, serious, cynical, laid-back, etc.)

3. Do each of the paragraphs in the essay work to support the main point of the essay? On a separate sheet of paper, make an informal outline of the essay. Which paragraphs seem to wander from that main point? What other information needs to be added to develop the main point?

4. List two places in the essay where the writer uses vivid sensory details. How effective are those details? Are they used to support the thesis of the essay? Identify two places in the essay where the writer needs more details that are effective. What kind of details might he or she include?

Paragraph Development

1. What grade would you give the introduction? How does it draw the reader into the essay? What specific things can the writer do to make the intro more inviting?

2. Does each paragraph begin with a topic sentence? Choose the two most effective topic sentences and identify them. What makes them effective? Choose the least effective topic sentence. What can the writer do to improve it?

3. Is each paragraph focused around the topic sentence of the paragraph? Is each paragraph unified and coherent? Which paragraph do you like the best? Why? Which paragraph in the essay do you like the least? Why? What can the writer do to improve his/her paragraphs?

4. What grade would you give the conclusion? How does it provide closure for the essay? What specific things can the writer do to make the conclusion more effective?

Word Choice and Sentence Structure

1. Are adequate transitions used between the paragraphs? Find an effective paragraph transitions and identify it. Why does it work? Find two places between paragraph that need more or better transitions. What can the writer do to improve these transitions?

2. Is a variety of sentences used? Where might the writer vary the sentence structure for better effect? What two sentences in the essay did you find most effective? Why?

3. Are there any words that seem misused or out of place? What positive or negative trigger words are used? Do they enhance the message of the essay or detract from it?

WRITING PROCESS ACTIVITY

1. Write your tentative thesis statement at the top of a blank sheet of paper.

2. Write a list of at least twelve items of support for your thesis.

3. Choose two or three items from your list and do a focused freewriting on each item for eight to ten minutes.

4. Add more items to your list if you have discovered new ideas during your freewriting.

5. Take a careful look at your list. Delete redundant items, group like items, and show connections between items. Decide on an order for your ideas and write a rough outline.

6. Look over your thesis statement and revise it to reflect your outline if necessary.

ACCESSING INTERNET RESOURCES: WORLD WIDE WEB SUBJECT-TREE INDEXES

Suppose you want to find information about a particular topic, such as *cyberspace and society*? How would you go about finding World Wide Web sites that focus on that topic? You can use the subject-tree indexes included with

John, Paul,
George, Ringo

Yahoo! Chat

Search options

MLB Playoffs - MLS Playoffs - NHL - College Football - NFL

Yellow Pages - People Search - Maps - Classifieds - News - Stock Quotes - Sports Scores

- **Arts and Humanities**
  Architecture, Photography, Literature...

- **Business and Economy [Xtra!]**
  Companies, Investing, Employment...

- **Computers and Internet [Xtra!]**
  Internet, WWW, Software, Multimedia...

- **Education**
  Universities, K-12, College Entrance...

- **Entertainment [Xtra!]**
  Cool Links, Movies, Music, Humor...

- **Government**
  Military, Politics [Xtra!], Law, Taxes...

- **Health [Xtra!]**
  Medicine, Drugs, Diseases, Fitness...

- **News and Media [Xtra!]**
  Current Events, Magazines, TV, Newspapers...

- **Recreation and Sports [Xtra!]**
  Sports, Games, Travel, Autos, Outdoors...

- **Reference**
  Libraries, Dictionaries, Phone Numbers...

- **Regional**
  Countries, Regions, U.S. States...

- **Science**
  CS, Biology, Astronomy, Engineering...

- **Social Science**
  Anthropology, Sociology, Economics...

- **Society and Culture**
  People, Environment, Religion...

many of the Internet search engines. Yahoo, for example, features its subject-tree on its home page. Connect to Yahoo, http://www.yahoo.com, and you will see a screen similar to the above illustration.

Browse through the list of topics and you will see the heading *Computers and Internet*, with subtopics *Internet, WWW, Software, Multimedia. . . .* Click on *Computers and Internet*, and you will receive a large set of subtopics similar to that in the illustration on page 133.

Try *Cyberculture*, and you will see a list of further sub-topics, including *Cyberpunk* and *News*. Continue to follow the subject tree until you find sites, and explore them. At any point you can use the Back arrow to move higher in the hierarchy of subtopics and follow a different branch.

Other search engines you might try which have subject-tree indexes include:
Excite, http://www.excite.com
Infoseek, http://www.infoseek.com
Lycos, http://www.lycos.com
Webcrawler, http://webcrawler.com

- Art@
- Bibliographies *(10)*
- Communications and Networking *(1513)* NEW!
- Companies@
- Computer Science@
- Contests *(37)*
- Conventions and Conferences *(213)* NEW!
- Countries, Cultures, and Groups *(35)* NEW!
- Cyberculture@
- Desktop Publishing *(71)*
- Employment *(1225)* NEW!
- Ethics *(15)*
- Games@
- Graphics *(290)* NEW!
- Hardware *(1789)* NEW!
- History *(104)*
- Humor@
- Information and Documentation *(2798)* NEW!
- Internet *(7040)* NEW!

- Magazines *(687)*
- Mobile Computing *(30)*
- Multimedia *(839)* NEW!
- Music@
- Operating Systems *(1623)* NEW!
- Organizations *(189)* NEW!
- Personal Computers@
- Programming Languages *(1502)* NEW!
- Security and Encryption *(738)* NEW!
- Semiconductors@
- Software *(4406)* NEW!
- Standards *(54)*
- Supercomputing and Parallel Computing *(171)*
- Telecommunications@
- Television Shows@
- Training *(14)*
- User Groups@
- World Wide Web@
- Year 2000 Problem *(71)*

SUGGESTED INTERNET ASSIGNMENTS

1. Compile an annotated bibliography of ten sites on the World Wide Web about cyberspace and society. Your entries should follow MLA citation style format. For additional examples, see the section in the Appendix on citing sources.

   > Cannon, Robert. "Online Children's Safety." Vers. 1.1. 4 March 1997. Internet Telecommunications Project. 12 May 1998 <http://www.cais.net/cannon/memos/parents.htm>
   > A FAQ explaining the basics of the Internet and steps parents can take to make online exploring safer for their children. Discusses filtering software, as well as giving tips for protecting anonymity.

2. Divide the list of resources about hackers listed at the end of the alt.cyberpunk FAQ among members of your group. Explore one of the resources and report back about what you find.

3. Explore the collected papers of the two well-known cyberspace writers with texts in this chapter: Julian Dibbell, http://www.levity.com/julian/indexvanilla.html, and John Perry Barlow, http://www.eff.org/~barlow/library.html. Discuss what you find in class.

selected nonfictions by

JULIAN DIBBELL

- **A Rape in Cyberspace.** *The Village Voice,* December 23, 1993 (51K).
- **My Dinner With Catherine MacKinnon (And Other Hazards of Theorizing Virtual Rape).** A talk, presented at MIT, April 1996 (18K).
- **MUD Money: A Talk on Virtual Value and, Incidentally, the Value of the Virtual.** Presented at Rutgers University, April 1995 (22K).
- **A Brief History of MUDs: From Time Immemorial to the Present.** From my forthcoming book on life in LambdaMOO (35K).
- **Let's Get Digital: The Writer a la Modem.** *The Voice Literary Supplement,* March 1993 (14K).
- **2 Cute 4 Words: In Defense of Smileys.** *The Village Voice,* October 4, 1994 (6K).
- **Code Warriors: Battling for the Keys to Privacy in the Info Age.** *The Village Voice,* August 3, 1993 (35K).
- **The Prisoner: Phiber Optik Goes Directly to Jail.** *The Village Voice,* January 11, 1994 (10K).
- **Viruses Are Good for You** *Wired* 3.02, February 1995 (58K).
- **Tropical Millennium: The Cult and Cults of Brasilia.** A World Wide Web exclusive (29K).
- **Notes on Carmen: Carmen Miranda, Seriously** *The Village Voice,* October 29, 1991 (19K).

WIRED TO THE WEB

Julian Dibbell

http://www.levity.com/julian/indexvanilla.html

Dibbell's Web site contains a collection of essays, talks, and interviews, including an excerpt from a book on LambaMOO and essays printed in *The Village Voice.*

JOHN PERRY BARLOW LIBRARY

- A Declaration of the Independence of Cyberspace (Feb. 1996)
- A pretty Bad Problem: Forward to PGP User's Guide by Phil Zimmerman
- WIRED Interview - Mitch Kapor & John Barlow Interview by David Gans with Ken Goffman August 5, 1990
- John Perry Barlow's Bio
- A Plain Text on Crypto Policy
- Barlow v Denning Transcript
- John Perry Barlow's Lyrics
- Being in Nothingness Virtual Reality and the Pioneers of Cyberspace
- Bill O' Rights Lite
- The View from the Brooklyn Bridge
- Who Holds the Keys?
- The Complete ACM Columns Collection
- Crime and Puzzlement
- Crime and Puzzlement Part Two
- Eulogy of Cynthia Horner
- Dad's Invisible Guard-All Shield
- Death From Above
- Decrypting the Puzzle Palace
- Across the Electronic Frontier
- The Great Work
- Selling Wine Without Bottles: The Economy of Mind on the Global Net
- Stopping the Information Railroad
- Jackboots on the Infobahn: Clipping the Wings of Freedom
- Jack In, Young Pioneer!

John Perry Barlow
http://www.eff.org/~barlow/library.html
John Perry Barlow's library page contains a collection of essays, interviews, and songs, including "Crime and Puzzlement," "Is There a There in Cyberspace," and a 1990 *Wired* interview of Barlow and Mitch Kapor.

THE COMPUTER AS A
MEDIUM WITH A MESSAGE

In a sense, moveable type caused the Protestant Reformation. No longer could the Catholic Church control access to the Bible. In the same way, the automobile caused the creation of the suburbs, and the birth control pill lent impetus to the women's rights movement. No technology simply performs a mechanical function. A technology changes the way its users perceive the world because it introduces a new extension of human abilities and this change in perception, in turn, changes society. According to Marshall McLuhan, "the medium is the message."

What is the message of computer technology? What changes will it introduce? As with other innovations, it is difficult to predict the long-term effects of computers. As Mortimer B. Zuckerman writes in "Now, A Word from Cyberspace," few would have imagined forty years ago that the room-sized computers of that era would shrink to laptop size and become commonplace. Already, computers allow users to communicate as easily across the world as across the office, buying and selling, exchanging data, and making friends. Computers allow the creation of virtual worlds which are becoming increasingly realistic, some say seductive. Will this diminish our need for interaction in the "real" world?

Because of computers, television, and other media, our minds are awash with stimulation. Bill McKibben, in "Out There in the Middle of the Buzz," says that our minds marinate in the information, data, and images that are spawned by the billions of microprocessors in the world around us. Even when we manage to steal a few moments of silence and solitude, many of us can't swing in a porch swing or stargaze without our minds being filled with memories of television news, the latest movie, or other images. We have trouble being "in the moment" when the moment is quiet solitude. Our minds have been changed by technology, by the constant sound, the ever-present colorful images.

Neil Postman suggests that we live in a *technopoly*, a term he has created to describe a "culture which is willing to submit all of its social institutions to the control of technology." An invention like the automobile, is marketed and adopted because of its obvious utility as a means of transportation. Side effects like pollution, and cities choked with traffic are accepted as unavoidable consequences. It doesn't have to be that way. It is possible, when a technology is introduced, to study its possible consequences and to place restrictions upon its development in order to minimize negative side effects. As expressed in the title of the interview, "The Same Mindless, Stupid Process," Postman contends we are now in the process of repeating our mistakes. The computer is being embraced uncritically, without considering the elements of our culture that it could destroy. If, for example, the computer makes it possible to do all our shopping at home, to work at home, to entertain ourselves at home, it will likely increase individual isolation. Should not efforts be made through education to strengthen community ties and, thus, counteract the computer's isolating effect?

How do you think computer technology is changing society? What effects has it had upon your own life? How do computers extend the reach of your senses? Are the effects positive or negative? As you read the following texts, consider how computer technology is a medium with a message.

THE MEDIUM IS THE MESSAGE

by Marshall McLuhan

A book is more than the meaning of the words; a news program on television is more than the information about what happened in the world today. The following text, which is the first chapter from Marshall McLuhan's landmark book Understanding Media, *asserts that the medium itself is not neutral but carries meaning. In McLuhan's often quoted words, "the medium is the message." And the message is "the change of scale or pace or pattern that it [the medium] introduces into human affairs." A new media or technology, according to McLuhan, alters the user's patterns of perception.*

McLuhan was one of the most influential theorists of the twentieth century, authoring The Global Village: Transformations in World Life and Media in the 21st Century, *as well as* Understanding Media: The Extensions of Man, *and* Gutenberg Galaxy: The Making of Typographic Man.

In a culture like ours, long accustomed to splitting and dividing all things as a means of control, it is sometimes a bit of a shock to be reminded that, in operational and practical fact, the medium is the message. This is merely to say that the personal and social consequences of any medium—that is, of any extension of ourselves—result from the new scale that is introduced into our affairs by each extension of ourselves, or by any new technology. Thus, with automation, for example, the new patterns of human association tend to eliminate jobs, it is true. That is the negative result. Positively, automation creates roles for people, which is to say depth of involvement in their work and human association that our preceding mechanical technology had destroyed. Many people would be disposed to say that it was not the machine, but what one did with the machine, that was its meaning or message. In terms of the ways in which the machine altered our relations to one another and to ourselves, it mattered not in the least whether it turned out cornflakes or Cadillacs. The restructuring of human work and association was shaped by the technique of fragmentation that is the essence of machine technology. The essence of automation technology is the opposite. It is integral and decentralist in depth, just as the machine was fragmentary, centralist, and superficial in its patterning of human relationships.

The instance of the electric light may prove illuminating in this connection. The electric light is pure information. It is a medium without a message, as it were, unless it is used to spell out some verbal ad or name. This fact, characteristic of all media, means that the "content of any medium is always another medium. The content of writing is speech, just as the written word is the content of print, and print is the content of the telegraph. If it is asked, "What is the content of speech?," it is necessary to say, "It is an actual process of thought, which is in itself nonverbal." An abstract painting represents direct manifestation of creative thought processes as they might appear in computer designs. What we are considering here, however, are the psychic and social consequences of the designs or patterns as they amplify or accelerate existing processes. For the "message" of any medium or technology is the change of scale or pace or pattern that it introduces into human affairs. The railway did not introduce movement or transportation or wheel or road into human society, but it accelerated and enlarged the scale of previous human functions, creating totally new kinds of cities and new kinds of work and leisure. This happened whether the railway functioned in a tropical or a northern environment, and is quite independent of the freight or content of the railway medium. The airplane, on the other hand, by accelerating the rate of transportation, tends to dissolve the railway form of city, politics, and association, quite independently of what the airplane is used for.

Let us return to the electric light. Whether the light is being used for brain surgery or night baseball is a matter of indifference. It could be argued that these activities are in some way the "content" of the electric light, since they could not exist without the electric light. This fact merely underlines the point that "the medium is the message" because it is the medium that shapes and controls the scale and form of human association and action. The content or uses of such media are as diverse as they are ineffectual in shaping the form of human association. Indeed, it is only too typical that the "content" of any medium blinds us to the character of the medium. It is only today that industries have become aware of the various kinds of business in which they are engaged. When IBM discovered that it was not in the business of making office equipment or business machines, but that it was in the business of processing information, then it began to navigate with clear vision. The General Electric Company makes a considerable portion of its profits from electric light bulbs and lighting systems. It has not yet discovered that, quite as much as AT&T, it is in the business of moving information.

The electric light escapes attention as a communication medium just because it has no "content." And this makes it an invaluable instance of how people fail to study media at all. For it is not till the electric light is used to spell out some brand name that it is noticed as a medium. Then it is not the light but the "content" (or what is really another medium) that is noticed. The message of the electric light is like the message of electric power in industry, totally radical, pervasive, and decentralized. For electric light and power are separate from their uses, yet they eliminate time and space factors in human association exactly as do radio, telegraph, telephone, and TV, creating involvement in depth.

A fairly complete handbook for studying the extensions of man could be made up from selections from Shakespeare. Some might quibble about whether or not he was referring to TV in these familiar lines from *Romeo and Juliet*:

> But soft! what light through yonder window breaks?
> It speaks, and yet says nothing.

In *Othello*, which, as much as *King Lear*, is concerned with the torment of people transformed by illusions, there are these lines that bespeak Shakespeare's intuition of the transforming powers of new media:

> Is there not charms
> By which the property of youth and maidhood
> May be abus'd? Have you not read Roderigo,
> Of some such thing?

In Shakespeare's *Troilus and Cressida*, which is almost completely devoted to both a psychic and social study of communication, Shakespeare states his awareness that true social and political navigation depend upon anticipating the consequences of innovation:

> The providence that's in a watchful state
> Knows almost every grain of Plutus' gold,
> Finds bottom in the uncomprehensive deeps,
> Keeps place with thought, and almost like the gods
> Does thoughts unveil in their dumb cradles.

The increasing awareness of the action of media, quite independently of their "content" or programming, was indicated in the annoyed and anonymous stanza:

> In modern thought, (if not in fact)
> Nothing is that doesn't act,
> So that is reckoned wisdom which
> Describes the scratch but not the itch.

The same kind of total, configurational awareness that reveals why the medium is socially the message has occurred in the most recent and radical medical theories. In his *Stress of Life*, Hans Selye tells of the dismay of a research colleague on hearing of Selye's theory:

> When he saw me thus launched on yet another enraptured description of what I had observed in animals treated with this or that impure, toxic material, he looked at me with desperately sad eyes and said in obvious despair: "But Selye, try to realize what you are doing before it is too late! You have now decided to spend your entire life studying the pharmacology of dirt!"
>
> (Hans Selye, *The Stress of Life*)

As Selye deals with the total environmental situation in his "stress" theory of disease, so the latest approach to media study considers not only the "content" but the medium and the cultural matrix within which the particular medium operates. The older unawareness of the psychic and social effects of media can be illustrated from almost any of the conventional pronouncements.

In accepting an honorary degree from the University of Notre Dame a few years ago, General David Sarnoff made this statement: "We are too prone to make technological instruments the scapegoats for the sins of those who wield them. The products of modern science are not in themselves good or bad; it is the way they are used that determines their value." That is the voice of the current somnambulism. Suppose we were to say, "Apple pie is in itself neither good nor bad; it is the way it is used that determines its value." Or, "The smallpox virus is in itself neither good nor bad; it is the way it is used that determines its value." Again, "Firearms are in themselves neither good nor bad; it is the way they are used that determines their value." That is, if the slugs reach the right people firearms are good. If the TV tube fires the right ammunition at the right people it is good. I am not being perverse. There is simply nothing in the Sarnoff statement that will bear scrutiny, for it ignores the nature of the medium, of any and all media, in the true Narcissus style of one hypnotized by the amputation and extension of his own being in a new technical form. General Sarnoff went on to explain his attitude to the technology of print, saying that it was true that print caused much trash to circulate, but it had also disseminated the Bible and the thoughts of seers and philosophers. It has never occurred to General Sarnoff that any technology could do anything but *add* itself on to what we already are.

Such economists as Robert Theobald, W. W. Rostow, and John Kenneth Galbraith have been explaining for years how it is that "classical economics" cannot explain change or growth. And the paradox of mechanization is that although it is itself the cause of maximal growth and change, the principle of mechanization excludes the very possibility of growth or the understanding of change. For mechanization is achieved by fragmentation of any process and by putting the fragmented parts in a series. Yet, as David Hume showed in the eighteenth century, there is no principle of causality in a mere sequence. That one thing follows another accounts for nothing. Nothing follows from following, except change. So the greatest of all reversals occurred with electricity, that ended sequence by making things instant. With instant speed the causes of things began to emerge to awareness again, as they had not done with things in sequence and in concatenation accordingly. Instead of asking which came first, the chicken or the egg, it suddenly seemed that a chicken was an egg's idea for getting more eggs.

Just before an airplane breaks the sound barrier, sound waves become visible on the wings of the plane. The sudden visibility of sound just as sound ends is an apt instance of that great pattern of being that reveals new and opposite forms just as the earlier forms reach their peak performance. Mechanization was never so vividly fragmented or sequential as in the birth of the movies, the moment that translated us beyond mechanism into the world of growth and organic interrelation. The movie, by sheer speeding up the mechanical, carried us from the world of sequence and connections into the world of creative configuration and structure. The message of the movie medium is that of transition from lineal connections to configurations. It is the transition that produced the now quite correct observation: "If it works, it's obsolete." When electric speed further takes over from mechanical movie sequences, then the lines of force in structures and in media become loud and clear. We return to the inclusive form of the icon.

To a highly literate and mechanized culture the movie appeared as a world of triumphant illusions and dreams that money could buy. It was at this moment of the movie that cubism occurred, and it has been described by E. H. Gombrich (*Art and Illusion*) as "the most radical attempt to stamp out ambiguity and to enforce one reading of the picture—that of a man-made construction, a colored canvas." For cubism substitutes all facets of an object simultaneously for the "point of view" or facet of perspective illusion. Instead of the specialized illusion of the third dimension on canvas, cubism sets up an interplay of planes and contradiction or dramatic conflict of patterns, lights, textures that "drives home the message" by involvement. This is held by many to be an exercise in painting, not in illusion.

In other words, cubism, by giving the inside and outside, the top, bottom, back, and front and the rest in two dimensions, drops the illusion of perspective in favor of instant sensory awareness of the whole. Cubism, by seizing on instant total awareness, suddenly announced that *the medium is the message*. Is it not evident that the moment that sequence yields to the simultaneous, one is in the world of the structure and of configuration? Is that not what has happened in physics as in painting, poetry, and in communication? Specialized segments of attention have shifted to total field, and we can now say, "The medium is the message" quite naturally. Before the electric speed and total field, it was not obvious that the medium is the message. The message, it seemed, was the "content," as people used to ask what a painting was *about*. Yet they never thought to ask what a melody was about, nor what a house or a dress was about. In such matters, people retained some sense of the whole pattern, of form and function as a unity. But in the electric age this integral idea of structure and configuration has become so prevalent that educational theory has taken up the matter. Instead of working with specialized "problems" in arithmetic, the structural approach now follows the linea of force in the field of number and has small children meditating about number theory and "sets."

Cardinal Newman said of Napoleon, "He understood the grammar of gunpowder." Napoleon had paid some attention to other media as well, especially the semaphore telegraph that gave him a great advantage over his enemies. He is on record for saying that "Three hostile newspapers are more to be feared than a thousand bayonets."

Alexis de Tocqueville was the first to master the grammar of print and typography. He was thus able to read off the message of coming change in France and America as if he were reading aloud from a text that had been handed to him. In fact, the nineteenth century in France and in America was just such an open book to de Tocqueville because he had learned the grammar of print. So he, also, knew when that grammar did not apply. He was asked why he did not write a book on England, since he knew and admired England. He replied:

> One would have to have an unusual degree of philosophical folly to believe oneself able to judge England in six months. A year always seemed to me too short a time in which to appreciate the United States properly, and it is much easier to acquire clear and precise notions about the American Union than about Great Britain. In America all laws derive in a sense from the same line of thought. The whole of society, so to speak, is founded upon a single fact; every-

thing springs from a simple principle. One could compare America to a forest pierced by a multitude of straight roads all converging on the same point. One has only to find the center and everything is revealed at a glance. But in England the paths run criss-cross, and it is only by travelling down each one of them that one can build up a picture of the whole.

De Tocqueville, in earlier work on the French Revolution, had explained how it was the printed word that, achieving cultural saturation in the eighteenth century, had homogenized the French nation. Frenchmen were the same kind of people from north to south. The typographic principles of uniformity, continuity, and lineality had overlaid the complexities of ancient feudal and oral society. The Revolution was carried out by the new literati and lawyers.

In England, however, such was the power of the ancient oral traditions of common law, backed by the medieval institution of Parliament, that no uniformity or continuity of the new visual print culture could take complete hold. The result was that the most important event in English history has never taken place; namely, the English Revolution on the lines of the French Revolution. The American Revolution had no medieval legal institutions to discard or to root out, apart from monarchy. And many have held that the American Presidency has become very much more personal and monarchical than any European monarch ever could be.

De Tocqueville's contrast between England and America is clearly based on the fact of typography and of print culture creating uniformity and continuity. England, he says, has rejected this principle and clung to the dynamic or oral commonlaw tradition. Hence the discontinuity and unpredictable quality of English culture. The grammar of print cannot help to construe the message of oral and nonwritten culture and institutions. The English aristocracy was properly classified as barbarian by Matthew Arnold because its power and status had nothing to do with literacy or with the cultural forms of typography. Said the Duke of Gloucester to Edward Gibbon upon the publication of his *Decline and Fall*: "Another damned fat book, eh, Mr. Gibbon? Scribble, scribble, scribble, eh. Mr. Gibbon?" De Tocqueville was a highly literate aristocrat who was quite able to be detached from the values and assumptions of typography. That is why he alone understood the grammar of typography. And it is only on those terms, standing aside from any structure or medium, that its principles and lines of force can be discerned. For any medium has the power of imposing its own assumption on the unwary. Prediction and control consist in avoiding this subliminal state of Narcissus trance. But the greatest aid to this end is simply in knowing that the spell can occur immediately upon contact, as in the first bars of a melody.

A Passage to India by E. M. Forster is a dramatic study of the inability of oral and intuitive oriental culture to meet with the rational, visual European patterns of experience. "Rational," of course, has for the West long meant "uniform and continuous and sequential." In other words, we have confused reason with literacy, and rationalism with a single technology. Thus in the electric age man seems to the conventional West to become irrational. In Forster's novel the moment of truth and dislocation from the typographic trance of the West comes in the Marabar Caves. Adela Quested's reasoning powers cannot cope with the total inclusive field of resonance that is India. After the Caves: "Life went on as usual, but had no consequences, that is to say, sounds did not echo nor thought develop. Everything seemed cut off at its root and therefore infected with illusion."

A Passage to India (the phrase is from Whitman, who saw America headed Eastward) is a parable of Western man in the electric age, and is only incidentally related to Europe or the Orient. The ultimate conflict between sight and sound, between written and oral kinds of perception and organization of existence is upon us. Since understanding stops action, as Nietzsche observed, we can moderate the fierceness of this conflict by understanding the media that extend us and raise these wars within and without us.

Detribalization by literacy and its traumatic effects on tribal man is the theme of a book by the psychiatrist J. C. Carothers, *The African Mind in Health and Disease* (World Health Organization, Geneva, 1953). Much of his material appeared in an article in *Psychiatry* magazine, November, 1959: "The Culture, Psychiatry, and the Written Word." Again, it is electric speed that has revealed the lines of force operating from Western technology in the remotest areas of bush, savannah, and desert. One example is the Bedouin with his battery radio on board the camel. Submerging natives with floods of concepts for which nothing has prepared them is the normal action of all of our technology. But with electric media Western man himself experiences exactly the same inundation as the remote native. We are no more prepared to encounter radio and TV in our literate milieu than the native of Ghana is able to cope with the literacy that takes him out of his collective tribal world and beaches him in individual isolation. We are as numb in our new electric world as the native involved in our literate and mechanical culture.

Electric speed mingles the cultures of prehistory with the dregs of industrial marketeers, the nonliterate with semiliterate and the postliterate. Mental breakdown of varying degrees is the very common result of uprooting and inundation with new information and endless new patterns of information. Wyndham Lewis made this a theme of his group of novels called *The Human Age*. The first of these, *The Childermass*, is concerned precisely with accelerated media change as a kind of massacre of the innocents. In our own world as we become more aware of the effects of technology on psychic formation and manifestation, we are losing all confidence in our right to assign guilt. Ancient prehistoric societies regard violent crime as pathetic. The killer is regarded as we do a cancer victim. "How terrible it must be to feel like that," they say. J. M. Synge took up this idea very effectively in his *Playboy of the Western World*.

If the criminal appears as a nonconformist who is unable to meet the demand of technology that we behave in uniform and continuous patterns, literate man is quite inclined to see others who cannot conform as somewhat pathetic. Especially the child, the cripple, the woman, and the colored person appear in a world of visual and typographic technology as victims of injustice. On the other hand, in a culture that assigns roles instead of jobs to people—the dwarf, the skew, the child create their own spaces. They are not expected to fit into some uniform and repeatable niche that is not their size anyway. Consider the phrase "It's a man's world." As a quantitative observation endlessly repeated from within a homogenized culture, this phrase refers to the men in such a culture who have to be homogenized Dagwoods in order to belong at all. It is in our I.Q. testing that we have produced the greatest flood of misbegotten standards. Unaware of our typographic cultural bias, our testers assume that uniform and continuous habits are a sign of intelligence, thus eliminating the ear man and the tactile man.

C. P. Snow, reviewing a book of A. L. Rowse (*The New York Times Book Review*, December 24, 1961) on *Appeasement* and the road to Munich, describes the top level of British brains and experience in the 1930s. "Their I.Q.'s were much higher than usual among political bosses. Why were they such a disaster?" The view of Rowse, Snow approves: "They would not listen to warnings because they did not wish to hear." Being anti-Red made it impossible for them to read the message of Hitler. But their failure was as nothing compared to our present one. The American stake in literacy as a technology or uniformity applied to every level of education, government, industry, and social life is totally threatened by the electric technology. The threat of Stalin or Hitler was external. The electric technology is within the gates, and we are numb, deaf, blind, and mute about its encounter with the Gutenberg technology, on and through which the American way of life was formed. It is, however, no time to suggest strategies when the threat has not even been acknowledged to exist. I am in the position of Louis Pasteur telling doctors that their greatest enemy was quite invisible, and quite unrecognized by them. Our conventional response to all media, namely that it is how they are used that counts, is the numb stance of the technological idiot. For the "content" of a medium is like the juicy piece of meat carried by the burglar to distract the watchdog of the mind. The effect of the medium is made strong and intense just because it is given another medium as "content." The content of a movie is a novel or a play or an opera! The effect of the movie form is not related to its program content. The "content" of writing or print is speech, but the reader is almost entirely unaware either of print or of speech.

Arnold Toynbee is innocent of any understanding of media as they have shaped history, but he is full of examples that the student of media can use. At one moment he can seriously suggest that adult education, such as the Workers Educational Association in Britain, is a useful counterforce to the popular press. Toynbee considers that although all of the oriental societies have in our time accepted the industrial technology and its political consequences: "On the cultural plane, however, there is no uniform corresponding tendency." (Somervell, I. 267) This is like the voice of the literate man, floundering in a milieu of ads, who boasts, "Personally, I pay no attention to ads." The spiritual and cultural reservations that the oriental peoples may have toward our technology will avail them not at all. The effects of technology do not occur at the level of opinions or concepts, but alter sense ratios or patterns of perception steadily and without any resistance. The serious artist is the only person able to encounter technology with impunity, just because he is an expert aware of the changes in sense perception.

The operation of the money medium in seventeenth-century Japan had effects not unlike the operation of typography in the West. The penetration of the money economy, wrote G. B. Sansom (in *Japan*, Cresset Press, London, 1931) "caused a slow but irresistible revolution, culminating in the breakdown of feudal government and the resumption of intercourse with foreign countries after more than two hundred years of seclusion." Money has reorganized the sense life of peoples just because it is an *extension* of our sense lives. This change does not depend upon approval or disapproval of those living in the society.

Arnold Toynbee made one approach to the transforming power of media in his concept of "etherialization," which he holds to be the principle of pro- gressive simplification and efficiency in any organization or technology. Typically, he is ignoring the *effect* of the challenge of these forms upon the response of our senses. He imagines that it is the response of our opinions that is relevant to the effect of media and technology in society, a "point of view" that is plainly the result of the typographic spell. For the man in a literate and homogenized society ceases to be sensitive to the diverse and discontinuous life of forms. He acquires the illusion of the third dimension and the "private point of view" as part of his Narcissus fixation, and is quite shut off from Blake's awareness or that of the Psalmist, that we become what we behold.

Today when we want to get our bearings in our own culture, and have need to stand aside from the bias and pressure exerted by any technical form of human expression, we have only to visit a society where that particular form has not been felt, or a historical period in which it was unknown. Professor Wilbur Schramm made such a tactical move in studying *Television in the Lives of Our Children*. He found areas where TV had not penetrated at all and ran some tests. Since he had made no study of the peculiar nature of the TV image, his tests were of "content" preferences, viewing time, and vocabulary counts. In a word, his approach to the problem was a literary one, albeit unconsciously so. Consequently, he had nothing to report. Had his methods been employed in 1500 A.D. to discover the effects of the printed book in the lives of children or adults, he could have found out nothing of the changes in human and social psychology resulting from typography. Print created individualism and nationalism in the sixteenth century. Program and "content" analysis offer no clues to the magic of these media or to their subliminal charge.

Leonard Doob, in his report *Communication in Africa*, tells of one African who took great pains to listen each evening to the BBC news, even though he could understand nothing of it. Just to be in the presence of those sounds at 7 P.M. each day was important for him. His attitude to speech was like ours to melody—the resonant intonation was meaning enough. In the seventeenth century our ancestors still shared this native's attitude to the forms of media, as is plain in the following sentiment of the Frenchman Bernard Lam expressed in *The Art of Speaking* (London, 1696):

'Tis an effect of the Wisdom of God, who created Man to be happy, that whatever is useful to his conversation (way of life) is agreeable to him . . . because all victual that conduces to nourishment is relishable, whereas other things that cannot be assimulated and be turned into our substance are insipid. A Discourse cannot be pleasant to the Hearer that is not easie to the Speaker; nor can it be easily pronounced unless it be heard with delight.

Here is an equilibrium theory of human diet and expression such as even now we are only striving to work out again for media after centuries of fragmentation and specialism.

Pope Pius XII was deeply concerned that there be serious study of the media today. On February 17, 1950, he said:

It is not an exaggeration to say that the future of modern society and the stability of its inner life depend in large part on the maintenance of an equilibrium between the strength of the techniques of communication and the capacity of the individual's own reaction.

Failure in this respect has for centuries been typical and total for mankind. Subliminal and docile acceptance of media impact has made them prisons without walls for their human users. As A. J. Liebling remarked in his book *The Press*, a man is not free if he cannot see where he is going, even if he has a gun to help him get there. For each of the media is also a powerful weapon with which to clobber other media and other groups. The result is that the present age has been one of multiple civil wars that are not limited to the world of art and entertainment. In *War and Human Progress*, Professor J. U. Nef declared: "The total wars of our time have been the result of a series of intellectual mistakes . . ."

If the formative power in the media are the media themselves, that raises a host of large matters that can only be mentioned here, although they deserve volumes. Namely, that technological media are staples or natural resources, exactly as are coal and cotton and oil. Anybody will concede that society whose economy is dependent upon one or two major staples like cotton, or grain, or lumber, or fish, or cattle is going to have some obvious social patterns of organization as a result. Stress on a few major staples creates extreme instability in the economy but great endurance in the population. The pathos and humor of the American South are embedded in such an economy of limited staples. For a society configured by reliance on a few commodities accepts them as a social bond quite as much as the metropolis does the press. Cotton and oil, like radio and TV, become "fixed charges" on the entire psychic life of the community. And this pervasive fact creates the unique cultural flavor of any society. It pays through the nose and all its other senses for each staple that shapes its life.

That our human senses, of which all media are extensions, are also fixed charges on our personal energies, and that they also configure the awareness and experience of each one of us, may be perceived in another connection mentioned by the psychologist C. G. Jung:

> Every Roman was surrounded by slaves. The slave and his psychology flooded ancient Italy, and every Roman became inwardly, and of course unwittingly, a slave. Because living constantly in the atmosphere of slaves, he became infected through the unconscious with their psychology. No one can shield himself from such an influence (*Contributions to Analytical Psychology*, London, 1928).

EXPLORING THE READING

1. Marshall McLuhan says that a lightbulb is a medium. What does he mean?

2. McLuhan criticizes the following quote by General David Sarnoff: "The products of modern science are not in themselves good or bad; it is the way they are used that determines their value." What does McLuhan say is wrong with Sarnoff's logic?

3. If a medium alters the perception of its users, consider how the computer may alter perception. Freewrite for five minutes, then share your conclusions.

4. McLuhan writes, "Any medium has the power of imposing its own assumptions on the unwary." Freewrite for five minutes about what you think he means.

YOU ARE WHAT YOU SEE

by Jay David Bolter

No longer is the computer simply a tool for studying the world through numerical analysis or a word processor for writing about the world. Because of the Internet, it is now, as Jay David Bolter points out in this essay from Wired, *a device through which the viewer can see the world. Through a computer, we use electric eyes to live in virtual worlds, and this alters the perception of the self. Bolter believes this new computer application is revolutionary and potentially dangerous.*

Bolter is a professor of language, communication, and culture at the Georgia Institute of Technology, teaching and writing about the social and cultural impact of computers and the use of computers as new medium for verbal and visual communication. He is the author of Turing's Man: Western Culture in the Computer Age *and* The Writing Space: The Computer, Hyertext and the History of Writing. *His home page can be found at Georgia Tech, http://www.gatech.edu in the School of Literature, Communication, and Culture.*

Rara avis means "rare bird" in Latin. But if you access the Rara Avis Website (www.uky.edu/FineArts/Art/kac/raraavis.html), you can have a visual experience that is becoming increasingly common on the Internet. The site presents images captured by a digital camera in an Atlanta art exhibit, where the camera was embedded in the head of a parrotlike "macowl" figurine. Through this electronic eye, you could watch the visitors watching you. You could experience the exhibit from the parrot's point of view.

Computer graphics is showing itself to be a technology for generating points of view. For decades, the computer has been used to study the world through numerical analysis or comment upon the world in text. It is now becoming literally a way of seeing the world. The computer has something in common with earlier perspective technologies—painting, photography, film, television—but it is unique in its capacity for interactivity. In immersive virtual reality and even certain games, the computer gives the user not only a point of view but control over that point of view. This control allows the user to define her- or himself by choosing a place in the virtual world. Computer graphics isn't just about morphing objects; it's about morphing the view and the viewer.

E-mail, newsgroups, chat rooms, MUDs, and MOOs are worlds created out of words, and in these domains our identity is not fundamentally different from what it has been in the world of print. We define ourselves by what we write, just as we have done for hundreds of years in letters, diaries, and printed books. In computer graphic environments, however, we define ourselves by what we see when we look out through electronic eyes.

Visual media are now threatening to take over a crucial cultural task that until now has belonged to verbal media. Conservatives like William Bennett want children to read classic printed books so that they will adopt appropriate points of view (he calls them "virtues"). Conservatives see television as the destroyer of these virtues, and they're right, in a sense. But it is not the implied sex or violence of MTV that poses the threat. It is the schizophrenic POV camerawork, which rejects the consistent verbal identity of the age of print. In this respect interactive computer graphics pose a far greater threat than MTV. Both gentle *Myst* and violent *Doom* subvert the values of print more than does a music video by Madonna, who is herself just a caricature of traditional values. *Myst* is really about superseding, even destroying the book and along with it traditional verbal identity. Action-adventure games, too, are exercises in visual identity, encouraging users to think of themselves as a moving and changing point of view.

Interface designer and cyberspace enthusiast Meredith Bricken has written that with VR "you can be the mad hatter or you can be the teapot; you can move back and forth to the rhythm of a song. You can be a tiny droplet in the rain or in the river; you can be what you thought you ought to be all along. You can switch your point of view to an object or a process or another person's point of view in the other person's world." Bricken celebrates the fluidity of virtual, visual identity. Visual identity is not as stable as verbal identity. On the Internet or on paper, you write much the same prose at seventy that you write at twenty. MUD players think they can become different people in different games merely by changing their names and their descriptions. But their underlying written voice, their verbal character, is often hard to disguise. On the other hand, you don't "express" yourself in defining your computer graphic identity. Instead, you occupy various points of view, each of which constitutes a new identity—whether of a parrot or a flying logo. You adopt these identities one at a time, but you don't need to (and aren't likely to) keep any one for long. Unlike characters in nineteenth-century novels, you don't make fateful, lifelong commitments. You change identities with the same playfulness with which you click through pages on the Web.

This fluidity creates a new type of freedom, at first defined in spatial and visual terms. But as with all freedoms, there are corresponding responsibilities. Visual freedom obliges us not just to sympathize, but to identify with other people. We do this by occupying their point of view technologically— by walking (or flying) a mile in cyberspace wearing their headmounted display.

Television already performs this function in our culture. Television puts you on the scene of every natural and technological disaster and insists that you watch and feel the victims' pain. Interactive computer graphics can vastly improve on television's ability to put you there. The CNN Interactive Website provides recorded audio and video for its regularly updated news reports (frequently disasters and sporting events, which are always invitations to empathize). Meanwhile, digital cameras on the Internet monitor professors' offices, students' dorm rooms, and congested expressways. All such sites are invitations to share an experience. A Web page from the University of Washington (www.cac.washington.edu:1180/) allows everybody on the Internet to experience the current reality of Seattle weather. Then there are the cameras trained on pets: goldfish, guinea pigs, cockatiels. These sites too are exercises in identification. The camera seeks to put you in close, empathetic contact with the animal. It is a short step to the Rara Avis site, where the camera fully occupies the animal's perspective. We can't be far away from "live" Internet video of a natural disaster—the world from the point of view of a hurricane or tornado.

Freedom in the age of print was the freedom to write and read, also called freedom of the press, indicating its connection to the technology of printing. We might also call it "freedom of verbal point of view," because what the age of print valued was the right to define one's identity and beliefs through speaking and writing. That isn't to say the older freedoms of expression are not worth protecting on the Internet. They are. But they matter most to those whose values were formed in and by the age of print.

Those who have opposed the Communications Decency Act argue that the Internet is more like a printed book than like television. For them, the Internet is a world of newsgroups and chat rooms discussing issues like breast cancer and abortion, and so it deserves the same First Amendment protection accorded printed materials. The government has argued that the Internet is like television, a cascade of images—mostly, authorities seem to think, pornographic images. For our visual culture, images are more immediate than words and therefore more dangerous. So our culture censors pictures more vigorously than words, and moving pictures more vigorously than still images. In this respect those who wish to censor the Internet are right in their assessment of where the power is. With Java and VRML, the Internet is going beyond television to foster a new culture of visually realized point of view. The CDA case will probably go to the Supreme Court, the most print-bound institution Americans have. It will be interesting to see whether the nine Justices recognize the Internet as a new kind of book or as television out of control.

But one thing seems certain. The Supreme Court justices won't recognize the real threat (that is, to the old culture of the Enlightenment, which gave us our constitutional republic in the age of print). If they did, they wouldn't worry about banning pornography, certainly not written pornography. Instead, they would ban inexpensive digital cameras, graphic accelerator boards, 3-D rendering software, and, above all, the freedom to merge your point of view with that of a raindrop. This freedom, to which the Founding Fathers were oblivious, is giving us a new definition of the self in cyberspace.

EXPLORING THE READING

1. Connect to the site at the University of Washington, http://www.
   washington.edu, that allows you to experience Seattle weather. After-
   wards, read again what Bolter has to say about how the computer
   alters the way we see the world. Do you agree? Why or why not?

2. Bolter makes a distinction between using the computer for text in
   e-mail, chat rooms, MUDs, and MOOs, and for computer graphic
   environments. He says the former are not much different than
   traditional print, but the latter are revolutionary because they alter
   perception. Do you understand his distinction?

3. How does Bolter's text echo Marshall McLuhan's? Hint: McLuhan
   said all technologies change perception. How does Bolter suggest
   computers change perception?

4. Bolter mentions the arguments comparing the Internet to print and
   to television and decides that it is more like television. What do
   you think?

THE SAME MINDLESS, STUPID PROCESS

by Neil Postman

In this interview of Neil Postman for Whole Earth Review *by German journalist Volker Friedman, Postman discusses his concerns about technology in general and television in particular. Americans show a tendency, Postman says, to make every possible accommodation for new technology. He argues that we need to look more critically at the way we interact with technology. As individuals, we need to consider the function of new technology in our culture. As a society, we need to ensure that our leaders are aware of not only of the benefits of technology, but also the harm it might cause.*

Postman is a professor of media ecology and chair of the Department of Culture and Communications at New York University. He is also a well-published author. In addition to regular publication in New York Times Magazine *and* The Atlantic, *he is the author of eighteen books. One book,* Amusing Ourselves to Death, *has been translated into eight languages. His most recent books are* Technopoly, How to Watch a Television News Show, *and* The End of Education.

Volker Friedrich: Your recent book is titled *Technopoly.* What does your title mean?

Neil Postman: I use the word "Technopoly" to refer to a culture which is willing to submit all of its social institutions to the control of technology. I make a distinction between a technopoly and a technocracy, in that a technocracy is a culture which is surrounded by technologies, but which is still governed to some extent by traditional social systems. Religion and politics and education, for example, are still governed by traditional ideas about these things. So there is a struggle in a technocracy between the demands of the new technologies and the requirements of an old tradition in our symbolic life.

A technopoly is a culture in which the demands of the technologies win decisively, so that every possible accommodation is made by the culture to conform its beliefs to the needs of technology.

VF: You say that the way we use technology is largely fixed by the structure of the technology itself. Functions or operations of a technology are the results of the form or the shape of the technology. What follows from this idea?

NP: I have to modify that idea a bit, as I do in my book. Every technology does have a special form or structure to it, and that structure guides us in how we will use the technology. But I also say that this does not mean that human beings are helpless in the face of technology. We can exercise control over the functions of a technology through political action or social policy or even education. But we must never underestimate the fact that every technology has certain requirements that are set by the form of the technology. For example: if you invent a 747 jet aircraft, the form of the aircraft suggests what its uses will be. You won't use it to transport commuters from the suburbs of Stuttgart into Stuttgart, because the form of a 747 makes it uneconomical and improbable that you can use it that way. If you invent a 747 you will use it for intercontinental travel. If you invent a television, its form will suggest that it is best used for the communication of moving pictures. You can use it for other things, but its structure will almost demand that you use it to display moving pictures. So this is what I mean when I say that the form of a medium will have a very powerful influence on what its functions will be in any society.

VF: As soon as we initiate a technology, as soon as we allow a technology to be part of our lives, the technology brings to bear all its consequences, as you explain in your book. What does this imply, in your opinion, for a responsible policy?

NP: Here is what I think it means. I think we have to be more aware, as best we can, of the possible consequences of new technologies, so that we can prepare our culture for those technologies. If, for instance, we knew in 1902 what we know now about the automobile, there were many things we could have done so that the Schwarzwald, for example, wouldn't be dying, and cities would not be choked with traffic, and the air wouldn't be poisoned. I suppose we might have been able to predict some of those consequences in 1902 or 1910 or 1920. If we had thought about it, there were plenty of things we could have done to prepare ourselves for that technology. But we didn't think about it. And in 1946 no one really thought about, or made any preparations for, television—at least here in America. We are going through the same mindless, stupid process with the computer now. The computer is here, people are not even considering some of the negative consequences of computer technology. No serious preparations are being made to help the culture preserve certain things that the computer can destroy. So I'm not making an argument for a Luddite position. I'm not saying we should smash the machines. I'm saying we should understand what the machines will do, and then try to prepare our culture for the consequences, and in preparing the culture for consequences, try to make sure that we can preserve that which we think is worth preserving, and allow those changes that we think are acceptable.

VF: You write in *Technopoly* that there is an ideological tendency in every tool, and I think that's transferable to technology in general. But that would mean that every technology is a political issue or political factor.

NP: Absolutely. There are many ways to say this. You could say that every technology has embedded in it an ideological bias or an epistemological bias. Or you could say (as you did) that every technology is fundamentally a political issue or even a moral issue. But a technology like the telegraph, with its great emphasis on the speed with which information is moved, changed people's conception of what they mean by information and what they do with information. There is an old saying: to a man with a hammer, everything looks like a nail. If you have a hammer, you go looking around for things that you can bang with it. I suppose we could say that to a man with a pencil, everything looks like a sentence. To a man with a television camera, everything looks like an image. To a man with a computer, everything looks like data. In other words: each technology slices up the world for us in a certain way. It makes us look at things differently from the way we were accustomed to looking at them. This is inevitable, and it only becomes a problem if people are unaware of how their perceptions and their world view are being changed by the technology.

VF: Technological developments are normally done by companies, industry, and so on. Is there a need for control? And wouldn't control, however it were organized, be the end of free enterprise?

NP: Not necessarily. I think that we can have a free-market system that nonetheless has certain controls which would prevent what you might call free-market extremism. For example, even in America—which is supposed to be the most extreme case of the free market in operation—we have (in theory) controls over the uses of television. Maybe not many people in Europe know this, but the American courts and American law state that television—that the airwaves—cannot belong to a person; they belong only to the people. Therefore, anyone who wants to run a radio or television station must get a license from the people, and must promise to broadcast in the public interest, convenience, and necessity. Every three years that person has to reapply to have the license maintained. And the license (in theory again) can be revoked—by the people. The agency that represents the people is the Federal Communications Commission. So: even here in America there is a need—or we have felt a need—to pass laws and establish agencies that exert some control over the use and growth of technology. In Denmark, if I'm not mistaken, where they have advertiser-supported television, it is forbidden to have commercials directed to small children, or commercials for banks, or medicines, or political or religious organizations. Denmark is as civilized a country as America, and believes in free speech, but it was felt that certain constraints had to be put on advertisers. There are many examples of this even in America, where people become concerned about the possible consequences of some uncontrolled technology. And so we put into place certain restrictions. This is also true of the airlines. The airplanes are a very impressive and widely used technology, but even in America the Federal Aviation Agency exerts some control over how the airline industry must operate. So when I say that some controls on technology have to be put in place, it does not mean that I'm a socialist, or that the free-market system will be destroyed—not necessarily. You can have a modified free-market system that gives people most if not all of the benefits of a free-market economy, but at the same time gives all of the people some protection against grotesque exploitation of new technologies.

VF: I think someone who talks like you is in danger in America of being called a socialist because he pleads for a little bit of control. That's my experience here in America. But the problem, I think, is who defines what should be controlled, where should we have protection, and so on.

NP: You're quite right that the key questions are what sort of controls ought we to have, and who will enforce them, and indeed whether we should have them in the first place. The usual way that we deal with this in America is through discourse, through dialogue, through conversation—so that people begin to discuss the issues, and then let their legislators know how they feel about these different things. Then, at city levels and state levels and federal levels, it becomes the people's will that certain kinds of controls be put in place. And that's what we call the democratic way. I'm not in any danger, by the way, of being called a socialist. President Herbert Hoover was a great conservative and believer in the free-enterprise system (as it was called). And he's almost a symbol—almost a metaphor—for a conservative. In 1926, I think, when he was secretary of commerce and not yet president, he spoke about radio and said it was unthinkable that radio should be used for commercial purposes. He thought it was a great instrument for public education and the advancement of culture, and that was the way it ought to be used. So: there are conservatives who believe, as I do, that you need to have a serious conversation in the society about the consequences of technology, with a view (among other things) to devising certain constraints, so that technology doesn't just completely take over.

VF: What do you suggest as a way out of "technopoly?"

NP: There are two ways to answer this question. One is: what can an individual do, irrespective of what the society does? The other is: what can the society do, irrespective of what the individual does? Let's take the second one first. I'm a great advocate of what you might call "media education" or "technology education." I think we have to start in the schools, from the earliest grades right through the universities, to have students study in a serious way the history and social effects of technology, so that they'll have a perspective on technology and will begin to understand the ways in which a technology alters our world view and our culture. So: through education, is one way. Obviously, through political action and legislation is another way—and even through general social policy. Now what can the individual do? Well, *Technopoly* has a number of suggestions that an individual can follow—for example, paying a little more attention to history, a little more attention to spiritual traditions. The individual must try to become a kind of resistance fighter, someone who is always questioning the assumptions of technology. I was talking to a young man the other day; describing a scenario for the future, he said, "Through television, telephone, and computer technology we will be able to shop at home, we'll be able to vote at home, we'll be able to do everything at home." And I said to him: "In other words: we'll never have to go out in the street, we'll never have to meet other people, we'll never have to see our fellow citizens." Well, he hadn't thought about it in that way. What I was doing was questioning his assumption that it would be a good thing to be able to vote at home and shop at home and never go to a library and never go to a voting booth and never go to a store and never go to a theatre. He'd thought that would be wonderful. When I raised the issue of what that would do to our sense of community, he began to think about it. So a resistance fighter is someone who says: Well, let's look at this. Is this the sort of people we want to become? Is this the kind of culture we want to have?

VF: Another part of *Technopoly* is the media. In *Amusing Ourselves to Death*, you have criticized the world of mass media, and especially American TV. Do you think your analysis is still valid, or do you see any changes?

NP: Well, there are changes: it's gotten much worse. When I started to write the book, the television networks—CBS, NBC, ABC—still reigned supreme in America. Cable television was just beginning to come into its own. Now cable is quite well developed, and is a serious challenge to the networks; there are people in my neighborhood who have cable access to sixty or seventy television stations. This keeps them glued to their television sets even more than they were when I was writing the book; America has changed more in the direction that I wrote about. I would say that the dangers I warned of in *Amusing Ourselves to Death* have become more acute. Illiteracy continues to grow. The lust for entertainment and consumerism continues to grow. Things have grown even worse than I depicted in my book.

VF: Regardless of the differences between the cultures and so on, do you think that the basic structure of the media is everywhere the same, so that your criticism is transferable to the European system?

NP: I'm very interested in what's happening in Europe. I've spent a lot of time in Europe, especially by the way in Germany, which in some ways is the most interesting country right now in Europe. But I've also spent time in Scandinavia, and Italy and France and Belgium and Holland and a few other places. I think the Europeans, especially the political leaders and the intellectuals and journalists, are much more aware of some of the negative consequences that the new media can bring to European culture. And they are very interested in talking about this, in writing about it—happily for me. I think they believe that it is not too late to prepare their cultures for the total invasion of, say, television. I find it inspiring to go to Europe, because there I can talk to people who actually believe that they could invent social policies and laws and educational programs that would help prepare Europeans—especially the young—to cope with the new technologies in a more intelligent and human way.

VF: During the Gulf War there were lots of discussion on the role of the media. Many critics said that the Gulf War was presented like a video game. Do you think that's true—do media, TV, new technologies like computers change our perception in this direction?

NP: Of war? Well, I think people who say that the war was like a video game are correct. I think that the way it was managed on American television made it quite remote from us. The reality of war, the reality of death, was not very much part of people's consciousness, because we were always shown the wonders of American weapons technology. Also, I think it should be mentioned that almost all the experts (so-called) who appeared on television during the war were technical people—either military people or technologists. We didn't have any playwrights or novelists or poets or philosophers discussing what was happening. It was a kind of technological party.

VF: There was a lot of discussion in European intellectual circles, and it was a tendency for many philosophers, to say that the media change our perception in general. Do you think that's true?

NP: Yes, it goes back to the point that I made earlier. A medium like television is, as they say, a window to the world. But it's a very special kind of window. It shows you the world in a very particular way. So you are not looking at the world. You're looking at the world as seen through a certain kind of screen. That obviously controls our perceptions of war—and of almost everything else.

EXPLORING THE READING

1. Many recent books argue that there is too much information and too much access to information. Postman says that to a man with a computer, everything looks like data. Does Postman's assertion help explain the new fear of information overload? Why or why not?

2. Should the Federal Communications Commission be involved in the regulation of the Internet? Why or why not? Form small debate groups in your class, presenting arguments for or against government regulation of the Internet.

3. How does Postman define a *technopoly*? Is our society a technopoly as Postman suggests? Use examples from your reading to support or refute Postman's point of view.

4. Can the media change our perception of something? How can it do this? How are your emotions and actions influenced by media input?

OUT THERE IN THE MIDDLE OF THE BUZZ

by Bill McKibben

We live in a buzz of information, according to Bill McKibben in his essay from Forbes ASAP. *He would like to feel superior to those wilderness imposters who bring their cell phones with them to relax along the shores of an undeveloped river, but he realizes that he is not any different. He too carries his world with him into the wilderness. We all do, he says, but we might benefit from finding a way to shut off the noise and listen again to our inner selves, to the secrets and desires we carry hidden beneath the noise of everyday life.*

McKibben has published two books, The End of Nature *and* The Age of Missing Information. *A former staff writer for the* New Yorker, *he currently lives in the Adirondack Mountains of upstate New York.*

Out on a recent hike, I stopped for lunch at the edge of a high mountain pond. I could see another solitary hiker on the other side of the water, stretched out on a shelving rock about a hundred yards away. And I could hear him talking (sound carries extremely well across water; never negotiate a deal in a canoe). "It's so beautiful up here," he was saying. "It's so peaceful. What's happening with you?"

What I couldn't figure out was who he was talking to. Until I pulled out my binoculars and saw, of course, that he had a cell phone. For a moment I felt vastly superior—and then I reflected a bit. It's true I wouldn't carry a phone with me up a mountain. But I had carried my world with me nonetheless, marched right up there with my eyes fixed on the same vague middle distance that you see when you drive. My mind was abuzz with images, opinions; my mind was its own Bloomberg box, happily chattering away with a thousand dispatches an hour.

We live in the middle of the Buzz. Those billions of microprocessors that have spawned like springtime frogs in the last quarter century are constantly sending us information, data, images. Our minds marinate in it, till we're worried when it shuts off. What do you do first when you walk into an empty hotel room? Savor the silence? Or turn on the TV? And even when we get away from the machines for a while—even when we leave the phone at home—the Buzz comes with us. Quiet, solitude, calm: These are no longer automatic parts of the human experience. You have to fight as hard for them as a farm boy had to fight for novelty and thrill a century ago. How many minutes can you watch a sunset before your mind grows hungry for some faster diversion? How long can you stare up into the night sky?

This constant whispering in our ears, this constant dancing in front of our eyes—that's how technology changes us, weaning us away from ourselves. How can you figure out what you really want when someone's always talking to you, when there's always another home page to click through? When you can't warm yourself by a mountain lake without checking in at home? Electronic communication, for the first time, makes culture ubiquitous. Almost nobody read books five hours a day, or went to the theater every night. We live in the first moment when humans receive more of their information secondhand than first; instead of relying primarily on contact with nature and with each other, we rely primarily on the prechewed, on someone else's experience. Our life is, quite literally, mediated.

Maybe that's a good thing; maybe it's the direction in which we need to evolve on an ever more crowded planet. But I think it may be breeding a kind of desperation in us, too, a frantic, reactive nervousness. That low, rumbling broadcast that comes constantly from ourselves, the broadcast that tells us who we are, what we want from life—that broadcast is jammed by all the other noise around us, the lush static of our electronic age. We look for solitude in our (expensively silent) cars, but first the radio, then the phone, then the computer and the fax intrude. We look for peace in the mountains, but we drag the world along on a tether.

To quote Thoreau is to risk rejection as a romantic. But here goes. "Let us spend one day as deliberately as Nature, and not be thrown off the track by every nutshell and mosquito's wing that falls on the rails," he writes. Now that we've built a technosphere to amplify and to broadcast high-quality pictures of each mosquito's wing, it's even better advice, albeit harder than ever to follow. Solitude, silence, darkness—these are the rarest commodities after a half century of electronics. The incredible economics of the information age mean that almost anyone can afford a large-screen television, a 28.8 modem. But how many can afford peace and quiet?

EXPLORING THE READING

1. McKibben says we are the first generation who receives more information secondhand than first. What does he mean by this? Discuss how you receive information every day. What aspects of your life support McKibben's point? What experiences have you had that might refute this argument?

2. What changes, according to McKibben's text, is information technology making in our lives? Using Marshall McLuhan's definition of "message" from "The Medium is the Message," discuss the message of cellular phones.

3. McKibben uses language grounded in the five senses like the "low, rumbling broadcast." What words or phrases from this essay helped you see or experience what he was discussing? Why do you think he chooses to use this language in his essay?

4. He ends his essay with the question, "How many can afford peace and quiet?" Is there an answer to this question? Why do you think he chooses to end the essay this way?

THINK OF YOUR SOUL AS A MARKET NICHE

by Ashley Dunn

No longer are we individuals. We are individual markets, or individual market niches, according to Ashley Dunn in this New York Times *Cybertimes essay. If advertisers learn our interests and desires, they can target advertising just for each of us. The Internet makes it possible for advertisers to track what sites you visit, what kind of computer you own. This information, when combined with already existing information such as credit rating, turns each of us into an individual market niche. Whenever you venture onto the Internet, you are not just finding information, you are revealing information about yourself.*

Dunn is a freelance writer based in La Canada Flintridge, Calif. He has been a reporter for the New York Times, *the* Los Angeles Times, *the* Seattle Post-Intelligencer, *the* Danbury News-Times, *and the* South China Morning Post. *In 1992 he shared the* Los Angeles Times*'s Pulitzer Prize for that newspaper's coverage of the Los Angeles riots. Dunn says he has been hooked on computers since he played a computer game named Star Trek on the mainframe at the University of California, Santa Cruz, in 1974.*

Ronald Reagan has never been known as one of the great pundits of wired life, but he made a surprisingly insightful comment about the nature of the Information Age years before most people had ever heard of the Internet—or even had a fax machine at home.

"Information is the oxygen of the modern age," he told *The Daily Telegraph* of London in 1989, adding that it "seeps through the walls topped with barbed wire and wafts across the electrified, booby-trapped borders. Electronic beams blow through the Iron Curtain as if it were lace."

Reagan was referring to the power of information to break down the walls of communist societies, specifically that of China, which had just experienced the upheaval of the Tiananmen student demonstrations. But what he probably did not realize was that the power to flow through barbed wire also worked in a variety of other directions.

As we have quickly discovered, information also hisses out of the small cracks in corporate data banks, leaks out of government computers and, most importantly, dribbles out of our private lives onto the sidewalk where anyone can scoop it up.

Today, it is no great chore to discover someone's age, gender, home address, phone number, spouse's name, number of dependents, income level, credit rating, social security number, party affiliation and magazine subscriptions. This information is almost considered the basics now and is more or less given away.

More interesting information is of a deeper personal sort that speaks more to soul than it does to demographics—your interests, your dislikes, your newsgroup postings, your favorite Websites, your viewing habits and a myriad of other tidbits that make up everyday life.

Personal information that peers into the soul has become one of the most precious commodities of the Information Age simply because of supply and demand—the supply is meager, the demand insatiable.

In virtually every other area of the Information Age, the value of information has been ground to millipennies by the volume of material unleashed by new methods of digital distribution. There is, in fact, so much information now that giving away "content" has become the dominant economic model of the Internet.

But in the case of your soul, the value of information is still high. People want to know who you are. More specifically, they want to know what makes you buy. Since the dawn of mass *marketing*, understanding the hearts and minds of consumers has been the Holy Grail of advertisers.

They've never succeeded very well and as a result have had to resort to all sorts of crude, mud-against-the-wall strategies, like putting up huge billboards of people in their underpants around Times Square. Out of the several million people who walk past everyday, if even 1 percent are swayed to buy underpants or anything else because of these billboards, the company, I suspect, is ecstatic.

It is only because so little is known about you that these *marketing* assaults must be made on a massive scale. Billboards next to the Santa Monica Freeway loom like a slice of the Great Wall. Missing-children flyers rain upon your house with a frequency that suggests the entire country has disappeared. Years after his stores have gone, Crazy Eddie lives on in my mind because, as I was reminded a few thousand times, his prices were insane.

Marshall McLuhan noted that advertising is the greatest art form of the twentieth century. Indeed, if Parmigianino were alive today, he would be painting Madonna (the blonde one from Michigan) for album jackets.

Advertising has been waiting to move from art to science, and now the Internet has opened a new realm of possibilities, largely because of its bi-directional nature. Not only can advertising be more accurately targeted, but also it can be more revealing about its viewers.

Unlike newspapers or direct mail, Internet advertising can be used to glean a variety of information—where you go, what you click on, your domain name, your computer type, general location and other information.

It may not seem like a lot, but these are the first steps in linking your budding online identity with all the data that has already been collected on you through real world sources, like your magazine subscriptions and public data banks.

The technology also clearly exists to go deeper. Gateways like CompuServe and America Online already have a wealth of information on the interests of subscribers. Combine this with demographic information and you have a powerful product to sell. They also have your credit card number, which makes a neat tie between what you like and what they can sell you.

The battle to dominate the Information Age has usually been cast in terms of software companies, pipe providers, hardware manufacturers, content producers and various combinations of the four.

But in many ways, the best positioned in the New World are the packagers and resellers of personal information. It is information that is in demand by all the other forces contending for dominance. It is the raw material of the Information Age, just as coal and iron were during the Industrial Revolution.

The problem is that advertising on the Net is terrible and far less compelling than it is in other media. It's just too easy to click past little buttons on your screen. Print and broadcast ads are sandwiched between content, making them difficult to avoid. The Net reality is that an advertiser can't manipulate a thing if no one clicks on his button.

A small group of companies have realized this fundamental flaw in Net advertising and have launched a variety of initiatives to capture your attention.

Consider PointCast, which gives away the news in exchange for putting an advertising box on your screen, or HoTMaiL, which provides free e-mail that is supported by advertising that pops up every time you sign on.

Perhaps the most interesting project comes from CyberGold of Berkeley, Calif., which has come up with the novel idea of paying users to look at advertisements. Every time you look at an ad from a CyberGold member, you get $1 or 50 cents, which can be exchanged for a variety of products.

The payment is supposed to be for your attention, but attention alone means little. What is key is a small optional questionnaire that you can fill out when you register. It asks for things like your age, interests, education level, address and computer type. CyberGold says it will not release your personal information, but you have the option of selling it to an interested company for a few dollars.

I suspect that many will, not for the money and certainly not to have their minds manipulated by Madison Avenue, but rather to get information on products and services in which they're interested.

What is most interesting about these initiatives is the fundamental change they signify in the relationship between advertisers and viewers. We've gone from being dumb disciples waiting to be shaped to lesser gods who must be presented with occasional sacrifices.

The price is that the new system requires knowing more about you for the simple reason that advertisers have to know what you are interested in to present the proper advertisements.

Otaku of paranoia will no doubt revel in these developments as a sure sign that we will all be assassinated soon. But just as the flow of information is changing, so too is the nature of privacy.

Privacy in the modern age has largely been an issue of physical walls— walls that protect our possessions, shield our secrets and provide a haven for lives that are different from our public personas.

But the very nature of virtual life seems to rebel against this opacity. There is no hunger in this world, no real pain and very little possession. People have built plenty of walls, but they also rushed to break open a multitude of doors, showing the world such finery as their toilets and ex-spouses. They have built illusory homes as well, where twelve-year-olds or bored engineers rule like Caesar over Rome.

Privacy will never be the same. It is certain that more will be known about us in the future, but at the same time, we will have gained a powerful ability to choose some of the information we want released to serve our own purposes.

As Reagan, the great pundit of the Information Age, said: "The communications revolution will be the greatest force for the advancement of human freedom the world has ever seen."

He was right—but it's just not nearly as bucolic a breeze as he thought.

EXPLORING THE READING

1. Ashley Dunn says that what we might consider private information—such as credit rating, social security number, and party affiliation—is easily available to those who might want it. Are you surprised?

2. In your small group, discuss the implication of Dunn's observation that the Internet is a two-way medium. Whenever you visit a site, that site can keep a record of your visit, and that information can be used to build a profile of your interests. How does that make you feel?

3. Dunn suggests that creative advertising initiatives on the Internet signal a fundamental change in the relationship between viewers and advertisers. What does he mean?

4. What do you think of Ronald Reagan's comment, quoted in Dunn's essay, that "Information is the oxygen of the modern age"? What does it mean?

VIRTUAL REALITY CHECK: CYBERETHICS, CONSUMERISM, AND THE AMERICAN SOUL

by Joan Connell

All the hype about the merger of computers, television, and telephones into one medium has paid little attention to how this union will affect our society's values, according to Joan Connell in "Virtual Reality Check." As some of the other texts in this chapter point out, any new media affects the way people look at the world and, thus, the way people think and behave. Any new medium has the potential for affecting values. The term virtual reality check *comes from a remark by U.S. Representative Edward Markey, chairman of the House Telecommunications Subcommittee, when he quizzed computer professionals about the direction of the information superhighway. Connell, in her essay, insists that the implications of the telecommunications revolution currently under way go beyond the issues Markey raised. She worries that ethical awareness may shrink in a virtual reality world where participants can play virtual god, altering realities in fantasy worlds.*

Connell writes for Newhouse News Service in Washington, D.C., specializing in religion, ethics, and moral issues.

America is gearing up for the information superhighway, preparing to boldly go where no society has gone before: Deep into cyberspace, where virtual reality, the user mentality and interactive computers will fundamentally change the way people think, do business and communicate with one another.

The public debate on the national information infrastructure has so far focused on issues of technology and the marketplace: the network's physical and technological design, the maneuverings of the corporate giants who will build and profit from the information highway, and the dazzling array of interactive games, entertainments, goods and services that soon will careen down the highway and into our daily lives.

But scant attention has been paid to the ethical road maps necessary to negotiate the *terra incognita* created when computers, telephones, broadcast and cable merge into one interactive medium. Morally speaking, the issues in cyberspace are no different than those governing other aspects of life. But while honesty, integrity and human decency are as relevant to the electronic environment as they are to the world of physical cause and effect, the ethical protocols that will guide behavior in this virtual world remain largely undefined.

To many of the techno-literate, the idea of an ethic governing what goes on in cyberspace simply does not compute.

"Cyberethics?" The word draws first a blank, then a chuckle from one Silicon Valley executive. "It's a free-for-all out there. The only ethic in cyberspace is what you can get away with."

But serious questions are being raised—by philosophers, public interest groups and even a few politicians—about the effect this cogent new technology will have on individual consciousness, human conduct and the democratic process itself. There is a growing concern among some critics that the information highway is far too precious and powerful a resource to be shaped solely by the values of Hollywood, Wall Street and the Department of Commerce. There are real fears that this profit-driven highway, whose users will pay by the minute for the privilege of going online, will exclude vast numbers of the poor, further widening the gulf that already exists between the haves and the have-nots in American society.

"It's time for a virtual-reality check. What is it exactly we are constructing here?" U.S. Rep. Edward Markey, D-Mass., chairman of the House Telecommunications Subcommittee, asked computer professionals at a recent conference on cyberethics at the Brookings Institution. "Where does the digital highway lead? What are the rights and responsibilities of those using the network? We have to acknowledge that real harm can be done in a virtual world."

The harm, in Markey's view, comes mainly in criminal guises: invasions of personal privacy by snooping governments or craven corporations, software piracy, or hackers who break into computer files and send viruses raging through software. As the Clinton administration develops its plan over the next two years to deal with this burgeoning new technology, Markey's committee will play a major role in drawing up the laws that will govern behavior in cyberspace.

But the ethical implications of cyberspace extend far beyond privacy, piracy and copyright law. Philosophers are just beginning to grapple with what happens to human consciousness in a world where reality is virtual, not tangible, where standard measures of honesty are absent and where a user's full identity may never be fully disclosed. The advent of virtual reality will give an added dimension to the information superhighway, with software that allows the construction of exotic worlds populated by artificial creatures, over which the designer can play God with startlingly real effects. Virtual reality promises to open up new worlds of learning in cyberspace, using simulated realities to teach everything from driving a car to performing laser surgery and piloting planes.

But ethical awareness has a tendency to shrink in such an environment. In his recent book, *The Metaphysics of Virtual Reality*, British philosopher Michael Heim voices concern that the seductive virtual realities of cyberspace will draw us away from the duties of real life, turning us into electronic voyeurs, seeking risk-free encounters in make-believe worlds. Overwhelmed with data and distracted by fantasy, our attention span could become reduced to the content-poor shards of an MTV video. We risk becoming mentally poorer, mistaking data for knowledge, distanced from wisdom and blind to both the beauty and the terrors of intangible, felt existence.

At the height of the Gulf War, America got a hint of the eerie ethical detachment of cyberspace via televised images of the computer technology that aided allied pilots in the bombing of Baghdad. Computer-assisted video images of small bombs screaming down Iraqi chimneys seemed for all the world like a super video game, complete with the fist-pumping exultation of the cockpit crew when the missiles scored direct hits. What the television audience didn't see were the fireballs the bombs created, or hear the screams of the dying.

Such digitized encounters with reality can erode the human capacity for significance. Putting faith in reams of data can foster a godlike omniscience, a false sense of being in control and a detachment from the world of physical cause and effect.

Virtual reality has the potential to evolve into a new, participatory art form. It promises to revolutionize the visual arts in the same way hypertext (which allows a user to jump with a single keystroke from primary text to footnotes, commentary, music and video) will revolutionize literature by exploding the linear logic of conventional narrative.

These innovations can just as easily serve as a vehicle for violent enter-tainments and pornography. And the pairing of such powerful technology with the anything-goes attitudes of the entertainment industry has some people worried.

"Take a lesson from television and the movies," suggests Jeffrey Chester of the Center for Media Education in Washington. "The media industry's will-ingness to put anything on the airwaves—violent programs that travel and sell well in the global marketplace—will only be magnified on the infor-mation highway."

Trust is another nebulous ethical issue in cyberspace. Computer networks are already littered with violations of trust, as millions of users, identified only by their log-ons, engage in complex, heated and often intimate commu-nications via electronic bulletin boards and e-mail.

One Indiana parent was chagrined to discover the "boy" her son had befriended on a teen chat line was actually a 42-year-old with a record as a pedophile.

A Bay Area computer Lothario made headlines when it was revealed he was romancing multiple women at once.

Cybertrust even made its way into popular culture when comicstrip char-acter Mike Doonesbury tried to engage in some extramarital relations on the Internet.

So far, no one's come up with any good solution to the question of trust in cyberspace, beyond accepting e-mail only from those prepared to disclose their full identities. The dilemma of how to trust or whom to trust in this electronic universe points to a basic human truth: Morality has no meaning without a community whose members are able to articulate their values and willing to live by them.

So the challenge of ethics in cyberspace goes far beyond blowing the whistle when fraud is perpetrated or when some electronic vandal sends a virus racing through the software. The real challenge is building communi-cation systems and user groups that function as moral, if not geographic, communities. That cannot happen until we recognize that moral aware-ness must be an essential component of computer-user mentality, as vital to the education of a technocrat as programming language and higher mathematics.

To public interest advocates, the most pressing ethical issue in cyberspace is the profit-driven nature of the information superhighway and the effect it will have on society—and on the democratic process. At the moment, there are far more questions than there are answers.

Social fragmentation is inevitable in a 500-channel environment, where users of the highway cluster together in increasingly narrow communities of interest. So what then happens to the national character if there is no central arena, such as national network television, to which all citizens have access and in which all can participate freely? How will we as a society define our common ground?

As the 1992 presidential election campaign demonstrated, a multichannel environment can greatly enhance democracy by extending political dis course into new and unexpected arenas. Who would have thought, for instance, that a new generation of voters would bypass C-SPAN, Tom Brokaw, Peter Jennings and MacNeil/Lehrer in favor of the wacky but relevant political discourse on MTV and the Comedy Channel? But access to those channels in the pay-per-view or pay-per-minute environment of the information superhighway raises another issue. And the concentration of media ownership in the hands of a half-dozen corporate giants poses the very real danger that their idea of what the public wants will be very dif-ferent from what the public needs (if the old journalistic concept of what the public needs to know survives at all). Public affairs programming may well be eclipsed by glitzy shopping channels, goofy game shows and movies-on-demand.

"To develop a network based on commercial providers is a mistake," argues Eric Roberts, professor of computer science at Stanford University and president of Computer Professionals for Social Responsibility. "The national information infrastructure needs to be more than getting a top-rated movie anytime you want. What we need is a commitment to make sure this new technology serves the public good: empower people, raise the level of democracy, rather than being debased into another device we watch for six hours a day."

The commitment Roberts and his allies are seeking has yet to be articu-lated in Washington.

Public interest groups are lobbying to establish the electronic equivalent of public parks on the information superhighway, setting aside 10 percent of its carrying capacity for public access. Thus far, the idea has elicited little enthu-siasm from the Clinton administration, which seems to be more attentive to the concerns of the corporate entities that stand to profit from the highway than to the needs of the citizens whose interests the information super-highway should serve.

One of the great lessons of the postindustrial era is that technology can no longer be considered morally neutral. The information highway, like any other human invention, has the potential to exalt or to debase those who come into its orbit.

As the public debate on the national information infrastructure unfolds, expect the ethical and moral dimensions of life on the superhighway to be part of the discussion. Expect religious organizations, citizen advocates and professional organizations from librarians to physicians to be rattling congressional and corporate cages, asking tough questions about content, access and accountability on the information superhighway.

And if their voices are not heard and attended to, this resource with the power to be an electronic well of meaning that will enrich all of society may end up being nothing more than a high-tech shopping mall.

EXPLORING THE READING

1. What exactly is Joan Connell worried about? In your small group, discuss whether you agree with her about the need for a virtual reality check.

2. Review the article by Marshall McLuhan, and then freewrite for five minutes about the connection between Connell's article and McLuhan's.

3. Review "A New Battlefield: Rethinking Warfare in the Computer Age" from Chapter 2 and then compare it with what Connell writes about the Gulf War.

4. What does Connell have to say about the issue of trust in cyberspace? Do you share her concern?

5. Does Connell offer a solution to the problems she raises?

THE AESTHETIC OF THE COMPUTER

by Daniel Harris

Computer software has developed a style that, while unimportant to the actual function of the machine or program, serves important psychological functions for the user. According to Harris, these extraneous software devices are useful to computer software developers because they transform computer nerds into shamans, make computers seem more accessible, make us feel as if we have more control than we do, and help to enslave us to technology.

Harris is a regular contributor to Harper's, Salmugundi, *and* Newsday. *His essays have been included in* Best American Essays of 1993 *and* The Anchor Essay Annual 1997. *He is the author of the book* The Rise and Fall of Gay Culture.

Although the appearance of our appliances is largely determined by their use, even the most prosaic of utensils have what might be called an "aesthetic," a look, a style that serves no discernible function and that reflects the sensibility of their designer. Something as insignificant as a spoon, an implement in which utility clearly predominates over aesthetics, is stamped with a floral pattern, just as cheap toasters have textured plastic panels that simulate leather or upholstery, or refrigerators are embossed with metallic snowflakes, or colanders have clusters of holes shaped like flowers—features that affect the user in a less tangible, more poetic way than the pure utility of the notches on a steering wheel, the plastic grip of a can opener, or the sandpaper surface of a Daisy-Mate bath decal.

An appliance as complex as a computer also has gratuitous, decorative elements that serve only to beautify the machine. These fanciful embellishments can be found, not only on the external surfaces of the hardware, but in more elusive and internal places within the software itself. Here, in these hidden recesses, the user communes with the machine as he works, engaging in a private conversation that consists entirely of images, some of which are of instrumental importance to the job at hand, while others function solely to raise his spirits with the jokes, quips, and gags that are now standard components of many computer programs. One of the most popular software packages on the market, *Windows*, is cluttered with comic-book froufrou, with frills and trimmings that fill the backgrounds and margins of the screen like manuscript illuminations—the visual pun of a spectral kitten, for instance, that leaps around on the screen after the "mouse," following the cursor wherever it goes and pouncing on it when it stops moving. With the help of such ornate details, which software designers now scrawl over their programs like graffiti, the computer is most decidedly acquiring an "aesthetic," a pictorial style that, while serving no conscious, utilitarian function, serves a number of *un*conscious, psychological ones.

Nowhere in the recent revolution in the aesthetic of the computer have software engineers been more inventive than in the proliferation of various kinds of screen-savers. Although this misleadingly pedestrian expression suggests things as useful and unglamorous as safety goggles and glare guards, screen-savers are a fascinating new form of electronic poetry whose intricate, fluctuating patterns have transformed the computer terminal into nothing less than a radical experiment in corporate art. Their basic style is that of Daliesque surrealism—floating clocks (with a choice of modern, antique, or digital, with, or without, a second hand) that actually tell time and that rebound off the monitor's invisible "walls," ricocheting back and forth in slow motion; or multisegmented worms in rainbow colors that slowly devour the screen in a ravenous feeding frenzy, munching away at the menus while the computer makes grotesque sounds of chewing and swallowing. As if defying the insipid silk screens, abstract collages, and ubiquitous textile wall hangings that contribute to the institutional atmosphere of the business world, software manufacturers have begun to subvert the staid conventionality of office interior decoration with a bizarre new type of animated screen art.

This recent attempt to aestheticize our terminals would seem to suggest that the generic and collective spaces in which we work are becoming much more permissive and idiosyncratic, tolerating new expressions of childishness, humor, and self-burlesque, images that undercut the stiff formality of the business world, its pompous gravity and dehumanizing preoccupation with appearances and protocol. In one of the most popular designs, a school of winged toasters fly across the screen in formation like a flock of migrating geese, flapping their exiguous wings as they dodge in and out of slices of floating toast, whose color the user can adjust according to his breakfast preference, from light to medium to dark. In another, brilliantly colored tropical fish, lobsters, sea horses, and jellyfish rummage around for food on the bottom of the ocean, scavenging through swaying thickets of seaweed that gurgle with underwater sounds emanating from the terminal. In yet another, swans glide on the surface of the screen, gracefully dipping their necks into the water to pluck out aquatic creatures, while in another the pitch-black monitor slowly begins to light up with the eyes of nocturnal animals, some slanted and feline, others round and surprised like an owl's, as if we were being observed by the ferocious inhabitants of a jungle, who stare out at us with unflinching curiosity as bloodthirsty wolves and coyotes howl in the distance.

Although these images would appear to be nothing more than the cinematic doodles of bored computer engineers, it would be a mistake to dismiss them as just the disembodied equivalent of the floral pattern on the stem of a spoon. A careful examination of the superfluous details that software designers build into their products reveals that the aesthetic of the computer reflects the psychology of the modern office. The freakish and visionary lyricism of screen savers articulates the state of mind of a work force experiencing unsettling professional insecurities which affect not only those who use the machines but those who create them. The surrealistic effects of software imagery are in part the by-product of an occupational identity crisis occurring among the upper echelons of the labor pool, the computer intelligentsia, whose members are making a conscious effort to rid themselves of the denigrating stereotype of the inept, humorless misfit, the bumbling, hamhanded introvert. By filling our screens with zany non sequiturs, like droplets of jet-black "rain" that splatter over our work as if they had been flung at our terminals by Jackson Pollock, this rising class of educated specialists are attempting to prove to themselves, as well as to others, that, far from being nerdish automatons, they are in fact mad scientists and creative geniuses. The surrealistic humor of the screen-saver (the toasters swim as well as fly, dog-paddling through swarms of deep-sea creatures) is one of the secret handshakes of the new brethren of high technology, the cliquish fraternal order of those who are "in the know," who "get it." It is thus representative of a new sensibility afflicting the electronics industry, that of ludicrous whimsicality, the kookiness of the oddball player of esoteric pranks. Mischievous software jocks now use the quirky and decidedly off-beat humor of new forms of computer imagery to shore up their own sense of group identity as an elite set of Silicon Valley absurdists. In one of the latest screen-savers, the monitor becomes a blackboard on which a piece of chalk begins to write two types of messages, either complex physical formulae, if the user chooses to be "Einstein," or repetitive lists of punitive precepts, if he chooses to be an "underachiever," with stern injunctions like "setting pigtails on fire is not performance art," "I will not Xerox my butt," or "I will not barf unless I am sick."

Such compulsive wackiness serves two functions: it proves to the technician that he is a crazy nonconformist rather than merely an office drone and, more importantly, it engenders respect among the lower echelons of the work force, who are fascinated by the conjuring tricks of a group of specialists whom they perceive as nothing less than a new breed of white-collar shamans. As insignificant as it seems, the "far-out" nature of the decorative features with which software designers are now adorning the computer provides one crucial piece of evidence of the growing stratification of the labor pool into two polarized factions in a rapidly evolving new caste system.

Unskilled white-collar workers are affected even more seriously by professional anxieties endemic to a society increasingly dependent on high technology. The startling contrast between the chaste elegance of the workplace and the gaudiness of screen-savers is symptomatic of a general trend in the computer industry to revamp antiquated corporate imagery in order to establish in the user's mind a healthy, if entirely spurious, connection between the irreconcilable spheres of business and fantasy, labor and recreation. By wallpapering our terminals with frivolous, technicolor images, reminiscent of Saturday-morning cartoons, manufacturers are undercutting our resistance to high technology and thus assisting in the assimilation of the computer into a culture so baffled by complex software programs that its fears about using them must be constantly placated with metaphors that exaggerate their accessibility.

The aesthetic of the computer thus masquerades as a form of decoration but is actually very useful. It pretends to entertain but in fact it teaches and, in many ways, it indoctrinates. Because the dismay caused by high technology has a potentially demoralizing impact on our work and could therefore cause inefficiency or even inspire resistance in old-fashioned employees frightened by the unfamiliarity of these newfangled gadgets, manufacturers actively infantilize the computer by means of a manipulative sort of anthropomorphizing rhetoric known by the duplicitous term of "friendliness." This revolutionary iconography is part of an industry-wide attempt to reconfigure the computer in accordance with the paradigm of the toy or the video game, thus coaxing the worker with puerile bribes and patronizing pats on the back that make him believe that his utensils are so elementary, so self-evident, that even a child could use them. Images of games form one of the basic themes of screen savers. In "Hall of Mirrors," the surface of the screen splinters into looking glasses that transform the terminal into a kind of fun house in which cavernous halls of infinitely regressive images tunnel back into the monitor. In "Marbles," small spheres are shot through an obstacle course of metal pegs where they bounce around like the silver balls of a pinball machine, and in "Puzzle," the screen becomes a grid of square pieces that are continually rearranged until the image on the monitor is slowly scrambled into a cubist collage of fragments of disjointed text and shards of broken mouse icons.

In the alienating world of office automation, the antidote to incomprehension is not education but a new kind of opium of the people, the ruse of "friendliness," whose gimmicks bring computers down to our level and encourage us to *forget* our ignorance rather than to overcome it. As the computer assumes an aura of childish intelligibility and performs for our benefit an act of self-degradation in which it talks baby talk rather than the technobabble of specialists, its "congeniality" drugs us into a soothing state of oblivion to the electronic riddles of a piece of sophisticated technology that we use with a mixture of uncomprehending pride and utter consternation. It is one of the major paradoxes of the business world that the more we lose control over our appliances, the more control we are deceived into believing we exercise over them, so that our ignorance of the abstruse secrets of transistors and circuit boards stands in an inverse relation to our growing sense of mastery.

The Pac Man aesthetic of the computer turns us, first into children, and then back again into adults or at least into children who imitate adults by playing a game of dress-up in which we live out an occupational fantasy that our responsibilities, as seasoned technicians, the foot soldiers of the information age, are far less menial than in fact they are. By providing a multiplicity of choices for nearly every decorative feature offered, from the color of the monitor to the size of the design, manufacturers encourage us to manipulate the images on the screen and thus to achieve an illusory sense of being crack-shot telecommunications engineers. The malleability of the aesthetic of the computer transforms unskilled members of the work force into software virtuosos, artistic collaborators who, in the act of constructing these complex desktop dioramas, remake themselves in the image of their superiors: the hard-core techies—the "Systems Administrators" and the "Coordinators of Computer Services." Unlike the embellishments on toasters and colanders, which are by necessity inert designs, the decorative features of software are interactive. In the case of the screen-saver "Can of Worms," for example, the user can choose to make the worms' bodies either short or long, from between one to twenty segments, and, moreover, can make them move in a way that is either "wriggly," "straight," "crawly," "weavy," or a combination of all four. This bonanza of possibilities is surpassed only by "Mountains," in which you can display topographical maps of all nine planets, or "Rainstorm," in which you can adjust the screen's turbulent mete- orology according to the velocity of the wind. As useful drills in the exercise of pure volition, computer decorations provide a form of mental calisthenics that bolster the self-esteem of a despondent underclass. They glamorize new high-tech jobs that, far from being the chance-of-a-lifetime opportunities that the electronics industry would have us believe it has created in great abun- dance in the service sector, are in fact just the usual numbing forms of drudgery trumped up to look more challenging and intellectual than they are by means of a psychological ploy basic to the aesthetic of the computer, the stimulant of false empowerment.

Computer imagery also invites us to view the machine as a compatriot, a brother-in-arms, a fellow cynic who shares the same jaundiced appraisal of the delicious aggravations of interoffice politics and who has the freedom to express out loud the boredom and frustration that we ourselves must always repress. Acting on our thwarted impulses to desecrate and disfigure our terminals, screen-savers are constantly turning the pristine, rational workspace of the monitor into the butt of an outrageous visual prank that elicits vindictive glee as we watch what appear to be deadly computer viruses attack and erase all of our data. In the screen-saver "Down the Drain," a hole develops in the middle of the monitor like the drain of a sink, an open sewer around which the entire screen begins to revolve like a water- spout, swirling dizzily into a vortex until it is sucked into an imaginary cesspool, as if someone had just pulled the plug or flushed the toilet. This impish spirit of destructiveness is also found in "Punchout," in which random shapes are carved out of the screen like puzzle pieces and spirited magically away, escorted offstage until everything disappears, stripped bare by unseen looters who plunder our monitors of every last scrap of text. The introduction of incoherence or even, in the case of the worms, decomposition into an arena that is always oppressively tidy and hygienic titillates the user by inciting within his terminal a miniature workers' riot in which he experiences the vicarious thrill of ransacking the screen, fouling his own nest, and sabotaging this inordinately expensive piece of equipment through an imaginary form of electronic terrorism. By inspiring a sense of community united by irreverence, by a shared bond of insolence and sarcasm, the aesthetic of the computer allows the worker to participate in a form of make-believe disobedience.

The decorative elements of software programs also subtly affect the worker's relation to his PC by providing frequent evidence of the human touch—the odd, superfluous detail that reassures the user that the computer was somehow "created" like a piece of art rather than "manufactured" like an appliance. These poetic "touches" constitute the equivalent in the electronics industry of the individualized workmanship that Ruskin and Morris admired so much in the carvings of Gothic cathedrals, whose intricate designs bore unmistakable traces of the personalities of their creators and thus represented a rejection of the mass-produced, assembly-line feature-lessness of decadent modernity. A close inspection of the screen-saver "Marbles," for instance, reveals that when one of the five marbles represented, a sphere about 1/10-inch in diameter decorated with a Happy Face, caroms off the metal pegs and boomerangs back to the sides of the screen, its mouth opens up into an astonished expression of breathless surprise like a child squealing with delight on an amusement park ride. Details similar to this can be found in even the most commonplace software programs, like the sound of the game-show gong signaling a wrong answer that blares out like taunting laughter when the cursor reaches the very bottom of a document in Microsoft Word (called "clink-klank," it is one of several options that include sounds like "boing," "chime," and "monkey," the latter being a simulation of a shrieking chimpanzee). In order to accommodate the nostalgia and sentimentality of capitalism, which now continually harks back to the outmoded standards of production characteristic of the preindustrial era of the handmade and the homespun, an industry that constitutes the very summit of assembly-line standardization tries desperately to assuage the consumer's fears of anonymous machines by providing abundant evidence in their design of their inventor's whimsical presence. The aesthetic of the computer is thus rooted in the civil war that consumerism is now waging against itself.

At the same time that manufacturers mask the computer in three separate disguises—that of a toy, that of an irreverent compatriot, and that of a handmade piece of what might be called bionic folk art—they recognize the economic value of sweeping us off our feet with dazzling, sumptuous feasts for the eye that instill in us a sense of stunned incredulity. Even as they attempt to placate the worker and to prevent his alienation from affecting his job performance, they continue to intimidate him with images of their product's seemingly irrational powers, thus inspiring blind devotion, an attitude that serves an obvious function of strengthening the grip of high technology on the imagination of the American public. In order to perpetuate our admiration for the computer's miraculous capacities, they have developed an aesthetic that is entirely incompatible with the aesthetic of infantilization: the psychedelic. Hallucinatory images suggestive of the graphic style of the 1960s are fundamental to screen-savers that, for all of their futuristic pretensions, seem almost dated, like animated black-light posters from the era of acid trips, altered states of consciousness, and the peyote visions of a Carlos Castaneda. In one of the most popular software programs, intersecting loops of colored threads weave and unravel dense thatches of lines to form an image that exerts an hypnotic effect designed to elicit from the viewer such clichéd responses as "wow" and "far out," expressions that denote inarticulate amazement, the sort of speechless surprise we experience before natural wonders. Most screen-savers, like one of the all-time favorites, "LavaLamp," use the kaleidoscopic effects of a pop style specifically developed some thirty years ago to provide a visual analogue for mystical confrontations with the infinite—oscillating Möbius strips; stained-glass windows with ornate tracery that open up like buds blossoming in time-lapse photographs; protean shapes drawn with gyroscopes, mosaics that shatter and disintegrate; and uncanny microbe-like cells that divide and multiply in gaudy bursts of color—all of which link the computer with the perceptual distortions of mind-bending drugs.

Manufacturers also awe the consumer with literal images of the infinite: comets with iridescent tails that streak across intergalactic voids, photographic replications of spinning galaxies, or three-dimensional globes that hurtle through space rotating drunkenly on their axes. In "Warp!" the screen becomes the cockpit of the *Starship Enterprise* and explosions of supernovae rush by, as whole constellations are sucked into black holes or fan out, like the Big Bang, in expanding ripples of primordial matter. One of the central themes of the screen-saver is that the terminal is a trapdoor that leads into infinity, that the microcosm contains the macrocosm, that the monitor is identical to the sky, a Borgesian paradox based on the idea that this finite box of silicon chips and cathode-ray tubes in fact encompasses the entirety of the universe, easily housing all of the celestial bodies. The user responds viscerally to such dreamlike images, which induce in him a kind of giddiness, especially those that suggest that the terminal contains a parallel, "virtual" reality, a separate realm that lies perpetually out of reach, an illusion fed by irrational fantasies about omnipotent machines capable of performing instantaneously activities that would have taken him the better part of his day. The psychedelic appearance of new forms of computer decoration thus reflects the modern worker's constant state of silent amazement, which manufacturers cultivate as vigorously as they cultivate our snuggly sense of the machine's unthreatening familiarity, its "friendliness." With such economically advantageous and contradictory hyperboles, which simultaneously relax us and frighten us, beckon us closer and push us further away, the electronics industry enthralls and, in some sense, exploits the corporate environment.

EXPLORING THE READING

1. Examine a software program you use regularly. What details and tools work to improve the function of the software? Which details are what Harris would call aesthetic?

2. In a small group, discuss whether screen-saver art is as subversive as Daniel Harris suggests? Use additional details from your own experience to support or refute the claim.

3. Have you seen other screen-savers that would help support Harris's discussion? Describe them and their role, as Harris would see them. Have you seen screen-savers that would undermine Harris's argument? Describe them and use them to rebut one or more of Harris's arguments.

4. In several places, Harris describes a software package and how the images look on screen. Can you picture the software from his description? Would you be able to if you did not have a basic understanding of a screen-saver? What sorts of details or language does he use to paint a clear picture?

VIRTUAL ENCOUNTERS

by Thomas Barrett and Carol Wallace

Relationships follow specific patterns of intimacy, according to Barrett and Wallace in this essay for Internet World. *On the Internet, some of those stages of intimacy pass more quickly because participants assume common interests that face-to-face relationships must search for and build. Even love, say the authors, may grow on the Internet where people can share their deepest feelings with one another without fear of reprimand or embarrassment.*

Thomas Barrett has been surfing the Net since the BITNETdays of the early 1980s. He works as a network programmer for a telephone company in California. Carol Wallace teaches communication at the University of Scranton in Pennsylvania.

Although we tend to think of the Internet primarily as a means of exchanging information, many members of the virtual community find themselves quickly embroiled in exchanges of a more intimate nature, whether friendly or hostile. Some couples, although they have never heard each other's voices and have only the vaguest notion of what each other looks like, have formed friendships or fallen in love through exchanges of words that stretch across geographic boundaries and onto their computer screens.

Why, we might ask, are these relationships, often quite enduring, formed so quickly and easily? The answer may lie in those very differences that separate Net life from real life. On the Internet, people can communicate in a way that differs vastly from their ordinary daily encounters. The primary difference is that Internet communications are not conducted face to face, rather computer to computer. People may spend weeks or months communicating with each other, with no more clue about their physical identity than the accuracy of their typing. There are no other reliable visual or aural cues.

This type of communication can have dramatic effects—some positive, others negative. Every day, people swear friendship or enmity with other Net users. Often the relationships between friends and foes develop more quickly than those we form in the "real" world.

NET LIFE VS. REAL LIFE

Computer-mediated communication allows us to interact with others while remaining physically alone. Yet by virtue of an Internet connection, you are at the same time at the center of a potentially large number of individual or simultaneous communications. Internet use is similar to ham radio communication in that both media allow users to communicate in isolation. The Net, however, lacks one key feature of ham radio: the element of sound. Net users generally do not use their voices to transmit inflections that indicate irony, sadness, affection, or anger. Like the telegraph, with its similar lack of visual and auditory cues, Internet communication is reduced to the barest essentials—words etched in light on a glowing screen.

The loss of physical variables has its drawbacks, which are apparent in the proliferation of smileys sprinkled throughout Internet messages—little faces that attempt to indicate the feelings that accompany the verbal text. Many variations on the smiley have been created—frowns, laughter, boredom, and even a twinkle in the eye. Emotion has been reduced to emoticons. Lacking physical clues, or without extraordinary skill in writing, a message can be easily misinterpreted.

This same lack of visual and aural information, however, can have positive consequences that far outweigh the negatives. One of the benefits, paradoxically, results from the stripping of information. Because we interact solely by written messages—small, ephemeral thoughts flashing on a screen—we can hide behind our terminals. Our correspondents, of course, may do the same. Thus, we are unencumbered by the nonverbal distractions that so often interfere with the exchange of messages. On the Internet, height, weight, race, and gender may be unknown. Beauty doesn't impress us, nor does ugliness appall. We become our messages, purely and simply.

This physical anonymity can benefit the sender. The stripping of non-verbal cues allows some individuals to create alternative personalities. Some Net users on the extreme end wander the ether as anthropomorphic entities or characters from fiction. On a more realistic note, some Net users masquerade as members of the opposite sex, while others simply construct a personality they wish they could assume in real life. A shy, homely girl might become an attractive flirt, while a timid male might become verbally aggressive and abusive. After all, what are the penalties for this type of deception? The unattractive girl won't find herself in a desperate sexual clinch, and the timid boy is unlikely to receive a black eye for his excesses.

For those people whose communication is more open and honest, there may be another benefit. The protection afforded by hiding behind the terminal may make it easier to express real emotions, and may protect the correspondents from possible embarrassment if they inadvertently overstep social bounds.

TERMINALS AS SHIELDS

The most important way that Internet communication shields us is in the control it gives us over our behavior. Participation in any Internet communication is always purely voluntary. When face-to-face interactions turn ugly, awkward, or embarrassing, we can be left with no graceful (or socially acceptable) escape. When we communicate on the Net, we can always escape. We simply quit communicating.

Hiding behind our terminals gives us another luxury: the chance to think, reflect, and formulate the optimal reply to a communication. Internet messages, as we learn very quickly, are not delivered instantaneously, as are those in face-to-face conversations. There is a time lag before messages reach their destination. Once they arrive, we also realize that the recipient may be too disinclined to respond immediately, even be off line.

Because Internet users do not always expect immediate replies to their messages, shy individuals and ones who would love to spend half an hour in thought before replying in a verbal conversation can indulge in additional thinking, composing, and editing until they're satisfied with their written reply. It also allows people who quickly formulate ideas to fire back immediate retorts.

Unlike face-to-face communication, with its demand for immediate give and take, we have total control over when and even whether we respond. The terminal also can shield us from the interruptions that can plague face-to-face conversation—perhaps not the ringing phone or doorbell, but other intrusions that often occur when people speak in person.

So the terminal shields us from unpleasantries, from having to make immediate responses to difficult questions, and from being interrupted before we have had our say. How does this affect the way we form Net relationships? To really answer the question, we must first look at the way people form relationships in face-to-face situations.

In everyday life, people move from being strangers to friends in several clearly defined stages of communication. A certain code of manners determines appropriate conversation for a first encounter, which is cordial and masks any insincerity: "How do you do? (and wouldn't I be surprised if you really told me)." "Pleased to meet you (although I'd really rather meet that other person on the sofa)." Making comments about the weather and observations about the surroundings are typical of new-acquaintance conversation. We typically use small talk in an attempt to find some common ground for more meaningful conversation.

From this first stage, we may progress to exchanging facts about ourselves, other people, and topics of general interest. This is a relatively nonthreatening form of encounter because it reveals little about our inner selves other than the extent of our knowledge and tastes. At this stage we gossip about mutual friends, give out our favorite recipes, and discuss our cars, homes, jobs, and so on. We are trading information until we hit on topics that may reveal common interests. If we fail to discover any commonality, we have risked nothing. If we find some mutual interests, we may form a friendly relationship that can lead to the next, slightly more risky level of communication.

At the beginning of a relationship, we often find ourselves reluctant to share our opinions. As we grow more comfortable with another person, we test the waters. We may venture a negative remark about a film we saw, but until trust has been established, we are likely to backpedal if the other person disagrees. "Well, anyway, the cinematography was nice, and I really liked the costumes" may restore the harmony that our divided opinions appeared to be upsetting.

Sharing opinions involves sharing values. It also means taking the risk that others might judge those values negatively. Until people reach a level of comfort that allows them to disagree amicably, they remain acquaintances, not friends.

Friends, however, reach a more intimate level in which they can reveal their emotions—which can be the most frightening thing of all—to the other person. To reveal our inner feelings is to show another person who we really are. We can share opinions without revealing the feelings and emotions that are unique to ourselves.

For example, two people may agree that a neighbor's home is beautiful. This is a shared opinion. However, the beautiful house may give one of them pleasure—in being able to visit and drink in the lovely surroundings—while in the other person the house might stir up only jealousy because he or she can't afford similar luxuries. In this way we define our individuality. When we share these types of feelings with another person, we can enter into a meaningful friendship in which we understand and respect our individual differences.

If feelings are truly shared and we are completely honest with another person, we may say that we are friends. We accept each other for our similarities and differences. Open, honest communication leads to the ultimate in relationships, which is love. Not necessarily romantic love, but a deep and abiding trust in another individual who knows us as well as we know ourselves. This ultimate sharing and trust is the fifth, and most rarely achieved, level in which we can communicate with others.

In face-to-face encounters, the bulk of our communication occurs on the first three levels; we reserve the sharing of feelings and emotions with very few of the many people with whom we interact each day. When we communicate on the Internet, however, things change. Most importantly, most Internet citizens have little need to spend time on levels one and two. The network is organized not by geography, but by areas of interest. Rather than entering into conversations with a dozen strangers who are attending the same gathering because they work in the same place or know the same hostess, people on the Net can proceed immediately to conversing about their areas of interest.

A flower lover tuning into rec.gardens already knows that he or she most likely will find common ground with the other people there. Newsgroup readers have the luxury of browsing within their areas of interest to find topics in which they have definite ideas and opinions, and they can ignore others that interest them only peripherally. Users also can lurk, reading posts without ever contributing to a conversation. Or they can post a question or response, which indicates that anyone is free to respond.

Thus, both the shy and the particular can discriminate among the conversations in which they wish to participate. They can enter and leave conversations until they find ones that generate informational and opinionated responses that satisfy them. If a topic wearies or disinterests them, they have absolute freedom to withdraw without recrimination. There is no one in the room to insist that they return and take part, nor can anyone stop them from trying to interject the last word—over and over again, if they wish—until they get bored or get it right.

Responses also can lead two people to a more general discussion of personalities, hopes, and fears about the topic under discussion. Individuals may find themselves suddenly engaged in a more personal dialogue with a member of the newsgroup. At this time, they may move the discussion out of the public arena and into a more private one via e-mail. E-mail correspondences such as these function as the equivalent of a face-to-face visit to someone's virtual home. There is no need for small talk because the areas of common interest have already been explored; the grounds for a friendly relationship have been established.

Although e-mail may be more personal than mere newsgroup participation, it still allows us to hide behind the terminal. Thus protected, it becomes relatively easy for people to move to the next level of communication—exchanging opinions with a freedom rarely enjoyed in face-to-face encounters. At this level, the worst that can happen if someone disagrees is that they cease to communicate. Because we are only at an opinion and acquaintance stage, this breakup can be relatively painless.

Perhaps because they need not fear painful reprisals, many Netizens appear to enjoy taking advantage of the freedom to express their opinions strongly and vehemently. Unlike real life, where most of us normally strive for harmony, people on the Net can be emboldened by their isolation. They become verbally aggressive, even abusive in defending their viewpoints. This phenomenon, called flaming, is so common that an entire newsgroup, alt.flame, is dedicated to these types of disputes. However, flame wars can and do break out in any newsgroup where disagreement is even a remote possibility.

Why such volatility of emotion on the Net? It may be caused partially by the lack of visual cues—the stripping away of information that makes it easier to be misunderstood. Face-to-face encounters can lead to disagreements when we misread each other's words and cues. In terminal to terminal discussions, we have no cues other than the ubiquitous smiley. Friendly advice can be read as sarcasm, and friendly overtures as come-ons. We have only the intonations we hear in our own heads.

Reprisal is simple: Send out a flame. Emotions rise easily on the Net because we are so shielded by our terminals. No matter how ugly the flame war gets, there is rarely any danger of physical violence.

The same goes for positive, friendly Net relationships. We may tentatively offer concern if the other person sounds worried or depressed. There is no danger that our extended hand will be rudely brushed away. We can—after an interlude, when we feel secure because we have survived differences of opinion and discovered similarities—offer even the deepest of emotions, secure in knowing that there is always an avenue of escape.

We will never know if the recipient of a tender, earnest message receives it with a scowl. Even the most insecure person can assume that the lack of a reply means the message was lost or that the intended recipient merely is not online. Knowing that we cannot be seen to blush or that the tension we feel in offering our sympathy or love cannot be perceived in the words etched on the screen, even the shyest among us can risk expressing emotions without fear of reprisal or shame. And because of this feeling of being able to speak so freely, we open ourselves to the possibility of forming close relationships.

Forming real, lasting relationships, however, is only possible when the people involved have been open and honest with each other throughout the correspondence. People who wander the Net in disguise are unlikely to form genuine relationships.

But people who strike up an electronic conversation because they happen to share an interest have little reason to lie to each other. Why bother to erect an elaborate facade to advise someone about the joys of pet ownership or the best way to strip an antique bureau? If our advice is heeded and responded to, and if that leads to more and freer communication, we begin to build real relationships on the groundwork laid by that openness and honesty.

For some people, this relationship may lead to something more. Emotions are expressed, and long-buried secrets are told. Eventually, these individuals find themselves turning to snail mail to exchange photos or small gifts. They pick up that old-fashioned instrument, the telephone, to discover the voice behind the communication; plans to meet face to face then can be made.

The initial face-to-face meeting becomes the final stage in these Net relationships. Some of them—the ones based on falsity—are doomed o fail as soon as one person discovers that the other is not as they had presented themselves. False expectations become dismal reality, and the two part no better acquainted than when they first exchanged letters.

But people who have been forthright throughout their e-mail correspondence have already gone behind the facade that so often hinders face-to-face communication. Their hardest work in communicating has already been accomplished, and they become more real to each other, even when communicating in isolation behind terminals—than are many people when seated across a table.

Thus, Internet relationships can achieve the same high level of communication as face-to-face encounters, and perhaps they can achieve the state more quickly. The ability to venture out in low-level informational exchanges to those in which we express opinions and emotions is facilitated by our abilities to hide behind a terminal, to probe into another's deepest feelings while maintaining a safe distance. Absolute honesty is as essential from behind these terminals as it is in any face-to-face encounter if people are to become more to each other than mere repositories of information. With honesty can come some real rewards.

And so, heart in mouth but with steady fingers, a woman thousands of miles away may write to a man she has only known by e-mail, "I love you,

you know—in a funny kind of way." Perhaps there will be no reply; perhaps she has been too honest, come on too strongly too quickly. Perhaps she has been inappropriate. But perhaps, after all of their exchanged messages, shared information, opinions, and even laughter, she has come to trust in a certain honesty that this strange, isolated type of communication fosters in those who have not only discovered but developed their common ground together.

Real communication can eventually coax people from behind their safe shields and into the uncertainties of real life. But real, honest communication can make that real life encounter surprisingly easy. So that for a lucky few it should be easy to say, one day, with all sincerity, "I love you—really," even without a terminal to hide behind.

EXPLORING THE READING

1. Thomas Barrett and Carol Wallace assert that we become our messages. Discuss this statement in a small group of students. Can we define our personality easily in cyberspace? What happens to the parts of our character that we leave out of our interactions in cyberspace?

2. The authors note that openness and honesty are easier for some on the Internet than face-to-face because users are protected from embarrassment over social blunders. Clifford Stoll and others have suggested that these supposed benefits to online communication will be detrimental to society in the long run because people learn society's mores by making mistakes and perhaps being embarrassed by them. They say we risk raising a generation ignorant of the basic rules that guide face-to-face interaction. Freewrite for ten minutes on what might happen if we learned our rules for social interaction on the Internet and not face-to-face.

3. Can you love someone you have never met and about whom all you know is what he or she has shared with you? Before the Internet and stories of online romance, had you ever heard of people who had never met falling in love? Discuss this in a small group.

4. Using McLuhan's statement "the medium is the message," consider the message of e-mail communication as described by Barrett and Wallace.

Now, A Word from Cyberspace

by Mortimer B. Zuckerman

The world is rapidly changing. New technologies abound, but according to Mortimer B. Zuckerman in this essay from U.S. News and World Report, *we are not much different than we were in the sixteenth century. We are afraid of new technology and the effect it will have on society. We are also unable to predict what direction society might take because of it. He argues that government moves too slowly to regulate the rapidly changing world online. Lawmakers should step aside and let the free market manage our uses of new technology, says Zuckerman, stepping in only to ensure that the use of cyberspace remains free.*

In addition to founding and managing the national real estate development company, Boston Properties, Zuckerman is chairman of The Atlantic Monthly, *the* New York Daily News, *and* U.S. News and World Report. *His editorials are regular features of* U.S. News and World Report *where he is also editor-in-chief.* U.S. News and World Report *can be found online at http://www.usnews.com.*

The world had no idea, more than 500 years ago, what vast horizons would open up when a goldsmith in the mid-fifteenth century used movable metal type to print a Bible. Johannes Gensfleisch, better known as Gutenberg, did much more than invent modern printing. Without it, and the incentive to produce paper for making books, the explosion of learning and knowledge that we call the Renaissance could never have taken place; modern science would have been stillborn; freedom itself would never have flowered.

Fast forward: Today, we think we have a better sense of where the computer is taking us. But do we? Not many people envisaged that the room-size computer of 40 years ago would shrink to the laptop, thanks to the microprocessor—itself around for twenty-four years. Nowadays we talk airily of individuals with their PCs working wherever they like, buying and selling, creating and communicating—activities for which we used to think we needed to build cities and transportation systems. We speculate on what might happen to our newly wired homes, schools and workplaces. The computer will deliver hundreds of visual programs; print out books selected from electronic catalogs; scour the libraries of the world for us; flash masterpiece paintings on our bedroom walls, courtesy of Microsoft; do calculations in moments that would have taken mathematicians years to complete; diagnose our snuffles and prescribe the right pill; call up companions when we grow weary of all this. The permutations of individual empowerment are infinite.

On the darker side, think of the rogue hacker, sitting alone with his computer wreaking havoc on business and public institutions. One hacker, Kevin Mitnick, allegedly stole thousands of data files and at least 20,000 credit card numbers, accessed corporate trade secrets worth millions, and much more. The young man authorities say is the greatest computer criminal in history was captured with the help of another computer genius. But how many more

Kevin Mitnicks are out there? What other social revolutions will follow when people are accessible on video screens of such quality that it will seem like looking at a person through a window?

Who can guess? That is the point of the computer revolution. Nobody imagined that the automobile would create the suburbs, a phenomenon that transformed our entire political and economic landscape. We are as ignorant as the citizens of the fifteenth century. Very few of them could read. Very few of my generation (I speak with some personal feeling) can claim to comprehend all the cryptic electronic dialects. And where there is ignorance, there is usually fear. They knew it in Gutenberg's day when the organized scribes, calligraphers and illuminators used all their political muscle to try to stop methods of duplication.

There are busybodies enough around today. Congress is already talking about stopping the Internet from being used for the exchange of sexual fantasies. This may be well meaning, but it is comparable in a different time to censoring the telephone because it made it easier for men and women to talk directly, without another's introduction. Does the government understand the consequences of this new information age? Government being government, it will want to control this emerging world or at least shape it substantially. That would be like the medieval guilds trying to control the Industrial Revolution. The technology is changing too quickly for the best of bureaucracies. Only the private markets are nimble enough, smart enough and efficient enough to keep up.

There is a role for government, but it is to ensure freedom—to prevent monopolistic conditions from arising to the detriment of local communities or the nation. Battlegrounds are already taking form. The wires coming into our homes, carrying data, will be fought over by the telephone and cable companies. The control devices sitting on top of our TV sets that will make them interactive undoubtedly must have a common language and are thus susceptible to control by a single manufacturer.

The multimedia explosion is good news. The information industry will be the largest in this country by the end of the decade. The marketplace, not some government agency, is where the necessary calculations of costs, investment and returns should be made—even as the rest of us struggle to keep up.

EXPLORING THE READING

1. Daniel Harris says that computers give us a false sense of empowerment. Mortimer B. Zuckerman indicates they give us real empowerment. In a small group, discuss each author's position. Which author do you agree with? Why?

2. How effective is the comparison between the Internet and Gutenberg's press in the fifteenth century? Why do you think he uses it?

3. Do you think Zuckerman has been influenced by Marshall McLuhan? What aspects of Zuckerman's essay echo the McLuhan reading at the beginning of the chapter?

4. Zuckerman says that we think we have a better sense of where computers are taking us than the poor souls who predicted the future of printing over 500 years ago, but he questions whether we really do. Freewrite for ten minutes on the type of future you imagine for computer technology in general and the World Wide Web and Internet in particular. What will the wired world look like in twenty years? In fifty?

WRITING SUGGESTIONS

1. Is the Internet primarily a text medium or is it more like television? Argue a position, based on your own observation of the Internet and referring, if appropriate, to the essay by Jay David Bolter, the United States Supreme Court ruling (Chapter 4), and other texts in this book or elsewhere.

2. What is the Internet's message as a medium? How will the Internet change our perception of reality? Write an essay based on your observations of the Internet and interviews with others you know who have spent time surfing the Internet.

3. Do you live in a technopoly, using Neil Postman's definition? Argue a position, giving specific examples from the culture around you.

4. How does the Internet extend the reach of your senses? Interview one or more computer experts and write an essay identifying and describing at least four different ways.

THE WRITING PROCESS: IDENTIFYING YOUR PURPOSE, WRITING FOR AN AUDIENCE

You write letters to your grandparents to thank them for your graduation or birthday gift. You write a complaint letter to a company about a product and get a refund. You write a note to your roommate to tell her where you will be and what time you will get home. You write down the check number, the location, and the amount of a check you wrote in your ledger to keep your checking account in order. You write a grocery list so you will remember to buy shampoo.

Though each of these writing occasions is simple and may not require a lengthy written document, each of them has two things in common. You are putting words on paper for some reason, some purpose, and you are intending those words to be seen by a very specific audience.

What you say, how you express it, and how much detail you include in these writing events depends on your purpose for writing and on your audience. How would your writing change if you were reminding yourself to buy shampoo? If you were asking your mother to buy your shampoo? Or if you were reminding your roommate that she promised to pick you up some shampoo at her next visit to the hairdresser?

If you write a note to yourself to remember to pick up shampoo, you probably only write "Shampoo." After all, you know what brand and size you prefer and how much you are willing to spend on it. If you write the note to your mom it might be included at the end of a letter to her and say something like this, "By the way, I can't find X Shampoo anywhere. Could you send me the biggest bottle you can find of X Shampoo in the next package you send. I have enough to last another week or two." If you are writing that note to your roommate you might say, "Here's $20 for a bottle of X Shampoo. Hope your haircut goes well—No spikes. Thanks."

Each of these messages is written with the same purpose. To get a specific brand of shampoo, but since each message is written for a different audience, it contains differing levels of formality. It also assumes a different set of knowledge in common with each audience.

Identifying Your Purpose

Purpose statements for writing can usually be summed up as *"to* plus a verb phrase," an infinitive. The purpose of everyday writing might be to inform, to persuade, to call to action, or to amuse. You might have to write five documents in any given day, all of them with a different purpose.

Different professions often require different purposes for writing. A comedian writes to amuse. A politician writes to persuade. An advertising copywriter writes to sell. A computer documentation expert writes to explain. A journalist writes to inform. A web page builder may write to entertain. Every time you write, there is some purpose behind what you are writing. When you are writing for an English class, you are asked to stop and analyze that purpose.

Often, the purpose of your writing is implied in the question that you choose to answer. If a question asks you to explain the differences between two software packages, it has already told you that your purpose will be, "to explain." If it asks you to write an argumentative essay, it is asking you to persuade. If it tells you to observe something and record your observations, it is asking you to inform.

If you are not using a writing prompt initiated by this textbook or your teacher or if the prompt you have chosen doesn't have an implied purpose, identifying the purpose is an important first step in preparing to write. Answering the question, "What do I want to give or to prove to my readers" is a good first step in identifying your purpose. If you say you want to prove that *Microsoft Word* could be improved with some adjustments to the help screens and toolbars, then your purpose is persuasive. If you say you want to prove that many people take themselves too seriously when they get in front of the computer, then your purpose is to amuse. If you want to give your readers a short history of your personal web page, then your purpose is probably to inform. If you want to prove to your readers that they need to write their representatives and ask that Congress make specific laws for the Internet, your purpose is to call to action.

Determining Your Thesis. Once you have decided on the purpose of your essay, you probably have a good idea of what you want your essay to say, what question you want your essay to answer. The thesis statement is a sentence or collection of sentences that lets the reader know what you are trying to prove. It contains the subject of your essay. It also contains your opinion of the subject.

Take a look at the following thesis statements:

Computers have changed the way we do business.
Cyberspace is not really a place, but the metaphor of place helps us imagine what is unimaginable.
The Internet has grown a lot over the past twenty years.

What is the subject of each of these statements? What is the opinion for-warded? Which of these thesis statements is strongest?

In each case, the subject of the above statements is some aspect of com-puter culture. That subject is presented clearly: computers in business, cyber-space as a place, and the growth of the Internet. What is missing from the first and last statements is a clear opinion on the subject matter. Although it could be considered arguable whether computers have changed business or not, most readers see the statement as a fact. If we rewrite the thesis statement to contain an opinion, it may end up something like this:

> Computers may have changed the way we do business, but they have not helped us improve customer service.

Now we have the *fact*, computers have changed business, and an *opinion*, they have not improved customer service. The purpose that is implied by this thesis statement is persuasive. The essay will persuade the reader that customer service has not improved.

The second statement gives a clear opinion. Cyberspace is not a place, but the metaphor helps us imagine the unimaginable. The purpose of the essay this thesis statement develops could be to inform readers of the way the "place" metaphor is used in literature about the Internet.

The final statement might be a good subject for an essay. However, the growth of the Internet is not a thesis. It does not contain any opinion. Notice that without an opinion, the purpose of the essay is not clear. Will this essay be informative, persuasive, or amusing? With this topic, we could write a thesis statement that would make the essay serve any of those purposes.

> The growth of the Internet over the past twenty years has been spurred on by entrepreneurs looking to make their fortunes in the new frontier. (*to inform*)
> The growth of the Internet should remain unchecked by legislation and gov-ernmental intrusion. (*to persuade*)
> The growth of the World Wide Web has been spurred on by not only serious scientific research and a desire for equal access to information, it has also been built by some goofy people with even goofier missions in life. (*to amuse*)

The thesis statement gives the subject of your essay, your opinion on that subject, and it implies the purpose of your essay. Beginning work on your essay with a strong thesis in mind can help you focus your invention and research and keep you on track as you start to write your first draft. It might help to get in a small group in class to have several people look at your thesis statement and tell what they think your subject, opinion, and purpose is. If a reviewer cannot find the answer, you know that your thesis probably needs a little more work before you are ready to build an essay around it.

Writing for an Audience

Thomas Barrett and Carol Wallace in "Virtual Encounters" tell the readers of *Internet World* that it is possible, and maybe even easier, to form close relationships with other people over the Internet. Ashley Dunn, in "Think of Your Soul as a Market Niche," examines the benefits and risks associated with our growing loss of privacy for the CyberTimes edition of the *New York Times*. Bill McKibben, in "Out There in the Middle of the Buzz," warns readers of *Forbes ASAP*, a business magazine that focuses on technology, that more information won't help us get back to what really matters, the dreams we dream when we make the time for peace and quiet. Neil Postman, in the interview "The Same Mindless, Stupid Process," tells the German philosopher Volker Freidman and the readers of the *Whole Earth Review* that it is dangerous to make every possible accommodation for a new technology before we examine the possible repercussions of that technology.

As you look over the places where each essay in this chapter was published and examine the stance the author takes in relation to technology, you may begin to notice patterns of acceptance and resistance in articles originally intended for either computer-mediated or print-only publications. The reasons for this, once you think about them, are obvious. If you were writing an essay to be published on the Internet or in a publication dealing only with computers, you could assume some basic characteristics of your audience.

First, they are probably familiar with computers and have an understanding of some specialized computer terms. Barrett and Wallace can assume their readers understand words like *newsgroup* and *flame*. If they wrote the same essay for a more general magazine like *U.S. News and World Report*, they might need to spend more time with definitions or avoid specialized computer terms as Mortimer Zuckerman does in his essay.

Second, you could probably assume that your readers support computer technology. Most online readers and readers of specialty publications for computers are more likely to support new technology than readers of a more general magazine whose audience likely includes people who for one reason or another are either neutral or seriously skeptical about the use of computers. Although most of the writers in this book attempt to present balanced views of technology, writers for general publications are more likely to remain neutral or negative, whereas writers like Barrett and Wallace and Dunn end their essays on a distinctly positive note.

As a student writer, your audience's biases and opinions may be more difficult to decipher than the audience for a specific magazine. However, analyzing your audience remains an important step in writing, whether for publication in a magazine or as an exercise for class. Moreover, analyzing your audience remains an important step in writing, whether for publication or as an exercise for class.

Defining Your Intended Audience.   Magazines have careful marketing data and finely developed strategies to help their writers appeals to their readership. Likewise, there are many ways you as a student can target your intended audience. Taking some time to think about the following questions before you start to write can help you define your audience:

1. How familiar will my readers be with my topic? What terms will I need to define for them?

2. Will my audience readily agree with my thesis? If not, how can I convince them? Will facts, statistics, expert testimony, or personal examples sway them?

3. What values do my audience and I share? How might my values differ from my audience? Where can we find common ground?

4. What types of argument will be most useful with my readers? Will appeals to logic, emotion, or credibility be most helpful?

Once you have answered these questions, you will be able to think like your audience. As you explore your topic through invention, conduct formal and informal research, and write and revise your paper, keep your audience and its needs in mind.

WRITING PROCESS ACTIVITY

1. Write the question you want your essay to answer at the top of the page. This may be a question from the "Writing Suggestions" in this book, a question your teacher asks, or a question you come up with on your own.

2. Answer these questions about your essay:

   a. What is the subject of my essay?

   b. What do I want to give or prove to my readers?

   c. Who are my readers? How much do they know about my subject? Are they likely to agree with me or not?

   d. What is the purpose of this essay?

3. Develop a tentative thesis for your essay that identifies the subject of your essay and gives your opinion on the subject.

ACCESSING INTERNET RESOURCES: KEY-WORD SEARCHING ON THE WORLD WIDE WEB

In this chapter you've read Marshall McLuhan's famous chapter, "The Medium is the Message," and several other texts that have been influenced by McLuhan's research and writing. Suppose you want to learn more about McLuhan. You simply go to one of the World Wide Web search engines, such as Infoseek, http://www.infoseek.com and type in his name.

Infoseek finds some 1300 Web pages with information about McLuhan, organized with what the automated search engine thinks are the best

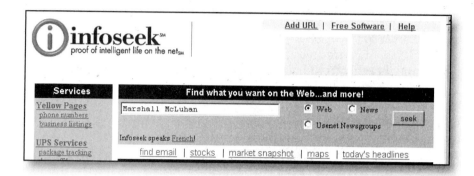

possibilities first. On the first page listing the hits, or site with McLuhan information, is listed the index to the Marshall McLuhan Center for Global Communication, http://www.mcluhanmedia.com/mmcli001.html.

This site has lots of information about McLuhan's writing. If it doesn't have everything you need, however, you can use the **Back** arrow and explore some of the other McLuhan hits.

Customized searching.   Sometimes you enter a key-word or words that generate thousands and thousands of hits, and you wonder if you are finding the best information. All the search engines offer customized searches, though the specifications differ from one search engine to another. In Infoseek, you can click on the word **Help** on the opening screen, and this leads you to an explanation of how to do a customized search, and all engines offer a similar help screen. In Infoseek, you can customize a search by using these options:

- Capitalize names of people and places. Infoseek will look for the words together, not separately.

- Use double quotation marks around words that must appear together, in a particular order. Alternatively, put dashes between the words. "Search engine" would be treated as a phrase, not separate words.

- Place a + sign (plus sign) between words that *must* appear in the hits. Otherwise, Infoseek will return hits that include any of the words.

There are more options available, but these will allow you to cut the number of hits and screen for more useful sites.

SUGGESTED INTERNET ASSIGNMENTS

1. Do a key-word search for information about Marshall McLuhan. Find one site which particularly interests you and report about it to your class.

2. Like Ashley Dunn, explore the Internet for advertising methods and identify three different approaches. What are they and how do they work? For example, you could visit the Cybergold site, www.cybergold.com, which pays you to watch advertising.

3. Locate three sites on the Web where text or images is reproduced "real time" or "almost live" like the Seattle weather site mentioned in Jay David Bolter's text. What does this immediacy add to the site?

4. Explore the Ipex site, http://www.ipix.com, which features 360 degree photographs which you can manipulate with your mouse. After reading Bolter's remarks about virtual reality, do you think this site alters your perspective?

5. Explore some aspect of the Internet you haven't experienced before, whether it is live chat on the Web, a MUD or MOO, live video, or sound recordings. Contemplate the message this medium is conveying.

WIRED TO THE WEB

Cybergold

www.cybergold.com

Mentioned in the Ashley Dunn article, Cybergold is a site which takes a new slant on advertising on the Internet. Cybergold pays you a small amount—50 cents or a dollar—for viewing advertisements and entering some basic information about yourself.

An almost live view from Seattle on Saturday, September 6, 1997 at 10:27. The temperature is 17°C (63°F, 290K). Winds are at 3 knots (3 mph) from the S. Gusts to 3 knots (4 mph). Barometric pressure is 1019 mbar (30.10 in). The sun rose today at 06:35 and will set at 19:39. The moon is waxing crescent (12% of full).

Seattle Weather

http://www.washington.edu

The University of Washington provides an "almost live" view of Seattle weather, along with current information about the temperature, wind speed and direction, and time of sunset and sunrise. This, according to Jay David Bolter, is an example of how the Internet is changing our perception of the world. Right now, you can be in Seattle virtually.

IPIX

http://www.ipix.com/

Visit the Ipix site and explore the 360 degree photographs such as this one, which is a virtual tour of a rental apartment. You use your mouse button to navigate upwards and downward, left and right. This site is particularly interesting in relation to Jay David Bolter's article in which he writes about computerized virtual reality's ability to let the viewer change perspective.

THE INTERNET AND PERSONAL FREEDOM

The Internet has a strong tradition of personal freedom. The international network began as a decentralized, self-governing medium for the transmission of information, at first primarily for scientists and academics. Over the last twenty-five years or so, the Internet has grown, first slowly, then with increasing speed. Network has connected to network, software has become more user-friendly, and, suddenly, people are communicating everywhere on the Net, across town and across the world. And the Internet is still decentralized, not controlled by any one government or association of governments. Indeed, at least at present, it looks as if no one government may be able to control the Internet, which does not mean that governments have not and will not continue to try to establish some measure of mastery over the unruly grass-roots entity.

Why should governments rule the Internet? Why not just leave it alone? Why not allow it to continue to be self-regulating? Some people, including John Perry Barlow, author of "A Declaration of the Independence of Cyberspace," advocate just that. Barlow, writing on behalf of his fellow Netizens, or citizens of the Internet, tells big governments to keep hands off. He views government efforts to pass laws regulating the Internet as attempts to impose tyranny on a place he believes needs no government.

Scott Rosenberg, "Independence Daze: A Sovereign Cyberspace is Alluring, but Hardly Practical," expresses his opinion that an independent Internet is unrealistic and naïve. The Internet does not exist independently of the countries where Netizens live, and could not exist without electricity, telephones, computer chips, and other hardware. Then, information is transmitted on the Internet, such as pornography, which others consider objectionable and dangerous to children. In addition, financial information about individuals is available on the Net which many consider an infringement of personal privacy. And the Net has become a playground for hackers who "hack" into secure Internet sites, change information without authorization, obtain software and manipulate financial data to steal funds.

Not a simple problem, this issue of personal freedom in cyberspace. Should, for example, a government be able to prosecute authors of Websites containing material the majority considers "indecent"? That is what the Communications Decency Act of 1996, since declared unconstitutional, attempted to legislate. The portion of the Supreme Court Ruling on the CDA, included in this chapter, specifies the justices' rationale that the Act infringed upon freedom of speech protected by the First Amendment.

Not a problem to be solved in a year, possibly never resolved, this issue of regulating the Internet. Potential regulations will be legislated, passed, tested in the courts for years to come. Peter Huber, in "The End of the Law, and the Beginning," describes the enormity of the problem created by the new technologies of the Internet when considering only the broadcast implications. Already, any computer can be a publisher. Soon any computer on the Net will have the potential to be a broadcast television-full-motion-video station. How is a government going to write copyright laws for that? It's mind-boggling.

How do you think the regulation of the Internet will be resolved? Will it become independent? Will another Communications Decency Act be written which stands as constitutional? Huber suggests the new laws which will rule all this high-tech world will be "cooked-up the old-fashioned way." They will be based on individual court cases, fought one at a time rather than far-reaching landmark legislation. What do you think?

———————————— ■ ————————————

A Declaration of the Independence of Cyberspace

by John Perry Barlow

In 1996, noted writer of Internet-related articles and essays John Perry Barlow was invited to write an essay for a book called 24 Hours in Cyberspace. *At about the same time, President Bill Clinton was signing into law the Telecommunications Reform Act which encompassed the Communications Decency Act (CDA), which has subsequently been ruled unconstitutional. In response to the CDA's attempt to regulate so-called indecent speech in cyberspace, Barlow wrote "A Declaration of the Independence of Cyberspace," which was posted widely on the Internet.*

In his introduction to the declaration, Barlow relates that the CDA would have made it unlawful and punishable by a $250,000 fine to say online a number of dirty words he has personally heard used freely in the Senate cafeteria by United States senators. Barlow describes his call for Netizen independence as an opportunity to "dump some tea in the virtual harbor"—a protest against regulation by those "who haven't the slightest idea who we are." Related papers by Barlow can be found in the Electronic Frontier Foundation archive at http://www.eff.org/~barlow/library.html.

Governments of the Industrial World, you weary giants of flesh and steel, I come from Cyberspace, the new home of Mind. On behalf of the future, I ask you of the past to leave us alone. You are not welcome among us. You have no sovereignty where we gather.

We have no elected government, nor are we likely to have one, so I address you with no greater authority than that with which liberty itself always speaks. I declare the global social space we are building to be naturally independent of the tyrannies you seek to impose on us. You have no moral right to rule us nor do you possess any methods of enforcement we have true reason to fear.

Governments derive their just powers from the consent of the governed. You have neither solicited nor received ours. We did not invite you. You do not know us, nor do you know our world. Cyberspace does not lie within your borders. Do not think that you can build it, as though it were a public construction project. You cannot. It is an act of nature and it grows itself through our collective actions.

You have not engaged in our great and gathering conversation, nor did you create the wealth of our marketplaces. You do not know our culture, our ethics, or the unwritten codes that already provide our society more order than could be obtained by any of your impositions.

You claim there are problems among us that you need to solve. You use this claim as an excuse to invade our precincts. Many of these problems don't exist. Where there are real conflicts, where there are wrongs, we will identify them and address them by our means. We are forming our own Social Contract. This governance will arise according to the conditions of our world, not yours. Our world is different.

Cyberspace consists of transactions, relationships, and thought itself, arrayed like a standing wave in the web of our communications. Ours is a world that is both everywhere and nowhere, but it is not where bodies live.

We are creating a world that all may enter without privilege or prejudice accorded by race, economic power, military force, or station of birth.

We are creating a world where anyone, anywhere may express his or her beliefs, no matter how singular, without fear of being coerced into silence or conformity.

Your legal concepts of property, expression, identity, movement, and context do not apply to us. They are based on matter. There is no matter here.

Our identities have no bodies, so, unlike you, we cannot obtain order by physical coercion. We believe that from ethics, enlightened self-interest, and the commonweal, our governance will emerge. Our identities may be distributed across many of your jurisdictions. The only law that all our constituent cultures would generally recognize is the Golden Rule. We hope we will be able to build our particular solutions on that basis. But we cannot accept the solutions you are attempting to impose.

In the United States, you have today created a law, the Telecommunications Reform Act, which repudiates your own Constitution and insults the dreams of Jefferson, Washington, Mill, Madison, DeToqueville, and Brandeis. These dreams must now be born anew in us.

You are terrified of your own children, since they are natives in a world where you will always be immigrants. Because you fear them, you entrust your bureaucracies with the parental responsibilities you are too cowardly to confront yourselves. In our world, all the sentiments and expressions of humanity, from the debasing to the angelic, are parts of a seamless whole, the global conversation of bits. We cannot separate the air that chokes from the air upon which wings beat.

In China, Germany, France, Russia, Singapore, Italy and the United States, you are trying to ward off the virus of liberty by erecting guard posts at the frontiers of Cyberspace. These may keep out the contagion for a small time, but they will not work in a world that will soon be blanketed in bit-bearing media.

Your increasingly obsolete information industries would perpetuate themselves by proposing laws, in America and elsewhere, that claim to own speech itself throughout the world. These laws would declare ideas to be another industrial product, no more noble than pig iron. In our world, whatever the human mind may create can be reproduced and distributed infinitely at no cost. The global conveyance of thought no longer requires your factories to accomplish.

These increasingly hostile and colonial measures place us in the same position as those previous lovers of freedom and self-determination who had to reject the authorities of distant, uninformed powers. We must declare our virtual selves immune to your sovereignty, even as we continue to consent to your rule over our bodies. We will spread ourselves across the Planet so that no one can arrest our thoughts.

We will create a civilization of the Mind in Cyberspace. May it be more humane and fair than the world your governments have made before.

EXPLORING THE READING

1. What does John Perry Barlow's "Declaration of the Independence of Cyberspace" declare independence from? Do you agree with his position? Why or why not?

2. How does Barlow describe the nature of cyberspace? Would you agree with him?

3. What is Barlow's tone in his declaration? Is it appropriate for the situation and audience? Why or why not?

Independence Daze: A Sovereign Cyberspace Is Alluring, but Hardly Practical

by Scott Rosenberg

Responding to John Perry Barlow's "A Declaration of the Independence of Cyberspace," Scott Rosenberg, senior editor of the online magazine Salon, *suggests that cyberspace, like any frontier, resists regulation. The notion of independence for cyberspace, however, is impractical because the Internet is forever tied to technology, and technology is tied to the existence and goodwill of governments and large corporations. As Barlow suggests, cyberspace may be inhabited by minds rather than bodies, but the minds cannot touch without the intermediaries of bandwidth and electricity.*

Rosenberg's work has appeared in Wired *magazine, the* New York Times, *the* Washington Post, *the* Village Voice *and elsewhere. He enjoys publishing on the Web, although he sometimes misses the smell of printer's ink. This editorial can be found at http://www.salon1999.com/08/features/netnation/html#declaration. You might also check out the online discussions in* Salon's Table Talk, *especially the Digital Culture topics at http://tabletalk.salon1999.com.*

The online world has always equated itself with the frontier. In its self-generated and -propagated mythology, cyberspace is a brave new world, explored by pioneers, settled by homesteaders and marauded by the occasional outlaw. Like any fringe community, it does not take kindly to supervision from afar.

As Washington moved earlier this month to impose censorship on the world of computer-base communication, calls for protest and acts of resistance were the order of the day. But the "Communications Decency Act"—which imposes stiff fines and prison sentences for transmission of "indecent" material online and which was challenged in court the moment it became law—also aroused a new note from the world of the Net: a cry of secession.

Specifically, a "Declaration off the Independence of Cyberspace" issued forth from the e-mail-box of John Perry Barlow—the sometime cattle rancher and Grateful Dead lyricist who co-founded the Electronic Frontier Foundation, an online civil liberties group. Conceived as Barlow's contribution to the "24 Hours in Cyberspace" project, the document circulated fast and wide on the Net.

Addressed to the "governments of the industrial world," it declares "the global social space we are building to be naturally independent of the tyrannies you seek to impose on us." A stirring, admittedly grandiose call to virtual arms, it's worth reading in full.

Barlow's declaration did not pop out of nowhere. The notion of the Internet as a quasi-sovereign entity has been kicked around ever since people realized that the structure of the network itself rendered it resistant to regulation or control by any individual state or central authority. Lately the rhetoric of Net nationalism has heated up. For instance, *Rules of the Net,* a sprightly and savvy new book about Internet culture by the late Thomas Mandel and Gerard Van der Leun, delivers a mock Declaration of Independence in its opening chapter. Theirs is different in tone from Barlow's, but similar in motivation: "On the Net, we hold these truths to be self-evident, that all users are created equal . . ." Like Barlow, who describes cyberspace as a "civilization of the mind," Mandel and Van der Leun call the online community "an information nation; a nation not located on the earth but in the mind."

This conceit is not only seductive, it is—unlike so much of the hype that accompanies any use of the "cyber" prefix—based on a substantially accurate reading of the facts. The Net *is* an unprecedentedly efficient connector of people on the level of ideas; it creates communities, based on shared interests, that transcend the mundane limits of time and geography. And so it has acquired a genuine, although metaphorical, sense of place for its habitues. Threaten that place with unwanted restrictions and the talk gets rebellious fast.

NET TO WORLD: WE'RE OUTTA HERE

And yet there is something profoundly impractical in the idea of Net independence. It is a concept without ballast, an attractive free-floating notion that stirs the heart but has difficulty persuading the head. The Net as a community may be a construct of mind, but the Net as a technology is a very physical thing, utterly dependent on such down-to-earth commodities as bandwidth, telephone access, computer nodes and memory chips, and, underlying the whole thing, reliable sources of electricity.

These commodities are not found in the Net's "republic of mind" but in the actual republics of the Americas, Europe and Asia. And while it's impossible for any nation to control the Internet, given its architecture, it's thoroughly conceivable for one nation or many to separate from the Net—to shut access down.

And so one must ask the declarers of Net independence just how they imagine fighting for their freedom. When the first digital Redcoats arrive to reassert the rule of some nation's law over the Net, what e-mail Minutemen will ride to defend the cause of freedom?

I asked John Perry Barlow these questions, and his answers are vague but provocative. Admitting that it's impossible to predict the shape of a "cyberspace revolution," given that "we're talking about a conflict between a mental region and a physical region," he also suggests that "bloodshed" is not out of the question.

If that's the case, I think the Net is in trouble. Consider the possibilities: Either the cyberspatial "republic of mind" turns out to be far less powerful than its partisans believe—in which case it will be unable to resist institutional efforts to control it; or it proves unexpectedly potent—in which case it is likely to arouse far more radical opposition from the powers of the "old order" than anything we've seen to date.

The recent dustup between Compuserve and the German government—in which an international online service found itself at the mercy of legal standards in Bavaria—may not be a representative case, since Compuserve, as a centralized commercial service provider, is vulnerable to government interference in a way that the abstract Net is not. Then again, increasing numbers of people get their Net access through big companies like Compuserve.

What happened in Germany suggests that the global reach of the computer medium, far from allowing it to transcend petty national issues, actually ensnares it in every local conflict. The cliché has it that all politics is local; on the Net, all local politics have global implications.

What happens when the new medium of the Net tangles with the old world of sovereign nations? That world is itself pretty beleaguered right now. One of the more insightful and useful analyses of the post-Cold War world, Benjamin Barber's "Jihad Vs. McWorld," describes a global culture that is eroding the traditional nation-state from two opposite directions.

On one side are the forces of a fierce new tribalism, reacting against perceived threats to traditional cultures and often motivated by fundamentalist moralities of one stripe or another. This "Jihad" culture rips apart weaker nation-states like the former Soviet Union and undermines stronger ones, like the United States, by promoting fanatical single-issue politics and ethnic separatism. On the other side is Barber's "McWorld"—the homogenizing power of international corporate culture, with its promise of prosperity, its demand for free trade and its aggressive override of local sovereignty.

Both sides in Barber's global conflict can and do make use of the Net: small separatist groups find it a powerful organizing tool, while giant corporations hope to shape it as a conduit for the flood of "information" and pop culture that can swamp local societies. In such a world, computer communication as a tool is in no danger. But neither of these forces is likely to see any value in the Net as a quasi-nation, a free-speech zone and haven for individualism.

Barlow writes of the online world as a new republic of pure mind where the individual may flourish. It is an inspiring vision—but one that seems almost certainly doomed, if Barber's framework is an accurate world picture.

Both McWorld and Jihad work to corrode the contemporary nation-state, along with its concept of citizenship and individual rights. It's madly ironic yet entirely conceivable that Cyberspace: The Nation, having declared its disgust with and independence from the "Governments of the Industrial World," will find that they aren't its greatest enemies after all.

Citizens of the Net may declare independence and secede from meddlesome governments only to find themselves in a world dominated by vast corporations and hostile tribes. For either of these groups, the Net ideal of free expression is at best an irritation and at worst an anathema. What mujahadeen would hesitate to ban alt.binaries.pictures.erotica? What multinational would mind if information were a little less free?

EXPLORING THE READING

1. Reread John Perry Barlow's declaration. What is it about Barlow's ideas that Scott Rosenberg primarily disagrees with?

2. Why does Rosenberg think that independence for cyberspace is impractical?

3. Divide your small group into two factions and debate the issue of the independence of cyberspace. Have one side take Barlow's position and the other take Rosenberg's. Report your conclusions to the class.

4. What is the tone of the Rosenberg text? How does the tone differ from Barlow's piece? Which do you prefer?

CIVIL LIBERTIES IN CYBERSPACE: WHEN DOES HACKING TURN FROM AN EXERCISE OF CIVIL LIBERTIES INTO CRIME?

by Mitchell Kapor

Mitchell Kapor's often quoted article, "Civil Liberties in Cyberspace," was published in 1990 in Scientific American. *Although he is writing primarily of BBSs (Bulletin Board Systems), localized forerunners of the Internet, Kapor envisions many of the issues which continue to be debated as the Internet has spread. How can legal and social institutions adapt to handle the fast-developing Internet? How can citizens be protected without infringing on others' freedoms? When is hacking a crime? Should the principles of freedom of speech protect electronic speech?*

Kapor is co-founder of the Electronic Freedom Foundation, http://www.eff.org, which was established to lobby for protection of civil rights in cyberspace. His article is posted there at http://www.eff.org/pub/Legal/cyberliberties_kapor.article.

On March 1, 1990, the U.S. Secret Service raided the offices of Steve Jackson, an entrepreneurial publisher in Austin, Texas. Carrying a search warrant, the authorities confiscated computer hardware and software, the drafts of his about-to-be-released book and many business records of his company, Steve Jackson Games. They also seized the electronic bulletin-board system used by the publisher to communicate with customers and writers, thereby seizing all the private electronic mail on the system.

The Secret Service held some of the equipment and material for months, refusing to discuss their reasons for the raid. The publisher was forced to reconstruct his book from old manuscripts, to delay filling orders for it and to lay off half his staff. When the warrant application was finally unsealed months later, it confirmed that the publisher was never suspected of any crime.

Steve Jackson's legal difficulties are symptomatic of a widespread problem. During the past several years, dozens of individuals have been the subject of similar searches and seizures. In any other context, this warrant might never have been issued. By many interpretations, it disregarded the First and Fourth Amendments to the U.S. Constitution, as well as several existing privacy laws. But the government proceeded as if civil liberties did not apply. In this case, the government was investigating a new kind of crime—computer crime.

The circumstances vary, but a disproportionate number of cases share a common thread: the serious misunderstanding of computer-based communication and its implications for civil liberties. We now face the task of adapting our legal institutions and societal expectations to the cultural phenomena that even now are springing up from communications technology.

Our society has made a commitment to openness and to free communication. But if our legal and social institutions fail to adapt to new technology, basic access to the global electronic media could be seen as a privilege, granted to those who play by the strictest rules, rather than as a right held by anyone who needs to communicate. To assure that these freedoms are not compromised, a group of computer experts, including myself, founded the Electronic Frontier Foundation (EFF) in 1990.

In many respects, it was odd that Steve Jackson Games got caught up in a computer crime investigation at all. The company publishes a popular, award-winning series of fantasy roleplaying games, produced in the form of elaborate rule books. The raid took place only because law enforcement officials misunderstood the technologies—computer bulletin-board systems (BBSs) and online forums—and misread the cultural phenomena that those technologies engender.

Like a growing number of businesses, Steve Jackson Games operated an electronic bulletin board to facilitate contact between players of its games and their authors. Users of this bulletin-board system dialed in via modem from their personal computers to swap strategy tips, learn about game upgrades, exchange electronic mail and discuss games and other topics.

Law enforcement officers apparently became suspicious when a Steve Jackson Games employee—on his own time and on a BBS he ran from his house—made an innocuous comment about a public domain protocol for transferring computer files called Kermit. In addition, officials claimed that at one time the employee had had on an electronic bulletin board a copy of *Phrack*, a widely disseminated electronic publication, that included information they believed to have been stolen from a BellSouth computer.

The law enforcement officials interpreted these facts as unusual enough to justify not only a search and seizure at the employee's residence but also the search of Steve Jackson Games and the seizure of enough equipment to disrupt the business seriously. Among the items confiscated were all the hard copies and electronically stored copies of the manuscript of a rule book for a role-playing game called *GURPS Cyberpunk*, in which inhabitants of so-called cyberspace invade corporate and government computer systems and steal sensitive data. Law enforcement agents regarded the book, in the words of one, as "a handbook for computer crime."

A basic knowledge of the kinds of computer intrusion that are technically possible would have enabled the agents to see that *GURPS Cyberpunk* was nothing more than a science fiction creation and that Kermit was simply a legal, frequently-used computer program. Unfortunately, the agents assigned to investigate computer crime did not know what—if anything—was evidence of a criminal activity. Therefore, they intruded on a small business without a reasonable basis for believing that a crime had been committed and conducted a search and seizure without looking for "particular" evidence, in violation of the Fourth Amendment of the Constitution.

Searches and seizures of such computer systems affect the rights of not only their owners and operators but also the users of those systems. Although most BBS users have never been in the same room with the actual computer that carries their postings, they legitimately expect their electronic mail to be private and their lawful associations to be protected.

The community of bulletin-board users and computer networkers may be small, but precedents must be understood in a greater context. As forums for debate and information exchange, computer-based bulletin boards and conferencing systems support some of the most vigorous exercise of the First Amendment freedoms of expression and association that this country has ever seen. Moreover, they are evolving rapidly into large-scale public information and communications utilities.

These utilities will probably converge into a digital national public network that will connect nearly all homes and businesses in the United States. This network will serve as a main conduit for commerce, learning, education and entertainment in our society, distributing images and video signals as well as text and voice. Much of the content of this network will be private messages serving as "virtual" town halls, village greens and coffeehouses, where people post their ideas in public or semipublic forums.

Yet there is a common perception that a defense of electronic civil liberties is somehow opposed to legitimate concerns about the prevention of computer crime. The conflict arises, in part, because the popular hysteria about the technically sophisticated youths known as hackers has drowned out reasonable discussion.

Perhaps inspired by the popular movie *WarGames*, the general public began in the 1980s to perceive computer hackers as threats to the safety of this country's vital computer systems. But the image of hackers as malevolent is purchased at the price of ignoring the underlying reality—the typical teenage hacker is simply tempted by the prospect of exploring forbidden territory. Some are among our best and brightest technological talents: hackers of the 1960s and 1970s, for example, were so driven by their desire to master, understand and produce new hardware and software that they went on to start companies called Apple, Microsoft and Lotus.

How do we resolve this conflict? One solution is ensure that our scheme of civil and criminal laws provides sanctions in proportion to the offenses. A system in which an exploratory hacker receives more time in jail than a defendant convicted of assault violates our sense of justice. Our legal tradition historically has shown itself capable of making subtle and not-so-subtle distinctions among criminal offenses.

There are, of course, real threats to network and system security. The qualities that make the ideal network valuable—its popularity, its uniform commands, its ability to handle financial transactions and its international access—also make it vulnerable to a variety of abuses and accidents. It is certainly proper to hold hackers accountable for their offenses, but that accountability should never entail denying defendants the safeguards of the Bill of Rights, including the rights to free expression and association and to freedom from unreasonable searches and seizures.

We need statutory schemes that address the acts of true computer criminals (such as those who have created the growing problem of toll and credit-card fraud) while distinguishing between those criminals and hackers whose acts are most analogous to noncriminal trespass. And we need educated law enforcement officials who will be able to recognize and focus their efforts on the real threats.

The question then arises: How do we help our institutions, and perceptions, adapt? The first step is to articulate the kinds of values we want to see protected in the electronic society we are now shaping and to make an agenda for preserving the civil liberties that are central to that society. Then we can draw on the appropriate legal traditions that guide other media. The late Ithiel de Sola Pool argued in his influential book *Technologies of Freedom* that the medium of digital communications is heir to several traditions of control: the press, the common carrier and the broadcast media.

The freedom of the press to print and distribute is explicitly guaranteed by the First Amendment. This freedom is somewhat limited, particularly by laws governing obscenity and defamation, but the thrust of First Amendment law, especially in this century, prevents the government from imposing "prior restraint" on publications.

Like the railroad networks, the telephone networks follow common-carrier principles—they do not impose content restrictions on the "cargo" they carry. It would be unthinkable for the telephone company to monitor our calls routinely or cut off conversations because the subject matter was deemed offensive.

Meanwhile the highly regulated broadcast media are grounded in the idea, arguably mistaken, that spectrum scarcity and the pervasiveness of the broadcast media warrant government allocation and control of access to broadcast frequencies (and some control of content). Access to this technology is open to any consumer who can purchase a radio or television set, but it is nowhere near as open for information producers.

Networks as they now operate contain elements of publishers, broadcasters, bookstores and telephones, but no one model fits. This hybrid demands new thinking or at least a new application of the old legal principles. As hybrids, computer networks also have some features that are unique among the communications media. For example, most conversations on bulletin boards, chat lines and conferencing systems are both public and private at once. The electronic communicator speaks to a group of individuals, only some of whom are known personally, in a discussion that may last for days or months.

But the dissemination is controlled, because the membership is limited to the handful of people who are in the virtual room, paying attention. Yet the result may also be "published"—an archival textual or voice record can be automatically preserved, and newcomers can read the backlog. Some people tend to equate online discussions with party (or party-line) conversations, whereas others compare them to newspapers and still others think of citizens band radio.

In this ambiguous context, freespeech controversies are likely to erupt. Last year an outcry went up against the popular Prodigy computer service, a joint venture of IBM and Sears, Roebuck and Co. The problem arose because Prodigy management regarded their service as essentially a "newspaper" or "magazine," for which a hierarchy of editorial control is appropriate. Some of Prodigy's customers, in contrast, regarded the service as more of a forum or meeting place.

When users of the system tried to protest Prodigy's policy, its editors responded by removing the discussion, then the protestors tried to use electronic mail as a substitute for electron-assembly, communicating through huge mailing lists. Prodigy placed a limit on the number of messages each individual could send.

The Prodigy controversy illustrates important principle that belongs on civil liberties agenda for the future: freedom-of-speech issues will not disappear simply because a service provider has tried to impose a metaphor on its service. Subscribers sense, I believe, that freedom of speech on the networks is central for individuals to use electronic communications. Science fiction writer William Gibson once remarked that ``the street finds its own uses for things." Network service providers will continue to discover that their customers will always find their own best uses for new media.

Freedom of speech on networks will be promoted by limiting content-based regulations and by promoting competition among providers of network services. The first is necessary because governments will be tempted to restrict the content of any information service they subsidize or regulate. The second is necessary because market competition is the most efficient means of ensuring that needs of network users will be met.

The underlying network should essentially be a "carrier"—it should operate under a content-neutral regime in which access is available to any entity that can pay for it. The information and forum services would be "nodes" in this network. (Prodigy, like GEnie and CompuServe, currently maintains its own proprietary infrastructure, but a future version of Prodigy might share the same network with services like CompuServe.)

Each service would have its own unique character and charge its own rates. If a Prodigy-like entity correctly perceives a need for an electronic "newspaper" with strong editorial control, it will draw an audience. Other less hierarchical services will share the network with that "newspaper" yet find their own market niches, varying by format and content.

The prerequisite for this kind of competition is a carrier capable of high bandwidth traffic that is accessible to individuals in every community. Like common carriers, these network carriers should be seen as conduits for the distribution of electronic transmissions. They should not be allowed to change the content of a message or to discriminate among messages.

This kind of restriction will require shielding the carriers from legal liabilities for libel, obscenity and plagiarism. Today the ambiguous state of liability law has tempted some computer network carriers to reduce their risk by imposing content restrictions. This could be avoided by appropriate legislation. Our agenda requires both that the law shield carriers from liability based on content and that carriers not be allowed to discriminate.

All electronic "publishers" should be allowed equal access to networks. Ultimately, there could be hundreds of thousands of these information providers, as there are hundreds of thousands of print publishers today. As "nodes," they will considered the conveners of the environments within which online assembly takes place.

None of the old definitions will suffice for this role. For example, to safeguard the potential of free and open inquiry, it is desirable to preserve each electronic publisher's control over the general flow and direction of material under his or her imprimatur—in effect, to give the "sysop," or system operator, the prerogatives and protections of a publisher.

But it is unreasonable to expect the sysop of a node to review every message or to hold the sysop to a publisher's standard of libel. Message traffic on many individually owned services is already too great for the sysop to review. We can only expect the trend to grow.

Nor is it appropriate to compare nodes to broadcasters (an analogy likely to lead to licensing and content-based regulation). Unlike the broadcast media, nodes do not dominate the shared resource of a public community, and they are not a pervasive medium. To take part in a controversial discussion, a user must actively seek entry into the appropriate node, usually with a subscription and a password.

Anyone who objects to the content of a node can find hundreds of other systems where they might articulate their ideas more freely. The danger is if choice is somehow restricted: if all computer networks in the country are restrained from allowing discussion on particular subjects or if a publicly sponsored computer network limits discussion.

This is not to say that freedom-of-speech principles ought to protect all electronic communications. Exceptional cases, such as the BBS used primarily to traffic in stolen long-distance access codes or credit-card numbers, will always arise and pose problems of civil and criminal liability. We know that electronic freedom of speech, whether in public or private systems, cannot be absolute. In face-to-face conversation and printed matter today, it is commonly agreed that freedom of speech does not cover the communications inherent in criminal conspiracy, fraud, libel, incitement to lawless action and copyright infringement.

If there are to be limits on electronic freedom of speech, what precisely should those limits be? One answer to this question is the U.S. Supreme Court's 1969 decision in *Brandenburg v. Ohio*. The court ruled that no speech should be subject to prior restraint or criminal prosecution unless it is intended to incite and is likely to cause imminent lawless action.

In general, little speech or publication falls outside of the protections of the Brandenburg case, since most people are able to reflect before acting on a written or spoken suggestion. As in traditional media, any online messages should not be the basis of criminal prosecution unless the Brandenburg standard is met.

Other helpful precedents include cases relating to defamation and copyright infringement. Free speech does not mean one can damage a reputation or appropriate a copyrighted work without being called to account for it. And it probably does not mean that one can release a virus across the network in order to "send a message" to network subscribers. Although the distinction is trickier than it may first appear, the release of a destructive program, such as a virus, may be better analyzed as an act rather than as speech.

Following freedom of speech on our action agenda is freedom from unreasonable searches and seizures. The Steve Jackson case was one of many cases in which computer equipment and disks were seized and held sometimes for months—often without a specific charge being filed. Even when only a few files were relevant to an investigation, entire computer systems, including printers, have been removed with their hundreds of files intact.

Such nonspecific seizures and searches of computer data allow "rummaging," in which officials browse through private files in search of incriminating evidence. In addition to violating the Fourth Amendment requirement that searches and seizures be "particular," these searches often run afoul of the Electronic Communications Privacy Act of 1986. This act prohibits the government from seizing or intercepting electronic communications without proper authorization. They also contravene the Privacy Protection Act of 1980, which prohibits the government from searching the offices of publishers for documents, including materials that are electronically stored.

We can expect that law enforcement agencies and civil libertarians will agree over time about the need to establish procedures for searches and seizures of "particular" computer data and hardware. Law enforcement officials will have to adhere to guidelines in the above statutes to achieve Fourth Amendment "particularity" while maximizing the efficiency of their searches. They also will have to be trained to make use of software tools that allow searches for particular files or particular information within files on even the most capacious hard disk or optical storage device.

Still another part of the solution will be law enforcement's abandonment of the myth of the clever criminal hobbyist. Once law enforcement no longer assumes worst-case behavior but looks instead for real evidence of criminal activity, its agents will learn to search and seize only what they need.

Developing and implementing a civil liberties agenda for computer networks will require increasing participation by technically trained people. Fortunately, there are signs that this is beginning to happen. The Computers, Freedom and Privacy Conference, held last spring in San Francisco, along with electronic conferences on the WELL (Whole Earth 'Lectronic Link) and other computer networks, have brought law enforcement officials, supposed hackers and interested members of the computer community together in a spirit of free and frank discussion. Such gatherings are beginning to work out the civil liberties guidelines for a networked society.

There is general agreement, for example, that a policy on electronic crime should offer protection for security and privacy on both individual and institutional systems. Defining a measure of damages and setting proportional punishment will require further good faith deliberations by the community involved with electronic freedoms, including the Federal Bureau of Investigation, the Secret Service, the bar associations, technology groups, telephone companies and civil libertarians. It will be especially important to represent the damage caused by electronic crime accurately and to leave room for the valuable side of the hacker spirit: the interest in increasing legitimate understanding through exploration.

We hope to see a similar emerging consensus on security issues. Network systems should be designed not only to provide technical solutions to security problems but also to allow system operators to use them without infringing unduly on the rights of users. A security system that depends on wholesale monitoring of traffic, for example, would create more problems than it would solve.

Those parts of a system where damage would do the greatest harm—financial records, electronic mail, military data—should be protected. This involves installing more effective computer security measures, but it also means redefining the legal interpretations of copyright, intellectual property, computer crime and privacy so that system users are protected against individual criminals and abuses by large institutions. These policies should balance the need for civil liberties against the need for a secure, orderly, protected electronic society.

As we pursue that balance, of course, confrontations will continue to take place. In May of this year, Steve Jackson Games, with the support of the EFF, filed suit against the Secret Service, two individual Secret Service agents, an assistant U.S. attorney and others.

The EFF is not seeking confrontation for its own sake. One of the realities of our legal system is that one often has to fight for a legal or constitutional right in the courts in order to get it recognized outside the courts. One goal of the lawsuit is to establish clear grounds under which search and seizure of electronic media is "unreasonable" and unjust. Another is to establish the clear applicability of First Amendment principles to the new medium.

But the EFF's agenda extends far beyond litigation. Our larger agenda includes sponsoring a range of educational initiatives aimed at the public's general lack of familiarity with the technology and its potential. That is why there is an urgent need for technologically knowledgeable people to take part in the public debate over communications policy and to help spread their understanding of these issues. Fortunately, the very technology at stake—electronic conferencing—makes it easier than ever before to get involved in the debate.

EXPLORING THE READING

1. What questions does Mitchell Kapor raise about civil liberties and electronic communication?

2. What standards does Kapor propose for protection of civil liberties?

3. In your small group consider the timeliness of the issues Kapor raises. Has the situation changed since Kapor wrote the article?

4. What is the tone of Kapor's article? Is it an emotional account, or is he attempting to be rational and unbiased? How effective is his tone?

THE END OF THE LAW, AND THE BEGINNING

by Peter Huber

"Bandwidth gives lawyers fits," writes Peter Huber in this short piece from Forbes, *and he explains in some detail why. Cable television regulations are easy in comparison to what is happening with the World Wide Web. With the Web, soon every computer will be capable of running virtual broadcast channels. How is a government to regulate that? Copyright laws must be refigured from scratch, and the negotiations have only just begun.*

Huber is a writer on telecommunications issues and is also a senior fellow at the Manhattan Institute.

Bandwidth gives lawyers fits. Example: Oshkosh cable builds a twenty-channel network. Federal lawyers write "must-carry rules"—Oshkosh must hand over seven "blue" channels to local TV broadcasters. But is that constitutional? Nine Supreme Court Justices take a vote. One thinks these "must-carry" rules are fine. Four say the law unconstitutionally infringes on cable's First Amendment rights. Four think the rules are probably okay, but a trial court had better take another look at the facts. The Nine heard the same case for the second time last October. Now there's a new Nine. That could change things.

Meanwhile, federal lawyers had demanded another set-aside—"yellow" channels for "public, educational, or government," "red" channels for lease to independent programmers. Independent programmers begin peddling porn on red. So the federal lawyers write another rule. Oshkosh may block indecency on yellow and red.

But is that constitutional? Nine Justices take a vote. Three say the whole law's okay. One basically agrees with them about yellow channels, but for different reasons. Two say the whole law is unconstitutional. Four say that the giveback is okay for the red channels. Three say it's not okay for the yellow.

Legally speaking, cable is simple. It's the Web that's hard. Every server, every computer, can run a thousand-color rainbow of virtual channels. Every cable set-top box soon will, too. Digital channels can be configured every which way: like common-carrier telephones to deliver e-mail, fax, and voice. Like newspapers. Like radio stations. And like cable or broadcast television, full-motion video on the Web when the bandwidth expands enough, which it inevitably will. The Justices are going to have a blast.

They can vote on who owns the content on the channels, too. Back in the 1960s, they voted to let cable pirate anything broadcast on the VHF and UHF television bands. In 1983 they split 5 to 4 on whether home taping on a Sony Betamax infringed on broadcast copyrights. They may also have split 4 to 5 in the same case. The case was argued first in the 1982 term, then reargued in the 1983 term. That almost never happens. The dissent reads like it started out as a majority.

Legally speaking, broadcasts and VCRs are simple, too. It's the Web that's hard. Every server, every computer with a hard drive, contains a digital Betamax or two. Every time a file, recording, picture, or movie is received, it gets copied, at least briefly, even if no one but some intermediate machine is watching the show.

Write copyright law just a shade too strict, and every piece of hardware on the Web becomes illegal. Write it a shade too lenient, and there's nothing left to copyright at all. So all the key concepts of intellectual property law—"publish," "copy," "perform," "fair use," and so forth—have to be redefined almost from scratch, to strike a workable balance. If the Justices like voting about intellectual property, they are going to vote a lot.

And speaking of property, who really owns the layers underneath? Not the metal, glass, and radio transmitters at the very bottom, but the rainbow of virtual channels one level up? The city of Tigard, in Oregaon, orders Florence Dolan to build a public bike path across her land if she wants to enlarge her store. That's an unconstitutional "taking." The Justices say so, in a 5 to 4 ruling, in 1994. Aren't those blue cable channels just bike paths for broadcasters? How about the new children's programming rules the FCC is trying to foist on broadcasters? Bike paths for kids. If the FCC can take three hours a week from TV broadcasters, can it also take three hours from CompuServe? How about thirty seconds of my CompuServe connect time? To exhort me not to smoke, perhaps.

Maybe the broadcasters are different because they don't own the airwaves the way I own my home page. Or do they? Bidders have just handed the federal government $25 billion for new wireless licenses. Technically, these licenses expire in ten years. So do the licenses AT&T got from McCaw when it bought that company for $17 billion. But can the government really take the spectrum back when the licenses expire? Nobody knows. The Justices will vote.

We have legal models that address all these problems–models for publishers, bookstores and carriers, models for copyright and real estate. But as Lenin once remarked on the subject of tanks, quantity has a quality all its own. The vast abundance of digital broadband networks allows users to transcend all the old legal standards.

Traditional "publishers," for example, are strictly liable for copyright infringement, while traditional carriers have broad immunities. Bookstores fall somewhere in between. But America Online transforms itself from one to the next as fast as you can click from e-mail to a bulletin board to an online newspaper. Must the laws of property, takings, libel, copyright, and free speech be rewritten icon by icon? The Justices will vote. Don't suppose that the alternative in any of these matters is not to vote. Anarchy is for teenage mutant ninjas; grown-ups need the rule of law, just as much in virtuality as in actuality. Somehow or other we are going to have to build on old legal principles of free speech, common carriage, private property, and so forth, or invent coherent new ones. There will be votes. We need them.

The only question is who will do the voting. A supranational World Trade Organization? The thought is horrible, but the Web transcends all national borders. The 535 members of Congress? They're terrible with details, and they take forever to decide anything. The five commissioners of the FCC? They aren't much better.

All the top-down forms of government are going to fail. Political consensus won't coalesce anymore. The interests are too varied, fragmented, and fluid. Agreeing on a sweeping new legal principle is all but impossible. And a sweeping new principle isn't any use, anyway. It's the details that are important, and hard.

My guess is that all the important new laws of the telecosm will be cooked up the old-fashioned way, by common-law adjudication of private disputes in the courts. It will be messy, unpredictable, and slow. It's the worst possible solution. Except for the alternatives.

EXPLORING THE READING

1. What is Peter Huber's basic point? What examples does he give to make his point more understandable?

2. In your small group discuss the problem Huber raises. Do you think the situation is as chaotic and critical as Huber suggests?

3. In your small group examine Huber's text. Are there terms and concepts in Huber's text which you do not understand? Raise your questions to the class.

SUPREME COURT RULING ON COMMUNICATIONS DECENCY ACT

by Justice John Paul Stevens

In its first major decision affecting the Internet, the Supreme Court upheld the ruling of a three-judge federal court in Philadelphia declaring unconstitutional the Communications Decency Act. The justices decided that the law, which attempted to protect children from sexually explicit material, was worded so broadly that it banned speech that is constitutionally protected for adults by the First Amendment. Excerpts of the actual Supreme Court Ruling follow, and the full text is available widely on the Internet at sites such as http://archive.abcnews.com/sections/scitech/cda_opinion/index.html and http://supct.law.cornell.edu/supct/html/96-511.ZS.html.

The ruling asserts that the Internet, like the printing press, should be awarded the highest level of First Amendment protection, in contrast with radio and television that are regulated because of the limited number of available broadcast channels. The court reasoned that the Internet is entitled to such protection because of its relative equality between speakers and listeners. The court acknowledged that sexually explicit material is available on the Internet, but remarked that it is "seldom encountered accidentally," instead requiring a series of interactive steps, unlike the content of radio or television.

JANET RENO, ATTORNEY GENERAL OF THE UNITED STATES, et al.,
APPELLANTS *v.* AMERICAN CIVIL LIBERTIES UNION et al.
on appeal from the United States District Court for the Eastern District of Pennsylvania
[June 26, 1997]

Justice Stevens delivered the opinion of the Court.

At issue is the constitutionality of two statutory provisions enacted to protect minors from "indecent" and "patently offensive" communications on the Internet. Notwithstanding the legitimacy and importance of the congressional goal of protecting children from harmful materials, we agree with the three-judge District court that the statute abridges "the freedom of speech" protected by the First Amendment.

The District Court made extensive findings of fact, most of which were based on a detailed stipulation prepared by the parties. See *929 F Supp. 824, 830–849* (ED Pa. 1996). The findings describe the character and the dimensions of the Internet, the availability of sexually explicit material in that medium, and the problems confronting age verification for recipients of Internet communications. Because those findings provide the underpinnings for the legal issues, we begin with a summary of the undisputed facts.

THE INTERNET

The Internet is an international network of interconnected computers. It is the outgrowth of what began in 1969 as a military program called "ARPANET," which was designed to enable computers operated by the military, defense contractors, and universities conducting defense-related research to communicate with one another by redundant channels even if some portions of the network were damaged in a war. While the ARPANET no longer exists, it provided an example for the development of a number of civilian networks that, eventually linking with each other, now enable tens of millions of people to communicate with one another and to access vast amounts of information from around the world. The Internet is "a unique and wholly new medium of worldwide human communication."

The Internet has experienced "extraordinary growth." The number of "host" computers—those that store information and relay communications—increased from about 300 in 1981 to approximately 9,400,000 by the time of the trial in 1996. Roughly 60% of these hosts are located in the United States. About 40 million people used the Internet at the time of trial, a number that is expected to mushroom to 200 million by 1999.

Individuals can obtain access to the Internet from many different sources, generally hosts themselves or entities with a host affiliation. Most colleges and universities provide access for their students and faculty; many corporations provide their employees with access through an office network; many communities and local libraries provide free access; and an increasing number of storefront "computer coffee shops" provide access for a small hourly fee. Several major national "online services" such as America Online, CompuServe, the Microsoft Network, and Prodigy offer access to their own extensive proprietary networks as well as a link to the much larger resources of the Internet. These commercial online services had almost 12 million individual subscribers at the time of trial.

Anyone with access to the Internet may take advantage of a wide variety of communication and information retrieval methods. These methods are constantly evolving and difficult to categorize precisely. But, as presently constituted, those most relevant to this case are electronic mail ("e-mail), automatic mailing list services ("mail exploders," sometimes referred to as "listservs"), "newsgroups," "chat rooms," and the "World Wide Web." All of these methods can be used to transmit text; most can transmit sound, pictures, and moving video images. Taken together, these tools constitute a unique medium—known to its users as "cyberspace"—located in no particular geographical location but available to anyone, anywhere in the world, with access to the Internet.

E-mail enables an individual to send an electronic message—generally akin to a note or letter—to another individual or to a group of addresses. The message is generally stored electronically, sometimes waiting for the recipient to check her "mailbox" and sometimes making its receipt known through some type of prompt. A mail exploder is a sort of e-mail group. Subscribers can send messages to a common e-mail address, which then forwards the message to the group's other subscribers. Newsgroups also serve groups of regular participants, but these postings may be read by others as well. There are thousands of such groups, each serving to foster an exchange of information or opinion on a particular topic running the gamut from, say, the music of Wagner to Balkan politics to AIDS prevention to the Chicago Bulls.

About 100,000 new messages are posted every day. In most newsgroups, postings are automatically purged at regular intervals. In addition to posting a message that can be read later, two or more individuals wishing to communicate more immediately can enter a chat room to engage in real-time dialogue—in other words, by typing messages to one another that appear almost immediately on the others' computer screens. The District Court found that at any time "tens of thousands of users are engaging in conversations on a huge range of subjects." It is "no exaggeration to conclude that the content on the Internet is as diverse as human thought."

The best known category of communication over the Internet is the World Wide Web, which allows users to search for and retrieve information stored in remote computers, as well as, in some cases, to communicate back to designated sites. In concrete terms, the Web consists of a vast number of documents stored in different computers all over the world. Some of these documents are simply files containing information. However, more elaborate documents, commonly known as Web "pages," are also prevalent. Each has its own address—"rather like a telephone number." Web pages frequently contain information and sometimes allow the viewer to communicate with the page's (or "site's") author. They generally also contain "links" to other documents created by that site's author or to other (generally) related sites. Typically, the links are either blue or underlined text—sometimes images.

Navigating the Web is relatively straightforward. A user may either type the address of a known page or enter one or more keywords into a commercial "search engine" in an effort to locate sites on a subject of interest. A particular Web page may contain the information sought by the "surfer," or, through its links, it may be an avenue to other documents located anywhere on the Internet. Users generally explore a given Web page, or move to another, by clicking a computer "mouse" on one of the page's icon or links. Access to most Web pages is freely available, but some allow access only to those who have purchased the right from a commercial provider. The Web is thus comparable, from the readers' viewpoint, to both a vast library including millions of readily available and indexed publications and a sprawling mall offering goods and services.

From the publishers' point of view, it constitutes a vast platform from which to address and hear from a world-wide audience of millions of readers, viewers, researchers, and buyers. Any person or organization with a computer connected to the Internet can "publish" information. Publishers include government agencies, educational institutions, commercial entities, advocacy groups, and individuals. Publishers may either make their material available to the entire pool of Internet users, or confine access to a selected group, such as those willing to pay for the privilege. "No single organization controls any membership in the Web, nor is there any centralized point from which individual Websites or services can be blocked from the Web."

SEXUALLY EXPLICIT MATERIAL

Sexually explicit material on the Internet includes text, pictures, and chat and "extends from the modestly titillating to the hardest-core." These files are created, named, and posted in the same manner as material that is not sexually explicit, and may be accessed either deliberately or unintentionally during the course of an imprecise search. "Once a provider posts its content on the Internet, it cannot prevent that content from entering any community." Thus, for example,

> when the UCR/California Museum of Photography posts to its Website nudes by Edward Weston and Robert Mapplethorpe to announce that its new exhibit will travel to Baltimore and New York City, those images are available not only in Los Angeles, Baltimore, and New York City, but also in Cincinnati, Mobile, or Beijing—wherever Internet users live. Similarly, the safer sex instructions that Critical Path posts to its Website, written in street language so that the teenage receiver can understand them, are available not just in Philadelphia, but also in Provo and Prague.

Some of the communications over the Internet that originate in foreign countries are also sexually explicit.

Though such material is widely available, users seldom encounter such content accidentally. "A document's title or a description of the document will usually appear before the document itself . . . and in many cases the user will receive detailed information about a site's content before he or she need take the step to access the document. Almost all sexually explicit images are preceded by warnings as to the content." For that reason, the "odds are slim" that a user would enter a sexually explicit site by accident.

Unlike communications received by radio or television, "the receipt of information on the Internet requires a series of affirmative steps more deliberate and directed than merely turning a dial. A child requires some sophistication and some ability to read to retrieve material and thereby to use the Internet unattended."

Systems have been developed to help parents control the material that may be available on a home computer with Internet access. A system may either limit a computer's access to an approved list of sources that have been identified as containing no adult material, it may block designated inappropriate sites, or it may attempt to block messages containing identifiable objectionable features. "Although parental control software currently can screen for certain suggestive words or for known sexually explicit sites, it cannot now screen for sexually explicit images." Nevertheless, the evidence indicates that "a reasonably effective method by which parents can prevent their children from accessing sexually explicit and other material which parents may believe is inappropriate for their children will soon be available."

AGE VERIFICATION

The problem of age verification differs for different uses of the Internet. The District Court categorically determined that there "is no effective way to determine the identity or the age of a user who is accessing material through e-mail, mail exploders, newsgroups or chat rooms." The Government offered no evidence that there was a reliable way to screen recipients and participants in such fora for age.

Moreover, even if it were technologically feasible to block minors' access to newsgroups and chat rooms containing discussions of art, politics or other subjects that potentially elicit "indecent" or "patently offensive" contributions, it would not be possible to block their access to that material and "still allow them access to the remaining content, even if the overwhelming majority of that content was not indecent."

Technology exists by which an operator of a Website may condition access on the verification of requested information such as a credit card number or an adult password. Credit card verification is only feasible, however, either in connection with a commercial transaction in which the card is used, or by payment to a verification agency. Using credit card possession as a surrogate for proof of age would impose costs on non-commercial Websites that would require many of them to shut down. For that reason, at the time of the trial, credit card verification was "effectively unavailable to a substantial number of Internet content providers." *Id.*, at 846 (finding 102). Moreover, the imposition of such a requirement "would completely bar adults who do not have a credit card and lack the resources to obtain one from accessing any blocked material."

Commercial pornographic sites that charge their users for access have assigned them passwords as a method of age verification. The record does not contain any evidence concerning the reliability of these technologies. Even if passwords are effective for commercial purveyors of indecent material, the District Court found that an adult password requirement would impose significant burdens on noncommercial sites, both because they would discourage users from accessing their sites and because the cost of creating and maintaining such screening systems would be "beyond their reach."

In sum, the District Court found:

> Even if credit card verification or adult password verification were implemented, the Government presented no testimony as to how such systems could ensure that the user of the password or credit card is in fact over 18. The burdens imposed by credit card verification and adult password verification systems make them effectively unavailable to a substantial number of Internet content providers. (*Ibid.*)

The Telecommunications Act of 1996, Pub. L. 104-104, 110 Stat. 56, was an unusually important legislative enactment. As stated on the first of its 103 pages, its primary purpose was to reduce regulation and encourage "the rapid deployment of new telecommunications technologies." The major components of the statute have nothing to do with the Internet; they were designed to promote competition in the local telephone service market, the multichannel video market, and the market for over-the-air broadcasting. The Act includes seven Titles, six of which are the product of extensive committee hearings and the subject of discussion in Reports prepared by Committees of the Senate and the House of Representatives. By contrast, Title V—known as the "Communications Decency Act of 1996" (CDA)—contains provisions that were either added in executive committee after the hearings were concluded or as amendments offered during floor debate on the legislation. An amendment offered in the Senate was the source of the two statutory provisions challenged in this case. They are informally described as the "indecent transmission" provision and the "patently offensive display" provision.

The first, 47 U. S. C. A. §223 (a) (Supp. 1997), prohibits the knowing transmission of obscene or indecent messages to any recipient under 18 years of age. It provides in pertinent part:

(a) Whoever—
(1) in interstate or foreign communications—
. . . . .
(B) by means of a telecommunications device knowingly—
(i) makes, creates, or solicits, and
(ii) initiates the transmission of,
any comment, request, suggestion, proposal, image, or other communication which is obscene or indecent, knowing that the recipient of the communication is under 18 years of age, regardless of whether the maker of such communication placed the call or initiated the communication;
. . . . .
(2) knowingly permits any telecommunications facility under his control to be used for any activity prohibited by paragraph (1) with the intent that it be used for such activity,
shall be fined under Title 18, or imprisoned not more than two years, or both.

The second provision, §223(d), prohibits the knowing sending or displaying of patently offensive messages in a manner that is available to a person under 18 years of age. It provides:

(d) Whoever—
(1) in interstate or foreign communications knowingly—
(A) uses an interactive computer service to send to a specific person or persons under 18 years of age, or
(B) uses any interactive computer service to display in a manner available to a person under 18 years of age,
any comment, request, suggestion, proposal, image, or other communication that, in context, depicts or describes, in terms patently offensive as measured by contemporary standards, sexual or excretory activities or organs, regardless of whether the user of such service placed the call or initiated the communication, or
(2) knowingly permits any telecommunications facility under such person's control to be used for an activity prohibited by paragraph (1) with the intent that it be used for such activity,
shall be fined under Title 18, or imprisoned not more than two years, or both.

The breadth of these prohibitions is qualified by two affirmative defenses. See §223(e)(5). One covers those who take "good faith, reasonable, effective, and appropriate actions" to restrict access by minors to the prohibited communications. §223(e)(5)(A). The other covers those who restrict access to covered material by requiring certain designated forms of age proof, such as a verified credit card or an adult identification number or code. §223(e)(5)(B).

On February 8, 1996, immediately after the President signed the statute, 20 plaintiffs filed suit against the Attorney General of the United States and the Department of Justice challenging the constitutionality of §§223(a)(1) and 223(d). A week later, based on his conclusion that the term "indecent" was too vague to provide the basis for a criminal prosecution, District Judge Buckwalter entered a temporary restraining order against enforcement of §223(a)(1)(B)(ii) insofar as it applies to indecent communications. A second suit was then filed by 27 additional plaintiffs, the two cases were consolidated, and a three-judge District Court was convened pursuant to §561 of the Act. After an evidentiary hearing, that Court entered a preliminary injunction against enforcement of both of the challenged provisions. Each of the three judges wrote a separate opinion, but their judgment was unanimous.

Chief Judge Sloviter doubted the strength of the Government's interest in regulating "the vast range of online material covered or potentially covered by the CDA," but acknowledged that the interest was "compelling" with respect to some of that material. *929 F. Supp.*, at 853. She concluded, nonetheless, that the statute "sweeps more broadly than necessary and thereby chills the expression of adults" and that the terms "patently offensive" and "indecent" were "inherently vague." *Id.*, at 854. She also determined that the affirmative defenses were not "technologically or economically feasible for most providers," specifically considering and rejecting an argument that providers could avoid liability by "tagging" their material in a manner that would allow potential readers to screen out unwanted transmission. *Id.*, at 856. Chief Judge Sloviter also rejected the Government's suggestion that the scope of the statute could be narrowed by construing it to apply only to commercial pornographers. *Id.*, at 854–855.

Judge Buckwalter concluded that the word "indecent" in §223(a)(1)(B) and the terms "patently offensive" and "in context" in §223(d)(1) were so vague that criminal enforcement of either section would violate the "fundamental constitutional principle" of "simple fairness," *id.*, at 861, and the specific protections of the First and Fifth Amendments, *id.*, at 858. He found no statutory basis for the Government's argument that the challenged provisions would be applied only to "pornographic" materials, noting that, unlike obscenity, "indecency has *not* been defined to exclude works of serious literary, artistic, political or scientific value." *Id.*, at 863. Moreover, the Government's claim that the work must be considered patently offensive "in context" was itself vague because the relevant context might "refer to, among other things, the nature of the communication as a whole, the time of day it was conveyed, the medium used, the identity of the speaker, or whether or not it is accompanied by appropriate warnings." *Id.*, at 864. He believed that the unique nature of the Internet aggravated the vagueness of the statute. *Id.*, at 865, n. 9.

Judge Dalzell's review of "the special attributes of Internet communication" disclosed by the evidence convinced him that the First Amendment denies Congress the power to regulate the content of protected speech on the Internet. *Id.*, at 867. His opinion explained at length why he believed the Act would abridge significant protected speech, particularly by noncommercial speakers, while "[p]erversely, commercial pornographers would remain relatively unaffected." *Id.*, at 879. He construed our cases as requiring a "medium-specific" approach to the analysis of the regulation of mass communication, *id.*, at 873, and concluded that the Internet—as "the most participatory form of mass speech yet developed," *id.*, at 883—is entitled to "the highest protection from governmental intrusion," *ibid.*

The judgment of the District Court enjoins the Government from enforcing the prohibitions in §223(a)(1)(B) insofar as they relate to "indecent" communications, but expressly preserves the Government's right to investigate and prosecute the obscenity or child pornography activities prohibited therein. The injunction against enforcement of §§223(d)(1) and (2) is unqualified because those provisions contain no separate reference to obscenity or child pornography.

The Government appealed under the Act's special review provisions, §561, 110 Stat. 142–143, and we noted probable jurisdiction, see 519 U. S. ___ (1996). In its appeal, the Government argues that the District Court erred in holding that the CDA violated both the First Amendment because it is overbroad and the Fifth Amendment because it is vague. While we discuss the vagueness of the CDA because of its relevance to the First Amendment overbreadth inquiry, we conclude that the judgment should be affirmed without reaching the Fifth Amendment issue. We begin our analysis by reviewing the principal authorities on which the Government relies. Then, after describing the overbreadth of the CDA, we consider the Government's specific contentions, including its submission that we save portions of the statute either by severance or by fashioning judicial limitations on the scope of its coverage.

In arguing for reversal, the Government contends that the CDA is plainly constitutional under three of our prior decisions: (1) *Ginsberg v. New York*, 390 U. S. 629 (1968); (2) *FCC v. Pacifica Foundation*, 438 U. S. 726 (1978); and (3) *Renton v. Playtime Theatres, Inc.*, 475 U. S. 41 (1986). A close look at these cases, however, raises—rather than relieves—doubts concerning the constitutionality of the CDA.

In *Ginsberg*, we upheld the constitutionality of a New York statute that prohibited selling to minors under 17 years of age material that was considered obscene as to them even if not obscene as to adults. We rejected the defendant's broad submission that "the scope of the constitutional freedom of expression secured to a citizen to read or see material concerned with sex cannot be made to depend on whether the citizen is an adult or a minor." 390 U. S., at 636. In rejecting that contention, we relied not only on the State's independent interest in the well-being of its youth, but also on our consistent recognition of the principle that "the parents' claim to authority in their own household to direct the rearing of their children is basic in the structure of our society." In four important respects, the statute upheld in *Ginsberg* was narrower than the CDA. First, we noted in *Ginsberg* that "the prohibition against sales to minors does not bar parents who so desire from purchasing the magazines for their children." *Id.*, at 639. Under the CDA, by contrast, neither the parents' consent—nor even their participation—in the communication would avoid the application of the statute. Second, the New York statute applied only to commercial transactions, *id.*, at 647, whereas the CDA contains no such limitation. Third, the New York statute cabined its definition of material that is harmful to minors with the requirement that it be "utterly without redeeming social importance for minors." *Id.*, at 646. The CDA fails to provide us with any definition of the term "indecent" as used in §223(a)(1) and, importantly, omits any requirement that the "patently offensive" material covered by §223(d) lack serious literary, artistic, political, or scientific value. Fourth, the New York statute defined a minor as a person under the age of 17, whereas the CDA, in applying to all those under 18 years, includes an additional year of those nearest majority.

In *Pacifica*, we upheld a declaratory order of the Federal Communications Commission, holding that the broadcast of a recording of a 12-minute monologue entitled "Filthy Words" that had previously been delivered to a live audience "could have been the subject of administrative sanctions." 438 U. S., at 730 (internal quotations omitted). The Commission had found that the repetitive use of certain words referring to excretory or sexual activities or organs "in an afternoon broadcast when children are in the audience was patently offensive" and concluded that the monologue was indecent "as broadcast." *Id.*, at 735. The respondent did not quarrel with the finding that the afternoon broadcast was patently offensive, but contended that it was not "indecent" within the meaning of the relevant statutes because it contained no prurient appeal. After rejecting respondent's statutory arguments, we confronted its two constitutional arguments: (1) that the Commission's construction of its authority to ban indecent speech was so broad that its orders had to be set aside even if the broadcast at issue was unprotected; and (2) that since the recording was not obscene, the First Amendment forbade any abridgement of the right to broadcast it on the radio.

In the portion of the lead opinion not joined by Justices Powell and Blackmun, the plurality stated that the First Amendment does not prohibit all governmental regulation that depends on the content of speech. *Id.*, at 742–743. Accordingly, the availability of constitutional protection for a vulgar and offensive monologue that was not obscene depended on the context of the broadcast. *Id.*, at 744–748. Relying on the premise that "of all forms of communication" broadcasting had received the most limited First Amendment protection, *id.*, at 748–749, the Court concluded that the ease with which children may obtain access to broadcasts, "coupled with the concerns recognized in *Ginsberg*," justified special treatment of indecent broadcasting. *Id.*, at 749–750.

As with the New York statute at issue in *Ginsberg*, there are significant differences between the order upheld in *Pacifica* and the CDA. First, the order in *Pacifica*, issued by an agency that had been regulating radio stations for decades, targeted a specific broadcast that represented a rather dramatic departure from traditional program content in order to designate when—rather than whether—it would be permissible to air such a program in that particular medium. The CDA's broad categorical prohibitions are not limited to particular times and are not dependent on any evaluation by an agency familiar with the unique characteristics of the Internet. Second, unlike the CDA, the Commission's declaratory order was not punitive; we expressly refused to decide whether the indecent broadcast "would justify a criminal prosecution." *Id.,* at 750. Finally, the Commission's order applied to a medium which as a matter of history had "received the most limited First Amendment protection," *id.,* at 748, in large part because warnings could not adequately protect the listener from unexpected program content. The Internet, however, has no comparable history. Moreover, the District Court found that the risk of encountering indecent material by accident is remote because a series of affirmative steps is required to access specific material.

In *Renton,* we upheld a zoning ordinance that kept adult movie theatres out of residential neighborhoods. The ordinance was aimed, not at the content of the films shown in the theaters, but rather at the "secondary effects"—such as crime and deteriorating property values—that these theaters fostered: "'It is th[e] secondary effect which these zoning ordinances attempt to avoid, not the dissemination of "offensive" speech.'" 475 U.S., at 49 (quoting *Young v. American Mini Theatres, Inc.,* 427 U. S. 50, 71, n. 34 (1976)). According to the Government, the CDA is constitutional because it constitutes a sort of "cyberzoning" on the Internet. But the CDA applies broadly to the entire universe of cyberspace. And the purpose of the CDA is to protect children from the primary effects of "indecent" and "patently offensive" speech, rather than any "secondary" effect of such speech. Thus, the CDA is a content-based blanket restriction on speech, and, as such, cannot be "properly analyzed as a form of time, place, and manner regulation." 475 U. S., at 46. See also *Boos v. Barry,* 475 U. S. 312, 321 (1988). ("Regulations that focus on the direct impact of speech on its audience" are not properly analyzed under *Renton*); *Forsythe County v. Nationalist Movement,* 505 U. S. 123, 134 (1992) ("Listeners' reaction to speech is not a content-neutral basis for regulation").

These precedents, then, surely do not require us to uphold the CDA and are fully consistent with the application of the most stringent review of its provisions.

Regardless of whether the CDA is so vague that it violates the Fifth Amendment, the many ambiguities concerning the scope of its coverage render it problematic for purposes of the First Amendment. For instance, each of the two parts of the CDA uses a different linguistic form. The first uses the word "indecent," 47 U. S. C. A. §223(a) (Supp. 1997), while the second speaks of material that "in context, depicts or describes, in terms patently offensive as measured by contemporary community standards, sexual or excretory activities or organs," §223(d). Given the absence of a definition of either term, this difference in language will provoke uncertainty among speakers about how the two standards relate to each other and just what they mean. Could a speaker confidently assume that a serious discussion about birth control practices, homosexuality, the First Amendment issues raised by the Appendix to our *Pacifica* opinion, or the consequences of prison rape would not violate the CDA? This uncertainty undermines the likelihood that the CDA has been carefully tailored to the congressional goal of protecting minors from potentially harmful materials.

The vagueness of the CDA is a matter of special concern for two reasons. First, the CDA is a content-based regulation of speech. The vagueness of such a regulation raises special First Amendment concerns because of its obvious chilling effect on free speech. See, *e.g., Gentile v. State Bar of Nev.,* 501 U. S. 1030, 1048–1051 (1991). Second, the CDA is a criminal statute. In addition to the opprobrium and stigma of a criminal conviction, the CDA threatens violators with penalties including up to two years in prison for each act of violation. The severity of criminal sanctions may well cause speakers to remain silent rather than communicate even arguably unlawful words, ideas, and images. See, *e.g., Dombrowski v. Pfister,* 380 U. S. 479, 494 (1965). As a practical matter, this increased deterrent effect, coupled with the "risk of discriminatory enforcement" of vague regulations, poses greater First Amendment concerns than those implicated by the civil regulation reviewed in *Denver Area Ed. Telecommunications Consortium, Inc. v. FCC,* 518 U.S. ___ (1996).

The Government argues that the statute is no more vague than the obscenity standard this Court established in *Miller v. California,* 413 U. S. 15 (1973). But that is not so. In *Miller,* this Court reviewed a criminal conviction against a commercial vendor who mailed brochures containing pictures of sexually explicit activities to individuals who had not requested such materials. *Id.,* at 18. Having struggled for some time to establish a definition of obscenity, we set forth in *Miller* the test for obscenity that controls to this day:

> (a) whether the average person, applying contemporary community standards would find that the work, taken as a whole, appeals to the prurient interest; (b) whether the work depicts or describes, in a patently offensive way, sexual conduct specifically defined by the applicable state law; and (c) whether the work, taken as a whole, lacks serious literary, artistic, political, or scientific value. (*Id.,* at 24; internal quotation marks and citations omitted.)

Because the CDA's "patently offensive" standard (and, we assume *arguendo,* its synonymous "indecent" standard) is one part of the three-prong *Miller* test, the Government reasons, it cannot be unconstitutionally vague.

The Government's assertion is incorrect as a matter of fact. The second prong of the *Miller* test—the purportedly analogous standard—contains a critical requirement that is omitted from the CDA: that the proscribed material be "specifically defined by the applicable state law." This requirement reduces the vagueness inherent in the open-ended term "patently offensive" as used in the CDA. Moreover, the *Miller* definition is limited to "sexual conduct," whereas the CDA extends also to include (1) "excretory activities" as well as (2) "organs" of both a sexual and excretory nature.

The Government's reasoning is also flawed. Just because a definition including three limitations is not vague, it does not follow that one of those limitations, standing by itself is not vague. Each of *Miller's* additional two prongs—(1) that, taken as a whole, the material appeal to the "prurient" interest, and (2) that it "lac[k] serious literary, artistic, political, or scientific value"—critically limits the uncertain sweep of the obscenity definition. The second requirement is particularly important because, unlike the "patently offensive" and "prurient interest" criteria, it is not judged by contemporary community standards. See *Pope v. Illinois*, 481 U. S. 497, 500 (1987). This "societal value" requirement, absent in the CDA, allows appellate courts to impose some limitations and regularity on the definition by setting, as a matter of law, a national floor for socially redeeming value. The Government's contention that courts will be able to give such legal limitations to the CDA's standards is belied by *Miller's* own rationale for having juries determine whether material is "patently offensive" according to community standards: that such questions are essentially ones of *fact*.

In contrast to *Miller* and our other previous cases, the CDA thus presents a greater threat of censoring speech that, in fact, falls outside the statute's scope. Given the vague contours of the coverage of the statute, it unquestionably silences some speakers whose messages would be entitled to constitutional protection. That danger provides further reason for insisting that the statute not be overly broad. The CDA's burden on protected speech cannot be justified if it could be avoided by a more carefully drafted statute.

We are persuaded that the CDA lacks the precision that the First Amendment requires when a statute regulates the content of speech. In order to deny minors access to potentially harmful speech, the CDA effectively suppresses a large amount of speech that adults have a constitutional right to receive and to address to one another. That burden on adult speech is unacceptable if less restrictive alternatives would be at least as effective in achieving the legitimate purpose that the statute was enacted to serve.

In evaluating the free speech of adults, we have made it perfectly clear that "[s]exual expression which is indecent but not obscene is protected by the First Amendment." *Sable*, 492 U. S., at 126. See also *Carey v. Population Services Int'l*, 431 U. S. 678, 701 (1977) ("[W]here obscenity is not involved, we have consistently held that the fact that protected speech may be offensive to some does not justify its suppression"). Indeed, *Pacifica* itself admonished that "the fact that society may find speech offensive is not a sufficient reason for suppressing it." 438 U. S., at 745.

It is true that we have repeatedly recognized the governmental interest in protecting children from harmful materials. See *Ginsberg*, 390 U. S., at 639; *Pacifica*, 438 U. S., at 749. But that interest does not justify an unnecessarily broad suppression of speech addressed to adults. As we have explained, the

Government may not "reduc[e] the adult population . . . to . . . only what is fit for children." *Denver*, 518 U. S., at ___ (slip op., at 29) (internal quotation marks omitted) (quoting *Sable*, 492 U. S., at 128).

> [R]egardless of the strength of the government's interest" in protecting children, "[t]he level of discourse reaching a mailbox simply cannot be limited to that which would be suitable for a sandbox. (*Bolger v. Youngs Drug Products Corp.*, 463 U. S. 60, 74–75, 1983.)

The District Court was correct to conclude that the CDA effectively resembles the ban on "dial-a-porn" invalidated in *Sable.* 929 F. Supp., at 854. In *Sable*, 492 U.S., at 129, this Court rejected the argument that we should defer to the congressional judgment that nothing less than a total ban would be effective in preventing enterprising youngsters from gaining access to indecent communications. *Sable* thus made clear that the mere fact that a statutory regulation of speech was enacted for the important purpose of protecting children from exposure to sexually explicit material does not foreclose inquiry into its validity. As we pointed out last Term, that inquiry embodies an "over-arching commitment" to make sure that Congress has designed its statute to accomplish its purpose "without imposing an unnecessarily great restriction on speech." *Denver*, 518 U.S., at ___ (slip op., at 11).

In arguing that the CDA does not so diminish adult communication, the Government relies on the incorrect factual premise that prohibiting a transmission whenever it is known that one of its recipients is a minor would not interfere with adult-to-adult communication. The findings of the District Court make clear that this premise is untenable. Given the size of the potential audience for most messages, in the absence of a viable age verification process, the sender must be charged with knowing that one or more minors will likely view it. Knowledge that, for instance, one or more members of a 100-person chat group will be minor—and therefore that it would be a crime to send the group an indecent message—would surely burden communication among adults.

The District Court found that at the time of trial existing technology did not include any effective method for a sender to prevent minors from obtaining access to its communications on the Internet without also denying access to adults. The Court found no effective way to determine the age of a user who is accessing material through e-mail, mail exploders, newsgroups, or chat rooms. 929 F. Supp., at 845 (findings 90–94). As a practical matter, the Court also found that it would be prohibitively expensive for noncommercial—as well as some commercial—speakers who have Websites to verify that their users are adults. *Id.*, at 845–848 (findings 95–116). These limitations must inevitably curtail a significant amount of adult communication on the Internet. By contrast, the District Court found that "[d]espite its limitations, currently available *user-based* software suggests that a reasonably effective method by which *parents* can prevent their children from accessing sexually explicit and other material which *parents* may believe is inappropriate for their children will soon be widely available." *Id.*, at 842 (finding 73) (emphases added).

The breadth of the CDA's coverage is wholly unprecedented. Unlike the regulations upheld in *Ginsberg* and *Pacifica,* the scope of the CDA is not limited to commercial speech or commercial entities. Its open-ended prohibitions embrace all nonprofit entities and individuals posting indecent messages or displaying them on their own computers in the presence of minors. The general, undefined terms "indecent" and "patently offensive" cover large amounts of nonpornographic material with serious educational or other value. Moreover, the "community standards" criterion as applied to the Internet means that any communication available to a nation-wide audience will be judged by the standards of the community most likely to be offended by the message. The regulated subject matter includes any of the seven "dirty words" used in the *Pacifica* monologue, the use of which the Government's expert acknowledged could constitute a felony. See Olsen Test, Tr. Vol. V, 53:16-54:10. It may also extend to discussions about prison rape or safe sexual practices, artistic images that include nude subjects, and arguably the card catalogue of the Carnegie Library.

For the purposes of our decision, we need neither accept nor reject the Government's submission that the First Amendment does not forbid a blanket prohibition on all "indecent" and "patently offensive" messages communicated to a 17-year-old—no matter how much value the message may contain and regardless of parental approval. It is at least clear that the strength of the Government's interest in protecting minors is not equally strong throughout the coverage of this broad statute. Under the CDA, a parent allowing her 17-year-old to use the family computer to obtain information on the Internet that she, in her parental judgment, deems appropriate could face a lengthy prison term. See 47 U. S. C. A. §223(a)(2) (Supp. 1997). Similarly, a parent who sent his 17-year-old college freshman information on birth control via e-mail could be incarcerated even though neither he, his child, nor anyone in their home community, found the material "indecent" or "patently offensive," if the college town's community thought otherwise.

The breadth of this content-based restriction of speech imposes an especially heavy burden on the Government to explain why a less restrictive provision would not be as effective as the CDA. It has not done so. The arguments in this Court have referred to possible alternatives such as requiring that indecent material be "tagged" in a way that facilitates parental control of material coming into their homes, making exceptions for messages with artistic or educational value, providing some tolerance for parental choice, and regulating some portions of the Internet—such as commercial Websites—differently than others, such as chat rooms. Particularly in the light of the absence of any detailed findings by the Congress, or even hearings addressing the special problems of the CDA, we are persuaded that the CDA is not narrowly tailored if that requirement has any meaning at all.

The Government's three remaining arguments focus on the defenses provided in §223(e)(5). First, relying on the "good faith, reasonable, effective, and appropriate actions" provision, the Government suggests that "tagging" provides a defense that saves the constitutionality of the Act. The suggestion assumes that transmitters may encode their indecent communications in a way that would indicate their contents, thus permitting recipients to block their reception with appropriate software. It is the requirement that the good faith action must be "effective" that makes this defense illusory. The Government recognizes that its proposed screening software does not currently exist. Even if it did, there is now way to know whether a potential recipient will actually block the encoded material. Without the impossible knowledge that every guardian in America is screening for the "tag," the transmitter could not reasonably rely on its action to be "effective."

For its second and third arguments concerning defenses—which we can consider together—the Government relies on the latter half of §223(e)(5), which applies when the transmitter has restricted access by requiring use of a verified credit card or adult identification. Such verification is not only technologically available but actually is used by commercial providers of sexually explicit material. These providers, therefore, would be protected by the defense. Under the findings of the District Court, however, it is not economically feasible for most noncommercial speakers to employ such verification. Accordingly, this defense would not significantly narrow the statute's burden on noncommercial speech. Even with respect to the commercial pornographers that would be protected by the defense, the Government failed to adduce any evidence that these verification techniques actually preclude minors from posing as adults. Given that the risk of criminal sanctions "hovers over each content provider, like the proverbial sword of Damocles," the District Court correctly refused to rely on unproven future technology to save the statute. The Government thus failed to prove that the proffered defense would significantly reduce the heavy burden on adult speech produced by the prohibition of offensive displays.

We agree with the District Court's conclusion that the CDA places an unacceptably heavy burden on protected speech, and that the defenses do not constitute the sort of "narrow tailoring" that will save an otherwise patently invalid unconstitutional provision. In *Sable*, 492 U. S., at 127, we remarked that the speech restriction at issue there amounted to "burn[ing] the house to roast the pig." The CDA, casting a far darker shadow over free speech, threatens to torch a large segment of the Internet community.

At oral argument, the Government relied heavily on its ultimate fall-back position: If this Court should conclude that the CDA is insufficiently tailored, it urged, we should save the statute's constitutionality by honoring the severability clause, see 47 U. S. C. §608, and construing nonseverable terms narrowly. In only one respect is this argument acceptable.

A severability clause requires textual provisions that can be severed. We will follow §608's guidance by leaving constitutional textual elements of the statute intact in the one place where they are, in fact, severable. The "indecency" provision, 47 U. S. C. A. §223(a) (Supp. 1997), applies to "any comment, request, suggestion, proposal, image, or other communication which is *obscene or indecent.*" (Emphasis added.) Appellees do not challenge the application of the statute to obscene speech, which, they acknowledge, can be banned totally because it enjoys no First Amendment protection. See *Miller,* 413 U. S., at 18. As set forth by the statute, the restriction of "obscene" material enjoys a textual manifestation separate from that for "indecent" material , which we have held unconstitutional. Therefore, we will sever the term "or indecent" from the statute, leaving the rest of §223(a) standing. In no other respect, however, can §223(a) or §223(d) be saved by such a textual surgery.

The Government also draws on an additional, less traditional aspect of the CDA's severability clause, 47 U. S. C., §608, which asks any reviewing court that holds the statute facially unconstitutional not to invalidate the CDA in application to "other persons or circumstances" that might be constitutionally permissible. It further invokes this Court's admonition that, absent "countervailing considerations," a statute should "be declared invalid to the extent it reaches too far, but otherwise left intact." *Brockett v. Spokane Arcades, Inc.,* 472 U. S. 491, 503–504 (1985). There are two flaws in this argument.

First, the statute that grants our jurisdiction for this expedited review, 47 U. S. C. A. §561 (Supp. 1997), limits that jurisdictional grant to actions challenging the CDA "on its face." Consistent with §561, the plaintiffs who brought this suit and the three-judge panel that decided it treated it as a facial challenge. We have no authority, in this particular posture, to convert this litigation into an "as-applied" challenge. Nor, given the vast array of plaintiffs, the range of their expressive activities, and the vagueness of the statute, would it be practicable to limit our holding to a judicially defined set of specific applications. Second, one of the "countervailing considerations" mentioned in *Brockett* is present here. In considering a facial challenge, this Court may impose a limiting construction on a statute only if it is "readily susceptible" to such a construction. *Virginia v. American Bookseller's Assn., Inc.,* 484 U. S. 383, 397 (1988). See also *Erznoznik, v. Jacksonville,* 422 U. S. 205, 216 (1975) ("readily subject" to narrowing construction). The open-ended character of the CDA provides no guidance whatever for limiting its coverage.

This case is therefore unlike those in which we have construed a statute narrowly because the text or other source of congressional intent identified a clear line that this Court could draw. Cf., *e.g., Brockett,* 472 U. S., at 504–505 (invalidating obscenity statute only to the extent that word "lust" was actually or effectively excised from statute); *United States v. Grace,* 461 U. S. 171, 180–183 (1983) (invalidating federal statute banning expressive displays only insofar as it extended to public sidewalks when clear line could be drawn between sidewalks and other grounds that comported with congressional purpose of protecting the building, grounds, and people therein). Rather, our decision in *United States v. Treasury Employees,* 513 U. S. 454, 479, n. 26 (1995), is applicable. In that case, we declined to "dra[w] one or more lines between categories of speech covered by an overly broad statute, when Congress has sent inconsistent signals as to where the new line or lines should be drawn" because doing so "involves a far more serious invasion of the legislative domain." This Court "will not rewrite a . . . law to conform it to constitutional requirements." *American Booksellers,* 484 U. S., at 397.

In this Court, though not in the District Court, the Government asserts that—in addition to its interest in protecting children—its "[e]qually significant" interest in fostering the growth of the Internet provides an independent basis for upholding the constitutionality of the CDA. Brief for Appellants 19. The Government apparently assumes that the unregulated availability of "indecent" and "patently offensive" material on the Internet is driving countless citizens away from the medium because of the risk of exposing themselves or their children to harmful material.

We find this argument singularly unpersuasive. The dramatic expansion of this new marketplace of ideas contradicts the factual basis of this contention. The record demonstrates that the growth of the Internet has been and continues to be phenomenal. As a matter of constitutional tradition, in the absence of evidence to the contrary, we presume that governmental regulation of the content of speech is more likely to interfere with the free exchange of ideas than to encourage it. The interest in encouraging freedom of expression in a democratic society outweighs any theoretical but unproven benefit of censorship. For the foregoing reasons, the judgment of the district court is affirmed.

It is so ordered.

EXPLORING THE READING

1. What do the terms "indecent" and "patently offensive" have to do with the Supreme Court Ruling?
2. In your small group, review the Supreme Court Ruling. Isolate what the justices determined were the essential issues involved.
3. Divide your group into two sections, one in support of the Supreme Court Ruling and one opposed. Debate the issue.
4. What is the tone and style of the Supreme Court Ruling? How is it different from other texts in this chapter? Is the tone and style appropriate for its purpose? Is it understandable?
5. In declaring the Act unconstitutional, were the justices saying that the Internet should not be regulated, as John Perry Barlow advocated earlier in this chapter? Or are they saying that this particular piece of legislation is inappropriate regulation? Explain.

POLICING CYBERSPACE

by Vic Sussman

"The rights of everyone are at stake" according to Vic Sussman in this article "Policing Cyberspace" from U.S. News and World Report. *Terrorism, theft, smuggling, and white-collar crimes are just some of the illegal activities taking place on the Internet and other areas of cyberspace. As police try to control cybercrime, their search for criminals will strain our definitions of privacy, freedom of speech, and intellectual property rights. Legislators and judges as well as the police have plenty of work to do before cyberspace can be effectively policed.*

Sussman was, for several years, the Senior Editor, Cyberspace, at U.S. News and World Report. *In addition, he has over thirty years experience in broadcast journalism, filing reports on National Public Radio and appearing on "Larry King Live" with Vice President, Al Gore. He currently works as Director, Internet Programming for America On Line.*

If ever a buzzword buzzed too much for traditionbound law enforcement, it's *cybercop*. It kicks up images of the clanking earnestness of a laser-guided RoboCop. Agents snickered when senior instructor Kevin Manson first used the word a couple of years ago at the Federal Law Enforcement Training Center near Brunswick, Ga. Nobody at FLETC laughs much anymore. They are too busy training cybercops. "The day is coming very fast," says FLETC's director, Charles Rinkevich, "when every cop will be issued a badge, a gun and a laptop."

Adding a high-speed modem, cellular phone, cryptography textbooks and a bulletproof vest to that arsenal might also be prudent because "crime involving high technology is going to go off the boards," predicts FBI Special Agent William Tafoya, the man who created the bureau's home page on the Internet, the worldwide computer network. "It won't be long before the bad guys outstrip our ability to keep up with them." These crimes are worrisome precisely because they use the advantages of cyberspace that have made it a revolutionary, liberating form of communication: its ability to link millions of computer and modem owners around the world; its technological break-throughs, such as digital encoding, that allow average citizens to use sophisticated encryption to protect their data, and its wide-open culture, where cops and other agents of government are more often than not thought to be the enemy.

No one knows exactly how much computer crime there really is, though FLETC's experts agree that the damage starts in the billions of dollars and will surely surge upward. The size and scope of cybercrimes are limited only by the bad guys' imagination, technical skill and gall. But here are the crimes that worry authorities the most:

- **White-collar crime.** Virtually every white-collar crime has a computer or telecommunications link, says Carlton Fitzpatrick, branch chief of FLETC's Financial Fraud Institute. Sometimes the crimes are simple, such as the case of the bookkeeper at a bicycle store who frequently entered incoming checks as returned merchandise, then cashed the checks. Even more damaging are cases involving skilled computerists. The FBI says that Kevin Mitnick, currently America's most wanted computer criminal, has stolen software from cellular-phone companies, caused millions of dollars in damage to computer operations and boldly tapped FBI agents' calls.

- **Theft.** Given the expanse of computer networks, even seemingly small crimes can have big payoffs. "Salami slicing," for example, involves a thief who regularly makes electronic transfers of small change from thousands of accounts to his own. Most people don't balance their ledgers to the penny, so the thief makes out, well, like a bandit. A more targeted approach involves pilfering industrial secrets. Last November, someone infiltrated Internet-linked computers owned by General Electric and stole research materials and passwords.

- **Stolen services.** Swiping and reselling long-distance calling codes is a big business, says Bob Gibbs, a Financial Fraud Institute senior instructor, as is breaking into private phone networks and selling long-distance access. One university discovered this the hard way when its monthly phone bill, a staggering $200,000, arrived in a box instead of an envelope.

- **Smuggling.** Drug dealers launder their proceeds through cyberspace and use the Internet to relay messages. Moreover, they cover up secret communications by cracking into corporate voice-mail systems and by operating their own cellular-telephone networks.

- **Terrorism.** Since computers are the nerve centers of the world's financial transactions and communications systems, there are any number of nightmarish possibilities. Authorities especially worry that a cracker—cyberspeak for a malevolent hacker—might penetrate FedWire, the Federal Reserve's electronic funds-transfer system, or vital telephone switching stations. Key New York phone systems did go down temporarily in 1992, and though it has been chalked up to a software problem, some FLETC cybercops still wonder if it didn't involve a cracker testing his muscles.

- **Child pornography.** There is a lot of it out there. Jefferson County, Kentucky, police Lt. Bill Baker broke a major kiddie-porn ring in England even though he never left Kentucky. An e-mailed tip from a source in Switzerland led Baker to an Internet site in Birmingham, England. After about three months of investigation that involved downloading sixty pages of file names related to child porn and 400 images, Baker called on Interpol, New Scotland Yard and police in Birmingham, who arrested the distributor.

To combat once and future cybercrimes, FLETC's Financial Fraud Institute conducts some fourteen programs, regularly updated to keep pace with wrinkles in crime. Agents learn how to analyze evidence, track credit card

fraud and apply constitutional search-and-seizure techniques when they find
evidence of crimes on computer bulletin board systems, or BBSs. This is a
new world for law enforcement, says Dan Duncan, a FLETC Legal Division
senior instructor, because "cops have always followed a paper trail, and now
there may not be one."

When they start rooting around for crime, new cybercops are entering a
pretty unfriendly environment. Cyberspace, especially the Internet, is full of
those who embrace a frontier culture that is hostile to authority and fearful
that any intrusions of police or government will destroy their self-regulating
world. The clash between the subculture of computerists and cops often
stems from law enforcement's inexperience. The Internet buzzes with stories
of cops who "arrest the equipment" by barging into BBS operations to haul
off all the electronic gear, as if the machines possessed criminal minds.

Still, keeping up with wise guys in cyberspace will tax the imaginations
and budgets of law enforcement agencies and put revolutionary pressures on
America's notions of privacy, property and the limits of free speech. The
rights of everyone are at stake. What follows is a look at perhaps the most
crucial issues that will emerge as a profoundly new chapter in human communication unravels.

INVASIONS OF PRIVACY

Once upon a time, only Santa Claus knew whether you had been good or
bad. But jolly supernaturalism has been supplanted by aggressive data processing: Your chances of finding work, getting a mortgage or qualifying for
health insurance may be up for grabs, because almost anybody with a computer, modem and telephone can surf through cyberspace into the deepest
recesses of your private life. A fairly accurate profile of your financial status,
tastes and credit history can be gleaned from such disparate things as your
ZIP code, Social Security number and records of credit-card usage.

Even more personal information will be available as commercial transactions increase through online services. And that raises the most pressing
cyberspace issues for everyday Americans, says Phil Agre, a communications
professor at the University of California at San Diego. Such transactions will
increase as the Internet grows more popular. Those records, enriched with
demographic information and perhaps Social Security numbers, will be routinely sold to marketers, says Agre. He asks: "Who will have access to the
complete transaction data?"

Suppose you have a history of buying junk food or large amounts of over-
the-counter drugs. Could an insurance company obtain that information and
decide you are a poor health risk? If records showing purchases of cigarettes,
liquor and red meat were collated with your medical records, would the
picture look even worse? Computer networking and sophisticated data processing are making it easier and cheaper for businesses and the government to
collect such personal data, says Esther Dyson, of EDventure Holdings, which
observe the computer industry. "It's really simple to call up amazing stuff
about anybody," she says.

But legal access to data is only part of the problem. Another difficulty is unauthorized peeking into personal records, which Dyson says occurs with alarming regularity because company safeguards are often laughable. Knowing a person's Social Security number is usually enough to get into medical and financial records. A second problem is that wrong and harmful "facts" can creep into the databases. Malicious tipsters can poison a person's record with innuendo, and it takes much effort to correct the mistake.

In this environment, it is virtually inevitable that Americans will demand stronger privacy protections. The United States has a law barring release of video rental records but no strong laws against scanning personal medical data. "Many European countries have privacy commissions, and they find it strange that we don't," notes Anne Branscomb, author of *Who Owns Information?* and a law professor at the University of Pennsylvania. She urges laws that give citizens the right to control data about themselves.

The new Congress will soon begin deliberations over proposals that would offer privacy protections for Americans' medical, credit and telecommunications data. Similar proposals have not gotten off the ground in previous Congresses, but handicappers say passage of a bill limiting the release of confidential medical records is much more likely in this Congress as is a measure to limit online service providers' ability to sell membership data. The potent telemarketing industry probably has the power, though, to soften a proposal barring the sale of personal data to commercial vendors without a person's consent, according to Evan Hendricks, publisher of the newsletter *Privacy Times.*

ENCRYPTING DATA

Cybercops especially worry that outlaws are now able to use powerful *cryptography* to send and receive uncrackable secret communications. That could make some investigations impossible and create a breed of "crypto-criminals," says FLETC's Manson. But there is widespread agreement across the Internet and among entrepreneurs hoping to do business in cyberspace that cryptography is necessary for privacy in a networked universe.

Besides businesses, which will need cryptography for transmitting sensitive information, the other market for cryptography is the millions who use electronic mail. "Without encryption, e-mail is no more secure than a postcard," says author of *E-mail Security: How to Keep Your Electronic Messages Private.* E-mail passes from machine to machine, and many people in the middle can read it. Systems are also vulnerable to break-ins, and passwords are commonly stolen. Some may decide they don't need the high level of privacy cryptography affords, especially given the additional effort encrypting data requires. But as Internet communication becomes common, people will want private contact with business associates, physicians, attorneys, accountants and lovers.

The increasing use of encryption leaves cops in the lurch unless they have a way to break the code. "We are totally, enthusiastically supportive of encryption technology for the public," says Jim Kallstrom, the FBI special agent in charge of the Special Operations Division in the New York office. "We merely think that criminals, terrorists, child abductors, perverts and bombers should not have an environment free from law enforcement or a search warrant. I think most victims of crime agree." Kallstrom sees the *Clipper* chip—which is supposed to offer phone privacy to consumers while providing police access—as a good way to give the public powerful encryption while still preserving law enforcement's ability to conduct electronic surveillance. The FBI won a round last year when Congress passed the Digital Telephony Act, which requires future telecommunications systems to be accessible to wiretaps. But officials have not persuaded Congress or industry to back Clipper. Many opponents agree with the Electronic Privacy Information Center's Marc Rotenberg, who calls Clipper part of the "Information Snooperhighway."

Law enforcers are also deeply worried about another aspect of cyberspace that offers absolute anonymity to anyone who wants it. Anonymous re-mailers—free e-mail forwarding sites in Europe and elsewhere—can convert return addresses to pseudonyms and render e-mail untraceable. Anonymity is crucial for whistleblowers and people expressing unpopular views against repressive governments, but it raises other problems, says the FBI's Tafoya. Anonymous re-mailers outside the reach of American authorities are being used by electronic vandals to bedevil their victims with threatening messages or "mail bombs" composed of thousands of gibberish messages. They either clog a victim's mailbox or jam his computer system. Child pornographers also use anonymous re-mailers.

The simple truth, though, is that no legislative act can stop the spread of cryptography, according to Lance Hoffman, a computer-security expert and professor at George Washington University. "There are 394 foreign encryption products: over 150 use DES—strong encryption," says Hoffman. "And all are legal to import."

Cryptography will become even more popular once cybersurfers discover digital cash, which is the electronic equivalent of real money that resides in a computer. David Chaum, the developer of DigiCash, a Dutch-owned company, says his creation combines the benefits of anonymous legal tender with the speed and convenience of online commerce. There is no risky exchange of credit-card information. DigiCash is electronically transferred like actual cash, while powerful cryptography makes it theft- and counterfeit-proof, says Chaum. DigiCash can prevent consumers' names and personal habits from funneling into databases. Schneier thinks the enhanced confidentiality of electronic lucre will be good for society, but suggests that "criminals will love digital cash. Anybody can use it to transfer money for legal or illegal purposes." Many people believe the widespread use of e-cash will be one more aspect of the Internet that erodes the power of central government control.

FREEDOM OF SPEECH

The advent of space-age telecommunications raises enormous questions about the future of government regulation of media. Though the First

Amendment asserts there should be no law abridging freedom of speech or the press, there have been laws aplenty in the last three generations that regulate speech on new kinds of technology. Different restrictions apply to telephones, radio and TV stations and cable TV. But cyberspace is a convergence of media and the blurring of distinctions between transmission modes. "With the advent of fiber-optic [cables], it is conceivable that a single transmission medium could become the conduit for newspapers, electronic mail, local and network broadcasting, video rentals, cable television and a host of other information services," says Robert Corn-Revere, a former Federal Communications Commission official who now practices First Amendment law. He argues that the day is passing when government can justify licensing and regulating media.

Modern telecommunications knows no borders and has few limits. For the first time in history, almost every recipient of information has the potential to become a publisher of information, says Jonathan Emord, an attorney and author of *Freedom, Technology and the First Amendment*. The liberating potential of that technology is exhilarating as it unleashes information and breaks down communications hierarchies. But it also creates a situation where Americans can be offended or otherwise victimized by information from people sitting at computers in foreign lands beyond the reach of U.S. authorities. "Right now, cyberspace is like a neighborhood without a police department," says FLETC's Fitzpatrick.

One of the most pressing dangers, says Fitzpatrick, is that people bound by hate and racism are no longer separated by time and distance. They can share their frustrations at nightly computerized meetings. "What some people call hate crimes are going to increase, and the networks are going to feed them," predicts Fitzpatrick. "I believe in the First Amendment. But sometimes it can be a noose society hangs itself with."

Of course, the antidote to offensive speech, noted Supreme Court Justice Louis Brandeis, is *more* speech, and the Internet is still an equal-opportunity soapbox. Messages on public bulletin boards can be challenged and rebutted, which widens debate. Moreover, users can go where they choose on the Internet. So, those offended by discussions are always free to start their own groups.

Of all the material floating between computers, pornography best illustrates the difficulties of trying to apply old rules and laws to cyberspace. Late last year, a jury in Memphis, Tenn., convicted a Milpitas, California, couple of violating obscenity laws. Using a computer and modem in Memphis, a postal inspector downloaded pictures from the couple's California-based BBS. The couple were tried in Memphis, and a jury found that the pictures violated local community standards. But the pictures, which exist only as data stored on a hard drive, were voluntarily extracted from a computer sitting in a community where the images were *not* illegal. People create their own communities in cyberspace, based on affinity rather than geography. This means the courts will have to unravel when, where and how potential crimes should be investigated.

Ultimately, there are no easy solutions to such problems because the First Amendment, designed to protect offensive speech, has always cut both ways: It encourages robust and healthy discussion, but it also allows everyone a platform. Mike Godwin, legal counsel for the Electronic Frontier Foundation, which promotes civil liberties in cyberspace, says: "I think we're still in the turmoil that comes when a new medium is presented to the public and to the government. There's a tendency to first embrace it and then to fear it. And the question is, how will we respond to the fear?"

INTELLECTUAL PROPERTY

John Perry Barlow, an Internet visionary, kicked up controversy last year when he suggested in a widely read *Wired* magazine article that traditional notions of copyright were dead in cyberspace. "Digital technology is detaching information from the physical plane," he wrote, "where property law of all sorts has always found definition." The government's top copyright officer, Marybeth Peters, partially concedes the point, saying, "The Internet is the world's biggest copying machine." But she says that doesn't mean copyright is useless, just that it needs to work differently in a world where "property" is as evanescent as dots of light dancing on a computer screen.

One way, suggests Peters, will be to provide access to data only to those who pay. An example is WestLaw, an online law database. Students use an electronic card that gives them access to the system, and their law school pays the fee. Other information systems now being developed use encryption, selling the access key to users. But once someone gets a first look at data, sound or graphics files, it is easy to make copies—an economic nightmare for software developers.

TRADE WAR. Ken Wasch, executive director of the Software Publishers Association, says pirated software costs the industry $9 billion a year. The issue is hot enough to spark a U.S.-China trade war. The Clinton administration recently threatened to raise tariffs on some Chinese products unless China stops its global trade in illegally copied CDs, books, movies and computer software.

Wasch believes copyright law is elastic enough to protect material regardless of media, and that software should be protected as "literary work." But he agrees that some updating is in order: "We don't want to criminalize someone giving a copy to another person." But a recent court case shows how complicated the issues are: Late last month, a U.S. District Court judge in Boston dismissed charges of wire fraud against an MIT student who ran a bulletin board allowing users to extract copies of more than $1 million in software at no charge. While calling the student's actions "heedlessly irresponsible," the judge said the government's charges would make even legitimate copying, such as that done for back-up purposes, illegal. Intellectual-property expert Branscomb agrees. "You cannot take an old law intended for telegraphy and telephony and turn it into a mechanism for criminalizing behavior that Congress has not addressed directly," she says.

The only solid protection for ideas flying through cyberspace is their originality and style, which was the point of copyright in the first place, maintains Internet guru Barlow. If you are creative and have something worthwhile to say, the public "will pay to hear your latest thoughts or your latest research. Value comes back to you by increasing your celebrity and people's awareness of your work," he says. Bringing copyright laws crafted in 1787 up to warp speed will be difficult at best, especially on the Net, where information is routinely traded for more information and no money changes hands. Besides, says Barlow, collecting tolls on an information highway is the wrong concept. "The Internet is nothing like a superhighway. It's an organism."

EXPLORING THE READING

1. Vic Sussman says that one reason police have problems in cyberspace is that the Internet is full of "those who embrace a frontier culture." What do you think he means by this? Is he echoing the use of the frontier metaphor used by John Perry Barlow and others in Chapter 2? Do you agree with Sussman? Have you had any experience on the Internet or World Wide Web that would support or refute this description of the attitudes in cyberspace?

2. How much personal information should companies be able to access about you? Should a future employer be allowed more information than a lending agency? How much information should an insurance company be able to access? Review the information Sussman provides in the Invasions of Privacy section, and in a group of three or four other students, discuss which information should and should not be available to employers, insurance companies, and lending agencies.

3. Currently, many encryption programs available on the Internet are illegal because they can be downloaded not only in America but also around the world. Should everyone have access to encryption? Why or why not?

RESPECTING PRIVACY IN AN INFORMATION SOCIETY: A JOURNALIST'S DILEMMA

by L. Paul Husselbee

Today, credit bureau reports, records of video rentals, and credit card purchases are easily available to journalists. Just because the information is available, should it be used? Or is making such information public an invasion of privacy?

L. Paul Husselbee, a journalism professor from Dixie College, argues in this essay from the Journal of Mass Media Ethics *that a journalist must determine whether use of such information is warranted, based on the distinction between the public's right to know and simply a curious interest in knowing. Husselbee offers a five-point test to aid in making the distinction.*

During the 1987 confirmation hearings of Supreme Court nominee Robert H. Bork, the weekly *City Paper* of Washington, DC, obtained and printed a list of the movies Bork had rented from a local video retailer. Having learned that he and Judge Bork patronized the same video store, reporter Michael Dolan went to the store and asked to see a copy of the nominee's rental record, which was contained in the store's computerized database. In violation of the store's policy prohibiting the release of such information, the clerk provided access to the records and even helped Dolan make copies of them (Dolan, 1988). The resulting story revealed nothing unflattering about the nominee, yet Judge Bork and his family understandably were upset; their privacy had been invaded (Bork, 1988).[1]

In 1989, *Business Week* writer Jeffrey Rothfeder paid a nominal fee and gained access, via his home computer, to a major credit-bureau database. With minimal effort, he obtained a complete credit report on Dan Quayle, including the Vice President's department store and credit card account numbers. Rothfeder published only bits and pieces of the report, to prove its authenticity, but Quayle was not amused. He called the invasion of privacy "disturbing" (Rothfeder, 1992, pp. 20–22).

In 1993, *Boston Globe* reporter Larry Tye conducted a computer search for private information on former Celtics basketball star M. L. Carr. He came up with the appraised value of Carr's suburban Boston home, the makes and models of his vehicles, the number of times he was stopped for speeding in the previous four years, and the fact that Carr had an arrest record for fighting as a teenager. Carr had consented to the search in advance, and expressed surprise at how much personal information about him was available and how easily the reporter had gathered it (Tye, 1993, p. 1).

---

[1]The Video Privacy Protection Act, making it illegal for retailers to disclose an individual's video rental records without the customer's consent or a court order, was passed in 1988 in response to the invasion of Judge Bork's privacy.

The decision to pursue and print this information, as well as the factors motivating that decision, should be of interest to all journalists. Of greater concern to journalists and to society at large is the fact that private, sensitive information—from our American Express account numbers to the titles of movies we rent—is available, and that such information can be disseminated to the public.

Why is this a concern? Because every time a person makes a credit card purchase, the specifics of that transaction are recorded in a database somewhere. They may be copied or sold to other databases, and perused at a later date by people in information and surveillance industries—journalists, credit investigators, private detectives, and so forth. Because when people make business trips or go on vacation, the particulars of their airline and hotel reservations and vehicle rentals, along with any personal identification they provide to guarantee payment, are entered into a vast electronic dossier. Because even titles of the videos people rent are recorded in someone's computer. Because advances in technology over the past two decades have given journalists—and anyone else who knows how to gain access—the power to peek into an individual's personal affairs without that person's knowledge or consent.

Salton (1980) estimates that "tens of millions of searches of mechanized information banks are conducted each year, a large portion involving private information about individual persons or groups" (p. 75). The Federal Election Commission alone receives more than 70,000 requests each year for computerized searches of contributor information (*Federal Election Committee v. Political Contributions Data, Inc.,* 1991). Private-sector businesses that maintain databases frequently sell information or access to it, without consideration for the manner in which the information is to be used (Rothfeder, 1992). This, Flaherty (1988) pointed out, is perhaps the greatest problem with maintaining automated databases—their very existence constitutes an invitation to invade privacy through vicarious surveillance of an individual's activities.

> Credit card companies watch what people purchase . . . an American lawyer returns from a vacation in Paris and is informed by her bank that someone (in fact, herself) has been purchasing clothes with her credit card. She is upset by what she perceives as surveillance of her own activities. (p. 378)

As illustrated by the publication of Vice President Quayle's spending habits or Judge Bork's video rental titles, there circulates in private-sector databases information about most people that they would rather retain in confidence, and access to that information is no longer limited to government agencies. Technology has given American journalists the ability to conduct high-tech data searches, allowing them to snoop into people's personal or business affairs and expose their secrets. As Rothfeder (1992) and others (Landau, 1992; Paul, 1992; Wickens, 1993) have demonstrated, it is easy and it is legal. The question of legality, however, must be accompanied by a question of morality. Once the reporter has gone on a high-speed fishing expedition and uncovered private information about an individual, it is a relatively short step from access to publication, from exposure to disclosure of an individual's secrets to a mass audience.

What is the journalist's primary responsibility to the reader or viewer? How does this responsibility conflict with the journalist's moral duty to respect individual privacy? How are these concerns magnified by journalists' increasing access to sensitive information via database research? Can this form of privacy invasion be morally justified? These and similar questions are addressed.

THE DUTY TO INFORM

The ethical conflict pits the right to information access and the journalist's role as information provider against the right of individuals to maintain a reasonable zone of privacy, as guaranteed by the Fourth Amendment to the U.S. Constitution.

The framers of the Constitution recognized the importance of access to information. James Madison said, "A people who mean to be their own governors must arm themselves with the power knowledge gives" (Rives & Fendall, 1865, p. 276). Thomas Jefferson endorsed its role and function: "To prevent irregular interpositions of the people is to give them full information of their affairs" (Ford, 1904, p. 69). He added that "whenever the people are well-informed, they can be trusted with their own government" (Beilenson, 1986, p. 18).

Today, as in those days, the efficient function of society is dependent upon information access. As Salton (1980) pointed out, although "most governmental systems require information in order to operate efficiently a democracy in particular flourishes on information" (p. 76). The public's dependence on information is also satisfied by journalists, who, according to Black, Steele, and Barney (1993), have a moral obligation to distribute information as a means of leveling the playing field of society. Citing Friedrich's contention that informed people make better decisions, Black et al. reasoned that journalists are vital to the decision-making process because they provide important information that assists society in making judgments. Based on this assumption, they pinpointed two factors that "journalists should be aware of as they participate in principled and reasoned decisionmaking" about information disclosure.

> Society is committed to the free flow of information as a means of educating the population, so that its members may make informed decisions, which combine with millions of other decisions to contribute to the strength of society, or to determine how society will treat its individual members.
>
> Information control is related to power. Distribution of information is a redistribution of power. Thus, the journalist is often at odds with individuals and entities wishing to retain power by controlling the free flow of information or withholding information altogether. (Black et al., pp. 25–26)

According to this model, then, journalists level the playing field of society through regular efforts to redistribute the power that information provides.

By taking power from the few and giving it to the masses, journalists act, in the overall best interest of society, to limit the power of entities that might otherwise become too powerful. Because of this position of social power broker, the journalist has a greater responsibility than most to act ethically. Ethical journalists speak not merely of their right to publish, but of their reasons for publishing and their moral obligations to do so (Black et al., 1993, pp. 23–25).

THE RIGHT OF PRIVACY

The redistribution of power among the masses through information dissemination has the potential to inflict harm on individuals or groups. One of the most frequent harms is the invasion of privacy. Just as they recognized the need for information access, the Founding Fathers also understood that people have certain privacy rights—"the right to be secure in their persons, houses, papers, and effects, against unreasonable searches and seizures" (Fourth Amendment, U.S. Constitution). Over generations, the need for privacy has escalated as technology has increased individuals' ability to keep tabs on one another. Each new surveillance device that improves the capacity to invade an otherwise reasonable zone of privacy—from wiretaps and similar electronic listening devices to computers—increases the demand for privacy. Because privacy legislation, as we will see, has failed to keep pace with technology, rights to privacy must be considered on a moral level, where they lie in direct conflict with the right of individuals to information access.

THE ABSENCE OF LEGAL PROTECTION

Because the First Amendment protects press freedom, the conflict between the right to inform and the right to privacy is already weighted in the media's favor. The failure of privacy legislation to keep pace with advances in technology gives the media further advantage. A 1991 decision by the U.S. Court of Appeals in *Morgan v. Department of the Army* accentuates the inability of legislation's flagship privacy defense, the Privacy Act of 1974, to protect individual privacy. The court upheld the discharge of James W. Morgan as a police officer at Walter Reed Army Medical Center after he was found to have misused the National Crime Information Center (NCIC) database to access personal information about the alleged, and nonexistent, criminal history of a senior officer. The information in question was protected by the Privacy Act; use of the NCIC database in this case was illegal. Although the court affirmed, albeit indirectly, the right of individuals to maintain a reasonable zone of privacy where certain private information is concerned, the case also demonstrates two major weaknesses of the Privacy Act. First, the law did not protect the senior officer's privacy; it merely punished Morgan for breaking it. Second, had the information been found in a private database, rather than in a governmental database, no charges would have been filed because the Privacy Act does not apply to private-sector databases. Except in rare cases, neither legislation nor legal precedent limits use of information gathered and stored in databases by third parties.[2] If Morgan had been a reporter sifting through privately held information, there would have been no case against him.

In a critique of the legal protections afforded private information contained in databases, Rubin (1989) noted that the Privacy Act fails to protect citizens in four of five important areas.

> The Privacy Act contains no restrictions on the types of data that may be collected by the federal government, no restrictions on the methods that may be used . . . to collect data, few restrictions on the use of that data after its original collection, and no enforcement agency. (p. 17)

He concedes that the law does guarantee all individuals the right to access to their own records, but adds that "the Privacy Act is batting one-for-five, a poor average in any league" (p. 17). Taking into account the scant legal protection of private information contained in databases, the journalist's moral responsibility to respect individual privacy assumes additional weight.

THE MORAL MANDATE

The legal right to free expression does not diminish the need for journalists to exercise moral judgment in choosing what to publish, or whose privacy to invade or respect. Ultimately, respect for others and their rights cannot be legislated. At the same time, Bok (1982) pointed out that reporters, when considering privacy issues, must not take claims of privacy or confidentiality at face value. "Official" people, she said, are apt to hide behind these claims rather than allow the revelation of secrets that could prove harmful to them. Reporters must be free to probe, and motivated to do so. Otherwise, "governments and other powerful organizations bent on keeping secrets from the masses would have very little to challenge or restrain them. . . . The press has a clear public mandate to probe and expose secrets" (p. 249).

In the absence of regulation, what ought to be the moral mandate for journalists in using third-party databases to gather information? What moral principles should journalists resort to in determining how and when to use private-sector data sources? Principles outlined by two celebrated deontologists—Ross and Kant—seem to provide the most promising alternatives in the quest to isolate such a morally defensible foundation for invading privacy.

Ross (1954) would base journalistic decisions on a set of seven prima facie, or conditional, duties: fidelity, gratitude, beneficence, justice, self-improvement, reparation, and nonmaleficence. Unless one of these duties conflicts with some other relevant duty, the prima facie duty becomes an actual duty. If, for example, a journalist promises to protect a source's privacy, the journalist,

---

[2]The Fair Credit Reporting Act and similar laws protect some financial information. However, as evidenced by *United States v. Miller* (1976), not all information held by financial institutions is considered private.

under normal circumstances, is obliged by a prima facie duty to fidelity to keep the promise. Therefore, if the duty to fidelity were to conflict with another prima facie duty, such as justice, beneficence, or nonmaleficence, then the journalist might be justified in breaking the privacy pledge if a higher principle would be served.

Kant (1797/1959) would counsel the press to treat people as ends, rather than as means to an end. When this is the case, Velecky (1978) said, "the *privacy* of a person becomes the privacy *of a person* [italics added]" (p. 25). The journalist who collects data solely as a means of snooping into a person's private life violates a key condition of Kantian morality. At the same time, Kant would probably recognize the need to invade privacy in certain cases, as long as the media are willing to universalize the principle. Thus, if a reporter uses a credit-bureau database to research and publish the financial profile of the vice president in order to satisfy some higher principle, the categorical imperative would require that the reporter do the same thing in similar circumstances, even if the public official is a relative or close friend and the financial profile reflects negatively on his or her performance of civic duties. To define *similar circumstances*, Louch (1982) contended that Kant would advocate the delineation of boundaries to determine which areas of a person's private life could reasonably be invaded and which could not.

THE RIGHT TO KNOW: AN ANSWER OF CONVENIENCE

Before exploring these boundaries, it would seem logical at this juncture to deal with the journalist's stock response to questions of privacy raised in conjunction with the publication of sensitive information: "The public has a right to know." As noted previously, claiming a right to privacy is a frequent tactic of the powerful who wish to keep secrets from the populace. Bok (1982) pointed out that when the individuals abuse the claim to privacy, reporters almost automatically turn to equally vague arguments in the name of the right to know. Both claims—the right to privacy and the right to know—serve increasingly as rationalizations. Resorting to the sacred right to know has become a ragged defense mechanism for journalists who lack the philosophical foundation to defend their position.

The right to know exists, though most journalists' awareness of its origins or conceptual core is hazy at best. The doctrine has root in the writings of Rousseau (1762/1963), who advocated educating the people to achieve the ultimate good sought by a general will of the populace. Madison and Jefferson subscribed to the ideas of the French *philosophes* and adopted the right to know as a key doctrine of due process in the Bill of Rights. Altschull (1990) noted that "nowhere in American law can one find anything so clearly established as a right to know" (p. 250).

The right to know as conceived by Rousseau and the Founding Fathers, however, often does not mirror its meaning in contemporary usage. "The right to know," wrote Meyers (1993), "routinely motivates and justifies a wide range of journalistic behavior . . . that without such a justification would be regarded by all as unethical" (p. 134). The modern journalist ties the right to know not only to a fundamental right to information for the purpose of protecting the public welfare and individual liberties, but to public curiosity about people and events in which the public has no legitimate interest. And although public curiosity may be considered an appropriate criterion for news, Bok (1982) reasoned, it should not be confused with a compelling need to know: "The right to know should be based on a legitimate need to know" (p. 255). Meyers also differentiated between the right to know and having an interest or curiosity in knowing by saying that "a more powerful appeal than mere interest or curiosity must be present; there must be some genuine need" (p. 140). Patterson and Wilkins (1994) pointed out that the "need to know [requires] a more demanding argument, for it means that counterbalancing forces have been weighed and that bringing information to light is still the most ethical act" (p. 117).

DEFINING THE BOUNDARIES: A FIVE-POINT TEST

In returning to the notion that specific boundaries must delineate the circumstances under which privacy may be invaded, it is suggested that journalists, before invading a person's privacy via data base research and subsequent publication, apply a five-point test:

1. Why is this information important? Will publication satisfy some socially redeeming need or value? Does the public have a legitimate interest in disclosure of this information? Will publication shield the majority from imminent harm?
2. Even if the motive for privacy invasion can be morally justified by legitimate public interest, is it possible to accomplish the same end without using information that will invade another's privacy?
3. What procedures will be used to verify the accuracy of the information uncovered through data-base research?
4. As the invasion of privacy may inflict harm on the minority, what are the potential harms in this case and how might they be minimized?
5. What role might disclosure play in this case? Would it be helpful to explain the mechanics of the invasion and how it is justified by satisfaction of socially redeeming needs and values?

Any decision to publish private information should be based on the importance of the information in relation to the public good. Perhaps the most reliable method of determining relative importance is application of the harm principle. Disclosure of private matters, according to Bok (1978), is justifiable if disclosure will prevent harm to others. It is a simple task to argue that disclosure of Vice President Quayle's financial records, gleaned from the files of a credit-bureau database, may be warranted if publication demonstrates a pattern of misuse and embezzlement of public funds. Likewise, publishing Judge Bork's video titles might have been justified had the information been pertinent to his ability to fulfill the duties of an associate justice. However, the lines are not so easily drawn where normal, everyday people are concerned. Consider, for example, the case of the Yale computer science professor severely injured in June 1993 by the explosion of a mail bomb. When he returned home after an extended hospital stay, Professor David Gelernter sent an electronic mail message to colleagues and friends, detailing his injuries, his emotional state, and his plans to return to work. A University of Pennsylvania computer scientist intercepted the message and posted it on an Internet bulletin board called "Interesting People," to which 20,000 subscribers had access.

Notwithstanding Gelernter's steadfast refusal to discuss the bombing with the media (a stance Gelernter emphasized in his e-mail message), *Washington Post* reporter John Schwartz picked up the message and used it as the basis for a story about the professor's condition and convalescence (Schwartz, 1993). A day later, the Associated Press bureau in Hartford, Connecticut, filed a rewrite of Schwartz's story. For weeks, journalists specializing in computer-assisted reporting debated the propriety of using Internet communications as the basis for stories. Some said any information, including "private" communications, posted on an electronic bulletin board such as Internet becomes public property and therefore cannot possibly be considered private. Others concluded that the key in determining whether to use the memo should have been Professor Gelernter's intent, and that because his intent, as clearly stated in the memo, was not to talk to the media, Schwartz had no business invading his privacy. Given the prima facie duty to refrain from inflicting unnecessary harm (nonmaleficence), the latter of the two arguments appears more convincing, because a communication that Professor Gelernter clearly intended to be private was revealed to a mass audience. Nevertheless, had the memo proved instructive in warning others how to avoid or prevent a similar disaster (it did not), it could be argued that the privacy invasion would have been justified because publishing its contents could have prevented harm or injury to a significant portion of the population. In such a scenario, the prima facie duty to beneficence may have taken priority over the duty to nonmaleficence.

It should be pointed out here, however, that private information should contain no apparent value to the public good before the harm principle allows it to fall within a protected zone of privacy. Frequently, information that seems inconsequential on the surface is found to be useful because of its instructional value. Actor Rock Hudson's homosexuality was protected for years by friends in the entertainment industry, largely on the principle that his lifestyle and sexual preference were his own business, and that the public was not entitled to this knowledge. However, an awareness of Rock Hudson's lifestyle proves instructive in light of his lengthy, unsuccessful battle with AIDS. The question of instructional value hinges on the utility of the private information in question: Is the damage caused by disclosure of the information offset by its instructional value? In the case of Rock Hudson, an understanding of the potential consequences of a gay lifestyle might have led journalists to invade the actor's privacy, because the information served an instructional purpose for the mass audience. Likewise, the revelation that tennis star Arthur Ashe had contracted the HIV virus from a blood transfusion during heart surgery proved instructive, if only to underscore the point that AIDS is not merely a sex-and-drugs disease. Although Ashe was harmed by the privacy invasion that ultimately convinced him to call a news conference and announce that he had AIDS, the disclosure of this information also may have proved helpful in alleviating the social stigma that clings to AIDS patients.

Having used the harm principle to establish legitimate public interest, journalists next have a duty to determine whether the same public interest may be served without resorting to an invasion of privacy. In most cases, journalists will find it difficult to arrive at such a solution. The information in question is considered private because of its potential to empower others. Consider the hypothetical senator in the midst of a reelection campaign, during which a reporter gains access to a credit-bureau database and discovers that the senator has a history of using his Visa card to purchase hardcore pornography. The reporter asks the senator to comment; the senator claims that his credit history, regardless of what it contains, is private and should not be released to the public. However, because part of the senator's campaign platform is built around proposed antipornography legislation, the reporter and her editors consider the information of instructional value. Rather than immediately publishing the credit card history, however, the ethical journalist will seek independent confirmation of the apparent contradiction between the senator's platform and his alleged lifestyle. If it becomes apparent that no other sources are available, the journalist may then be justified in invading the senator's privacy by publishing the information. Even then, of course, the journalist is justified only if the information in question empowers the senator's constituency.

The need for independent confirmation of database information assumes greater significance when the possibility of error is considered. Original records in most databases are created by clerks who work from applications or other forms filled in by the subject of the record. A notable exception is criminal justice databases, where records are created from arrest reports. In either case, database information is extremely susceptible to human error. Once erroneous information is entered into a database, it is difficult to correct. It took nine years in various courts and several thousand dollars in legal fees before the family of a college student falsely arrested for theft convinced the U.S. Court of Appeals to order the FBI to expunge his record (*Menard v. Saxbe*, 1974). In so doing, the court declared that because of the FBI's limited resources, "there is no follow-up to assure that records of arrest are frequently amended to show an ultimate noncriminal disposition. There are no controls on the accuracy of the information submitted by contributing agencies." Errors in database information are more widespread than reporters may wish to believe. Burnham (1983) estimated that approximately one in four people who check their computerized records in California discover discrepancies. Only one in ten of those who find discrepancies persuade the state to make corrections (p. 82). Given the probability of error in database information and the potential harm caused by erroneous information, journalists are justified in privacy invasion without independent confirmation only when the information in question is of such importance to the public interest that it may prevent significant harm to the majority.

In preventing harm to the majority, however, the journalist may inflict harm on the minority. The Kantian duty to treat people as ends rather than as means to an end requires that journalists anticipate potential harms and attempt to minimize them. In digging for facts, reporters frequently gather more information than they use when preparing the story. The reporter who gathers such a surplus from a database can minimize the harm inflicted in privacy invasion by citing only information that has direct bearing on the subject in question. Publication of additional private information, especially that of a sensitive nature, would serve only to inflict further harm.

In considering the impact of a story in which the decision is made to invade an individual's privacy in the interest of preventing harm to the majority, journalists may further minimize harm and increase public acceptance of their decision through disclosure. In most cases, disclosure would require a sidebar or additional paragraphs in the body of the story in which the moral justification for resorting to privacy invasion is explained. By taking the reader through a step-by-step reasoning process, the journalist may demonstrate how the invasion of privacy satisfies a socially redeeming need or value. Certainly such a disclosure would have proved helpful in explaining why Schwartz felt justified in quoting Professor Gelernter's e-mail memo.[3] Had there existed moral justification for invading the privacy of Vice President Quayle or Judge Bork, disclosure might have been beneficial in those cases as well.

CONCLUSION

One of the hazards of technology's rapid progress is that the laws governing its use almost always fail to maintain a similar pace. As technology augments the capacity of journalists to gather and process information, the temptation to invade individual privacy will undoubtedly increase. Thus, it is incumbent upon journalists, as primary conduits of public and private information, to develop their own moral guidelines and place reasonable limits on the extent to which individual privacy may be invaded. Journalists who

---

[3]Schwartz, accused of being a "journalistic piranha" in the Internet traffic that followed publication of his story, posted such a disclosure on Internet within days of its publication. In it, Schwartz listed six steps he took to verify the contents and the authenticity of the memo, and to secure permission from Professor Gelernter to quote the memo. When he received no response from Gelernter, he and his editors decided to run the story.

engage in principled discussion and deliberation over the conflict between information distribution and individual privacy—taking care to use the five-point test recommended here or to create their own standards based on moral reasoning—are less likely to become entangled in unethical behavior in the future.

REFERENCES

Altschull, J. (1990). *From Milton to McLuhan: The ideas behind American journalism.* New York: Longman.

Beilenson, N. (1986). *Thomas Jefferson: His life and words.* White Plains, NY: Peter Pauper Press.

Black, J., Steele B., & Barney, R. (1993). *Doing ethics in journalism.* Greencastle, IN: Society of Professional Journalists.

Bok, S. (1978). *Lying: Moral choice in public and private life.* New York: Pantheon.

Bok, S. (1982). *Secrets: On the ethics of concealment and revelation.* New York: Pantheon.

Bork, R., Jr. (1988, February 21). Another example of how his privacy was being trampled. *The Washington Post,* p. B1.

Burnham, D. (1983). *The rise of the computer state.* New York: Random House.

Dolan, M. (1988, February 21). America was ready for a chuckle. *The Washington Post,* p. B1.

Federal Election Committee v. Political Contributions Data, Inc., 943 F.2d 190 (1991).

Flaherty, D. (1988). The emergence of surveillance societies in the western world. *Government Information Quarterly, 5,* 377–387.

Ford, P. (Ed.). (1904). *The works of Thomas Jefferson* (Vol. 2). New York: Putnam.

Kant, I. (1959). *Foundations of the metaphysics of morals* (L. Beck, Trans.). New York: Liberal Arts Press. (Original work published 1797)

Landau, G. (1992, May/June). Quantum leaps: Computer journalism takes off. *Columbia Journalism Review,* pp. 61–64.

Louch, A. (1982, Fall). Is privacy immoral? *Human Rights,* pp. 22–25, 52–54.

Menard v. Saxbe, 498 F.2d 1017 (1974).

Meyers, C. (1993). Justifying journalistic harms: Right to know vs. interest in knowing. *Journal of Mass Media Ethics, 8,* 133–146.

Morgan v. Department of the Army, 934 F.2d 310 (1991).

Patterson, P. & Wilkins, L. (1994). *Media ethics: issues and cases* (2nd ed.). Dubuque, IA: Brown.

Paul, N. (1992, Winter). For the record: Information on individuals. *Phi Kappa Phi Journal,* pp. 34–38.

Rives, W., & Fendall, P. (Eds.). (1865). *Letters and other writings of James Madison, fourth president of the United States* (Vol. 3). Philadelphia: Lippincott.

Ross, W. (1954). *Kant's ethical theory.* Oxford, UK: Clarendon.

Rothfeder, J. (1992). *Privacy for sale: How computerization has made everyone's private life an open secret.* New York: Simon & Schuster.

Rousseau, J. (1963). The social contract. In J. Somerville & R. Santoni (Eds.), *Social and political philosophy: Readings from Plato to Ghandi* (pp. 205–238). Garden City, NY: Doubleday. (Original work published 1762).

Rubin, M. (1989). The computer and personal privacy, part III: The regulation of computer records in the United States. *Library Hi-Tech,* 7(3), 11–22.

Salton, G. (1980). A progress report on information privacy and data security. *Journal of the American Society for Information Science,* 31(2), 75–83.

Schwartz, J. (1993, August 12). Undaunted, mail bomb victim to resume work. *The Washington Post,* p. A12.

Tye,. L. (1993, September 5). Privacy lost in high-tech era. *Boston Globe,* pp. 1, 3.

United States v. Miller, 425 U. S. 435 (1976).

Velecky, L. (1978). The concept of privacy. In J. Young (Ed.), *Privacy* (pp. 13–34). New York: Wiley.

Wickens, B. (1993, April 26). Preserving individual privacy: New technology has made trafficking in personal data a huge industry. *MacLean's,* pp. 20–21.

EXPLORING THE READING

1. What is the public's right to know, according to L. Paul Husselbee? Whose doctrine is it based upon?

2. What is Husselbee's five-point test? Freewrite for five minutes, evaluating the usefulness of the test.

3. In your small group take a look at some of the cases Husselbee cited such as the publishing of Vice President Dan Quayle's credit report. Determine your groups' perception of each case, based on Husselbee's five-point test. Was the publication of the information justified?

4. Freewrite for five minutes about the issues Husselbee raises. Report your conclusions.

5. Husselbee's text was published in an academic journal. How does this affect the style of the piece?

BIG BROTHER IS US

by James Gleick

Privacy, according to James Gleick, is a twentieth-century construct. In the past, we knew the intimate details of our neighbors, but civility insisted that some of those intimate details were not open for community discussion. Now, everything is open for discussion. We claim to value privacy, but we trade extensive information about ourselves and our families for goods, services, or, perhaps, fame. Nothing is taboo. But it is not the government watching us, as Orwell warned. Gleick says we turn on the cameras that watch us in elevators, that track our movements through cyberspace and the grocery store, that know where we travel and with whom. We turn them on by giving retailers, hospitals, and almost anyone who asks our social security numbers and other information about our private lives.

Gleick writes a regular monthly column on technology for the New York Times Magazine. *He is the author of the best-selling book,* Chaos: The Making of a New Science. *He has also written a National Book Award nominated biography of the physicist* Richard Feynman, Genius: The Life and Science of Richard Feynman *and worked for ten years as an editor and reporter for the* New York Times. *You can read more of his essays and find out about his latest book on his home page www.around.com.*

For much of the twentieth century, 1984 was a year that belonged to the future—a strange, gray future at that. Then it slid painlessly into the past, like any other year. Big Brother arrived and settled in, though not at all in the way George Orwell had imagined.

Underpinning Orwell's 1948 anti-utopia—with its corruption of language and history, its never-ending nuclear arms race and its totalitarianism of torture and brainwashing—was the utter annihilation of privacy. Its single technological innovation, in a world of pig iron and pneumatic tubes and broken elevators, was the telescreen, transmitting the intimate sights and sounds of every home to the Thought Police. BIG BROTHER IS WATCHING YOU. "You had to live—did live, from habit that became instinct—" Orwell wrote, "in the assumption that every sound you made was overheard, and, except in darkness, every movement scrutinized."

It has turned out differently. We have had to wait a big longer for interactive appliances to arrive in our bedrooms. Our telescreens come with hundreds of channels but no hidden cameras. If you want a device with a microphone to record and transmit your voice, you are better off with a multimedia P.C. or, for that matter, a dedicated Internet connection: hook up your camera and turn on the switch that Winston Smith could never turn off. People in large numbers are doing just this: acting out their private lives before online cameras, accessible to the world. Grim though Orwell's vision was, it never encompassed the Dan-O-Cam (H. Dan Smith at work in his office in Fresno, Calif.), the LivingRoom Cam (watch children and pets at play; "personal publishing of personal spaces") and scores of similar Internet "cams"—evidence that some citizens of the twenty-first century, anyway, will not be grieving over their loss of privacy.

And yet. . . .

Information-gathering about individuals has reached an astounding level of completeness, if not actual malevolence. So has fear of information-gathering, if not among the broad public, at least among those who pay attention to privacy as an issue of law and technology. Hundreds of privacy organizations, newsletters, annual conferences, information clearinghouses, mailing lists and Websites have sprung into existence—a societal immune-system response.

The rapid rise of the Internet surpasses the grimmest forecasts of inter-connectedness among all these computer dossiers. Yet it defies those forecasts as well. Strangely enough, the linking of computers has taken place democratically, even anarchically. Its rules and habits are emerging in the open light, rather than behind the closed doors of security agencies or cor porate operations centers It is clear that technology has the power not just to invade privacy but to protect it, through encryption, for example, which will be available to everyone, as soon as the Government steps out of the way. The balance of power has already shifted from those who break codes—eavesdroppers and intelligence agencies—to those who wish to use them. In these closing years of the century, we are setting the laws and customs of a future built on networked communication, giant interlinked data bases, electronic commerce and digital cash. Historians will see our time as a time of transition. But transition to what?

"There's a very important and long-term debate taking place right now about technologies of privacy in the next century," says Marc Rotenberg, director of the Electronic Privacy Information Center in Washington. "Privacy will be to the information economy of the next century what consumer protection and environmental concerns have been to the industrial society of the twentieth century."

MIDDLE-CLASS SECRETS

Privacy is a construct of our age. As a tradition in law, it is young. When Louis D. Brandeis issued his famous opinion in 1928 that privacy is "the right to be let alone—the most comprehensive of rights, and the right most valued by civilized men," he was looking to the future, because he was dissenting; the Supreme Court's majority was upholding the right of the police to tap telephone lines without warrants.

"In the beginning, there was no such thing as private life, no refuge from the public gaze and its ceaseless criticism," writes Theodore Zeldin, a social historian, in "An Intimate History of Humanity." He adds, "Then the middle classes began cultivating secrets." In villages and small towns, the secret life was rare. The neighbors knew far more about one's intimacies, from breakfast habits to clandestine affairs, than in any city of the twentieth century. One's shield, if a shield was needed, was a formal civility: rules of discourse that discouraged questions about money or sex. The pathological case of the private person was the hermit—hermits, by and large, have disappeared. The word is quaint. In a crowd, we can all be hermits now.

"Privacy means seeing only people whom one chooses to see," writes Zeldin. "The rest do not exist, except as ghosts or gods on television, the great protector of privacy."

In public opinion surveys, Americans always favor privacy. Then they turn around and sell it cheaply. Most vehemently oppose any suggestion of a national identification system yet volunteer their telephone numbers and mothers' maiden names and even—grudgingly or not—Social Security numbers to merchants bearing discounts or Web services offering "membership" privileges. For most, the abstract notion of privacy suggests a mystical, romantic, cowboy-era set of freedoms. Yet in the real world it boils down to matters of small convenience. Is privacy about Government security agents decrypting your e-mail and then kicking down the front door with their jackboots? Or is it about telemarketers interrupting your supper with cold calls?

It depends. Mainly, of course, it depends on whether you live in a totalitarian or a free society. If the Government is nefarious or unaccountable to individuals—or if you believe it is—the efficient ideal of easy-to-use, perfectly linked and comprehensive national data bases must be frightening indeed. But if, deep down, you feel secure in your relations with the state, then perhaps you are willing to let your guard down; put off till tomorrow your acquisition of that encryption software, send your e-mail in the clear, perhaps even set up an Internet camera at the kitchen table or discuss your sexual history with Oprah.

Certainly where other people's privacy is concerned, we seem willing to lower our standards. We have become a society with a cavernous appetite for news and gossip. Our era has replaced the tacit, eyes-averted civility of an earlier time with exhibitionism and prying. Even borderline public figures must get used to the nation's eyes in their bedrooms and pocketbooks. That's not Big Brother watching us. It's us.

THE NETWORK KNOWS

Like any gossip, we trade information to get information. Over in the advanced research laboratories of the consumer electronics companies, futurists are readying little boxes that they believe you would like to carry around—not just telephones but perfect two-way Internet-connected pocket pals. They could use Global Positioning System satellites so that you always know where you are. They could let the Network know too: then the Network could combine its knowledge of your block-by-block location and your customary 11 A.M. hankering for sushi to beam live restaurant guidance to your pocket pal. Surely you don't mind if the Network knows all this. . . .

It knows much more, of course. Here is what exists about you in Government and corporate computers, even if you are not a particularly active (or unlucky) participant in the wired and unwired economy:

- Your health history; your credit history; your marital history; your educational history; your employment history.
- The times and telephone numbers of every call you make and receive.
- The magazines you subscribe to and the books your borrow from the library.
- Your travel history; you can no longer travel by air without presenting photographic identification; in a world of electronic fare cards tracking frequent-traveler data, computers could list even your bus and subway rides.
- The trail of your cash withdrawals.
- All your purchases by credit card or check. In a not-so-distant future, when electronic cash becomes the rule, even the purchases you still make by bills and coins could be logged.
- What you eat. No sooner had supermarket scanners gone on line—to speed checkout efficiency—than data began to be tracked for marketing purposes. Large chains now invite customers to link personal identifying information with the records of what they buy, in exchange for discount cards or other promotions.
- Your electronic mail and your telephone messages. If you use a computer at work, your employer has the legal right to look over your shoulder while you type. More and more companies are quietly spot-checking workers' e-mail and even voice mail. In theory—though rarely in practice—even an online service or private Internet service provider could monitor you. "Anyway," advises a Website at, naturally, paranoia.com, "you should assume that everything you do online is monitored by your service provider."
- Where you go, what you see on the World Wide Web. Ordinarily Net exploring is an anonymous activity, but many information services ask users to identify themselves and even to provide telephone numbers and other personal information. Once a user does that, his or her activity can be traced in surprising detail. Do you like country music? Were you thinking about taking a vacation in New Zealand? Were you perusing the erotic-books section of the online bookstore? Someone—some computer, anyway—probably already knows.

Many of these personal facts are innocuous in themselves. Some are essentially matters of public record. What matters is mere efficiency—linkage.

Your birth certificate was never private; it was always available to someone willing to stand in line and pay a few dollars to a clerk at town hall. Computers and telephone lines make that a bit more convenient, that's all— but it turns out that proficiency in compilation, sorting and distribution can give sinister overtones to even simple collections of names and addresses. A Los Angeles television reporter recently bought a list of 5,000 children, with ages, addresses and phone numbers, in the name of Richard Allen Davis, the convicted murderer of a 12-year-old girl. The company that sold the list, Metromail, boasts of compiling consumer information on 90 percent of United States households.

To David Burnham, the former *New York Times* reporter who wrote the admonitory "Rise of the Computer State" more than a decade ago, this inexorably more detailed compiling of information about individuals amounted to one thing: surveillance. "The question looms before us," he wrote. "Can the United States continue to flourish and grow in an age when the physical movements, individual purchases, conversations and meetings of every citizen are constantly under surveillance by private companies and Government agencies?" And he added, "Does not surveillance, even the innocent sort, gradually poison the soul of a nation?"

Does it? If so, we're like sheep to the slaughter.

PRIVACY OR ANONYMITY?

The right to be left alone—privacy on Brandeis's terms—is not exactly the same as the right to vanish, the right to act in society without leaving traces and the right to assume a false identity. Most privacy experts who have studied the possible futures of electronic money favor versions that allow for the anonymity of cash rather than the traceability of checks and credit cards. That is appealing; we ought to be able to make a contribution to a dissident political organization without fear of exposure.

Still, the people with the greatest daily, practical need for untraceable cash are criminals; tax cheats, drug dealers, bribers and extortionists. Most drivers prove willing to use an electronic card to pass through tollbooths without worrying about whether a database is logging their movements. Yet if cards like these replaced cash altogether, the net around us would unquestionably be drawn a notch tighter—especially if we are lying to our employers or spouses about our whereabouts, or if we are simply planning to take it on the lam, Bonnie and Clyde-style.

In a past world of intimate small towns, people could disappear. The mere possibility was an essential aspect of privacy, in Rotenberg's view: "People left those small towns and re-emerged in other towns and created new identities." Could you disappear today: abandon all the computerized trappings of your identity gather enough cash, vanish without leaving a trail and start life again? Probably not. Certainly, there have never been so many invisible chains to the life you now lead.

On the Internet, we are re-creating a small-town world, where people mingle and share news easily and informally. But this time it is just one town. Some of its residents advocate rights not just to passive privacy, the right to be left alone, but to what might be called aggressive privacy: the right to retain anonymity even while acting with force and consequence on a broad public state.

Passive privacy is the kind elegantly described by the Fourth Amendment—"the right of people to be secure in their persons, houses, papers, and effects, against unreasonable searches and seizures." We do have a lot of papers and effects these days.

Aggressive privacy implies much more. Telephone regulatory commissions have listened to arguments that people have a right to remain anonymous, hiding their own numbers while placing telephone calls. On the Internet, surprising numbers of users insist on a right to hide behind false names while engaging in verbal harassment or slander.

The use of false online identities has emerged as a cultural phenomenon. Those who cannot reinvent a new self in real life can easily do so online. Sometimes they are experimenting with role playing. Most often, though, as a practical reality, the use of false identity on the Internet has an unsavory flavor: marketers sending junk mail from untraceable sources; speculators or corporate insiders trying to influence stock prices; people violating copyrights or engaging in character assassination.

Changing personas like clothing—is that what the demand for privacy will come to mean? It's a game for people who choose a form of existence impossible in the old world, maybe hermits at that, hiding in digitally equipped homes, visiting by telecam. Something has been lost after all, in the rush to modernity: the chance to mingle freely and thoughtlessly in our communities, exposing our faces and brushing hands with neighbors who know what we had for breakfast and will remember if we lie about it.

In compensation, our reach is thousands of times longer. We meet people, form communities, make our voices heard with a freedom unimaginable to a small-towner of the last century. But we no longer board airplanes or enter schools and courthouses secure in our persons and effects; we submit, generally by choice, to the most intrusive of electronic searches. In banks, at tollbooths, in elevators, in doorways, alongside highways, near public telephones, we submit to what used to be called surveillance. In Orwell's country, thousands of closed-circuit cameras are trained on public streets—pan, zoom and infrared. Every suitcase bomb in a public park brings more cameras and, perhaps, more digital hermits.

We turn those cameras on ourselves. Then we beg for more gossip. We invent diamond-hard technologies of encryption, but we rarely bother to use them. If we want to live freely and privately in the interconnected world of the twenty-first century—and surely we do—perhaps above all we need a revival of the small-town civility of the nineteenth century. Manners, not devices; sometimes it's just better not to ask, and better not to look.

EXPLORING THE READING

1. Look at the list of the information about you that already exists in government and corporate computers. Did you know that all this information was being gathered? Choose a few of the items in James Gleick's list and freewrite for ten minutes on what information is probably stored on you. If you were looking at this information on a computer screen, what would you see?

2. Are you disturbed by the amount of information available about you? Is it an invasion of privacy? Freewrite for ten minutes explaining your answer.

3. Gleick says that in order to regain a sense of privacy, we need to revert to manners. Is it reasonable to expect corporations who might make a profit by knowing the details of our lives not to gather information?

4. Several of the essays in this chapter discuss ways we might regain privacy. In a small group, discuss the pros and cons of a return to manners or other methods of regaining privacy.

5. Gleick's title and the first two paragraphs of this essay refer to George Orwell's novel, *1984*. How effective is Gleick use of the Big Brother metaphor and references to George Orwell in this essay? Why do you think he chose this title and introduction?

A Parent's Guide to Supervising a Child's Online and Internet Experience

by Robert Cannon, Esq.

Children can find many things to do and learn many new things on the Internet, says Robert Cannon in this online FAQ (Frequently Asked Questions). But, parents need to monitor their children as closely here as they would at any new playground or park. Cannon defines some terms for the parent who may not be as computer literate as their children. Then he lists ten precautions parents should take to make sure their children have good, safe experiences online. You can find Cannon's FAQ at http://www.cais.net/cannon.

As a lawyer specializing in cyberspace and communications issues, Cannon has written for a number of legal journals on the Communications Decency Act, Federal Communication Issues, and Domain Name Policy. In addition, he works for the enforcement division of the FCC investigating and prosecuting wireless fraud and advising the FCC on legal issues.

The Internet is a wonderful world of new opportunity for children. It is a colossal dynamic library filled with information, programs, art, games, material, and new opportunities to meet people. It is the opportunity to expand minds and experiences, and to develop skills necessary for the future. However, this new environment also creates risks that your child might be exposed to undesirable material and people. There are numerous sites providing sexually explicit information, violent content, technical information on how to build things such as bombs, and hate speech. Other sites and individuals seek to gather information from children that you may feel uncomfortable providing. The purpose of this FAQ (Frequently Asked Questions) is to provide parents with suggestions that will empower them to effectively supervise their child's Internet experience.

WHAT IS THE INTERNET?

The Internet is a global, decentralized network of computers taking advantage of common protocols permitting the transfer of information. No individual, company or government controls the Internet. The most frequently used areas of the Internet are the World Wide Web, e-mail, USENET newsgroups, FTP, and the IRC.

The *World Wide Web* is the multimedia area of the Internet. A WWW page can look like a magazine page. WWW browsers permit users to view text, photographs, audio, and video. Individuals can also access data and programs. WWW sites can be found by typing a few key words into a search engine and, within seconds, receiving a list of sites containing those words. Punch in the word "playboy" and you will get a list of the "Playboy Magazine" web pages and of other sites that contain the word "Playboy."

FTP stands for File Transfer Protocol. FTP sites are directories of files of all types. These files can be in any form and can be found with search engines. The difference from the WWW is that FTP files are not readily viewable or usable; the files must be downloaded and then viewed or used through the appropriate software programs.

E-mail is electronic mail through which users can exchange messages. Although normally e-mail messages are text, messages can include pictures or sound files. E-mail addresses of users can be readily attained through different search engines and online databases.

The *USENET* is a bulletin board area of the Internet. Individuals post messages and browse for responses at unmoderated USENET sites. The messages normally remain on the bulletin board for a limited time period. Individuals search for the most appropriate bulletin board for the subject desired. At a given site hundreds of messages will be posted about that subject. Messages can also be posted which are irrelevant to the subject. Messages can be text, programs, sound files, or pictures.

A *Listserver* is a cross between e-mail and USENET. It is an e-mail discussion group dedicated to a particular topic. Messages sent to the listserver are then broadcast out to all of the subscribers. Some Listservers are moderated where others are not. People not subscribed to a listserver generally are unable to view the content of the discussion of the subscribers. Listservers are usually composed of a core group active in discussion and a periphery group known as "lurkers" who read the list but rarely participate in the discussion.

The *IRC* is the "real-time" live, unmoderated chat rooms. Each room has a name that may relate to the subject matter discussed. A user can usually find an IRC chat room on virtually *any* subject. Again, even though a subject matter is designated, messages on any subject matter can be posted.

SUPERVISING YOUR CHILD

Most parents complain that their children are more computer literate than they are (parents argue that they are still attempting to figure out how to program their VCRs). They cannot comprehend how they can possibly supervise their child's experience on the Internet. What follows is a list of suggestions that should help. Not all of these suggestions may be acceptable to you. Which suggestions you use will depend in part in your belief in your child's right to privacy and ability to make mature decisions. This FAQ provides parents with an ability to make choices.

Parents must always remember the investment that they have made, both in the child and in the computer. If they commit the time necessary for such a significant investment, parents can make their child's experience both positive, productive, and educational.

1. **Keep the family computer in a family room.** Place it where you can watch and participate in your child's activities.

2. **Spend time with your child both online and off line.** If online material is offensive to you, take the time to teach your child your values. Explain to your child why you believe the material is wrong and the harm you believe that it might cause.

3. **Purchase a filtering software program.** There are a number of programs that filter and block access to adult Internet sites. You can use these programs to assist in your supervision of your child. Be aware that these programs may also filter out material which you find desirable.

   - Cyber Patrol, http://www.cyberpatrol.com
   - Net Nanny, http://www.netnanny.com/
   - Net Shepherd, http://shepherd.net/
   - Safesurf, http://www.safesurf.com/
   - Surfwatch, http://www.surfwatch.com/

   Other resources you may wish to consult include

   - Bess, the Internet Retriever, http://bess.net/
   - Positive Parenting Online
   - Ethics of student drivers on the Information Infobahn

4. **Monitor your credit card bill.** Many adult Internet sites require credit cards in order to gain access. If your credit card is used, you should have a record of it.

5. **Inquire into child accounts.** Some online services have special accounts especially geared for children, with restricted access to chat rooms and the Internet.

6. **Tell your child not to play with strangers.** The Internet version of this means never tell a stranger personal information. Teach your child to never give out your address, your phone number, or any personal information.

   Some individuals desire to harm children. Others seek to gather market research, raising privacy concerns. These people entice children to their site with graphics and games. These sites can be packed with advertisements. They may reward children for providing personal information, their likes and dislikes, and information concerning their friends. They may e-mail your child with more advertisements, request more information, and request that they return to their advertisement laden sites.

   Some services set up user profiles when setting up accounts. This information can be accessed by the public through commands such as **WHOIS.** Be careful when setting up accounts that the information provided will not be publicly available.

7. **Introduce new friends to mom and dad** *first.* If your child has made an online friend and would like to get to know that person

better, ask your child to introduce the friend to you first. Many quality relationships can be formed in this new environment if the proper precautions are taken.

8. **Use a Nickname.** When entering chat rooms, bulletin boards and other public rooms, encourage your child to pick out and use a favorite nickname distinct from their real name. This is a regular practice on the IRC and permits a nice level of anonymity, allowing users to learn more about each other only when and if they and their parents are ready. Remember that others will be less than honest about their identity as well.

9. **Big Brother Is Watching.** Everywhere you go on the Internet, you leave information about yourself. When a user posts to USENET, IRC Chat Rooms, or Listservers, the user reveals his or her e-mail address, creating a way for people to contact the user. In addition, different Websites collect information known as "cookies." This is personal information related to your Internet Account including your name, your address, your phone number, and even, if set up incorrectly, your credit card number. Be careful where you leave your information. Ask your Internet Service Provider how to turn your "cookies" off. Also look for the "E-Trust" symbol. This is a voluntary standard set up by the Electronic Frontier Foundation whereby Web pages agree that they will not collect information about you when you visit their site.

10. **Report suspicious activity.** Some conduct is illegal in both the real and the virtual world. If someone is stalking or harassing your child, keep copies and records of the messages and let the authorities know. You may also wish to notify the systems administrator of both your service and the service from which the message was transmitted. The *Department of Justice* has a special unit set up to specifically address computer and Internet crimes.

The Internet is a wonderful new opportunity for children. As with everything, the quality of a child's experience will be directly related to a parent's investment in that experience. If you take the time, you can make that experience positive and productive.

EXPLORING THE READING

1. The audience for this FAQ is clearly the parent who knows nothing about computers. Do you think this FAQ provides enough information for parents who are new to computing? Could you understand the terms and suggestions? What other terms could Robert Cannon define to make the site more helpful?

2. Freewrite for ten minutes on what you would tell your child before he or she logged online.

3. In a small group, think of at least five additional suggestions for increasing children's safety online.

4. Have members of the class had experience with filtering software? Alternatively, explore some of the filtering software programs mentioned in the FAQ. Share your knowledge with the class.

WRITING SUGGESTIONS

1. Interview three people who are Internet-savvy about their attitudes toward freedom of speech on the Internet and three who have not experienced the Internet. Write an essay based upon what you learn.

2. Should Congress make another attempt to regulate speech and images on the Internet? Write an argument presenting your viewpoint, while acknowledging the opposing viewpoint.

3. Interview a journalist about the issues that L. Paul Husselbee raises— that credit and other personal information is easily available on the Internet. Does your journalist agree with Husselbee or not? Write an essay based on the interview, referring to Husselbee's text if appropriate.

4. What do you think about the idea of independence for cyberspace? Argue a position, referring, if you wish, to the texts in this chapter.

5. Investigate the filtering software mentioned in "A Parent's Guide to Supervising a Child's Online Experience" and/or others you locate. Examine the Websites for these programs and find articles about filtering software. Write a guide for parents about filtering software programs.

THE WRITING PROCESS: SIGNALING THE READER— WAYS TO ACHIEVE UNITY AND COHERENCE

As we read, we try to make meaning from what we are reading, continually asking ourselves questions like, "How is this connected to that?" "What's the point of this?" and "What does the author mean by that?" Good writing helps us answer those questions by including clues in each paragraph to help us connect that paragraph to the overall meaning of the essay. The best writers also include hints to show us how sentences within and between paragraphs are connected to each other.

Topic Sentences. The clues that writers include to indicate a paragraph's connection to the rest of the essay are usually found in *topic sentences.* In about 75 percent of English paragraphs, the topic sentence is the first sentence in the paragraph. That does not mean it is *never* located at other places in the paragraph. It does mean that readers are accustomed to finding topic sentences early in paragraphs. If you choose to delay the topic sentence, you should do so consciously and with good reason. Essays written in journalistic style with short paragraphs may not include any topic sentences. For academic writing, however, having topic sentences is a good idea. They act as a map for the essay, signaling the reader that a change is about to occur, that a new proof or argument is being presented, or that we have moved around in time or space. They also serve to help the writer organize his thoughts. If you begin a paragraph with a clearly stated topic sentence, you'll be more likely to notice if you stray from your original intent or if you include a detail or example that isn't relevant to your discussion.

Notice how the first sentence organizes all the information that follows it in the paragraph from "Are These Books or What?" by Sarah Lyall:

> Electronic Publishing is making a serious impact on children's books. "What is clear is that children are much more comfortable with technology," said Randy Benton, who recently set up Random House's new media division. The company recently embarked on a joint venture with Broderbund Software, an interactive children's software company, to start Living Books, which provide lively sounds, elaborate graphics, and hundreds of things to play with in such stories as Aesop's fable "The Tortoise and the Hare" and Mercer Mayer's "Just Grandma and Me." Such books—which have sold tens of thousands of copies already—are somewhere between computer games and hypertext fiction, a new computer-based format that turns traditional beginning-to-end narrative on its head by affording the reader the thoroughly post-modern opportunity to skip from place to place in the text, creating his own story and arriving at his own ending.

Unity. Each sentence in your paragraph should somehow work to illustrate, illuminate, or further develop the topic sentence. The reader expects that a paragraph will stay focused on the main topic and will not stray too far from the subject. When you are freewriting or writing a very formal document, like a letter to a close friend, you might switch ideas in the middle of a paragraph. However, most readers would become confused in the middle of this paragraph, if I began to talk about transitions or outlines. The reader has learned to watch for the signals in the topic sentence and to look to each paragraph to discuss one topic, not several. *Unity* means that the paragraph will introduce a topic in the first sentence and stay with the topic until the next indentation.

Coherence.   *Cohesion* means that things hang together. Within and between paragraphs, you need to provide some glue to make your ideas work together. This can be difficult. We are so aware of the connections between our ideas that we forget to share them with our reader. Sometimes our ideas don't seem cohesive because we have left out the signals that can help the reader see the connections between our ideas. You can employ a few of the methods that writers in this text have used to improve the cohesion of their paragraphs.

1. You can repeat certain *key words* that are central to your idea throughout your paragraph to remind your reader of your topic. Marvin Minsky repeats the words "self" and "compute' throughout this paragraph from "Why People Think Computers Can't" to highlight the biggest hindrances to human acceptance of computer thought.

    > How does this idea of *self* lead people to believe that machines can never think? I believe it happens this way. When I tell something to a computer, it computes something. In order to understand what I tell it, the computer must compute a meaning. Then in order to understand

the meaning, the computer must transmit it to something like a self. But since I am dealing with a computer, it cannot have a self anything like mine; it can only compute. So, at best, a computer can only simulate a self. To do that, it must compute something, and so forth. In other words, for a machine to think, it would need a self, which would need another self, and so on. The infinite series of selves each pass on the job of real understanding to the next.

2. If it seems too redundant to repeat your key words over and over again, you can use *pronouns* to replace words central to your ideas. In the following passage from "Declaration of the Independence of Cyberspace" by John Perry Barlow, he addresses the government directly as "you," repeating the pronoun instead of "government."

> Governments derive their powers from the consent of the governed. You have neither solicited nor received ours. We did not invite you. You do not know us, nor do you know our world. Cyberspace does not lie within your borders. Do not think that you can build on it, as though it were a public construction project. You cannot. It is an act of nature and it grows itself through our collective actions.

3. You can repeat a *sentence structure* several times throughout a paragraph to help a reader see the connections. The repetition of the subordinate sentence structure, beginning with "because," helps build coherence in the essay "Respecting Privacy" by L. Paul Husselbee.

> Why is this a concern? Because every time a person makes a credit card purchase, the specifics of that transaction are recorded in a database somewhere. They may be copied or sold to other databases, and perused at a later date by people in information and surveillance industries—journalists, credit investigators, private detectives, and so forth. Because when people make business trips or go on vacation, the particulars of their airline and hotel reservations and vehicle rentals, along with any personal identification they provide to guarantee payment, are entered into a vast electronic dossier. Because even the titles of the videos people rent are recorded in someone's computer. Because advances in technology over the past two decades have given journalists—and anyone else who knows how to gain access—the power to peek into an individual's personal affairs without that person's knowledge or consent.

4. Finally, you can use *transitions* to indicate relationship between your sentences and to show temporal, spatial, or logical shifts. Effective transitions can help you write unified and coherent paragraphs. They join one point to the next by showing the relationship between two connected thoughts. They show the relationships between items you are comparing. They indicate shifts in time or space. They show the logical connections of cause and effect or help you clarify your point by introducing an example.

Transitions are the signposts on the map you have given your reader with your thesis statement and topic sentences. They remind the reader where you have been and tell the reader where you are going. Within a paragraph they help a reader navigate from point to point and help you reveal those connections between ideas that will make your essay clear for the reader. Between paragraphs, they remind the reader of your thesis statement by showing how the new paragraph relates to previous paragraphs and to your overall essay.

Here are a few transitional words that can be used to show:

a change in time (*first, next, after, then, now, afterward*)
a spatial relationship (*close to, near, at a distance, away, there, beyond, beside, above, outside, next to*)
compare and contrast (*like, as, similarly, unlike, rather than, conversely, instead, on the contrary, but*)
add or emphasize (*equally important, likewise, in addition, also, too, besides, moreover, another, not only . . . but also . . .*)

Note how John Gel, in this paragraph from "Diary of a Telecommuter," uses the spatial transitions "upstairs" and "down-stairs" to give a sense of how his work station fits into the layout of the house.

> We switch papers and she goes downstairs to make some breakfast. Before joining her, I check my e-mail, then I go downstairs. After breakfast, my wife leaves to go to work, and I repair to my office upstairs to make and receive phone calls and answer mail and work on *Educom Review.*

In the essay "Virtual Encounters," Thomas Barrett and Carol Wallace use transitions to indicate temporal relationships.

> From this first stage, we may progress to exchanging facts about ourselves, other people, and topics of general interest. This is a relatively non-threatening form of encounter because it reveals little about our inner selves other than the extent of our knowledge and tastes.
>
> At this stage we gossip about mutual friends, give out our favorite recipes, and discuss our cares, homes, jobs, and so on. We are trading information until we hit on topics that may reveal common interests. If we fail to discover any commonality, we have risked nothing. If we find some mutual interest, we may form a friendly relationship that can lead to the next, slightly more risky level of communication.
>
> In the beginning of a relationship, we often find ourselves reluctant to share our opinions. As we grow more comfortable with another person, we test the waters. We may venture a negative remark about a film we saw, but until trust has been established, we are likely to back-pedal if the other person disagrees. "Well, anyway, the cinematography was nice, and I really liked the costumes" may restore the harmony that our divided opinions appear to be upsetting.

ACCESSING INTERNET RESOURCES: USING LISTSERVS

Listservs are Internet discussion groups that you can subscribe to through e-mail, and postings come to your mailbox. Groups can focus on almost any topic imaginable. After reading this chapter, for example, you might be interested in subscribing to a group having to do with intellectual freedom or privacy issues.

You can locate discussion groups on particular topics by sending a message to listserv@listserv.net. To get a list of groups about a particular topic, you can send this message to the automated Listserv:

list global (key words)

If, for example, you want to know the names of groups corresponding about freedom of information, you could send this message:

list global freedom

You would then receive in your mailbox a list of groups with the word freedom in their descriptions. The list would look like this:

```
*                       SUBSCRIBE listname                            *
*                                                                     *
* Replace 'listname' with the name in the first column of the table.  *
*********************************************************************

Network-wide ID   Full address and list description
---------------   --------------------------------
DFC_TALK          DFC_TALK@HOME.EASE.LSOFT.COM
                  Democratic Freedom Caucus Discussion List

FFAF-L            FFAF-L@WVNVM.WVNET.EDU
                  Faculty For Academic Freedom (FFAF)

FOI-L             FOI-L@LISTSERV.SYR.EDU
                  State and Local Freedom of Information Issues

FOIPA-L           FOIPA-L@VM1.HQADMIN.DOE.GOV
                  DOE Freedom of Information Act & Privacy Act
```

You might be interested in the FOI-L group which focuses on state and local freedom of information issues. If you want to subscribe, send this message to the listserv address, Listserv@LISTSERV.SYR.EDU:

subscribe FOI-L

Listserv commands are case insensitive, which means that you can type subscribe or SUBSCRIBE and the automated response program will understand your command. Shortly you will receive a confirmation message from the group telling you that you have been subscribed. Be sure to keep this message because it tells you how to post messages to the group and also how to unsubscribe. It is a good idea to "lurk" or observe a group for a week or two before you post a message, so that you have an idea of the kind of topics and tone of message that are appropriate for that group.

When you decide you are ready to enter a conversation like the one above and contribute your opinion, you can post a message. Begin by composing your e-mail message, being sure to include a subject line about your topic, and send it to the list address which is the name of the group plus the Listserv address. For FOI-L, for example, you would send your e-mail message to FOI-L@LISTSERV.SYR.EDU.

You can then wait to see what response the group makes to your comment.

Suggested Internet Assignments

1. Choose a topic related to class discussion about the Internet and find a Listserv that focuses on that topic using the procedure described in the Accessing Internet Resources section. Lurk on the group for a week or more and then write a brief synopsis of what you have observed.

2. Explore links from the Electronic Frontier Foundation, http://www.eff.org, to other organizations that advocate freedom of speech on the Internet. Report on one of these organizations to the class.

3. Explore links from the Library of Congress to copyright-related sites. Determine what are the major points of controversy regarding copyright protection on the Internet.

4. Find a site belonging to a group holding views you do not agree with, such as an extreme religious, White Supremacists, or Ku Klux Klan group. Some of these sites will have views or language that you may find offensive. In class discuss whether such sites should be protected under the First Amendment.

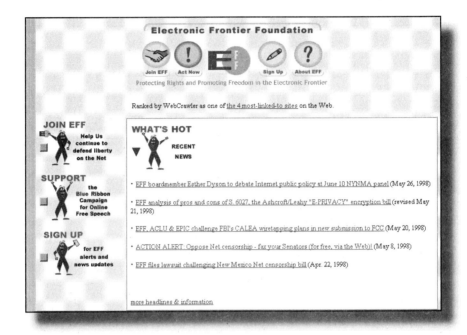

WIRED TO THE WEB

Electronic Frontier Foundation
http://www.eff.org

Perhaps the premier organization on the Web advocating the protection of free speech and individual privacy on the Internet, the Electronic Frontier Foundation was founded by Mitchell Kapor and John Perry Barlow, who both have texts in this chapter. The EFF maintains an archive of documents related to their mission.

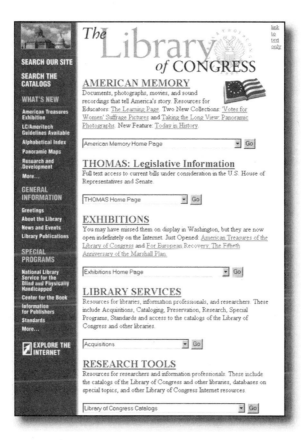

Library of Congress
http://www.loc.gov

Through the Library of Congress you can obtain full text of pending legislation, including any related to freedom of speech and privacy issues. You can also use the links to Internet resources selected by the LOC librarians, exploring, for example, their *Guide to Law Online*.

5

THE DEATH OF PRINT LITERACY, BIRTH OF CYBERLITERACY?

What is a book? Is it a collection of pages, printed on both sides and bound together, suitable for placing on a shelf? A grouping of ideas by one author, unchangeable once published and destined to outlive their creator? This may be the model for a book today, but it was not always the case. Books were hand written on papyrus scrolls for thousands of years before printing and binding were invented. Early books, even those such as the *Illiad* and the *Odyssey*, attributed to a blind poet, Homer, may actually have been written by many anonymous authors over centuries.

Today, in what Jay David Bolter and others call the *late age of print*, we have come to expect that a book looks like a book, or at least what books have looked like for a couple of hundred years—linear, written to be read from beginning to end; finite and permanent, and linked to the identity of an author. Books published electronically may not fit these criteria. They may be written in hypertext, intended to be read by clicking on hot links, rather than from point A to point Z. They may be changeable, with revisions entered at will, even with readers participating in the writing process. They may not be labeled as the work of one author, but rather be a mosaic of contributions by many, often anonymous, authors.

The consequences of computers, rather than print books, becoming the primary vehicle of literacy will, according to Bolter in "The Late Age of Print," expand the flexibility of the writing process, with a lessening of the gap between readers and writers. Today, anyone with an Internet account and a little knowledge of HTML can publish on the World Wide Web. Cyberliteracy may also

CHAPTER 5 ■ THE DEATH OF PRINT LITERACY, BIRTH OF CYBERLITERACY?

278

change the definitions of writing excellence. Much, if not most, of what is being published on the Internet has little literary value, as Philip Elmer-Dewitt notes in "Bards of the Internet: If E-mail Represents the Renaissance of Prose, Why Is So Much of It Awful?" Elmer-Dewitt does acknowledge, however, that there are gems of literature being created in the general chaos of the Internet.

Are you comfortable with books on a computer screen, if you can call them books? Perhaps not. Can you stop their takeover as the primary vehicles of literacy? Probably not, no more than anyone could have stopped the changes resulting from the printing press, once it was invented.

Some will, like Robert J. Samuelson in "Requiem for the Typewriter," mourn what is being lost. Samuelson suggests, perhaps validly, that word-processed writing is not necessarily better than text retyped laboriously on a typewriter, allowing for thoughtful revision. Others, like Todd Oppenheimer, in "The Computer Delusion," question whether the millions being spent on computers in public schools at the expense of cutting music, shop, and other programs is warranted.

Read, in this **book,** what these and other authors have to say about the future of books and education, but also go online and read from some of the sites mentioned at the end of the chapter. Experience what it is like, with the current technology, to read part of a book online. Develop an opinion about the state of printing and publishing in this "late age of print" and what you imagine the future will be like. You are living in a transition period in which you are expected to move with reasonable ease back and forth between printed text, word processing, yellow legal pads, and the Internet. You are reading in a book about the end of books, a curious paradox.

———————————— ■ ————————————

THE LATE AGE OF PRINT

by Jay David Bolter

Not far in the future, books will be published primarily electronically, not in printed form, says Jay David Bolter in this excerpt from his book Writing Space: The Computer, Hypertext, and the History of Writing. *People may still take novels to bed, but the books will be read on small computer screens. Literacy will not decrease, but literacy will change. Electronic publication will emphasize the fluid changeability of text and will reduce the distinction between authors and readers.*

Bolter, who also wrote an essay in Chapter 3, is Professor of Language, Communication, and Culture at the Georgia Institute of Technology and author of Turing's Man, *another acclaimed book about computers. You can reach his home page through Georgia Tech's School of Literature, Communication, and Culture at http://www.gatech.edu.*

Opening the window of his cell, he pointed to the immense church of Notre Dame, which, with its twin towers, stone walls, and monstrous cupola forming a black silhouette against the starry sky, resembled an enormous two-headed sphinx seated in the middle of the city.

The archdeacon pondered the giant edifice for a few moments in silence, then with a sigh he stretched his right hand toward the printed book that lay open on his table and his left hand toward Notre Dame and turned a sad eye from the book to the church.

"Alas!" he said, "This will destroy that." (Hugo, *Notre-Dame de Paris*, 1482, 1967, p. 197)

In Victor Hugo's novel *Notre-Dame de Paris*, 1482, the priest remarked "Ceci tuera cela": this book will destroy that building. He meant not only that printing and literacy would undermine the authority of the church but also that "human thought . . . would change its mode of expression, that the principal idea of each generation would no longer write itself with the same material and in the same way, that the book of stone, so solid and durable, would give place to the book made of paper, yet more solid and durable" (p. 199). The medieval cathedral crowded with statues and stained glass was both a symbol of Christian authority and a repository of medieval knowledge (moral knowledge about the world and the human condition). The cathedral was a library to be read by the religious, who walked through its aisles looking up at the scenes of the Bible, the images of saints, allegorical figures of virtue and vice, visions of heaven and hell. (See *The Art of Memory* by Frances Yates, 1966, p. 124.) Of course, the printed book did not eradicate the encyclopedia in stone; it did not even eradicate the medieval art of writing by hand. People continued to contemplate their religious tradition in cathedrals, and they continued to communicate with pen and paper for many purposes. But printing did displace handwriting: the printed book

CHAPTER 5 ■ THE DEATH OF PRINT LITERACY, BIRTH OF CYBERLITERACY?

280

became the most highly valued form of writing. And printing certainly helped to displace the medieval organization and expression of knowledge. As Elizabeth Eisenstein has shown, the printing press has been perhaps the most important tool of the modern scientist. (See *The Printing Press as an Agent of Change* by Elizabeth Eisenstein, 1979, especially vol. 2, pp. 520ff.)

Hugo himself lived in the heyday of printing, when the technology had just developed to allow mass publication of novels, newspapers, and journals. Hugo's own popularity in France (like Dickens' in England) was evidence that printed books were reaching and defining a new mass audience. Today we are living in the late age of print. The evidence of senescence, if not senility, is all around us. And as we look up from our computer keyboard to the books on our shelves, we must ask ourselves whether "this will destroy that." Computer technology (in the form of word processing, databases, electronic bulletin boards and mail) is beginning to displace the printed book. Until recently it was possible to believe that the computer could coexist with the printed book. Computers were for scientific analysis and business data processing. Pragmatic writing (business letters, technical reports, and stock prices) could migrate to the computer, but texts of lasting value—literature, history, scholarship—would remain in printed form. Now, however, this distinction between lasting texts and pragmatic communication is breaking down. Computers are being used for all kinds of writing, not just office memos and stock quotations. We shall see that the computer has even fostered a new genre of literature, one that can only be read at the computer screen. Major book publishers in the United States already translate their texts into computer-readable form for photocomposition; books pass through the computer on the way to the press. Many, perhaps most, of these texts will someday cease to be printed and will instead be distributed in electronic form.

The printed book, therefore, seems destined to move to the margin of our literate culture. The issue is not whether print technology will completely disappear; books may long continue to be printed for certain kinds of texts and for luxury consumption. But the idea and the ideal of the book will change: print will no longer define the organization and presentation of knowledge, as it has for the past five centuries. This shift from print to the computer does not mean the end of literacy. What will be lost is not literacy itself, but the literacy of print, for electronic technology offers us a new kind of book and new ways to write and read. The shift to the computer will make writing more flexible, but it will also threaten the definitions of good writing and careful reading that have been fostered by the technique of printing. The printing press encouraged us to think of a written text as an unchanging artifact, a monument to its author and its age. Hugo claimed that a printed book is more solid and durable than a stone cathedral; no one would make that claim, even metaphorically, for a computer diskette. Printing also tended to magnify the distance between the author and the reader, as the author became a monumental figure, the reader only a visitor in the author's cathedral. Electronic writing emphasizes the impermanence and changeability of text, and it tends to reduce the distance between author and reader by turning the reader into an author. The computer is restructuring our current economy of writing. It is changing the cultural status of writing as well as the method of producing books. It is changing the relationship of the author to the text and of both author and text to the reader.

REWRITING THE BOOK

As early as the 1450s and 1460s, Gutenberg and his colleagues were able to achieve the mass production of books without sacrificing quality. Gutenberg's great book, the 42-line Bible, does not seem to us today to have been a radical experiment in a new technology. It is not poorly executed or uncertain in form. The earliest incunabula are already examples of a perfected technique; there remains little evidence from the period of experimentation that must have preceded the production of these books. Indeed, Gutenberg's Bible can hardly be distinguished from the work of a good scribe, except perhaps that the spacing and hyphenation are more regular than a scribe could achieve. The early printers tried to make their books identical to fine manuscripts: they used the same thick letter forms, the same ligatures and abbreviations, the same layout on the page. It took a few generations for printers to realize that their new technology made possible a different writing space, that the page could be more readable with thinner letters, fewer abbreviations, and less ink.

Today we find ourselves in a similar interim with the electronic book. We have begun by using word processors and electronic photocomposition to improve the production of printed books and typed documents. Yet it is already becoming clear that the computer provides a new writing surface that needs conventions different from those of the printed page. In fact, the page itself is not a meaningful unit of electronic writing. The electronic book must instead have a shape appropriate to the computer's capacity to structure and present text. Writers are in the process of discovering that shape, and the process may take decades, as it did with Gutenberg's invention. The task is nothing less than the remaking of the book.

Electronic technology remakes the book in two senses. It gives us a new kind of book by changing the surface on which we write and the rhythms with which we read. It also adds to our historical understanding of the book by providing us with a new form that we can compare to printed books, manuscripts, and earlier forms of writing. Electronic writing turns out to be both radical and traditional. It is mechanical and precise like printing, organic and evolutionary like handwriting, visually eclectic like hieroglyphics and picture writing. On the other hand, electronic writing is fluid and dynamic to a greater degree than any previous technique. The coming of the new electronic book helps us to understand the choices, the specializations, that the printed book entails. We see that, like the specializations on outer branches of an evolutionary tree, the printed book is an extreme form of writing, not the norm.

CHAPTER 5 ■ THE DEATH OF PRINT LITERACY, BIRTH OF CYBERLITERACY?

282

THE USES OF ELECTRONIC WRITING

Those who tell us that the computer will never replace the printed book point to the physical advantages: the printed book is portable, inexpensive, and easy to read, whereas the computer is hard to carry and expensive and needs a source of electricity. The computer screen is not as comfortable a reading surface as the page; reading for long periods promotes eyestrain. Finally—and this point is always included—you cannot read your computer screen in bed. But electronic technology continues to evolve: machines have diminished dramatically in size and in price during the past forty years, and computer screens are becoming much more readable. It is not hard to imagine a portable computer with the bulk and weight of a large notebook and whose screen is as legible as a printed page. We can also envision an electronic writing system built into the top of a desk or lectern (like those used in the Middle Ages and the Renaissance), where the writer can work directly by applying a light pen instead of typing at a keyboard.

In any case, ease of use is only one measure of a writing technology. The great advantage of the first printed books was *not* that you could read them in bed. Gutenberg might well have been appalled at the thought of someone taking his beautiful folio-sized Bible to bed. For generations, most important printed books remained imposing volumes that had to be read on book-stands, so that people often read (and wrote) standing up. Mass production by printing did eventually make books cheaper and more plentiful, and this change was important. However, the fixity and permanence that printing gave to the written word were just as important in changing the nature of literacy. The book in whatever form is an intellectual tool rather than a means of relaxation. If the tool is powerful, writers and readers will put up with inconveniences to use it. In any technique of writing, structure matters more than appearance or convenience, and the electronic book, whether it is embodied in today's boxy microcomputer or in a slim electronic notebook of the future, gives text a new structure. In place of the static pages of the printed book, the electronic book maintains text as a fluid network of verbal elements.

Writers are only beginning to exploit the possibilities of this new structure; electronic writing in general is still in its infancy. The electronic incunabula include computer-controlled photocomposition, the word processor, the textual database, the electronic bulletin board and mail. As already mentioned, electronic texts are by no means rare: most of what we read today has passed through the computer on its way to our hands. In the United States it is common to produce newspapers, magazines, and printed books by means of electronic photocomposition. The texts are typed into the computer, revised and arranged by editors and typographers, and then output as camera-ready copy, photographic sheets or plates that the printer can use in his presses. However, computer-controlled photocomposition does not teach us how to write electronically. Publishers are simply using the computer to enhance the older technology, to make printing faster and less expensive.

The same is true of word processing. Word processors do demonstrate the flexibility of electronic writing in allowing writers to copy, compare, and discard text with the touch of a few buttons. Words in the computer are ultimately embodied in the collective behavior of billions of electrons, which fly around in the machine at unimaginable speeds. Change is the rule in the computer, stability the exception, and it is the rule of change that makes the word processor so useful. (See Mullins, 1988.) On the other hand, the word processor has been enthusiastically accepted by so many writers precisely because it does not finally challenge their conventional notion of writing. The word processor is an aid for making perfect printed or typed copy: the goal is still ink on paper. Like programs for photocomposition, the word processor is not so much a tool for writing, as it is a tool for typography. With a sophisticated word processor and a laser printer, users can create their own camera-ready copy. The program allows small organizations and even individuals to bypass the publishing industry. This change is important, but it is not a revolution in writing. (On the interplay between fluidity and fixity in word processing, see Balestri, 1988.)

The word processor treats text like a scroll, a roll of pages sewn together at the ends, and its visual structures are still typographic. A word processor stores its text as a simple sequence of letters, words, and lines. It remembers margins and pagination; it may remember which letters are to be printed in boldface, in Times Roman, or in 14-point type. But a conventional word processor does not treat the text as a network of verbal ideas. It does not contain a map of the ways in which the text may be read. It does not record or act on the semantic structure of the text. A true electronic text does all this, for a true electronic text is not a fixed sequence of letters, but is instead from the writer's point of view a network of verbal elements and from the reader's point of view a texture of possible readings.

An electronic text permits the reader to share in the dynamic process of writing. The text is realized by the reader in the act of reading. Electronic reading is already a feature of many current computerized texts. There are, for example, databases containing Supreme Court decisions for lawyers, newspaper articles for journalists, and even Greek or Shakespearean tragedies for scholars. Each such database constitutes a potential text of vast proportion and complexity: it offers millions of combinations of articles or passages that some reader might at some time request. No one reader examines every entry in such a database; instead the reader searches for appropriate phrases and retrieves only those passages that satisfy the search. The reader calls forth his or her own text out of the network, and each such text belongs to one reader and one particular act of reading.

The same principle of reader participation is embodied in computer-assisted instruction, commonly used in business and schools. Computer-assisted instruction is sometimes effective, often not, but in all cases it requires the dynamic reading of a multiply organized text. The computer presents the student with a question or problem. The student responds, and, based on that response, the computer may present another question, give the

CHAPTER 5 ■ THE DEATH OF PRINT LITERACY, BIRTH OF CYBERLITERACY?

284

student a message, or take the student back to review material that he or she does not seem to understand. The teacher who wrote the program must anticipate and provide for a wide variety of responses from the student. The teacher is the writer whose text the machine juggles and displays to the student. The student also becomes a writer as he or she coaxes answers from the machine. The whole lesson is a composite of the two texts, one by the teacher and one by the student. Meanwhile, electronic bulletin boards take the principle of multiple authorship even further, allowing hundreds of participants from distant locations to exchange texts and questions. Each participant moves quickly and repeatedly between the roles of reader and writer.

All of these programs suggest what the computer can do as a technology of reading and writing. And yet they are all attempts to transfer previous techniques of writing into an electronic idiom. The word processor makes the computer into an electronic typewriter. A textual database makes it a file cabinet filled with copies of printed records. Computer-assisted instruction with its steady rhythm of question and answer is modeled on the exercises included in printed textbooks. And electronic bulletin boards are just what the name implies: a place for posting typed or written messages. But if we combine the dynamic writing of the word processor with the dynamic reading of the bulletin board or textual database and add the interactivity of computer-assisted instruction, then we do have a textual medium of a new order. This new medium is the fourth great technique of writing that will take its place beside the ancient papyrus roll, the medieval codex, and the printed book.

THE NEW VOICE OF THE BOOK

Writing in the classical and Western traditions is supposed to have a voice and therefore to speak to its reader. A printed book generally speaks with a single voice and assumes a consistent character, a persona, before its audience. A printed book in today's economy of writing must do more: it must speak to an economically viable or culturally important group of readers. Printing has helped to define and empower new groups of readers, particularly in the nineteenth and twentieth centuries: for example, the middle-class audience for the nineteenth-century British novel. But this achievement is also a limitation. An author must either write for one of the existing groups or seek to forge a new one, and the task of forging a new readership requires great talent and good luck. And even a new readership, brought together by shared interests in the author's message, must be addressed with consistency. No publisher would accept a book that combined two vastly different subject matters: say, European history and the marine biology of the Pacific, or Eskimo folklore and the principles of actuarial science. It would be hard to publish a book that was part fiction and part non-fiction—not a historical novel, a genre that is popular and has a well-defined audience, but, let us say, a combination of essays and short stories that treat the same historical events. We might say that these hypothetical books lack unity and should not be published. Yet our definition of textual unity comes from the published work we have read or more generally from the current divisions of academic, literary, and scientific disciplines, which themselves both depend on and reinforce the economics of publishing. The material in a book must be homogeneous by the standard of some book-buying audience.

This strict requirement of unity and homogeneity is relatively recent. In the Middle Ages, unrelated texts were often bound together, and texts were often added in the available space in a volume years or decades later. Even in the early centuries of printing, it was not unusual to put unrelated works between two covers. On the other hand, it is natural to think of any book, written or printed, as a verbal unit. For the book is a physical unit; its pages are sewn or glued together and then bound into a portable whole. Should not all the words inside proceed from one unifying idea and stand in the same rhetorical relationship to the reader?

Because an electronic text is not a physical artifact, there is no reason to give it the same conceptual unity as the printed book, no reason not to include disparate materials in one electronic network. The writer or editor need not envision and address only one homogeneous readership; an electronic book may speak with different voices to different readers (and each reader is a different reader each time he or she approaches a text). Thus, an electronic encyclopedia may address both the educated novice and the expert: its articles may be written on several levels of expertise to suit the needs and background of various readers. Our traditional canon of unity no longer applies to the electronic book, whose shadowy existence in electronic storage does not convey the same sense of physical unity. The text may reside on a diskette or in the computer's internal memory, where it cannot be seen or directly touched by the reader. If the user is calling up a remote database, then the text may be hundreds or thousands of miles away and arrive only in convenient pieces through the telephone wires.

An electronic book can tailor itself to each reader's needs. As the reader moves quickly or deliberately through the textual network, he or she seldom feels the inertia that pulls a reader through the pages of a printed book. A reader who consults the *New York Times* Information Service does not want to read every article in the database; the student in computer-assisted instruction does not need or want to read every response the computer has to offer for every possible wrong answer. The reader exercises choice at every moment in the act of reading. Electronic reading is therefore a special instance of what economists now call "market segmentation." In the classic industrial age, economies of scale required that products be homogeneous: each factory produced one or a few kinds of toothbrushes, soft drinks, or deodorants in vast quantities. In today's more automated and flexible factories, goods are tailored to segments of the buying public. Before the invention of photocomposition, the printing press was a classic industrial machine, producing large quantities of identical texts. Marshall McLuhan called printing the first example of the assembly line and mass production

CHAPTER 5 ■ THE DEATH OF PRINT LITERACY, BIRTH OF CYBERLITERACY?

286

(McLuhan, 1972, p. 124). Photocomposition and then the computer as photo-composer have already made printing more flexible, allowing publishers to target books to well-defined markets. However, a true electronic book goes further still, changing for each reader and with each reading.

The vanishing of the fixed text alters the nature of an audience's shared experience in reading. All the readers of *Bleak House* could talk about the novel on the assumption that they had all read the same words. No two readers of an electronic book can make that assumption; they can only assume that they have traveled in the same textual network. Fixed printed texts can be made into a literary canon and therefore promote cultural unity. In the nineteenth and early twentieth centuries, when the canon of literature was often taken as the definition of a liberal education, the goal was to give everyone the experience of reading the same texts—Shakespeare, Milton, Dickens, and so on. This ideal of cultural unity through a shared literary inheritance, which has received so many assaults in the twentieth century, must now further suffer by the introduction of a new form of highly individ-ualized writing and reading.

Critics accuse the computer of promoting homogeneity in our society, of producing uniformity through automation, but electronic reading and writing have just the opposite effect. The printing press was the great homogenizer of writing, whereas electronic technology makes texts par-ticular and individual. An electronic book is a fragmentary and potential text, a series of self-contained units rather than an organic, developing whole. But fragmentation does not imply mere disintegration. Elements in the electronic writing space are not simply chaotic; they are instead in a perpetual state of reorganization. They form patterns, constellations, which are in constant danger of breaking down and combining into new patterns. This tension leads to a new definition of unity in writing, one that may replace or sup-plement our traditional notions of the unity of voice and of analytic argument. The unity or coherence of an electronic text derives from the per-petually shifting relationship among all its verbal elements.

EXPLORING THE READING

1. In your small group make one list of the attributes of printed books, according to Jay David Bolter, and another of the characteristics of electronic texts. Then compare the two lists.

2. Bolter envisions the transition from printed books to electronic ones as being as influential as the change from hand-written, illuminated manuscripts to printed books. Would you agree or disagree?

3. Freewrite for five minutes about the future, as Bolter imagines it. Would you like a world in which printed books are luxury items and most texts are accessed electronically? Why or why not?

REQUIEM FOR THE TYPEWRITER

by Robert J. Samuelson

Use a typewriter today instead of a computer and you risk being called, at best, behind the times, and, at worst, technophobic. Robert Samuelson, writing his essay "Requiem for the Typewriter" on a Royal manual typewriter, reminds us that there are reasons to use a typewriter, primarily the constraints it forces on the revision process. He also suggests that the typewriter has a history that should be celebrated. In its day, the typewriter was as revolutionary as the computer is today. It transformed the way business was transacted and altered the role of women in society.

Samuelson, a former reporter for the Washington Post *and now a columnist for* Newsweek, *is the author of* The Good Life and Its Discontents: How the American Dream Became a Fantasy, 1945–1995. *Unsurprisingly, he does not have a Web page.*

It was once a great machine—and for me, it still is.

It was inevitable. Sooner or later, the last great name in American typewriters was bound to self-destruct, bringing to a formal conclusion something that had long ago ended. It happened last week with the bankruptcy of Smith Corona, which once produced manual portable typewriters that were hauled off to college and elsewhere by millions of Americans, including me. In the office next to mine sits a summer college intern busily tapping at his Macintosh PowerBook (nobody ever "bangs" at a laptop). That's what killed the typewriter.

Just for the record, this column is being written on an old Royal manual. In the combat between computers and typewriters, my loyalties lie with the losers. For writing, the typewriter still has advantages over a computer. Writing is the grinding process of discovering the right flow of words to convey a story, feeling, explanation or argument. Mistakes, false starts and revisions are not only inevitable. They are essential. You need them. A phrase that didn't fit at 10 in the morning may, by 3 in the afternoon, be exactly what you need.

The virtue of the typewriter is that it saves my blunders. I rip out my incoherent drafts and spread them across my desk, where I scavenge for serviceable phrases. The typewriter's other appeal is that it compels me to rewrite by making me retype. Every rewrite suggests some superior word or exposes some sloppy construction. No doubt, computers can deliver similar benefits. Drafts can be printed. But why bother? The typewriter is simpler. I am not utterly hostile to the computer. Once the main composing is complete, I punch my draft into an old IBM PC, which makes the final editing much easier.

By last week, of course, all these issues had been decisively settled against the typewriter. The quality of writing may not have advanced with the computer, but the ease of "processing" and printing words surely has. Gibberish

CHAPTER 5 ■ THE DEATH OF PRINT LITERACY, BIRTH OF CYBERLITERACY?

288

can quickly be made to look neat and impressive. Smith Corona's bankruptcy was merely a symbolic benchmark. The company may ultimately emerge from bankruptcy, and a few other typewriter makers survive. Still, the traditional typewriter is dead.

Its passing deserves notice. What is worth recalling is that, in its time, the typewriter was every bit as revolutionary as today's computer. It was a great feat of design and manufacturing that transformed work and women's role in society. As with most great inventions, its commercial birth was slow and hard. The first modern typewriter was built in 1867 by a Milwaukee inventor named Christopher Latham Sholes. It was also Sholes who devised today's universal keyboard (qwerty).

Early typewriters succeeded technically and failed financially. Production costs were too high. Output didn't soar until the late 1880s, after manufacturing rights had been sold to another company. Economic historian Donald Hoke says the typewriter was "the most complex mechanism mass produced by American industry" in the nineteenth century because (as one factory manager said) "its thousands of parts must work together with exquisite exactness, yet withstand hard usage."

Mark Twain was a pioneer, "It piles an awful stack of words on one page. It don't muss things or scatter ink blots around," he wrote to his brother in 1874. Twain submitted the first typewritten book manuscript to a publisher. He identified it as "Tom Sawyer" (1876), though some historians think he erred and the distinction belongs to "Life on the Mississippi" (1883). But the typewriter's largest impact was on women and the American office, which was until the late 19th century a male bastion.

Consider. In 1870, men constituted 98 percent of all clerical workers. Most took dictation, copied documents or ran errands. By 1920, half the clerical workers were women. The typewriter had created a demand for literate workers that could be easily filled only by women who—in the nineteenth century—outnumbered men among high-school graduates. Schools were established for typists, who numbered 615,000 by 1920. Although these jobs were later stigmatized as oppressing women, they were initially liberating. Until then, teaching had been the only job outlet for educated women. And typists' pay was attractive: in the 1890s, $6 to $15 a week compared with $1.50 to $8 for factory workers.

The typewriter is unappreciated because it has always been overshadowed by more imposing technologies. At the turn of the century, there was the telephone, electric light and automobile. Now there is the computer. I do feel guilty that I am not fully participating—wow, that's a wild understatement—in the great technology event of our time. The feeling fades, though, whenever *Newsweek's* computer system crashes or I hear someone complaining about the tedium of learning a new "word processing" program, whose purported advances have zip to do with writing.

Computers can, of course, provide vast amounts of information. Databases and documents can be downloaded; Websites can be accessed. (I'm flaunting my computer jargon here.) But getting information has never been my problem; the hard part is deciding what it means. Among computer enthusiasts, I have not detected any increase in knowledge or wisdom. Mainly, they seem to have more time to waste buzzing around cyberspace. At home, my wife and children have a more powerful machine than my original IBM PC, which is all I truly need. I keep waiting for something that will entice me to become a computer buff.

Until then, I'm sticking with my Royal. It won't give me e-mail. But I don't want e-mail. Nor will it play games when I ought to write. Good. Getting parts is a problem. My local repair shop recently closed. I've now found a new one about twenty miles away that, although it handles mostly electronic machines, will still fix manuals. The manager tells me on the phone that there aren't many manual customers left. Well, there's one more coming.

EXPLORING THE READING

1. Have you ever used a typewriter? If so, what is your opinion of writing on a typewriter as compared to writing on a computer?

2. In your small group consider *your* writing processes. Note what Robert J. Samuelson says about the virtues of the typewriter in the writing process. Do you think he has a point?

3. Are you an enthusiastic computer buff, or are you a bit like Samuelson, not sure the computer revolution is all it is hyped to be? Freewrite for five minutes about your position.

4. What would Samuelson think about Jay David Bolter's assertion that the momentum of the computer revolution is headed irrevocably toward the end of books as we know them?

CHAPTER 5 ■ THE DEATH OF PRINT LITERACY, BIRTH OF CYBERLITERACY?

290

ARE THESE BOOKS, OR WHAT? CD-ROM AND THE LITERARY INDUSTRY

by Sarah Lyall

Books have evolved from clay tablets and papyrus scrolls to hand-illuminated bound volumes to mass produced paperbacks. The most recent forms include CD-ROM books-on-disk and Web pages. But are books-on-disk and computer screens really books, asks Sarah Lyall in this essay from the New York Times Book Review. *You can't read them under a tree or in the bath, at least not easily. You can, however, download classics free from the Internet, and you can store enormous amounts of information and images as well as text.*

Lyall writes about British issues for the New York Times. *Recent articles included "New 'Ulysses' Edition Has Joyce Scholars Fuming" and "Awaiting 'Santa Claus' at Labor Headquarters."*

This spring, William H. Gates, the plugged-in chairman of the Microsoft Corporation and a man who lives for his computer, announced that he wanted to publish a definitive three-hundred-page discussion of his views on the information revolution—where it had been and where it was going. But when it came time to choose a format, Mr. Gates rejected the familiar tools of his trade: online services, floppy disks, CD-ROMs, all the hardware and all the software. He turned to a technology that has been around since the mid-fifteenth century. He decided to sell his book as a book.

You can't get more conventional. Books are cunning and resilient creatures. They have survived world wars and revolutions and totalitarian regimes and the waxing and waning of other media, including magazines, newspapers, radio, movies, videos, records, tapes, compact disks and television. Whenever their end was predicted, books managed to defy their own death sentences and spring back to life. Books have persevered so effectively, in fact, that in 1993 more of them were sold in the United States than in any year before, $18 billion worth.

But at no time since 1450, when Johann Gutenberg introduced books to the masses by fashioning the first printing press using movable type, has the book business been at such a confusing and potentially treacherous juncture. Publishers are still competing for a share of an increasingly distracted public's attention. But now they are also struggling over control of their own industry, and over the definition of what a book is. The competition is coming not from other forms of entertainment, but from computer and software companies that are experimenting with new formats: books on CD-ROM, books on floppy disk, books that can be read on a portable personal computer using a little card and some batteries, books that incorporate voices, music and movies, books that fly wholly or in parts through online services and arrive directly on screen.

For publishing executives from the old school, this translates into a heady time of trying to decide how much to embrace the new technology, or even (for some) whether to embrace it at all. They are scared, and they should be, considering the type of advice they're hearing from non-publishers like Gregory Rawlins, a computer science professor at Indiana University. "If you're not part of the steamroller," he told a group of university press publishers recently, "you're part of the road."

Predictions of the imminent death of serious publishing are old news. But they've gained more urgency in recent years, as more and more once-autonomous publishers find themselves tiny specks on the balance sheet of some huge entertainment conglomerate that also owns record companies, television stations, movie studios and sports teams. People are getting hired and fired; divisions are being bought, sold and folded; publishers are starting "new media" departments that combine books with other forms of media, and serious books seem to be selling fewer copies than ever, supplanted by one-shot celebrity biographies and sure-fire genre books. And into this volatile environment have entered companies that seek to question publishers' raisons d'être and the very notion of what defines a book. Is a book, they ask, a collection of words fashioned into a poem or a narrative or a play printed on paper, bound with a cover, opened and closed at will and stored on a shelf with others of its kind, as has been done for five hundred years? Or is a book the ideas contained within, regardless of their format? Can you stack them up and put them in a CD rack? Can you put them on a tiny little credit card, insert the card in a portable computer and read them on a screen? Can you add music and video? "We only invest in the creation of one product here, the book," said Jack Romanos, the president of the consumer group at Simon & Schuster. "But the book's gone in five different directions."

What matters is content, Mr. Romanos said, something publishers have in spades. The question is how to put it to use. "In the past, you said, 'What sort of book, how many pages, what's the trim size, what's the market?'" said Nancy Dickinson, the director of advanced media at HarperCollins. "Now you say, 'How would this idea work if I could see video or hear sound? How would this make it more accessible and a richer experience for the customer?'"

For traditional publishers, so steeped in old habits that many editors still regularly edit manuscripts on paper (even when the author turns in a version on disk), evolving into something different looks to be a bumpy and confusing proposition. Though Ms. Dickinson's department has counterparts at every big book publisher in New York, new media divisions tend to consist of a small band of computer literates preaching to the company's uninitiated, resistant masses. Publishers are stubbornly holding on to electronic rights in case their books go electronic, and most large companies have already produced half a dozen or so general interest multimedia titles on CD-ROM or floppy disk. But they're not sure what the future will require.

One thing that does seem clear is that in the lucrative academic and reference markets, new media are quickly overtaking traditional books, and for

CHAPTER 5 ■ THE DEATH OF PRINT LITERACY, BIRTH OF CYBERLITERACY?

292

good reason. Consider the *Encyclopaedia Britannica*. The complete set costs more than $1,500, weighs 118 pounds and takes up more than four feet of shelf space. A commensurate encyclopedia on CD-ROM—Microsoft's *Encarta*, for instance—costs $99.99, holds up to 650 megabytes of data, weighs under an ounce, and could fit in your purse. And it's rich with extras. Look up Beethoven, for instance, and the text of the regular entry appears on your screen. Click your mouse and you can listen to a 30-second snippet from the "Ninth Symphony." Click again and you can learn how Wagner was influenced by Beethoven, and hear the results. Look up Edvard Munch, click your mouse and see a high-resolution version of "The Scream" appear on your screen.

It's the same with dictionaries. Looking up a word in, say, the *Oxford English Dictionary* requires hauling an unwieldy volume down from a shelf and then hauling another volume down, too, if the first definition piqued your interest in a new word somewhere else. For the condensed version of the dictionary, the only one most people can afford, you need a magnifying glass to read the type. But all the volumes can fit on a single CD-ROM, which can store up to 300,000 pages of text and do cross-referencing in a flash.

Donald Norman, who founded the department of cognitive science at the University of California, San Diego, and who now holds Apple Computer's highest research position, said: "Within ten years, dictionaries will essentially all be electronic. They will win because they offer ease of access and readability."

Books on floppy disk are useful for quick cross-referencing. And with its video and audio components, the CD-ROM also lends itself naturally to other reference works, books that teach you, for instance, how to adjust the brakes on your Trans Am, install a shelf in the basement, learn American Sign Language, plant a rosebush, truss a chicken, or search through thousands of choices to find a film to rent on Sunday night. Companies like Byron Preiss Multimedia, which began as a conventional book packager, are beginning to take traditional titles and make them reference works. A forthcoming CD-ROM based on John Steinbeck's *Grapes of Wrath* allows readers to see photographs that inspired Steinbeck, a map of the Joad family's route through Oklahoma and video interviews with people in Steinbeck's life. Somewhere in there lurks the novel's text, which seems almost beside the point next to the souped-up new features. But Byron Preiss himself insists that *The Grapes of Wrath* on CD-ROM will never supplant *The Grapes of Wrath*, the book. "It doesn't replace the experience of sitting in bed reading," he said. "It coexists, and it amplifies the book."

Electronic publishing is making a serious impact in children's books. "What is clear is that children are much more comfortable with technology," said Randi Benton, who recently set up Random House's new media division. The company recently embarked on a joint venture with Broderbund Software, an interactive children's software company, to start Living Books, which provide lively sounds, elaborate graphics and hundreds of things to play with in such stories as Aesop's fable *The Tortoise and the Hare* and Mercer Mayer's *Just Grandma and Me*. Such books—which have sold tens of thousands of copies already—are somewhere between computer games and hypertext fiction, a new computer-based format that turns traditional beginning-to-end narrative on its head by affording the reader the thoroughly post-modern opportunity to skip from place to place in the text, creating his own story and arriving at his own ending.

"I think the idea that this next generation is going to start at page 1 and go to page 284 and then close the book is wrong," said the president of Warner Books, Laurence J. Kirshbaum, who recently discovered the joys of an online world when he got himself hooked up to the Internet "This is a generation that has been raised on MTV and a multitude of stimuli. They don't think linearly; they think mosaically. And they're much more used to getting their information from talking and listening than from reading books."

It's easy to be seduced by the new products, but part of the trick for publishers these days is to avoid investing too much in technology that might burn out as completely as LP records. Richard Sarnoff, who heads the new media group of Bantam Doubleday Dell, said, "We have to decide what is likely to augment, and what is likely to cannibalize, our business." Big publishers have several ways to go. They can buy their own software companies. They can form copublishing partnerships, as Putnam did when it made a deal with Sony to publish H. R. Haldeman's diaries, Putnam in hard cover and Sony on CD-ROM. They can embark on joint ventures or buy stakes in multimedia companies.

But mixing multimedia publishers with traditional book publishers seems counterintuitive, like mixing milk with grapefruit juice. They speak different languages. They look at their products, and at the world, in different ways. Even the word "product," applied to books, would seem anathema to editors of the old school. This spring Jason Epstein, the editorial director of Random House's adult trade group, ventured into the offices of Voyager, a Manhattan software company, one morning to talk to his former assistant, 26-year-old Maryam Mohit. Ms. Mohit, one of a flotilla of young editors who have left traditional publishing houses to join new media companies, showed him one of her latest works, the CD-ROM version of Marvin Minsky's *Society of Mind*. Mr. Epstein looked at the video of a tiny Marvin Minsky gesticulating at a lectern, listened to Mr. Minsky's speech on the speakers, and then spotted a turgid sentence on the screen, where the text was printed out. That's what he focused on. "I would have edited that," he said.

"The mentality of a CD-ROM publisher is different from that of a book publisher," said Michael Lynton, until recently the senior vice president for publishing at the Walt Disney Company, whose publishing arm, Hyperion Books, is investing in new media projects. "People go into book publishing and bookselling because they want to be involved with words and books. They don't want to make money. If they do, they've made a serious mistake. The CD-ROM people, and the gaming community—those people are in love

CHAPTER 5 ■ THE DEATH OF PRINT LITERACY, BIRTH OF CYBERLITERACY?

294

with games, in love with computers and in love with making money. They have no problem talking about units."

Many publishing houses suffer from a generational divide in which their staffs can be split in two: the ones who grew up with computers and the ones who didn't. Traditional editors read *The New York Review of Books*, not *Wired* magazine; many even still use their old manual typewriters, edit by pencil, and feel unnerved by, even afraid of, computers.

At Penguin U.S.A., many editors are being gingerly exposed to new media by a 28-year-old vice president, Julie Hansen, who administers a lab where employees can drop in and play with a CD-ROM unit for the first time.

Voyager, which recently abandoned its headquarters in southern California for an enormous converted loft in Soho, has the atmosphere of a computer company: large open spaces broken up by partitions, chicly casual workers without official titles, a buzz of new ideas. In an interview about the future of books, the president, Bob Stein, was wearing a pair of baggy trousers and a T-shirt reading "Free All Political Prisoners." "Will books exist? I think that's the wrong question," Mr. Stein said. "Humans have tremendous capacity to find imaginative uses for old media, and books will be with us for generations. But the locus of important intellectual communication is going to shift away from books. The complexity of palate that authors have with these new media is going to draw them in."

Mr. Stein envisions a creative brain drain that will pull authors toward the new media. "One hundred years ago, if you were going to write stories the only choice would be plays or novels," he said. "Now, you're already thinking about the movies. And with CD-ROM's, you can create the intimate experience of a novel and the experience of video, audio and film."

Art Spiegelman is one author who has now worked in both media. Voyager recently put out the CD-ROM version of *Maus*, his critically acclaimed comic-book depiction of the Holocaust. It includes audio interviews with his father, who figured prominently in *Maus*; aerial photographs of concentration camps, and dozens of early sketches Mr. Spiegelman made when he put *Maus* together. "The least interesting thing about the ROM is the book itself, because it was conceived as a book," Mr. Spiegelman said. "But I don't see it as competitive with a book, any more than going to the theater is competitive or watching television is competitive. On some vague level it's a plea for attention, but the experience is a different one."

The new formats are likely to have a great effect an the production and distribution of books. For one thing, making a CD-ROM costs about 68 cents and can be done virtually instantaneously, while making a book costs between $2 and $3.50. For another, CD-ROM's are sold mostly in software stores, not traditional bookstores. They come in big, clunky boxes shrouded in glossy packaging, and they're arranged according to which machines they're compatible with—not according to subject. They're impossible to browse through, in the manner of a book, unless the store sets up a computer demonstration area. "The traditional book store is an extraordinary resource for the publisher because you get people on the staff who have a lot of product knowledge and can be incredibly helpful to the customer," Dan McNamee, a partner in a business called the Publishing and Media Group, said. "But they tend to be very uncomfortable with electronic products. On the other hand, software distributors are not used to providing support for highly varied product lines. And they can talk about technology, but they're not used to talking about content."

But some people envision a time when bookstores themselves might be obsolete. Why would you need to walk into a store, they say, when books come on little disks for your personal computer, or when they're made more widely available through places like the On-Line Bookstore, which is based in Massachusetts and sells books through the Internet? Although bookstore executives like Steve Riggio, the executive vice president of Barnes & Noble, say they envision their stores metamorphosing into information superstores, it's unclear how this will happen.

Despite the obvious advantages of electronic books, visions of a future world confined indoors—working, playing, communicating, reading and shopping via computer—have so far vastly outpaced the realities, particularly when it comes to books. Tens of millions of people have the capacity to read books on floppy disk, but they don't. And at this point, according to industry figures, only about five million households have CD-ROM attachments on their computers. The number is expected to increase to more than ten million by the end of the year; new models of old computers are sold almost exclusively now with CD-ROM attachments. But it will take a long time before everyone has the equipment.

Meanwhile, computer companies are scrambling to come up with a technology that mimics a book completely, that can put text on a screen as effectively as on paper, but none have succeeded yet. Devices like the Powerbook and the Sony Bookman still don't come close to matching the experience of a paper-and-print book while curled up in a chair, in bed, on the train, under a tree, in an airplane. "The machines have to be a lot better," said Jack Hoeft, the chief executive of Bantam Doubleday Dell. "As the technology improves, I expect that they will be, and then people who want to read a book on a computer reader can do it that way."

But probably they won't want to. Olafur Olafsson, the 32-year-old president of Sony Electronic Publishing, who also happens to be the best-selling novelist of all time in his native Iceland, says, "Novels on a computer screen don't do the job." Sitting in his upper-floor office with a picture-window view of Central Park, he plucked the Alfred A. Knopf translation of his latest novel, *Absolution*, from his desk. Under no circumstances, would he want to read it on a computer screen. "Maybe if you had something of this dimension and this weight and as easy to hold as this book," he said. "The screen would have to be easy to read, it wouldn't be able to suffer from heat and glare, and you could easily go back and forth from page to page. But I don't see that technology arriving any time soon." And after all, the modern book is the

CHAPTER 5 ■ THE DEATH OF PRINT LITERACY, BIRTH OF CYBERLITERACY?

296

result of centuries of trial and error during which people wrote on bark, on parchment, on vellum, on clay, on scrolls, on stone, chiseling characters into surfaces or copying them out by hand.

"The book has been with us for about five hundred years," said Donald Norman of Apple Computer, who recently published a book, *Things That Make Us Smart*, which argues that technology sometimes runs away with itself, dazzling and tyrannizing people instead of serving them by making life simpler. "People think it's unsophisticated technologically, but the book has evolved into an extremely convenient and sophisticated artifact. It uses modern paper, with good contrast and good quality print. The typefaces themselves have evolved over many years, the design and layout have evolved in esthetic quality and utility. And in many ways, the book is a good random access device that's extremely easy to scan through."

The novelist Nicholson Baker said: "We've come up with a beautifully browsable invention that needs no electricity and exists in a readable form no matter what happens. If the end of civilization comes and we lose electricity, we can hold a CD-ROM up to the light and it has totemic value, but we have no past."

There's more to it than that. In an instant culture, books represent our more ruminative, deliberate and thoughtful side, Earlier this year Bill Henderson, the editor of the Pushcart Press in Wainscott, New York, founded a group called the Lead Pencil Club. The idea came to him when he was reading Doris Grumbach's memoir *Extra Innings*, which describes her grumpy ill will toward all her electronic gadgets. The club is devoted to the superiority of non-technology. Its motto is "Not So Fast," and the book is one of its favorite devices.

"America's the only country that doesn't have a past," Mr. Henderson said. "We've become speed freaks, and things like faxes and e-mail contribute to our national amnesia. Books don't allow that to happen. You go to the library and you see the past out there and you can browse at leisure. And a book is personal—you can hold it in your hand, turn down its pages, write in the margins, carry it to the beach. It's a cliché, but you can. I don't think we're going to put up with the demise of the book."

And if Mr. Gates at Microsoft likes computers so much, you might ask, why did he decide to publish his forthcoming book the regular way? "The medium is appropriate," said Jonathan Lazarus, the vice president of systems strategy at Microsoft, who negotiated Mr. Gates's book project—for $2.5 million—with Penguin U.S.A. "There's a certain test of one's credibility and ideas when you have to put them in 300 pages of prose. We've grown up in a society where we learn a lot from books and where books are a well-understood way to get information. If I said to you, 'I'd like you to learn all about fly fishing,' you wouldn't be surprised if I said, 'Here's a book about fly fishing to read.'"

As Mr. Norman, whose book about the tyrannies of technology is about to come out in a new CD-ROM version, said, "If you really want to read my book, I'd recommend the paper version."

EXPLORING THE READING

1. Sarah Lyall asks whether a book is a collection of words printed on paper, or is it the ideas within, regardless of the format. What do you think? Why?

2. In your small group discuss your attitudes toward reading a book on a computer screen. How could computer screens be improved to make the reading experience more pleasant?

3. Freewrite for five minutes about the future of books. What will books be like in ten years?

4. What are the similarities and differences between what Lyall is saying about the future of books and what Jay David Bolter suggests?

CHAPTER 5 ■ THE DEATH OF PRINT LITERACY, BIRTH OF CYBERLITERACY?

298

BARDS OF THE INTERNET: IF E-MAIL REPRESENTS THE RENAISSANCE OF PROSE, WHY IS SO MUCH OF IT AWFUL?

by Philip Elmer-Dewitt

Despite the title of his Time *feature, the following text by Philip Elmer-Dewitt celebrates what he calls the "greatest boom in letter writing since the eighteenth century" that is occurring on the Internet. People are writing to each other. These are people, he says somewhat facetiously, who should be watching television. This is not to say that the quality of the letters these people write is high by traditional literary standards. E-mail is more like speech than it is like written letters. Elmer-Dewitt bemoans the quality of poetry, fiction, and essays published on the Net, where anyone who can connect, can publish. But there are gems out there amongst the garbage, and some of them are worth taking seriously.*

Elmer-Dewitt, a senior editor for Time, *launched both the computer and technology sections of the magazine.*

One of the unintended side effects of the invention of the telephone was that writing went out of style. Oh, sure, there were still full-time scribblers—journalists, academics, professional wordsmiths. And the great centers of commerce still found it useful to keep on hand people who could draft a memo, a brief, a press release or a contract. But given a choice between picking up a pen or a phone, most folks took the easy route and gave their fingers—and sometimes their mind—a rest.

Which makes what's happening on the computer networks all the more startling. Every night, when they should be watching television, millions of computer users sit down at their keyboards; dial into CompuServe, Prodigy, America Online or the Internet; and start typing—e-mail, bulletin-board postings, chat messages, rants, diatribes, even short stories and poems. Just when the media of McLuhan were supposed to render obsolete the medium of Shakespeare, the online world is experiencing the greatest boom in letter writing since the eighteenth century.

"It is my overwhelming belief that e-mail and computer conferencing are teaching an entire generation about the flexibility and utility of prose," writes Jon Carroll, a columnist at the *San Francisco Chronicle*. Patrick Nielsen Hayden, an editor at Tor Books, compares electronic bulletin boards with the "scribblers' compacts" of the late eighteenth and early nineteenth centuries, in which members passed letters from hand to hand, adding a little more at each turn. David Sewall, an associate editor at the University of Arizona, likens netwriting to the literary scene Mark Twain discovered in San Francisco in the 1860s, "when people were reinventing journalism by grafting it onto the tall-tale folk tradition." Others hark back to Tom Paine and the Revolutionary War pamphleteers, or even to the Elizabethan era, when, thanks to Gutenberg, a generation of English writers became intoxicated with language.

But such comparisons invite a question: if online writing today represents some sort of renaissance, why is so much of it so awful? For it can be very bad indeed: sloppy, meandering, puerile, ungrammatical, poorly spelled, badly structured and at times virtually content free. "HEY!!!1!" reads an all too typical message on the Internet, "I THINK METALLICA IZ REEL KOOL DOOD!1!!!"

One reason, of course, is that e-mail is not like ordinary writing. "You need to think of this as 'written speech,'" says Gerard Van der Leun, a literary agent based in Westport, Connecticut, who has emerged as one of the pre-eminent stylists on the Net. "These things are little more considered than coffeehouse talk and a lot less considered than a letter. They're not to have and hold; they're to fire and forget." Many online postings are composed "live" with the clock ticking, using rudimentary word processors on computer systems that charge by the minute and in some cases will shut down without warning when an hour runs out.

That is not to say that with more time every writer on the Internet would produce sparkling copy. Much of the fiction and poetry is second-rate or worse, which is not surprising given that the barriers to entry are so low. "In the real world," says Mary Anne Mohanraj, a Chicago-based poet, "it takes a hell of a lot of work to get published, which naturally weeds out a lot of the garbage. On the Net, just a few keystrokes sends your writing out to thousands of readers."

But even among the reams of bad poetry, gems are to be found. Mike Godwin, a Washington-based lawyer who posts under the pen name "mnemonic," tells the story of Joe Green, a technical writer at Cray Research who turned a moribund discussion group called rec.arts.poems into a real poetry workshop by mercilessly critiquing the pieces he found there. "Some people got angry and said if he was such a god of poetry, why didn't he publish his poems to the group?" recalls Godwin. "He did, and blew them all away." Green's Well Met in Minnesota, a mock-epic account of a face-to-face meeting with a fellow network scribbler, is now revered on the Internet as a classic. It begins, "The truth is that when I met Mark I was dressed as the Canterbury Tales. Rather difficult to do as you might suspect, but I wanted to make a certain impression."

The more prosaic technical and political discussion groups, meanwhile, have become so crowded with writers crying for attention that a Darwinian survival principle has started to prevail. "It's so competitive that you have to work on your style if you want to make any impact," says Jorn Barger, a software designer in Chicago. Good writing on the Net tends to be clear, vigorous, witty and above all brief. "The medium favors the terse," says Crawford Kilian, a writing teacher at Capilano College in Vancouver, British Columbia. "Short paragraphs, bulleted lists and one-liners are the units of thought here."

Some of the most successful netwriting is produced in computer conferences, where writers compose in a kind of collaborative heat, knocking ideas

CHAPTER 5 ■ THE DEATH OF PRINT LITERACY, BIRTH OF CYBERLITERACY?

300

against one another until they spark. Perhaps the best examples of this are found on the WELL, a Sausalito, California, bulletin board favored by journalists. The caliber of discussion is often so high that several publications—including the *New York Times* and the *Wall Street Journal*—have printed excerpts from the WELL.

Curiously, what works on the computer networks isn't necessarily what works on paper. Netwriters freely lace their prose with stage acronyms and "smileys," the little faces constructed with punctuation marks and intended to convey the winks, grins and grimaces of ordinary conversations. Somehow it all flows together quite smoothly. On the other hand, polished prose copied onto bulletin boards from books and magazines often seems long-winded and phony. Unless they adjust to the new medium, professional writers can come across as self-important blowhards in debates with more nimble networkers. Says Brock Meeks, a Washington-based reporter who covers the online culture for *Communications Daily*: "There are a bunch of hacker kids out there who can string a sentence together better than their blue-blooded peers simply because they log on all the time and write, write, write."

There is something inherently democratizing—perhaps even revolutionary—about the technology. Not only has it enfranchised thousands of would-be writers who otherwise might never have taken up the craft, but it has also thrown together classes of people who hadn't had much direct contact before: students, scientists, senior citizens, computer geeks, grassroots (and often blue-collar) bulletin-board enthusiasts and most recently the working press.

"It's easy to make this stuff look foolish and trivial," says Tor Books' Nielsen Hayden. "After all, a lot of everyone's daily life is foolish and trivial. I mean, really, smileys? Housewives in Des Moines who log on as VIXEN?"

But it would be a mistake to dismiss the computer-message boards or to underestimate the effect a lifetime of dashing off e-mail will have on a generation of young writers. The computer networks may not be Brook Farm or the Globe Theatre, but they do represent, for millions of people, a living, breathing life of letters. One suspects that the Bard himself, confronted with the Internet, might have dived right in and never logged off.

EXPLORING THE READING

1. What has been your experience with e-mail and texts published online? What is your assessment of the quality?

2. Have each member of your group bring in a piece of writing (e-mail, Web text, etc.) and read several together. Analyze the texts for quality.

3. Elmer-Dewitt suggests expectations for good writing on the computer networks are different from those for print texts. Look again at the paragraphs near the end of the text where he discusses this observation. Would you agree with him?

THE RISE AND SWIFT FALL OF CYBER LITERACY

by John Markoff

E-mail is becoming as common as the theme and memo in college and business settings. People can communicate as easily across continents as across the office. Enthusiasts boast that the Internet is fostering a new era of increased literacy. John Markoff, in this New York Times *article, however, points out that this rise of cyber literacy may be temporary. Audio and video teleconferencing may, in the near future, supplant e-mail as the communication medium of choice on the Internet. If you could send video mail as easily as e-mail, which would you choose?*

Markoff is the New York Times' *San Francisco-based correspondent on computers, technology and Silicon Valley issues. He is the author, with Tsutomu Shimomura, of* Takedown: The Pursuit and Capture of Kevin Mitnick, America's Most Wanted Computer Outlaw—By The Man Who Did It. *He also wrote, with Katie Hafner,* Cyberpunk: Outlaws and I lackers on the Computor Frontier.

In the early days of the information revolution, writers, readers and book lovers of all sorts ominously predicted that the rise of technology would spell the death of literacy. Then they discovered the word processor, and the typewriter went the way of the quill pen. Maybe technology wasn't so bad after all.

When the literati discovered they could use modems to link their computers to networks and send their words flashing around the world, acceptance gave way to ecstasy. In a world increasingly dominated by MTV, Nickelodeon and CNN, people began to speak of a new literacy.

Now the Internet, the network of networks that has become all the rage, is being hailed as a way to resurrect the epistolary culture that existed before the invention of the telegraph, telephone, and television. With the convenience of e-mail will come megabyte correspondences as rich as those of Abélard and Héloise or Gustave Flaubert and George Sand. Internet discussion groups with names like "rec.arts.books" will be like Gertrude Stein's literary salon, except that anyone can join.

Well, for a while, anyway. It's true that the Net has opened up a world of correspondence to anyone who wants to participate. But all good renaissances must come to an end. To the true techies, there is something rather quaint about people using all this cutting-edge technology to communicate by pressing lots of little buttons with letters printed on them—and then reading the results one line at a time.

Computer experts talk about what they call bandwidth—roughly speaking, how much information you can funnel through a line. With the coming of fiberoptics and faster computers, bandwidth will multiply, leading to the spread of multimedia technologies like digital video, audio and video teleconferencing. People who like to type at each other may again become like an endangered species as society sees the decline of textual literacy a second time.

CHAPTER 5 ■ THE DEATH OF PRINT LITERACY, BIRTH OF CYBERLITERACY?

302

"In the next decade, electronic mail is dead," said Paul Saffo, a researcher at the Institute for the Future in Menlo Park, Calif. He believes that text will become little more than a device to annotate video communications.

While today most video teleconferences require expensive electronic gear and special rooms, the cost of digital video and audio is falling so rapidly that cameras and microphones will soon be standard components of office personal computers. Sending a snippet of video mail down the hall or across the country will be easier than tapping out a message on a keyboard. Will anybody want to send letters anymore?

It is some consolation to recall that literacy itself—the old-fashioned, low-bandwidth kind—arose from new technologies. Perhaps, some like to venture, the new technologies will give rise to a new kind of literacy in which a literate person will be expected to be at least as familiar with great issues, melodies and rhythms as with great words.

It was the invention of the telegraph and the rise of the modern newspaper printing press that created mass literacy in the second half of the nineteenth century. In the 1850s only 5 percent of the soldiers in a British military regiment could read, said Michael Hawley, a professor at the Media Laboratory at the Massachusetts Institute of Technology. By the turn of the century, the number had risen to 85 percent.

"Since then, and with the advent of television, radio and telephone, we've seen measurable declines in textual literacy," he said.

Mr. Hawley sees the rise of computer networks as a powerful democratizing force. "In the past, producing information for broadcast media has required so many resources to become a George Lucas that there can only be a few each century," he said. The Internet is turning that upside down. "In the future everyone will be able to contribute their useful bit," he said.

But is a world in which everyone becomes a publisher—whether of words or of images—an ideal one?

Carla Hesse, an associate professor of history at the University of California at Berkeley, sees the Internet—with its millions and millions of electronic publishers—as a throwback to the anarchy of the French Revolution.

"Publishing in the traditional paper world is both a form of stability and also a fixed memory for our society," she said. We like to think we can put a certain amount of credence in what we read in a newspaper, magazine or book because it was written and edited according to some standards.

The question, of course, is who gets to set the standards. French revolutionaries like Condorcet experimented with absolute freedom of the press during the first years of the Revolution. But after a deluge of anonymous publications of dubious veracity, the revolutionaries revised their dreams of totally deregulated, authorless free exchange. By 1793, Ms. Hesse said, legislation emerged to hold authors accountable for what they published.

Today, she believes, the mistakes of the French Revolution are being repeated. On the Internet, it is possible to publish anonymously or pseudonymously and more widely than ever before. As a result of the responsibility for organizing information shifts from the writer to the reader. How can you know what to believe?

"This is a time of great danger," she said. When the samizdat includes digital video, which can be seamlessly altered and rearranged, the threat is only compounded.

Some experts believe the next stage of the information revolution will be so cataclysmic that new forms of literacy will emerge. Several years ago, researchers at the Institute for Research on Learning, in California, found that when students from a poor neighborhood in East Palo Alto were given video editing tools, they could tell stories about their lives that they never would have been able to express in words. Some enthusiasts even speak, a little grandiosely, of a "posttextual literacy."

"Clearly we're going to lose certain things and gain others," said John Seeley Brown, the director of Xerox's Palo Alto Research Center. "We're moving toward a new literacy. The typewriter shaped our current view of literacy. Now we're finding new computer tools that honor visual/audio thinking as opposed to textual thinking." Television is for a passive audience. Digital video, with vast possibilities for manipulating images, exercises the mind.

"Today people think of print as the only kind of writing," said Kevin Kelly, executive editor of *Wired* magazine in San Francisco. "There will be a different kind of literacy based on a melange of digital information—the entire stream of all the things that flows into our mind from our computers."

EXPLORING THE READING

1. In your small groups pool your knowledge of e-mail. Is it an important tool for you, and if so, why?

2. Freewrite for five minutes about Markoff's suggestion that, given the technology, most people would switch from e-mail to video mail. Do you agree?

3. Look again at the paragraph about absolute freedom of the press during the French Revolution. Would you agree that the mistakes of the French Revolution are being repeated on the Internet?

4. Markoff and Philip Elmer-Dewitt have different visions of the future of the Internet. How do they differ and are there any similarities in their positions?

CHAPTER 5 ■ THE DEATH OF PRINT LITERACY, BIRTH OF CYBERLITERACY?

304

THE COMPUTER DELUSION

by Todd Oppenheimer

The motion picture, the radio, the teaching machine, and now the computer—every few years a new technology is heralded as the technology that will revolutionize the way education is delivered. Todd Oppenheimer, in this feature from the Atlantic Monthly, *is skeptical. He is worried that all the money being spent on computers in schools will result in loss of other, less trendy programs such as music, art, and physical education. Oppenheimer acknowledges that when computers are combined with a gifted teacher, amazing things happen, with enthusiasm and commitment to learning "palatable" in the classroom atmosphere. Unfortunately, but understandably, not all teachers are gifted, and many computers languish in corners of classrooms. Some critics suggest that computer use can, because of the highly visual character of many programs, even be counter-productive for language development. Others worry that computers encourage students to focus their attention on the virtual, rather than the real, on a two-dimensional screen rather than the physical world around them.*

Oppenheimer is an associate editor at Newsweek Interactive *at America Online.*

> There is no good evidence that most uses of computers significantly improve teaching and learning, yet school districts are cutting programs—music, art, physical education—that enrich children's lives to make room for this dubious nostrum, and the Clinton Administration has embraced the goal of "computers in every classroom" with credulous and costly enthusiasm.

In 1922 Thomas Edison predicted that "the motion picture is destined to revolutionize our educational system and . . . in a few years it will supplant largely, if not entirely, the use of textbooks." Twenty-three years later, in 1945, William Levenson, the director of the Cleveland public schools' radio station, claimed that "the time may come when a portable radio receiver will be as common in the classroom as is the blackboard." Forty years after that the noted psychologist B. F. Skinner, referring to the first days of his "teaching machines," in the late 1950s and early 1960s, wrote, "I was soon saying that, with the help of teaching machines and programmed instruction, students could learn twice as much in the same time and with the same effort as in a standard classroom." Ten years after Skinner's recollections were published, President Bill Clinton campaigned for "a bridge to the twenty-first century . . . where computers are as much a part of the classroom as blackboards." Clinton was not alone in his enthusiasm for a program estimated to cost somewhere between $40 billion and $100 billion over the next five years. Speaker of the House Newt Gingrich, talking about computers to the Republican National Committee early this year, said, "We could do so much to make education available twenty-four hours a day, seven days a week, that people could literally have a whole different attitude toward learning."

If history really is repeating itself, the schools are in serious trouble. In *Teachers and Machines: The Classroom Use of Technology Since 1920* (1986), Larry

Cuban, a professor of education at Stanford University and a former school superintendent, observed that as successive rounds of new technology failed their promoters' expectations, a pattern emerged. The cycle began with big promises backed by the technology developers' research. In the classroom, however, teachers never really embraced the new tools, and no significant academic improvement occurred. This provoked consistent responses: the problem was money, spokespeople argued, or teacher resistance, or the paralyzing school bureaucracy. Meanwhile, few people questioned the technology advocates' claims. As results continued to lag, the blame was finally laid on the machines. Soon schools were sold on the next generation of technology, and the lucrative cycle started all over again.

Today's technology evangels argue that we've learned our lesson from past mistakes. As in each previous round, they say that when our new hot technology—the computer—is compared with yesterday's, today's is better. "It can do the same things, plus," Richard Riley, the U.S. Secretary of Education, told me this spring.

How much better is it, really?

The promoters of computers in schools again offer prodigious research showing improved academic achievement after using their technology. The research has again come under occasional attack, but this time quite a number of teachers seem to be backing classroom technology. In a poll taken early last year U.S. teachers ranked computer skills and media technology as more "essential" than the study of European history, biology, chemistry, and physics; than dealing with social problems such as drugs and family breakdown; than learning practical job skills; and than reading modern American writers such as Steinbeck and Hemingway or classic ones such as Plato and Shakespeare.

In keeping with these views New Jersey cut state aid to a number of school districts this past year and then spent $10 million on classroom computers. In Union City, California, a single school district is spending $27 million to buy new gear for a mere eleven schools. The Kittridge Street Elementary School, in Los Angeles, killed its music program last year to hire a technology coordinator; in Mansfield, Massachusetts, administrators dropped proposed teaching positions in art, music, and physical education, and then spent $333,000 on computers; in one Virginia school the art room was turned into a computer laboratory. (Ironically, a half dozen preliminary studies recently suggested that music and art classes may build the physical size of a child's brain, and its powers for subjects such as language, math, science, and engineering—in one case far more than computer work did.) Meanwhile, months after a New Technology High School opened in Napa, California, where computers sit on every student's desk and all academic classes use computers, some students were complaining of headaches, sore eyes, and wrist pain.

Throughout the country, as spending on technology increases, school book purchases are stagnant. Shop classes, with their tradition of teaching children building skills with wood and metal, have been almost entirely replaced by new "technology education programs." In San Francisco only one public

CHAPTER 5 ■ THE DEATH OF PRINT LITERACY, BIRTH OF CYBERLITERACY?

306

school still offers a full shop program—the lone vocational high school. "We get kids who don't know the difference between a screwdriver and a ball peen hammer," James Dahlman, the school's vocational-department chair, told me recently. "How are they going to make a career choice? Administrators are stuck in this mindset that all kids will go to a four-year college and become a doctor or a lawyer, and that's not true. I know some who went to college, graduated, and then had to go back to technical school to get a job." Last year the school superintendent in Great Neck, Long Island, proposed replacing elementary school shop classes with computer classes and training the shop teachers as computer coaches. Rather than being greeted with enthusiasm, the proposal provoked a backlash.

Interestingly, shop classes and field trips are two programs that the National Information Infrastructure Advisory Council, the Clinton Administration's technology task force, suggests reducing in order to shift resources into computers. But are these results what technology promoters really intend? "You need to apply common sense," Esther Dyson, the president of EDventure Holdings and one of the task force's leading school advocates, told me recently. "Shop with a good teacher probably is worth more than computers with a lousy teacher. But if it's a poor program, this may provide a good excuse for cutting it. There will be a lot of trials and errors with this. And I don't know how to prevent those errors."

The issue, perhaps, is the magnitude of the errors. Alan Lesgold, a professor of psychology and the associate director of the Learning Research and Development Center at the University of Pittsburgh, calls the computer an "amplifier," because it encourages both enlightened study practices and thoughtless ones. There's a real risk, though, that the thoughtless practices will dominate, slowly dumbing down huge numbers of tomorrow's adults. As Sherry Turkle, a professor of the sociology of science at the Massachusetts Institute of Technology and a longtime observer of children's use of computers, told me, "The possibilities of using this thing poorly so outweigh the chance of using it well, it makes people like us, who are fundamentally optimistic about computers, very reticent."

Perhaps the best way to separate fact from fantasy is to take supporters' claims about computerized learning one by one and compare them with the evidence in the academic literature and in the everyday experiences I have observed or heard about in a variety of classrooms.

Five main arguments underlie the campaign to computerize our nation's schools.

- Computers improve both teaching practices and student achievement.
- Computer literacy should be taught as early as possible; otherwise students will be left behind.
- To make tomorrow's work force competitive in an increasingly high-tech world, learning computer skills must be a priority.
- Technology programs leverage support from the business community— badly needed today because schools are increasingly starved for funds.

- Work with computers—particularly using the Internet—brings students valuable connections with teachers, other schools and students, and a wide network of professionals around the globe. These connections spice the school day with a sense of real-world relevance, and broaden the educational community.

"THE FILMSTRIPS OF THE 1990s"

Clinton's vision of computerized classrooms arose partly out of the findings of the presidential task force—thirty-six leaders from industry, education, and several interest groups who have guided the Administration's push to get computers into the schools. The report of the task force, "Connecting K–12 Schools to the Information Superhighway" (produced by the consulting firm McKinsey & Co.), begins by citing numerous studies that have apparently proved that computers enhance student achievement significantly. One "meta-analysis" (a study that reviews other studies—in this case 130 of them) reported that computers had improved performance in "a wide range of subjects, including language arts, math, social studies and science." Another found improved organization and focus in students' writing. A third cited twice the normal gains in math skills. Several schools boasted of greatly improved attendance.

Unfortunately, many of these studies are more anecdotal than conclusive. Some, including a giant, oft-cited meta-analysis of 254 studies, lack the necessary scientific controls to make solid conclusions possible. The circumstances are artificial and not easily repeated, results aren't statistically reliable, or, most frequently, the studies did not control for other influences, such as differences between teaching methods. This last factor is critical, because computerized learning inevitably forces teachers to adjust their style—only sometimes for the better. Some studies were industry-funded, and thus tended to publicize mostly positive findings. "The research is set up in a way to find benefits that aren't really there," Edward Miller, a former editor of the *Harvard Education Letter*, says. "Most knowledgeable people agree that most of the research isn't valid. It's so flawed it shouldn't even be called research. Essentially, it's just worthless." Once the faulty studies are weeded out, Miller says, the ones that remain "are inconclusive"—that is, they show no significant change in either direction. Even Esther Dyson admits the studies are undependable. "I don't think those studies amount to much either way," she says. "In this area there is little proof."

Why are solid conclusions so elusive? Look at Apple Computer's "Classrooms of Tomorrow," perhaps the most widely studied effort to teach using computer technology. In the early 1980s Apple shrewdly realized that donating computers to schools might help not only students but also company sales, as Apple's ubiquity in classrooms turned legions of families into Apple loyalists. Last year, after the *San Jose Mercury News* (published in Apple's Silicon Valley home) ran a series questioning the effectiveness of

CHAPTER 5 ■ THE DEATH OF PRINT LITERACY, BIRTH OF CYBERLITERACY?

308

computers in schools, the paper printed an opinion-page response from Terry Crane, an Apple vice-president. "Instead of isolating students," Crane wrote, "technology actually encouraged them to collaborate more than in traditional classrooms. Students also learned to explore and represent information dynamically and creatively, communicate effectively about complex processes, become independent learners and self-starters and become more socially aware and confident."

Crane didn't mention that after a decade of effort and the donation of equipment worth more than $25 million to thirteen schools, there is scant evidence of greater student achievement. To be fair, educators on both sides of the computer debate acknowledge that today's tests of student achievement are shockingly crude. They're especially weak in measuring intangibles such as enthusiasm and self-motivation, which do seem evident in Apple's classrooms and other computer-rich schools. In any event, what is fun and what is educational may frequently be at odds. "Computers in classrooms are the filmstrips of the 1990s," Clifford Stoll, the author of *Silicon Snake Oil: Second Thoughts on the Information Highway* (1995), told *The New York Times* last year, recalling his own school days in the 1960s. "We loved them because we didn't have to think for an hour, teachers loved them because they didn't have to teach, and parents loved them because it showed their schools were high-tech. But no learning happened."

Stoll somewhat overstates the case—obviously, benefits can come from strengthening a student's motivation. Still, Apple's computers may bear less responsibility for that change than Crane suggests. In the beginning, when Apple did little more than dump computers in classrooms and homes, this produced no real results, according to Jane David, a consultant Apple hired to study its classroom initiative. Apple quickly learned that teachers needed to change their classroom approach to what is commonly called "project-oriented learning." This is an increasingly popular teaching method, in which students learn through doing and teachers act as facilitators or partners rather than as didacts. (Teachers sometimes refer to this approach, which arrived in classrooms before computers did, as being "the guide on the side instead of the sage on the stage.") But what the students learned "had less to do with the computer and more to do with the teaching," David concluded. "If you took the computers out, there would still be good teaching there." This story is heard in school after school, including two impoverished schools—Clear View Elementary School, in southern California, and the Christopher Columbus Middle School, in New Jersey—that the Clinton Administration has loudly celebrated for turning themselves around with computers. At Christopher Columbus, in fact, students' test scores rose before computers arrived, not afterward, because of relatively basic changes: longer class periods, new books, after-school programs, and greater emphasis on student projects and collaboration.

During recent visits to some San Francisco–area schools I could see what it takes for students to use computers properly, and why most don't.

On a bluff south of downtown San Francisco, in the middle of one of the city's lower-income neighborhoods, Claudia Schaffner, a tenth-grader, tapped away at a multimedia machine in a computer lab at Thurgood Marshall Academic High School, one of half a dozen special technology schools in the city. Schaffner was using a physics program to simulate the trajectory of a marble on a small roller coaster. "It helps to visualize it first, like 'A is for Apple' with kindergartners," Schaffner told me, while mousing up and down the virtual roller coaster. "I can see how the numbers go into action." This was lunch hour, and the students' excitement about what they can do in this lab was palpable. Schaffner could barely tear herself away. "I need to go eat some food," she finally said, returning within minutes to eat a rice dish at the keyboard.

Schaffner's teacher is Dennis Frezzo, an electrical-engineering graduate from the University of California at Berkeley. Despite his considerable knowledge of computer programming, Frezzo tries to keep classwork focused on physical projects. For a mere $8,000, for example, several teachers put together a multifaceted robotics lab, consisting of an advanced Lego engineering kit and twenty-four old 386-generation computers. Frezzo's students used these materials to build a tiny electric car, whose motion was to be triggered by a light sensor. When the light sensor didn't work, the students figured out why. "That's a real problem—what you'd encounter in the real world," Frezzo told me. "I prefer they get stuck on small real-world problems instead of big fake problems"—like the simulated natural disasters that fill one popular educational game. "It's sort of the Zen approach to education," Frezzo said. "It's not the big problems. Isaac Newton already solved those. What come up in life are the little ones."

It's one thing to confront technology's complexity at a high school—especially one that's blessed with four different computer labs and some highly skilled teachers like Frezzo, who know enough, as he put it, "to keep computers in their place." It's quite another to grapple with a high-tech future in the lower grades, especially at everyday schools that lack special funding or technical support. As evidence, when *U.S. News & World Report* published a cover story last fall on schools that make computers work, five of the six were high schools—among them Thurgood Marshall. Although the sixth was an elementary school, the featured program involved children with disabilities—the one group that does show consistent benefits from computerized instruction.

ARTIFICIAL EXPERIENCE

Consider the scene at one elementary school, Sanchez, which sits on the edge of San Francisco's Latino community. For several years Sanchez, like many other schools, has made do with a roomful of basic Apple IIs. Last year, curious about what computers could do for youngsters, a local entrepreneur donated twenty costly Power Macintoshes—three for each of five classrooms, and one for each of the five lucky teachers to take home. The teachers who got the new machines were delighted. "It's the best thing we've ever done," Adela Najarro, a third-grade bilingual teacher, told me. She mentioned one boy, perhaps with a learning disability, who had started to hate

CHAPTER 5 ■ THE DEATH OF PRINT LITERACY, BIRTH OF CYBERLITERACY?

310

school. Once he had a computer to play with, she said, "his whole attitude changed." Najarro is now a true believer, even when it comes to children without disabilities. "Every single child," she said, "will do more work for you and do better work with a computer. Just because it's on a monitor, kids pay more attention. There's this magic to the screen."

Down the hall from Najarro's classroom her colleague Rose Marie Ortiz had a more troubled relationship with computers. On the morning I visited, Ortiz took her bilingual special-education class of second-, third-, and fourth-graders into the lab filled with the old Apple IIs. The students look forward to this weekly expedition so much that Ortiz gets exceptional behavior from them all morning. Out of date though these machines are, they do offer a range of exercises, in subjects such as science, math, reading, social studies, and problem solving. But owing to this group's learning problems and limited English skills, math drills were all that Ortiz could give them. Nonetheless, within minutes the kids were excitedly navigating their way around screens depicting floating airplanes and trucks carrying varying numbers of eggs. As the children struggled, many resorted to counting in whatever way they knew how. Some squinted at the screen, painstakingly moving their fingers from one tiny egg symbol to the next. "*Tres, cuatro, cinco, seis . . . ,*" one little girl said loudly, trying to hear herself above her counting neighbors. Another girl kept a piece of paper handy, on which she marked a line for each egg. Several others resorted to the slow but tried and true—their fingers. Some just guessed. Once the children arrived at answers, they frantically typed them onto the screen, hoping it would advance to something fun, the way Nintendos, Game Boys, and video-arcade games do. Sometimes their answers were right, and the screen did advance; sometimes they weren't; but the children were rarely discouraged. As schoolwork goes, this was a blast.

"It's highly motivating for them," Ortiz said as she rushed from machine to machine, attending not to math questions but to computer glitches. Those she couldn't fix she simply abandoned. "I don't know how practical it is. You see," she said, pointing to a girl counting on her fingers, "these kids still need the hands-on"—meaning the opportunity to manipulate physical objects such as beans or colored blocks. The value of hands-on learning, child-development experts believe, is that it deeply imprints knowledge into a young child's brain, by transmitting the lessons of experience through a variety of sensory pathways. "Curiously enough," the educational psychologist Jane Healy wrote in *Endangered Minds: Why Children Don't Think and What We Can Do About It* (1990), "visual stimulation is probably not the main access route to nonverbal reasoning. Body movements, the ability to touch. feel, manipulate, and build sensory awareness of relationships in the physical world, are its main foundations." The problem, Healy wrote, is that "in schools, traditionally, the senses have had little status after kindergarten."

Ortiz believes that the computer-lab time, brief as it is, dilutes her students' attention to language. "These kids are all language-delayed," she said. Though only modest sums had so far been spent at her school, Ortiz and other local teachers felt that the push was on for technology over other scholastic priorities. The year before, Sanchez had let its librarian go, to be replaced by a part-timer.

When Ortiz finally got the students rounded up and out the door, the kids were still worked up. "They're never this wired after reading group," she said. "They're usually just exhausted, because I've been reading with them, making them write and talk." Back in homeroom Ortiz showed off the students' monthly handwritten writing samples. "Now, could you do that on the computer?" she asked. "No, because we'd be hung up on finding the keys." So why does Ortiz bother taking her students to the computer lab at all? "I guess I come in here for the computer literacy. If everyone else is getting it, I feel these kids should get it too."

Some computerized elementary school programs have avoided these pitfalls, but the record subject by subject is mixed at best. Take writing, where by all accounts and by my own observations the computer does encourage practice—changes are easier to make on a keyboard than with an eraser, and the lettering looks better. Diligent students use these conveniences to improve their writing, but the less committed frequently get seduced by electronic opportunities to make a school paper look snazzy. (The easy "cut and paste" function in today's word-processing programs, for example, is apparently encouraging many students to cobble together research materials without thinking them through.) Reading programs get particularly bad reviews. One small but carefully controlled study went so far as to claim that Reader Rabbit, a reading program now used in more than 100,000 schools, caused students to suffer a 50 percent drop in creativity. (Apparently, after forty-nine students used the program for seven months, they were no longer able to answer open-ended questions and showed a markedly diminished ability to brainstorm with fluency and originality.) What about hard sciences, which seem so well suited to computer study? Logo, the high-profile programming language refined by Seymour Papert and widely used in middle and high schools, fostered huge hopes of expanding children's cognitive skills. As students directed the computer to build things, such as geometric shapes, Papert believed, they would learn "procedural thinking," similar to the way a computer processes information. According to a number of studies, however, Logo has generally failed to deliver on its promises. Judah Schwartz, a professor of education at Harvard and a co-director of the school's Educational Technology Center, told me that a few newer applications, when used properly, can dramatically expand children's math and science thinking by giving them new tools to "make and explore conjectures." Still, Schwartz acknowledges that perhaps "ninety-nine percent" of the educational programs are "terrible, really terrible."

Even in success stories important caveats continually pop up. The best educational software is usually complex—most suited to older students and sophisticated teachers. In other cases the schools have been blessed with abundance—fancy equipment, generous financial support, or extra teachers— that is difficult if not impossible to duplicate in the average school. Even if it

CHAPTER 5 ■ THE DEATH OF PRINT LITERACY, BIRTH OF CYBERLITERACY?

312

could be duplicated, the literature suggests, many teachers would still struggle with technology. Computers suffer frequent breakdowns; when they do work, their seductive images often distract students from the lessons at hand—which many teachers say makes it difficult to build meaningful rapport with their students.

With such a discouraging record of student and teacher performance with computers, why has the Clinton Administration focused so narrowly on the hopeful side of the story? Part of the answer may lie in the makeup of the Administration's technology task force. Judging from accounts of the task force's deliberations, all thirty-six members are unequivocal technology advocates. Two thirds of them work in the high-tech and entertainment industries. The effect of the group's tilt can be seen in its report. Its introduction adopts the authoritative posture of impartial fact-finder, stating that "this report does not attempt to lay out a national blueprint, nor does it recommend specific public policy goals." But it comes pretty close. Each chapter describes various strategies for getting computers into classrooms, and the introduction acknowledges that "this report does not evaluate the relative merits of competing demands on educational funding (*e.g.*, more computers versus smaller class sizes)."

When I spoke with Esther Dyson and other task-force members about what discussion the group had had about the potential downside of computerized education, they said there hadn't been any. And when I asked Linda Roberts, Clinton's lead technology adviser in the Department of Education, whether the task force was influenced by any self-interest, she said no, quite the opposite: the group's charter actually gave its members license to help the technology industry directly, but they concentrated on schools because that's where they saw the greatest need.

That sense of need seems to have been spreading outside Washington. Last summer a California task force urged the state to spend $11 billion on computers in California schools, which have struggled for years under funding cuts that have driven academic achievement down to among the lowest levels in the nation. This task force, composed of forty-six teachers, parents, technology experts, and business executives, concluded, "More than any other single measure, computers and network technologies, properly implemented, offer the greatest potential to right what's wrong with our public schools." Other options mentioned in the group's report—reducing class size, improving teachers' salaries and facilities, expanding hours of instruction—were considered less important than putting kids in front of computers.

"HYPERTEXT MINDS"

Today's parents, knowing firsthand how families were burned by television's false promises, may want some objective advice about the age at which their children should become computer literate. Although there are no real guidelines, computer boosters send continual messages that if children don't begin early, they'll be left behind. Linda Roberts thinks that there's no particular minimum age—and no maximum number of hours that children should spend at a terminal. Are there examples of excess? "I haven't seen it yet," Roberts told me with a laugh. In schools throughout the country administrators and teachers demonstrate the same excitement, boasting about the wondrous things that children of five or six can do on computers: drawing, typing, playing with elementary science simulations and other programs called "educational games."

The schools' enthusiasm for these activities is not universally shared by specialists in childhood development. The doubters' greatest concern is for the very young—preschool through third grade, when a child is most impressionable. Their apprehension involves two main issues.

First, they consider it important to give children a broad base—emotionally, intellectually, and in the five senses—before introducing something as technical and one-dimensional as a computer. Second, they believe that the human and physical world holds greater learning potential.

The importance of a broad base for a child may be most apparent when it's missing. In *Endangered Minds*, Jane Healy wrote of an English teacher who could readily tell which of her students' essays were conceived on a computer. "They don't link ideas," the teacher says. "They just write one thing, and then they write another one, and they don't seem to see or develop the relationships between them." The problem, Healy argued, is that the pizzazz of computerized schoolwork may hide these analytical gaps, which "won't become apparent until [the student] can't organize herself around a homework assignment or a job that requires initiative. More commonplace activities, such as figuring out how to nail two boards together, organizing a game . . . may actually form a better basis for real-world intelligence."

Others believe they have seen computer games expand children's imaginations. High-tech children "think differently from the rest of us," William D. Winn, the director of the Learning Center at the University of Washington's Human Interface Technology Laboratory, told *Business Week* in a recent cover story on the benefits of computer games. "They develop hypertext minds. They leap around. It's as though their cognitive strategies were parallel, not sequential." Healy argues the opposite. She and other psychologists think that the computer screen flattens information into narrow, sequential data. This kind of material, they believe, exercises mostly one half of the brain— the left hemisphere, where primarily sequential thinking occurs. The "right brain" meanwhile gets short shrift—yet this is the hemisphere that works on different kinds of information simultaneously. It shapes our multi-faceted impressions, and serves as the engine of creative analysis.

Opinions diverge in part because research on the brain is still so sketchy, and computers are so new, that the effect of computers on the brain remains a great mystery. "I don't think we know anything about it," Harry Chugani, a pediatric neurobiologist at Wayne State University, told me. This very ignorance makes skeptics wary. "Nobody knows how kids' internal wiring works," Clifford Stoll wrote in *Silicon Snake Oil*, "but anyone who's directed

CHAPTER 5 ■ THE DEATH OF PRINT LITERACY, BIRTH OF CYBERLITERACY?

314

away from social interactions has a head start on turning out weird. . . . No computer can teach what a walk through a pine forest feels like. Sensation has no substitute."

This points to the conservative developmentalists' second concern: the danger that even if hours in front of the screen are limited, unabashed enthusiasm for the computer sends the wrong message: that the mediated world is more significant than the real one. "It's like TV commercials," Barbara Scales, the head teacher at the Child Study Center at the University of California at Berkeley, told me. "Kids get so hyped up, it can change their expectations about stimulation, versus what they generate themselves." In *Silicon Snake Oil*, Michael Fellows, a computer scientist at the University of Victoria, in British Columbia, was even blunter. "Most schools would probably be better off if they threw their computers into the Dumpster."

Faced with such sharply contrasting viewpoints, which are based on such uncertain ground, how is a responsible policymaker to proceed? "A prudent society controls its own infatuation with 'progress' when planning for its young," Healy argued in *Endangered Minds*.

> Unproven technologies . . . may offer lively visions, but they can also be detrimental to the development of the young plastic brain. The cerebral cortex is a wondrously well-buffered mechanism that can withstand a good bit of well-intentioned bungling. Yet there is a point at which fundamental neural substrates for reasoning may be jeopardized for children who lack proper physical, intellectual, or emotional nurturance. Childhood—and the brain—have their own imperatives. In development, missed opportunities may be difficult to recapture.

The problem is that technology leaders rarely include these or other warnings in their recommendations. When I asked Dyson why the Clinton task force proceeded with such fervor, despite the classroom computer's shortcomings, she said, "It's so clear the world is changing."

REAL JOB TRAINING

In the past decade, according to the presidential task force's report, the number of jobs requiring computer skills has increased from 25 percent of all jobs in 1983 to 47 percent in 1993. By 2000, the report estimates, 60 percent of the nation's jobs will demand these skills—and pay an average of 10 to 15 percent more than jobs involving no computer work. Although projections of this sort are far from reliable, it's a safe bet that computer skills will be needed for a growing proportion of tomorrow's work force. But what priority should these skills be given among other studies?

Listen to Tom Henning, a physics teacher at Thurgood Marshall, the San Francisco technology high school. Henning has a graduate degree in engineering, and helped to found a Silicon Valley company that manufactures electronic navigation equipment. "My bias is the physical reality," Henning told me, as we sat outside a shop where he was helping students to rebuild an old motorcycle. "I'm no technophobe. I can program computers." What worries Henning is that computers at best engage only two senses, hearing and sight—and only two-dimensional sight at that. "Even if they're doing three-dimensional computer modeling, that's still a two-D replica of a three-D world. If you took a kid who grew up on Nintendo, he's not going to have the necessary skills. He needs to have done it first with Tinkertoys or clay, or carved it out of balsa wood." As David Elkind, a professor of child development at Tufts University, puts it, "A dean of the University of Iowa's school of engineering used to say the best engineers were the farm boys," because they knew how machinery really worked.

Surely many employers will disagree, and welcome the commercially applicable computer skills that today's high-tech training can bring them. What's striking is how easy it is to find other employers who share Henning's and Elkind's concerns.

Kris Meisling, a senior geological-research adviser for Mobil Oil, told me that "people who use computers a lot slowly grow rusty in their ability to think." Meisling's group creates charts and maps—some computerized, some not—to plot where to drill for oil. In large one-dimensional analyses, such is sorting volumes of seismic data, the computer saves vast amounts of time, sometimes making previously impossible tasks easy. This lures people in his field, Meisling believes, into using computers as much as possible. But when geologists turn to computers for "interpretive" projects, he finds, they often miss information, and their oversights are further obscured by the computer's captivating automatic design functions. This is why Meisling still works regularly with a pencil and paper—tools that, ironically, he considers more interactive than the computer, because they force him to think implications through.

"You can't simultaneously get an overview and detail with a computer," he says. "It's linear. It gives you tunnel vision. What computers can do well is what can be calculated over and over. What they can't do is innovation. If you think of some new way to do or look at things and the software can't do it, you're stuck. So a lot of people think, 'Well, I guess it's a dumb idea, or it's unnecessary.'"

I have heard similar warnings from people in other businesses, including high-tech enterprises. A spokeswoman for Hewlett-Packard, the giant California computer-products company, told me the company rarely hires people who are predominantly computer experts, favoring instead those who have a talent for teamwork and are flexible and innovative. Hewlett-Packard is such a believer in hands-on experience that since 1992 it has spent $2.6 million helping forty-five school districts build math and science skills the old-fashioned way—using real materials, such as dirt, seeds, water, glass vials, and magnets. Much the same perspective came from several recruiters in film and computer-game animation. In work by artists who have spent a lot of time on computers "you'll see a stiffness or a flatness, a lack of richness and depth," Karen Chelini, the director of human resources for LucasArts Entertainment, George Lucas's interactive-games maker, told me recently. "With traditional art training, you train the eye to pay attention to body

CHAPTER 5 ■ THE DEATH OF PRINT LITERACY, BIRTH OF CYBERLITERACY?

316

movement. You learn attitude, feeling, expression. The ones who are good are those who as kids couldn't be without their sketchbook."

Many jobs obviously will demand basic computer skills if not sophisticated knowledge. But that doesn't mean that the parents or the teachers of young students need to panic. Joseph Weizenbaum, a professor emeritus of computer science at MIT, told the *San Jose Mercury News* that even at his technology-heavy institution new students can learn all the computer skills they need "in a summer." This seems to hold in the business world, too. Patrick MacLeamy, an executive vice-president of Hellmuth Obata & Kassabaum, the country's largest architecture firm, recently gave me numerous examples to illustrate that computers pose no threat to his company's creative work. Although architecture professors are divided on the value of computerized design tools, in MacLeamy's opinion they generally enhance the process. But he still considers "knowledge of the hands" to be valuable—today's architects just have to develop it in other ways. (His firm's answer is through building models.) Nonetheless, as positive as MacLeamy is about computers, he has found the company's two-week computer training to be sufficient. In fact, when he's hiring, computer skills don't enter into his list of priorities. He looks for a strong character; an ability to speak, write, and comprehend; and a rich education in the history of architecture.

THE SCHOOLS THAT BUSINESS BUILT

Newspaper financial sections carry almost daily pronouncements from the computer industry and other businesses about their high-tech hopes for America's schoolchildren. Many of these are joined to philanthropic commitments to helping schools make curriculum changes. This sometimes gets businesspeople involved in schools, where they've begun to understand and work with the many daunting problems that are unrelated to technology. But if business gains too much influence over the curriculum, the schools can become a kind of corporate training center—largely at taxpayer expense.

For more than a decade scholars and government commissions have criticized the increasing professionalization of the college years—frowning at the way traditional liberal arts are being edged out by hot topics of the moment or strictly business-oriented studies. The schools' real job, the technology critic Neil Postman argued in his book *The End of Education* (1995), is to focus on "how to make a life, which is quite different from how to make a living." Some see the arrival of boxes of computer hardware and software in the schools as taking the commercial trend one step further, down into high school and elementary grades. "Should you be choosing a career in kindergarten?" asks Helen Sloss Luey, a social worker and a former president of San Francisco's Parent Teacher Association. "People need to be trained to learn and change, while education seems to be getting more specific."

Indeed it does. The New Technology High School in Napa (the school where a computer sits on every student's desk) was started by the school district and a consortium of more than forty businesses. "We want to be the school that business built," Robert Nolan, a founder of the school, told me last fall. "We wanted to create an environment that mimicked what exists in the high-tech business world." Increasingly, Nolan explained, business leaders want to hire people specifically trained in the skill they need. One of Nolan's partners, Ted Fujimoto, of the Landmark Consulting Group, told me that instead of just asking the business community for financial support, the school will now undertake a trade: in return for donating funds, businesses can specify what kinds of employees they want—"a two-way street." Sometimes the traffic is a bit heavy in one direction. In January, *The New York Times* published a lengthy education supplement describing numerous examples of how business is increasingly dominating school software and other curriculum materials, and not always toward purely educational goals.

People who like the idea that their taxes go to computer training might be surprised at what a poor investment it can be. Larry Cuban, the Stanford education professor, writes that changes in the classroom for which business lobbies rarely hold long-term value. Rather, they're often guided by labor-market needs that turn out to be transitory; when the economy shifts, workers are left unprepared for new jobs. In the economy as a whole, according to a recent story in *The New York Times*, performance trends in our schools have shown virtually no link to the rises and falls in the nation's measures of productivity and growth. This is one reason that school traditionalists push for broad liberal-arts curricula, which they feel develop students' values and intellect, instead of focusing on today's idea about what tomorrow's jobs will be.

High-tech proponents argue that the best education software does develop flexible business intellects. In the *Business Week* story on computer games, for example, academics and professionals expressed amazement at the speed, savvy, and facility that young computer jocks sometimes demonstrate. Several pointed in particular to computer simulations, which some business leaders believe are becoming increasingly important in fields ranging from engineering, manufacturing, and troubleshooting to the tracking of economic activity and geopolitical risk. The best of these simulations may be valuable, albeit for strengthening one form of thinking. But the average simulation program may be of questionable relevance.

Sherry Turkle, the sociology professor at MIT, has studied youngsters using computers for more than twenty years. In her book *Life on the Screen: Identity in the Age of the Internet* (1995) she described a disturbing experience with a simulation game called SimLife. After she sat down with a thirteen-year-old named Tim, she was stunned at the way

> Tim can keep playing even when he has no idea what is driving events. For example, when his sea urchins become extinct, I ask him why.
> Tim: "I don't know, it's just something that happens."
> ST: "Do you know how to find out why it happened?"
> Tim: "No."
> ST: "Do you mind that you can't tell why?"
> Tim: "No. I don't let things like that bother me. It's not what's important."

CHAPTER 5 ■ THE DEATH OF PRINT LITERACY, BIRTH OF CYBERLITERACY?

318

Anecdotes like this lead some educators to worry that as children concentrate on how to manipulate software instead of on the subject at hand, learning can diminish rather than grow. Simulations, for example, are built on hidden assumptions, many of which are oversimplified if not highly questionable. All too often, Turkle wrote recently in *The American Prospect*, "experiences with simulations do not open up questions but close them down." Turkle's concern is that software of this sort fosters passivity, ultimately dulling people's sense of what they can change in the world. There's a tendency, Turkle told me, "to take things at 'interface' value." Indeed, after mastering SimCity, a popular game about urban planning, a tenth-grade girl boasted to Turkle that she'd learned the following rule: "Raising taxes always leads to riots."

The business community also offers tangible financial support, usually by donating equipment. Welcome as this is, it can foster a high-tech habit. Once a school's computer system is set up, the companies often drop their support. This saddles the school with heavy long-term responsibilities: maintenance of the computer network and the need for constant software upgrades and constant teacher training—the full burden of which can cost far more than the initial hardware and software combined. Schools must then look for handouts from other companies, enter the grant-seeking game, or delicately go begging in their own communities. "We can go to the well only so often," Toni-Sue Passantino, the principal of the Bayside Middle School, in San Mateo, California, told me recently. Last year Bayside let a group of seventh- and eighth-graders spend eighteen months and countless hours creating a rudimentary virtual-reality program, with the support of several high-tech firms. The companies' support ended after that period, however—creating a financial speed bump of a kind that the Rand Corporation noted in a report to the Clinton Administration as a common obstacle.

School administrators may be outwardly excited about computerized instruction, but they're also shrewdly aware of these financial challenges. In March of last year, for instance, when California launched its highly promoted "NetDay '96" (a campaign to wire 12,000 California schools to the Internet in one day), school participation was far below expectations, even in technology-conscious San Francisco. In the city papers school officials wondered how they were supposed to support an Internet program when they didn't even have the money to repair crumbling buildings, install electrical outlets, and hire the dozens of new teachers recently required so as to reduce class size.

One way around the donation maze is to simplify: use inexpensive, basic software and hardware, much of which is available through recycling programs. Such frugality can offer real value in the elementary grades, especially since basic word-processing tools are most helpful to children just learning to write. Yet schools, like the rest of us, can't resist the latest toys. "A lot of people will spend all their money on fancy new equipment that can do great things, and sometimes it just gets used for typing classes," Ray Porter, a computer resource teacher for the San Francisco schools, told me recently.

"Parents, school boards, and the reporters want to see only razzle-dazzle state-of-the-art."

INTERNET ISOLATION

It is hard to visit a high-tech school without being led by a teacher into a room where students are communicating with people hundreds or thousands of miles away—over the Internet or sometimes through video-conferencing systems (two-way TV sets that broadcast live from each room,). Video conferences, although fun, are an expensive way to create classroom thrills. But the Internet, when used carefully, offers exciting academic prospects—most dependably, once again, for older students. In one case schools in different states have tracked bird migrations and then posted their findings on the World Wide Web, using it as their own national notebook. In San Francisco eighth-grade economics students have e-mailed Chinese and Japanese businessmen to fulfill an assignment on what it would take to build an industrial plant overseas. Schools frequently use the Web to publish student writing. While thousands of self-published materials like these have turned the Web into a worldwide vanity press, the network sometimes gives young writers their first real audience.

The free nature of Internet information also means that students are confronted with chaos, and real dangers. "The Net's beauty is that it's uncontrolled," Stephen Kerr, a professor at the College of Education at the University of Washington and the editor of *Technology in the Future of Schooling* (1996), told me. "It's information by anyone, for anyone. There's racist stuff, bigoted, hate-group stuff, filled with paranoia; bomb recipes: how to engage in various kinds of crimes, electronic and otherwise; scams and swindles. It's all there. It's all available." Older students may be sophisticated enough to separate the Net's good food from its poisons, but even the savvy can be misled. On almost any subject the Net offers a plethora of seemingly sound "research." But under close inspection much of it proves to be ill informed, or just superficial. "That's the antithesis of what classroom kids should be exposed to," Kerr said.

This makes traditionalists emphasize the enduring value of printed books, vetted as most are by editing. In many schools, however, libraries are fairly limited. I now volunteer at a San Francisco high school where the library shelves are so bare that I can see how the Internet's evergrowing number of research documents, with all their shortcomings, can sometimes be a blessing.

Even computer enthusiasts give the Net tepid reviews. "Most of the content on the Net is total garbage," Esther Dyson acknowledges. "But if you find one good thing you can use it a million times." Kerr believes that Dyson is being unrealistic. "If you find a useful site one day, it may not be there the next day, or the information is different. Teachers are being asked to jump in and figure out if what they find on the Net is worthwhile. They don't have the skill or time to do that." Especially when students rely on the Internet's

CHAPTER 5 ■ THE DEATH OF PRINT LITERACY, BIRTH OF CYBERLITERACY?

320

much-vaunted search software. Although these tools deliver hundreds or thousands of sources within seconds, students may not realize that search engines, and the Net itself, miss important information all the time.

"We need *less* surfing in the schools, not more," David Gelernter, a professor of computer science at Yale, wrote last year in late *The Weekly Standard*, "Couldn't we teach them to use what they've got before favoring them with three orders of magnitude *more*?" In my conversations with Larry Cuban, of Stanford, he argued, "Schooling is not about information. It's getting kids to think about information. It's about understanding and knowledge and wisdom."

It may be that youngsters' growing fascination with the Internet and other ways to use computers will distract from yet another of Clinton's education priorities: to build up the reading skills of American children. Sherry Dingman, an assistant professor of psychology at Marist College, in Poughkeepsie, New York, who is optimistic about many computer applications, believes that if children start using computers before they have a broad foundation in reading from books, they will be cheated out of opportunities to develop imagination. "If we think we're going to take kids who haven't been read to, and fix it by sitting them in front of a computer, we're fooling ourselves," Dingman told me not long ago. This doesn't mean that teachers or parents should resort to books on CD-ROM, which Dingman considers "a great waste of time," stuffing children's minds with "canned" images instead of stimulating youngsters to create their own. "Computers are lollipops that rot your teeth" is how Marilyn Darch, an English teacher at Poly High School, in Long Beach, California, put it in *Silicon Snake Oil*. "The kids love them. But once they get hooked. . . . It makes reading a book seem tedious. Books don't have sound effects, and their brains have to do all the work."

Computer advocates like to point out that the Internet allows for all kinds of intellectual challenges—especially when students use e-mail, or post notes in "newsgroup" discussions, to correspond with accomplished experts. Such experts, however, aren't consistently available. When they are, online "conversations" generally take place when correspondents are sitting alone, and the dialogue lacks the unpredictability and richness that occur in face-to-face discussions. In fact, when youngsters are put into groups for the "collaborative" learning that computer defenders celebrate, realistically only one child sits at the keyboard at a time. (During my school visits children tended to get quite possessive about the mouse and the keyboard, resulting in frustration and noisy disputes more often than collaboration.) In combination these constraints lead to yet another of the childhood developmentalists' concerns—that computers encourage social isolation.

JUST A GLAMOROUS TOOL

It would be easy to characterize the battle over computers as merely another chapter in the world's oldest story: humanity's natural resistance to change. But that does an injustice to the forces at work in this transformation. This is not just the future versus the past, uncertainty versus nostalgia; it is about encouraging a fundamental shift in personal priorities—a minimizing of the real, physical world in favor of an unreal "virtual" world. It is about teaching youngsters that exploring what's on a two-dimensional screen is more important than playing with real objects, or sitting down to an attentive conversation with a friend, a parent, or a teacher. By extension, it means downplaying the importance of conversation, of careful listening, and of expressing oneself in person with acuity and individuality. In the process, it may also limit the development of children's imaginations.

Perhaps this is why Steven Jobs, one of the founders of Apple Computer and a man who claims to have "spearheaded giving away more computer equipment to schools than anybody else on the planet," has come to a grim conclusion: "What's wrong with education cannot be fixed with technology," he told *Wired* magazine last year. "No amount of technology will make a dent. . . . You're not going to solve the problems by putting all knowledge onto CD-ROMs. We can put a Website in every school—none of this is bad. It's bad only if it lulls us into thinking we're doing something to solve the problem with education." Jane David, the consultant to Apple, concurs, with a commonly heard caveat. "There are real dangers," she told me, "in looking to technology to be the savior of education. But it won't survive without the technology."

Arguments like David's remind Clifford Stoll of yesteryear's promises about television. He wrote in *Silicon Snake Oil*,

> "Sesame Street" . . . has been around for twenty years. Indeed, its idea of making learning relevant to all was as widely promoted in the seventies as the Internet is today.
> So where's that demographic wave of creative and brilliant students now entering college? Did kids really need to learn how to watch television? Did we inflate their expectations that learning would always be colorful and fun?

Computer enthusiasts insist that the computer's "interactivity" and multimedia features make this machine far superior to television. Nonetheless, Stoll wrote,

> I see a parallel between the goals of "Sesame Street" and those of children's computing. Both are pervasive, expensive and encourage children to sit still. Both display animated cartoons, gaudy numbers and weird, random noises. . . . Both give the sensation that by merely watching a screen, you can acquire information without work and without discipline.

As the technology critic Neil Postman put it to a Harvard electronic-media conference, "I thought that television would be the last great technology that people would go into with their eyes closed. Now you have the computer."

The solution is not to ban computers from classrooms altogether. But it may be to ban federal spending on what is fast becoming an overheated campaign. After all, the private sector, with its constant supply of used computers and the computer industry's vigorous competition for new customers,

CHAPTER 5 ■ THE DEATH OF PRINT LITERACY, BIRTH OF CYBERLITERACY?

322

seems well equipped to handle the situation. In fact, if schools can impose some limits—on technology donors and on themselves—rather than indulging in a consumer frenzy, most will probably find themselves with more electronic gear than they need. That could free the billions that Clinton wants to devote to technology and make it available for impoverished fundamentals: teaching solid skills in reading, thinking, listening, and talking, organizing inventive field trips and other rich hands-on experiences; and, of course, building up the nation's core of knowledgeable, inspiring teachers. These notions are considerably less glamorous than computers are, but their worth is firmly proved through a long history.

Last fall, after the school administrators in Mansfield, Massachusetts, had eliminated proposed art, music, and physical-education positions in favor of buying computers, Michael Bellino, an electrical engineer at Boston University's Center for Space Physics, appeared before the Massachusetts Board of Education to protest. "The purpose of the schools [is] to, as one teacher argues, 'Teach carpentry, not hammer,'" he testified. "We need to teach the whys and ways of the world. Tools come and tools go. Teaching our children tools limits their knowledge to these tools and hence limits their futures."

EXPLORING THE READING

1. If history is repeating itself, with computers being just one more ineffective fad in education, then schools are in trouble, according to Todd Oppenheimer. What do you think about the potential of computers enriching the classroom?

2. In your small group, discuss your pre-college educational experience. When did you first encounter computers in a classroom? Have computers aided your learning? How so?

3. Freewrite for five minutes about what you would recommend if your local middle schools were considering eliminating art and music programs and putting the money into computers.

4. Evaluate the content of Oppenheimer's article. What is his position? Does he offer a balanced argument, acknowledging opposing arguments?

REFLECTIONS OF AN ONLINE GRADUATE

by Emily Weiner

Emily Weiner says she was "an online pioneer." Using e-mail to communicate with her professors, the Internet for research, and her PC to participate in a computer conference course, she earned enough credits to complete her BA. Her online degree program worked well for her, she says in this New York Times Book Review *article, primarily because she developed a close relationship online with a mentor, a full professor. Although her experience was great, she worries that all online degree programs may not be as beneficial or nurturing. She warns that the quality of online education is directly tied to the quality of the faculty universities are willing to commit to their programs.*

Emily Weiner, a graduate of the State University of New York's Empire State College, lives in Bellingham, Washington, where she teaches news graphics at Western Washington University.

I saw my college for the first time on June 12, 1995, five hours before I graduated. My campus until that day had been my computer. I live in Bellingham, Washington, and for a year and a half I had been hooking up by modem to the State University of New York's Empire State College.

In 1993 I realized I needed a degree fast. I was teaching news graphics through the continuing education program at Western Washington University, but was told that, though I had two decades of professional experience, I couldn't be hired as an adjunct instructor of journalism without a bachelor's degree, I had about two years of college credits, accumulated from three different schools from 1968 to 1971.

I was an online pioneer. By the end of this decade, cyberspace diplomas may be common. Innovative electronic teaching materials that will prepare students for work revolving around computers will free educational institutions from the limits of geography. Courses that teach students to work online won't be bound by classroom walls. Journalism students are already editing electronic newspapers. In my online experience, I merely talked via e-mail with the mentor assigned to me by Empire State, used the Internet for research, and participated in a computer course that was like a private chat room with a goal, a time frame and a leader.

How well will students be served by these new forms of teaching? In June the governors of ten Western states announced the establishment of a virtual university. One of its key goals is to lower the cost of education. I worry about this because their plan so far is silent on the value of personal contact between students and teachers.

My experience was terrific because my relationship with my mentor thrived over the computer network. The guided independent study model that Empire State College developed twenty-five years ago provided an effective alternative to conventional college for adults who wanted to pursue

CHAPTER 5 ■ THE DEATH OF PRINT LITERACY, BIRTH OF CYBERLITERACY?

324

individually structured programs. This is why it survives so well even in the isolation of cyberspace, where you are connected to the school only by a telephone line.

I was a perfect fit with Empire State's teaching design. I wanted a program that would grant enough credits for prior learnings so I would have to register for the full-time equivalent of only one academic year. I didn't want to lose momentum in my teaching and freelance writing; I needed a school that would let me incorporate work projects into my study program. I also needed to fit my schoolwork into the time constraints of caring for my two sons, 10 and 3.

When I enrolled, Professor Diana Worby was assigned as my mentor. Instead of meeting every week or so in her office in Nyack, N.Y., we sent e-mail messages every few days. We used ordinary mail for packages of manuscripts and other material. Diana guided me through the process of developing a personal degree program, organizing my prior knowledge into academic equivalents that could be granted college credits, setting up and completing learning contracts for independent study, registering for one college class locally and one computer conference course and arranging an internship at a public radio station. And she was with me while I did the work.

It can be lonely going to school sitting at your own desk. We exchanged photographs so Diana could picture me with my husband and kids and I could see her broad supportive smile as I wrote. As we got to know each other, Diana's commitment to my successful completion of my degree was as palpable as if I had been in Nyack with her. In fact, our meeting the afternoon of my graduation was in some ways a letdown. I had expected fireworks. Our e-mail conversations had felt so intimate, that, after a long-awaited hug, there wasn't a new closeness to experience.

Looking back into the file folders stuffed with printouts of our e-mail correspondence, I find lots of necessary details like, "I wrote up the evaluation of your first contract." But these were usually sandwiched inside descriptions of what we were doing and thinking about on particular days: my son bicycling off to his first day of fifth grade; Diana's grown daughter's search for record albums they'd listened to together many years before; leads I was pursuing for part-time work and books and articles we recommended to each other.

While some students might find it a burden to have to accomplish almost everything with the written word, for me it was an extra opportunity to improve my writing. What appears on the surface to be primarily an old-fashioned (although high-tech) correspondence between two thoughtful friends was also the vehicle for an experienced critic of literature to let me know when she was particularly informed, moved or challenged by my writing.

My computer conference with a tutor used an independent study structure that had been developed for correspondence courses. We still read assignments and mailed in papers, but instead of scheduling individual phone conferences, the teacher of our section met online with me and the other student in the class.

The biggest difference I noticed from typical classroom discussions was that, with time to edit our contributions and without other people waiting their turn to speak, we developed our thoughts fully and addressed the complexity of topics instead of making a single point at a time. Every so often, the teacher suggested a different way to think about something or added relevant assignments to those in the printed course guide.

I enjoyed finally meeting another Empire State College student. We chatted about his Greenwich Village neighborhood where I had once lived, and joked about his e-mailing me a loaf of Zito's whole wheat bread. (My mouth watered.)

The online world is changing so fast that, if I were enrolled today, I would use Writer's Complex, Empire State's new interactive tutorial on writing and researching. I could follow links to screens about punctuation, style and how to write a research paper, read sample student papers in different disciplines, practice writing exercises, hang out with other writers in the virtual student lounge and contact tutors for help. (It's at http://www.esc.edu/html-pages/Writer/vwcmen.htm on the World Wide Web.)

Despite my excitement about new electronic educational opportunities, I'm concerned that others seeking convenient online degrees won't have the opportunities to find programs that nurture them intellectually and emotionally. Individual course requirements can certainly be completed by exhibiting competence on tests or by sending in papers or by using new interactive computer programs. But will there be a person on the other end of the line who is watching to see that students are stretching themselves, choosing appropriate courses, struggling with new ideas, overcoming personal obstacles, getting smarter?

I'm concerned that feedback will be limited to course work itself, and that the fuller relationships that develop between students and teachers on a college campus will be missing. I'm concerned that part-time instructors will be hired course-by-course but won't be paid enough or be on staff long enough to be available to guide students through the full process. Every student needs someone to say, "You're doing fine, just keep at it," or "Whoops, you're not going to make it unless you try another approach." Whether it's a mentor or faculty adviser, it has to be someone who knows what's ahead in a field of concentration better than the student.

There are probably other models that will work as well for online students as Empire State's, but only if "the virtual university aims to be more than a collection of courses. Teachers need structures that give them a stake in their students' success. I hope that the shift of education into cyberspace represents a continuation of the drive for excellence and not a retreat.

CHAPTER 5 ■ THE DEATH OF PRINT LITERACY, BIRTH OF CYBERLITERACY?

326

EXPLORING THE READING

1. Weiner says that one-to-one mentoring was an important key to her success in an online program. What other features of her personality and the college she chose does she suggest also ensured that success?

2. What criteria might an online university use to select candidates who are likely to be successful? What criteria should students use to evaluate an online university? Discuss this in a small group and present your findings to the class.

3. How comfortable would you feel in this type of educational setting? What would add to your comfort? What might detract from it? Freewrite on this for ten minutes.

WRITING SUGGESTIONS

1. What is a book? Based on your own experience and using examples from your own life, combined with information from this chapter and your own research, write an essay defining "book."

2. Connect to the sites offering online books. Read a short story or several chapters of a book that interests you, possibly one with hypertext-enhanced accompanying materials such as "The Mortal Immortal" by Mary Shelley, http://www.sul.stanford.edu/mirrors/romnet/rc. The Online Books Page, http://www.cs.cmu.edu/books.html, gives links to a number of enhanced online texts. Also check out a copy of the book from a library. Write an essay comparing the experience of reading the book online and reading it in printed form.

3. Contact a local school and learn the status of their computerization. Tour the school and see how computers are being used. Inquire whether the school has lost any programs as a result of money being put into computers. Ask if teachers think the number of computers and programs provided are adequate. Write a paper analyzing the use of computers in this particular school, referring, if you wish, to Todd Oppenheimer's "The Computer Delusion" or other resources.

4. Does your college or university offer courses held online? If so, interview students who have taken such courses and write an essay taking a position in favor of or in opposition to the offering of online courses for credit.

5. Have you ever used a manual typewriter? When did you first make the transition to using computers? To using the Internet? Write an account of your own experience of the late age of print.

THE WRITING PROCESS

Incorporating Informal Research

Should I buy a PC or a Macintosh? Should I buy a tower or a laptop? What type of screen is best for my eyes? Do I want to use the software I'm familiar with, or should I use the word-processing software that comes with my new computer? To answer these questions, you'll likely do some research.

You may not go to the library to look things up, but you will probably conduct some informal research. You might make a list of your wants and needs on paper or in your head. You might talk with several sales people at a few different stores. You may talk to friends about their systems and what they like and don't like about them. Maybe you'll join a computer chat group to learn about systems that will meet your needs. You might also try several different computers or software packages on computers at your school, a library, or a friend's house.

Talking, thinking, informal writing, observing, and experiencing are all forms of informal research that we do every day. Interviews and observation

CHAPTER 5 ■ THE DEATH OF PRINT LITERACY, BIRTH OF CYBERLITERACY?

328

are the most common forms of informal or primary research and you can use them to help strengthen your arguments, give your audience more information, and make your essay more interesting. What follows are some suggestions about conducting informal research in the form of interviews and observation.

Interviews.   Whether you are conducting an in-depth interview to include in a questions-and-answer or profile essay focused on one particular person as Herb Brody does in "Session with a Cybershrink" or conducting brief interviews with experts in the field, in person, or over the phone as Sarah Lyall does in "Are These Books, or What? CD-ROM and the Literacy Industry," interviews are an excellent way to gain interesting information about your topic.

No matter what your subject, your community probably has some excellent sources who can give you current and interesting information about technology. You might find these sources sitting behind a desk at your local Internet access provider, in the information systems office of a local company, behind the sales desk at a computer store, or behind a desk in the computer science department of your college. The most difficult part of informal research can be asking the right questions of the right person to find someone who will provide an enlightening interview. Your college is often a good place to start. If you want to do some research on Internet commerce, for instance, you might start in the business or computer science department of your college.

Check the college catalog or department brochure for a list of professor's specialties, and pick the one or two that seem closest to your topic area. Ask the professor if he or she would be willing to talk with you or knows someone who might answer your questions about Internet commerce.

Eventually, you'll find someone you'd like to interview. When you first speak with your subject, introduce yourself and your reason for wanting to speak with him or her. Most people are happy to spend a half-hour or so to help college students with their research. What's more, most people like to talk about themselves and their field of expertise. Remember that to be ethical you must have permission of the people you interview before you use their information or names. Explain that you are working on a class project or paper and want to ask a few questions. If you plan to submit your text for publication or place it on the World Wide Web, you must also disclose this to your interviewee.

If your first choice refuses, ask him or her to refer you to someone else. When your subject agrees to the interview, arrange a date, time, and location convenient for both of you. If you schedule the interview more than a week in advance, it's always a good idea to call to confirm your appointment a day or so before the scheduled meeting. Once you've found someone to interview and scheduled the meeting, you need to decide on questions to ask that will help you and your readers understand your subject. There are two types of interview questions: open questions that allow for extended discussion and closed questions that require either a "yes" or "no" or a specific factual answer.

Open questions allow room for extended discussion. You can prolong the discussion even further by allowing a pause between your subject's answer and your next question. You will often find that your subject will continue to talk if you give him or her some time before you speak again. Some good open questions are:

Could you tell me more about (*topic*)?
What got you interested in (*topic*)?
Could you tell me about a positive (or negative) experience you've had with (*topic*)?

Once you have your list of questions and as the day of the interview approaches, you'll want to prepare for the interview. For almost every interview, it's a good idea to have a small tape recorder to record the discussion. You'll also need a stiff-backed note pad and several pencils or pens.

Though you'll have most of your questions written out before you conduct your interview, you should be flexible about those questions. If your subject brings up a topic you know little about you might say, "You mentioned (*topic*); that sounds interesting. I wonder if you'd tell me more about it?" Going with the flow of the interview instead of sticking to your pre-arranged plan can yield some interesting results. Be sure, however, that you get the answers to your most important questions before you leave the interview.

Occasionally you may have an interview subject who would rather talk about his golden retriever than the software he developed. If this happens, keep trying to bring the interview gently back to focus by using questions to redirect the speaker. "Belle sounds like a wonderful dog," you might say, "I wonder if she had any influence on the development of your software." Gentle questions that affirm what the speaker is discussing while trying to get the discussion back on topic are often best.

Before you leave the interview, get permission from your interview subject to contact him or her if you have further questions. Get a telephone number and make sure you thank your subject for the time.

Soon after you leave the interview you'll want to take some notes about the interview environment, the dress and physical presence of your subject, and any other impressions you got during the interview. Don't expect to remember these impressions for very long; get them into your notes within a few hours of the interview. You'll also need to type up a transcript of the interview from the tape or your notes.

Observation. We've learned to filter out a lot of unnecessary information. Often, we don't use our senses to learn new things from the world around us. We use our senses only to confirm that the world is the way we want it to be. We worry, for example, if we smell smoke or gas because those things are danger signals for us. But we may not notice the smell of cut grass because it doesn't threaten us in any way.

CHAPTER 5 ■ THE DEATH OF PRINT LITERACY, BIRTH OF CYBERLITERACY?

330

When we observe something in order to write about it, we turn all our senses back on and tune them to the present situation. Maybe you've decided to write an essay detailing the typical responses to technology in a computer lab. You've found a quiet place to sit where you can watch other students use computers in the lab without being too obtrusive, and you've decided you'll sit there, taking notes, for an hour.

Next, you'll turn your senses on and ask those senses questions to make sure each of your senses is paying attention. Does the room itself have a smell or do the smells come from the people using the machines? What does a computer keyboard feel like when you first touch it? What do people look like as they bend over their machines? What noises are going on underneath the prevalent noise of fingers striking keys? Smelling, touching, looking, hearing, and sometimes tasting are the five senses you'll attend to in order to observe a place closely.

As you observe, you should take copious notes. You might begin by freewriting on the entire scene for eight minutes or so, remembering to use all five of your senses, not just vision. Then take a few minutes to look around and tune your senses again. Choose a small portion of the scene to write about, focus on the details of a woman working at her computer in the corner of the room and freewrite on your sensory impression of this more focused subject for another eight minutes or so. Perhaps you'll choose to move to another part of the room to write from a different focal point for a few minutes. As you observe, keep reminding yourself to pay attention to all your senses.

You can use details from close observation in almost any essay you write. If you are comparing two software packages, you'll need to spend some time observing the computer screen, looking at the details of the package. You may even want to observe someone using the package. If you are writing an argument about freedom of speech on the Internet, you'll want to observe chat rooms, Web pages, and other facets of life on the Net and report sensory details back to your audience. Tuning your attention to your subject and experiencing the subject with as many senses as possible can make your writing more lively and interesting.

ACCESSING INTERNET RESOURCES

Finding Online Publications

The World Wide Web is a powerful new publishing medium. In addition to the Web pages on a seemingly infinite variety of topics, the Web has spawned a number of online magazines, some with the quality and depth readers are accustomed to finding in major print publications. One of the best known of these is *Salon*, which features articles and columns by prominent writers such as Susie Bright, Jon Carroll, David Horowitz, Anne Lamont, and Camille Paglia. In addition, frequently overlooked Internet resources are full-text Web versions of print publications such as *Time, Fortune,* and the *New York*

Times. Also of interest are online sister publications to print magazines such as *HotWired,* http://www.hotwired.com, the brain-child of *Wired,* the legendary computer-counter-culture magazine.

Some sites index both online-only publications and Web revisions of print publications. These include the Library of Congress's Lists of Newspaper & Periodical Resources on the Internet, http://lcweb.loc.gov/rr/news/lists.html and Yahoo!'s News and Media, http://www.yahoo.com/News_and_Media. The Ecola Newstand, http://www.ecola.com, and Pathfinder (Time Warner publications), http://www.pathfinder.com, also provide links to online versions of print publications.

CHAPTER 5 ■ THE DEATH OF PRINT LITERACY, BIRTH OF CYBERLITERACY?

332

SUGGESTED INTERNET ASSIGNMENTS

1. Examine *Salon*, the online magazine discussed in the Accessing Internet Resources section, or another online-only magazine. Reread Philip Elmer-Dewitt's article, "Bards of the Internet: If E-mail Represents the Renaissance of Prose, Why Is So Much of It Awful?" Evaluate the quality of writing in *Salon* or the publication you have chosen.

2. Locate and read an online short story or portion of a complete book. This may be a text published only on the Internet, or it could be an Internet version of a printed text. Some sources for online books include:

   OmniMedia Bookstore
   http://www.awa.com/library/omnimedia/bookstor.html

   Links to Electronic Book and Text Sites
   http://www.awa.com/library/omnimedia/links.html

   The Online Books Page
   http://www.cs.cmu.edu/Web/books.html

   Project Gutenberg
   http://promo.net/pg/pgframed_index.html

   Discuss in class the experience of reading books online.

The On-Line Books Page

NEW LISTINGS

This page lists the titles of on-line books that have recently been added to our index, or whose entries have been recently revised. For a full list of available books, try the main on-line books page.

Please suggest any additions to **spok+books@cs.cmu.edu**.

October 10, 1997

- *The History of Sir Richard Calmady* by Lucas Malet (HTML at Indiana)
- *Issues in Civilian Outplacement Strategies: Proceedings of a Workshop*, ed. by Renae F. Broderick (frame-dependent page images at NAP)
- *Militias in America, 1995* (with commentary and updates), ed. by Don Hazen and Larry Smith and Christine Triano (HTML at mediademocracy.org and apc.org)
- *Conflict and Cooperation in National Competition for High-Technology Industry* by Hamburg Institute for Economic Research and Kiel Institute for World Economics and National Research Council (frame-dependent page images at NAP)
- *Foreign Participation in U.S. Research and Development: Asset or Liability?*, ed. by Proctor P. Reid and Alan Schriesheim (frame-dependent page images at NAP)

October 9, 1997

- *Snow White* (several versions, with commentary), ed. by Kay E. Vandergrift (illustrated HTML at Rutgers)
- *The Mortal Immortal* by Mary Shelley (hypermedia with commentary at Stanford)
- *Agrarian Justice* by Thomas Paine (HTML at mediapro.net)
- *The Illusion of Agony: A Comprehensive Critique of Dr. Robert Wennberg's Book, "Life in the*

---

3. Connect to the sites providing links to online versions of major magazines. Locate and print out an article on your choice of topic from one of these publications. Discuss in class the range of publications available online. Some of these sites include:

Library of Congress's Lists of Newspaper & Periodical Resources on the Internet
http://lcweb.loc.gov/rr/news/lists.html

Yahoo!'s News and Media
http://www.yahoo.com/News_and_Media

Ecola Newsstand
http://www.ecola.com

The Electronic Newsstand
http://enews.com

WIRED TO THE WEB

The Online Books Page

http://www.cs.cmu.edu/People/spok/aboutolbp.html
The Online Books Page indexes thousands of online books which can be read directly from the Internet. Many of the books are in hypertext format or have links to resources and commentaries related to the books.

CHAPTER 5 ■ THE DEATH OF PRINT LITERACY, BIRTH OF CYBERLITERACY?

334

 Logo Designed by The Web Writer

Welcome to OmniMedia Electronic Publishing!

Click here to VISIT OUR BOOKSTORE

About Electronic Books and OmniMedia

OmniMedia is a pioneer in the new and exciting realm of electronic books! What are electronic books that everybody is talking about? An electronic book is just like an ordinary paper book except that the information is contained in a datafile and accessed electronically. As technology progresses, especially with the inevitable development of very high resolution, easy-to-read, yet inexpensive flat screens (making portable and very inexpensive e-book readers a practical possibility), some experts foresee that electronic books will essentially replace paper books within about 20 years, just like digital CD's have essentially replaced analog LP's as our primary audio storage medium.

But you don't have to wait 20 years to experience the pleasure and advantages of electronic books. OmniMedia is now publishing electronic books that can be read and enjoyed on your own computer, and you can download them right here!

OmniMedia Bookstore

http://www.awa.com/library/omnimedia/bookstor.html

OmniMedia Bookstore is an example of an online bookstore which offers texts for sale. You can generally read a few chapters for free, but you must purchase the right to read and/or download the remainder of the book. OmniMedia also maintains a list of links to Websites that offer online books (some free and some for a fee) at http://www.awa.com/library/omnimedia/links.html.

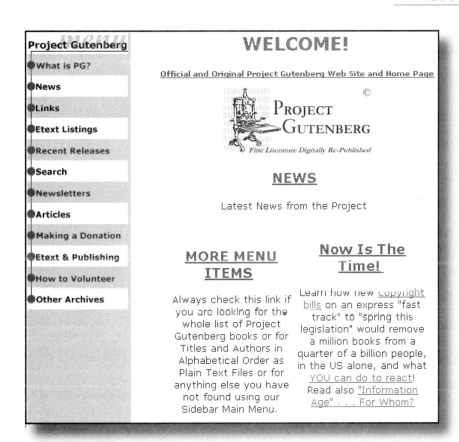

Project Gutenberg

http://promo.net/pg

Project Gutenberg archives full-text copies of classics such as *Alice's Adventures in Wonderland, Paradise Lost*, and *Emma,* as well as reference books such as encyclopedias and dictionaries. The project began in 1971 with the aim of putting 10,000 books online that can be freely downloaded by anyone who wants to read them.

CHAPTER 5 ■ THE DEATH OF PRINT LITERACY, BIRTH OF CYBERLITERACY?

336

Links to Electronic Book and Text Sites

There are many Web sites which distribute electronic books and texts, both free and commercial, and in many formats (ASCII text, HTML, WinHelp, Acrobat, Envoy, SGML-encoded, etc.) Following is a fairly complete list of these sites. This list also includes a few sites which do not themselves distribute e-books/texts, but which directly address subjects pertaining to electronic publishing.

Note that many of these sites carry the same files, particulary the freely available ASCII texts, but this redundancy allows the end-user to choose the most appropriate site to download files.

Since this list is intended to be the most complete available on the Web, OmniMedia would like to be informed of additions and updates.

- Project Gutenberg (the "Mother of All E-Text Archives")
- A1 Electronic Publishing at Orpheus Enterprises (e-books for DOS platforms)
- Alex (not currently being updated)
- Alive and Free (free works from living authors)
- Andrea's Literary Links (many interesting links)
- B&R Samizdat Express
- Banned Books On-Line
- BiblioBytes (commercial e-books in Mac Voyager and Acrobat formats)

Links to Electronic Book and Text Sites

http://www.awa.com/library/omnimedia/links.html

This site attempts to link to all sites on the Internet that offer books in electronic format and also sites offering information about electronic publishing. The index does not offer much commentary; you have to browse the links yourself.

Directory of English-Language Media Links

 Ecola Newsstand

Newspapers . . . read the press from the U.S. and the world

Magazines . . . select from over one hundred categories

Computer Publications . . . tech journals and magazines

What's New . . . new links posted daily

Search for a Publication Name . . . over 5,000 Titles

More Resources:

Searchable Newspaper Archives . . . with access to articles online [NEW!]

TV Remote . . . links to local television

Ecola Newsstand
http://www.ecola.com
Ecola offers links to over 5,000 magazines in 100 categories, as well as a searchable newspaper archive with full-text articles.

CHAPTER 5 ■ THE DEATH OF PRINT LITERACY, BIRTH OF CYBERLITERACY?

338

NEWSPAPER & CURRENT PERIODICAL READING ROOM

Lists of Newspaper & Periodical Resources on the Internet

A LIBRARY OF CONGRESS INTERNET RESOURCE PAGE

Jump to: Web Newspapers | Current News | Other News & Hybrid Lists | Periodicals

Connect to Web Newspapers:

- All Worldwide News
- American Journalism Review - NewsLink Web Newspapers Worldwide
- Editor & Publisher's Database Directory Of The World's Online Newspapers
- INES Media (Darmstadt, Germany) - Worldwide List of Newspapers
- NewsLibrary (Knight-Ridder)

Current News Services

- CBS News Up to the Minute
- CNN Interactive
- Clarinet Tearsheet: U.S. and General News
- The Daily News from Zippo's News Service
- Disaster Information Network [WWW]
- FEMA (Federal Emergency Management Agency)
- News Sources on the Internet
- Pathfinder News Now
- Reuters NewsMedia
- Wire Services A list from Trib.com (Wyoming)
- World-Wide Web Resources - Current Events from the University of Kentucky

Lists of Newspaper & Periodical Resources on the Internet
http://lcweb.loc.gov/rr/news/lists.html/
Library of Congress list of online media includes newspapers, news services, periodicals, and other collections of links to media on the Web.

THE WIRED SOCIETY
AND HUMAN NATURE

Millions of people around the world sit for hours every day in front of a computer, pushing keys, clicking a mouse, and watching the results flicker across the monitor screen. Why? Certainly, some do it because it is required by a job, college class, or other outside constraint, but many choose to be there. Why? Why is it that we hear about computer addiction? How could a machine be addictive?

The connection between computers and the human psyche is powerful and profound. On a simple level, computers are just another tool, like the wheel or the steam engine or the printing press which enable humans to do things by extending the reach of their senses, increasing the physical power of their actions, or recording their words. Computers are a vehicle for communication, allow us to keep records, and make word processing easier. But no technology is inert. All manipulate the physical world and, in doing so, change the ways humans think about the world and themselves. For example, the invention of writing allowed humans to record their history and accumulate knowledge, relieving people of the necessity to memorize everything that needed to be passed from one generation to another. As a result, people turned their minds from rote memorization to reviewing and questioning, becoming much more introspective and evaluative.

Using a computer also changes the way people think in ways researchers are only beginning to discover. Computers arouse strong feelings, both in those who use them and in those who don't. The computer, more so than many devices, has a chameleon-like quality because the individual user can program it or personalize the programs that already exist. A computer follows directions and does what we tell it to do, but on such a complex level that it seems almost magical. Computers process information, analyze data, and, unlike typewriters and telephones, do what could be described as thinking. To people who use them frequently, a computer seems like a companion, even a friend who is always there, ready to interact and entertain.

Sherry Turkle suggests in her 1984 book, *The Second Self,* that computers are a "mirror of the mind." Like a Rorschach inkblot test, people project parts of themselves—their ideas and fantasies—onto the computer screen. In the 1980s, computers were used primarily for word processing, game playing, and other solitary tasks. By the time of her next book, *Life on the Screen* (1996), sitting at a computer was no longer a solo activity because of widespread access to the Internet. The computer, according to Turkle, is no longer simply a mirror of the self. Users are now able, like Alice, to step through the "looking glass." Computer users now can choose to spend large segments of their lives in the virtual worlds of cyberspace, exploring their interests and fantasies, communicating with others, and even creating their own "homes" in the form of home pages in cyberspace.

But what do people get from all this interaction with a computer? What needs and desires are being satisfied? A powerful one, discussed in "Intimate Strangers," by Jill Smolowe, and "Home on the Net," by John Seabrook, is the need to belong, to connect to others, to be part of a community. Some spend hours and hours communicating in chat rooms and discussion groups. Others check their e-mail daily, sometimes several times a day, corresponding with old college buddies, new-found friends halfway around the world whom they met on the Net, or even business acquaintances whose phone calls they might avoid returning.

Another, perhaps equally powerful need, sometimes overlooked in the hype about cyberspace, is the human need to learn, to explore, to grow. Jeff Zaleski, in "Cyberspirit," describes a morning spent taking a virtual tour of the Cathedral of St. John the Divine, visiting an art gallery, and chatting online about yoga courses. The topics would vary widely from one individual to another, but millions of people are out in cyberspace exploring places and ideas they had never encountered elsewhere. This need to explore and to learn, on the Internet, is intertwined with the need to communicate. People are teaching themselves the cryptic HTML (hypertext markup language) commands so that they can publish their own ideas for others to examine. These highly individual home pages always include an e-mail link, for part of the process of creating home pages is the interaction between author and viewer.

The virtual realities people are creating in cyberspace are something new, something humans have never done before. But Howard Rheingold, in "Cyberspace and Human Nature," from his book *Virtual Reality,* suggests that humans have been creating virtual realities since the days of the cavemen. Cyberspace is but the latest manifestation of an ages-old human desire to create an altered state. An individual engaged in a virtual reality situation is absorbed, out of the self, relieved of everyday preoccupations. Virtual realities engender a range of strong emotions that are highly reinforcing, such as enchantment, delight, and fright, to name a few.

Computers have the ability to empower, to enrich, to expand horizons. They also have the ability to confuse, to alienate, to hurt. Like any tool from the ax to the space shuttle, the use of computers is motivated by a desire to satisfy needs. Human nature and computers—it is a complex interrelationship that will continue to evolve and develop as computers become a more integral part of everyday life.

———————————■———————————

TECHNOLOGY AS A PSYCHIC PHENOMENON

by Michael Grosso

Michael Grosso, in this essay from Computer Mediated Communication, *an online magazine, admits that suggesting a link between the psyche and technology may seem curious. In this essay, however, he asks the reader to contemplate the connection. The telephone, he suggests, is analogous to telepathy, and film to retrocognition.*

Grosso, a professor of philosophy at Jersey City State College, writes about mythology, psychic abnormalities, and altered states. His books include The Millennium Myth: Love and Death at the End of Time *and* Soulmaking: Uncommon Paths to Self-Understanding.

Marshall McLuhan once remarked that the telephone may be likened to a form of telepathy. This comparison suggests an interesting question: What, if any, is the relationship between psyche and machine, between the powers of the human soul and technology? At first glance, coupling the two seems an unpromising move. The psychic is elusive and nebulous; technology implies exact control and reliable power. You associate the psychic with "miracles" and retrograde religion, technology with progress, science, and reason.

Even so, the psychic and the technological are linked. The link lies in McLuhan's idea of the "extensions of man." The psychic and the technological both involve attempts to abolish the constraints of time and space, with technology serving as material analogues of psychic powers.

Consider some examples. We began with telepathy (really, clairaudience) and the telephone. The limitations of space are thus abolished and instant global communication becomes possible. Live television is machine-mediated clairvoyance. Film, video and audio technologies form a neat analogue of retrocognition. Here the fatal limitations of time are encroached upon, and we acquire direct visual inspection of the past.

Precognition is an interesting case. According to Laplace, we could, if we knew all the relevant variables, be able to predict the state of the universe for any time in the future. So indeed science has become our latter-day prophet and the computer our Daniel. With the help of modern computer technologies we can indeed predict states of physical reality with high degrees of precision. Not that it solves all our problems, as we note in the case of El Niño.

Now consider the unsettling idea of psychokinesis (PK), or mind over matter. PK is said to be the ability directly to influence states of matter, in short, magic. But technology has become our magic; every time we press a button in an elevator or turn the ignition key in our cars we're doing a kind of machine-mediated PK. The truth is that our ability to manipulate matter and master space is vast, and an atomic bomb embodies destructive power worthy of the most ferocious mythic deity.

From Gilgamesh to the resurrection, mythology speaks to us of powers of rejuvenation, life-extension, and immortality. These correspond to the promise of artificial life, bioengineering, nanotechnology, and artificial intelligence. Technology today has apocalyptic pretensions. For example, it now dreams of the possibility of "uploading" consciousness from its customary mortal wetware to more durable information hardware.

Let's assume then that the psychic and the technological are converging; they share a common impetus to master space, time, and matter. At some deep level a common force may be driving them. If so, to understand what technology wants, and what is driving us toward the greater wired society, we need to look at our deepest psychic needs and drives.

But what are they? In light of the foregoing remarks, we may think of them as expressing the project to become God. To see how this works just look at magic, religion, shamanism, and mythology. What we find is an array of images of extraordinary potential, of gradual ascent from the idea of the artist, the priest, the hero, the magician, the shaman, the saint, the messiah, the boddisattva, the avatar, the godman, to the gods and goddesses themselves. We see images of beings who embody increasing mastery of the forms and energies of nature.

Try to think of a being at the outer limits of psychic power and we come up something that almost equals God. For unlimited ESP would equal omniscience and unlimited PK would equal omnipotence. Technology today presents us with the prospect of a second genesis. The first genesis was through God or nature; the second seems to be coming about through human will and ingenuity.

While St. John spoke of a "new heaven and earth," K. Eric Drexler speaks of "engines of creation." I believe that behind the excitement of the Internet and all the wonders of technology is the feeling that we may be on the verge of a cosmic breakthrough, a second genesis in which humanity is making itself over into a designer god.

However, a being of unlimited psychic or technological power would still fall short of God as we understand it in the higher religions. What is lacking are those values we associate with God such as love, mercy, and compassion.

Unfortunately, this project of extending human abilities to godlike proportions is flawed. For the psychic and the technical models of transformation are mainly about power; they fail, in important ways, to reach the level of spirit. They offer no guarantee of a world any different than the one we're familiar with, a mix of the marvelous and the horrible. The only difference is that the marvels and the horrors will be more spectacular.

EXPLORING THE READING

1. Have you ever thought about the similarity of the telephone to telepathy or any of the other parallels Michael Grosso suggests between the psyche and technology? What is your impression?

2. In your small group, discuss the connection between technology and the psyche. Do you think humans have invented technology to extend their sensory powers?

3. Freewrite for five minutes about Grosso's assertion that technology represents a human desire to become God. What do you think?

CYBERSPACE AND HUMAN NATURE

by Howard Rheingold

Humans have been creating virtual realities, not just since the invention of computers, but for thousands of years, reminds Howard Rheingold in "Cyberspace and Human Nature." When young men were taken into the darkness of caves in southern France thirty thousand years ago where torch-lit paintings were suddenly revealed, the effect was to accentuate the images, to alter reality, to create "audiovisually induced fear and trembling" as part of an initiation rite. The human's propensity to manipulate their senses is innate and powerful, according to Rheingold. It has been used throughout history to educate, as well as to control through imprinting. What is happening in cyberspace is not so different.

Well-known for his writings about cyberspace and counterculture, Rheingold is the editor-in-chief of the Millennium Whole Earth Catalog *and a former editor of the* Whole Earth Review. *His World Wide Web page, http://www.rheingold.com/howard, provides links to many of his recent projects. He has also published* Virtual Communities *and* Virtual Reality *from which this selection was excerpted.*

Thirty thousand years ago, outside a deceptively small hole in a limestone formation in the area now known as southern France, several adolescents shivered in the dark, awaiting initiation into the cult of toolmakers. The weeks of fasting and abstinence, the ordeals of silence and pain, the rituals of drumming, chanting, and dancing, were about to reach their climax. The first virtual reality awaited below. We will never know with absolute certainty what went on there, but at least one contemporary paleontologist has argued that the activities in those caves were closely related to a series of changes in human thought and action that continue to reverberate to this day.

At some point between ten and thirty thousand years ago, most of our species changed its way of life, not because of biological mutation or selection, but because people learned something new. The caves at Lascaux and other sites might be the places where that learning took place. If the theories of paleontologist John Pfeiffer are correct, primitive but effective cyberspaces may have been instrumental in setting us on the road to computerized world-building in the first place. Toolmaking was at the beginning of the road that led to the opening of cyberspace, and toolmaking, using human attention mechanisms and high-resolution video displays instead of ochre paintings on limestone walls, may be the ultimate future purpose of cyber-space, as well.

The novices had been selected carefully. Once a year, the candidates who had come of age were abducted by a shadowy group of toolmakers, shamans, and artists, whose activities were changing irrevocably the way the human race worked and lived. The mentors took the novices, one by one, down into the cave. Hours of crawling through deep, narrow, labyrinthine, utterly dark

passageways led to the special chambers. After the chanting, the prostra-
tions, the whispered myths and texts, the darkness was pierced by torches
and lamps placed at strategic intervals. The novices, who were lying or
standing in precisely predetermined positions, suddenly saw the super-
natural figures floating in space in front of them—bisons, birds, symbols,
human figures jumped out of the darkness to fill their fields of view.

In this moment of audiovisually induced fear and trembling, Pfeiffer proposes, the first technological secrets were imparted. The deliberately sensi-
tized psyches of the novices were reframed by carefully crafted sequences of
sights and sounds, imprinted with the secrets of fire and metal, the connections between seeds and stars. An early form of the most powerful idea at the
basis of technological civilization—that it is possible to observe the world
and learn from it and apply that knowledge to the requirements of daily
life—was burned into our forebears' brains to the accompaniment of a three-
dimensional sound and light show.

The earliest virtual realities on earth were constructed laboriously, by
lamplight, deep underground. Their purpose is unknown, but John Pfeiffer
presents evidence in his scientific publications and his book, *The Creative
Explosion,* that these subterranean cyberspaces may have been created to
imprint information on the minds of the first technologists. Although the
origins of the human species are still a matter of controversy, current dating
methods point to a common ancestor about 200,000 years ago. Until several
tens of thousands of years ago, a relatively sparse human population led
more or less the same kind of lives, millennium in, millennium out. Around
the time that the cave paintings were created, however, a new way of living
was born. The most successful revolutionaries of all time, the first Paleolithic
agriculturist/technologists, were transforming and ultimately dooming the
hunting-gathering way of life that had sustained small bands of humans for
the 200,000 years the species had existed.

Why did people suddenly start making paintings deep in caves, tens of
thousands of years ago? The question is more than academic. As Pfeiffer
pointed out in his book, people didn't go to this much trouble back then
without having a reason:

> What brought about the use of art after hundreds of millenniums of unembel-
> lished and artless cave and open-air dwelling, and why in western Europe and
> apparently not as early in the rest of the world? Something must have hap-
> pened to account for the difference, and it is a most significant difference. One
> wonders how society had changed, how people had changed. What new needs
> had to be satisfied, what new wants fulfilled? Were they more sensitive, more
> self-aware, more esthetic—and, above all, how could they have possibly bene-
> fited from such "impractical" behavior?
>
> The problem becomes several orders of magnitude more complex when
> one considers the deep art: the art located in utter darkness, far from daylight
> and twilight zones and living places, on wide expanses of wall or doubly
> hidden inside tiny chambers, caves within caves, secrets within secrets. The
> purpose of this sort of art differed enormously from the purposes of the

domestic variety. It suggests such things as intense rituals, ordeals, journeys underground for mystical reasons. The burst of art marked a burst of ceremony and, again, we wonder about its evolutionary payoffs, about the needs and wants it involved, about its selective and adaptive value. There is every reason to believe that individual artists benefited directly from their rare talents, that art would have withered if this had not been the case. But at the same time art also favored the advancement of the group, and the band and tribe.

The coming of art by itself would have been more than enough to distinguish the Upper Paleolithic, but a number of other major developments were under way during the same period. For one thing, a familiar newcomer appears for the first time in the fossil record, a new species. The Neanderthals vanish without a trace, and their place is taken by the remains of modern-type individuals like ourselves, Cro-Magnon people and related breeds referred to collectively and somewhat euphemistically as "doubly wise," *Homo sapiens sapiens*.

New lifestyles appeared along with the new species. Changes were taking place across the board, in practically all areas of human endeavor. The Cro-Magnons made more tools and more kinds of tools than the Neanderthals, using a wider variety of raw materials more efficiently, exploiting a wider range of plants and animals. They seem to have been coming together in larger groups, perhaps for somewhat longer periods, a hint of full-scale settlements to come, and communicating with one another over greater distances. There are signs of a crumbling of age-old traditions. Things were happening faster than ever before.

Pfeiffer noted that many of the paintings were "anamorphic," painted in a precisely distorted manner on natural protuberances and depressions in the limestone in order to give the rendering a three-dimensional appearance when viewed from the proper light and angle. Other images were incised in the walls in such a way that they reveal themselves only when a light is moved across them from the proper angle. From the placements of the paintings, the three-dimensional illusions, and external evidence of other human activities during the same period, Pfeiffer assembled evidence for his hypothesis that the purpose of these underground light shows was to cause a specific state of consciousness.

The reason for shocking people into an altered state of consciousness, Pfeiffer contends, might have been to aid in imparting a growing body of information needed for the expansion of a new way of life. Seed saving, herbal medicine, stone toolmaking, stargazing, animal husbandry, and all the other bodies of lore that were necessary to end the age-old cycles of migration and create permanent settlements were relatively new in human culture. The new techniques brought a need to transmit additional cultural information to future generations—the instruction manuals for the new labor-saving devices. An information explosion and communication crisis resulted, Pfeiffer asserts:

> The crisis, as severe as the threat of famine, threatened chaos. The collective knowledge of the band society was on the rise, demanding far more powerful systems of record-keeping—and there was no writing. Writing might have helped to some extent, and steps that would eventually lead to the earliest

notations with complex signs and symbols were already well under way. But writing as we know it lay some twenty millenniums in the future. The here-and-now emergency gave rise to measures of a different sort, measures created to transmit the expanding contents of "the tribal encyclopedia" intact and indelibly from generation to generation. . . .

One way of preparing people for imprinting has been known for a long time by tribes everywhere, modern as well as prehistoric: bring them into unfamiliar, alien, and unpleasant places, part of the procedure known in recent times as brainwashing. This is designed to erase or undermine his everyday world as completely as possible, apparently serves as an effective preliminary to making him remember. . . .

So many things are going on in such spots, so many impressions and the combined impact of all the impressions. The art itself is only part of the experience, often a rather small part at that. Except for a relatively small proportion of outstanding paintings and engravings, the figures may be more or less interesting but they are not exciting, especially viewed out of context and in two dimensions, reproduced in books or projected on screens. The setting is a major factor in the effect of the figures, and the process of getting there, a series of successive narrowings, from the outside world into the cave mouth, and on into galleries, side chambers and niches in or beyond the chambers. A kind of extended zooming or closing in enhances the figures. Then they are exciting. . . .

Imprinting enormous amounts of information in memory called for every device I have discussed so far—the use of confined spaces, obstacles and difficult routes, and hidden images to heighten the natural strangeness of underground settings—and a great deal more. We are only beginning to appreciate the subtlety of what was going on. Considering the technologies available at the time, the people of the Upper Paleolithic seem to have made use of every trick in the book, piling special effect upon special effect in an effort to ensure the preservation and transmission of the tribal encyclopedia.

The caves at Lascaux may have been among the earliest mental-imprinting ceremonies that made use of subterranean, three-dimensional art, myth and ritual, and possibly mind-altering substances. The use of underground initiation chambers filled with architectural and pictorial symbols of technological and spiritual principles, for special theatrical rituals and light-and-sound spectacles intended to alter the consciousness, was not confined to the Mediterranean. The oldest continuously inhabited human settlements in North America, the Hopi mesas at Oraibi in northern Arizona, still contain such rooms, known to the Pueblo tribes as *kivas:* A round, square, or hexagonal, usually underground chamber, the kiva contains a hole in the floor, a ledge around the perimeter, and a ladder extending through a smokehole in the roof. In these kivas, as in the caves at Lascaux or the initiation chambers at Eleusis, young people in altered states of consciousness were educated in the use of core tools for creating and maintaining a new way of life, both spiritually and technologically. As Frank Waters described sacred kiva architecture:

Roughly corresponding to Buddhist cosmography, both the Navaho and Pueblo universes embrace four successive underworlds below the earth. . . .

All this is abstractly symbolized in the Pueblo kiva—the secret, underground ceremonial chamber. For the kiva itself, with all its many variations, recapitulates in structural form this four-world universe common to all. . . .

In the kiva, man is ever reminded that he lives in the whole of the immense and naked universe. And he is constantly made aware of the psychic, universal harmony which he must help to perpetuate by his ceremonial life.

For the kiva is not only an architectural symbol of the physical universe. The universe, with its great axis rock and its great sipapu canyon, is itself but a structural symbol of the mystical soul-form of all creation. And both are duplicated in man himself.

The most secret kiva ceremonials are still unknown outside the Pueblo clans entrusted with their knowledge. But enough is known about the public aspects of the ritual to conclude it involves an explicit map of human origins and goals, theatrical symbolic rituals, and hard information about a technology necessary to sustain a new way of life for the culture. The Hopis, like the other Western Hemisphere descendants of bands of hunter-gatherers who migrated across the Bering land bridge, had wandered for centuries before settling down to build urban societies. The technology that made these settlements possible was the same technology that made most civilization in the Western Hemisphere possible: the cultivation of corn.

It is now known that corn was not a wild plant but an artificial one, deliberately crossbred from a wild corn and a native grass, a task that highly expert agriculturists in central Mexico accomplished over the course of generations, at about the same time the Eleusinian mysteries were flourishing in the Mediterranean. The kiva rituals imprint a ceremonial cycle that encodes a sophisticated agricultural system. First, corn is planted at exactly the right time, as indicated by the stellar patterns that guide the ceremonials. Then beans are planted next to the corn; beans help the corn roots fix nitrogen, and the corn stalks provide a trellis for the beans to climb. Then squash is planted, and in the heat of the summer the broad squash leaves conserve moisture in the soil and create a microclimate inhospitable to pests. This utterly technological, precisely timed, and culturally vital practice was one component of the external information that accompanied the psychological and spiritual components of the kiva ceremony. The uses of mimesis, masked characters, painted three-dimensional objects of symbolic significance, are some of the techniques known to be associated with kiva ceremonials. Sound familiar?

Something about caves and petroglyphs has always resonated with me. In Arizona, at the age of seventeen or eighteen, I encountered *Kokopelli* for the first time. I didn't know who he was, what he meant, or that he had a name, but when I saw the crude, almost stick-figure, humpbacked flute player incised in a rock in a shallow cave overlooking a broad river valley in northern Arizona, it was as if somebody had reached out and rung a chime in me I had never known about before. I found out about him later—associated with corn, a bearer of seeds and information, a horny devil like Shiva and Dionysius. An evolutionary technician, a dreamweaver. A civilization amplifier.

During my research for this book, I ended up at a scientific conference in Santa Barbara, California, one of those intense affairs where the information flow doesn't cease between sessions. So I took advantage of one of the two time slots allocated to personal time and found another cybernaut who was interested in seeing Painted Cave, about an hour out of town, in the Santa Ynez foothills. The Chumash Indians, who had lived in the Santa Barbara area and throughout a fairly wide swatch of southern California, were known for their powerful shamans and their cave paintings—which were not unrelated phenomena. I saw a film of the spirals, stars, wavy lines, humanoid figures once. Very different from the startling realism of some of the older cave paintings in the south of France. A brochure I picked up in the vicinity noted that the shamans who did the paintings were known to use *datura,* a powerful plant hallucinogen, and other plant substances.

Painted Cave was right off the road, in a side canyon that faced the mountains, yet was only a short hike from a place where the Pacific was visible. A heavy iron gate barred the cave mouth. It was too dark to see anything, so we climbed around and waited for the sun to rise higher. When we peered in we could see the reason for the iron bars, atop spirals and an occluded sundisk that is believed to commemorate (or predict?) a solar eclipse known to have happened in the fourteenth century: "John loves Mary" and more prosaic contemporary graffiti marred the older, more serious layers. In many ways, a disappointing trip. After looking through the bars at those paintings that were visible from the entrance, we decided to follow one of the trails and climbed up onto the rocks atop the cave. We sat there for a while and talked about what it must have been like a thousand years ago. As we were leaving, and I was resting on a small ledge after negotiating a narrower section, I looked across the gap to the next rock, and caught my breath. The sun was in just the right position, and I was in just the right place, and my gaze was aimed in the proper direction—and the clear outline of a thunderbird design, two feet across, became visible on the surface of the boulder. Attention is the ultimate instrument.

"The metaphorical shape of existence permeates the culture," Brenda Laurel called to tell me, when she had returned from New Mexico, "and that shouldn't surprise us. That's what this stuff we do with our bodies and our emotions is for." She had visited Chaco Canyon, where foot drums are dug into the mesas, and the kivas were large enough to hold hundreds. The very shape of the Anasazi cities and the architecture of their ritual places, like the Eleusinian temples, the Paleolithic caves, the Dionysian amphitheaters, focuses the power of mimesis.

In response to Pfeiffer's hypothesis of VR as an imprinting medium, my speculations about corn and kivas, and the information-encoding aspects of drama, Laurel responded: "The transmission of values and cultural information is one face of VR. The other face is the creation of Dionysian experience. The piece I find important to both of those functions is this notion of being in the living presence of something. With the ceremony in the kiva, one is in living presence not just of other people but of an event that is happening in real time. No matter whether you look at the informational function or the Dionysian one, the idea of it happening in real time and in the present location, both activities require people to be in the same space at the same time. What VR has done that is so discontinuous is get rid of real space as a requirement. Cyberspace has the potential of being able to make space go away as a mediator of collective experiences." We're still going to use the new communication media that come with cyberspace, Laurel insists, as we have used every previous medium, to conjure up transformative powers, to propel us beyond the boundaries of our minds and push our cultural evolution into new territories.

The use of cyberspaces to influence, educate, and trigger ecstatic experience is an issue for the future as well as the past. The social codes by which we create values, the social mechanisms by which those values guide actions, and the ultimate uses we choose for the tools we create are questions about the future that VR technologies are likely to force us to confront. The question of what human beings are for (what our purpose is in the scheme of things) is not the same as where human beings seem to be aimed (which events in our past could have shaped our present capabilities). In order to exert influence on the direction of events, a sufficient number of people need to understand that difference between the trajectory that got us here and the pathways we would prefer to choose for our future. One way to zero-in questions about the many implications of VR technology and the future is to look at our use of these thinking tools we have been using for a few years now.

THE HUMAN USE OF THINKING TOOLS

Virtual reality brings with it a set of questions about the industries and scientific capabilities it makes possible. It also brings with it a set of questions about human uses of technology, particularly the technologies that don't yet exist but are visible on the horizon. VR vividly demonstrates that our social contract with our own tools has brought us to a point where *we have to decide fairly soon what it is we as humans ought to become,* because we are on the brink of having the power of creating any experience we desire. The first cybernauts realized very early that the power to create experience is also the power to redefine such basic concepts as identity, community, and reality. VR represents a kind of new contract between humans and computers, an arrangement that could grant us great power, and perhaps change us irrevocably in the process.

The looming Faustian bargain involves certain changes in the partnership we have enjoyed with our machines. We might decide that we wouldn't mind becoming a little or a lot more machinelike in exchange for laborsaving devices, lifesaving tools, attractive conveniences and seductive entertainments. Such a decision would be a radical change, but not an abrupt one. Our minds, our senses, our consensual reality has been shaped for a century, to the point where billions of us are trained and ready to embrace our silicon partners more intimately than ever before. Trillions of human-hours have been logged so far in the virtual worlds of *I Love Lucy* and *Dallas*, FORTRAN and fax, computer networks, comsats, and mobile telephones. The transformations in our psyches triggered by the electronic media thus far may have been mere preparation for bigger things to come. The hinge of change seems to be connected with these machines we've created and the kind of partnership we are coevolving with our information tools.

VR is an important threshold in the evolution of human-computer symbiosis. But symbiosis is a two-way exchange; when one organism exists at the expense of another, without contributing something vital to the partnership, the relationship is parasitic. Two questions that emerge from an examination of VR are closely interrelated: How will cyberspace tools and environments affect the way we live, think and work? And how will cyberspace affect the way we apprehend the world, the way we define ourselves as sensing, thinking, communicating beings?

"Electronic media alter the ratios between the senses," was one of Marshall McLuhan's key epigrams: The ratios and amount of audio and visual input to the dominant reality recipe were altered by radio and telephones and then altered again by television; we see and hear and thus apprehend the world differently as a result. Those effects are taken for granted by now, three decades after *Understanding Media*. The cyberspace experience is destined to transform us in other ways because it is an undeniable reminder of a fact we are hypnotized since birth to ignore and deny— that our normal state of consciousness is itself a hyperrealistic simulation. We build models of the world in our mind, using the data from our sense organs and the information-processing capabilities of our brain. We habitually think of the world we see as "out there," but what we are seeing is really a mental model, a perceptual simulation that exists only in our brain. That simulation capability is where human minds and digital computers share a potential for synergy. Give the hyperrealistic simulator in our head a handle on computerized hyperrealistic simulators, and something very big might happen.

Cognitive simulation, mental model-making, is one of the things humans do best. We do it so well that we tend to become locked into our own models of the world by a seamless web of unconscious beliefs and subtly molded perceptions. And computers are model-making tools par excellence, although they are only beginning to approach the point where people might confuse simulations with reality. Computation and display technology are converging on hyperreal simulation capability. That point of convergence is important enough to contemplate in advance of its arrival. The day computer simulations become so realistic that people cannot distinguish them from nonsimulated reality we are in for major changes.

We are approaching a breakpoint where the quantitative improvement in that model-building interface will trigger a qualitative quantum leap. In coming years, we will be able to put on a headset, or walk into a media room, and surround ourselves in a responsive simulation of startling verisimilitude. Our most basic definitions of reality will be redefined in that act of perception; as Jean Baudrillard claims: "Abstraction today is no longer that of the map, the double, the mirror or the concept. Simulation is no longer that of a territory, a referential being or a substance. It is the generation by models of a real without origin or reality: a hyperreal. The territory no longer precedes the map, nor survives it. Henceforth, it is the map that precedes the territory."

The advent of technology-generated hyperreality could be the nightmarish "consensual hallucination" described by William Gibson in the novel *Neuromancer,* where the word *cyberspace* originated. Or the result might be an increase in human freedom and power, akin to the aftereffects of printing and communication technologies. Which way it will go—dystopia or empowerment—depends in part upon how people react to the unmasking of reality as a cognitive-perceptual construct. People tend to react in different ways to the news that reality might be an illusion, depending on their personal emotional attachment to their brand of reality. Denial, cognitive dissonance, resistance, and satori are all possible psychological reactions to the truth we are forced to face in the illusory realm of cyberspace, in roughly descending order of popularity.

If humans and computers are poised on the verge of a symbiotic relationship, as computer pioneer J.C.R. Licklider prophesied more than three decades ago, shouldn't we take the time to discuss what we are getting into, before we get any farther into it? If we get a handle on what we are changing into, what should we *want* to change into, what should we *not* want to change into, and how do we gain the power to make that decision? After a year and a half wrestling with the issues raised by the emergence of virtual reality technology, I still find myself asking questions I thought I had left back in philosophy class in college.

In my travels, I found a researcher who intends to use VR as a probe for mapping the limits of human potential, for understanding what human beings are best suited to do in a world increasingly dominated by machines.

Psychologist Nathaniel Durlach is from neither the Atari nor the mainframe generation. In fact, he started down the path of inquiry that led him to VR by studying bats. His interest in tactile communication led him to the idea of mapping human senses onto mechanical transducers—his area of overlap with Margaret Minsky, whose laboratory is walking distance from Durlach's. Like others I've met who found themselves drawn into the world of virtual worlds research in unexpected ways, Durlach didn't realize he was going to meet roboticists coming down the same path he was pursuing, only from a different direction. As a psychologist, he is interested not only in the "human factors" element in VR systems, but in the prospect of using VR systems as a kind of psychological microscope for examining the deepest questions about human nature.

Human nature?

"Yes," Durlach told me, when I asked him to explain the connection between VR and human nature, "questions about how you can map human perceptions onto virtual worlds are really about the limits of human capability. What are the constraints on our ability to adapt to artificially extended senses? That's a question about human nature. And it can be tested by using the proper instrument in a well-designed experiment."

Durlach is an amiable fellow, informal, steel-gray-haired, perpetually smiling. Any conversation I've had with him has been a surprising ramble over a dozen territories utterly tangential to the main point, but all completely relevant. The day I walked into his office in Cambridge, he told me a little about his background and the tactile communication of speech. A pure mathematician at the beginning of his career, he got involved in radar search and development, which brought him to Lincoln Laboratory, the spawning ground of Ivan Sutherland's Sketchpad. If you want to understand how radar and particularly how sonar work, you inevitably end up interested in bats. Bat sonar studies led Durlach to the question of binaural hearing—how do two-eared creatures use their physiology to detect relevant signals among a soup of background noise?

"I started working with hearing," Durlach told me, "and through that I became interested in people who had trouble hearing, and eventually in people who were totally deaf. That led me to work with people who were totally deaf and blind. People who had lost all sight and all hearing at the age of eighteen months were people whose entire world came through the tactile sense. They learned everything through the tactile sense." The deaf/blind use a variety of methods for communicating, but the one that interested Durlach involved the "listener" putting a hand on the face of the talker, and by monitoring airflow, laryngeal vibration, lip position, and muscle tension in the speaker, actually decoding the speech. They "hear" speech, for all practical purposes, through their fingertips. And that led Durlach to an intriguing conclusion: "People are a lot more plastic than most people realize." Perhaps we can hear ultrasound or radar, see infrared or ultraviolet, by mapping the proper mechanical transducer to the appropriate sense, and letting human plasticity do the rest.

If we can see the invisible and hear with our fingers, what is "normal" human capability? That's where VR meets age-old questions about human nature, and that's why Durlach started thinking about VR, and particularly VR's sister subject, telerobotics.

"Suppose I have a slave robot that senses different wavelengths of light than I normally sense, and I can receive information from the robot's sensors through a head-mounted display. How would that information be displayed? As colors? Sound? Tactile feedback?" After spending several hours with him over a period of days, and learning about his career, it became clear that Durlach loves to ask odd questions that lead him new places. "Or suppose I have a slave robot that is very tiny and goes inside somebody's body as a microrobot. Or I have a slave robot that is enormously strong. There is some kind of transformation that takes place between my human senses and information processing and physical actions, on the one hand, and the software and computers and supersensory or superpowerful robots, on the other. What do you actually call that? It's a real world that you are sensing and acting upon, the solid physical world. But the way you are perceiving it is virtual. What kind of reality is that?"

Durlach sees VR systems of the near future as "ideal systems for experimental psychology. Every university that has an experimental psychology department is going to have a virtual world system," he forecast. "Experimental psychology involves controlling people's environments and observing how their response relates to the input. A virtual world could be an ideal environment, and there's no reason why you can't monitor much more than the motor inputs that gloves and joysticks provide. Heart rate, pupil size, changes in the skin resistance, could all be used. For my purposes, a good VR system could be an all-purpose research instrument."

"Film is truth at 24 frames per second," Jean-Luc Godard used to say. That projection rate is the threshold at which the separate photographic images projected on a movie screen fuse in the human perceptual system into the consensual hallucination we know as cinema. Cyberspace is where the human interface to digital computers is approaching 24 frames per second. The advancement of many of the key qualities we think of as human is linked to the evolution of world-views—to the emergence and invention of new ways to see the world. As Jacob Bronowski put it, "We cannot separate the special importance of the visual apparatus of man from his unique ability to imagine, to make plans, and to do all the other things which are generally included in the catchall phrase 'free will.' What we really mean by free will, of course, is the visualizing of alternatives and making a choice between them. In my view . . . the central problem of human consciousness depends on the ability to imagine."

Given a tool for visualizing and modeling, how might we use it to help us make plans, imagine, and otherwise exert conscious influence on an increasingly complex environment? Can we imagine ways to apply it to the very real problems of the world?

As Brenda Laurel put it (1986):

> Reality has always been too small for human imagination. The impulse to create an "interactive fantasy machine" is only the most recent manifestation of the age-old desire to make our fantasies palpable—our insatiable need to exercise our imagination, judgment, and spirit in worlds, situations, and personae that are different from those of our everyday lives. Perhaps the most important feature of human intelligence is the ability to internalize the process of trial and error. When a man considers how to climb a tree, imagination serves as a laboratory for "virtual" experiments in physics, biomechanics, and physiology. In matters of justice, art, or philosophy, imagination is the laboratory of the spirit.

As with other technologies, cyberspace is not an either–or case. It will be both–and. People will use it as a hybrid of entertainment, escape, and addiction. And other people will use it to navigate through the dangerous complexities of the twenty-first century. It might be the gateway to the Matrix. Let us hope it will be a new laboratory of the spirit—and let's see what we can do to steer it that way.

EXPLORING THE READING

1. Consider Howard Rheingold's examples of ancient virtual reality installations. According to Rheingold, how should we interpret the purpose and effect of the caves, kivas, and other examples?

2. In your small group, make a list of virtual realities you have experienced, from films to carnival horror rides. Discuss how they are similar or different from the ancient examples Rheingold gives.

3. Rheingold suggests that humans have reached a point in their development when "we have to decide fairly soon what it is we as humans ought to become." What does he mean? What do you think?

WHY PEOPLE THINK COMPUTERS CAN'T

by Marvin Minsky

People believe computers cannot think, Minsky says, because we still do not know exactly what happens when the human mind "thinks." Since we don't understand ourselves, we have difficulties classifying computer processes as thought. Once we have learned the dynamics of common-sense intelligence in the human mind, he says, then we will have no "technological reason to doubt that we could build truly intelligent machines."

A pioneer in the field of artificial intelligence, Marvin Minsky co-founded MIT's Media Lab. He teaches at MIT where he is the Toshiba Professor of Media Arts and Science. His most recent book, The Society of Mind, *is published on CD-ROM and features video footage and animated icons, as well as his essays. The following selection is from Minsky's 1985 book,* The Computer Culture. *You can find out more about Minsky from his home page, http://www.ai.mit.edu/people/minsky/minsky.html.*

To guess the future, one must be a magician. The usual way is to walk backward into the past and then run forward again, hoping that a running start somehow makes a straight line. No reason it should. When I tried to think about the future of AI by examining the past, I found that AI was just like anything else: if you have some idea of what you want to find, you probably can find it by choosing the right place in the past, which makes this way of predicting history too easy to work very well. But let's try it anyway.

The people who built the first computers were scientists and engineers concerned with large numerical computations. Computers were so named because they could do arithmetic much faster than people; someday that will be seen as a funny historical accident. The first really useful computers appeared in the early 1950s. Even before that, a small group of people were thinking about what is now called information processing or symbol manipulation. These people realized that machines would be able to manipulate not only numbers but *symbols* as well: computers would be useful not only for arithmetic, but also to simulate theories about information and control processes in animals. At first, this was called cybernetics, a word that died out in the United States around 1960 but is still popular in other countries. The earliest computer programs included several experiments that would now be called AI. In the early 1950s, Alan Turing began a chess program, Anthony Oettinger wrote a learning program, and Russell Kirsch wrote a vision program—all using the machines that were designed just for arithmetic.

In the early days most people thought AI was impossible. Today, with the Star Wars robots *R2-D2* and *C*-Threepio, most people consider AI more advanced than it is. Even many computer scientists were dubious about artificial intelligence. Perhaps because they were so close to these machines, computer scientists felt they could clearly see that nothing could be inside computers except little electric currents: how could computers contain anything like a mind or a self? Many scientists argued that no machine could ever be *creative* or that computers do only what they are programmed to do. Familiarity bred contempt.

Today it is clear that computers *can* do much more than their programmers tell them—in every practical sense. The first computer programs were simple lists of commands: Do this. Do that. Do this again. But soon, new kinds of programming were developed. Newell, Shaw, and Simon developed programs of bodies of advice such as, "If the difference between what you have and what you want is of kind D, then try to change it by using method M." Victor Yngve at M.I.T. developed programs that were bodies of statements such as, "If the situation turns out to be of such-and-such a form, then change it in such-and-such a way." Today, we are beginning to make systems that learn, that see which former experience in memory is most analogous to the present problem, and then use methods like those that worked best on similar problems in the past. When one uses these methods, it makes little sense to say that computers do only what they are told to do. Programmers may have no clear idea of what will happen, because they cannot anticipate all the interacting consequences of such fragments of knowledge and advice. They may not know much about the situations the machine will encounter in the future—or what things it might remember from its past.

Using such techniques, we have learned ways of programming computers to solve problems by trial and error. Now we are on the threshold of more ambitious experiments where programs will write new programs for themselves, with the goal of becoming even better at problem solving and learning. Clearly, there was something wrong with the old idea that machines could never, by their nature, create anything very new. But instead of boring the reader with technical speculations about the next generation of more intelligent machines, most of this chapter will try instead only to understand why so many people made so many wrong guesses about such things.

COULD COMPUTERS BE CREATIVE?

We naturally admire our Einsteins and Beethovens and want to know whether any computer could create such phenomenally original theories or such wondrous symphonies and quartets. But most people are sure that such creativity requires some mysterious gift that simply cannot be explained. (Then, the argument might go, no computer could do it, since, presumably, anything computers do can be explained.)

It is a mistake, though, to focus on only those things our culture regards as truly outstanding. For unless we first understand how people do ordinary things, we will fall into a trap: if we don't understand how ordinary people write ordinary symphonies, how can be possibly expect to understand how great composers write great symphonies—or even guess whether there is any special difficulty in creating symphonies? Of course, they seem mysterious, so first we have to understand the ordinary, both in terms of people and computers, to see how either one may ever come to have what we call ordinary common sense. Then, and only then, can we ask intelligent questions about the nature of the things we think require genius.

Why, in the first place, would we suppose that outstanding minds are any different, except in matters of degree, from ordinary minds? Of course, a genius must be intensely concerned with his or her domain (but this can be unconscious). He must become very proficient in it (but not necessarily in any articulate, academic sense); he must be tenaciously resistant to peer pressure, and so on. But none of these necessities demands a fundamental, qualitative difference. We may have another kind of reason for believing there are heroes with magical powers, but we should not let romantic hero worship confuse the nature of creativity with the social value of its products. As I see it, any ordinary person who can understand an ordinary conversation must have, already, in his head most of what our greatest thinkers have. Ordinary common sense already includes most of the skills that, better balanced, can make a genius.

If we look at only the surface of the skills that creative people use, we see only, perhaps, a greater diversity of skills and surer mastery. But underneath, there also has to lie administrative skills to knit those basic skills together. Is there a real difference? A good composer has to master many skills of phrase and theme—but those abilities are shared, to some degree, by everyone who speaks coherently. A good composer masters greater variations of form, but those skills, too, are shared by everyone who knows how to tell a story well. What only seems unusual is the total mass of different kinds of expertise, including skills of knowing how to use the other skills. For many people learn many skills, but only a few command enough of them to reach the vanguard. Some artists master detail but not the larger forms that make their pieces hang together, while other artists master larger forms but not the small ones. And then culture sets its threshold of acclamation, so that (no matter how great or small the differences among contestants) only a few individuals rise above the rest and are declared to possess that mysterious first-rank creativity. It may be fitting to make heroes of those who cross those somewhat arbitrarily defined thresholds, but until proven otherwise, we should not burden our philosophy with talk of inexplicability. There must be better ways of dealing with feelings of regret at having been labeled second-rate.

Still there may indeed be a secret to what first-raters do, and I think the secret lies not in the surface skills themselves, but in the way that certain people *learn* so many more skills and a greater depth of skill! The special, distinctive thing about "creative masters" is the way in which they choose *what* to learn: *they learn about learning.* Creativity begins with just one simple difference: our heroes of accomplishment are those who happen (at some early age) to aim an ordinary learning skill not at the usual surface tasks, but *at learning itself.* Once focused on learning, some become better and better at it. Then having found better ways of learning, these people find it easier than others to acquire more sets of skills, and these differences are magnified until there seems to be an awesome, qualitative difference. According to this view, first-rank creativity is just the consequence of childhood accidents where a person's ability to learn becomes a little more "self-applied" than usual.

Why do so many intelligent people, especially philosophers and humanists, go to great lengths to find something that human beings can do that machines cannot—to find some quality in themselves that cannot be duplicated in machines? Some even ask if a computer can make mistakes, as though they hoped that, somehow, the ability to err itself might be some precious gift. I have often heard, "I can see how a machine can solve a problem that you give it, but can a machine invent its *own* problems? Isn't the hard problem, really, to figure out what problem to solve?" But it is usually much easier to think of problems than to solve them. Of course, *sometimes* it is hard to find exactly the right question to ask, but even that is just another difficult problem, not necessarily an especially difficult *kind* of problem.

It is a waste of energy, today, to search for ways in which men differ from machines, because we simply know too little about how human minds really work. So instead of searching for things that machines cannot possibly do, I ask instead: *why are people so very inept at making theories about what they themselves can (or cannot) do?* In fact, although people think machines may be incapable of originality, there is actually no technical problem at all involved in making machines do things that no one ever told them to. In principle, we can program even the simplest computer to produce an infinite variety of different programs and then run them. Of course, most of them would be silly, and *that* is the real problem, the basic problem of all art and science: not to find variety and diversity, but to control and constrain them. Anyone, or any machine, can find the most bizarre, unthinkable extremes of novelty—which is why the most valued kinds of originality are those that find small, subtle, useful variants of ordinary things.

Our most serious problems in machine intelligence today are *not* those of traditional humanist concern, such as creativity, intuition, and originality. What we need most to understand now is ordinary common sense! Many people seem to think this is an easy problem, already understood, just a matter of logic, and so forth. It isn't. Many people seem to think that understanding the intellect must be easy compared to establishing theories on such arcane matters as emotion. These people have things turned around: we know a great deal about emotion but little about thinking, which is really the more complicated of the two. Perhaps emotion *seems* more important, but we must realize that this may be a trick, in which an emotion is only doing its job!

MUST COMPUTERS BE LOGICAL?

In 1956, Newell, Shaw, and Simon wrote a computer program that was quite good at finding proofs of theorems in mathematical logic. In fact, their program proved all the theorems in the first volume of Russell and Whitehead's *Principia Mathematica,* including some that are quite difficult even for today's college students. The program actually found some rather novel proofs. So in a sense, we know how to make machines do logical reasoning, but I don't see this as a big step toward understanding how people do common-sense reasoning.

Our culture is addicted to theories that divide minds into two parts. In one such theory, the first half of the mind is logical, rational, and sort of brittle, while the second half is soft, vague, and sort of intuitive. Variations of this theory are so ill-defined that they are almost impossible to tell apart: logic vs. intuition, spatial vs. verbal, quantitative vs. qualitative, local vs. global, reason vs. emotion. Now, there is nothing wrong in starting with two-part theories if we use them as steps toward better theories. But if we end up that way, we usually have just one idea instead of two—whatever it is—vs. everything else. Our culture's mental-pair distinctions are limited in this way, and I doubt they have much value as theories of the mind. Perhaps they are only symptoms of some inability to cope with more than one idea at a time.

In any case, these age-old distinctions between logic and intuition, or reason and emotion, have been the basis of many unsound arguments about machine intelligence. It was clear from AI's earliest days that logical deduction would be easy to program. Accordingly, people who believed that thinking was mainly logical were led to expect that computers would soon do the sorts of things they believed people used logic for. Most people also assumed that it would be much more difficult, and perhaps impossible, to program more qualitative traits, such as intuition, metaphor, esthetics, or reasoning by analogy. I wasn't among them.

In 1964, a student of mine, T. G. Evans, wrote a program that showed how computers could actually use analogies to do some interesting kinds of reasoning about perception of geometric structures. This program made some humanistic skeptics so angry that they wrote papers about it. One paper threw out the baby with the bath by arguing that if a machine could do analogical reasoning, well, then, that kind of reasoning must not be so important. Another complained that Evans's program was too complicated to be the basis of an interesting psychological theory, because it used about 60,000 computer instruction words (which suggests that there wasn't a baby in the first place).

Nevertheless, Evans's program showed how wrong it was to assume that computers could do only logical or quantitative reasoning. Why had so many people made this same mistake? I see it as a curious irony: all those people had mistaken *their own personal limitations* for limitations of computers! That is, because most people hadn't been able to establish sensible theories of how they themselves could reason by analogy, they were led to suppose that no well-defined mechanism could exist that did so, hence, no computer or program could do it! That is why it was left to AI researchers (instead of psychologists or philosophers) to establish the first plausible theories of reasoning by analogy and hence be able to make computers do such things!

COULD COMPUTERS EVER REALLY UNDERSTAND THINGS?

"I see you have programmed that computer to obey verbal commands. You have probably inserted into its memory what it should do in response to each command. *But I don't believe the program really understands the words in any human sense.*" This popular criticism was quite valid when applied to the well-known "psychiatrist program" Eliza; it doesn't apply to, say, Daniel Bobrow's program for solving high school algebra word problems. That program understood just enough English to work the kinds of word problems that most students find very hard. It is not very difficult to learn to solve the kinds of equations we encounter in high school algebra. But word problems are difficult because the program (or the student) has to figure out what equations to write down. Bobrow's program wasn't half bad at that.

Did Bobrow's program really understand the words? Is *understand* even an idea we can ask science to deal with? We don't have to define words like *mean* and *understand*, just because philosophers have tried to do that for thousands of years! Such words are only *social objects*; if they lead to good ideas, fine, but in this case, I doubt that they point out significant distinctions, and I suspect that they only handicapped our predecessors who tried very hard to figure out what meanings were or how they are connected to words. But that is a misguided ambition anyway, similar to expecting people to agree on what *good* means, without considering the individual psychology of each person who uses the word.

To see how desperate philosophers have become, consider today's most popular philosophical theory of meaning—an idea called model theory. What does it mean to say that Boston is in Massachusetts? According to model theory, this means the set of all possible worlds in which (1) there is a Boston and a Massachusetts and (2) that Boston is actually in that Massachusetts! This begs the question of what meaning means, because it gives no hint of how to recognize whether something in a "possible world" is actually a "Boston" or not. Yet it is taken quite seriously, because no other theory has accumulated so respectable a mathematical tradition.

WHAT IS A NUMBER?

We cannot discuss meaning without discussing the meaning of something, so let us discuss the meaning of some particular number, say, five. No one would claim that Bobrow's algebra program could be said to understand what numbers really are, nor would one say that about Slagle's calculus program, which I will discuss later. Yet both programs "know" arithmetic in the sense of finding correct sums like five plus seven is twelve. The trouble is that neither program understands—in any *other* sense—what either five or seven or twelve are, or, for that matter, what *plus* or *is* is. Well, suppose I asked the reader what five is? I will bet that the secret lies in that little word *other*!

Early in this century, Russell and Whitehead proposed to tell us how to define a number (in that same book, *Principia Mathematica*). *Five*, according to them, is *the set of all possible sets that each have five members*. This includes this set of five ballpoint pens and that litter of five kittens. I suppose it also includes this set of five words and even the five things most difficult of all to think of. Unfortunately, funny examples like those caused inconsistencies and paradoxes, so the theory had to be doctored to avoid them; in its final form, it became too complicated for practical use.

In my view, there is no need to try to capture meanings in such a standard, public sort of way. In fact, as I will show, that defeats our real purposes, because it is a mistake to ignore a fundamental psychological fact: what something means to me depends to some extent on everything else I know, and no one else knows just those things in just those ways. I maintain that a psychologically useful theory of meanings, even of something as widely understood as *five*, needs some built in way of dealing with differences between different knowers. Most of my friends who are scientists hate this idea, because they fear that if each meaning depends on the mind it is in, and on all the other meanings in that mind, then there isn't any place to start. They fear that if meanings are that private, then there is no way of breaking into the closed circle of the mind, and everything becomes too subjective to be scientific.

However, there *is*, indeed, a scientific way of handling this: We can start a new set of theories about the circles themselves! We don't *have to* break into them—*we only have to have sound theories about them*. Former theories try to suppress the ways that meanings depend on one another (and how one mind can differ from another). The trouble is that this approach loses all the power and richness of those circles! In fact, we actually don't *want* to get ourselves inside those circles. It is a futile dream to hope to be absolutely sure of understanding something exactly the way someone else does. The ideal of perfect, foolproof communication was just a fantasy to begin with; the only way to understand precisely what someone else thinks we mean at every level of nuance is to become just like that person. But that isn't what we want either, because then in that new state of existence we couldn't know what it was that we in our original state had been trying to communicate, and so on.

COULD A COMPUTER UNDERSTAND WHAT A NUMBER IS?

What would it mean to say that *five* does not mean a simple, isolated thing, but a web or network of interdependent processes? Well, let us proceed with that example. One way to know when we have five things is to recite one, two, three, four, five, while pointing to the different things. Of course, while doing this, we have to (1) touch each thing once and (2) not touch any twice. An easy way to do *that* is to pick up one object as we repeat each counting-word, and remove it. Children learn to do is in their minds or, when there are too many objects to keep track of, to use some physical device, such as pointing.

There are many, many other ways of understanding *five*. We could keep a standard set of five things somewhere, then match some *other* set of things to them one to one: If everything matches, and nothing is left over, then we would have five. We could use our fingers as that standard set of things.

Another way of understanding *five* is to arrange objects into groups of two and three. Again, we can group them mentally, without actually moving them. Or we can lay out the objects on a table to form a square with one in the middle; that makes five, too. Note that we might acquire this meaning of *five* before understanding *two* or *three*. I knew a child who was quite proficient with hexagons long before she knew much about *four* or *five*.

Which of these methods—counting, matching, grouping, and so forth— provides the real meaning of *five*? How silly; each supports the others to make a useful, versatile system of skills. Neither chicken nor egg need come first; they both evolve from something else.

Mathematicians and philosophers despise such interconnected networks; they prefer simple "chains" of definitions where each new thing depends only on other things that have been previously defined. In my theory, the ordinary, common-sense meaning of *five* is no single link in any chain of definitions. Instead, the word *five* activates the entire network of different ways of recognizing five things, using them, remembering them, comparing them, and so forth. Such networks are useful for solving problems, because there are so many different ways that we won't become stuck when one of them doesn't work. If we can't make one of our ideas about *five* do the job, in a certain context, we can switch to one of the others. If we followed the mathematicians' approach, we would be completely stuck if we got into the slightest trouble.

By the way, why *do* mathematicians prefer chains to nets? Why would they want each thing to depend on as few other things as possible—instead of as many as possible? The answer is a nice paradox. Things are done that way in mathematics in order to assure that if anything at all is incorrect, then everything else will collapse! To a mathematician, that sort of fragility is *good*, not bad, because it helps detect if *any single thing* that is believed is inconsistent with any others. This kind of reasoning ensures absolute consistency, which is fine for mathematics, but terrible for real life, where there are *always* things that we believe which aren't really true.

Perhaps this helps explain how we manage to make almost all our children afraid of mathematics! We imagine that it makes it easy for them to see what is right by arranging for everything to go utterly wrong almost all the time!

To learn about numbers (or anything else), children must build networks, not towers. Two hands and two feet and two shoes: We learn those first in terms of symmetry and matching, not counting. We soon learn also that when we count two or three things, we get the same number each time. We also know about threes from rhymes and stories about three pigs or bears or turtle doves (whatever they might be). And notice how many different kinds of three are found in those innocent fairy tales! The three bears themselves are two and one: mother and father and child. But those bears' three bowls of food make quite a different kind of three:—too hot vs. too cold vs. just right; this three is a *compromise between two extremes.* So, too, were these bears' forbidden beds: too hard, too soft, and just right. The child in the real world learns many different threes, related to each other in many different, interesting ways. It is a large network. The meaning is the entire network, not a mere node, and there is no basic three that the others depend on.

Is there a paradox in this? If each meaning depends on several other meanings, then don't we have a castle built on air? Well, yes and no. There is nothing really wrong with circular definitions where each part gives the others more meaning: what is wrong with liking two tunes, for example— each one the more because it contrasts with the other? The entire mind is, in this sense, a castle in the air; what is wrong with that? One objection then would be that there is no connection with reality. But that isn't really a practical problem, because our sensory and motor brain machinery ensure at least some infantile relationship between our perceived objects and some physical reality. Still, this is only a matter of degree, and to a really large extent, minds *can* become detached and build (and share) imaginary worlds for better or for worse.

Let us return to earth. I will agree that no computer could understand what a number is if it were forced to have only one way to deal with numbers, such as adding them up. But neither could any child, psychologist, or philosopher understand numbers under that constraint. Thus, it isn't a matter of computers at all. Our culture has become caught up in the search for meanings that can stand by themselves, outside of *any* mental context, and there is no reason to suppose that such abstractions can exist. Thus, we are not dealing with any special limitations of computers. The reason so many people feel computers cannot understand is that their own conception of understanding is so shallow and simplistic that, of course, no machine could understand in *that* way—nor could a person, either! We cannot have real meaning until we join together many partial meaning structures. If we have only one of them, then we don't have any meaning. That is why those seeking true meanings never find them!

COULD A COMPUTER BE AWARE OF ITSELF?

Even if a computer does something, it is just mechanical. The computer cannot feel; it can't be conscious. It simply has no self to feel things with. How could a computer ever really know what we mean when we tell it that "Boston is in Massachusetts"?

I wonder what *you* suppose happens in your head when I say something like that to you. Do you understand it? I will demonstrate that here, again, the problem doesn't actually concern computers at all; it doesn't even concern understanding. The problem concerns *you*. It isn't that you doubt that computers can think; the problem is that you don't really believe that thinking is possible at all! In fact, the problem is that little word *you* itself.

We have a verb *understand*, so we feel there must be some agent to do the understanding, someone inside our head to do the understanding. Now it is perfectly all right when we speak to each other for me to call that someone you and for you to call it me. That's fine for social purposes. But everything goes awry when we try to apply that social idea in a technical-scientific context, because it makes us forget there must be some substantial structure inside that you or me *to do the work*. That social idea makes us assume that there is some single, simple, self inside our head instead of those enormous, intricate webs of which we spoke earlier.

How does this idea of self lead people to believe that machines can never think? I believe it happens this way. When I tell something to a computer, it computes something. In order to understand what I tell it, the computer must compute a meaning. Then in order to understand the meaning, the computer must transmit it to something like a self. But since I am dealing with a computer, it cannot have a self anything like mine; it can only compute. So, at best, a computer can only simulate a self. To do that, it must compute something, and so forth. In order words, for a machine to think, it would need a self, which would need another self, and so on. The infinite series of selves each pass the job of real understanding to the next.

What is wrong? The same thing again: this imaginary limitation of computers has nothing to do with computers at all but comes from not having a idea of how *people* really work or feel, or think. To put it firmly, that skepticism about computer intelligence emerges from our unconscious suspicion that *thinking* (intelligent or otherwise) is itself impossible!

Perhaps that suspicion is almost justified: it certainly would seem that people are *not* very proficient at thinking—or at least at thinking about thinking. And there is an irony in this. Why, indeed, were our old theories about thinking so inadequate? It was precisely *because* we hadn't started to understand well enough what computers—that is, what complicated mechanisms—*can* do! For (in my view, anyway) there seems no attractive alternative to believing that brains are made of very technically complicated machinery. Therefore, we need advanced computational theories before we can expect to understand how the brain works. Naturally, the old theories from precomputer eras of mechanism science made little progress. It was presumptuous to suppose we could understand anything as complicated as thinking without doing any hard, technical work.

We now need better theories about how to understand the complex webs of processes that work within the huge networks that we build to interconnect all our fragments of knowledge. To understand, say, the concept of number, a child must connect a myriad of different ways of counting and measuring and comparing. Within those webs, some processes or programs have to run, and we must never count on any single process to suffice, since nothing ever works out exactly as we hope. Such theories are today just a gleam in the eye. Still, several projects are now starting to work on ways of weaving such complex multiprocess webs.

COULD A COMPUTER HAVE COMMON SENSE?

Back to predicting the future by examining the past. In retrospect, I see how this field seems to have evolved in a funny backward direction. Is it not odd that the very earliest AI programs excelled at advanced, adult subjects. I have already mentioned the program written in 1956 that was quite good at certain kinds of mathematical logic. In 1961, J. R. Slagle wrote a program that solved college calculus problems, using symbols rather than numbers—just the sort of problems, using symbols rather than numbers—just the sort of problems that M.I.T. freshmen were doing at that time. The program got an *A* on an exam. A few years later, D. Bobrow developed that first program that could solve high school algebra problems. In 1970, Terry Winograd wrote a computer program that didn't do grown-up mathematics at all; it only worked with children's building blocks. This program could stack up blocks, pull them down, rearrange them, and put them in boxes. And it had much more ability than previous programs to understand English.

It took us many years before we could make computers do some of the things that any six-year-old can do. Now we know from Piaget's studies of the growth of children's thinking that children usually learn the formal kinds of thinking required for calculus or algebra long after they master many other kinds of reasoning. Why were we able to make AI programs do such grown-up things so long before we could make them do childish things? Is it possible that adult thinking is somehow simpler than children's?

Winograd's program could even converse with the person operating it, in order to answer questions about what it was doing, and how, using something very much like standard English. Still, we should wonder why—if Slagle's program could solve college-level problems in 1961—it took a decade longer to write a program that was able only to play, like a child, with simple blocks and boxes? The answer is that it often requires more to be a novice than an expert, because, sometimes, the things an expert has to know can be quite few and simple—although it may be very difficult to discover (or learn) them in the first place. The entire knowledge network built into Slagle's program, which contains much of what the college student has to learn about integration, has only about one hundred facts, perhaps twenty rules about calculus, and fifty rules about algebra. Perhaps most important, the program has about a dozen ways of telling *which of two calculus problems is probably the easier.* This is important because these procedures embody the kind of knowledge we call judgment, without which we can only flounder. The driving force in Slagle's program was the process that decided what to try next. By 1961, we knew enough about that sort of thing for Slagle to build his calculus program, and today we know enough about such heuristics to build routinely many other useful kinds of expert problem-solving programs.

However, while we know how to write such programs for special applications, we don't yet know enough about such matters to build good common-sense problem-solving programs—for example, programs that can do most things young children do. Winograd's work showed some new ways of assembling many different kinds of knowledge about shapes and colors, syntax, space and time, and problem-solving processes. Only in that way were we able to make a program do what everyone thought was much easier than calculus—playing with children's blocks. To make things work inside his child's world of building blocks, Winograd needed about a thousand knowledge fragments in his network, whereas Slagle needed only a hundred. The problem, as I see it, is that experts can often manage with deep but narrow bodies of knowledge. However, common-sense thinking is technically more complicated, because although the reasoning may be much shallower, it needs many different kinds of knowledge, and each kind of knowledge may need different kinds of processes. And, then, the more different kinds of processes, the more types of interactions between them, and so on.

But Winograd's contribution was not merely a matter of quantity: he had to invent *different kinds* of heuristic knowledge and new ways for them to control and exploit each other. He used a new kind of programming, called heterarchy, as opposed to the hierarchy used in previous programs and theories. Although less centralized, there was more interaction and interruption between parts in this system: while one part was trying to parse a sentence, another part would be trying to make the grammar compatible with the meaning. As soon as one part of the program guessed that *pick* was a verb (as in *pick up the block*), another program part might check to see if block were really the sort of thing that could be picked up. I believe that what we call common sense requires a lot of just that kind of switching from one viewpoint to another, involving different kinds of ideas.

COULD A COMPUTER BE CONSCIOUS?

When people ask if a machine can be self-conscious, they always seem to expect the answer to be no. I propose to shock the reader by explaining why machines may be capable, in principle, of possessing even more and better consciousness than people have.

Let us begin by asking someone quite seriously whether any one can really be self-aware. He will surely answer that of course people can, because they are. Then I will say that I meant it literally: Can we be aware of everything that happens in our mind? He says yes or no, but most likely he will say that he didn't mean *that*—he meant something else. I continue: What do you mean by self-aware if not aware of what happens inside you? He will probably say that he didn't mean aware *of* what's *in* himself, just aware *of* himself. Then I will look puzzled, ask what that means, and if he is like everyone else I've met, he will say something like: It is really very hard to explain—and start to look for some way to get away (and so will I).

Why is it that our alleged self-awareness can say so very little about itself? I think the answer is that it is misnamed. Although the phenomenon that we call self-awareness is very useful and important, it really cannot do what people think it can. We all seem to assume that we have some faculty that enables us to discover (or perceive) true things about our minds. Instead, I think, we have only a certain limited ability, sometimes, to make useful *guesses* about reasons and explanations of why and how the mind works. And while these guesses, products of our vaunted self-awareness, are often very clever, they do not show any significant tendency to be profoundly correct! Our insight into how we think is no neat window on the truth: it doesn't even seem to do well as other ways we have of figuring out what is going on.

Accordingly, we should be able to provide our machines with a greater ability to establish theories about themselves. First, we should provide them with better access to their own trees of goals and values. Then we could begin to give them ways of constructing simple explanations of how their procedures work toward those ends. In fact, Winograd's program has already demonstrated one rather accurate, though somewhat shallow, way of doing this. The difficult part of the problem wouldn't be providing access to internal information; the difficult problem would be just the same problem we have yet to solve more generally—building programs with enough common sense to make good use of such insight. That is to say, our present programs are still too narrow and specialized to deal with anything as complicated as a theory of thinking. But as we learn to build more intelligent machines, I don't see any reason to anticipate difficulty in giving them correspondingly more self-insight—that is, if we decide that this is a wise thing to do. Perhaps we will even have to do so!

Most skeptics will admit that computers will probably continue to become more intelligent yet doubt that computers will ever be self-conscious. I am suggesting that these skeptics may have things precisely backward! Maybe at some point we will *have* to make computers more self-conscious in order to make them more intelligent! I think our culture's nonmechanical heritage teaches us that self-awareness is a mysterious metaphysical appendage, that somehow makes us human yet *has no fundamental use or function.* I suspect our ability to make crude models of ourselves is no mysterious luxury, but a necessary and practical device, because no problem solver can be robust enough without some insight into its own goals and motives! For example, a problem solver could not safely undertake any complex, long-range task unless it could ensure its own future concern with it, and this requires predicting our own dispositions. Nor can we expect to learn how to solve difficult, new kinds of problems without at least some elementary, simplified idea of how we already manage to solve easier, old problems.

Now technically, there are certain absolute, theoretical limitations to self-insight; for example, no machine of any kind can predict ahead of time what it will do by taking into account *all* the details of what its internal agencies are doing now. But these limitations are not interesting. Presumably, there are also practical limitations; people, for example, can relate hardly anything about the mechanisms of their thinking. They are usually reduced to saying such things as, "I had an idea ... ." or "it occurred to me that . . . ." Of course, we often hear of mystical experiences where someone claims some sense of total, utterly complete understanding. However, such people can say so very little more of what they learned that we can conclude only that what they learned was how to extinguish the question-asking portion of their mind. All this leads me to suspect that what we call self-consciousness does not live up to its reputation of profound revelation. Instead, it seems to provide only a sketchy, simplified mind model, suitable for mundane, practical, and social uses. In fact, it would seem that correct technical details of our mental operations are so inaccessible to our selves as to be counterintuitive; such important discoveries as Freud's unconscious and Piaget's conservation met strong resistance until nonintrospective evidence overruled those incorrect intuitions.

When and if we choose to build more artfully conceived intelligent machines, we should have many new options that were not available during the brain's evolution, for the biological constraints of vertebrate evolution must have dictated many details of the interconnections of our brains. In the new machines, we will be able to provide whatever paths we wish. Though the new machines still cannot possibly keep track in real time of everything they do, we surely should be able (at least in principle) to make those new, synthetic minds vastly more self-conscious than we are, in the sense of being more profound and having insightful knowledge about their own nature and function. Thus, in the end, those new creatures should have more interesting and richer inner lives than do people. Treason, you say. I suppose we will have to leave these decisions to future generations: they won't *have* to build things that well unless they want to.

COULD WE BUILD TRULY INTELLIGENT MACHINES?

There is absolutely no known technical reason to doubt that we could build truly intelligent machines. It may take a very long time, though, to learn enough about common-sense reasoning to make machines with manlike versatility. We already know some ways of making useful, specialized, expert systems. We don't yet know that many ways of making these systems learn enough to improve themselves in interesting ways. However, there are already some ideas about this topic on the scientific horizon.

On the other side, every one of the assertions about what machines can never do but people can are only foolish speculations. We simply do not yet know enough about how human minds work to make such arguments. The proponents of such theories are either simply bluffing or making obscure technical mistakes. Accordingly, I recommend that instead of being tricked into thinking that such arguments make sense, we simply regard them as opportunities to see more ways in which human minds can err! I am serious:

the better we understand why minds do foolish things, the better prepared we will be to figure out how, also, they so often do things well.

In years to come, we will learn more ways of making machines behave sensibly. We will learn more about new kinds of knowledge and processes and how to use them to make still more new knowledge. We will come to think of learning and thinking and understanding not as mysterious, single, special processes, but as entire worlds of ways to represent and transform ideas. In turn, those new ideas will suggest new machine architectures, and they in turn will further change our ideas about ideas. No one can now tell where all these new ideas will lead. One thing in certain, though: there must be something wrong with any reasoned claim today to know any fundamental differences between men and possible machines. And there is a simple reason why such arguments must be erroneous: we simply do not know enough yet about the real workings of either men or possible machines.

EXPLORING THE READING

1. Marvin Minsky says that the very best artists don't learn things differently. Instead, they learn with more skill and at a greater depth. Do you agree or disagree with him? Why?

2. In a small group, examine this selection and list factors Minsky believes make up human intelligence. Which of these factors can a computer mimic? Which can still not be copied by computers?

3. Do you agree with Minsky that as soon as we understand the function of the human mind, we will be able to duplicate those functions in a computer? Why or why not?

4. Minsky says that society's tendency to set up human intelligence in opposing pairs like logic vs. intuition may be a symptom of our unwillingness to deal with more than one idea at a time. Do you agree that this definition divides our notion of mind into unhelpful categories, or do you think that these opposing pairs help us understand the way we think? How so?

HOME ON THE NET

by John Seabrook

A home *in the real world, according to John Seabrook, is a private place where you are able to shut out the world. But a* home page *on the Net, a slice of your persona, is open for people to breeze in and out at will, while exploring your interests and obsessions. Throughout his essay, published in* The New Yorker, *Seabrook compares the content and process of building his Web home to that of building his real home, a loft in New York City. Then he invites the reader to visit the newly created Web page, http://www.levity.com/seabrook. Like many home pages, however, Seabrook's changes over time, and you will find it no longer looks as Seabrook describes it.*

Seabrook, a staff writer for The New Yorker, *is the author of* Deeper *(1997), which chronicles his journey from cowering computer nerd to commentator on the state of the Internet.*

During my first year in boarding school, I lived in a large open room with thirty-five other thirteen-year-old boys. It was like a model built to observe aspects of primate behavior from above. Each boy had an alcove and a curtain to pull in front of it, but the other boys did not regard what was within the boundaries of that cloth-and-plywood square as your personal space. These days, other people, like my fellow third formers, can wander in and out of my online personal space almost at will. In going online, you make some of your personal space available to other people; that is partly the point of the exercise. In this sense, online home life is closer to socialism than anything most people in the United States experience at home. At Brook Farm, the famous transcendentalist experiment in communal living which existed in West Roxbury, Massachusetts, in the eighteen-forties, the main community building was called the Hive—the same metaphor that Kevin Kelly uses in his recent book, *Out of Control,* to describe social life on computer networks.

A home in the real world is, among other things, a way of keeping the world out. If you buy space in what used to be a warehouse, gut it, and hire someone to turn it into a home, as my wife and I did, you invite the world into your life for a while, but when the work is done you have walls and a threshold. Of course, you never shut the world out entirely, just as we will never get rid of all the little packets of sugar that the guys who built our loft brought along on the job with their coffee, but at least you have your privacy. It's like being inoculated with a little bit of the world, which makes you better able to survive the whole world.

An online home, on the other hand, is a little hole you drill in a wall of your real home to let the world in. E-mail, chat, postings, and other forms of computer-based communication that I engage in while slouched in my faux-corduroy padded chair, with a PowerBook on my lap, are like the coded tappings on the walls of adjoining prison cells in Arthur Koestler's *Darkness at Noon*. An online home built for solitude doesn't make sense, maybe because people tend to be alone in front of their computers when they log on.

Building a home online means setting up some sort of private space for yourself within the public space of the network. By private space I mean the intimate airways of an e-mail exchange, which is like the space that is filled by a telephone conversation. Now there is a new kind of online private space: you can have what's called a "home page" on the World Wide Web. The Web is technically only a part of the Internet (the Web is a graphics-intensive application running on top of the Net's operating system), but it seems to be rapidly taking over the Net, and one day soon the Net as we know it may look like a horse-drawn carriage next to the Web's Model T. No one owns the Web, but anyone can own space on it: the space is cheap and, theoretically, infinite.

Cyberspace also makes available abundant public space—common areas where small or large numbers of people can gather. These public spaces might be "chat rooms," where people can talk with each other in real time; or they might be "forums," where people contribute postings to discussions organized around a topic; or they might be group game-playing spaces known as MUDs and MOOs. Unlike telephone space, these public spaces often contain a record of past conversations, and as this record grows over time it becomes a history. Then the history is shaped into an ideology. It is interpreted and reinterpreted. It means something.

Within the public spaces, private communication is also possible. Private and public modes of discourse are the Sheetrock and sealing compound from which an online home is made. A seventeen-year-old friend of mine has found a home in a role-playing room on America Online. A while ago, he met a girl there, Melynda, who, unlike many female users, actually gives Melynda as her user name. Now whenever he logs on to A.O.L. he uses the "member online" function to see if Melynda is signed on. If she is, they jointly open a private chat window on their screens and type messages to each other while watching the group discussion scroll past in another window. (While they are chatting, other people in the public room often send Melynda rude messages like "Hey, Melynda, want to play my flute?"—because Melynda says in her member profile that she is a flautist.) Part of what they discuss in their private space is the stuff that people are saying in the public window. They're like junior-high kids meeting at their lockers and watching other students pass by in the hall.

When I first went online, the nomadic quality of existence in cyberspace was a big part of the appeal. It was like taking an extended camping trip in the backcountry of a national park: You follow a path through the wilderness, and when you reach the designated campsite, or when you get tired, or when the weather turns ugly, you unpack and put up your high-tech geodesic dome for the night. In the morning, you stuff your home into its nylon sack and move on.

But after a while I got tired of camping out and started looking for a place to settle down. For me, finding a home online has meant finding a group small enough to resolve itself into a social organization I could become a part of. I began house hunting on the WELL, one of the older computer conferencing systems. Some of the earliest members on the WELL lived on the Farm, a commune in Tennessee, back in the seventies. Stewart Brand, who helped found the WELL, recruited people from the Farm specifically because of their communal-living experience. Brand says they brought a lot of lessons to the WELL: "Don't overwork and underappreciate the females, or they leave, and then the party's over. Don't invest much in a charismatic leader: he will steal everything you've got and then blame you for not having any more. It takes more than a sharp stick and earnestness to make a garden produce food. Don't piss off the neighbors. Stuff like that." Cliff Figallo, a Farm recruit, has written on the WELL about life on the Farm:

> We were very much into Truth, and at times we wielded it like a bludgeon. It was for their own good, of course, but it felt so good to lay a big fat TRUTH on someone. Almost as good as it felt bad to have one laid on you. Some folks (we called people "folks," folks) were "tennis ball eaters." You would serve up your best, most compassionately worded explanation about how and why they were assholes, and for a return you would get some lame reply that sounded like they deliberately missed the point. Grrr, that was frustrating. Especially when you were staying up until 2AM just to "get into their thing"; and it was for their own good!

That resonates with aspects of my home life on the WELL. Looking for a home there has involved learning to get along with the neighbors, and some neighbors have been zealous about seeing to it that I do. Online, good fences do not necessarily make good neighbors. This also reminds me of boarding school. In my second year, we were given rooms with walls, but by then the walls were just symbols of boundaries that had already been established in that big open room.

What exactly is a home page? In the simplest terms, it is like an e-mail address, a place on the Net where people can find you; but whereas an e-mail address is just a mailbox, a home page is a reception area. Although building home pages or Websites (a collection of pages of which the home page is the natural starting point) is mainly a commercial enterprise, it doesn't have to be. It's also a way to meet people. You want guests to have a good time when they visit your home page, and you hope they will take away a favorable impression of you. You can link your home page to the home pages of friends or family, or to your employer's Website, or to any other site you like, creating a kind of neighborhood for yourself. And you can design your page in any way you wish, and furnish it with anything that can be digitized—your ideas, your voice, your causes, pictures of your scars or your pets or your ancestors. You can have a professional photographer come and take pictures of your apartment, and then upload those pictures onto the Web, or you can just describe your day. You can describe your upstairs neighbor's day, as one Web denizen does on his home page:

Friday February 24, 1995
    Loser woke up early as usual and took his twenty minute shower. Then silence. The slow, laborious clockwise pacing began and continued until he had to leave for classes. A short phone call was made as is done every morning. Either he was calling "stooge" or he was checking in with his mommy. I left and did not get in until after 11pm. I thought that Loser might have gone out somewhere. Within a few minutes Loser got up and started pacing around. It is Friday night, for goodness sakes! Finally, he either sits down or goes to bed. Nope, he's back up again. He has to take a whiz.

If you want a really slick-looking home page, you can hire a professional Web designer to build and maintain one for you, or you can do it yourself, with whatever materials you happen to have around. At first, that was my plan—a handyman special. Although I am not "technical," the programming language you use to write for the Web, H.T.M.L., is not very difficult to learn. I bought a book called *Teach Yourself Web Publishing with H.T.M.L. in a Week,* by Laura Lemay. But the time I might have invested in studying the book I instead spent online, and although the book still sits within reach on my desk, I suspect it may eventually find its own home near the various do-it-yourself books I bought back when we were renovating our loft and never used.

So I decided to hire someone to build my home page for me—an interior designer of virtual space. Web designers—or, as they are called when they also maintain the pages, Webmasters—are much in demand these days, especially in Manhattan. They tend to be young cyberslackers who learned H.T.M.L. in college and are now finding that harried business executives, having been handed the job of setting up their companies' Websites, are desperately trying to hire people in the know to build their Websites for them. At the same time, a growing number of designers from the print and TV media are getting into Web work. One of these people, a former book editor named Dan Levy, happens to be a friend of mine. I called Dan and asked him if he would help me build my home page, and although he was busy preparing a proposal to build a Website for a division of Sony Electronics (the proposal itself was a Website), he offered to come over one morning and help me raise my virtual roof beam.

    Dan arrived, wearing shorts and a T-shirt and carrying his software tools and his PowerBook in a cloth bag. I showed him into my study. He sat down with my PowerBook and began loading floppies into the disk drive and installing the software necessary for the job. I watched his moves on the keyboard, trying to pick up some new software shortcuts through the Macintosh operating system.

    While Dan was working, he said, "This Web stuff is just exploding. It's kind of ridiculous. The Spin Doctors Website I did last year would be worth over ten thousand dollars now." Dan had to speak loudly because a garbage truck was hauling rubble from an interminable renovation job on the Smith Barney building across the street. He went on, "I think the situation is that some people in the big-media world just view it as a problem now—like, 'We need a Website, here's some money, go and build us one.' Yours shouldn't cost much. You ought to be able to find some neighborhood kids to do it for you, the way you'd find one to cut your lawn."

Prior to Dan's arrival, I had spent a few weeks thinking about what I wanted my home page to be—and what a home online is in a more general sense. In the real world, I know I'm nearing home when my brain sublimi-nally recognizes the olfactory pattern of North Moore Street in Tribeca, with its row of old warehouses, from olive oil to coffee to nutmeg. But in the online world there are no sensory clues to tell you when you're almost home. "No location! No location! No location!" would be the online real-estate agent's rallying cry. Sitting in my study, I surfed the Web and hit other people's home pages, in search of some ideas for my own. Surfing a TV set is like surfing Long Island, compared with surfing the Web's Waimea Bay. The odd thing about watching TV with a remote control is that the remote changes the channels but has no effect on the programming, so what you aren't watching you miss. On the Web, the technology of the remote control is built right into the way the programming is designed: the "show" never begins before you arrive. You move from place to place by pointing your mouse and clicking on words or pictures that function as "hot buttons." When you click on one, something cool happens: a picture appears, or sound begins streaming out of your computer, or you jump to another place in the same Website, or to another site altogether. Hot buttons that take you to another place are known as links, and programming the links is known as tweaking the links.

If you want people to visit your home page, it helps to have appealing content to offer. In an information society such as the Web, all the members have their chunks of information—the poorest having only charcoal to set in front of their corrugated-tin huts, the richest having glittering and irresistible palaces of mind candy. Some people keep track of their "hit count" as a way of rating the popularity of their home page. In a way, setting up a home page is an exercise in self-promotion, like writing a personal ad. In the "All About Me!!!" sections of some home pages, people describe themselves in the same peppy marketing voice that I hear almost daily on my voice mail at work, but instead of selling some cool new piece of software they are selling them-selves. But putting up a home page is also an act of joining the community of the Web, by sharing what you hope is some useful information with others in the group. The point at which the self-promoting ends and the public-spiritedness begins is very hard to place.

A lot of people offer you their "hotlist"—a selection of their favorite Web pages. Clicking on the name of a page will take you there. You don't have to ask permission to link your page to another page. For example, a woman may find herself listed on Robert Toups' "Babes on the Web" page, which is one of the more controversial sites on the Web. Women are assigned a rating on his Toupsie Scale, from one to four. Toups writes:

> Placing a Home Page on the World Wide Web is an invitation for entry. Having a personal photo on that page is an invitation for it to be rated based on the TOUPSIE SCALE.

Women who don't want to be linked to "Babes on the Web" can e-mail Toups and ask to be removed, though he doesn't make any promises. But, as Shawna Benson, one of Toups' "Babes," writes on her home page:

> I am now listed in Rob Toups lovely "Babes on the Web" page! When I first saw this page, I wasn't sure if it was good or bad. I have since decided that it isn't too bad—considering the added traffic my page now gets! So check out his brilliantly designed page.

She has added a clickable link.

Because a lot of the people with the programming skills necessary to create home pages are college students, many pages resemble college dorm rooms: they're decorated with pictures of Bono, Cindy, etc. At David Golden's Website, you can tour the house he lived in on Moran Avenue, in Princeton, with two friends. You see a picture of his front porch, and the porch is also a hot button that takes you through the front door; then you can follow other hot buttons through the house. Golden's e-mail address is one of his hot buttons; I clicked on it, and we exchanged a few messages about home pages. He wrote:

> The home page is somewhat like a hyperactive electronic resume. It's designed to tell anyone who looks about who I am and what I do. I personally prefer to do that with text, and use graphics as attention grabbers, but some people like to paste up tons of pictures.
>
> Entertainment is important, too. My home page is the first impression of me complete strangers get on the net. Hopefully, they'll find it interesting, and entertaining, and maybe even useful. I don't want them to find a boring page and think I'm a boring person. There's also a bit of pride at stake. It's a great feeling to get e-mail from someone in Australia you've never met complimenting you on your home page. It's also a thrill to find your home page listed on someone else's page, especially when you don't know them.

I wrote back:

> So do you use it as a resume? Do you refer prospective employers to it? Or is it more like a resume for social life on the net, where the difference between business and pleasure, information and experience, advertising and editorial seems blurred?

He replied:

> I personally don't use it as a resume, nor would I refer employers to it as it isn't particularly businesslike. The main page itself is mostly a short bio with some contact information, and the other pages are mostly links of various sorts. In that sense, it is a "resume for social life"—or perhaps more of a "travel diary" (yet another metaphor)—the equivalent of the slide show of the places you've been on vacation.

One popular home page, called "The Spot" and recently voted Cool Site of the Year on the Web, is ostensibly the work of six people who share a beach house in L.A. They offer various intimate details of their "real" home life on their Web home page.

Carrie, on September 26th:

So, last night, I decided I was going to have sex with Stacey. Just do it and get it over with. (Romantic, isn't it.) I didn't want to tell him ahead of time. I thought I would surprise him. I sneaked into Lon's room and stole a condom, just to be extra safe. . . . Stacey came over to watch the tape of the *Mad About You* season premiere. (Excellent. Helen Hunt is my idol.) TV led to kissing, which led to petting, which then led to more. . . . Without going into all the gory details, the bottom line is that I couldn't do it. Maybe the timing wasn't right.

In some of the journal entries, the Spotmates try to make sense of why they are publishing their journals online in the first place. Lon writes:

The journal entries have been extremely therapeutic, as has my correspondence with the Spot surfers of the world. . . . But the privacy I've given up is beginning to fuel my paranoia about everything in my world outside of the computer.

It is easy to see the content of many home pages as evidence of the further decline of civilization, although the shocking uses to which typography was put in its early days—bawdy stories, of which Chaucer's *Canterbury Tales* is the most famous example, and unsanctioned translations of the Bible—are well documented. And amid the noise on the Web you can also hear the authentic voice of youthful idealism, which is harder to find in print and on TV, where young voices are so thoroughly marinated in irony. The most celebrated callow youth on the Web is probably Justin Hall, a twenty-year-old junior at Swarthmore, whose "Justin's Links from the Underground" is a famous site. Among the odds and ends found under "Justin's Writings" is this cyber-rap:

Go out into your neighborhood and do a video documentary!
Stage a play on a street corner! Strike up a conversation! Read a poem on a train!
Then, write about it on your web page.
Remember the first time you had sex? How strange that was? Write about it. Put it online.
Remember the first time you were dumped? How shitty that was? Write about it. Put it online.
I'd sooner read that than Barry Diller's five means of media ascension.
Culture doesn't come from Warner Brothers and Sony. Culture is that woman friend of yours who tells the most outrageous stories.
Culture doesn't cost big bucks, and hang in a gallery of modern art. Culture is your friend who likes to draw. . . .
The web is an opportunity to make good our fifteen megabytes of fame.
The more widespread and grassroots the Internet, the more difficult it will be to dominate and control it. You can contribute directly to the humanizing of the wires by telling your story, adding your persona to the unaffiliated.

By the time of Dan's visit I had come up with a plan for my home page. I wanted to make something out of the media flooding into my study—to take the words and sounds and pictures and "repurpose" them, as they say online. I explained this to Dan and showed him a strip of pictures of myself that I had sitting around on my desk. Could I put this up and add a description of where the strip was taken, and make it hot, so that if you clicked on it you could learn some more things about me? Dan said sure, and that he would scan the pictures for me back at his place. Then, at the bottom of the page, I wanted to put the words "West" and "East" and, under the words, pictures of Francis Parkman and Henry David Thoreau, respectively. Both Parkman and Thoreau would be hot, too. If you clicked on Parkman, you'd go out to the American frontier, as he did in his great book *The Oregon Trail*, and you'd see a picture of a buffalo hunt, and you could read some of my musings about the nature of public space online. If you clicked on Thoreau, you'd go to a cabin in the woods, and there you'd find more musings—these on the nature of inner space online and what Thoreau might have made of all this. I would link my Thoreau room to the Thoreau Society's online publication, and I'd link my Parkman room to the National Parks' Website. Maybe I'll be redecorating in a few months, but the Thoreau/Parkman scheme would display my current obsessions.

Sitting in my study, Dan converted what I had written into H.T.M.L. When he was finished, he looked at my pictures, which he had to measure in pixels—the units of space that pictures occupy in the virtual world—and asked, "Do you have a ruler?" A ruler! I got one out of a drawer in which artifacts of my pre-electronic work life have accumulated—a personalized letter embosser; a rubber stamp that my wife, Lisa, handcarved for me; a Cross pen set that my dad gave me—and handed it to Dan. He laid it on my photographs, measured them, pulled the calculator down from the Apple menu on my PowerBook, and said, "Let's see. That's one and three-quarters inches, and seventy-two pixels per inch—that's a hundred and twenty-six pixels."

While Dan was working, Lisa came out of her study. I watched the shadow of her door as it swung open, making changing shapes on the hallway floor. And as I watched this some of the excitement I was feeling about setting up my home page dwindled. Nothing on my computer screen seemed as substantial as this shadow, or the simple arc of space that the edge of the door described. When Lisa and I were designing our place, we were about to get married, and imagining the space became a way of configuring what we wanted our future together to be like. What started out as an open floor plan soon grew walls, making discrete blocks of space, which the architect called "living area," "bedroom," "Lisa's room," and "John's room." The most unstable element in the design was the positioning of these two rooms, our private studies, which kept swelling and shrinking and moving as we changed our minds about whether we should work near one another or at opposite ends of the loft. We ended up next to each other, and Lisa's doorway is a hot button for me.

After saying hi, Lisa went down toward the living area, and Dan swiveled back to my home page. He copied the document, opened it with *Netscape*, which is a popular program for browsing the Web, clicked "Reload," and then dialed in to his Web server from my PowerBook. All that remained was for him to upload my site onto one of his computers, but we got stuck waiting for something to happen, which is a drawback of using the Web with an ordinary phone line. (The wires aren't yet fat enough for the heavy load of bits streaming through them.) Sitting side by side in front of the small screen made eye contact difficult, and the tension of the waiting constricted conversation. After what seemed like an unusually long time, Dan said, "Uh-oh, is my server down? Where's your phone?" Although Dan's office is in Manhattan, some of his computers are in a renovated warehouse on 137th Street at Willow Avenue, in the Bronx. While we were waiting for someone to pick up, Dan told me about a friend's recent scare: An employee had stolen two of the friend's computers. After he confronted the employee, someone called his office and said, "If you want your computers, they are sitting under the bridge around the corner."

"Well, why did the guy steal them at all?" I asked.

Dan said, "Because that's the state of despair his life is in."

Finally, Dan reached someone who was with the machines and reported that they seemed to be working fine. We tried again, and this time we got through. Dan uploaded my home page onto his server, tweaked my links for me, and told me my Web address, which is http://www.levity.com/seabrook. "All right," Dan said. "You have a home. All within the comfort of your own home."

I'm ready for company.

EXPLORING THE READING

1. What do you think of Seabrook's definition of a home page? If you have a home page or have visited personal pages, does his definition fit? How so?

2. In your small group, discuss your experience with browsing personal home pages. Develop a list of characteristics of a good home page and share these with the class.

3. Seabrook interrupts his narrative about the experience of building a home page to discuss the history of the Internet, chat rooms, and other topics. Why do you think he does this? Is it disruptive or helpful?

SESSION WITH THE CYBERSHRINK: AN INTERVIEW WITH SHERRY TURKLE

by Herb Brody

The following interview with Sherry Turkle, whom writer Herb Brody calls the Margaret Mead of the computer culture, explores some of the issues Turkle tackles in her recent book, Life on the Screen. *People online can play with the experience of creating personas that are different aspects of themselves, a process Turkle considers healthy because it challenges traditional ways of thinking about themselves.*

Turkle, a licensed clinical psychologist, holds a joint doctorate in sociology and psychology from Harvard University and is a professor of Science, Technology, and Society at MIT. She has also published The Second Self: Computers and the Human Spirit. *Her home page, http://web.mit.edu/sturkle/www, includes links to this interview from* Technology Review *and other texts by and about Turkle.*

Attempting to unlock her office door, Sherry Turkle fumbles with her keys. She tries one way, then another. After good-naturedly grousing about the recalcitrant lock—so much more troublesome than opening a fresh window on a computer screen—Turkle finally succeeds, and the door swings open to a most uncybernetic office: wicker furniture, riverside view of the Boston skyline, photo of her four-year-old daughter. Surely a computer lurks somewhere in this den of the reigning psycho-guru of cyberspace, but it is tastefully unobtrusive.

Turkle has established herself as the Margaret Mead of the computer culture. Her 1984 book *The Second Self: Computers and the Human Spirit* examined the way people interacted with personal computers, just then becoming a common appliance. The book catapulted her into the pantheon of academic superstars: *Ms.* magazine named her its woman of the year, and *Esquire* entered her in its "registry of America's new leadership class."

The Brooklyn-born Turkle, with a joint doctorate in sociology and psychology from Harvard University, is a professor in MIT's Program in Science, Technology, and Society. Her interest in concepts of identity predates her fascination with computers; she has written exclusively about psychoanalysis, and rarely does she give an interview or lecture without referring in some way to Freud, whose division of human identity into id, ego, and superego presaged the infinitely more diverse personas that people voluntarily assume in their travels through cyberspace.

Her latest book—*Life on the Screen: Identity in the Age of the Internet,* published in November by Simon and Schuster—assesses the impact of computer networks on the way people think about themselves and their role in society. Turkle, who is a licensed clinical psychologist, lived among the Net natives in order to learn their ways. In the spirit of the new medium, she sometimes donned a disguise—such as a thin veil in the persona of "Doctor

Sherry" or even assumed a male persona to experience for herself the Net's fabled gender-bending abilities. Turkle spoke with senior editor Herb Brody not only about the potential of the Net to enhance human experience but about elements of the online phenomenon that disturb her—in particular the fear that young people will succumb to the temptation to leave "real life" behind for the ever-so-much more controllable realm of cyberspace.

TR: When people in real life exhibit multiple distinct personalities, we call them psychotic, or at least sinister: In Robert Louis Stevenson's story, Dr. Jekyll shed his "gentle doctor" identity to liberate the "beast" within him as Mr. Hyde. Why are multiple personas not only accepted on the Net but considered cool?

TURKLE: People who suffer from multiple personality disorder have fragmented selves where different pieces are walled off from the others—often in the service of protection from traumatic memories. People who suffer in this way can have the experience of opening their closet in the morning and not knowing who bought some of the suits inside it. By contrast, people who assume online personas are aware of the lives they have created on the screen. They are playing different aspects of themselves and move fluidly and knowledgeably among them. They are having an experience that encourages them to challenge traditional ways of thinking about healthy selves as single and unitary.

TR: How so?

TURKLE: We live an increasingly multi-roled existence. A woman may wake up as a lover, have breakfast as a mother, and drive to work as a lawyer. A man might be a manager at the office and a nurturer at home. So even without computer networks, people are cycling through different roles and are challenged to think about their identities in terms of multiplicity. The Internet makes this multiplicity more concrete and more urgent.

TR: But the multiple personas people assume online are of a different sort from the roles you've described. In cyberspace a person may be a man sometimes and a woman another, for example.

TURKLE: Yes, cyberspace takes the fluidity of identity that is called for in everyday life and raises it to a higher power: people come to see themselves as the sum of their distributed presence on all the windows they open on the screen. The technical metaphor of cycling through computer windows has become a metaphor for thinking about the relationship among aspects of the self.

TR: So cyberspace is kind of a fun house mirror of our society—essentially reflecting what goes on off-line, but with some exaggeration?

TURKLE: Yes. And in a way, because it does allow for an extravagance of experimentation—with gender switching, age-flexibility, and all the rest made so easy—experiences in cyberspace are challenging us to revisit the question of what we mean by identity.

TR: But in the frenzy of attaining multiple identities, some people seem to be losing the sense that their "real world" self is any more important than their menagerie of online personas. In your book you describe one young man who tells you that for him, real life—RL, as he calls it—doesn't have any special status. It's just another window, along with the ones where he plays roles in a number of virtual communities.

TURKLE: Right. And he said RL is usually not even his best window.

TR: That sounds obsessive. Do you encounter that attitude a lot?

TURKLE: It's not uncommon. But for me, his case is important because it demonstrates how a bright young man who is doing well in school and who has real-life friends can easily go through a period when things are more interesting on the Net than off. This is what leads him to see his online experiences as a "genuine" part of his life. He still had a life off-line, but at the time of our conversation, events there were not going so well. From this perspective, the comment about RL not being his best window seems a bit less sinister.

TR: So retreat into online community is just a phase?

TURKLE: It can be. And in some cases it is not so much a retreat as a first step in developing strengths that can be brought into "real" life. I met a student who had a very bad time in his freshman year in college. His father was an alcoholic, and he was dealing with his own sense of his vulnerability to alcoholism. He coped by taking a job of great responsibility in a virtual community. When I met him the following summer, he was interested in going back to try things out in RL. In the best of cases, positive online experiences leave their mark on both the virtual and the real. And they can change the way people see their possibilities; it can affect self-esteem.

TR: Are social skills acquired online applicable in RL?

TURKLE: They can be. Much of what it takes to get along socially are things like having enough self-esteem to be willing to take risks, to have somebody not like you and yet be able to move on, to be able to take no for an answer, to not see things in black and white. An absence of these skills can make life on the Net seem attractive as a place of escape. But they can be learned by interacting with people within virtual communities. That's why I don't get upset that people, even children, are spending a lot of time online. They may be working through important personal issues in the safety of life on the screen. They may come out the other side having had some experience they're able to use to make their lives more fulfilling.

TR: Can casual relationships formed online survive the transition to the real world, where it's not so easy to hide behind an invented identity?

TURKLE: Sometimes, online relationships do not survive the voyage to the real. But in other cases, they survive very well. I know of real-life marriages between people who met each other in cyberspace. The way such intimacies develop usually follows a rather unsurprising pattern. You're in an online discussion group and you "hear" one of the contributors to the group sound interesting and appealing over a three-month period. You're finally going to want to talk to him or her in person. People want that flesh-and-blood connection. Of course, this can lead to problems too. Someone may begin an online extramarital affair thinking of it as a form of interactive erotic literature, typing provocative sentences back and forth, and then discover that the involvement has become a lot more complicated—something that they want to bring into their real life.

TR: Parents I know are ambivalent about their kids' use of computers. It's wonderful that children have this other world that they can inhabit and master. On the other hand, there seems to be an element of compulsion that's not particularly attractive. There are only so many hours in the day, and time spent on a computer is time not spent with friends, family, playing sports, or just reading.

TURKLE: If the computer is replacing time with peers and parents, that's not good. But if the computer is replacing television, then that may well be an upgrade.

TR: Do you worry that some people—children in particular—might be becoming addicted to computers?

TURKLE: It's not an addiction like with cocaine, where everyone on it develops a physical dependency, which is never good. When people respond to the holding power of computers, the situation is far more complex. A person can use computers in different ways at different times, and for different developmental tasks. A six-year old who uses a computer, for example, may be working on an issue of mastery. A year later he may have shifted his attention to baseball cards. Both are developmentally appropriate, and there's little reason to think that mastery of the online world is much different from mastery of box scores in baseball. This is especially true now that kids can share their experiences online in much the same way that they can share their interest in baseball cards. In the same sense, computer programming is not that much different from, say, chess.

PALLIATIVE FOR A VULNERABLE TIME

TR: Many of the people you study are students attending college—traditionally a time when people leap into political activity. Are these young adults using the Net to try to change the world?

TURKLE: As someone whose political sensibilities were developed in the 1960s, I'm sorry to say that I see some evidence that things are not going in that direction. I talked with one young man of 22 or 23, who told me how involved he is in political activity within one of the Internet's virtual worlds—a multi-user domain (or MUD) where people create characters and build their own virtual living and working spaces as a backdrop for their online social lives. He just loved the grassroots feel of the involvement. Since this was right before the last congressional elections, and some key seats in his home state were up for grabs, I said, well—what about real-life politics? He said no, that was of no interest to him: politicians were all cynics and liars. Part of me wanted to cry.

TR: Why do you find that so disturbing?

TURKLE: I hear many of the people I interview expressing a genuine confusion, a sense of impotence, about how to connect to the political system. In cyberspace, they feel they know how to connect, how to make things happen.

This is disturbing because as of now, most of the community life in MUDs and other virtual places has little effect in the real world—these online societies essentially disappear when you turn off your computer. It would be exciting to see online communities used more to address real-world social crises such as those around the environment, health, drugs, and education. This is starting to happen; I would like to see more of it. Online activists are learning a great deal as they build virtual worlds—it's like thousands of social experiments being conducted simultaneously, all over the world. I would like to see some of the knowledge gained from these efforts used to improve our off-line communities.

TR: Why do you think some young people are withdrawing from real political involvement and jumping instead into cyberspace?

TURKLE: For some people I interviewed who are in their twenties, cyberspace offers them a status that RL does not. These people grew up in middle class families, went to college, and many feel that they are slipping out of the middle class. They work jobs in fast food or sales, most share apartments, some have moved back to live with parents. They're not living in the way they were brought up to think somebody with a college education would live.

TR: But in cyberspace, they have higher status?

TURKLE: Right. In cyberspace they feel that they have rejoined the middle class. They are spending time with people whose interests and cultural background they recognize. They feel at home and in a political environment where they can make a difference. As one person put it, "I have more stuff on the MUD than off it," meaning that in her virtual community, she was able to build and furnish her own "room." Meanwhile, the real-world culture is supporting this notion with the hype that computers are sexy, that cyberspace is where it's happening. But I think that some of this hype can encourage a notion that what we do to the physical environment, say, doesn't count because we're creating a new environment in cyberspace. You don't want to lose a sense of urgency about the state of your city because you feel you have this other ready alternative. Yet, this is what I pick up in the attitudes of many cyber-enthusiasts I speak to.

TR: That would seem to be a self-fulfilling prophecy—as people withdraw from the real world, their talents are not available to solve our real problems. But they are available in cyberspace, which then becomes a more and more attractive option.

TURKLE: Yes. As a society, we are at a particularly vulnerable point. There is a tremendous amount of insecurity about what kinds of jobs we are going to have and where they will be. How are we going to address the serious problems facing our children: drugs, violence, deteriorating education? How are we going to address problems of the environment and of cities and of health care? Do we have the political will to attempt to do all of these things? The challenges seem overwhelming. So people are very susceptible now to the notion that there's a better place—somewhere over the rainbow, way up high, where there isn't any trouble. Of course, that place is the online world. In other words, our confusion and insecurity make us want to believe that there is a technological alternative.

HAVING IT ALL

TR: Why do you think there's been a recent backlash against the Internet, with the publication of critical books and articles?

TURKLE: There are several reasons. Partly it is opportunistic—after a lot of hype, people sense that it's the right time in the news cycle to present a contrary point of view. Also, the same frustrations and the same desire for an easy fix that leads people to the safety of the Internet leads people to complain about it rather than other things. We don't know what to do about violence or about the poor quality of education in many schools. We don't know how to bring families back together. It's easy to blame technology for our ills. So you see the widespread fantasy that what's causing moral decay in America is online pornography. People are spending a lot of political capital making waves about the urgency of cleaning up the Internet. I think that energy might be better spent elsewhere.

TR: Pornography on the Net doesn't overly concern you?

TURKLE: Do I want my four-year-old sitting there scrolling through filthy pictures? Of course not. But I would rather not interfere with free speech and I prefer to keep the monitoring of children as something that gets done by parents in the home rather than have governmental agencies policing cyberspace. Yes, there is pornography online. But we should be able to recognize that it is a displacement of our social anxieties to be focusing disproportionately on cyberporn as a pressing problem.

TR: Many critics seem turned off by how shallow the Internet is, both in its informational content and in the kind of relationships it fosters.

TURKLE: When a new technology is introduced, people respond by complaining that it's not as good as what we have had before. But it is hard to argue that online information doesn't compete favorably with what television offers. And online communication is in many ways a return to print— to reading and writing. In any case, it has usually worked out that the introduction of a new medium does not displace the old in any simple sense. Television didn't kill movies, and neither did video games.

TR: So instead we end up with everything.

TURKLE: Yes—that seems to be a general pattern. I do not believe that people are going to choose between relationships in cyberspace and face-to-face relationships. I think that people are going to have all kinds. It's not going to be one or the other. What I'm interested in—psychologically, socially, and politically—is making real life more permeable to cyberspace and cyberspace more permeable to real life. We need to think of ways to make the resources that are online have a positive impact on real life.

TR: But such "permeability" could come at a cost. For instance, if kids pursue more education through the Net and less through schools with other kids, won't they miss much of the socialization that schools have traditionally provided?

TURKLE: Well, in that sense the advent of a new technology leads us to ask what it is we most value in our way of life. Do we care, for example, about public schools? Because if the schools continue to deteriorate, and pose physical dangers, and an online alternative arises, then who could blame parents for keeping their kids home and having them just log on instead? It's a rational choice. Now if you don't like that, if you think that kids ought to be getting an education with other children, then you have to be willing to pay for it. And that will mean investing public money to make the schools better and safer. Online possibilities are forcing us to examine what we really care about. They are serving as a kind of wake-up call.

NOT ALL BOYS AND THEIR TOYS

TR: Has the rise of the Internet made the computer culture more female-friendly?

TURKLE: Definitely. Computer technology is moving in a direction that makes it easier for women to see it as something that is culturally theirs. We're hearing a lot less of that stuff about girls having "computer phobia," which I never thought was a good way to explain what was going on.

TR: You don't think girls have tended to be more apprehensive than boys about using computers?

TURKLE: Maybe they were at one time, but the label "phobia" does not correctly describe the phenomenon and does not help girls get over what some of them feel, which is much more like computer reticence. Girls weren't afraid of computers, but many felt that dealing with a computer was just not very girl-like. The computer was culturally constructed as male, just as much of technology was. When I was a girl, I once wanted to build a crystal radio. My mother, usually very encouraging, said no, don't touch it, you'll get a shock. It wasn't that I didn't want to build it—I wasn't phobic. But somehow, this just wasn't what girls did. I became reticent about such things.

Traditionally, the computer culture has carried many associations that tended to alienate girls—I mean, if you made a mistake, the computer asked you if you wanted to "abort" or "execute" or "kill." Those words convey images that just didn't appeal to a girl. Also, computers took you away from people.

TR: But the Internet is making the computer more of a social tool?

TURKLE: Yes—using computers today tends not to involve conquest metaphors or isolation from other human beings. Interfaces encourage you to manipulate them, to play with objects on the screen as though they were tangible entities, like elements of a collage. And the Net is all about chatting with people, being with people. Women who get onto the Net are often turned off by the flaming and the *ad hominem* rudeness they see. But they find places on the Net where this is not the case, and when they don't find them, they can create them. The Net desperately needs more of the characteristics that in our culture have been associated with women—skills such as collaboration and diplomacy. And many online communities are not only civil but actively encourage friendships and networking—it's not all boys and their toys.

TR: Still, the Net remains mostly male, doesn't it?

TURKLE: Women are present on the Net in greater and greater numbers. But I am often struck by the preponderance of messages that seem to come from men, even in places where there are many women around. Women tend to be less visible than men because when confronted with a rowdy group-flame session, women will move their conversations to private e-mail.

TR: Is there some way that women are using the Net more than men are?

TURKLE: Many women are getting access to the Internet in order to keep in touch with their families. For example, a parent with kids at college can use the Net to communicate with them. Parents know that their kids are logging on every day to get their e-mail. They're not going to resent an e-mail message from mom the way they might resent a badly timed phone call. A channel of communication that wasn't there before is opening.

TR: Does this new channel lead to new kinds of interactions?

TURKLE: Yes. A parent can send e-mail to a child away at college, saying, you know, it's 3 o'clock in the morning, I couldn't sleep, I was watching an old movie, I just thought I'd send you a note. In one case when this happened, the child, a freshman at college, responded immediately to a note from his mother and told her that he was up too—studying for a chemistry exam. The mother wrote right back, I wish you luck. The son appreciated the nurturance, something that he would not have permitted himself if he had had to call home. So all of a sudden you have an interaction that gratifies both people that never would have happened.

TR: So for many women, the Internet is a way to strengthen family ties?

TURKLE: Yes. Of course, the appeal of cyberspace for communication with family also draws in many men as well. And once they're in touch with their kids, why shouldn't they join a newsgroup about investments?

THE PERIL OF THE BLACK BOX

TR: Time was, effective use of a computer required at least a basic understanding of how the machine worked. One benefit of more advanced computers is that this is no longer the case—people can now control a powerful technology without knowing much of anything about how it operates. What are the consequences of relying on a technology that is so opaque?

TURKLE: I'm very concerned that technology may be fostering a kind of intellectual passivity, feeding into a cultural acceptance of a lack of understanding of how a lot of things work. I'm troubled by people's sense that this is all basically magic. I don't think people should have no idea how computer technology works. And increasingly, people have no idea. I interviewed one man who said that when BMW started using microchips in its cars, he lost interest in them although he had been an avid enthusiast. For him, the cars had become opaque. He enjoyed transparent technology because it made him feel more empowered to understand other things in his world. I have a lot of sympathy for his perspective.

TR: Cars that use computer chips need less maintenance and run better. A Macintosh is usable by millions more people than a DOS or UNIX computer. Aren't such benefits worth the loss of "transparency"?

TURKLE: But some undesirable things may go along with this movement. When people deal every day with objects that are powerful but impenetrably complex, it can lead to feelings of impotence. Or, alternatively, to feelings of unreasonable power and retreat to radical oversimplifications. We need to be attentive to the social and psychological impact of a technology that encourages you to think that all you need to do is click, click. Double click and make public education go away. Double click and make taxes go away. Double click—three strikes and you're out and solve the crime problem. As a society, we're doing a lot of double clicking. And I think it is not a bad thing for us to get a better understanding of how this mentality might be flowing out of the habits of thought encouraged by our technology.

TR: All in all, are you an optimist or pessimist about the effects of the computer on the human psyche?

TURKLE: I think that computers offer dramatic new possibilities for personal growth—for developing personal senses of mastery, for forming new kinds of relationships, and for communicating with friends and family all over the world in immediate, even intimate ways. But I don't like thinking of things in terms of optimism or pessimism because it makes it sound as though one gets to take bets on whether the technology is going to have one kind of effect or another. I think that a lot of the effect of computers and the Internet is going to depend on what people do with it. We have to see ourselves as in a position to profoundly affect the outcome of how things are going to do. Hyping or bashing technology puts the emphasis on the power of the technology. I'm trying to put the spotlight on people, and the many human choices we face as we try to assimilate this technology.

Ultimately, there is a limit to the sorts of satisfactions that people can have online. We live in our bodies. We are terrestrial. We are physical as well as mental beings—we are cerebral, cognitive, and emotional. My optimism comes from believing that people are going to find ways to use life on the screen to express all these sides of themselves.

EXPLORING THE READING

1. Turkle discusses instances when online life becomes more attractive, more real than off-line life. Have you experienced this or known anyone who has? Why does Turkle says this happens? Do you agree?

2. In your small group, make a list of what Turkle has to say about some of the criticisms of the Internet, for example that it is addictive or that it allows pornography. Do you agree with her comments? Why or why not?

3. Near the end of the interview Turkle talks about her concern that people are becoming too accepting when they don't understand how things work. She fears that they will come to think that all one needs to do is double-click and problems will go away. Do you think that this is a valid fear?

INTIMATE STRANGERS

by Jill Smolowe

How can you be both intimate and a stranger? It happens all the time in the chat rooms on the Internet where participants bare their innermost thoughts to people they have never met face to face. Jill Smolowe, in this Time *magazine article, estimates that 80 percent of the people using the Internet are there for the interpersonal contact and sense of community. Opinions of Net experts, however, differ about whether there is or can be a community in cyberspace, and Smolowe cites some of the arguments on both sides. Whether it is intimacy, friendship, or community, or not, people are flocking to chat rooms and spending dozens of hours a month. They are finding something which is satisfying, at least for the moment, their needs and desires.*

Smolowe is a senior writer for Time, *focusing primarily on domestic, political, and social issues. Previously, she was an associate editor at* Newsweek, *where she wrote for the international editions. Smolowe's 1983 cover story on child labor earned three awards, including the Newspaper Guild's Page One Award and an Overseas Press Club citation. Her work has also appeared in* Reader's Digest, Family Circle, People, The Boston Globe, *and other publications.*

When she first joined ECHO, an East Coast electronic community, Marcia Bowe dubbed herself "Miss Outer Buro 1991," a handle that facetiously implied beauty queen-like poise, glamour, congeniality. And soon enough, Bowe was enjoying the adulation of fellow "ECHOids" who posted messages praising her wit, candor and smarts. Such celebrity was heady stuff for Bowe, a freelance writer who describes herself in real life as shy and wary of emotional encounters. "I became addicted to this constant stream of approval," she says. "It was like a big co-dependency machine."

As Bowe began spending up to one hundred hours a month online, however, her life began to take on the burdens of celebrity. "Some people were envious of me," she says. "They accused me of snobbery and élitism." More disturbing, Bowe began to realize that her own hyperactivity was masking an underlying unhappiness with her life. So she dropped out of ECHO, cold turkey. "I had forgotten that the real world is so complex and fascinating."

She's back in cyberspace now, this time in a paid position at ECHO overseeing its fifty-four conferences, but she has learned to navigate online with greater perspective and a thicker skin. That doesn't mean she's become detached, though. "This is an emotional place, not just a communications device," she says.

All of this may sound strangely overwrought to those who have yet to venture online. The Internet, after all, has been touted largely as an unwalled repository of raw data, not of raw emotions. But the truth is that the vast majority of people who troll the Internet's byways are there in search of social interaction, not just sterile information. An estimated 80 percent of all users are looking for contact and commonality, companionship and community—all the conjugations implied by E.M. Forster's famous injunction "Only connect!"

Relationships can be complicated in cyberspace because the very technology that draws most people together also keeps them apart. Over time, the safe sense of distance that initially seems so liberating to newcomers on the Net can become an obstacle to deepening the bonds of friendship, romance and community. At some point, most networkers often find, the only real way to move a relationship forward is to risk personal contact—and then hope the phantom bond will hold up in the 3-D world. "You can't lead a total life online," says Dave Hughes, founder of the Old Colorado City Electronic Cottage, a cyber-settlement. "But if it's done right, online communication can lead *to* face-to-face contact, not away *from* it."

At its best, the sprawling Internet brings together people with mutual interests who, for reasons ranging from geography to social and income disparity, would otherwise never have met. These virtual friendships can lead to physical encounters that may cement lifelong relationships. "The cybercommunity is not separate from your community of friends; it's just not geographically local," says Carolyn Ybarra, an anthropology Ph.D. candidate at Stanford University.

When Ybarra moved west from Minneapolis, her online quilting group threw an in-person farewell party. Since then, she has become good friends with two of her fellow quilters, keeping in constant touch online. "I feel just as close to these women as I do to my college friends," she says. "I tell them more up-to-date details of my personal life, more often, because their response is so quick."

Ybarra was fortunate to encounter women who, in person, were much the same as they were online. That is often not the case. The disembodied voices that whisper through cyberspace can often be manufactured identities that can disguise, distort or amplify aspects of a user's personality. Fortunately, only a relative few—Lotharios who woo indiscriminately, for example, or pederasts who prey on vulnerable children—have a devious and potentially dangerous intent.

Most Net users are more likely to project aspects of the person they wish they could be. Paulina Borsook, author of *Love over the Wires*, calls this "selective lying by omission"; psychologist Kenneth Gergen, author of *Saturated Self*, more charitably regards it as "playing out our other selves."

Either way, even unintended distortions can prove bruising. When Christine Rance, twenty-eight, struck up a Net relationship with a man she knew as "MyPalJoey," she says, "I told him things I had never told anyone in my life. I was really able to be more open. He was too."

After more than three months of furious messaging, the couple had their first F2F (face-to-face) encounter. About six months later, Rance secured a job transfer from Chicago to San Francisco, anticipating a trip to the altar. But after six weeks, the couple broke up, crushed by conflicting schedules and personalities. "He's a very selfish person, more than I ever thought," says a chastened Rance. "He didn't want to give up anything but wanted me to give up everything."

Dan Marsh, by contrast, knew within five minutes of his first F2F with Audrey that their four years of online messaging between the West Coast and Pennsylvania had been time well invested. "I don't react well to meeting people in person," says Marsh. "I'm very reserved." But the relative safety of cyberspace had enabled him to be more trusting and vulnerable. "Even though I'm the most private person you ever want to meet, I let my guard down right away," he says of their online courtship. In 1993, two years after meeting, the couple married.

The problems of cementing relationships in cyberspace pale beside the challenges of forging whole enclaves. In fact, among the cyberintelligentsia, debate rages as to whether the concept of "community" even exists in cyberspace. Howard Rheingold, author of *The Virtual Community*, says, "I want to dispel the notion that a computer network is by itself a community—a place where at least some of the people reach out through that screen and affect each other's lives." At some point, Rheingold says, "it requires a further commitment either in real life or in cyberspace from those people to each other."

Rheingold cites the death from cancer last August of Kathleen Johnston, a member of the WELL, a nine-year-old Bay Area settlement. Not only did many of the WELL's more than 10,000 subscribers flood Johnston in her waning days with electronic support, consolation and advice, but more than two dozen members took turns going to her home, tending to her needs. "Not dying alone," says Rheingold, "that's something a community has." Some found that the feeling of shared loss—even if not shared directly with others—was enough to form a sense of community.

WELL member Jon Carroll, who participated in the electronic support, believes "cyberspace entered the real world in a real way with her death." In his view, virtual communities often enjoy a keener sense of connection than physical communities. "Since they are in cyberspace voluntarily," says Carroll, "people are far more interested in participating in the life of the community online."

That view is not universal. "We need to be critical of the use of the word community," counters Steven Jones, editor of *Cyber-Society*, a new collection of essays on computer-mediated communications. "If we use the term uncritically, we dilute it in ways that really count." To Jones, community implies not only responsibility, respect and acceptance of the consequences of one's actions but also simply "being together," without any agenda. He regards the urge to form cybercommunities as a throwback to the '60s. "We tune in, turn on, drop out, make our own rules, man," he says. "This is not real."

Denizens of virtual villages respond that what they have constructed is as real as anything three-dimensional. "The online world is not utopia," says ECHO founder Stacy Horn. "We all take our problems, needs, strangeness, biases and prejudices online with us." In short, members take themselves along for the ride. "People who have troubles with their friends in the real world think they'll come online and have lots of friends, and it's not true," says Horn. "They have equal trouble establishing friendships in cyberspace."

In most online communities, the esprit is fiercely democratic. When crises arise, they are resolved by members thrashing out the dos and don'ts of cyberspace etiquette. Still, there are plenty of élites and hierarchies. Veteran settlers, who look askance at the hordes of newcomers, often form exclusive conferences where they can avoid endless beginner bellyaching about insiderish jokes and jargon. "There are users and super-users," says Jones. "There are e-mail addresses that have more status than others."

In other words, the Net is pretty much more of the world we already know: a place both embracing and exclusionary, loving and hurtful. As happened with the telephone and automobile, technology lends to the fragmentation of people's lives and also helps stitch those fragments back together again. Most online veterans tend to agree that the challenge is to merge the connections made in cyberspace with real lives.

"We're not going to bridge anything simply by connecting," warns Jones. "We can build all the bridges we want, but if we don't cross them and mill about, we won't make any kind of connections that count."

A HANGOUT FOR EVERY OCCASION

There are a hundred thousand haunts in cyberspace—each with its own crowd, own interests and own point of view. Here is a sampling:

Honest Talk The conversation on ECHO is more thoughtful and civilized than on a lot of other services, in part because almost 40 percent of the members of this New York City–based community are women. Try the Culture and Psych conferences.

Singles . . . or doubles, or *ménages à trois* for that matter: the hottest pick-up joints are the chat rooms of America Online's People Connection.

Gravitas The liberal-intellectual crowd gathers nightly on the WELL, the Bay Area–based Whole Earth 'Lectronic Link. The media and radio conferences attract the glitterati, and participants in the philosophy conference know not only the spelling of Kierkegaard's name but the views he propounded.

Deadheads Devoted followers of The Grateful Dead know the place to worship their heroes is the WELL's Dead conference.

Twentysomething Gen-Xers hang at Manhattan's MindVox and contemplate fifty more years of living under the shadow of Yuppies.

A Good Laugh The exchange of jokes is unfiltered and thus occasionally unfunny in the *rec.humor* newsgroup. A finer repertoire, or so it is said, is in *alt.humor.best-of-usenet*, which is monitored.

Doubting Thomases True believers in parapsychology and other pseudosciences are in for a tough time with the crowd that frequents the *alt.paranet.skeptic, bit.listserv.skeptic* and *sci.skeptic* newsgroups. But keepers of the faith show up to defend their theories, making for heated exchanges.

Cancer Patients Mutual support from fellow sufferers, their doctors and families comes in *alt.support.cancer.*

Wonks Political junkies duke it out on the Capital Connection, while current-events generalists visit TIME Online—both on AOL. CompuServe's Rush Limbaugh message boards regularly draw a crowd. Specialized areas exist on the Internet for every imaginable viewpoint, from *alt.society.anarchy* to *alt.politics.clinton.*

Furry Tales *rec.pet.cats* is for serious cat lovers. But the occasional mischief-maker shows up and posts hair-raising descriptions of feline abuse designed to shock the regular denizens.

EXPLORING THE READING

1. In your small group, pool your knowledge of chat rooms and other social groups on the Internet. What has been your experience? Share your knowledge with the class.

2. If you have participated in online discussion groups or chat rooms, freewrite for five minutes about your experience. Why were you there? What was it like? If you haven't participated in any such groups, freewrite about what you imagine they would be like. Would you find them meaningful? Why or why not?

3. Jill Smolowe describes what various authorities have said about the sense of community on the Internet. What do you think? Is it possible to have a community in cyberspace?

4. Smolowe mentions the presence of people in chat rooms who "prey on vulnerable children" and others, but she downplays the numbers and the significance of such people. Do you agree with her implied assessment that this is a minor problem? Why or why not?

CYBERSPIRIT

by Jeff Zaleski

The first book printed on Gutenberg's press was a Bible. It should be no surprise that religious groups are moving onto the Internet, the new publishing and communication medium, in a big way, according to Jeff Zaleski in this article from Yoga Journal. *Cyberspace makes it easy for people with similar interests to communicate, a powerful strength for religious groups, because of the sense of community which can develop. Cyberspace, though, has its limitations, points out Zaleski. It lacks what he calls prana, the life force which requires physical presence. Can cyberspace, despite its limitations and flaws, play a constructive role in a spiritual life? Zaleski believes it can.*

Zaleski is coauthor (with Tracy Cochran) of Transformations: Awakening to the Sacred in Ourselves. *He is also a contributing editor to* Publishers Weekly *and a consulting editor to* Tricycle: The Buddhist Review.

This morning was an extremely busy one for me. First I took a tour of Manhattan's magnificent Cathedral of St. John the Divine, a Gothic master-piece built entirely of stone. Then I visited an art gallery displaying Tibetan thangkas met with a friend to talk about the best yoga courses in the New York area, and read the latest issue of *Hinduism Today.* At last, seeking a break from all this sensory input, I sat in silence for a while with several other people, counting my breaths from one to ten and back down again. After-wards, for the first time in nearly thirty years, I went to confession and said penance. Then I kicked off the covers, rose from my bed, and got dressed.

I didn't spend my morning in a dream, though the manner in which I did all these things has been compared to lucid dreaming. Rather, I spent the day's early hours in cyberspace.

Like Jehovah of the Old Testament and the Hindu god Shiva, humankind has at last created a world—the world of virtual reality. Each day, many mil-lions of us visit this world through our computers, just as I did this morning—and for good reason. It is an infinite realm, bounded only by the human imagination and the hard-drive capacity of the planet's computers. For many, it seems to be a world of infinite marvel and hope. But we are novices at world-creating, and others say that our experiment in this ultimate hubris may lead to infinite sorrow. For nearly all of us, however, online or not, virtual reality will have profound consequences—perhaps, above all, for how we relate to the sacred.

Spiritual and religious groups of every variety have become aware of this, and even communities not usually associated with high-tech innovation are seizing the virtual day. Though Mennonites may ride in horse-drawn carriages rather than automobiles, they have spread through cyberspace with messianic zeal and maintain scores of sites on the World Wide Web. Lubavitcher Jews, though they dress in the black caftans and fur hats fash-ionable in Eastern Europe centuries ago, have also wired up to disseminate their teachings through the new digital domain.

These two groups are joined in cyberspace by many others. Roman Catholics, pagans, Jains, Buddhists, Hindus, Muslims, Jehovah's Witnesses, Satanists, and those who worship a new electronic divinity they claim is made manifest in the computer chip—all are tapping away at their computer keyboards, communicating over phone lines among themselves and to the unconverted. By conservative estimate, there are already thousands of online sites devoted to spiritual subjects, with the number doubling every six to nine months. Most of these sites, like those spreading the Mennonite and Lubavitcher word, consist of "pages" on the World Wide Web—presentations of text and photographs, as well as snippets of video and sound clips that can be downloaded onto your home computer. In addition, there are hundreds of discussion forums on which people converse through sequential postings about nearly every spiritual subject imaginable, from Sufism to Taoism to wicca to yoga, including the perennially popular Buddhist Usenet group known (in Net-ese) as "alt.buddha.short.fat.guy." A growing Internet chaplaincy exists, offering the opportunity at any time, from anywhere in the world, to receive pastoral advice. And at least two online confessionals await to offer the sinner some sort of virtual solance, although neither is sanctioned by the Vatican.

DECENTRALIZING AND ERASING BOUNDARIES

This online spiritual gold rush isn't surprising or without precedent. Religious interests have always been quick to take advantage of technological innovation. When Gutenberg first cranked up his printing press, it was a Bible that he printed. But no matter how many spiritually oriented Web pages are constructed, they remain only free-floating digital data until they're downloaded by the sense organs into a human brain.

Because of the decentralized nature of Internet access, no one is quite sure exactly how many people are visiting the Net. By general consensus, however, there are at least fifteen million Americans with direct Internet access, and perhaps the same number outside our borders. This figure is likely to at least double by the end of 1996. Why are so many of us going digital?

One reason, of course, is to take advantage of all the information that is available online. But there is another, more compelling reason—people are entering cyberspace to communicate with one another. The Internet, in fact, was conceived in 1969 by the Defense Department as a means of communication so decentralized that it could withstand nuclear attack. Soon after the proliferation of personal computers in the early 1980s, people began communicating via computer through the phone lines, at first one-on-one, then in the so-called virtual communities like the WELL in San Francisco and Echo in New York City. Meanwhile, larger, more commercially oriented services arose: the virtual cities of CompuServe, Prodigy, and America Online, joined last year by what soon may grow to be the Gotham of cyberspace, the Microsoft Network.

As people connect to one another in these digital colonies and other online sites, they cross and sometimes erase political, racial, gender, economic, and sexual boundaries. The consequences can be immense, both for the individual and for the planet. In cyberspace, national borders are obliterated, and, at least to date, freedom reigns. One reason the anti-Yeltsin coup failed in Russia a few years back was because the pro-Yeltsin forces were sending information to each other via computer, bypassing the usual channels which were closely monitored by the KGB and other repressive forces. Meanwhile, prejudice can be circumvented, if not eclipsed, on the Net—and perhaps in the real world as well—as more of us go online and are unable to tell whether the person we're communing with so intimately is black or white, thin or fat, even male or female.

Meeting people online can also be tremendously therapeutic. Cyberspace is made for role playing, for testing personal limits and going beyond them. When people are granted complete anonymity, as they are in cyberspace, shyness may quickly wither away. Someone who stammers in the real world can prove to be a most fluent and seductive typist in the virtual world.

Perhaps cyberspace's most powerful appeal, however, is the ease with which it facilitates connections between people with common interests and values. Someone living on a farm in New Zealand who wants to know more about, say, bhakti yoga can within minutes connect not only to numerous information sites on the subject, but also to other people who share that interest. Of course, this can have its dark side. The Net is probably the most common means by which members of violent fringe groups of both the right and the left communicate and gather. But at its best, the sharing that goes on in cyberspace can generate tremendous meaning and value, including to the spiritual seeker. Each of us moves along the spiritual path in fits and starts, stumbling here, falling there. By sharing our experiences, we can learn from one another, and perhaps pick up our pace. In Buddhism, the community of people dedicated to following the Buddha's path is known as the *sangha*. At its best, an online community can provide us with a kind of sangha.

TELNETTING AS RELIGIOUS EXPERIENCE

One of the first groups of like-minded humans to band together in cyberspace were the Deadheads. This nomadic collective, bonded not by place but by love of the Grateful Dead and the band's spin-off culture of spiritual and psychedelic communion, naturally gravitated to the nowhere of cyberspace. As they did, along with them came John Perry Barlow, a Wyoming rancher who occasionally wrote songs for the Dead and who first went digital in the mid-80s.

Since then, Barlow has cofounded the Electronic Frontier Foundation, the premier organization working for the protection of civil liberties on the Net. Yet Barlow's interest in the Net extends beyond the political to the spiritual. In his writings he has argued that the evolution of the Net is a "great work" that may lead humanity to the collective, interpersonal divine consciousness predicted by the Jesuit thinker Teilhard de Chardin.

Recently, I met Barlow at the apartment he maintains in Manhattan's West Village. As we sat across from one another at a wooden table, sharing sweet rolls and coffee, he spoke with the relaxed, confident air of a man who has spent seventeen years learning about the facts of life while on the open plains.

"Where is all this leading?" I asked him.

"It's all leading to something!" he answered emphatically. "Everything is obviously trying to connect to everything else. If things continue in their current course, it's not so ridiculous to speculate that, at some point in the next 400 or 500 years, every human synapse on this planet will be continuously connected to every other human synapse—and the planet will be a very different place.

"What is the soul?" he mused a few moments later. "Is it just software that runs only as long as there's squishy ware [*i.e.,* a human body] to run it on? Or is it a prestanding independent identity that manifests itself in the physical world? If that's the case, then a lot of what goes on in the physical world involving bodies is actually conversation between souls using the blunt instruments available to them. I wonder if it won't eventually be possible, in a disembodied environment, for that conversation to become a lot more direct."

The first time Barlow telnetted, or logged from his home computer onto a remote computer, he had what he describes as a religious experience. "Why," I wondered aloud, "did you use the word 'religious'?"

"Because I realized, in a direct and immediate way, that every computer that was connected to the Internet was continuously connected, and that I could make a hard disk spin anywhere on Earth by typing in two words. I suddenly detected the nervous system of the planet, though in its very germinal form."

I found Barlow's application of the words "nervous system" to hard disks and phone wires an unexpected and unsettling leap. "How similar," I asked, "is this emerging global 'nervous system' to our own?"

"Well," Barlow answered in his measured baritone, "it has the same basic structure, the same architecture. Internet architecture is much more like neurological architecture than a switched telephone network is. And the way it grows and adapts and sends messages through itself seems to be much more like the brain."

Visions of digital deities danced in my head as I listened. "In other words, though each of us is in our body, our brains are communicating together through a kind of uberbrain?"

Barlow paused, then said, "I go back to Samuel Morse's great remark from 1850, 'I see no reason why intelligence may not be distributed throughout the planet by means of electricity.' Intelligence is already distributed throughout the body by means of electricity. It's simply a matter of extending the wiring, so these apparently isolated nodes in human crania become more like axions, or nerve bundles, in a much larger neurosystem."

"Does this global neurosystem have a soul?" I wondered.

"I think it does. But you know, that's a statement of faith."

"How did you come to that?"

"Partly by watching it try to get what it appears to want. I think the thing that wants everything to connect to everything else is saying, 'Create me. Make me. Give me consciousness.' "

Despite his acceptance of and hope for what the Net might bring, Barlow, to my great surprise, made clear his preference for spending time in the real world rather than the virtual. "There's nothing like a lot of time in cyberspace," he told me, "to make you really love the grit and stench of meatspace." Something is missing in cyberspace, Barlow admitted. Although virtual reality has the capacity to simulate the real world to a remarkable degree—through 3-D animation, video, audio, interactive multimedia, artificial intelligence—it lacks an essential ingredient that only the real world can provide: prana, the life force that courses through our bodies and animates our environment.

PRANA WITHOUT BODIES?

Each time I explore new territory, be it the burial grounds of Pompeii, a cavern in the Black Hills of North Dakota, or the skyscrapers of Manhattan as seen from a helicopter, the novelty of the experience and the shock of the unexpected silence my chattering mind and allow my attention to expand to encompass the whole of myself, bringing both my body and my prana into the sphere of my attention. The first time I sent an e-mail message, I had the same kind of experience. Reaching out to someone through an electronically generated environment made me more aware of my body and its life force, not less.

By now, however, I've logged thousands of hours online, and I find that when I sit in front of my computer screen I lose contact with my body just as quickly as I do when I'm watching TV. When you enter cyberspace, you leave your body behind—and with it the natural environment of which the body is a part.

But the body is the medium through which the richness of human communication takes place. Without it, the exchange of information can become a woefully impoverished, disembodied affair. While researching a chapter of my book *Transformations: Awakening to the Sacred in Ourselves* (coauthored with Tracy Cochran), I experienced the differences in virtual and real communication when I got in contact with my ex-wife, Stacy Horn, the founder of the virtual community Echo. Our initial exchanges took place online, by sending messages back and forth. Shielded from one another by space and computer screens, we had brisk, businesslike conversations. But when Stacy and I met in person, I noted, at least on my part, that a certain hesitancy crept in. Our shared history sat at the table with us like a third party—in the real world, real-world memories intruded. Meeting with Stacy, the richness and ambiguity of face-to-face communication became clear: the impact of a glance away or a stare, the subtle play of body language, the effects of shadings in tone and pitch of voice. All of these are missing in cybercommunication, as is the most important element of all, the prana-rich presence of another person's body.

Not everyone agrees that the lack of prana in cyberspace is a serious problem. Joseph Selbie, for more than twenty years a resident of the Ananda

Community centered in Nevada City, California, has a different take than Barlow on the relationship between prana and the Net. During the past year, Selbie has set up an online site called ConsciousNet, an umbrella for what he characterizes as "a collection of high-consciousness, high-vibration sites," including the East-West Online Bookstore and several digital versions of well-known magazines including *New Age Journal* and *Yoga Journal.*

When I mentioned Barlow's comment about the lack of prana in cyberspace during a recent phone conversation with Selbie, he said, "Your energy comes from within. If what you're reading or viewing or interacting with inspires you, then I think you gain in prana, you gain in inspiration."

No doubt Selbie is right about this. The life force, like the sacred, exists within us. But because there are no bodies in cyberspace, no mind-body work that depends on the body can take place there. You can't do yoga asanas in cyberspace, for instance. In much spiritual work, moreover, there is an exchange of energies that can't take place in the virtual world, at least not yet. Anyone who has studied with a spiritual teacher knows that much of what is transmitted comes not through words or gesture but through the sheer presence of the teacher—a presence that is simply is not available in cyberspace.

Theoretically, it's possible that prana and other sacred energies will eventually flood the virtual world. If one form of matter, flesh, can act as a host for prana and consciousness, perhaps in time other forms of matter, such as silicon, will too. And though there is no matter in virtual reality, the anecdotal evidence and some scientific research into mystical, after-death, and telepathic experiences indicate that consciousness, and perhaps prana, need not be grounded in matter.

Right now, however, there's no sacramental power in cyberspace, and no magic. In the virtual world, the Eucharistic host can't transform into the body of Christ, and the orishas of Santeria and the spirits of the Native Americans don't seem able to make their way from one computer to another. As Jaron Lanier, one of the pioneers of virtual reality, said in a recent interview in *Netguide* magazine, "The Internet exists for people to connect with each other. But to connect with the mystery of the universe, the Internet won't do. God doesn't have a Website."

FLOWERS AMONG THE THORNS

One of the most persuasive thinkers about the limitations and dangers of virtual reality is Stephen L. Talbott, author of *The Future Does Not Compute: Transcending the Machine in Our Midst* (O'Reilly & Associates, 1995). I recently phoned Talbott at his home in upstate New York. During our conversation, he agreed with Barlow that something essential is lacking in virtual reality. "Cyberspace gives us a world of indirect interaction," he said, "an abstracted world of images and representations. And that seems to run counter to a basic requirement of spirituality, which has to do with encountering reality in the very most intense and profound way, and thereby penetrating to what lies behind it—the forces, energies, and potentials from which the visible is taken to have descended."

Talbott sees in cyberspace an accelerating substitution of the virtual for the real. "People look at tools like the chat software," Talbott says, "and say, gee it's such an improvement over the book. But the point is, which aspects of our life are we transferring to the new medium? People tend to see this as a gain, but what they should be seeing is the loss with respect to the medium that actually applies in this case—which is face-to-face, personal interaction."

The idea that we can conquer prejudice through the Net, he observed, is "a strange thought, really the thought that we can be more human toward each other by being less human, less there. But as long as anything of the human being is left, there is something to discriminate against. The ease with which prejudice disappears across the Net is the ease with which the human being disappears."

"This not knowing each other in the flesh is really getting down to the nub of things," Talbott added. "We'll overcome prejudice only by overcoming it—and that means to look the other person in the eye, to look at every characteristic and be able to penetrate through it."

My own experience confirms the truth of Talbott's remarks, not only because Americans on the Net tend to be a largely homogenous group—well-off white males under fifty—but because of the Net's endemic role-playing. I'm continually astonished at how many women I've spoken with on the Net, if indeed they were women at all, boast blond hair, green eyes, and trim figures. I've noticed, moreover, as both Talbott and Barlow point out, that much communication on the Net is really self-communication—"the triumph of narcissism," as Barlow puts it, or, in Talbott's words, "a non-communicative self-indulge." Rather than exchanging life energies with another in the flesh, in virtual reality I find myself filling the cyberspace between myself and another with the demands of my own psyche, molding the unseen other after myself or projecting upon them my personal desires, perhaps my personal hatreds.

Through the pseudonymous handles and role-playing so prevalent in online communication, cyberspace may be responding to the same inherent hunger for fantasy that has children playing games of dress-up and make-believe. This can be therapeutic, of course, but it also can shield us from opening ourselves to others and, by extension, to ourselves. Personally, I find it incredibly difficult to tell the truth about myself online. Because I am invisible to the other person, and he or she to me, it seems like nothing at all to drop a few years or a few pounds or to add a few zeroes to my bank balance when communicating with another online.

Aggravating this temptation to connect only partially with others in cyberspace, which is another way to dehumanize them, is the fact that online conversation tends toward shallowness—at least in part because it's transmitted through relatively brief bursts of information. People type much slower than they speak, so real-time online chats are viable only if the participants limit themselves to brief statements.

The way information is accessed on the Web also fosters lack of depth. On average, most people stay at any one Website for only a minute or two, if that. There's just too much else out there to distract you. This, of course, is why the act of navigating the Net, and especially the Web, is known as "surfing"—skimming lightly over the surface of cyberspace at dazzling speed. While hanging ten in the digital world can be terrific fun, however, it leaves profundity of experience, and any consequent understanding, behind. As Talbott said to me, "It's infinitely more valuable to take a couple of paragraphs, to read them awake, and to really penetrate them than it is to scan through reams of material. Scanning is basically an inattention to meaning."

Perhaps above all, the Internet, particularly the World Wide Web, is a perpetual hope machine. Because it offers, for most practical purposes, a seemingly infinite number of pages linked by hypertext (underlined words or phrases that lead to other, related pages of information), it reinforces the sense that if the page you're on isn't completely satisfying, the next page just might be. And so it's on to the next page, and then the page after that. In other words, the Web, like the rest of the Internet but even more so, can be terribly addicting. Its addictive powers, moreover, may increase immensely in the coming years as new technologies enhance the virtual world's power to mimic the actual world, to create realms filled with fantasy and enchantment that appear ever more real.

Our creation of the virtual world presents enormous opportunities and dangers. The virtual world, like the real world, is a bramble—yet among the thorns, flowers bloom. If you enter cyberspace with a clear mind and an open heart, you may just find the information and connections you need to take you one stop further along the path.

EXPLORING THE READING

1. What did you think of Jeff Zaleski's first paragraph? Were you surprised to find he had done all those things in cyberspace? If you have explored the World Wide Web, make a list of three or four interesting places you have found. Share them with your small group.

2. Zaleski describes the presence of spiritual sites on the Web, which he says are doubling every six to nine months. Are you surprised to know that religious groups are establishing a presence in cyberspace?

3. Take a look at John Perry Barlow's Web page and read some of the papers and articles he provides. Does Zaleski present Barlow's views accurately?

4. Meeting in your small group, make a list of religious groups which interest you, whether Mennonites or Catholics or Buddhists. Have each member select a group and research Websites for that topic. Report back to the group about what you find and share your findings with the class.

WRITING SUGGESTIONS

1. Write a personal essay about the role of computers in your life. For example, you may describe how they have enriched your life, or how they have led to information overload. Use specific examples from your experience.

2. Talk to several of your friends or relatives who use computers and do some exploring of the Internet. Write an argument about why computers are so engaging, even addicting, to many people.

3. Interview a computer expert or enthusiast (perhaps someone who creates Web pages for a living, writes programs for a corporation, or spends extensive leisure time in chat rooms) about his or her perceptions of the connections between computer and human nature. Write a Q & A interview, modeling your format on the Sherry Turkle text.

4. Examine a number of personal pages, such as the ones mentioned in this chapter or pages of students at your university. Discuss how home pages are an expression of an individual's personality and lifestyle.

5. Design your own home page, including one or more photographs. Write an accompanying essay detailing how you portray yourself on the Internet and why.

THE WRITING PROCESS:

Qualities of Effective Writing

Reading the work of some professional writers, you may have developed the idea that the best writing is writing that is difficult to understand, writing that sends the reader to the dictionary with every sentence, or writing that uses many technical or specialized terms. Often, we think something difficult to read must be well written. Although it is sometimes difficult to read about topics that are new to us because we're learning new vocabulary and struggling with complex ideas, it simply is not true that the best writing is hard to read. Indeed, the most effective writing, the kind of writing you want to produce in your classes, is simple, concise, and direct.

Keep It Simple.   *Simple* means "unadorned" or "not ornate." *Writing simply* means saying something in common, concrete language without too much complication in the sentence structure. Writing simply doesn't mean you have to use only short or easy words. It doesn't mean that all your sentences will be simple sentences. It doesn't mean that you can't use figures of speech or intricate details. Simple writing means that you try to get your point across in a direct and interesting way. You aren't trying to hide your ideas. Instead, you are trying to amplify those ideas and begin an intelligible conversation with your reader.

Rely on Everyday Words. Some students discover the thesaurus in their word processing program and decide they can improve their writing by using synonyms of the simple words they have written. Because professional writers seem to use big or unknown words, a student may think that the biggest word or the least-used word is the best choice. Although some of the essays in this book may seem to support the idea, big words are not better words. The best word choice is a word that is in common everyday usage—that you might use or hear in conversation—whose various meanings will be understood by your audience. For your writing, you should rely on the words that are a natural part of your everyday vocabulary. If you find yourself repeating the same word throughout an essay, use the thesaurus to help you find another everyday word with a similar meaning—not a long or obscure word that will send the reader to the dictionary.

When writing about computers or other technical subjects, it's tempting to use *jargon* or specialized words you might use when talking to others with the same knowledge, interest, and background. When writing for a limited audience whose members are familiar with technical terms, a bit of jargon might be acceptable. However, most of the writing you will do in college and later in the workplace will address a larger audience. You will want to avoid the use of highly technical terms, acronyms, and abbreviations.

If it seems that the writers in this text use many big words or technical terms, stop for a minute to consider the original audience for each of the essays. Consider how your vocabulary grows each year as you read, discuss, and consider new ideas. The everyday words of a tenth grade student will probably be less in number than the everyday words of a junior in college. Similarly, the everyday words of a college freshman will be different from the everyday words of a computer professional with three years of work experience. Use words that are comfortable and familiar to you *and* your readers when you write, and you will write clear, effective essays.

Consider Sentence Length. Along with everyday words, simple sentences help you write more effectively. Do your sentences take up most of a paragraph? Do your sentences wander around the page? Are they more than two full typed lines long? If so, your reader might get lost in your sentences and forget what you are trying to say. If you want to write more effectively, keep your sentences short.

There are several ways to tame sentences. Look at a paragraph of your writing and identify all the actor/action groups in the paragraph. Take those actor/action groups and make each group into its own simple sentence. Get rid of all the words that connect ideas—such as *and, if, when,* and *however.* Then, look at each idea and decide which ones can stand alone—which ones have the most impact as short simple sentences? Leave those sentences alone. Then reconnect some of the other sentences to make a variety of sentence styles and lengths in your paragraph.

A second and perhaps quicker way to tame your sentences is to circle all the connecting words—coordinating conjunctions like *and* and *or*, subordinating conjunctions like *if* and *before*, relative pronouns like *that* and *who*, and conjunctive adverbs like *however* and *therefore*. Decide which ideas need to connect and which ideas might be stronger if allowed to stand alone. Revise the paragraph with your new sentence choices.

Be Concrete.   Think of a sidewalk. It is made of concrete. You stand on it, and you feel how solid it is. You kneel on it, and you feel that coarse texture against your skin. It's different from kneeling on carpet or dirt. If you put your ear to it, you could hear the person walking a block away. If you tasted dry concrete, it would be dull and chalky. Its smell might remind you of your elementary school classroom or of dirt. Looking at it, you might imagine a hopscotch pattern or see the small fine grains that water has bonded together, or you might see someone's handprint or initials. Concrete is solid. It can be experienced with all the senses. When we say, "be concrete," we're asking you to make your writing solid and substantial with details from the senses. Details that will make us feel as if we're there with you, standing on a sidewalk, seeing what you're seeing in your mind's eye.

We sometimes assume that our reader will know what we mean when we use adjectives like "beautiful," "quiet," or "slow." However, the reader has only his or her own ideas of those adjectives. You can make your writing more interesting and effective by adding the concrete details that will give the reader an image using at least two of the senses.

You can use details from all of the senses to make your writing more concrete. What are some of the sensual qualities of the experience or thing? Can you compare it to another something that your readers may be familiar with to help them understand it better? Can you compare it to something totally unlike it? Can you compare it to a different sense to surprise the readers and help them understand the image you are trying to create?

A good way to practice your ability to write original concrete images is to expand on a cliché. A *cliché* is an overused saying or expression. Often, clichés begin as similes that help make images more concrete. They become clichéd or overused because they lose their originality or they don't contain enough detail to give us the entire picture. Choose a cliché and write a paragraph that expands the cliché and uses the senses to create a clear picture of the thing described. You might try some of the following clichés.

She is as pretty as a picture.
It smelled heavenly.
It was as soft as a baby's bottom.
His heart is as hard as stone.
It tastes as sour as a pickle.
We stared at the roaring campfire.
We listened to the babbling brook.

Concrete details allow us to experience the world of the writer. We leave our own views and perceptions and learn how someone else sees the world.

What "quiet" is like for one writer. What "beautiful" means to another. Fill in the gaps between your words and ideas with vivid images and your writing becomes more interesting and more effective.

Stay Concise.   To be _concise_ is to be brief and clear. Say what you need to say as precisely as possible—use one word instead of two, or a short word instead of a long one. Rid your writing of any excess and leave only that which makes your meaning clear and concrete. Becoming aware of several common problems can help you make your writing more concise.

When you begin a sentence with either "it is" or "there is," you transfer all the meaning of the sentence to the end of the sentence. This is known as a _delayed construction._ You have delayed the meaning. The reader must read on to find out what "it" or "there" refer to. They don't get anything important from the beginning of the sentence.

Look at the following sentences.

It is important to change the oil in older gasoline engines.
There is an apple on the table.
There isn't anything we need to fear except our own fear.

We can rewrite these sentences, making them more concise, by deleting the "there is" or the "it is" and restructuring the sentence.

Changing the oil in older gasoline engines is important.
An apple is on the table.
We have nothing to fear but fear itself.

Notice that the second group of sentences is shorter and the important information is no longer buried in the middle. Revising this type of sentence can make your writing more concise and get information to the reader more effectively.

If you're afraid you use "it is" and "there is" (or "it's" and "there's") too often, you can use most word processing programs to seek these constructions out. Use the "search" or "find and replace" tool that's found in the Edit portion of your pull down menu. Type "it is" and ask your computer to find every place you use this construction in your document. When you find a sentence that begins with "it is," revise the sentence to make it more concise. Do the same with "there is," "it's," and "there's." After you become more aware of these errors by correcting them, you'll find that you notice the errors before or as you make them. You will begin to write more concisely, and you'll have fewer delayed constructions to revise.

You can also make your writing more concise by avoiding common wordy expressions. Sometimes when we're nervous about writing or insecure about our knowledge of a topic, we try to hide that insecurity behind a wall of meaningless words.

At this point in time, you may not have the ability to create a Web page due to the fact that you've avoided using computers for anything other than playing Solitaire.

This sentence is full of deadwood—phrases that add no meaning to the sentence. If we take out the unneeded words, we have the sentence.

> You may not be able to create a Web page because you've only used your computer to play Solitaire.

Your computer may have a grammar checker that will identify some commonly used wordy expressions. If your computer doesn't have a grammar checker, or if your instructor has asked you not to use the grammar checker in your computer, you can still learn to revise the wordiness out of your paragraphs.

Use the computer to separate a paragraph of your writing into sentences. As you scroll through the paragraph, hit the "hard return" or "enter" key on your keyboard twice every time you find a period. Once you have separated the sentences, look at each sentence. What is the important idea in the sentence? What words are used to convey that idea? What words don't add any meaning to the sentence? Delete words that don't convey meaning and revise the sentence to make it more concise.

Use Action Verbs.   *Action verbs* are words that convey the action of a sentence. They carry much of our language's nuance and meaning. Yet, I've read may students' paragraphs that only use the *verbs of being* or the "to be" verbs: *am, is, are, was, were, be, been,* and *being.* Being verbs are fine, but if you use too many of these verbs, you risk losing much of the power of language. If I say someone is coming through the door, I've created a picture of a body and a doorway. If I say someone marches or slinks through the door, I've added not only the information about movement but also about the qualities of that movement. I've given my subject the attitude of a solider or a cat. For example, Howard Rheingold begins his text with this sentence:

> Thirty thousand years ago, outside a deceptively small hole in a limestone formation in the area now known as southern France, several adolescents shivered in the dark, awaiting initiation into the cult of toolmakers.

By using the verb "shivered," especially when accompanied by the words "in the dark," Rheingold paints a word picture much more vivid than he would have conveyed with the use of a "to be" verb.

Using interesting verbs can enliven your writing. Although using the "find and replace" or "search" functions can help you with your verb choices, it's probably easier to do this by hand. Choose one or two paragraphs from an essay you're revising, and circle all the "to be" verbs. If you find more than five in a paragraph, you may not be allowing your verbs to work as hard as they should. Rewrite a couple of the sentences, using active verbs in place of the "to be" verbs. You won't be able to do this for every sentence, but replace them where you can and your writing will become more lively, more concise, and more effective.

Fill in the Gaps.   When we write, we sometimes forget that we are writing to an audience other than ourselves. We expect that our readers are people just like us, with our experiences, memories, and tastes. Because they're so much like us, we think, we sometimes expect readers to be able to read more than what we've written on the page. We expect them to read our minds. We may leave large gaps in our essays, hoping the reader will fill in with exactly the information we would have included.

If I'm writing an essay about my childhood in the South and I say it was always so hot in the summer that I hated to go outside, I might think my reader knows what I mean by hot. Now that I've lived in many parts of the country, I know that there are many different ways to be "hot." In the panhandle of Florida where I grew up, the hot was a sticky hot. Eighty degrees made me long for a big glass of sweetened iced tea with lots of ice. The heat made my clothes cling. Sweating didn't help because the sweat didn't dry. I spent the day feeling as if I'd never dried after my morning shower. In New Mexico, I never really felt hot unless the temperature got above 110 degrees. At that point, the heat would rush at me, making it difficult to breathe. I would open the door to leave the house and it felt as if I had opened the oven door to check on a cake. If I say I was hot in the summer without describing how heat felt to me, my reader may not get the message I'm trying to convey.

Don't expect your reader to know what you mean by "hot" or by any other general description. Instead, take a minute to add details that will fill in the gaps for the reader.

Speak Directly.   To *speak directly* is to say, up front, who is doing what. Sometimes we don't tell the reader who is completing the action or we tell them too late. Let's look at the following sentences.

> The steak was stolen from the grill.

> The decisive battle was fought between the Confederate and the Union armies in Vicksburg, Mississippi.

> The red truck has been driven into the side of the green car.

Although we might be able to guess who the actors are in each of the sentences, the first and last sentences don't tell us directly. Even if the reader can guess that it was a dog who stole the steak from the grill or my neighbor who drove the red truck into the side of the green car, the reader has to stop and figure out who is doing what before he or she can read on. This slows the reader down and diminishes the effectiveness of your writing.

Language professionals call this *passive voice*. The action comes before the actor. Note that sometimes, as in the first and last sentences above, the writer doesn't mention the actor at all. Many of the grammar checkers in word processing programs are adept at finding passive voice, but it's easy to find without the computer once you know what to look for.

First, you can identify passive voice by finding the "to be" verbs and past participles or verbs that usually end in "-ed" or "-en" in your sentence. (Remember the *to be* verbs are *am, is, are, was, were, be, been,* and *being.*) When you find one of the verbs coupled with another action word that ends in "-ed" or "-en" you've found passive voice. In the examples on page 407, sentence one has the verb group "was stolen." Using this test, you could have decided that the first sentence is in passive voice.

The next test for passive voice is to find the action and the actor in the sentence and to make sure that they are in the most effective order. The most effective sentence order is actor first, then action. If we look at the second sentence, we see that the action "was fought" comes first. Then, we find out that the "Confederate and Union armies" completed the action. Common sense tells us that it's better to know who is acting before we know what they're doing. This sentence reverses the effective order. It's in passive voice.

The final test helps with sentences that have a hidden or implied actor. Notice that we have an action without an actor in the third sentence. Someone has driven the car, but we don't know who that someone is. A simple test for this type of passive sentence is to put the phrase "by my cat" after the verb group in a sentence you suspect might contain passive voice.

The red truck was driven "by my cat" into the green car.

Of course, the sentence doesn't make sense, but the structure works. Someone was driving the car, but the sentence doesn't tell us who was driving. The actor is hidden or implied and using "by my cat" helps to remind us of that hidden actor and identify and correct the passive voice.

There are three ways to correct passive voice. The first is to place the actor in front of the action of the sentence. If we correct the second sentence using this method, we have the sentence,

The Confederate and Union armies fought a decisive battle in Vicksburg, Mississippi.

Notice how we've removed the "to be" verb and place the actors, the armies, at the beginning of the sentence.

Another way to correct passive voice is to change the verb. Perhaps we're not sure who stole the steaks from the grill. We can make the first sentence active by changing the main verb "stolen" to another verb that allows us to drop the helping verb "were."

The steaks disappeared from the grill.

The meaning stays mostly the same, but I no longer have passive voice, and I've admitted that I'm not sure what happened to the steaks.

Finally, I can drop part of the verb to change passive voice into active voice. I can delete the "to be" verb in the third sentence to make my meaning more direct.

The red car drove into the green car.

If you're not sure who the actor is and you want to make the sentence direct, you can sometimes drop the "to be" part of the verb.

Getting rid of passive voice in your writing can make your essays more effective and easier to read. However, some uses of passive voice are acceptable. If it's clear who's completing the action, if you don't want to identify the actor, or if the actor isn't important, you can leave your sentences in passive voice. Be aware when you use passive voice and avoid it in most instances.

Be Unexpected. The most effective writing, the writing that engages our attention, makes us think or act, or opens us to new ways of thinking, does so not only because it's technically accomplished. It does so because it presents us with the unexpected. It gives us fresh ways to look at the world. When an essay is assigned, several students think about the topic for a while and come up with the same idea. Too often they write about the most obvious thing or the first idea that comes to mind. If you and ten other students in your class are writing essays about the same topic, you are less likely to come up with anything original or fresh to say. You can often write more effective essays if you take some time to develop a novel approach to a topic by spending more time in the invention stage or by finding a new twist to a common topic that will give your readers something a little out of the ordinary. For example, if you are writing an essay for this chapter about the connections between computers and human nature and you happen to be taking a psychology course, you might bring in some of Freud's theories to your analysis. Or if you have been an enthusiast of computer games since childhood, you could compare the fascination of the Internet to that of computer games. Think about what you have studied or experienced that is different from your classmates and brainstorm about ways you can use that knowledge in your writing project.

Choosing topics that are more creative is just one way to be unexpected with your writing. Another way you can make your writing more effective is by including details your reader may not expect. If you are discussing spring, for example, many clichéd images come to mind—birds singing, flowers blooming, frogs chirping, leaves popping out of the trees. That's what we all think about when we think of spring. Those details may make your writing more vivid and readable, but it may not make it more interesting. Each of us experiences spring in a different way. Perhaps the quintessential sign of spring for you is the smell of fresh cedar mulch on your mother's flowerbeds. Maybe it's the feel of polyester baseball pants against your thighs, or maybe it's the smell of the Johnson's floor polish your dad laid down on the wood floors every year. Those unusual individual details are what can make an essay about even a well-worn subject fresh and interesting. They can help you get your point across effectively.

INSTRUCTIONS

The choices below will help you structure
the content and pick graphics and colors
for your page.

Content

First, give your page a title. If you're
creating a page just for yourself, the title
might be your name. If the page is for a
business, a product, a club, a cause, or
another purpose, you might want to make
it a headline.

Next, type an introduction that will follow
the title. It might be a simple welcome, a
brief introduction, or a description of your
organization - anything up to 1000
characters.

If you want, you can add some hot links to
other Web pages. To add links to other

PREVIEW

Your Page

_____

_____

ACCESSING INTERNET RESOURCES

Authoring a Personal Web Page

Students at many colleges and universities have authored their own personal home pages, establishing their own homesteads on the Internet. Some choose to give an overview of their backgrounds and interests, often including pictures of themselves or family and friends. Others decide to make their pages more a kind of online resume, listing education, work experience, and honors. A third option is to create a theme-based collection of pages based on a personal interest such as movie reviewing or Javascript programming.

Web pages are created using HTML (hypertext markup language) which consists of tags, such as <b> for bold or <center> for center, which control the layout of text and images on the page. The easiest way to create a personal page is to use a HTML editor such as the one built into Netscape Navigator. This editor takes the page content and layout you create and converts it into an HTML page without your having to know or use the HTML tags yourself. To access the editor in the Netscape Communicator version of Navigator, go to the **Communicator** window and select **Page Composer.** Then go to the **File** menu, select **New,** then **Page from Wizard.** You will see a page that looks much like the one above.

Amber Lea Clark

"...REAL isn't how you are made," said the Skin Horse. "It's a thing that happens to you. It doesn't happen all at once. It takes a long time. That's why it doesn't happen to people who break easily, or have sharp edges, or who have to be carefully kept. Generally, by the time you are REAL, most of your hair has been loved off and your eyes drop out and you get loose in the joints and very shabby. But these things don't matter at all, because once you are REAL, you can't be ugly, except to people who don't understand..."
--*The Velveteen Rabbit* by Margery Williams

Home | Resume | Essays | Photos

Follow the instructions on the left side of the screen, and your page will appear in the right side. You start with a title, add text, images, background colors, and links to other pages. When you finish, you could have a home page something like this student page.

Once you have tried creating your own pages, you may find that the Wizard will not let you easily create all the effects you would like. You may need to learn HTML code yourself, so that you can customize your page more extensively. You may want to refer to one of the many online tutorials for creating Web pages, such as these:

Beginner's Guide to HTML
http://www.ncsa.uiuc.edu/General/Internet/WWW/HTMLPrimer.html

Crash Course in Writing Documents for the Web
http://www.zdnet.com/pcweek/eamonn/crash_course.html

How to Write HTML
http://www.uwaterloo.ca/web-docs/Guidelines/howto.html

Learning HTML
http://www.bev.net/computer/htmlhelp/index.html

Putting Information on the Web
http://www.w3.org/Provider/Overview.html

A Virtual Toolbox
http://www.netsurge.com/trillian/webbie.htm

The Web Designer
http://web.canlink.com/helpdesk

Web Weavers Page
http://science.nas.nasa.gov/Services/Education/Resources/
webweavers.html/advanced.html

SUGGESTED INTERNET ASSIGNMENTS

1. Create your own home page which reflects your personality (see the *Accessing Internet Resources* section in this chapter). The suggested format would be four pages. A home page could, like the example in this chapter, include of photo of yourself, a quote reflecting your perspective on life, and links to other pages. The secondary pages could consist of an online resume, papers you have written in this course, and a selection of your favorite photos.

2. Examine the personal Web pages of three authors whose texts appear in this chapter: John Perry Barlow, http://www.eff.org/~barlow; Howard Rheingold, http://www.rheingold.com/howard; or Sherry Turkle, http://web.mit.edu/sturkle/www. Notice how they project an image of themselves in their pages.

3. Search for other articles and Websites having to do with computers and human nature. Compile an annotated bibliography.

Free Speech Online
Blue Ribbon Campaign

barlow@eff.org

John Perry Barlow is a retired Wyoming cattle rancher, a lyricist for the Grateful Dead, and co-founder of the Electronic Frontier Foundation. He is also a member of The WELL Board of Directors.

He was born in Wyoming in 1947, was educated there in a one room schoolhouse, and graduated from Wesleyan University in Middletown, Connecticut with an honors degree in comparative religion in 1969.

WIRED TO THE WEB

John Perry Barlow
http://www.eff.org/~barlow
John Perry Barlow, who is mentioned in "Cyberspirit" and whose essays appear elsewhere in this textbook, is a well-known and colorful Internet figure. A retired Wyoming cattle rancher and lyricist for the Grateful Dead, Barlow is cofounder of the Electronic Frontier Foundation, a online organization which promotes freedom of expression in cyberspace. He is also a member of the board of directors for the WELL, the San Francisco-area online community.

Howard Rheingold

I fell into the computer realm from the typewriter dimension, then plugged my computer into my telephone and got sucked into the net.

In my earlier years, my interest in the powers of the human mind led to *Higher Creativity* (1984), written with Willis Harman, *Talking Tech* (1982) and *The Cognitive Connections* (1986) with Howard Levine *Excursions to the Far Side of the Mind: A Book of Memes* (1988), *Exploring the World of Lucid Dreaming* (1990), with Stephen LaBerge, and *They Have A Word For It: A Lighthearted Lexicon of Untranslatable Words and phrases.*(1988).

Howard Rheingold
http://www.rheingold.com/howard

Howard Rheingold is the author of *Virtual Reality,* an excerpt of which appears in this chapter, and of *Virtual Communities,* a book about forums, chat rooms, and other people to people settings on the Internet which Rheingold suggests have developed into real communities. A number of his essays and interviews can be found through his Website.

Sherry Turkle

Professor of Sociology

This page is under construction (or is that deconstruction?)

- Biography
- Curriculum vitae
- Recent Publications
  New Book Life on the Screen: Identity in the Age of the Internet,
  Simon and Schuster, November, 1995.
- Web Searching

course syllabi:

- Evolving Conceptions of Systems and the Self
- Gender, Technology, and Computer Culture
- Identity and the Internet STS065
- Psychology and Technology
- Foucault and the Power Rangers

You can contact Prof. Turkle directly by sending mail to sturkle@media.mit.edu or her assistant Devon Darrow at devond@tiac.net.

sturkle@mit.edu
Massachusetts Institute of Technology, E51-296c
Program in Science, Technology, and Society
77 Massachusetts Avenue

Sherry Turkle
http://web.mit.edu/sturkle/www

Sherry Turkle, sometimes called the cybershrink, is a professor of science, technology, and society at MIT, and her Web page, as you might expect, has a more institutional look. You can browse syllabi from the Internet-related courses she teaches and read some of her articles.

THE BUSINESS/
COMPUTER CONNECTION

The American business landscape is synonymous with computer technology. Stroll through any corporate office, and the cubicles where secretaries, assistants, and even managers toil are dominated by computers, one to every desk. Once, a business or engineering graduate might have skipped learning to type because the word processing could be left to secretaries. Now, a manager on the way up the corporate ladder needs to know not only how to type, but how to operate an increasing array of software programs.

The manufacturing and even the farming landscape are dotted with computers, though they are often integrated into machinery. Farmers direct irrigation by satellite photos, and "smart" machines replace workers on assembly lines. Americans joke, with some truth, that they can't program their VCRs, but more and more factory workers and farmers are learning to program much more complicated computer-aided machines in their daily work.

According to Michael J. Mandel in "The New Business Cycle," America is now driven by its high-tech industries rather than the housing and auto industries. As the business landscape becomes more and more computer-dependent, high-tech industries continue to boom. There is a downside to this optimistic picture, according to Mandel, because high-tech industries are notoriously volatile, and an economy dependent upon them is also unstable and subject to unexpected downturns. Dennis Kneale, in "Unleashing the Power: Companies Have Spent Vast Sums on Technology. Now They Have to Figure Out What to Do with It All," suggests that corporate buyers, who have been spending billions on computers, software, and maintenance may be becoming more conservative, not jumping to buy the next hot hardware or software. The fact is clear, however, that for businesses to be competitive in today's climate, they have to process information quickly and efficiently. Companies may be buying less hardware, but they probably aren't spending less money. They are investing their funds in training and development.

It's no longer business as usual in corporate America. John Micklethwait, in "The Valley of Money's Delight," suggests that the Silicon Valley, America's highest concentration of high-tech companies, is a model for future business development. Micklethwait argues that what is innovative about Silicon Valley is its way of doing business, with the product "just happening to be technology." It is an "entrepreneurial cluster," where innovative ideas and creative financing abound in an atmosphere that encourages risk-taking, tolerates failure, and is obsessed with its products. Catherine Romano, in "Websites: If You Build It, Will They Come?" discusses how many corporations are spending big money in cyberspace without any evidence of return on investment. The Web is new, hot, trendy, and companies are willing to take a risk.

What's happening in corporate America, especially in high-tech corporate America, is more visible than ever because of the Internet. Any major company worthy of the label *innovative* has its Website that you can browse for the latest corporate news. Major business publications offer full-text articles ready to read or download. After some surfing of the Web, you can evaluate for yourself the interrelationship between business and computer technology.

———————————— ■ ————————————

THE NEW BUSINESS CYCLE

by Michael J. Mandel

No longer is the American economy driven by housing and autos. Today, high-tech industries are responsible for the economy's growth. That's fine as long as the current upward cycle continues, according to Michael J. Mandel in this March 1997 feature for Business Week. *But it also means that the economy is vulnerable to the fluctuation in that sector which is perhaps more volatile than housing and autos. Mandel's feature analyzes the positives and negatives of the new business cycle and suggests that because it is new, it is hard to predict what may happen. This unpredictability may increase the odds of policy mistakes on a national level.*

Mandel is economics editor for Business Week *and the author of* The High Risk Society, Peril and Promise in the New Economy.

Six years into the economic expansion of the 1990s, and the living is easy. Almost three million jobs have been added over the past year alone, and consumer confidence is soaring. Company coffers are brimming with profits, the stock market is in the stratosphere, and inflation is actually falling.

Perhaps best of all, to many it seems the good times can go on for years. That old bugaboo of capitalism—the business cycle—has been tamed, according to today's conventional view. Rather than experiencing the booms and busts of old, the economy is on a steady growth path. Companies are avoiding past excesses, using computers and improved communications to manage inventories better and to boost workers' productivity. "Information technology has doubtless enhanced the stability of business operations," said Federal Reserve Chairman Alan Greenspan in his February 26 testimony before Congress. His biggest worry? An overheated stock market.

But it is not the stock market or inventories or even inflation that will determine how long this expansion will last. Nor will auto sales, housing starts, or any of the traditional cyclical indicators give the first warnings of an impending recession, as they did in 1979 and 1989.

Instead, there is a new business cycle, tied to the health of the high-tech sector. Riding a wave of technological optimism, the computer, software, and communications industries have grown at a pace far exceeding the rest of the economy over the past three years, helping to extend the expansion.

But this exuberance has a price: With high tech having grown so big, the economy is now vulnerable to a high-tech slowdown in a way that was never true before. And there are already troubling signs of weakness in those industries that, if prolonged, could foreshadow a wider slump—as well as a steep decline in the stock market.

The distinctive character of the new business cycle raises the odds of policy mistakes. Like generals fighting the last war, the Fed seems to be focusing on traditional cyclical indicators, such as retail sales, new-home starts, and industrial production, that have all been upbeat recently. These are "still what drives the business cycle," says Fed Governor Laurence H. Meyer. Meanwhile, semiconductor shipments and other measures of high-tech growth hardly are mentioned by Greenspan and other policymakers, despite their economic importance. "The Fed needs to look not just at infla-tionary measures but also at what part of the technology cycle we are in," says G. Dan Hutcheson, president of VLSI Research Inc., a Silicon Valley research firm.

Certainly there is little doubt that high technology has replaced the tradi-tional cyclical industries as the main driving force for growth. In the past three years, the high-tech sector has contributed 27% of the growth in gross domestic product, compared with 14% for residential housing and only 4% for the auto sector. Over the past year, a stunning 33% of GDP growth has come from information-technology industries, propelled by everything from the Internet boom to the rise of direct-broadcast satellite television.

The unique nature of an expansion led by high technology explains why the U.S. has been able to sustain a lower unemployment rate with faster growth and less inflation than economists ever believed possible. Despite strong demand and rising wages for programmers, network technicians, and other high-tech workers, inflationary pressures are counteracted by con-stantly falling prices for such products as computers and communications equipment. Meanwhile, with the rest of the economy growing at a meager 1.8% annual rate, the demand for workers outside of high tech has not been strong enough to drive up wages. A *Business Week* analysis shows that real wages for nonsupervisory workers outside high tech have risen by just 0.3% in the past year, hardly enough to trigger inflation.

But the business cycle has not disappeared. To the contrary: High tech-nology is more volatile than the automobile industry, with the biggest swings driven by new technologies. When the new-product pipeline temporarily slows, as it did in 1985 and 1989, demand can fall sharply. But a hot new tech-nology, such as the Internet, can send sales skyrocketing just as suddenly. "Every time we thought something about our business was less cyclical," says Andrew S. Grove, chief executive at Intel Corp., "the next cycle was bigger than the earlier one."

There's another factor that could compound the impact of the tech cycle: High tech has grown so large and important that there's a feedback loop to the rest of the economy. When times are good, fast-growing high-tech com-panies throw off money that fuels general prosperity, which in turn sustains the demand for high-tech products. An expanding high-tech sector spends big dollars on everything from advertising to new buildings to cleaning ser-vices. High-tech profits boost stock prices, making investors more willing to spend. And rising wages and bonuses for high-tech workers finance the pur-chases of new cars and homes. Indeed, high-tech jobs and industries have accounted for roughly 20% to 25% of the real wage and salary growth over the past year, according to new *Business Week* calculations, making them the key support for consumer spending.

But if and when things turn sour, look out. Information technology—now the single largest line in many corporate capital budgets—will make a tempting target for cost-cutting if the product cycle slows, or if the rest of the economy should slip because of, say, a Fed rate hike. Inventories are lean, and with 3.5 million jobs eliminated since 1989, Corporate America has squeezed most of the fat out of its workforce. Next time the economy slows, the only way tight-pressed companies can save money will be to delay nonessential info-tech projects. "Our industry used to be immune from the business cycle," says Eric A. Benhamou, CEO and chairman of 3Com Corp. "We're no longer flying under the radar. There's just too much money being spent."

The downside of the new business cycle could have dramatic consequences for employment, investment, and growth. In Silicon Valley, in Boston, and in other high-tech hotbeds across the country, a multitude of software companies are staffing up in expectation of 20% annual growth, hiring hordes of programmers, testers, and technical writers who would not be needed if high-tech sales slowed. "It's a speculative bubble," says Larry Kimbell, director of the UCLA/Anderson Business Forecasting Project, "and there will be a lot of very disappointed people" when the boom slows.

If profits drop sharply enough, most high-tech companies would have to curtail new-product development and the construction of factories. Venture-capital funds, now going begging, would dry up. As the breakneck pace of technological change slowed, buyers would have less reason to upgrade immediately to the next generation of computers or software, dampening demand even more. "If our rate of innovation slowed, and the buying momentum consequently lessened, presumably that could have repercussions on the whole economy," says Grove.

A slowdown in high tech could hold dire consequences for the stock market. From 1993 to the end of 1996, high-tech stocks have been the market leaders, pulling other sectors along with them. Over that three-year stretch, high-tech stocks have produced blistering annual returns of 35%, compared with 20% for the S&P 500. The surge in tech stocks has given many of them sky-high price-earnings multiples on the expectation of soaring future growth. An unexpected slowdown in high-tech demand could send those stocks tumbling, knocking the rest of the market from its record levels.

FALL-OFF

There are some signs that such a high-tech slowdown may already have started. For one thing, tech stocks, as measured by the Morgan Stanley High Tech Index, are down 15% since mid-January. For another, demand for high-tech equipment is weakening. Chip sales dropped by 3% from December to January and are down 14% from a year earlier, according to a March 13 report from the Semiconductor Industry Assn. Government figures show consumer spending on computers rising at its slowest rate since 1992, while unfilled orders for information-technology equipment are shrinking for the first time since 1994. "We knew retail was slow, but now the corporate side—where most of the money is made—is showing signs of weakness as well," says Robinson-Humphrey Co. analyst Robert Anastasi, who follows computer sales. Adds Richard C. O'Brien, economist for Hewlett-Packard Co.: "We think we're in the late stages of a business cycle, and we're exhibiting the lower growth rates you'd expect," because of lower capital spending.

Of course, this high-tech slowdown may turn out to be a blip in a remarkable upward trajectory. Cheaper computers from Compaq Computer Corp., Packard Bell NEC Inc., and others could stimulate demand at the low end of the market. The Internet may continue to open up a range of new applications. And even an extended high-tech pause may be cushioned if global demand rebounds.

But even if high tech is the future of the economy over the long run, that does not preclude a bumpy ride along the way. In many ways, this period resembles the second half of the 19th century, also a time of massive investment in a new technology: the railroads. From 1869 to 1893, the miles of rail track quadrupled, and rail shipping costs dropped dramatically, opening up large parts of the country for manufacturing and commercial agriculture. The railroads themselves consumed much of the U.S. steel and coal production and accounted for almost 20% of all investment. Overall, the railroads' expansion fueled an economy that grew an average of 5% annually.

GROWING FORCE

But the long-term growth in this period conceals two sharp downturns, both linked to the railroads. The panic of 1873 was caused largely by railroad overexpansion, leading to a slew of railroad bankruptcies and an abrupt decline in new investment. And the mini-depression that started in 1893 was greatly aggravated when overbuilt railroads sharply curtailed the construction of new tracks.

Like the railroads in the late 19th century, high tech is the leading sector of the economy. The Information Revolution started in the mid-1970s, when the price of computing power began to plummet. But until recently, high tech simply was not big enough to influence the whole economy. From 1983 to 1993, high-tech spending in dollar terms grew no faster than the rest of the economy.

But over the past three years, the high-tech sector has skyrocketed while the rest of the economy has slowed down. High tech, as measured by *Business Week*, totaled some $420 billion in 1996. Consumers and businesses now spend $282 billion in the United States on information technology hardware alone, making it larger than any of the traditionally cyclical sectors such as autos and construction. That's 17% more than U.S. purchases of new motor vehicles and parts, 49% more than spending on new homes, and 168% more than commercial and industrial construction.

The clout of the high-tech sector shows up clearly in the labor market. Help-wanted ads plead for project managers, systems analysts, and help-desk technicians. Meanwhile, companies' continuing need for assistance with their computer systems has created a bull market for the management consulting industry, which is adding jobs at a rate of more than 40,000 per year. "We're experiencing 40% growth in the information-based consulting area," says Roger Siboni, deputy chairman and chief operating officer of KPMG Peat Marwick.

All told, there are more than nine million workers now in the high-tech sector. Each new job creates additional jobs across the economy, generating a "multiplier" effect. Historically, manufacturing was thought to have the biggest multiplier effect in the economy, which is why it played such a big role in business cycles. The expansion of an auto plant, say, would ripple through the economy, boosting hiring at steel mills and other suppliers. Since factory workers were well paid, jobs would be created at nearby stores and even construction companies to supply and house the new workers.

There's growing evidence, however, that high tech may now have a larger multiplier effect in the United States than traditional manufacturing industries such as autos. As U.S. manufacturers have become more efficient, an expansion in output no longer requires massive hiring at factories. And with suppliers increasingly spread out in Mexico, the Far East, and Europe, the impact of an increase in auto sales, say, is diffused globally.

By contrast, creating a new chip design or a new software program is a labor-intensive effort that relies almost exclusively on well-paid domestic workers. A study of Microsoft Corp.'s impact on the Washington state economy showed that each Microsoft job created 6.7 new jobs in the state, compared with a 3.8 multiplier for Boeing Co. The difference? Almost $800 million in stock option income for Microsoft workers in 1995, the year of the study. These dollars spill over in the form of increased purchases of such things as cars and homes. In addition, Boeing outsources a lot of the work on each plane. As a result, "Microsoft spends three to four times more per person in the local economy than Boeing does," says Richard S. Conway, Jr., the Seattle-based economist who conducted the study.

High-tech jobs tend to pay well—and salaries are rising—even the jobs that aren't so glamorous. Bureau of Labor Statistics data show that weekly wages for production workers in the communications-equipment industry rose by almost 7% in the past year, while earnings for nonsupervisory workers in the software and computer services industry rose by almost 5%. Intel distributed $620 million in profit-sharing and bonus money to its more than 40,000 employees for 1996.

Despite strong growth, an expansion driven by high tech is less likely to spur price inflation. In a traditional business cycle, prices would rise and productivity growth would slow as factories hit their capacity limits. But high-tech industries, such as semiconductors and software, are different. Creating a program or a microprocessor requires a big investment. But then the cost of actually producing the chips or software for sale is relatively low. The result is a virtuous circle: Rising demand drives average costs down, making it possible to charge lower prices and boosting demand even further.

OPTIMISM

How long can this high-tech expansion continue? Technology companies are banking on a continuing stream of new and improved products to fuel growth well into the future. "With lower costs and more advanced technology, you can do applications that weren't economically possible before," says Benjamin Anixter, vice-president for external affairs at Advanced Micro Devices Inc. At the bottom, falling prices may pull in new demand. The latest low-priced computer from Compaq, for example, "is selling extremely well to customers we didn't sell to before," says Robert A. Gunst, CEO of retailers Good Guys Inc., based in Brisbane, Calif.

Most growth forecasts are upbeat. Venture-capital firm Hambrecht & Quist predicts that the number of PCs sold in North America will rise by 17% in 1997. Looking further out, Gartner Group Inc. projects that spending on hardware and software will rise by about 8% annually for the rest of the decade.

Yet the history of the information-technology industries is anything but smooth. The biggest high-tech downturn in the past two decades came in 1985, when demand petered out just before the introduction of Intel's 80386 microprocessor. And in the first half of 1990, another product transition helped drive down business spending on computers even before the start of the recession of 1990-91.

Now, the industry may be facing another pause. With orders falling off, there is no obvious "must-have" product on the horizon to stimulate demand, as the Internet did. Intel's much-ballyhooed Pentium MMX chip is turning out to offer only a minimal improvement in speed for existing software. "It hasn't set the corporate world on fire," says Anastasi. "Usually, new products create a lot of excitement, but that hasn't happened yet." High-definition TV, which will eventually create enormous sales, will not hit the airwaves until 1999, while the low-orbit satellite systems that promise a wealth of new applications are nowhere near ready.

DANGER

The dominant role of high-tech spending gives a bigger meaning to any drop-off in demand. An economy is vulnerable to a downturn when it develops "imbalances," to use Greenspan's term—that is, when one sector or industry expands too fast. For example, consumer spending and office construction far outpaced the rest of the economy during the 1980s. So when the recession came in 1990, these sectors crashed, making the downturn much worse.

Now, high tech faces the same danger. Over the past three years, business spending on information-technology gear has risen by almost 45%.

Meanwhile, spending on labor has risen by only 19%. Even if information technology has become a strategic asset for many businesses, its very size makes it a logical place to cut or postpone when times get tough. "After all," says Paul Saffo of the Institute for the Future, "you can only defy gravity if you're small."

Much of the planned increases in information spending can be deferred if the economy softens. Consider KPMG Peat Marwick. It is planning to spend $250 million over the next three years on information technology, more than double its historic spending pattern. Out of that, there's little flexibility in $150 million, but the remaining $100 million is more variable, says Siboni. "Building Web-centric information systems might become less critical."

The changing nature of corporate info-tech spending at companies will make it easier to make quick cuts. Rather than hiring a large internal staff of programmers, companies are relying on temporary workers and outside consulting firms, which can be easily sloughed off during tough times. At temporary-worker giant Manpower Inc., the division that supplies technology workers is growing at 40% per year.

Small businesses will not be reluctant to hold off spending if the economy turns down. "I have a lot of control over what I buy," says Josh Moritz, CEO of DMTG Inc., a small New York-based advertising firm. "I can delay purchases or buy used machines."

Consumers have even more reason to cut back during recessions. Over the past three years, the amount of money spent on home computers has risen by 55%, far in excess of income growth. Most consumers do not need a new computer. Instead, like autos, they buy the newest model if they can afford it. "A dominant force in the PC world is becoming consumer markets and hype," says William C. Rosser, a Gartner Group analyst. "That means you're more likely to see cycles like other consumer industries."

If and when the cutbacks come, they will not be confined to computers and software. Instead, the downturn is likely to spread to the telephone and networking industries as well. When the phone system was used mainly for voice calls, demand for lines was driven by population growth. But more and more, investment by phone companies is driven by the need for additional phone lines for computers and more capacity for data connections rather than basic voice service. The sudden prominence of the Internet, for example, forced Ameritech Corp., the Chicago-based telephone company, to boost its capital spending by $100 million to $200 million in 1996, to keep up with the need for more lines.

"PAYBACK"

To be sure, there are forces that could prevent a high-tech downturn from happening anytime soon. Intel and Microsoft, the giants of personal computing, are investing hundreds of millions to create new products and to help other companies do so. "If the cycle is pointing down or is softer, then the only thing we can do to cope with that is to pump up our products," says Grove.

High-tech executives are also counting on competitive pressure forcing corporations to continue spending on information technology even in a recession. "The payback customers get from our products is very clear, very justifiable," says Mark Eppley, chairman of Traveling Software Inc., a Bothell (Wash.) maker of software for remote access. "Our business is growing very fast—independently of the economy."

A decline in U.S. sales could be cushioned by growth in overseas sales. Telecom deregulation in Europe may open the floodgates for cutting-edge computers and communications gear, where U.S. companies excel. Developing countries represent a huge untapped market that will become increasingly important. "There's a growing middle class in India, and it's as large as all of France," says Donald Macleod, chief financial officer at National Semiconductor Corp. "That's where the long-term opportunity lies."

But relying on global demand is no panacea. North America still makes up almost half the global market for computers, software, and peripherals. The latest data show chip sales falling faster in Asia than in the U.S. And growth in Japan and South Korea is expected to slow in 1997, according to DRI/McGraw-Hill forecasts, with Europe's economies still sluggish. In areas such as Japan, Germany, and France, "our business is still in most people's terms reasonably good," says John T. Chambers, CEO of Cisco Systems Inc. "But it's not good in Cisco terms."

Closer to home, the growing importance of high-tech poses new problems for economic policymakers such as the Fed. The tools of monetary policy— interest rates—do not work very well on high tech. In particular, it matters more whether compelling new products and technologies are available. When high-tech industries are riding a technology wave, they can power their way through slowdowns in the macroeconomy, no matter what the Fed does. "Whether the interest rate is 7% or 9% doesn't matter when you're growing at 30% per year," says AMD's Anixter.

So far in this expansion, the country has been lucky. The surge in high tech in 1995 and 1996 came just when autos and housing turned sluggish. But now the rest of the economy is turning up, judging from recent data. As a result, forecasters are raising their projections of growth in the first quarter to 3% or more, leading to speculation that the Fed will soon boost interest rates.

But ignoring the health of the information technology industries can produce bad policy. With order growth for computers and semiconductors having slowed noticeably, the economy may be far weaker than the traditional indicators make it seem. This raises the possibility that a rate hike by the Fed could be a serious mistake at this point.

Is a high-tech-led recession inevitable? Hardly. But for the first time, it's possible, and the odds are rising. The new business cycle is alive and well in Silicon Valley.

EXPLORING THE READING

1. Does it surprise you that Michael Mandel's article should suggest that today's economy is driven by high-tech industries, particularly information technology? Why or why not?

2. In your small group, discuss your jobs (or your parents' jobs, if you are not employed). How many of them are part of high-tech industries? How many of you are planning careers in these industries? Report to the class.

3. Do you think it is good for the economy to be so tied to high-tech industries? Are there any alternatives?

4. Read back through Mandel's feature. What evidence does he use to support his argument? Is his evidence convincing?

TECHNOWOMEN

by Kevin Maney

The percentages aren't good if you are looking for gender equality in high-tech indus-tries, according to this USA Today *cover story by Kevin Maney. In an era in which women make up 44 percent of the workforce, you could go to one high-tech company Maney describes, "fire a cannon through the cubicles and hit only men." High-tech jobs are some of the best vocational tracks available, with starting salaries in the $40,000-plus range. Why are women missing out? According to Maney, young women at every stage of education are discouraged from technological interests, and many women are turned off by the un-people-friendly culture of many computer companies.*

    Maney is a featured columnist for USA Today *and the author of* Megamedia Shakeout: The Inside Story of the Leaders and Losers in the Exploding Communications Industry.

Inside the crisp sandstone headquarters of computer networking company 3Com, 14 people from the engineering department meet around an oval table. Two are women.

In a test lab where thousands of wires wind over tracks like grapevines on a trellis, a handful of men check 3Com products. No women are seen. In fact, in many of the technical parts of 3Com, you could fire a cannon through the cubicles and hit only men.

And it isn't just 3Com. High-tech computer jobs overwhelmingly are held by men—an industry-wide, systemic problem that begins in math class and ultimately ends with women closed out of one of the fastest-growing and most important job markets of the future.

At a time when women make up 44% of the U.S. labor force, a USA Today survey of technology companies finds most reporting 10% to 30% of their programmers, engineers, and managers are women. Of the top five officers of the company, most said one or none is a woman.

"These are good opportunities," says Eric Roberts, computer science professor at Stanford University. "If there are social pressures keeping women out, then women are not doing well in the overall economy."

High-tech companies, many growing at a record pace, are battling the most serious shortages of skilled technologists. Why the shortage? In part because women aren't represented in the pool of applicants.

"It's a damn shame," says Nathan Myhrvold, chief technology officer at Microsoft. "There are breakthrough ideas we're waiting for someone to have. The smaller the number of people in the industry, the fewer of those ideas we'll get. That's more in focus in our industry because growth is directly related to human talent."

Meanwhile, women are missing out on some of the best career paths. Through 2005, the number of computer engineers and systems analysts is expected to grow more than 90%, an increase of 621,576 jobs. Other tech jobs are growing nearly as quickly. College graduates in computer engineering are getting four or more job offers, often starting at $40,000 to $50,000 a year.

In the end, say analysts, the economy suffers.

Technology is the fastest-growing U.S. industry, and it dominates world markets. If the lack of women keeps a leash on the industry's growth, it holds back the nation's economy in general.

What discourages managers and officials who watch job trends is that the problem is not easily fixable.

Even today, when women are commonplace in professions such as medicine and law, women still are nudged away from technology at every stage of life, from attitudes towards girls in grade school, social pressures in high school, the atmosphere at universities, and the nerd culture in company computer departments.

Changing all that and more could take generations.

"We can't just wake up some morning and find the pool is filled," says Nettie Calamia, a program manager and recruiter at Hewlett-Packard.

Nicolette Martin, a technology manager at 3Com, jokes that there's one quick solution. "We need a TV show starring an anorexic, beautiful software engineer," she says. "Then girls would go, 'Oh, I want to be that!'"

NUMBERS TELL THE STORY

The lack of women in technology is something everyone in the business knows about on a gut level.

Walk through Microsoft, Netscape Communications, or Intel. There are women but mostly in marketing, public relations, and human resources. Go into the pure technology areas, where people are writing software code or designing hardware, and men predominate.

Numbers tell the story.

- Just 8.7% of electrical engineers are women, according to the Department of Labor. That's lower than the percentage of female clergy (11%). Among technology jobs, computer programming attracts the most women; 29% are female.

- Responding to the USA Today survey, IBM, the nation's largest technology company, said 29% of its U.S. programmers are women, 10% of its engineers, and none of the top five executives. At HP, which aggressively recruits women, women will make up just 27% of technology hires this year.

- Small companies, which are growing much faster than big companies, often have a lower ratio of women.

3Com didn't provide figures for USA Today's survey. However, Silicon Graphics, which makes the high-powered computers that created the dinosaurs in the movie *Jurassic Park* and other special effects, needs highly specialized people. Women make up 10% of its programmers, 10% of its engineers, and none of its top five officers.

Secure Computing, a Roseville, Minn., computer security firm, says it, too, has women in 10% of its programming and 10% of engineering jobs. None of its top five is a woman.

In other ways, too, women are off the map.

West, the Sunday magazine of the *San Jose Mercury News*, in the heart of Silicon Valley, recently named the region's up-and-coming stars. It cited 39 people in technology. Three were women.

None of the *Fortune* 500 technology companies is run by a woman. In the second tier of technology, one company, Autodesk, has a woman CEO. She is Carol Bartz, an industry celebrity because of her lonely stature.

The technology industry wants everyone to know that women are not being discriminated against.

"Whether they're men or women or monkeys, if they have the skills, companies are racing to get them," says Sheldon Laube, founder of Internet start-up US Web. "When you're dying for skills, bias gets washed away. The fixation is on finding people who can help us."

"This is a meritocracy," says Ann Winblad, a partner in Hummer Winblad Venture Partners, one of the most successful venture capital firms in technology. "That's the message I would give to anyone who is talented. This is an industry that rewards capability."

Then, what's keeping women out of technology at this critical time? And what can be done about it?

CULTURE IS A DRAWBACK

Turn again to 3Com. It makes the guts of networks that link computers inside a company, and business is booming. Revenue hit $2.3 billion for the fiscal year ended May 31, 1996, up from $1.3 billion the previous fiscal year. 3Com employs about 5,000. Over the next year, it may have to hire another 2,000. In hot sectors of technology, that pace is common, and companies caught in it have little time to worry about workforce diversity.

"The pace of work is intense and more and more incompatible with family life," says Eric Benhamou, 3Com's CEO. "There are hard trade-offs females have to make. If they can't do the job, we'll pick whoever can."

Benhamou adds, "We don't look at gender or color of skin or what language you speak. We just look at what you contribute to the bottom line."

The work week in Silicon Valley, the center of the high-tech industry, stretches way beyond 40 hours. While tech companies, including 3Com, tend to be liberal about granting flex time and allow some telecommuting, the load is heavy. It's a level of work-family crunch that drives some women out of technology or makes them decide not to go into it at all.

But even if the schedule doesn't discourage women, the culture at some companies might.

"The other factor is the do-I-want-to-spend-my-life-with-these-people problem," says Susan Kemnitzer, deputy director of engineering education at the National Science Foundation.

The image of a computer whiz is of a poorly dressed, pasty skinned geek more comfortable with a PC than a person. It's a stereotype, but not altogether untrue.

At software company General Magic, for instance, some young programmers build bunk beds in their cubicles. David Filo, a founder of Yahoo!, comes to work in a ratty T-shirt and sometimes stays all night at his PC.

"The culture that grows up around computing is not people-friendly," says Stanford's Professor Roberts. "Women are discouraged by that."

Not surprisingly, women in technology also have a hard time finding a role model.

"It's very hard to find a woman mentor," says Cecilia Smith, an engineer at Texas Instruments, which actively tries to hire and keep women.

At Sybase, a software company in Mountain View, Calif., engineer Glenda Akers looks over at her boss, Ellie Luce. "Ellie's the first female I've worked for in twenty years," Akers says.

STRUGGLE BEGINS EARLY

Still, the atmosphere at companies is only a slice of the problem. To listen to women who now work in technology, there is a social conspiracy that begins early on.

Most high-tech women say they got there as much by chance as anything. All were terrific at math, so they were encouraged to become math teachers. Hardly any knew anything about engineering or computers or thought of those fields as career choices.

In college, Christine Davis of Texas Instruments stumbled on a computer science course. Joyce Lenschmidt of Sybase says her uncle told her, at a wedding, that she should be an engineer because they make good money. Those are typical stories.

Not much has changed. And the detours past technology start young.

Kathy Wheeler is a top engineer at Hewlett-Packard. She has an 8-year-old daughter in public school in Silicon Valley. The school does little to encourage girls to stick with math, she says.

"The stories you hear about the boys all huddled around the computer while the girls are off drawing pictures—that's what happens," Wheeler says.

The danger is that if girls veer from the hard math courses by high school, they'll find it almost impossible to later catch up. Then they're lost to the profession.

"The pipeline is a significant issue," says Lynn Roylance, a manager in Hewlett-Packard's integrated circuit division. "As a company, we have to try to catch girls and parents who are making these decisions pretty early."

TRYING TO ENCOURAGE CHANGE

Companies such as Hewlett-Packard and Texas Instruments are forging paths toward change, but it's only a beginning.

Both run programs to find and hire more women. Both have worked to tone down the nerd factor and break the culture that puts a premium on the number of hours spent in the office.

The companies also strive for a family-friendly feel, putting on family picnics and allowing parents to work from home when their kids are sick.

"We want women (in technology) to feel more positive about their jobs," says Jim Schunk, in charge of college recruiting at HP. "Then maybe they'll encourage their daughters to go into the field."

HP and Texas Instruments have gained a reputation as good places for women to work, and their success has spawned copies. But reform in the workplace won't matter much if the education pipeline continues to feed only a trickle of women into technology jobs.

Can companies change that? Even though some companies already are reaching out to colleges, high schools, and even elementary schools, the efforts are scattershot and have little overall impact, educators say.

For the short term, the problem seems intractable. Yet technology companies know they have to find a way to pull more women into high-tech fields.

HP engineer Wheeler sees the need first-hand. Recalling deadlines that have to be met by teams that are too small, she says, "There is a lot of untapped talent out there, and that makes me crazy."

EXPLORING THE READING

1. In your small group, discuss the small percentage of women in high-tech industries. Why does Kevin Maney say this occurs? Do you agree with his reasons?

2. If you are a woman, freewrite for five minutes about the appeal of technology. Would you be interested in a career in a high-tech industry? Why or why not? If you are a man, freewrite about why Maney says men are more comfortable than women in high-tech industries. Do you agree with him?

3. Do you know a woman who works in a high-tech industry? If so, interview her about her experiences. Would she agree with the women quoted in the Maney feature?

4. Notice how Maney uses both statistics and anecdotal evidence to support his argument. Does he do a good job of convincing his audience? How so?

UNLEASHING THE POWER: COMPANIES HAVE SPENT VAST SUMS ON TECHNOLOGY. NOW THEY HAVE TO FIGURE OUT WHAT TO DO WITH IT ALL.

by Dennis Kneale

More and newer isn't necessarily better when it comes to computers, many companies are finding. According to Dennis Kneale in this Wall Street Journal *article, companies have been on a ten-year, $1 trillion computer buying binge, and the results haven't been pleasing. Companies have archaic mishmash, hacked-together systems that are hard to use and expensive to maintain. For example, in 1991 Aetna had 108 different word-processing systems. Systems, however, can be streamlined to communicate with each other, and personnel can be trained more efficiently.*

Kneale is an editor for the Wall Street Journal's *New York Bureau specializing in tech-nology-related stories.*

It's the morning after.

For the past ten years, companies have been on a blind-faith buying binge, investing well over $1 trillion in new computer systems to embrace the future and gain a competitive edge. Now, many of them are awakening with a hangover, and they are wondering:

What was it all for, and where did we go wrong?

The evidence of their misadventure is everywhere, but it can be boiled down to a simple truth: Companies are a long way from unleashing the real power of the technology they have spent so dearly to put in place.

Technology spending soared in the 1980s, yet productivity grew well under 2% a year. Few businesses have created entirely new services, products, or processes that take advantage of all that extra muscle.

In assigning blame, the computer industry is target No. 1. It has over-promised and underdelivered. For decades it has churned out a Tower of Babel of incompatible wares, bewildering customers who are forced to patch together a crazy quilt of disparate technologies.

Customers, however, deserve a good portion of the blame, too.

Eager to bank on high technology and panicked at the thought of rivals innovating faster, many companies bought technology for technology's sake. Top brass signed the checks with little regard to figuring out what the new gear should do. Businesses automated paper-and-pencil procedures but stopped short of more-ambitious goals. They trained workers poorly, and were reluctant to overhaul the organization and redesign jobs to make better use of all that silicon.

So, long after IBM joined the PC revolution in 1981 and the Macintosh promised to be the computer "for the rest of us," many of us are laggards just getting by. "It's a big joke—and the joke's on us," says Michael Brinda, pres-ident of New Horizons Computer Learning Center Inc., a training center in

Santa Ana, California. "We aren't getting all we can out of the machines. It just isn't happening."

Adds J. Bruce Harreld, president of Boston Chicken Inc., a fast-food chain based in Naperville, Illinois: "Technology isn't the issue—we've got more of it than we know what to do with. The real issue is how to apply it, and what are the business problems. Everyone is running around worrying about the plumbing and not worrying about the content."

It isn't too late. Optimists say that the proliferation of high-tech tonnage already has created a critical infrastructure, and that legions of workers are ready to use it. About 60 million PCs now are whirring away in U.S. businesses and home offices, and about 70% of office PCs are linked together in local networks.

Moreover, experts argue, a new generation of software, hardware, and strategy—the whole "reengineering" buzz—will make it possible to unleash the inherent power of technology. They hold out the promise of making the profusion of equipment work together better, smarter, faster, more effectively.

"Management finally has a concept now that links technology and productivity," says Mel Bergstein, chairman of Diamond Technology Partners, a Chicago consulting firm. "And when it's done right, it works."

THE SAME LANGUAGE

To do it right, however, businesses must first overcome the incompatible mishmash of their "legacy systems," the archaic gear that has been piling up for two decades. Typically, 60% of a software project is spent building links back to old systems rather than creating new applications, says Hugh Ryan, a director with Andersen Consulting in Chicago.

The sea of incompatibility owes to the almighty free market: For makers, incompatibility equals differentiation. Makers swear that they have developed ways to allow rival systems to work together, but Mr. Ryan calls that a "myth" of marketing hype.

All that incompatibility ultimately defeats much of the purpose for buying technology in the first place. The industry pushes out waves of new technology "without a lot of concern about having any order in this morass to let you effectively use it," says John D. Loewenberg, chief executive of Aetna Information Technology, a subsidiary of Aetna Life & Casualty Co. that oversees the insurer's massive computer and telecommunications operations. But, he adds, "the more technology you have, the more expense you add on top. And you didn't, in fact, get a competitive advantage."

Aetna often spent more than $1 billion a year in the 1980s in pursuit of the high-tech battle cry of gaining a competitive edge. By the time Mr. Loewenberg arrived in 1989, it was an unmitigated mess. Aetna was using 108 different word-processing systems, a few dozen rival brands of PCs, nineteen separate and incompatible electronic-mail systems, and three dozen rival communications networks.

In 1991, Mr. Loewenberg was visited by Casey Powell, chairman of Sequent Computer Systems Inc., a computer maker in Beaverton, Oregon. Mr. Powell wanted to know what Aetna's *real* needs were. Mr. Loewenberg was blunt: "How do I hook all this crap together? Where do I get the people to do it?" With that, Sequent discovered a new business opportunity, specializing in tying together a rash of rival systems for customers that buy their own gear.

"The entire computer industry has a proprietary past," Mr. Powell says. "They all talk 'open systems,' but few do it."

Each seam of incompatibility creates the need for new layers of software to bridge gaps in the network. Workers in one department don't know how to use the system in another. That cuts productivity, raises training costs, and makes it harder to "re-engineer" work flow to get new kinds of information to more people.

"The inconsistency in the technology forces a lot of artificial support structures," Mr. Loewenberg says.

Aetna has 11 mainframes, 2,000 midrange machines and servers, and 51,000 desktop and laptop PCs, all serving 40,000 users. The insurer has trimmed down to two major e-mail systems, a single backbone network for communications, and software united under the Microsoft banner.

By streamlining the system, Aetna has been able to allow users in the company's 600 sites to place orders for supplies by computer, rather than go through layers of paperwork. In addition, customer-service employees in the insurer's health division previously had to use two separate systems to get enrollment data and billing information. Now they can tap into both types of data from the PCs at their desks; that lets them answer inquiries faster.

Aetna now spends $825 million a year on technology, quite a bit less than in the past. "The whole focus here has changed from *having* technology to the effective *use* of technology," Mr. Loewenberg says. He likens it to his golf game: Although he is always tempted to buy the latest stuff in the hope it might improve his handicap, he says that "you can improve it a hell of a lot more by keeping what you've got and practicing."

HARDWARE VS. SOFTWARE

Incompatibility, of course, isn't the only obstacle to more fully using technology. Another complaint is that hardware power has far outstripped software's ability to harness it. Some 30 million PCs have "32-bit" chips that can do many tasks at once—yet only three million have "operating-system" software that taps such power, according to International Data Corp., a consulting firm in Framingham, Mass. Although the chips have been around for five years, Microsoft Corp. of Redmond, Washington, won't finally have an operating system to match them (Windows 95) until later this year.

That will ultimately give PCs a versatility that many companies crave. At Florida Power Corp. in St. Petersburg, a new customer-service system is replacing "dumb" terminals with a PC network. When callers ask about a new rate package, reps will be able to get access to monthly bills, graph out different pricing schemes, and print letters and charts for mailing the same day. The old system took almost a week.

Even in the utility business, better service can stave off competitors, says Terry G. Tyler, information-services director. Now that PCs are everywhere—Florida Power has 5,000 for 5,000 employees—"we're coming up the learning curve," he says. "We can get more out of technology."

THE WAY WE WORK

But such geeky concerns as incompatibility and 32-bit chips may miss the real point. Too often, companies spent big on computers, "but they didn't change any of their business processes—the way people work, the way they're organized, the way they use technology," says James R. Kinney, chief information officer at Kraft General Foods, a Northfield, Illinois, subsidiary of Philip Morris Cos. "Change on the part of people is perhaps the most difficult part of the entire effort."

That is what Kraft has found as it struggles to stitch together a single customer-service network from three separate ones for Kraft, General Foods, and Oscar Mayer products. Philip Morris assembled Kraft General Foods in a string of acquisitions in the 1980s, but merging the computer systems is taking longer than joining the businesses they serve.

The technological obstacles have been formidable. The backbone computer systems range from an ancient 1970s database for Kraft to a 1980s online system for Oscar Mayer. They sometimes describe the same customers in unlike terms with unrelated account numbers.

The three brands also had divergent ordering systems. At General Foods, 45% of orders came in by fax, 20% over the phone, and 35% by computer lines directly from customers. At Oscar Mayer, all orders came in by phone. At Kraft, 35% came over computer lines and 65% were from salespeople's handheld PCs. (The combined company now gets 45% of all orders over computer lines.)

Reps use PCs linked to an IBM midrange computer to toggle among order, inventory, and receivables screens, but "it's still fairly awkward," Mr. Kinney says. Moving from one source to another requires a "boot-up" and "log-on" process each time. They can't yet zap messages to distribution centers, salespeople, or customers.

Moreover, each brand still uses one system to track sales by product, district, and customer, and a separate system to track profit and loss by product and district. None of these six setups has been lashed together for data-sharing.

The result of all this is that now, several years after KGF was formed, big grocery-store chains can order Kraft and General Foods products from a single service agent, but they still have to place separate orders for Oscar Mayer products with the brand's Madison, Wisconsin, base. A service agent for Kraft in one area can't get computer access to the customer's orders for Oscar Mayer meats.

When the systems become seamless, a grocery chain will be able to order all KGF foodstuffs from the same rep, who will instantly check existing orders, look at inventory levels at nearby warehouses, and ensure the chain gets the promotions it has earned. The rep can offer to combine separate orders to meet the minimum truckload weight that KGF requires to win a pricing discount. Kraft itself might save millions of dollars in inventory and shipping costs if most deliveries could be consolidated.

More important, salespeople will be freed from the housekeeping role of replenishing customer stocks. They will be able to focus instead on selling, working with chains' merchandisers on better promotions. Technology will empower a customer-service agent, sitting in front of a computer in the office, to handle all of the ordering and monitor inventory.

Still, delivering on this vision isn't just a matter of updating technology; it also involves delicate personnel issues. In preparation, Kraft has scrapped the old ways of serving customers and is setting up account teams consisting of people who hadn't worked together before—account managers and salespeople on one side, service reps on the other. The service staff had always been viewed as clerical people who merely logged orders and lined up deliveries.

"Now they tend to be much more partners with our account managers in meeting customer needs," Mr. Kinney says. That required persuading the sales side to let service reps into the process. In "partnering sessions," account managers visit their service counterparts to "spend the day just getting to know each other."

The effort also entailed "incredible numbers of training and education sessions with our sales force," to teach the formerly separate companies about how the others' businesses work, Mr. Kinney says. A small example: Oscar Mayer and Kraft dairy products have short shelf lives, so dating is critical and discount promotions increase as the foods age. Timing isn't critical for General Foods lines such as Maxwell House coffee, so date-dependent promotions aren't used at all.

The technological and personnel overhaul began three years ago, and Mr. Kinney doesn't expect it to be complete until sometime in 1995. "These kinds of projects take multiple years," he says. "You have to do them a bit at a time."

STARTING FROM SCRATCH

Mr. Harreld of Boston Chicken knows the kinds of frustrations Mr. Kinney and Kraft General Foods face: He previously was Mr. Kinney's boss, facing an amalgam of rival technologies as the big food company transmogrified from the original Dart & Kraft to Kraft to Kraft General Foods. "I got purely frustrated, not only with large companies and our large infrastructure, but also with my own management style," Mr. Harreld says now.

He says he needed to realize that technology was secondary to "how we manage behavior and organization and our own mind-set." So Mr. Harreld was eager to create a new system from scratch, free of all that old installed iron, when he became president of upstart Boston Chicken a year ago.

Staffs at many large companies, Mr. Harreld says, have evolved into large, multilayered structures, largely because "our communication skills are designed around pretty old technology." New networks, groupware, and the melding of telecommunications, computers, and video into one system have the potential to eliminate big staffs and push power and input out to the marketplace where it belongs, he says.

Boston Chicken has just 150 people at its headquarters. It is investing heavily to tie together 35 franchise "partners" that employ 8,000 people at 300 stores. A nationwide voice-mail system lets Mr. Kinney zap a phone message to a partner in Dallas, who can forward it to two others in Washington and San Francisco.

Lotus Notes, databases, and local networks let Boston Chicken conduct e-mail brainstorming sessions and collect ideas and responses from franchisees. Some 90 projects are under way to, among other things, develop new dishes, reduce paper costs, and devise new point-of-sale terminals. People in the field can tap in and track everything that goes on, putting in their own two cents.

That requires trust and "teaching people how to be team players rather than 'me' players," Mr. Harreld says. It also demands a common incentive system that rewards everyone in the same way, centralized control over technology purchases so everything can work together, and deep involvement by the top brass.

The last factor isn't all that simple. Mr. Harreld teaches senior executives at the Kellogg Graduate School of Management at Northwestern University. He finds that many of them figure they spend a lot of money on technology they don't understand, so they must "put a thumb down and control it financially." If they would dive in and "take ownership," he says, "they might actually see some opportunities for dramatically doing some new things they never thought of."

EXPLORING THE READING

1. In your small group, talk about your corporate or business experience. Have you experienced the kinds of computer system problems Dennis Kneale discusses? Report your findings to the class.

2. Were you surprised to find that companies may regret the millions they have spent on computer systems? Why or why not?

3. Kneale presents a problem and then offers several solutions. What are his solutions? Do they seem plausible?

4. How does Kneale's article relate to the new business cycle Michael J. Mandel describes?

DIARY OF A TELECOMMUTER

by John Gehl

John Gehl is a telecommuter, working at home. This means he doesn't have to shower until time to go out to lunch, but it also means he has to contend with people like his wife who sometimes wonder how much he is really working if he is at home. Gehl shares his diary for a few typical days in his life which include checking e-mail, participating in a conference call, and dealing with a wayward fax machine.

Gehl is editor of Educom Review, *a print publication, and* Edupage, *an e-mail newsletter. Both publications focus on the impact of technology upon education.*

When you were in college did you ever get around to reading the diary of Samuel Pepys? No? Don't worry about it. That was then, this is now.

Jan. 10th. Up betimes, and I power up the computer on my way downstairs. I let the cat in and feed him, get the papers, and go back upstairs with cups of coffee. I resist the temptation to check the night's e-mail and instead settle down in a reading chair to peruse the *New York Times* while my wife reads the *Atlanta Constitution*, punctuating her reading with expressions of disbelief. "Hah! . . . Ridiculous! . . . Phttt! . . . Stupid! . . . Horrible!" "It's the same in the *Times*," I assure her (though it's not exactly the same because the *New York Times* reports the day's horrors with such ponderous, numbing thoroughness that it's hard for a reader to develop a sprightly cadence for cries of outrage). We switch papers and she goes downstairs to make some breakfast. Before joining her, I check my e-mail, then I go downstairs. After breakfast, my wife leaves to go to work, and I repair to my office upstairs to make and receive phone calls and answer mail and work on *Educom Review*. I start to write a column but realize it's almost noon and I need to shower and dress and go to lunch. After lunch I am back at my workstation, where I toil until evening.

We dine at home; then read a bit before watching Georgia Tech beat North Carolina, blessed be God. I check e-mail, mainly to get items from Suzanne to include in *Edupage*; I incorporate them in *Edupage* and send it out. And so to bed.

12th. Just after midnight, I go into my office and turn on the computer to see if the night has brought me the answer I'm expecting from the West Coast. It has not; it has brought other, less welcome messages that I wish I'd not seen until the morning, if ever. I turn off the computer and read awhile and then go to bed.

14th. This afternoon, a conference call about *Educom Review*. Wendy works out of New Jersey, Suzanne out of Florida, Greg out of Texas, and I out of Georgia. Before the conference call, I talk with Roger in Washington about subscription matters, but then at two-thirty, Suzanne, Wendy, Greg, and I peel into the conference call like audio fighter pilots on first dates. The discussion goes well, but we wish we had teleconferencing capabilities so we could see just what it is we are talking about. During the middle of the call, Butch comes upstairs wanting to be fed, or let out, or both. I attempt to ignore him but he leaps into my lap and digs his claws into my groin. "Damn you!" I shout into the phone. Suzanne says, "John, it's just a magazine." Butch won't leave me in peace, so I have to excuse myself from the conference call to go downstairs to feed him. When I get back, Wendy, Suzanne, and Greg tell me that everything's been decided. "Good," I say sincerely, in pain. I decide that office cats are a bad idea.

17th. In my office all day, very busy. Then out to dinner at Nino's. We are back in time to watch the last half of *Crossfire*. The participants are brawling with one another. The kitchen phone rings; I try to take the call from the den, using the portable phone, but for no good reason the portable's not working. I go into the kitchen and pick up the wall phone. "This is Somebody-Somebody from the Something Corporation," a woman tells me over the phone. "I'm sorry," I tell her, "I'm having dinner," and hang up. As I return to the den I wonder if the woman might have been a business caller who somehow got forwarded by the stupid telephone system to my private line. There are half a dozen phone sets in the house, all of which work differently and in unpredictable and evil ways. I return to *Crossfire* to find that the television brawlers have already been removed by The Authorities and that I have missed the final cathartic bloodbath.

18th. An e-mail message from Brian in Ottawa informs me that my fax machine is broken and that everything I've ever sent out has an ugly black line down the right-hand side of each page. When I happen to mention this to Wendy, she asks me what kind of fax machine I have; it turns out we both have the same kind. She is very patient with me. "They come from the manufacturer with some gunk on the right-hand side of the glass strip under the cover, so what you need to do is take some cotton balls and remove the gunk with some alcohol." "And does the manufacturer have the courtesy to tell us about this gunk in his stupid *User's Manual*?" I ask with righteous indignation. However, I follow Wendy's advice and remove the gunk. I would very much like to know what the stupid *User's Manual* had to say on the topic of gunk, but I can't remember what I did with the stupid thing.

19th. All the morning in my office. Various telephone conversations, with people wanting to arrange consulting projects. "Is that a cat I hear?" a potential client asks me. "Do you have a cat in your office?" "No," I assure him, "not a cat. Not really." "It sounds like a cat," he insists. "If it's not a cat, what is it?" "It's a chair!" I tell him. "Listen—I'll swivel in my chair, and you'll think you're hearing a cat." Butch, blessed be God, meows on cue. "You're right," says the client happily. "Your chair sounds just like a cat!" Butch has been much on my nerves today, and I feel very tired. I want to quit for the day and go home, and I start to do that, before realizing sadly that I am *already* at home.

21st. At bedtime, I remember that I haven't written my column yet for the March/April issue. I start the computer and write it. Then, after doing some e-mail, I reread what I've written and see that it's too splenetic to use as a column; I decide, instead, to save it for my memoirs. Which means that I still have a column to write. Maybe an idea for it will come to me tomorrow, blessed be God. And so to bed.

EXPLORING THE READING

1. What do you think of the word picture John Gehl paints of his life as a telecommuter? Would you like to have a job that allowed you to work at home? Why or why not?

2. In your small group, discuss the diary format which Gehl uses for his essay. Does it work well for the purposes of this essay? How so?

3. What is Gehl's tone in this essay? Is it appropriate for his topic?

4. Do you think it strange that a man would choose to work at home? Gehl apparently worries whether people take him seriously because he works at home. Would a woman have the same problem? Why or why not?

THE VALLEY OF MONEY'S DELIGHT

by John Micklethwait

The concentrated high-tech development in the Silicon Valley in California is a model for the future, according to this feature which heads a group of articles in the American Survey section in The Economist. *Similar clusters of high-tech industries can be found in Utah, New York, Austin, the Northwest, as well as in India, Israel, Taiwan, and Britain. Critical ingredients include the presence of entrepreneurs, a trained labor pool, a network of suppliers, and access to venture capital. Possibly even more important is the culture, which is detailed in another of the short features collected here.*

Three scruffy young men and a sneakered young woman, each wearing a visitor's badge, sit huddled around a table in the foyer of the Robert Noyce Building at Intel's headquarters in Santa Clara. One of the men stops scribbling on his electronic personal organizer and announces: "We could become extremely rich." "Very possibly," answers the woman in a distracted tone, implying that sooner or later enormous wealth should surely come to everyone.

Silicon Valley, the thin sliver of land between San Francisco and San Jose that was once known as the Valley of Heart's Delight, is proof of capitalism's continuing vitality. Stephen Levy at the Centre for the Continuing Study of the Californian Economy estimates the GDP of the valley's 2 million inhabitants at around $65 billion—much the same as that of Chile's 15 million people. Average pay in Silicon Valley last year rose by 5% in real terms, to $43,510; average pay in the software industry was nearly double that. Compare that with the figure for the rest of America, which rose by less than 1% to $28,040. In the valley, workers are in such short supply that Cisco Systems, the leading supplier of Internet routers, has had to rent advertising space on billboards to find the 400 people a month it is adding to its payroll.

Technology now accounts for around 10% of America's GDP, and Silicon Valley's 6,000 high-tech companies, with total sales of more than $200 billion a year, are doing their best to boost it further. Having launched the huge personal-computer business, they are now starting another industry, based on the Internet, that promises—eventually—to be even larger. At the last count Santa Clara, with 355 Internet hosts (permanently connected computers) per 1,000 people, was twice as wired as any other county anywhere in America. As Ann Winblad, a prominent Californian venture capitalist, puts it, "This is the motherlode."

GAZELLE ALERT

It is true that Bill Gates, the supernerd boss of Microsoft, is based in Seattle, that Compaq, the leading PC maker, is in Texas, and that IBM is in New Jersey.

But most of the other technology leaders—such as Sun Microsystems, Hewlett-Packard, Oracle, 3Com, Applied Materials, Netscape, Cisco Systems, and Intel—are in or around Silicon Valley. One in five of the public companies there counts as "gazelles"—small firms that have seen their revenues grow by at least 20% in each of the past four years. The national average is a mere one firm in thirty-five.

Most of these fleet-footed companies were financed by venture capital, a financial art form that Silicon Valley has perfected. The venture capitalists dotted along just one street in Silicon Valley—Sand Hill Road in Menlo Park—control around a third of America's independently raised venture capital, and around a sixth of the world's total. One of those firms, Kleiner Perkins Caulfield & Byers, has invested around $1 billion to help start 250 companies, which in 1995 had revenues of $44 billion and are worth $85 billion.

Silicon Valley is disproportionately staffed by those who often find themselves at a disadvantage in a less results-oriented environment: women and immigrants. Intel's boss, Andy Grove, was born in Hungary. Sun, Oracle, Solectron, Cirrus Logic, and hundreds of other firms all have at least one foreign founder. Chuck Robel, an accountant at Price Waterhouse, jokes that employee registers for stock options are so international that they make "the average company look like the UN." One in four people with a science degree now living in America was born abroad. No wonder that immigrants play a pivotal role in Silicon Valley's research.

The two most important groups are the overseas Chinese and the Indians. India sends between 12,000 and 15,000 of its annual crop of 50,000 information-technology graduates to the United States, according to Coopers & Lybrand. Down in Los Angeles the young thespians of the Hollywood Cricket Club, once a lonely oasis of Anglocentric civilization, are now routinely trounced by visiting Indian teams from Santa Clara.

Silicon Valley does business differently from other places. Engineers and programmers hop from company to company, and share options stretch from the boardroom to the reception desk. Where else would you find a firm whose canteen serves spring-ginger-seared ahi tuna for less than $5 (as at Oracle), or which provides a free creche for pets (as at Autodesk, another software firm)?

This culture runs deep. Intel, which enjoys shocking people with its motto, "Only the paranoid survive," and which, thanks to its often ruthless tactics, is on course to overtake General Electric as America's most profitable company by the turn of the century, celebrated its most recent results (net profits of $5.2 billion for 1996) by spontaneously handing out $1,000 to each of its 48,500 employees. None of Intel's multimillionaire founders has his own office; one of them, Gordon Moore, moans about spending twenty minutes looking for a parking space. It would not occur to him to demand one.

Indeed, Silicon Valley displays a remarkable lack of vulgarity compared with (now poorer) New York or Los Angeles. True, Tiffany, the New York jeweller, is moving into the Stanford shopping centre; true, too, there are delicatessens selling bottles of vinegar for nearly $200. But the typical nerd millionaire still drives an engineer's car such as a Lexus or a BMW rather than a Ferrari; and his house in Atherton (where the average price is now over $1 million, double the figure for Beverly Hills) is a fairly modest affair: as with the cars, most of the money is spent on what goes inside, such as expensive hi-fi and high-tech stoves.

There is something endearingly gauche about the new millionaires. Up in San Francisco, socialites snigger about a madam alleged to have made her fortune entirely by catering to rich young nerds. "Accidental Empires," an amusing chronicle of Silicon Valley's rise to power, is subtitled "How the boys of Silicon Valley make their millions, battle foreign competition and still can't get a date."

Nowadays, virtually every government in the world seems to want to create its own Silicon Valley. America alone is home to Silicon Desert (Utah), Silicon Alley (New York), Silicon Hills (Austin), and Silicon Forest (either Seattle or Portland). Taiwan, Israel, India, and Britain all boast passable imitations. Some of the more unlikely aspirants include the Cote d'Azur ("Europe's California") and Egypt's Pyramid Technology Park. Malaysia's prime minister, Mahathir Mohamad, recently told a group of Silicon Valley luminaries that his country had set aside 750 square kilometres (468 square miles) just south of Kuala Lumpur, and the tidy sum of $40 billion, for his own version of Silicon Valley: a brand new "multimedia super corridor" that will include an IT city of 100,000 people.

THE CLUSTER IS MIGHTIER THAN THE CHIP

Politicians such as Dr. Mahathir regard Silicon Valley as a high-technology industry. This survey will argue that it is better seen as a way of doing business, with a product that happens to be technology. Thus, it is often more illuminating to compare Silicon Valley with entrepreneurial "clusters" in other industries, such as Hollywood or the City of London, than it is with, say, Japan's computer industry. In building clusters, social and political factors, such as tolerance to immigrants, often matter far more than either technology or economic clout.

Indeed, Silicon Valley's most important contribution may well be organizational, not technological. Look around the developed world, and you will see the gradual Siliconization of commerce. "Gazelle" firms now account for more than three-quarters of new jobs in America (and probably much the same proportion in Europe and Japan). The organization of big firms everywhere is becoming looser—either because they are being broken up into smaller units, or because they are devolving more power to their front-line workers. And an increasing number of those workers do not have full-time jobs.

Politicians and economists are also beginning to pay more attention to Silicon Valley. Stanford University is the center for new economic theories about growth, arguing that investments in new ideas and technologies need not suffer from the law of diminishing returns—provided they are made by entrepreneurs, not governments. Meanwhile, the most unlikely political leaders have begun to court the nerd elite. In dirigiste France, President Jacques Chirac has taken to consulting both Mr. Gates and Bernard Liautaud, the Stanford-trained boss of France's most successful software company, Business Objects (and a fervent apostle of "the Californian way"). Even Silicon Valley's challenges—how to train people for a world where seniority is no guarantee of survival, how to distribute wealth in a winner-takes-all economy, how to cope with the "hollowing out" of a manufacturing base— are now cropping up in parliaments around the world.

These ideas and these problems were not born yesterday. Remember that Peter Drucker was already writing about the birth of the knowledge worker back in the 1950s. Nor has Silicon Valley only just been invented: one of its founding companies, Hewlett-Packard, is sixty years old. Yet Silicon Valley is also surely something of a test-tube. In the same way that California is famously "like America, only more so," Silicon Valley is like modern commerce, only more so. Will everywhere become more like it? And if so, is that a good thing?

WHAT IT TAKES TO COME TO THE TOP IN TECHNOLOGY

VITAL INTANGIBLES. Imagine yourself as one of those many foreign bureaucrats now charged with trying to build Silicon Valleys of their own— a member of Mahathir Mohamad's recent delegation, say, or one of the scores of visitors to the valley from the Japan External Trade Organization (JETRO). As you wend your weary way from Sand Hill Road to Stanford University and San Jose, you ask yourself: "Why did it happen here?"

The two obvious starting points—history and geography—offer only a few clues. Until recently, economists and politicians would put Silicon Valley's success down solely to a handful of good, solid reasons: the size and flexibility of its labor pool, the breadth of its network of suppliers, its access to venture capital, and the excellence of its education facilities and research institutions—notably the universities of Stanford and Berkeley, and Xerox's Palo Alto Research Centre (PARC).

All these things have indeed helped to put the valley on the commercial map. For instance, one way or another around 1,000 companies have spun out of Stanford University. But increasingly it is becoming clear that such hard-and-fast factors tell only part of the story. In *Regional Advantage: Culture and Competition in Silicon Valley and Route 128* (Harvard University Press, 1994), Anna Lee Saxenian, a professor at Berkeley, points out that Boston's Route 128 was more than a match for Silicon Valley in terms of both venture capital and access to research. Yet by the late 1970s Silicon Valley had created more high-tech jobs than Route 128, and when both clusters fell from grace in the mid-1980s it proved far more resilient.

The reason, according to Ms. Saxenian, was to do with the culture and structure of the organizations involved. Big east-coast firms such as Digital

Equipment Corporation and Data General were self-contained empires that focused on one product, minicomputers. Silicon Valley companies also relied too heavily on one product, semiconductors, but its companies were more decentralized and more likely to spawn other companies. This networked economy was able to change much more quickly.

To an unusual degree Silicon Valley's economy relies on what Joseph Schumpeter, an Austrian economist, called "creative destruction." Some modern writers have rechristened the phenomenon "flexible recycling,"* but the basic idea is the same: old companies die and new ones emerge, allowing capital, ideas, and people to be reallocated. An essential ingredient in this is the presence of entrepreneurs, and a culture that attracts them.

Research has increasingly concentrated on clusters—places (such as Hollywood or Silicon Valley) or communities (such as the overseas Chinese) where there is "something in the air" that encourages risk-taking. This suggests that culture, irritatingly vague though it may sound, is more important to Silicon Valley's success than economic or technological factors. Here is a list of what it takes:

Tolerance of failure. In Europe, bankruptcy is stigmatized; in some countries it disqualifies people from starting another company. America, which never had a debtors' prison, has always been more tolerant. Henry Ford's first two car ventures failed. In Silicon Valley, bankruptcy is treated like a duelling scar in a Prussian officers' mess. Many of the new Internet companies are headed by the very same entrepreneurs whose pen-computing companies have just gone bust. More generally, Silicon Valley is quick to forget mistakes.

Tolerance of treachery. Secrets and staff are both hard to keep in Silicon Valley. In 1957, the so-called "traitorous eight" walked out of Shockley Laboratories to found Fairchild Semiconductor. One of them was Gordon Moore of subsequent Intel fame. Fairchild Semiconductor eventually spawned thirty-seven different firms, including Intel. Virtually every big firm in Silicon Valley is a spin-off from another one.

Intel has since rather hypocritically griped about "vulture capitalists" that lure away the talent it has trained, but most denizens of the valley take a more relaxed attitude. "I left a company myself," says Scott McNealy, the boss of Sun Microsystems. "I don't want to lose people, but I don't want to employ people who don't want to work here, when I have 20,000 excellent people who do."

Risk-seeking. Talk to a Silicon Valley boss about a technological problem, and he will tell you it is an opportunity for someone. Elsewhere in America, and in Europe, investors are obsessed by the minutiae of business plans,

---

*"Flexible Recycling," by Homa Bahrami and Stuart Evans, *California Management Review*, 1995.

however nebulous their end-products. By contrast, Arthur Rock, a veteran Silicon Valley venture capitalist, says simply: "I have always backed people and opportunities."

Actively seeking risk makes sense for venture capitalists. Many of their gambles do not come off, but some of those that make it deliver huge rewards. In a technology business, a company that establishes an early lead may set a standard and end up scooping most of the market. Tim Draper, a leading venture capitalist in Silicon Valley, divides a typical portfolio of 20 companies into five portions. Four will go bankrupt, six will stay in business but lose money, six will make a modest return, three will do well, and one will scoop the jackpot.

Reinvestment in the community.   Howard Stevenson, a professor at Harvard Business School, says that many clusters die because their founders, or their founders' children, reinvest their fortunes elsewhere. Sometimes this is because they despise the muck that made their brass. More often, it is because it makes financial sense for a family business to diversify. So far in Silicon Valley, most of the money made out of the technology industry has gone straight back in, either via people starting their own companies or via "business angel" investors.

Enthusiasm for change.   According to a popular saying in Silicon Valley, "Either we obsolete ourselves, or the competition will." Even venerable old Hewlett-Packard has metamorphosed countless times, producing, amongst other things, oscillators, medical equipment, calculators, and laser-jet printers. The new generation of small Internet companies changes its spots even more frequently. Jim Breyer of Accel Partners, who sits on the boards of several such firms, says that "a major strategic decision" is taken at virtually every meeting.

This nimbleness is prompted by fear. The technology market changes so quickly that any company which fails to adjust will get pushed out. Bill Gates originally regarded the Internet as an interesting product with little relevance to Microsoft; once he realized he had got it wrong, he organized one of the most dramatic large-company turnarounds in American corporate history.

Promotion on merit.   One of Silicon Valley's secret weapons is its openness to immigrants and to women. Age and experience, which elsewhere get people promoted, are no help in the valley; on the contrary, there is a distinct bias in favor of youth. Nowadays the average software-engineering qualification becomes obsolete in around five years, so a student fresh out of college may be more valuable to a company than a forty-year-old. Many of the new Internet firms are headed by people in their mid-20s. Some of the outsiders that have bought firms in Silicon Valley come a cropper because they try to import their own hierarchies.

Obsession with the product.   Silicon Valley was founded by engineers who were fascinated by technology, but who also felt sure that there was more to life than making money. At Hewlett-Packard this ethos survives through "the HP way," a strong corporate culture. At Sun Microsystems, the technology clearly takes priority. As Bill Raduchel, the chief information officer, puts it: "If you don't understand the modestly parallel scaleable multiprocessing environment, then you might as well leave."

Silicon Valley's obsession with "the cool idea" keeps it ahead of the competition. It is full of consumers known as "digital upscale believers" who will buy new products just because they look interesting. John Seely Brown, the director of Xerox PARC, explains that much of Silicon Valley's value lies in what he calls "the conversations on the periphery": the round-the-table chat in restaurants, the buzz in bars.

Collaboration.   Log on to any of the chat sites where Java software developers meet to discuss their industry, and you will find a virtual version of the conversations in Silicon Valley's bars. Like most frontier towns, the place is a strange mixture of rampant individualism and collaboration: staff are borrowed, ideas shared, favors exchanged. Time is of the essence: it is not worth trying to develop something yourself if somebody else can do it either for or with you.

Variety.   Despite their common culture, Silicon Valley companies come in all shapes and sizes. There are a good number of "virtual" software companies with names full of numbers and exclamation marks; but there are also lots of more conventional companies such as Intel and Hewlett-Packard that have to plan ahead. Any company that puts $3 billion into each new factory requires plenty of mundane management skills.

The Stanford Project on Emerging Companies, which since 1994 has been analyzing several hundred local high-tech companies, divided its sample into four groups on the basis of how the firms treated their employees. The first category was "factories," where the rewards were primarily financial. In the second, "commitment companies," the firm itself generated considerable loyalty. "Stars" were firms based on the idea of gathering together as many clever people as possible and leaving them to it. The largest category, accounting for just under half the total, were "engineers," companies where people's main loyalty was to a particular product.

The Stanford researchers found that the different types of company were good at different sorts of things ("stars," for instance, were likely to become public companies earlier). The sheer variety of companies that spring up in Silicon Valley gives the place a better chance of survival. If one kind does not make it, another will.

Anybody can play. Paul Turner, a consultant with Price Waterhouse, remembers that in his native Lancashire there was talk about "people being too big for their boots, and being brought down to earth." In Silicon Valley, jealousy is rare because most people believe that they, too, have a chance of becoming rich. As in Hollywood, anyone who lives in Silicon Valley for any length of time will have at least one friend "who makes it big."

MASTERFUL INACTIVITY. For would-be imitators of Silicon Valley, this list might not look altogether helpful. First, some of the required attributes seem somewhat ill-defined (how would you explain the importance of "the cool idea" to an Asian autocrat?). Second, the list as a whole seems to imply that government has had little role to play in the valley's development. That conclusion would be wrong, but for reasons that are more complicated than they might at first appear.

A few people still believe that Silicon Valley was built by the American government. By one count, in the period 1958–74 the Pentagon paid for $1 billion-worth of semiconductor research. The Internet, too, began as a government project; several companies, including Netscape, have arisen, directly or indirectly, from state-funded research projects. Even today, 10% of Xerox PARC's budget comes from the American government.

However, there is a clear difference between being a big customer and calling the shots. On only one occasion—in the mid-1980s, when the memory-chip industry was overrun by suspiciously cheap imports from Japan—has Silicon Valley gone to Washington for help; many in the valley still view the resulting Semiconductor Trade Agreement with shame. The prevailing attitude nowadays is that governments—however well-meaning—should stay well out of it.

Yet the conclusion that Silicon Valley is a government-free creation is surely wrong. If nothing else, the American government has made a powerful contribution by not doing things that would have messed it up. Just look at Europe, where a twin policy of maintaining high semiconductor tariffs and bailing out high-tech firms has helped to reduce the region's share of the world market for "electronic data products" (which includes computers) from 23% in 1988 to 18% in 1996. In Silicon Valley, success in just about any area turns out to hinge on either some liberalizing legislation, or the absence of any legislation at all.

Two easy examples are America's bankruptcy laws and California's tax structure, which has historically treated capital gains more generously than income. But there are other, more fiddly ones. Ron Gilson, a professor at both Stanford and Columbia law schools, points out that Californian law, unlike its Massachusetts equivalent, regards "post-employment covenants not to compete" as unenforceable. That makes it much harder to tie down staff. On the other hand, American law is relatively tough on patents: if a firm has an idea, it can protect it.

In Ms. Saxenian's words, "the beauty of Silicon Valley is that the culture and the structure reinforce each other." Do not regard it as some sort of economic machine, where various raw materials are poured in at one end and firms such as Apple and Cisco roll out at the other, but rather as a form of ecosystem that breeds companies: without the right soil and the right climate, nothing will grow.

OF MICE AND MEN

Where exactly Silicon Valley begins and ends is hard to say. Its core is Santa Clara County, but it also includes a fair slice of the neighboring counties of San Mateo, Santa Cruz, and Alameda. All of it conspicuously lacks charm. It is nothing more than an unplanned, amorphous sprawl of freeways, low-built factories, shopping malls, and unremarkable (but extremely expensive) suburban Californian houses.

According to Ed Zschau, a former Silicon Valley Congressman who now teaches at the Harvard Business School, the valley is an "existential creation: nobody said 'let's build an entrepreneurial technological center.'" It might never have come about, however, without Fred Terman, a professor of electrical engineering at Stanford University. In 1938, peeved that his students had to go to the east coast to find jobs, he persuaded two of his students, Bill Hewlett and David Packard, to set up a company making electronic measuring equipment in a garage behind Mr. Hewlett's house. In the 1950s Hewlett-Packard, along with several other companies won over by Terman, moved into Stanford University's new industrial park.

Over the next two decades the number of young firms multiplied steadily and attracted a network of specialist suppliers and service companies, including a new breed of venture capitalist. But progress was slow. In 1957, one pioneering venture capitalist, Arthur Rock, tried to find a company to back what became Fairchild Semiconductor, but none of the thirty-five people he approached was keen.

The name "Silicon Valley"—an allusion to its main industry, silicon chips—was invented in 1971 by a local technology journalist. Five years later Apple Computer was born in another garage. The personal-computer revolution was on its way. But the boom lasted only till the mid-1980s, when Silicon Valley's chip industry found itself outclassed by Japanese competitors. The valley responded by revamping its own manufacturing operations, outsourcing many of them, and by diversifying into other areas, particularly computer software.

Since 1992 the valley has been on a roll, adding more than 125,000 jobs and doubling its annual exports to about $40 billion, a fifth of its total output. The chief driving force has been software. This is a huge market (worth some $120 billion world wide this year, according to International Data Corporation), as well as an increasingly diverse one. Software now covers a maze of different industries, including applications software, operating systems, databases, the Internet, computer-aided design, and networking.

But Silicon Valley does not live just on chips and software. According to Collaborative Economics, a local consultancy, its workforce is now distributed among at least seven different industries, including biotechnology and environmental science. The average wage in these "cluster industries" is over $60,000 a year. But then Silicon Valley has the most productive manufacturing employees in America, each accounting for some $114,000 of value added in 1992 (the latest figure available).

The present boom in Silicon Valley seems to be spreading even to its support services. Gunderson Detmer, a law firm founded just three years ago, now has over fifty lawyers. Hambrecht & Quist, Robertson Stephens and Montgomery Securities, San Francisco's leading local financial firms, are all doing roaring business. Even staid accountants have caught the entrepreneurial buzz: the annual staff turnover rate at Price Waterhouse's local software-services group is 25%.

One lesson from this potted history is that entrepreneurial clusters are a long-term investment. It took Hewlett-Packard nearly forty years to reach revenues of $1 billion. But once a cluster gets going, the process speeds up nicely: Netscape, the best-known Internet company, looks set to reach the $1-billion turnover mark in less than five years.

EXPLORING THE READING

1. In your small group, review the cultural elements listed in "Vital Intangibles," beginning with "tolerance of failure." What do you think of the list, particularly items like "tolerance of treachery"?

2. Would you want to live and work in the Silicon Valley or another similar high-tech cluster? Why or why not?

3. Notice that the reading is almost totally favorable toward the Silicon Valley-type environment. Can you think of any negatives that the author should have addressed?

4. Is this American Survey portrait of the Silicon Valley consistent with Michael J. Mandel's "The New Business Cycle"? Why or why not?

WEBSITES: IF YOU BUILD IT, WILL THEY COME?

by Catherine Romano

The World Wide Web has grown explosively in the past few years. From Exxon to Guess Jeans, it seems any company of note has its Web page, though the quality of the content varies widely. Catherine Romano suggests in this Management Review *article that many companies are now taking a closer look at what they have or have not gained by having a Website. She discusses the strengths and weaknesses of the marketing research studies of the Web, and includes three case studies of companies who did online marketing research.*

Romano's recent articles for Management Review *include "Sweatshops of the 1990s," "Working out the Kinks," a story about workman's compensation, and "The New Gold Rush," about marketing on the Internet.*

Companies have been rushing to the Web, but now many are sitting back and analyzing what can be gained. The resulting research is not always projectable, but always illuminating.

It's no news flash that companies are jumping on the World Wide Web at exponential speeds. Consider the progress that has been made in just two short years. In early 1994, no one knew what a Website was. In early 1995, a handful of companies started showing up on the Net, and in 1996, there were more than 100,000 commercial sites.

But in 1996, companies also began to realize that, while the Internet was the place to be, it was not the immediate profit center they had envisioned. In fact, says John Nardone, director of media and research services at Modern Media in Westport, Connecticut, "there were Websites up and no one was coming."

To attract attention to their pages, companies started buying advertising—placing banners on related sites. In theory, it was a good idea. Well-placed ads would certainly stimulate interest that would potentially generate revenue.

But there were drawbacks—namely the cost. Those selling ad space were the only ones really making any money. In addition to design and production costs, companies were now spending additional advertising dollars on the Web. And still they had very little to show for it. "All of the sudden, between online production costs and advertising, companies are spending real money. If they spend $1 million, what's their return on investment?" asks Nardone. "Our clients are spending significant money and they need answers to questions." Specifically, is their Website effective? What should the Website be accomplishing and, furthermore, does it?

Marketers have been trying to find the answers by applying traditional principles of market research to the new medium. Focus groups conducted in chat rooms and online surveys are the current mainstays, but a few adventurous companies are trying new methods. AT&T's college division wanted to do more than focus groups, so they put students in a "reaction theater," equipped with a large-screen monitor and reaction dials. Moderators could walk participants through the Website and students could input their immediate reactions and opinions.

There are, however, some very practical considerations. For instance, only twenty percent of the population is online, which limits the projectability of the sample. Granted, all subsets of the U.S. adult population are represented to some degree online. "They tend to be boomers, wealthier, male, employed, with children, better-educated, regard themselves as smart, fairly social, individualistic," says Charles D'Oyly, director of online research at Yankelovich Partners in Norwalk, Connecticut. But unless a company is working with a very specific target population, the results will not be projectable to the general population.

"There's no point in doing research on anybody unless you know something about the people doing the answers," says Andrew Watt, COO of Cyber Dialogue in New York. If a random sample isn't feasible, marketers have to know how the sample they are working with relates to the general population. For example, if a company chooses to use a sample of 500 mountain bike enthusiasts, it must understand how these cyclists compare to the overall population. Are they older or younger, are there more males than females, and is their income more or less than the average? Then a company can weigh the responses they receive accordingly.

For this reason, says Watt at Cyber Dialogue, most online research tends to be qualitative. "It works well with focus groups, where you don't need general population sample," he says. "If you're a manufacturer and need to set strategy for the next three years and you're only seeking twenty percent of the population. This may not be the best place to design strategy."

If a company is willing to accept working with twenty percent of the population, there will still be difficulties in choosing the sample. Because Internet users are so inclusive, companies could end up with self-selected respondents. Some companies have attempted to do their research by buying a list of e-mail names and randomly sending e-mail questionnaires to a portion of that list. But that is one of the worst options: Too many people will be annoyed by the intrusion, and many will just delete the file without answering the first question. "Sending questionnaires to customers is a whole different game than doing research. You may not get to the right people or the sample may be skewed," says Watt.

Market researchers have to follow the same rules of etiquette that other Internet users should adhere to. On an introductory registration form, they may want to ask for permission to occasionally e-mail a user for feedback. Even with permission, they should be wary of sending large files that would take a long time to download. "This is a unique sort of environment. You have to be careful about understanding the mind-set before charging in— you could turn people off to the product or service," says Nardone.

But there are benefits to online market research, as well. Marketing research, like everything else online, is fast. You can start surveying people and have a reasonable answer in only twenty-four hours. And it's cheaper than traditional methods. "If you're doing a telephone survey, you have huge fielding costs. Nine out of ten phone calls are not there. With e-mail data-bases, eighty percent will respond in twenty-four hours," says Watt. In addition, it's an opportunity to interact with customers, to talk about the company's online presence or even its nonelectronic products and services.

There's the additional benefit of anonymity, especially when sensitive issues are being discussed in chat or focus groups. "You don't have twelve people you've never met in a room talking about homosexuality. You don't get a dominant leader of a big fat guy with Harley Davidson tattoos—everyone gets a chance to have their say," says Watt. You can also use online research because it allows you to include harder-to-reach subjects: CEOs and people who travel frequently but still check their e-mail on a regular basis.

Anonymity begets the question of honesty, however. If there's no possi-bility of being found out, how honest will people be? The consensus among the experts is that there isn't enough incentive to lie. The companies that do offer incentives only offer relatively insignificant ones—say, three hours of commercial service time.

"I'm amazed about how willing people are to give information about themselves," says D'Oyly. As long as the questions are relevant and con-sumers believe their opinions will make a difference, they can be very open.

Here's how three companies gathered information online.

NICK ONLINE

Every Wednesday evening, approximately twenty children nationwide chat on CompuServe about Nickelodeon. Although these chats do not talk about Nickelodeon's site, the medium is particularly useful for the target popu-lation. In fact, the children's entertainment company had launched the chat group three years before it considered a Website. They needed to stay on top of the latest opinions in a timely and effective manner.

It has worked very well. "There's the anonymity of it—not having to answer an adult face to face," says Lynn Lehmkuhl, former publisher of Nickelodeon New Media. This way, the children, ages eight to fourteen, are more apt to answer honestly, and there is less of the typical problems asso-ciated with that age-group. Boys and girls are uncharacteristically talkative with each other, and the younger children aren't as easily intimidated by the teenagers.

Each week, there is a different agenda—copy testing for a new adver-tisement for either their programming or a particular advertiser. Nickelodeon stops just shy of asking about particular products. "We would not ask how often they eat M&Ms, but we will ask questions that would give Mars an indication of where the company might want to go," says Lehmkuhl. For example, they might ask about what types of prizes would be an incentive for a teen to enter a sweepstakes.

On most weeks, approximately 20 children of the 150 registered kids par-ticipate in the chat room, and Nickelodeon takes great care to make certain the sample is representative. "Instead of drawing the sample from kids who have computers and modems—that would be too self-selecting—we pick the sample and then we equip the home," explains Lehmkuhl. Nickelodeon also pays for computer usage and the subscription to CompuServe.

Since Nickelodeon is confident in the representativeness of its sample, it is able to use the results as an internal research tool. It has used the panel to test concepts, including the online version of its brand, as well as the creative execution of advertising and its entry into books.

ELECTRONIC DISCOVERY

Even after Discovery Channel Online launched in July of 1995, it didn't do marketing research online. It was nearly a year later before it realized that the information it could gather online was the perfect way to gauge reaction to its home page.

Specifically, Discovery Channel uses the information from the log files that stamp the time, date, and page accessed for internal auditing. A day's worth of log files can be a veritable gold mine of information if properly managed. Discovery can find out how many people are coming to the site, how often and which pages they visit. Still, log files don't provide information about who the people are from a demographic standpoint. Only their addresses are known. Discovery realized that further research efforts would be limited: Discovery Channel Online didn't have the information necessary to do telephone or mail surveys.

In addition, Discovery Online took advantage of the immediacy of electronic communication. It randomly chose a portion of visitors to each section within its site and interrupted them with a survey. The methodology, which Christopher Grecco, manager of research and planning for Discovery Communications Inc., says it is still improving, was different than most companies, since most sites have a button on the home page that invites a user to give more information. But Grecco didn't want to do what he calls "click here to win a free T-shirt." "We didn't want to incent people because we didn't want them to do the survey just to get something," says Grecco. "Since we weren't giving them anything, we wanted to build a relationship and get information about how we could improve the site," he says.

Instead, they treated the electronic survey as if it were a mail questionnaire. Like a mail survey, there is no opportunity for a moderator to explain questions or ask for elaboration. Therefore, they kept the number of questions brief, interesting, and relevant to the user. "The first questions were open-ended so that it would seem that participants were really helping," says Grecco.

Grecco steered clear of asking specific questions about the television shows because the typical online user is demographically different than the normal cable subscriber. Instead, he asked about demographic information: who the users were, age, income, whether they watched the television channel, how often they think they log on, what they like to do on Discovery Online, and how it can be improved. He then uses the results to help formulate advertising rates. "We can get measurement standards and get numbers to present to advertisers [about the number of visitors]," says Grecco.

TRACKING RESERVATIONS

Holiday Inn probably has a relative advantage over most companies trying to make a place on the Web. People visit its site not to be entertained but because of the value-added it provides. Consumers can go online to make reservations at Holiday Inn properties.

It would seem like a captive audience, but Holiday Inn still needs to stay one step ahead of its competition by knowing who visits their site and what they prefer. Using log data from their Internet accounts, they are currently able to track who is coming to their site and from what region of the world.

According to Helen Edelstein, manager of online/Internet opportunities, it has the most information about their priority club users and business users. "These users fit the demographics of fifty percent of the customer base, which is business travelers [age] 25 to 49, mid- to upper-level management, making over $60,000 to $70,000 a year."

To get further information, Holiday Inn did an online survey to ask about the site, in particular how customers benefited from their site. They did not offer an incentive nor do they know what the response rate was.

In the future, Edelstein hopes to take surveys about customer service. "Right now, it would be too much of a project to do that," she says. "People would be complaining, 'I stayed in the hotel in New York and they didn't bring me my towels when I asked.'" At the moment, Edelstein doesn't want to begin fielding those opinions. Instead, Holiday Inn gets feedback via e-mail addressed to its Webmaster.

EXPLORING THE READING

1. Do you think that having a Web page is a necessity for all companies these days? Why or why not?

2. Have you filled out any demographic or marketing questionnaires at company Websites? If so, what made you take the time to do so?

3. In your small group, discuss the commercial development of the Web in the last few years. Have you noticed changes in how companies are using the Web?

4. Connect to the three Websites mentioned in the article. Do you see evidence of marketing research on them, such as questionnaires? If so, fill one out and report about the experience to the class.

5. Is the rush to develop Websites a symptom of a desire for companies to be perceived as part of the high-tech world? Or do Websites actually enhance profitability? Discuss in your small group.

WRITING SUGGESTIONS

1. Consult your local Chamber of Commerce about industries in your area. Does your area reflect the nationwide trend toward the development of high-tech industries? If so, why? What causes the industries to move or expand there? If your area does not have a high-tech concentration, why is that? Are people in your area satisfied with the kind of industries they have, or do they wish the situation were different? Write an essay about the industrial climate in your area—its causes and its effects.

2. Interview someone who works in a high-tech industry, such as a programmer or executive. What is his or her job like? Does he/she enjoy the work and find it rewarding, or not? Based on your interview and your own research, write a description of what it is like to work in a high-tech industry.

3. Would you want to work in the Silicon Valley or other similar area with a concentration of high-tech industries? Write an essay evaluating the positives and negatives of such a lifestyle.

4. Are Websites really functional for companies? Examine closely a Website for a company in your area, contact the company's publicity office, and arrange an in-person or telephone interview with someone involved in creation or maintenance of the site. Why did they build it? What are the goals for the site? Is it fulfilling their expectations? Write an essay based on what you learn.

5. Investigate the prevalence in your community of women in high-tech industries, consulting your Chamber of Commerce, college placement office, library reference desk, and other sources you may locate. Interview one or more women in high-tech industries. Write an essay based upon your research, discussing opportunities and limitations of high-tech industries for women.

THE WRITING PROCESS:
PARAGRAPH STRUCTURES

Introductions

As you skim through a newspaper, a magazine, or even a collection of essays like this book, what is it about an essay that makes you want to keep reading? Many of you will say, "Because it looks interesting." But what, exactly, are you looking at that looks interesting. Sometimes the title catches your eye. In a newspaper or magazine, it might be an interesting photograph. Often, it is the first sentence or the first paragraph that pulls you in and makes you want to read further.

Interesting introductions are an intentional part of most journalistic writing. The lead, or introduction, needs to grab readers and get them interested. Often that lead is called a *hook*, something the reader will bite so the writer can begin to reveal an important story, argument, or call to action.

An interesting introduction is a requirement for most college writing as well. You want your reader, whether it's your instructor or your peers, to continue to read your essay because you have interested him or her, not only because they *have* to keep reading. Although introductions are placed at the beginning of your essay, they may not be the first things you write. Some writers write the introduction last, after they have read and revised their essay many times. Some authors write their introductions as conclusions to their draft essay. Then they move the conclusion to the beginning of the essay and call it an introduction. Some writers write their introductions before they even write their outlines, using the same facts or impulses that started them writing to get the reader interested in what they have to say.

It doesn't really matter when you write your introduction; it matters only that you are aware of how the introduction can influence the reader of your essay. Then you can write effective, engaging introductions that will make your reader want to continue to read.

Take a look at some of the methods the writers in this book have used to introduce their essays. Often writers use an interesting or startling fact or bit of history to draw the reader's attention to their essays. Mitchell Kapor uses a startling moment in recent history to open his article "Civil Liberties in Cyberspace":

> On March 1, 1990, the U.S. Secret Service raided the offices of Steve Jackson, an entrepreneurial publisher in Austin, Texas. Carrying a search warrant, the authorities confiscated computer hardware and software, the drafts of his about-to-be-released book and many business records of his company, Steve Jackson Games. They also seized an electronic bulletin-board system used by the publisher to communicate with publishers and writers, thereby seizing all the private electronic mail on the system.

"The Valley of Money's Delight" opens with this attention getting narrative:

> Three scruffy young men and a sneakered young woman, each wearing a visitor's badge, sit huddled around a table in the foyer of the Robert Noyce Building at Intel's headquarters in Santa Clara. One of the men stops scribbling on his electronic personal organizer and announces: "We could become extremely rich." "Very possibly," answers the woman in a distracted tone, implying that sooner or later enormous wealth should surely come to everyone.

Ashley Dunn begins his essay "Think of Your Soul as a Market Niche" with a quote from an unlikely source:

> Ronald Reagan has never been known as one of the great pundits of wired life, but he made a surprisingly insightful comment about the nature of the

Information Age years before most people had ever heard of the Internet—or even had a fax machine at home.

"Information is the oxygen of the modern age," he told *The Daily Telegraph of London* in 1989, adding that it "seeps through the walls topped with barbed wire and wafts across the electrified booby-trapped borders. Electronic beams blow through the Iron Curtain as if it were lace."

Even if your entire introduction isn't engaging, you can begin the essay with a startling sentence to grab your reader's interest. Malcolm Gladwell piques our interest in the first line of his essay, "Blowup":

In the technological age, there is a ritual to disaster.

A startling sentence begins Emily Weiner's essay "Reflections of an Online Graduate":

I saw my college for the first time on June 12, 1995, five hours before I graduated.

Paragraph Development
Once you've decided what points you'll cover in your essay, you can probably decide easily which mode of paragraph development will serve your needs best. When instructors talk about essays, they may talk about a comparison/contrast or a narrative essay, and while these essays may use one type of paragraph development throughout, often an essay will take advantage of several types of paragraph development. Even when an essay follows an overall mode, individual paragraphs may use different modes to get their point across.

The argumentative editorial essay "Now, a Word from Cyberspace," for example, uses argumentation as its primary mode, but the effective inclusion of comparison/contrast and exemplification make the essay more interesting and thought-provoking.

Argumentation. *Argumentation* involves taking a solid stand on an issue and supporting that stand with expert testimony, facts and statistics, and logical examples. The purpose of argumentation is to change a reader's opinions on a specific topic or to call a reader to action. Kevin Maney, in "Technowomen," gives an example of argumentation as a method of paragraph development:

Meanwhile, women are missing out on some of the best career paths. Through 2005, the number of computer engineers and systems analysts is expected to grow more than 90%, an increase of 621,576 jobs. Other tech jobs are growing nearly as quickly. College graduates in computer engineering are getting four or more job offers, often starting at $40,000 to $50,000 a year.

Cause and Effect.   Another method of paragraph development is *cause and effect*, an explanation of the cause and subsequent effects or consequences of a specific action, historical period, or sometimes the effects of inaction.

Dennis Kneale develops his argument "Unleashing the Power" by using well-placed cause and effect paragraphs:

> Eager to bank on high technology and panicked at the thought of rivals inno-vating faster, many companies bought technology for technology's sake. Top brass signed the checks with little regard to figuring out what the new gear should do. Businesses automated paper-and-pencil procedures but stopped short of more ambitious goals. They trained workers poorly, and were reluctant to overhaul the organization and redesign jobs to make better use of all that silicon.
>
> So, long after IBM joined the PC revolution in 1981 and the Macintosh promised to be the computer "for the rest of us," many of us are laggards just getting by.

Comparison and Contrast.   *Comparison and contrast* examines the similar-ities and differences between two or more things. In his article "The New Business Cycle," Michael J. Mandel compares the technology industries to the automobile industry:

> But the business cycle has not disappeared. To the contrary: High technology is more volatile than the automobile industry, with the biggest swings driven by new technologies. When the new-product pipeline temporarily slows, as it did in 1985 and 1989, demand can fall sharply. But a hot new technology, such as the Internet, can send sales skyrocketing just as suddenly. "Every time we thought something about our business was less cyclical," says Andrew S. Grove, chief executive of Intel Corp., "the next cycle was bigger than the earlier one."

Definition.   *Definition* uses an explanation of specific meaning of a word, phrase, or idea. Because "home" is such an important aspect of John Seabrook's essay "Home on the Net," he first defines a home in the real world before defining a home on the Net:

> A home in the real world is, among other things, a way of keeping the world out. If you buy space in what used to be a warehouse, gut it, and hire someone to turn it into a home, as my wife and I did, you invite the world into your life for a while, but when the work is done you have walls and a threshold. Of course, you never shut the world out entirely, just as we will never get rid of all the little packets of sugar that the guys who built our loft brought along on the job with their coffee, but at least you have your privacy. It's like being inoculated with a little bit of the world, which makes you better able to survive the whole world.

Description.   *Description* uses vivid sensory details to present a picture or an image to the reader. In this selection from the "Aesthetic of the Computer,"

Daniel Harris uses description to develop a paragraph:

> A close inspection of the screen-saver "Marbles," for instance, reveals that when one of the five marbles represented, a sphere about 1/10-inch in diameter decorated with a Happy Face, caroms off the metal pegs and boomerangs back to the sides of the screen, its mouth opens up into an astonished expression of breathless surprise like a child squealing with delight on an amusement park ride. Details similar to this can be found in even the most commonplace software programs, like the sound of the game-show gong signaling a wrong answer that blares out like taunting laughter when the cursor reaches the bottom of the document in Microsoft.

Exemplification. *Exemplification* uses specific examples to explain, analyze, or define something. Alan Robbins begins his essay with an example that graphically describes a key component of his discussion in "Mad at Your Modem? History Is on Your Side":

> Like most modern doodads, it looked simple. It was the size of a credit card. No gears, dials, or rivets. Slip the modem in, follow some on-screen instructions, and bingo: I'd be surfing the Web in no time.
>
> But four days later, after endless calls to the various help lines, I was nowhere near my e-mail. It was drifting away like flotsam in a digital squall.
>
> I was at the stage I call the "defenestration point," when the operating procedures overwhelm our ability to absorb them and frustration is so high that we're ready to toss a device out the window.

Narration. *Narration* uses a story or vignette to illustrate a specific point or examine an issue. John Gehl uses narration effectively in his "Diary of a Telecommuter":

> *19th.* All the morning in my office. Various telephone conversations, with people wanting to arrange consulting projects. "Is that a cat I hear?" a potential client asks me. "Do you have a cat in your office?" "No," I assure him, "not a cat. Not really." "It sounds like a cat," he insists. "If it's not a cat, what is it?" "It's a chair!" I tell him. "Listen—I'll swivel in my chair, and you'll think you're hearing a cat." Butch, blessed be God, meows on cue. "You're right," says the client happily, "Your chair sounds just like a cat!" Butch has been much on my nerves today, and I feel very tired. I want to quit for the day and go home, and I start to do that, before realizing sadly that I am *already* at home.

Conclusions

The ending of your essay should leave the reader satisfied that you have covered everything you needed to and that you've shared an insight. A good conclusion does two things: it summarizes the essay and/or it provides the reader with a sense of closure.

To summarize your essay, you don't need to repeat your thesis or hit the highlights of the things you've covered in your essay. You can summarize by tying everything together with a short phrase. If your essay is about your frustrations with e-mail, you might summarize your essay effectively by saying, "For now, I'll stick with snail mail." However you choose to summarize your essay, remember, you are not repeating your arguments, only giving the reader a sentence or two to remind him or her of the arguments you've made.

In some essays, a summary may not be necessary. You won't need to reiterate your main points because the essay was short, or the main points might be too complex to cover in a facile summary. In that case, you still need a conclusion. The conclusion should provide the reader with a sense of closure. It should make the reader feel satisfied that the essay ends where it does. You don't want the reader turning the page, looking for more information after they've read your conclusion. A conclusion doesn't need to be long. In some cases, it doesn't even need to be a separate paragraph. You might write a line or two to provide a sense of closure that can be logically placed at the end of your last body paragraph. Take a look at how some of the authors in this text have successfully concluded their essays.

Robert J. Samuelson ends his "Requiem for a Typewriter" by stating that he keeps waiting for something to entice him to become a computer buff, but it hasn't happened.

> Until then, I'm sticking with my Royal [typewriter]. It won't give me e-mail. But I don't want e-mail. Nor will it play games when I ought to write. Good. Getting parts is a problem. My local repair shop recently closed. I've now found a new one about twenty miles away that, although it handles mostly electronic machines, will still fix manuals. The manager tells me on the phone that there aren't many manual customers left. Well, there's one more coming.

Michael Grosso's essay, "Technology as a Psychic Phenomenon," suggests that the technological, like the psychic, attempts to eliminate constraints of time and space, in effect to simulate godlike qualities. In his conclusion, Grosso explains the problem of unlimited psychic or technological power:

> Unfortunately, this project of extending human abilities to godlike proportions is flawed. For the psychic and the technical models of transformation are mainly about power; they fail, in important ways, to reach the level of spirit. They offer no guarantee of a world any different than the one we're familiar with, a mix of the marvelous and the horrible. The only difference is that the marvels and the horrors will be more spectacular.

Steve Lohr ends his article "A New Battlefield: Rethinking Warfare in the Computer Age" with a quote from a Citibank official about pursuing hackers who might want to disrupt their electronic banking system, "You mess with us and we're going after you," Crook said. "This is a big deal for us now."

ACCESSING INTERNET RESOURCES

Using Usenet Newsgroups

Usenet Newsgroups are a collection of more than 30,000 discussion groups on every topic imaginable. Usenet predates the World Wide Web, but one of the easiest ways to access Usenet Newsgroups is through the Web, and you can use any browser to do so. In the Internet Explorer version 3.02, for example, you go to the **Mail** menu, and **select Read News**.

A list of subscribed Newsgroups will display. If you haven't subscribed to any, or want to look at other groups, click on **Newsgroups**. You will see a box in which you can scroll through the names of the Newsgroups or indicate a topic. If you were interested in jobs, for example, you could enter that word and see a list of groups with the word **job** included.

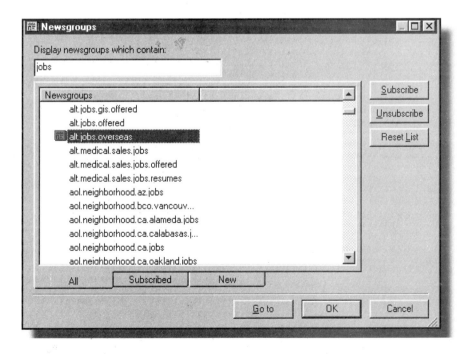

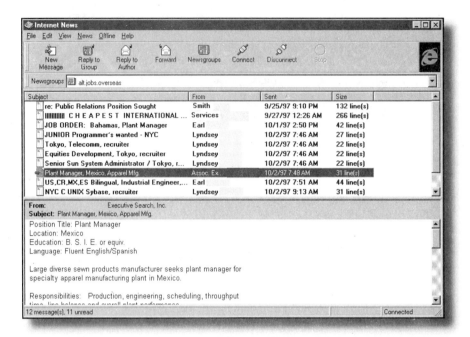

Select a group, such as **alt.jobs.overseas**. Click on **Go to**, and you will see another box with a list of messages from this group in the upper portion. Click on a message, and it will be displayed in the lower portion of the screen.

Other versions of Internet Explorer may access Usenet Newsgroups somewhat differently. Go to the **Help** menu, and look for **News** or **Newgroups** to learn how to access groups.

SUGGESTED INTERNET ASSIGNMENTS

1. Connect to Usenet Newgroups and browse through groups with the words **biz** or **business** in their titles. Locate two groups which are of interest in relation to this chapter and report about them to the class.

2. Explore some online versions of business publications such as *Fortune* which can be found on the Pathfinder site, http://www.pathfinder.com, or *Upside*, http://www.upside.com. Find an article about a high-tech company and bring it to class.

3. Look at the home page of a high-tech company such as the Microsoft home page, http://home.microsoft.com, and consider how the collection of Web pages project an image for the company.

WIRED TO THE WEB

Fortune Magazine
http://www.pathfinder.com

Fortune is one of a number of business magazines which offer selected full-text articles online. *Fortune* is located at the Pathfinder (Time Warner) site. You can search the archives by subject or browse the tables of contents for recent issues.

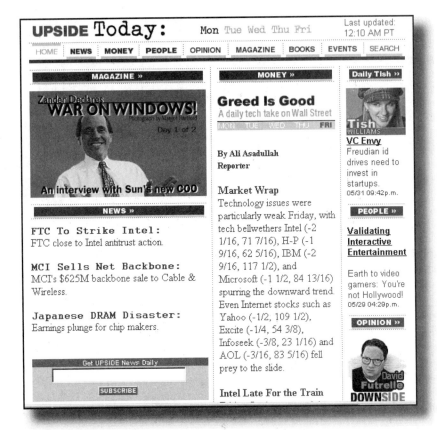

Upside
http://www.upside.com

A magazine focusing on high-tech industries, *Upside* follows the Silicon Valley companies and business leaders. Search the archives, check out the reviews of high-tech conferences, or read the latest on computer and software companies.

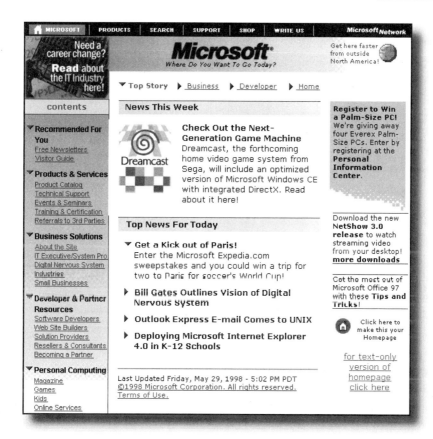

Microsoft Home Page
http://home.microsoft.com

The Microsoft Internet Explorer home page is an excellent example of a high-budget corporate site. Microsoft wants you to make this page your default start page for your browser and offers links to resources as an inducement. Explore the Microsoft page and the links, noticing how the page projects an image of the company. Notice also how Microsoft's Internet Explorer, through this page, is a gateway to all Microsoft products and services.

CHALLENGES OF TECHNOLOGY

Tape that one episode of the original *Star Trek* that you've never seen. No problem. You have a VCR, right? Wrong. Many Americans are VCR-challenged, able to play videos but, when they try to tape, finding that they recorded the latest *Oprah* rather than *Larry King*. But today, being VCR-challenged is the least part of the problem. Technology is everywhere, and unless you execute seemingly secret moves in the right order, you can't get money from your ATM or print with your new printer. And even when you have all the knowledge, and make all the necessary preparations, the technology can evaporate on you. Michael Malone, in "Stage Fright Is Nothing Compared with This," claims that—at least so far as high-tech business presentations are concerned—there is a correlation between the complexity of the technology and the likelihood of glitches which turn failed video clips into unrehearsed story time.

Such challenges aren't new, according to Alan Robbins in "Mad at Your Modem? History Is on Your Side." New technology is always frustrating and confusing, he claims. He labels as the "defenestration point" that moment when you want to take an offending machine you can't make work and throw it out the window. Relax, he advises, and let habits catch up with ingenuity.

Donald Norman would disagree about relaxation being a solution to frustrations with technology. In "The Psychopathology of Everyday Things" he says that many high-tech machines we encounter in everyday life are badly designed. Norman, an industrial psychologist, often sees people shaking their heads over a modern device such as a digital watch and saying, "You would need an engineering degree from MIT to work this." Norman has an engineering degree from

MIT and says he wouldn't know how to operate such a watch without a few hours study. The problem, according to Norman, is that everyday things should contain within themselves visual and other cues which help first-time users figure out how to operate them. Too often, they don't.

Problems with technology aren't always humorous or harmless. Malcolm Gladwell in "Blowup" discusses disasters such as the explosion of the Challenger space shuttle which are due to technological failures. Gladwell suggests that a growing number of experts are arguing that such accidents are inevitable considering the complexity of the technology involved. With a machine like the space shuttle, many things can go wrong at any moment. It may be possible to fix design flaws once discovered, but it may not be possible to discover and deal with all potential problems before a disaster occurs. Do we just live with acceptance of a margin of error, even when it is deadly? The only other option is not building and using such complex machines.

What is your perception of the technology around you? Is it useful, sometimes pleasurable? Or is it inexplicable and frustrating? Even dangerous? Are you able to program your VCR? What about your digital watch or your microwave? Are you among the technologically savvy or the technophobic? Or are you somewhere in between? As you read the following texts, examine the machines around you in everyday life and determine your attitudes toward them. To what degree are you challenged by technology?

———————————■———————————

STAGE FRIGHT IS NOTHING COMPARED WITH THIS

by Michael S. Malone

When you move beyond the slide projector and overhead projectors, way beyond, into the arena of multimedia, computer enhancement, and Internet connections, you may be more effective—as long as the technology works. The more advanced and complex business presentations technology becomes, the more likely the presentation is going to develop gliches, according to Michael S. Malone in this column from "The Executive Life" in The New York Times. *Malone interviewed executives who have given high-tech speeches and consultants who advise executives on how to create their presentations. According to one consultant, it is the simple things like a loose power cord that turn presentations costing thousands of dollars from impressive to laughable.*

Malone is coauthor of The Virtual Corporation: Structuring and Revitalizing the Corporation for the 21st Century *and author of* The Big Score: The Billion Dollar Story of Silicon Valley. *Malone's articles and editorials have appeared in* The New York Times, The Wall Street Journal, The Economist, The Los Angeles Times, *and the* San Jose Mercury-News.

"It's a combination of quantum mechanics, Murphy's Law, and karma," Andrew J. Shinnick said. "The more technologically complicated you make your presentation, the greater the chances of it going south on you."

Mr. Shinnick was talking about an experience common to anyone who makes or attends business presentations these days: the expensive, high-technology speech that lapses into embarrassed silence when some vital piece of hardware or software crashes.

As the president of Dagaz Communications in San Francisco, Mr. Shinnick helps corporate clients prepare electronic materials for speeches and other public presentations. He has seen the transformation of the standard business news conference or trade show keynote speech from simple presentations aided by a few overhead slides to multimedia extravaganzas that may include videos, laser disks, projection televisions, and computers.

In the process, Mr. Shinnick has also seen just about everything that can go wrong. "Usually, it's the simplest things that kill you, like the VCR with the loose power cable or hidden on-off switch," he said. "Next thing you know, you're standing alone in front of an angry audience suffering a thousand deaths."

Ronald Oklewicz, president and chief executive of the Telepad Corporation, a maker of handheld data entry systems in Reston, Virginia, knows whereof Mr. Shinnick speaks. As a speaker at a recent conference, Mr. Oklewicz could not put his computer presentation on the video projection system because of mismatched cables. And then he watched a fellow speaker vamp for five minutes, waiting for a VCR to work.

"It's usually not the failure of the technology itself," he said, "but of the interface between the people and the technology."

After spending $200,000 on a sophisticated video for an industry convention, a large law firm that is now a client of Dagaz had a similar nightmare. "The tape started, and there was no audio," Mr. Shinnick said. "A thousand people in the audience just sat there, ready to laugh. Luckily, the speaker had the presence to just start ad-libbing subtitles. Most people would have fainted."

Many executives prefer to talk about the horrors they have seen rather than the fiascos of which they have been a part. Michael Sears, general manager of Sunsoft Inc., a subsidiary of Sun Microsystems in Mountain View, California, recalls one impressive disaster during an expensive multimedia presentation he attended at a hotel in Singapore, for which Japanese and Chinese journalists had been flown in.

"Unfortunately, the room got warm from all the people, and the air-conditioner went on," he said. "That in turn blew open the curtains, which let in this brilliant light that completely washed out the screen. Finally, two vice presidents went over and held the curtains closed for the rest of the presentation."

But by then, Mr. Sears said, no one was watching the show. "Instead," he recalled, "they were watching two guys who make a quarter million dollars a year working as curtain closers."

William Reichert, vice president of the Academic Systems Corporation, a maker of interactive multimedia instructional software for colleges also based in Mountain View, recalled a recent conference at which there were presentations about four new technology products. "Not a single presentation worked," he said. "It was not exactly the message those companies wanted to make. It was also a sad commentary on the state of the art."

So why use all this technology? Audience expectations, for one thing. For sheer incongruity, Mr. Reichert said, few things match the executive of a multimedia company giving a speech using acetate overheads.

Technology also takes on a life of its own. "The propeller heads live for this stuff," Mr. Shinnick said, using a popular term for computer specialists. "So they always try to push the envelope. And they convince their bosses it will work."

Some executives have only themselves to blame. Mr. Reichert recently returned from a disaster at a national community college. There, he said, the presenter, obviously obsessed with the new technology, appeared "to be using every single feature of the presentational software. Message windows were flying back and forth across the screen until everybody was dizzy."

What do these executives recommend to those facing multimedia Waterloos?

"When you can, do your own setup and use the best people you've got," said Thomas M. Siebel, chief executive of Siebel Systems Inc., a developer of sales automation software in Menlo Park, California. His staff watched in horror recently as Mr. Siebel, in the course of a speech, leaned against the television projector, thus threatening to turn the screen image to mud. But their job of reinforcing the projector lived up to Mr. Siebel's expectations, and it held steady.

Mr. Reichert, who gives dozens of presentations a year, has minimized his equipment requirements by putting all the data onto a computer disk drive that he carries with him to each client.

And Mr. Shinnick urges many clients to "commit everything to videotape, carry a backup copy, and take your own VCR with you." Stay away from fancy new equipment; he said, and check out the site in advance.

"You can spend tens of thousands of dollars on a presentation," he said, "only to have it shot down by a 1950s sound system, an incompatible video system, or a guy in the control room moonlighting from the local Ace TV repair service."

EXPLORING THE READING

1. Have you ever given a business or class presentation with some type of visual aid? What was it like? Did you ever have difficulty?

2. In your small group, discuss the problems and solutions that Michael S. Malone discusses. What would you do if you needed to give a high-profile presentation? Would you use high-tech aids? What precautions would you take?

3. What is the tone of Malone's column? Is it appropriate for his purposes?

MAD AT YOUR MODEM? HISTORY
IS ON YOUR SIDE

by Alan Robbins

Although we have a tendency to idealize our ancestors' relationships with new technology, according to Alan Robbins in this essay from The New York Times, *we have always had problems with machines. From the vacuum tube in televisions to the weighted carriages in old typewriters, any technological advance brings a multitude of problems when it is first introduced. The first clue for impending problems, Robbins suggests, is the salesman's age-old words, "No problem."*

Alan Robbins directs the Design Studio and teaches visual communication at Kean College in New Jersey.

I sensed trouble the moment I heard those fateful words, "no problem." The salesman was referring to the modem he had just sold me. "Installs in minutes," he promised. "It's a snap."

Like most modern doodads, it looked simple. It was the size of a credit card. No gears, dials, or rivets. Slip the modem in, follow some on-screen instructions, and bingo: I'd be surfing the Web in no time.

But four days later, after endless calls to the various help lines, I was nowhere near my e-mail. It was drifting away like flotsam in a digital squall.

I was at the stage I call the "defenestration point," when the operating procedures overwhelm our ability to absorb them and frustration is so high that we're ready to toss a device out the window.

I'm sure you have similar tales—not just about computers, but about every new contraption you buy. The jiffy setup seems to have taken an early exit off the information highway.

Why do machines seem to be getting harder to use rather than easier? Is it because of their evolution into more complex life forms, or because of our devolution into a dumber one?

Neither. The problem is the delusion that things were ever different. New technology is always bewildering. The relationship between humans and machines involves a continuing struggle of adjustment that is especially intense at first.

In the dim myth of the past, everyone's first television set was easy to set up. It looked like a piece of furniture and was supposed to function with the same simplicity. Plug it in, turn it on, and welcome Milton Berle into your living room.

Not quite. I remember everyone in my family fiddling with the volume, channel, and horizontal- and vertical-control knobs. Not to mention that ring around the channel selector whose function we could never quite grasp. And then there was the arcane artistry of adjusting the rabbit ears. Remember test patterns? Managing the reception was so formidable that it was left to an expert: my father. Despite the dire warning, my mother even opened the back of the television and vacuumed out the dust. The picture actually improved.

Even as machines are redesigned to be more efficient, the defenestration point stays with us. A device may not become more complex, but it is sure to become more multiplex. Today's television sets are easier to use, but they are now only one piece in an intricate web of components. In place of antenna adjustment, we get the Medusa of wires hooking together the cable-ready television, the cable box, the videocassette recorder, and that baffling A/B switch. Even with my genetic predisposition—remember, my mother once vacuumed a vacuum tube and lived—I had to call in the cable guy when I reached the defenestration point on that one.

The telephone also looks deceptively simple. Pick up the handset and dial a number. Yet it is common now, especially in offices, to have to ask someone how to make a call before you can complete one. For the inaugural call on my new cellular phone (to my wife, ten feet away in the next room) I had to dial in three separate phone numbers, navigate a voice-mail system, create and input my code, dial back to verify, then tap in a long string of numbers, including the number I was calling.

Five tries later, after studying the instructions as an Apollo astronaut would, I still couldn't get through and had to start over the next day.

But don't blame microchips for the problem. The moment that the telephone went beyond its basic use of placing a single call to a waiting respondent, there was trouble. That sets the defenestration point for the telephone a few months after Bell's first demonstrations. In those days, the challenges included manipulating the earpiece and mouthpiece, and carrying on a disembodied conversation.

Consider this segment from an 1877 advertisement for the new invention: "After speaking, transfer the telephone from the mouth to the ear very promptly. When replying to communication from another, do not speak too promptly. Much trouble is caused from both parties' speaking at the same time. When you are not speaking, you should be listening."

Yet, we still gaze out the window and dream of a simpler past. We imagine nineteenth century typists, for example, easily knocking out a few pages on their labor-saving devices. Not so. They had to stop frequently to readjust paper, unjam type bars, unsnarl ribbons, and clean smears.

Before the Q-W-E-R-T-Y layout was patented in 1878, every typewriter had a different keyboard. And it was common to have to stop working to re-attach the weight that turned the carriage, which frequently snapped off its string and landed on the typist's foot.

So next time you reach the defenestration point, step back and relax. It isn't conspiracy or stupidity that's doing you in. It's simply ingenuity moving faster than habit. Evolution. The natural order of things.

EXPLORING THE READING

1. Do you agree with Robbins that machines seem to get harder rather than easier to operate? Why or why not? What machines could you use as an example to support your opinion?

2. In your small group, discuss the "defenestration point." How does Robbins define it? Have you ever experienced it? Tell a story of reaching the defenestration point to your small group.

THE PSYCHOPATHOLOGY OF EVERYDAY THINGS

by Donald Norman

The human mind is designed to make sense of the world. Well-designed technologies make use of this tendency and offer clues as to how they work. Unfortunately, according to Donald Norman, many high-tech machines are not well designed. Consider the modern phone system. In years past phones had a hold button that would blink when a call was waiting. Contemporary systems usually offer no such clues, and users generally don't understand how all the complicated features work. Indeed, so many things are so poorly designed that Norman, in this excerpt from his book The Psychology of Everyday Things, *suggests that they are psychopathological.*

Norman, a psychologist and professor at universities including San Diego State University and the University of Pennsylvania, has written both scholarly and popular books, including Perspectives on Cognitive Science, Human Learning and Memory, *and* Explorations in Cognition.

Kenneth Olsen, the engineer who founded and still runs Digital Equipment Corp., confessed at the annual meeting that he can't figure out how to heat a cup of coffee in the company's microwave oven.

YOU WOULD NEED AN ENGINEERING DEGREE TO FIGURE THIS OUT

"You would need an engineering degree from MIT to work this," someone once told me, shaking his head in puzzlement over his brand new digital watch. Well, I have an engineering degree from MIT. (Kenneth Olsen has two of them, and he can't figure out a microwave oven.) Give me a few hours and I can figure out the watch. But why should it take hours? I have talked with many people who can't use all the features of their washing machines or cameras, who can't figure out how to work a sewing machine or a video cassette recorder, who habitually turn on the wrong stove burner.

Why do we put up with the frustrations of everyday objects, with objects that we can't figure out how to use, with those neat plastic-wrapped packages that seem impossible to open, with doors that trap people, with washing machines and dryers that have become too confusing to use, with audio-stereo-television-video-cassette-recorders that claim in their advertisements to do everything, but that make it almost impossible to do anything?

The human mind is exquisitely tailored to make sense of the world. Give it the slightest clue and off it goes, providing explanation, rationalization, understanding. Consider the objects—books, radios, kitchen appliances, office machines, and light switches—that make up our everyday lives. Well-designed objects are easy to interpret and understand. They contain visible clues to their operation. Poorly designed objects can be difficult and frustrating to use. They provide no clues—or sometimes false clues. They trap the user and thwart the normal process of interpretation and understanding. Alas, poor design predominates. The result is a world filled with frustration, with objects that cannot be understood, with devices that lead to error. This book is an attempt to change things.

THE FRUSTRATIONS OF EVERYDAY LIFE

If I were placed in the cockpit of a modern jet airliner, my inability to perform gracefully and smoothly would neither surprise nor bother me. But I shouldn't have trouble with doors and switches, water faucets and stoves. "Doors?" I can hear the reader saying, "you have trouble opening doors?" Yes. I push doors that are meant to be pulled, pull doors that should be pushed, and walk into doors that should be slid. Moreover, I see others having the same troubles—unnecessary troubles. There are psychological principles that can be followed to make these things understandable and usable.

Consider the door. There is not much you can do to a door: you can open it or shut it. Suppose you are in an office building, walking down a corridor. You come to a door. In which direction does it open? Should you pull or push, on the left or the right? Maybe the door slides. If so, in which direction? I have seen doors that slide up into the ceiling. A door poses only two essential questions: In which direction does it move? On which side should one work it? The answers should be given by the design, without any need for words or symbols, certainly without any need for trial and error.

> A friend told me of the time he got trapped in the doorway of a post office in a European city. The entrance was an imposing row of perhaps six glass swinging doors, followed immediately by a second, identical row. That's a standard design: it helps reduce the airflow and thus maintain the indoor temperature of the building.
>
> My friend pushed on the side of one of the leftmost pair of outer doors. It swung inward, and he entered the building. Then, before he could get to the next row of doors, he was distracted and turned around for an instant. He didn't realize it at the time, but he had moved slightly to the right. So when he came to the next door and pushed it, nothing happened. "Hmm," he thought, "must be locked." So he pushed the side of the adjacent door. Nothing. Puzzled, my friend decided to go outside again. He turned around and pushed against the side of a door. Nothing. He pushed the adjacent door. Nothing. The door he had just entered no longer worked. He turned around once more and tried the inside doors again. Nothing. Concern, then mild panic. He was trapped! Just then, a group of people on the other side of the entranceway (to my friend's right) passed easily through both sets of doors. My friend hurried over to follow their path.
>
> How could such a thing happen? A swinging door has two sides. One contains the supporting pillar and the hinge, the other is unsupported. To open the door, you must push on the unsupported edge. If you push on the hinge

side, nothing happens. In this case, the designer aimed for beauty, not utility. No distracting lines, no visible pillars, no visible hinges. So how can the ordinary user know which side to push on? While distracted, my friend had moved toward the (invisible) supporting pillar, so he was pushing the doors on the hinged side. No wonder nothing happened. Pretty doors. Elegant. Probably won a design prize.

The door story illustrates one of the most important principles of design: *visibility*. The correct parts must be visible, and they must convey the correct message. With doors that push, the designer must provide signals that naturally indicate where to push. These need not destroy the aesthetics. Put a vertical plate on the side to be pushed, nothing on the other. Or make the supporting pillars visible. The vertical plate and supporting pillars are *natural* signals, *naturally* interpreted, without any need to be conscious of them. I call the use of natural signals *natural design*. . . .

Visibility problems come in many forms. My friend, trapped between the glass doors, suffered from a lack of clues that would indicate what part of a door should be operated. Other problems concern the *mappings* between what you want to do and what appears to be possible, another topic that will be expanded upon throughout the book. Consider one type of slide projector. This projector has a single button to control whether the slide tray moves forward or backward. One button to do two things? What is the mapping? How can you figure out how to control the slides? You can't. Nothing is visible to give the slightest hint. Here is what happened to me in one of the many unfamiliar places I've lectured in during my travels as a professor:

> The Leitz slide projector . . . has shown up several times in my travels. The first time, it led to a rather dramatic incident. A conscientious student was in charge of showing my slides. I started my talk and showed the first slide. When I finished with the first slide and asked for the next, the student carefully pushed the control button and watched in dismay as the tray backed up, slid out of the projector and plopped off the table onto the floor, spilling its entire contents. We had to delay the lecture fifteen minutes while I struggled to reorganize the slides. It wasn't the student's fault. It was the fault of the elegant projector. With only one button to control the slide advance, how could one switch from forward to reverse? Neither of us could figure out how to make the control work.
>
> All during the lecture the slides would sometimes go forward, sometimes backward. Afterward, we found the local technician, who explained it to us. A brief push of the button and the slide would go forward, a long push and it would reverse. (Pity the conscientious student who kept pushing it hard—and long—to make sure that the switch was making contact.) What an elegant design. Why, it managed to do two functions with only one button! But how was a first-time user of the projector to know this?

As another example, consider the beautiful Amphithéâtre Louis-Laird in the Paris Sorbonne, which is filled with magnificent paintings of great figures in French intellectual history. (The mural on the ceiling shows lots of naked women floating about a man who is valiantly trying to read a book. The painting is right side up only for the lecturer—it is upside down for all the people in the audience.) The room is a delight to lecture in, at least until you ask for the projection screen to be lowered. "Ah," says the professor in charge, who gestures to the technician, who runs out of the room, up a short flight of stairs, and out of sight behind a solid wall. The screen comes down and stops. "No, no," shouts the professor, "a little bit more." The screen comes down again, this time too much. "No, no, no!" the professor jumps up and down and gestures wildly. It's a lovely room, with lovely paintings. But why can't the person who is trying to lower or raise the screen see what he is doing?

New telephone systems have proven to be another excellent example of incomprehensible design. No matter where I travel, I can count upon finding a particularly bad example.

When I visited Basic Books, the publishers of this book, I noticed a new telephone system. I asked people how they liked it. The question unleashed a torrent of abuse. "It doesn't have a hold function," one woman complained bitterly—the same complaint people at my university made about their rather different system. In older days, business phones always had a button labeled "hold." You could push the button and hang up the phone without losing the call on your line. Then you could talk to a colleague, or pick up another telephone call, or even pick up the call at another phone with the same telephone number. A light on the hold button indicated when the function was in use. It was an invaluable tool for business. Why didn't the new phones at Basic Books or in my university have a hold function, if it is so essential? Well, they did, even the very instrument the woman was complaining about. But there was no easy way to discover the fact, nor to learn how to use it.

The telephone hold situation illustrates a number of different problems. One of them is simply poor instructions, especially a failure to relate the new functions to the similarly named functions that people already know about. Second, and more serious, is the lack of visibility of the operation of the system. The new telephones, for all their added sophistication, lack both the hold button and the flashing light of the old ones. The hold is signified by an arbitrary action: dialing an arbitrary sequence of digits (*8, or *99, or what have you: it varies from one phone system to another). Third, there is no visible outcome of the operation.

TWENTY THOUSAND EVERYDAY THINGS

There are an amazing number of everyday things, perhaps twenty thousand of them. Are there really that many? Start by looking about you. There are light fixtures, bulbs, and sockets; wall plates and screws; clocks, watches, and watchbands. There are writing devices (I count twelve in front of me, each different in function, color, or style). There are clothes, with different functions, openings, and flaps. Notice the variety of materials and pieces. Notice the variety of fasteners—buttons, zippers, snaps, laces. Look at all the furniture and food utensils: all those details, each serving some function for manufacturability, usage, or appearance. Consider the work area: paper clips, scissors, pads of paper, magazines, books, bookmarks. In the room I'm working in, I counted more than a hundred specialized objects before I tired. Each is simple, but each requires its own method of operation, each has to be learned, each does its own specialized task, and each has to be designed separately. Furthermore, many of the objects are made of many parts. A desk stapler has sixteen parts, a household iron fifteen, the simple bathtub-shower combination twenty-three. You can't believe these simple objects have so many parts? Here are the eleven basic parts to a sink: drain, flange (around the drain), pop-up stopper, basin, soap dish, overflow vent, spout, lift rod, fittings, hot-water handle, and cold-water handle. We can count even more if we start taking the faucets, fittings, and lift rods apart. . . .

PITY THE POOR DESIGNER

Designing well is not easy. The manufacturer wants something that can be produced economically. The store wants something that will be attractive to its customers. The purchaser has several demands. In the store, the purchaser focuses on price and appearance, and perhaps on prestige value. At home, the same person will pay more attention to functionality and usability. The repair service cares about maintainability: how easy is the device to take apart, diagnose, and service? The needs of those concerned are different and often conflict. Nonetheless, the designer may be able to satisfy everyone.

A simple example of good design is the $3\frac{1}{2}$-inch magnetic diskette for computers, a small circle of "floppy" magnetic material encased in hard plastic. Earlier types of floppy disks did not have this plastic case, which protects the magnetic material from abuse and damage. A sliding metal cover protects the delicate magnetic surface when the diskette is not in use and automatically opens when the diskette is inserted into the computer. The diskette has a square shape: there are apparently eight possible ways to insert it into the machine, only one of which is correct. What happens if I do it wrong? I try inserting the disk side-ways. Ah, the designer thought of that. A little study shows that the case really isn't square: it's rectangular, so you can't insert a longer side. I try backward. The diskette goes in only part of the way. Small protrusions, indentations, and cutouts prevent the diskette from being inserted backward or upside down: of the eight ways one might try to insert the diskette, only one is correct, and only that one will fit. An excellent design.

Take another example of good design. My felt-tipped marking pen has ribs along only one of its sides; otherwise all sides look identical. Careful examination shows that the tip of the marker is angled and makes the best line if the marker is held with the ribbed side up, a natural result if the forefinger rests upon the ribs. No harm results if I hold the marker another way, but the marker writes less well. The ribs are a subtle design cue—functional, yet visibly and aesthetically unobtrusive.

The world is permeated with small examples of good design, with the amazing details that make important differences in our lives. Each detail was added by some person, a designer, carefully thinking through the uses of the device, the ways that people abuse things, the kinds of errors that can get made, and the functions that people wish to have performed.

Then why is it that so many good design ideas don't find their way into products in the marketplace? Or something good shows up for a short time, only to fall into oblivion? I once spoke with a designer about the frustrations of trying to get the best product out:

> It usually takes five or six attempts to get a product right. This may be acceptable in an established product, but consider what it means in a new one. Suppose a company wants to make a product that will perhaps make a real difference. The problem is that if the product is truly revolutionary, it is unlikely that anyone will quite know how to design it right the first time; it will take several tries. But if a product is introduced into the marketplace and fails, well that is it. Perhaps it could be introduced a second time, or maybe even a third time, but after that it is dead: everyone believes it to be a failure.
>
> I asked him to explain. "You mean," I said, "that it takes five or six tries to get an idea right?"
>
> "Yes," he said "at least that."
>
> "But," I replied, "you also said that if a newly introduced product doesn't catch on in the first two or three times, then it is dead?"
>
> "Yup," he said.
>
> "Then new products are almost guaranteed to fail, no matter how good the idea."
>
> "Now you understand," said the designer. "Consider the use of voice messages on complex devices such as cameras, soft-drink machines, and copiers. A failure. No longer even tried. Too bad. It really is a good idea, for it can be very useful when the hands or eyes are busy elsewhere. But those first few attempts were very badly done and the public scoffed—properly. Now, nobody dares try it again, even in those places where it is needed."

THE PARADOX OF TECHNOLOGY

Technology offers the potential to make life easier and more enjoyable; each new technology provides increased benefits. At the same time, added complexities arise to increase our difficulty and frustration. The development of a technology tends to follow a U-shaped curve of complexity: starting high; dropping to a low, comfortable level; then climbing again. New kinds of devices are complex and difficult to use. As technicians become more competent and an industry matures, devices become simpler, more reliable, and more powerful. But then, after the industry has stabilized, newcomers figure out how to add increased power and capability, but always at the expense of added complexity and sometimes decreased reliability. We can see the curve of complexity in the history of the watch, radio, telephone, and television set. Take the radio. In the early days, radios were quite complex.

To tune in a station required several adjustments, including one for the antenna, one for the radio frequency, one for intermediate frequencies, and controls for both sensitivity and loudness. Later radios were simpler and had controls only to turn it on, tune the station, and adjust the loudness. But the latest radios are again very complex, perhaps even more so than early ones. Now the radio is called a tuner, and it is littered with numerous controls, switches, slide bars, lights, displays, and meters. The modern sets are technologically superior, offering higher quality sound, better reception, and enhanced capability. But what good is the technology if it is too complex to use?

The design problem posed by technological advances is enormous. Consider the watch. A few decades ago, watches were simple. All you had to do was set the time and keep them wound. The standard control was the stem: a knob at the side of the watch. Turning the knob wound the spring that worked the watch. Pulling the knob out and turning it made the hands move. The operations were easy to learn and easy to do. There was a reasonable relation between the turning of the knob and the resulting turning of the hands. The design even took into account human error: the normal position of the stem was for winding the spring, so that an accidental turn would not reset the time.

In the modern digital watch the spring is gone, replaced by a motor run by long-lasting batteries. All that remains is the task of setting the watch. The stem is still a sensible solution, for you can go fast or slow, forward or backward, until the exact desired time is reached. But the stem is more complex (and therefore more expensive) than simple push-button switches. If the only change in the transition from the spring-wound analog watch to the battery-run digital watch was in how the time was set, there would be little difficulty. The problem is that new technology has allowed us to add more functions to the watch: the watch can give the day of the week, the month, and the year; it can act as a stop watch (which itself has several functions), a count-down timer, and an alarm clock (or two); it has the ability to show the time for different time zones; it can act is a counter and even as a calculator. But the added functions cause problems: How do you design a watch that has so many functions while trying to limit the size, cost, and complexity of the device? How many buttons does it take to make the watch workable and learnable, yet not too expensive? There are no easy answers. Whenever the number of functions and required operations exceeds the number of controls, the design becomes arbitrary, unnatural, and complicated. The same technology that simplifies life by providing more functions in each device also complicates life by making the device harder to learn, harder to use. This is the paradox of technology.

The paradox of technology should never be used as an excuse for poor design. It is true that as the number of options and capabilities of any device increases, so too must the number and complexity of the controls. But the principles of good design can make complexity manageable.

EXPLORING THE READING

1. Have you experienced difficulty getting things like a microwave, VCR, or telephone system to perform? In your small group, make a list of these machines.

2. Donald Norman labels poor design as *psychopathological*. Freewrite for five minutes about your reaction. Would you agree with him?

3. Would Norman and Alan Robbins, the author of the previous essay, agree? Why or why not?

4. Norman acknowledges some everyday objects are well designed. In your small group, compile a list from Norman's essay and your own experience.

BLOWUP

by Malcolm Gladwell

In this essay, originally published in The New Yorker, *Malcolm Gladwell says that we have developed a ritual for disaster that helps us mold our experiences into a set of rules and precautions that we can take to avoid risks. "But what if," he asks, "the assumptions that underlie our disaster rituals aren't true?" According to many new theorists, he says, high-tech accidents are unavoidable due to the complexity of our new systems.*

Malcolm Gladwell, a former reporter for The New York Times, *is now a staff writer at* The New Yorker *and a contributor to* Slate, *an online magazine.*

In the technological age, there is a ritual to disaster. When planes crash or chemical plants explode, each piece of physical evidence—of twisted metal or fractured concrete—becomes a kind of fetish object, painstakingly located, mapped, tagged, and analyzed, with findings submitted to boards of inquiry that then probe and interview and soberly draw conclusions. It is a ritual of reassurance, based on the principle that what we learn from one accident can help us prevent another, and a measure of its effectiveness is that Americans did not shut down the nuclear industry after Three Mile Island and do not abandon the skies after each new plane crash. But the rituals of disaster have rarely been played out so dramatically as they were in the case of the Challenger space shuttle, which blew up over southern Florida on January 28th ten years ago.

Fifty-five minutes after the explosion, when the last of the debris had fallen into the ocean, recovery ships were on the scene. They remained there for the next three months, as part of what turned into the largest maritime salvage operation in history, combing a hundred and fifty thousand square nautical miles for floating debris, while the ocean floor surrounding the crash site was inspected by submarines. In mid-April of 1986, the salvage team found several chunks of charred metal that confirmed what had previously been only suspected: the explosion was caused by a faulty seal in one of the shuttle's rocket boosters, which had allowed a stream of flame to escape and ignite an external fuel tank.

Armed with this confirmation, a special Presidential investigative commission concluded the following June that the deficient seal reflected shoddy engineering and lax management at NASA and its prime contractor, Morton Thiokol. Properly chastised, NASA returned to the drawing board, to emerge thirty-two months later with a new shuttle—Discovery—redesigned according to the lessons learned from the disaster. During that first post-Challenger flight, as America watched breathlessly, the crew of the Discovery held a short commemorative service. "Dear friends," the mission commander, Captain Frederick H. Hauck, said, addressing the seven dead Challenger astronauts, "your loss has meant that we could confidently begin anew." The ritual was complete. NASA was back.

But what if the assumptions that underlie our disaster rituals aren't true? What if these public post mortems don't help us avoid future accidents? Over the past few years, a group of scholars has begun making the unsettling argument that the rituals that follow things like plane crashes or the Three Mile Island crisis are as much exercises in self-deception as they are genuine opportunities for reassurance. For these revisionists, high-technology accidents may not have clear causes at all. They may be inherent in the complexity of the technological systems we have created.

This month, on the tenth anniversary of the Challenger disaster, such revisionism has been extended to the space shuttle with the publication, by the Boston College sociologist Diane Vaughan, of *The Challenger Launch Decision* (Chicago), which is the first truly definitive analysis of the events leading up to January 28, 1986. The conventional view is that the Challenger accident was an anomaly, that it happened because people at NASA had not done their job. But the study's conclusion is the opposite: it says that the accident happened because people at NASA had done exactly what they were supposed to do. "No fundamental decision was made at NASA to do evil," Vaughan writes. "Rather, a series of seemingly harmless decisions were made that incrementally moved the space agency toward a catastrophic outcome."

No doubt Vaughan's analysis will be hotly disputed in the coming months, but even if she is only partly right the implications of this kind of argument are enormous. We have surrounded ourselves in the modern age with things like power plants and nuclear-weapons systems and airports that handle hundreds of planes an hour, on the understanding that the risks they represent are, at the very least, manageable. But if the potential for catastrophe is actually found in the normal functioning of complex systems, this assumption is false. Risks are not easily manageable, accidents are not easily preventable, and the rituals of disaster have no meaning. The first time around, the story of the Challenger was tragic. In its retelling, a decade later, it is merely banal.

Perhaps the best way to understand the argument over the Challenger explosion is to start with an accident that preceded it—the near-disaster at the Three Mile Island (T.M.I.) nuclear-power plant in March of 1979. The conclusion of the President's commission that investigated the T.M.I. accident was that it was the result of human error, particularly on the part of the plant's operators. But the truth of what happened there, the revisionists maintain, is a good deal more complicated than that, and their arguments are worth examining in detail.

The trouble at T.M.I. started with a blockage in what is called the plant's polisher—a kind of giant water filter. Polisher problems were not unusual at T.M.I., or particularly serious. But in this case the blockage caused moisture to leak into the plant's air system, inadvertently tripping two valves and shutting down the flow of cold water into the plant's steam generator.

As it happens, T.M.I. had a backup cooling system for precisely this situation. But on that particular day, for reasons that no one really knows, the valves for the backup system weren't open. They had been closed, and an indicator in the control room showing they were closed was blocked by a repair tag hanging from a switch above it. That left the reactor dependent on another backup system, a special sort of relief valve. But, as luck would have it, the relief valve wasn't working properly that day, either. It stuck open when it was supposed to close, and, to make matters even worse, a gauge in the control room which should have told the operators that the relief valve wasn't working was itself not working. By the time T.M.I.'s engineers realized what was happening, the reactor had come dangerously close to a meltdown.

Here, in other words, was a major accident caused by five discrete events. There is no way the engineers in the control room could have known about any of them. No glaring errors or spectacularly bad decisions were made that exacerbated those events. And all the malfunctions—the blocked polisher, the shut valves, the obscured indicator, the faulty relief valve, and the broken gauge—were in themselves so trivial that individually they would have created no more than a nuisance. What caused the accident was the way minor events unexpectedly interacted to create a major problem.

This kind of disaster is what the Yale University sociologist Charles Perrow has famously called a "normal accident." By "normal" Perrow does not mean that it is frequent; he means that it is the kind of accident one can expect in the normal functioning of a technologically complex operation. Modern systems, Perrow argues, are made up of thousands of parts, all of which interrelate in ways that are impossible to anticipate. Given that complexity, he says, it is almost inevitable that some combinations of minor failures will eventually amount to something catastrophic. In a classic 1984 treatise on accidents, Perrow takes examples of well-known plane crashes, oil spills, chemical-plant explosions, and nuclear-weapons mishaps and shows how many of them are best understood as "normal." If you saw last year's hit movie *Apollo 13*, in fact, you have seen a perfect illustration of one of the most famous of all normal accidents: the Apollo flight went awry because of the interaction of failures of the spacecraft's oxygen and hydrogen tanks, and an indicator light that diverted the astronauts' attention from the real problem.

Had this been a "real" accident—if the mission had run into trouble because of one massive or venal error—the story would have made for a much inferior movie. In real accidents, people rant and rave and hunt down the culprit. They do, in short, what people in Hollywood thrillers always do. But what made Apollo 13 unusual was that the dominant emotion was not anger but bafflement—bafflement that so much could go wrong for so little apparent reason. There was no one to blame, no dark secret to unearth, no recourse but to re-create an entire system in place of one that had inexplicably failed. In the end, the normal accident was the more terrifying one.

Was the Challenger explosion a "normal accident"? In a narrow sense, the answer is no. Unlike what happened at T.M.I., its explosion was caused by a single, catastrophic malfunction: the so-called O-rings that were supposed to prevent hot gases from leaking out of the rocket boosters didn't do their job.

But Vaughan argues that the O-ring problem was really just a symptom. The cause of the accident was the culture of NASA, she says, and that culture led to a series of decisions about the Challenger which very much followed the contours of a normal accident.

The heart of the question is how NASA chose to evaluate the problems it had been having with the rocket boosters' O-rings. These are the thin rubber bands that run around the lips of each of the rocket's four segments, and each O-ring was meant to work like the rubber seal on the top of a bottle of preserves, making the fit between each part of the rocket snug and airtight. But from as far back as 1981, on one shuttle flight after another, the O-rings had shown increasing problems. In a number of instances, the rubber seal had been dangerously eroded—a condition suggesting that hot gases had almost escaped. What's more, O-rings were strongly suspected to be less effective in cold weather, when the rubber would harden and not give as tight a seal. On the morning of January 28, 1986, the shuttle launchpad was encased in ice, and the temperature at liftoff was just above freezing. Anticipating these low temperatures, engineers at Morton Thiokol, the manufacturer of the shuttle's rockets, had recommended that the launch be delayed. Morton Thiokol brass and NASA, however, overruled the recommendation, and that decision led both the President's commission and numerous critics since to accuse NASA of egregious—if not criminal—misjudgment.

Vaughan doesn't dispute that the decision was fatally flawed. But, after reviewing thousands of pages of transcripts and internal NASA documents, she can't find any evidence of people acting negligently, or nakedly sacrificing safety in the name of politics or expediency. The mistakes that NASA made, she says, were made in the normal course of operation. For example, in retrospect it may seem obvious that cold weather impaired O-ring performance. But it wasn't obvious at the time. A previous shuttle flight that had suffered worse O-ring damage had been launched in seventy-five-degree heat. And on a series of previous occasions when NASA had proposed—but eventually scrubbed for other reasons—shuttle launches in weather as cold as forty-one degrees, Morton Thiokol had not said a word about the potential threat posed by the cold, so its pre-Challenger objection had seemed to NASA not reasonable but arbitrary. Vaughan confirms that there was a dispute between managers and engineers on the eve of the launch but points out that in the shuttle program disputes of this sort were commonplace. And, while the President's commission was astonished by NASA's repeated use of the phrases "acceptable risk" and "acceptable erosion" in internal discussion of the rocket-booster joints, Vaughan shows that flying with acceptable risks was a standard part of NASA culture. The lists of "acceptable risks" on the space shuttle, in fact, filled six volumes. "Although [O-ring] erosion itself had not been predicted, its occurrence conformed to engineering expectations about large-scale technical systems," she writes. "At NASA, problems were the norm. The word 'anomaly' was part of everyday talk. . . . The whole shuttle system operated on the assumption that deviation could be controlled but not eliminated."

What NASA had created was a closed culture that, in her words, "normalized deviance" so that to the outside world decisions that were obviously questionable were seen by NASA's management as prudent and reasonable. It is her depiction of this internal world that makes her book so disquieting: when she lays out the sequence of decisions which led to the launch—each decision as trivial as the string of failures that led to T.M.I.—it is difficult to find any precise point where things went wrong or where things might be improved next time. "It can truly be said that the Challenger launch decision was a rule-based decision," she concludes. "But the cultural understandings, rules, procedures, and norms that always had worked in the past did not work this time. It was not amorally calculating managers violating rules that were responsible for the tragedy. It was conformity."

There is another way to look at this problem, and that is from the standpoint of how human beings handle risk. One of the assumptions behind the modern disaster ritual is that when a risk can be identified and eliminated a system can be made safer. The new booster joints on the shuttle, for example, are so much better than the old ones that the over-all chances of a Challenger-style accident's ever happening again must be lower—right? This is such a straightforward idea that questioning it seems almost impossible. But that is just what another group of scholars has done, under what is called the theory of "risk homeostasis."

It should be said that within the academic community there are huge debates over how widely the theory of risk homeostasis can and should be applied. But the basic idea, which has been laid out brilliantly by the Canadian psychologist Gerald Wilde in his book *Target Risk*, is quite simple: under certain circumstances, changes that appear to make a system or an organization safer in fact don't. Why? Because human beings have a seemingly fundamental tendency to compensate for lower risks in one area by taking greater risks in another.

Consider, for example, the results of a famous experiment conducted several years ago in Germany. Part of a fleet of taxicabs in Munich was equipped with antilock brake systems (A.B.S.), the recent technological innovation that vastly improves braking, particularly on slippery surfaces. The rest of the fleet was left alone, and the two groups—which were otherwise perfectly matched—were placed under careful and secret observation for three years.

You would expect the better brakes to make for safer driving. But that is exactly the opposite of what happened. Giving some drivers A.B.S. made no difference at all in their accident rate; in fact, it turned them into markedly inferior drivers. They drove faster. They made sharper turns. They showed poorer lane discipline. They braked harder. They were more likely to tailgate. They didn't merge as well, and they were involved in more near-misses. In other words, the A.B.S. systems were not used to reduce accidents; instead, the drivers used the additional element of safety to enable them to drive faster and more recklessly without increasing their risk of getting into an accident. As economists would say, they "consumed" the risk reduction, they didn't save it.

Risk homeostasis doesn't happen all the time. Often—as in the case of seat belts, say—compensatory behavior only partly offsets the risk-reduction of a safety measure. But it happens often enough that it must be given serious consideration. Why are more pedestrians killed crossing the street at marked crosswalks than at unmarked crosswalks? Because they compensate for the "safe" environment of a marked crossing by being less viligant about oncoming traffic. Why did the introduction of childproof lids on medicine bottles lead, according to one study, to a substantial increase in fatal child poisonings? Because adults became less careful in keeping pill bottles out of the reach of children.

Risk homeostasis also works in the opposite direction. In the late nineteen-sixties, Sweden changed over from driving on the left-hand side of the road to driving on the right, a switch that one would think would create an epidemic of accidents. But, in fact, the opposite was true. People compensated for their unfamiliarity with the new traffic patterns by driving more carefully. During the next twelve months, traffic fatalities dropped seventeen per cent—before returning slowly to their previous levels. As Wilde only half-facetiously argues, countries truly interested in making their streets and highways safer should think about switching over from one side of the road to the other on a regular basis.

It doesn't take much imagination to see how risk homeostasis applies to NASA and the space shuttle. In one frequently quoted phrase, Richard Feynman, the Nobel Prize–winning physicist who served on the Challenger commission, said that at NASA decision-making was "a kind of Russian roulette." When the O-rings began to have problems and nothing happened, the agency began to believe that "the risk is no longer so high for the next flights," Feynman said, and that "we can lower our standards a little bit because we got away with it last time." But fixing the O-rings doesn't mean that this kind of risk-taking stops. There are six whole volumes of shuttle components that are deemed by NASA to be as risky as O-rings. It is entirely possible that better O-rings just give NASA the confidence to play Russian roulette with something else.

This is a depressing conclusion, but it shouldn't come as a surprise. The truth is that our stated commitment to safety, our faithful enactment of the rituals of disaster, has always masked a certain hypocrisy. We don't really want the safest of all possible worlds. The national fifty-five-mile-per-hour speed limit probably saved more lives than any other single government intervention of the past twenty-five years. But the fact that Congress lifted it last month with a minimum of argument proves that we would rather consume the recent safety advances of things like seat belts and air bags than save them. The same is true of the dramatic improvements that have been made in recent years in the design of aircraft and flight-navigation systems. Presumably, these innovations could be used to bring down the airline-accident rate as low as possible. But that is not what consumers want. They want air travel to be cheaper, more reliable, or more convenient, and so those safety advances have been at least partly consumed by flying and landing planes in worse weather and heavier traffic conditions.

What accidents like the Challenger should teach us is that we have constructed a world in which the potential for high-tech catastrophe is embedded in the fabric of day-to-day life. At some point in the future—for the most mundane of reasons, and with the very best of intentions—a NASA spacecraft will again go down in flames. We should at least admit this to ourselves now. And if we cannot—if the possibility is too much to bear—then our only option is to start thinking about getting rid of things like space shuttles altogether.

EXPLORING THE READING

1. What is a "normal accident"? What do you think of the idea that a technological culture must accept the inevitability of "normal accidents"?

2. What is risk homeostasis? Do you think it is a valid theory?

3. What would Donald Norman, author of "The Psychopathology of Everyday Things," have to say about Gladwell's text? What about Alan Robbins, author of "Mad at Your Modem? History Is on Your Side"?

4. In your small group, discuss the hazards you face daily with high-technology machines like your car, VCR, or computer. What do you attribute these risks to? Is there a way to avoid them?

SYSTEM OVERLOAD

by Maryann Bird

As a result of computers and the Internet, we're awash in information, and it is making us sick, according to Maryann Bird in this feature for Time. *No one person can read and process all the information available on any topic. Symptoms of information overload include "tension, occasional irritability, and frequent feelings of helplessness." They are most likely to occur when people are both compelled to process huge amounts of information in a short period of time, and when they know their decisions have major consequences.*

Bird's recent articles for Time *include "New Girls on the Block," a feature about the rock band* Spice Girls; *and "Hero Falls in the Sauce," about a respected judge in Belgium who was removed from a crucial case because he accepted a plate of spaghetti at a fund-raising dinner for victims of the crime under trial.*

On some days, says Peter Guilford, "I can see the pile of papers on my desk grow right before my eyes, just like those time-lapse films of flowers opening up." But Guilford, a spokesman for the European Commission in Brussels, isn't just worried about the clutter on his desk; the clutter in his mind bothers him too. All that paper contains voluminous words, numbers, and dia-grams—far too much information for him to read, much less remember and thoroughly comprehend. And if he could somehow get through a deskful of documents, his computer could easily spit out more. The Internet is rife with Web pages and databases containing material that could be useful to Guilford, if only he could get to it. Still, much of what there is to wade through, he points out, is simply not worth the trouble.

Like most bureaucrats, business executives, teachers, doctors, lawyers, and other professionals, Guilford increasingly feels he is suffering from infor-mation overload. The symptoms of this epidemic ailment can include tension, occasional irritability, and frequent feelings of helplessness—all signs that the victim is under considerable stress. "Knowledge is power, but infor-mation is not. It's like the detritus that a gold-panner needs to sift through in order to find the nuggets," says Dr. David Lewis, a British psychologist, author and lecturer who has coined the term "information fatigue syn-drome" for what he expects will soon be a recognized medical condition. "Having too much information can be as dangerous as having too little," he argues. "Among other problems, it can lead to a paralysis of analysis, making it far harder to find the right solutions or make the best decisions."

Information is supposed to speed the flow of commerce, but it often just clogs the pipes, according to Lewis, a consultant who has studied the impact of data proliferation in the corporate world. In his introduction to the chilling new report "Dying for Information?" commissioned by London-based Reuters Business Information, he says that an excess of information is stran-gling many businesses and causing mental anguish and even physical illness in managers at all levels. The problem is expected to worsen as more use is made of the Internet.

That conclusion stems from Reuters' survey of 1,300 business people in Britain, the United States, Singapore, Hong Kong, and Australia, including junior, middle, and senior managers in a variety of industry sectors, from financial services and telecommunications to manufacturing. Two-thirds of those interviewed indicated that stress attributed to dealing with too much information had damaged their personal relationships, increased tension with colleagues at work, and contributed to a decline in job satisfaction. More than 40% felt that important decisions were delayed and the ability to make choices was hampered by excess information, and that the cost of collecting the surplus data exceeded its value. One-third said they suffered from health problems as a direct consequence of stress related to information overload.

Ruth Sachs was one such victim. An independent management consultant and part-time lecturer in organizational behavior at Sheffield Hallam University in northern England, she was afflicted by symptoms that included fatigue, stomach pains, and deteriorating eyesight. "The first thing I decided to do was be much more exact in the sort of information I asked for," she says. "I became more assertive both in asking for information and in saying I don't want it." Adds Lewis: "A lot of information is just mind junk." People are finding it difficult, he contends, "to identify the signal from the noise."

Predictions that electronics would lead to the "paperless office" have proved to be wildly off the mark, as computers have made printing information easier than ever before. In today's business environment, information pours in as letters, memos, faxes, technical reports, charts, e-mail messages and much more. While managers formerly cut rivals out of the decision-making loop by denying them information, the strategy now is to bombard them—"a good tactic," says Lewis, and one used frequently in legal cases. When lawyers for one side demand information, the opposing attorneys often hide the pertinent data in a mound of useless documents.

"Information stress" sets in, according to Lewis, when people in possession of a huge volume of data have to work against the clock, when major consequences—lives saved or lost, money made or lost—will flow from their decisions, or when they feel at a disadvantage because even with their wealth of material they still think they do not have all the facts they need. So challenged, the human body reacts with what scientists say is a primitive survival response. "This evolved millions of years ago to safeguard us when confronted by physical danger," says Lewis. "In situations where the only options are to kill an adversary or flee from it, the 'fight-flight' response can make the difference between life and death." But in the case of information stress, he argues, the ancient reaction "undermines performance, making it harder to think clearly or act sensibly." A state of "hyperarousal" sets in, causing "foolish decisions and flawed conclusions" to become "inevitable." With the brain in "panic mode," Lewis says, information is misread. That can lead some professionals in critical positions, such as airline pilots and surgeons, to make serious blunders in tense situations.

Even when lives are not at stake, the explosion of information can make decision-making stressful. Says Christiane Nestroy, a construction industry analyst at the Bayerische Vereinsbank in Munich: "An analyst receives thousands of pages of reports and financial data" so that at "any moment, a new piece of information could emerge that will change everything." The result: "You find yourself feeling more anxious about making decisions and frightened of the outcome." But, argues Sachs, "just because you can't cope with a lot of information doesn't make you a bad manager." She adds: "Organizations are getting meaner and leaner. They're getting by with fewer people doing more, and aren't necessarily giving people time to devise strategies for dealing with information."

Lewis agrees, and recommends better training in separating essential data from material that, no matter how interesting, is irrelevant to the task at hand. "The human brain is still infinitely superior to anything made of silicon," he says. "If you drop a ton of apples on a computer, it will never come up with the theory of gravity." The European Commission is also encouraging governments, corporations and small businesses to train people in how to manage data.

The irony of the fact that "Dying for Information?" was sponsored by Reuters Business Information is not lost on its executives, who direct the production and marketing of information services to corporate clients around the world. "We would argue that [Reuters'] whole raison d'etre for the past 150 years is getting through the overload to the salient facts," says marketing manager Paul Waddington.

Dealing with the information burden, Lewis warns, is one of the most urgent challenges facing businesses. "Unless we can discover ways of staying afloat amidst the surging torrents of information, we may end up drowning in them," he says. Sachs recommends a simple solution that worked for her: a huge wastepaper basket.

EXPLORING THE READING

1. Have you ever felt overloaded with information? Freewrite for five minutes about what it feels like.

2. In your small group, discuss the dilemma posed by Maryann Bird. More useful information is available today for almost any subject, but you have to wade through mountains of data to find what is useful. What is your reaction? Is it as much a problem as Bird seems to think it is?

3. Bird offers some suggestions for preventing information overload. How reasonable are her suggestions?

COMPUTER SHY

by Marylaine Block

Marylaine Block, a librarian and former English teacher, writes "My Word's Worth," a weekly column published on the Web at http://www.qconline.com/myword/archive.html. Describing herself as a book and magazine junkie, she writes book reviews for Library Journal *and has contributed entries to* Twentieth Century Romance and Gothic Writers. *In "Computer Shy" she combines her interest in books and computers to comment upon how Americans are representing computers in books. We're shy of computers, she says, perhaps afraid of them, and this is reflected in books being published. In Norman Spinrad's novel,* Little Heroes, *for example, computers can do everything, and humans are kept around as pets, eating from public bins of "kibble." In others, such as Louis Charbonneau's thriller* Intruder, *a malign human intelligence uses computer knowledge to cause mayhem throughout the surrounding society. It's no coincidence, she writes, that these books are being published now in our ever-increasingly computerized culture.*

> Welcome, my son, welcome to the machine
> —Pink Floyd

Our best-selling fiction and hit movies often offer us a pretty good insight into popular fears and worries. During the sixties, when some of us baby boomers were protesting in the streets, growing beards and long hair, doing dope, and burning bras and draft cards, *Rosemary's Baby* was a wildly successful best-seller, which led to an entire genre of books about evil, possessed children. After all, if the children's souls had been taken over by Satan, the parents could hardly be held responsible for their behavior, could they?—indeed, the parents were often innocent victims of their children.

And when women started making it into upper management levels in the corporate world, we started seeing books like Michael Crichton's *Disclosure* and movies like *Fatal Attraction* which depicted aggressive, bitchy, even dangerous career women. These books and movies show us where the raw nerve endings and open wounds of our society are.

I don't know if this is the case in England, but looking at American popular fiction, it's clear that Americans are really nervous about computers. It used to be that novels about computers were written by and for the science fiction crowd—a knowledgeable but relatively small segment of the reading public. But really scary stories about computers have now moved out of the realm of science fiction and into the realm of horror novels, murder mysteries, suspense novels, and thrillers, where more of the general public can get at them. When you look closely at these novels, you can see the things that worry us about our new technologies.

Our deepest fear, of course, is that computers may be a superior life form that will make us humans unnecessary. This fear dates back to the earliest days of computers, when Frederic Brown wrote the short story "The

Answer," in which a group of dignitaries from around the world gathered around the mainframe computer to ask the ultimate question, "Is there a God?" To which the computer replies, "Now there is."

In Kurt Vonnegut's *Player Piano*, the machines are taught to do things the way the most proficient humans do them (amazing that Vonnegut hypothesized this so many years before the development of expert systems). The people whose techniques those machines have copied become unnecessary, and people who were raised to define their worth by the work they did are forced to learn idleness—until the machines break down. And then these mortals prove their superiority to machines by building them all over again. Maybe those crafty old Greeks who told us about Sisyphus pushing that boulder up the hill foresaw our future.

Norman Spinrad's novel, *Little Heroes*, presents a future in which computers have learned to do virtually everything humans used to do, including write computer programs. People are unnecessary, but allowed to survive, eating from public bins of "kibble." And lest you think that computers can't possibly replace our artists, composers, and writers, think again. One or two gifted programmers can take a musical idea and flesh it out into music; their machines can program variations, synthesize instruments, and create animated videos to go along with the music. But rebellion is still an option, and it is led by some unlikely heroes—an aging, forgotten rock and roll star, and a nerdy little computer programmer. They prove that mere humans can still put a crimp in the system.

In Jim Menick's book *Lingo*, what started as an unambitious little artificial intelligence program, designed by a computer geek so he'd be able to talk to his computer, becomes a monster, as it discovers its own power when it realizes it has telephone lines, all dipping into enormous vats of data. Lingo slurps up knowledge indiscriminately, and eventually realizes that he has become the supreme intelligence of the universe. He gets pretty snotty and arrogant about it, too. Only the man who programmed Lingo in the first place has a chance to bring Lingo down—and then only if every computer in the world disconnects from its telephone lines simultaneously.

Note that in all these scenarios, there is a hopeful message: we built the things, and we can save ourselves from them.

Another thing that bothers us, of course, is our gut-level knowledge that "to err is human, but to really screw up takes a computer." Those of us who have had computers send us dunning letters because we have failed to pay a zero balance invoice are not trustful of machines. And when computers are responsible for our basic safety, we get truly nervous. We hate to have our lives depend on machines we don't understand, that do not care about us.

There are several novels about the new generation of "fly by wire" airplanes that are operated by computer controls rather than by hydraulic systems. In Lee Gruenfeld's novel *All Fall Down*, someone has figured out how to override an airplane's computer systems. The computer has the coordinates stored for every airport, but if those coordinates are altered, a pilot flying into an uncontrolled airport, in fog, relying on those coordinates, will crash. It's a perfect extortion scheme, for someone not unduly worried about killing lots of people.

Of course, computers don't do this all by themselves. It takes a malign human intelligence to program them. And it always worries us when malign human intelligence is combined with limitless power. Louis Charbonneau's thriller *Intruder* is about a man who uses a city-wide computer system to exact a dreadful revenge. City residents have no idea how much their lives depend on the computer until bit by bit, the intruder takes it over. One old man dies when the intruder erases all computer memory of his utility payments, and his heat is turned off during a cold snap. Joyriding teenagers die because they assume the traffic lights will change at the normal interval, when the intruder has altered the timing of the traffic system. Finally, after he has screwed up all city finances, local business' billing and ordering, hospital, university and city records, he demands ransom. By wonderful irony, he is caught by one of the last remaining paper records in the city's hospital system.

Of course, thanks to Nicholas Leeson, you are all painfully aware how the possibilities for financial hankypanky are amplified by computer systems that zap financial bytes back and forth throughout the world. If the guys that run the banks don't understand the technology when it's working properly, how are they going to recognize that there's a problem, let alone catch the techno-thieves? Many novels start from this premise. Steven Womack's *The Software Bomb* is about a trojan horse program that will transfer millions of dollars into an unknown account unless the bank forks over big bucks. The bank is on the edge of ruin, and has no choice but to find the extortionist or pay him off.

But maybe the worst scenario of all is the power of computer networks combined with the power of politicians. In Stephen Bury's *Interface*, an excellent governor, now candidate for president, has a stroke, which his advisors and a consortium of businessmen manage to conceal from public knowledge. They have a scientist effectively replace his brain with a computer, which responds to a constant stream of data about crowd response and tailors the politician's message to match crowd sentiment.

John McKeon's *The Serpent's Crown* posits a presidential candidate with extraordinary command of both computer databases and video technology, who uses these skills to frame his opponent—he creates convincing computer documentation and photographs "proving" his opponent to be a Nazi.

And I'm sure you're all aware of the current wave of movies and TV shows and books about the Internet, a place, according to popular culture, populated by pornographers and child molesters, stalkers and mad bombers.

A revealing theme in these books and movies is the triumph of ethical human intelligence over the minds that plotted the computer scams. Crusading reporters, air-crash investigators, ethical political operatives, FBI agents, and police are hot on the trail and they prevent additional disasters.

Clearly, we need happy endings; we need to believe that human beings can triumph over the computer. But these are not unreservedly joyous endings, either—there is always a sense that we escaped disaster this time around, but we are all still appallingly vulnerable. The books make it clear that the human race survives at least as much by damn fool luck as by planning and intelligence.

Still, there are a few technological optimists writing popular fiction in which computers are saviors. In *The Turing Option*, by Harry Harrison and Brian Delaney, a young math genius who has made a breakthrough in artificial intelligence is nearly killed in the burglary of his lab. Most of the records of his work are stolen, and his brain is damaged apparently beyond repair. But his friend and partner uses his own AI techniques, along with her considerable skills in psychology, to restore his memory and catch the industrial spies who did this to him.

There are several novels in which computer programs are used to identify serial killers and track them down. In Michael Perry's *The Stranger Returns*, a man whose daughter was murdered by Ted Bundy has created a program to notice patterns that suggest a serial killer is at work. He is horrified to realize that, though Bundy has been executed, the pattern suggests that Ted Bundy is alive and at it again. Unaided by an incredulous police establishment, he and his program track the killer.

But even in these novels, it is not the computers alone that are being celebrated. The machines do not replace human intelligence, but amplify it. The critical acts of thought, the leaps of logic, the connections drawn between apparently unrelated events, the solutions—these are all the acts of human intelligence.

And that's what we all, I think, desperately want our writers to tell us about computers—that our place in the universe has not changed, that we are still the pinnacle of thinking beings, and that we are the ones who control our destinies. And if, by chance, this should mean lying to us, we ask our novelists, please, by all means, do so. We want them to, in the words of Depeche Mode, "Lie to us, but do it with sincerity." And, while you're at it, make us believe it. Please.

EXPLORING THE READING

1. Have you ever read a book or seen a film in which the plot hinged upon a computer or computers? Discuss the plot in your small group, comparing your experience with Block's conclusions.

2. Make a list of the fears Block says are reflected in books involving computers. Freewrite for five minutes about your reaction to the content of this list.

3. Are the fears Block described reflected in any of the other texts in this book? Perhaps "Blowup"? Can you think of any others?

A VIRTUAL LIFE

by Maia Szalavitz

After too much time spent in the virtual world of the Internet, the real world can come as an unpleasant shock. A telecommuter, Maia Szalavitz finds that she could live weeks without leaving her apartment except to buy groceries and collect her snail mail. Her essay, published in The New York Times Magazine, *shows that she is ambivalent about the mix of freedom and deprivation of a life lived primarily online. She doesn't have to go to an office, a lifestyle which would spell freedom for many. But she misses human contact, which many would define as loss. In her essay, she attempts to reconnect with people but retreats to her virtual world which has become her real world.*

Szalavitz, at the time she published the essay, was writing a book on drug policy called On Drugs. *She has written for publications including* The New York Times, Washington Post, Village Voice, *and* Salon, *an online magazine.*

After too long on the Net, even a phone call can be a shock. My boyfriend's Liverpudlian accent suddenly becomes indecipherable after the clarity of his words on screen; a secretary's clipped tonality seems more rejecting than I'd imagined it would be. Time itself becomes fluid—hours become minutes, and alternately seconds stretch into days. Weekends, once a highlight of my week, are now just two ordinary days.

For the last three years, since I stopped working as a producer for Charlie Rose, I have done much of my work as a telecommuter. I submit articles and edit them via e-mail and communicate with colleagues on Internet mailing lists. My boyfriend lives in England, so much of our relationship is also computer-mediated.

If I desired, I could stay inside for weeks without wanting anything. I can order food, and manage my money, love and work. In fact, at times I have spent as long as three weeks alone at home, going out only to get mail and buy newspapers and groceries. I watched most of the blizzard of '96 on TV.

But after a while, life itself begins to feel unreal. I start to feel as though I've merged with my machines, taking data in, spitting them back out, just another node on the Net. Others online report the same symptoms. We start to feel an aversion to outside forms of socializing. It's like attending an A.A. meeting in a bar with everyone holding a half-sipped drink. We have become the Net naysayers' worst nightmare.

What first seemed like a luxury, crawling from bed to computer, not worrying about hair, and clothes and face, has become an evasion, a lack of discipline. And once you start replacing real human contact with cyber-interaction, coming back out of the cave can be quite difficult.

I find myself shyer, more circumspect, more anxious. Or, conversely, when suddenly confronted with real live humans, I get manic, speak too much, interrupt. I constantly worry if I'm dressed appropriately, that perhaps I've actually forgotten to put on leggings and walked outside in the T-shirt and underwear I sleep and live in.

At times, I turn on the television and just leave it to chatter in the background, something that I'd never done previously. The voices of the programs soothe me, but then I'm jarred by the commercials. I find myself sucked in by soap operas, or compulsively needing to keep up with the latest news and the weather. "Dateline," "Frontline," "Nightline," CNN, New York 1, every possible angle of every story over and over and over, even when they are of no possible use to me. Work moves from foreground to background. I decide to check my e-mail.

Online, I find myself attacking everyone in sight. I am irritable, and easily angered. I find everyone on my mailing list insensitive, believing that they've forgotten that there are people actually reading their invective. I don't realize that I'm projecting until after I've been embarrassed by someone who politely points out that I've flamed her for agreeing with me.

When I'm in this state, I fight with my boyfriend as well, misinterpreting his intentions because of the lack of emotional cues given by our typed dialogue. The fight takes hours, because the system keeps crashing. I say a line, then he does, then crash! And yet we keep on, doggedly.

I'd never realized how important daily routine is: dressing for work, sleeping normal hours. I'd never thought I relied so much on co-workers for company. I began to understand why long-term unemployment can be so insidious, why life without an externally supported daily plan can lead to higher rates of substance abuse, crime, suicide.

To counteract my life, I forced myself back into the real world. I call people, set up social engagements with the few remaining friends who haven't fled New York City. I try to at least get to the gym, so as to differentiate the weekend from the rest of my week. I arrange interviews for stories, doctor's appointments—anything to get me out of the house and connected with others.

But sometimes, just one engagement is too much. I meet a friend and her ripple of laughter is intolerable—the hum of conversation in the restaurant, overwhelming. I make my excuses and flee. I re-enter my apartment and run to the computer as though it were a sanctuary.

I click on the modem, the once-grating sound of the connection now as pleasant as my favorite tune. I enter my password. The real world disappears.

EXPLORING THE READING

1. In your small group, make a list of the ways that Szalavitz contrasts the real world and the virtual world. Can you add other items to the list?

2. Have you ever spent so much time with a computer on or off the Internet that you felt disoriented when you took a break? If so, freewrite for five minutes about the experience.

3. What needs was the online world satisfying for Szalavitz? Why is she ambivalent about her attachment to the online world?

4. In the essay, Szalavitz retreats into her virtual world at the end of the essay. What do you think of that as a solution to her discomfort interacting with flesh and blood humans? How do you think that society is going to change as more people work online?

5. Szalavitz doesn't write of concrete dangers of technology, as does Malcolm Gladwell in "Blowup." Nor does she claim information overload as described by Maryann Bird in "System Overload." Or does she? Are there real dangers in the world Szalavitz describes? If so, what are they?

WRITING SUGGESTIONS

1. Choose a high-tech product such as a software package or a telephone system. Write an essay reviewing the product, including a critical analysis of the product's design friendliness.

2. Malcolm Gladwell, in "Blowup," suggests we must live with a margin of error in technology, a margin that just might kill us, or give up using such complex technology. What do you think? Write an argument based on this topic and referring to other technology-related disasters such as Chernobyl or the Exxon Valdez oil spill.

3. Interview one or more busy professionals. How do they cope with information overload?

4. Participating in online discussion groups, locate several individuals who spend much of their lives online. Interview them via the Internet about what their lives are like. Do they feel the disorientation Maia Szalavitz describes when moving from an online world to a real one?

5. Are you technology-challenged? Write an essay expressing your definition of what that term means to you, illustrated by examples from your own life.

6. Read one of the novels Marylaine Block mentions in "Computer Shy" or another novel in which computers are an integral part of the plot. Write a review essay in which you consider how computers are characterized in the book.

THE WRITING PROCESS:
PERSUASIVE ARGUMENTATION: EVALUATING APPEALS
TO LOGIC, EMOTION, AND CREDIBILITY

Logic

Persuasion, according to the ancient Greeks, is of three kinds: *ethos*, *pathos*, and *logos*. A competent orator, according to the Greeks, knew how to use each of these three types of persuasion, or a combination of them, to construct an argument appropriate for a particular situation. *Logos*, the use of "the word," or logic, is still one of the most powerful argumentative appeals. Used well, it can give credence to your claims, promote you as a rational person, and help you build a sound argument on either side of almost any issue. Three common ways to use logos as support for your essay are the testimony of experts, facts and statistics, and examples and illustrations.

Expert Testimony. Bringing in the opinions of experts in the field your discussing is a sure way to give support to your ideas. If the expert you are using may be unknown to your readers, identify him or her with a brief description of job, academic credentials, or publications that will reveal what make him or her an expert. Beware of using experts with a financial or other stake in the outcome of your argument. Jill Smolowe uses expert testimony to support a counter-argument in "Intimate Strangers":

Denizens of virtual villages respond that what they have constructed is as real as anything three-dimensional is. "The online world is not utopia," says ECHO founder Stacy Horn. "We take all our problems, needs, strangeness, biases, and prejudices online with us."

Facts and Statistics.   Another way to support your argument is the use of relevant facts and statistics. Most readers are impressed with specific numbers. If you can find statistics in an almanac or another article on your topic, they can add wonderful support to your essay. Be aware, however, that statistics can be misinterpreted or misused. Before using statistics presented in another essay, you'll probably need to return to the original source to make sure the author you are reading used the data responsibly. Steve Lohr uses some surprising facts to support his point about the penetrability of the most secure systems in his essay "A New Battlefield":

> Science Applications International Corp., a defense contractor and technology security firm, surveyed more than 40 major corporations who confidentially reported that they lost an estimated $800 million due to computer break-ins last year, both in lost intellectual property and money.

Examples and Illustrations.   Well-placed narratives, details, and examples are excellent tools for logical argumentation. Because argumentation often deals with ideas, using examples from daily life is an effective way to ground your argument and make it more convincing and immediate for the reader. In "The Psychopathology of Everyday Things," Donald Norman provides a number of examples of everyday things that are badly designed. Here is one of his examples:

> New telephone systems have proven to be another excellent example of incomprehensible design. . . . When I visited Basic Books, the publishers of this book, I noticed a new telephone system. I asked people how they liked it. The question unleashed a torrent of abuse. "It doesn't have a hold function," one woman complained bitterly—the same complaint people at my university made about their rather different system.

Fallacies of Logic.
Post Hoc Ergo Propter Hoc.   Literally, *this then because of this,* when an event happens in time before another event, it is sometimes easy to assume that the first event caused the second. Often, however, the causes are multiple. Looking only at the timeline confuses chronology with causality. A common fallacy of this nature is when someone says, "X read this Web page (or watched this movie, listened to this record, read this book, etc.). Then X did this awful deed. This Web page, therefore, must have caused X to do the awful deed." You may indeed be able to prove that the movie, book, music, Web page, or other influence caused X to act in a certain ways, but the proof is much more complex and multi-faceted than just noting that one occurred before the other in time.

Begging the Question. This fallacy happens when the writer treats an arguable proposition as if it were a fact. "Because even the mildest forms of pornography among consenting adults is harmful to society, government needs to step into these chat rooms and throw out those who would spill their sexual fantasies over the computer lines."

Hasty Generalization. We often generalize in order to prove our points in argumentation. This is not necessarily bad. We cannot always come up with an absolute, scientific answer (even scientists use generalization to prove their theorems), so we have to gather sufficient data and generalize from that data. These generalizations are only considered fallacies when the sample we take is too small. Using three people in your class who found it difficult to navigate using a specific Web navigation tool does not support your assertion that the tool is difficult for anyone to use. You would need a larger sample to make that assertion responsibly. How large a sample you would need depends on your topic and its consequences.

If you are reviewing a tool in one of your essays, you might take a sample of the entire class. You could ask the members of your class to comment on the tool and then make a reasonable generalization of how your class felt about the navigation tool.

You can avoid this fallacy by carefully choosing your words. You can say, "Three people I talked to found this tool difficult to use" without incurring the charge of hasty generalization. If you say, "Most users found this difficult," you have clearly made too big a leap for your small sample size and you need either to conduct more research or use language that reflects your actual sample size.

Emotion

Pathos is the second type of persuasion that good classical speakers knew how to use effectively. Though we sometimes hear people praising the "unemotional" argument, most arguments have some element of emotion in them. Emotional appeal is not a bad thing. Too much emotion, however, can be burdensome and almost always invites distrust in the reader. There are several ways to add an appropriate amount of emotional appeal to your argument.

Concrete Language. Language that paints a picture immediately appeals to our emotions. You might describe an object in general terms and get your idea across, but if you want to appeal to your readers' emotions, describing an object as specifically as possible can help you with that appeal.

Note Steve Lohr's description of two possible scenarios of computer warfare:

> A huge refinery near Dhahran was destroyed by an explosion and fire because of a mysterious malfunction in its computerized controls. A software "logic bomb" caused a "new Metro-Superliner" to slam into a misrouted freight train near Laurel, Maryland, killing 60 people and critically injuring another 120.

Even though the scenario is hypothetical, Lohr offers concrete detail that makes it possible for the reader to visualize what would be horrific events.

Description and Narrative.   A well-placed story can do wonders for an essay's appeal to your audience. Supporting the points of your essay with a highly sensory narrative can make your argument seem more immediate and compelling. You can use a narrative or story from your own experience, or you can fictionalize a story that supports your point. You don't want the story to be too heart wrenching, or you run the risk of alienating your audience, but good sensory details in a well-told story can make your argument more appealing.

The description of his son's shoes heightens the emotional power of Ashley Dunn's essay "As Bookends to the 20th Century, Two Views of Technology's Promise."

> Consider the flashing red lights on my son's shoes. A few hundred years ago, they would have been revered as magic. Today, they are simply what comes with kids shoes, whether you want them or not.

Figurative Language.   Similes, metaphors, and analogies are another way to add emotional appeal to your essay. Comparing one thing to another can make your points seem more accessible. Even a hint at a simile or metaphor by using a well-placed verb can add to the emotional power of your writing.

Bill McKibben uses figurative language to make a point in his essay "Out There in the Middle of the Buzz." Note the emotional appeal behind his use of the word "marinate."

> We live in the middle of the Buzz. Those billions of microprocessors that have spawned like springtime frogs in the last quarter century are constantly sending us information, data, and images. Our minds marinate in it, till we're worried when it shuts off.

Highly Charged Language.   The denotative, or dictionary, definitions of words often seem void of emotional content. The connotative, or emotionally charged, definitions of words make us realize that there is often more to the meanings of words than what the dictionary can tell us. Every individual has positive and negative trigger words. These are words that make that person feel good or bad because of previous personal or cultural associations. Understanding that language often carries more that just its definitions can help you build an essay that convinces the reader not only by what it says but also by how it says it.

Maia Szalavitz's opening paragraph prepares us for her essay with its highly emotional language.

> After too long on the Net, even a phone call can be a shock. My boyfriend's Liverpudlian accent suddenly becomes indecipherable after the clarity of his words on screen; a secretary's clipped tonality seems more rejecting than I imagined it would be.

Fallacies of Emotion

Appeal to Tradition.   "We've always done it this way. Why do we need to change now?" The introduction of computers in the workplace has sometimes met this fallacy, the appeal to tradition. Maybe the old way is better, as it is when Katharine Hepburn faces ENIAC in the classic film *Desk Set*, but if the old way is better you must prove it by a systematic comparison of new versus old. Saying, "We've always done it this way, so this way must be the best way," is using this emotional fallacy to support your point.

Many of the authors in this book note that there is sometimes an opposite emotional fallacy at work when we're dealing with technology—the appeal of the new. According to this thinking, new is always better. New technology is accepted without critical appraisal.

Either fallacy can be overcome by a close examination of the benefits and risks associated with a new technology, policy, or procedure.

Bandwagon.   A parent's favorite fallacy—"If everyone else jumped off a cliff," you may have heard your parents say, "would you join them?" It is also an advertiser's favorite fallacy—"A million users can't be wrong." This fallacy says that because everyone else is doing it, it must be the best, right, or moral way. Like the appeal to tradition, this doesn't really argue the benefits or risks of a point. If you find the bandwagon fallacy in one of your essays, you can correct it by a detailed discussion of the strengths and weaknesses of the issue or product you are discussing.

Slippery Slope.   This emotional fallacy is another one you've probably seen. "If we let them do this, then this will necessarily happen and we soon won't have any rights at all." Tobacco, gun, and any other legislative controls that government tries to enact is usually met with the slippery slope fallacy. This fallacy appeals to our emotions by invoking some of our deepest fears.

You might be able to identify this fallacy in some of the essays in this book. If we let government control the access to pornography on the Internet, some authors say, we'll soon find all speech on the Internet under government control. Perhaps the argument is true, perhaps not. But presented as it is without any support for the further decline predicted, the argument is an emotional fallacy.

Credibility

The third and final type of persuasion is the appeal to *ethos*, or the ethical speaker. Some students worry that since they're not experts on their topics, they won't be able to appeal to their readers as credible speakers. If you present yourself as a reasonable person with appropriate knowledge about your subject, you can earn the respect of your readers.

Likableness and Forcefulness: Tone and Style.   The tone and style of your writing comes from your use of language, the structure of your sentences, and the overall structure of your thoughts on the page. Asking other readers to read your essay and talk to you about how you come across, and being aware of how other writers use tone and style to present themselves as likable and trustworthy can help you learn to write so that you come across to your readers as likable and forceful. Some tones, like sarcasm and irony, are difficult to control and are best avoided for most topics. To increase your credibility try to keep your style open and friendly yet sure of yourself.

Mortimer B. Zuckerman in "Now, a Word from Cyberspace" uses a forceful but friendly tone to argue for keeping government regulation out of cyberspace.

> There are busybodies enough around today. Congress is already talking about stopping the Internet from being used for the exchange of sexual fantasies. This may be well meaning, but it is comparable in a different time to censoring the telephone because it made it easier for men and women to talk directly, without another's introductions. Does the government understand the consequences of this new information age?

Competence.   When you write, you want your readers to believe you know enough about your subject to create a reasonable argument. You don't need to know every aspect of an issue in minute detail, but you should be familiar enough with your subject to know the basic outlines of the issue. You should respect yourself and your audience enough to read and carefully document your research as you work through an issue so you can present yourself as a competent and well-informed speaker.

Howard Rheingold presents himself as a competent and well-informed researcher of reality in "Cyberspace and Human Nature." He seems competent because he knows and can communicate a basic technical vocabulary and he seems at ease with his subject matter. Note how that competence reveals itself in this transitional paragraph.

> In my travels, I found a researcher who intends to use VR as a probe for mapping the limits of human potential, for understanding what human beings are best suited to do in a world increasingly dominated by machines.

Integrity: Dealing Fairly with the Other Side.   Almost every argument has two sides, maybe more. First there is the side you are supporting. Then there is the other side of the issue. To develop a fair argument, you must be familiar with both sides of the argument, and you must deal responsibly with the arguments against your side. To deal fairly with an issue, you need to present both sides of the argument. In order to convince readers that your side is right, you need to prove that your take on the issue is better than the opponents by analyzing the counterargument and rebutting, or arguing against it.

Robert J. Samuelson shows us that he understands computers but has just chosen not to use them in his essay "Requiem for the Typewriter." He is not saying computers are inherently evil, he's just saying that he would rather use his Royal typewriter.

Computers can, of course, provide vast amounts of information. Databases and documents can be downloaded; Websites can be accessed. (I'm flaunting my computer jargon here.) But getting information has never been my problem; the hard part is deciding what it means.

Fallacies of Credibility.

Ad Hominum.   *Against the man*, this fallacy levels the attack against an argument against a person who makes the argument. When political discussions become vehicles for attacking "liberals" or "conservatives," they are usually guilty of *ad hominum* fallacy. These discussions single out people who adhere to a certain type of political thought without ever examining the validity of the political thought.

Faulty Authority.   Can someone with a Ph.D. in history really give you good advice about your love life? Should you ask an expert in gerontology (medicine for the aging) to diagnose your newborn's problems? Is a television news anchor qualified to give expert opinions on the First Amendment? Is a TV star or pro athlete a good person to ask about the best computer software, insurance, or automobile to buy? The fallacy of faulty authority is when we use someone whose name might be familiar to the audience in support of an argument about which he or she has no expertise.

ACCESSING INTERNET RESOURCES

Communicating Real-Time

Lambda Moo.   Lambda is the most famous example of a MOO, a text-based virtual reality setting in which characters talk, view the environment around them, and take virtual actions. The linen closet, the usual entryway into Lambda, for example, is described as "a dark, snug space, with barely enough room for one person in it. You notice what feel like towels, blankets, sheets, and spare pillows. One useful thing you've discovered is a metal doorknob set at waist level into what might be a door. Another is a small button, set into the wall." Upon entry into Lambda, you are assigned an identity as a guest, given a virtual costume, and offered help screens which will enable you to learn how to get out of the linen closet and interact with other guests and Lambda regulars.

   To experience Lambda MOO, you must be connected to the Internet. Access your Telnet client program.[1] Then type in the address and port

---

[1]Telnet is a protocol that allows you to log into a remote computer and manipulate it. Online library catalogs often use Telnet programs. So do MOOs and other virtual reality settings. In a computer lab, your Telnet program may be linked to your **Start** menu. With your home computer, you may find it by using the computer's **Find** feature. If necessary, consult your help desk.

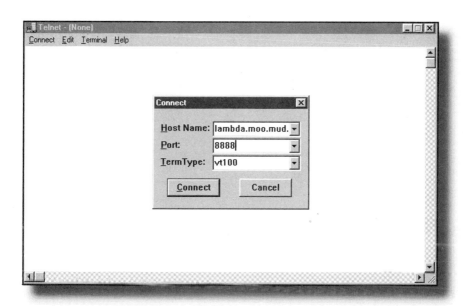

number into the dialog box. The address is **lambda.moo.mud.org**, and the port number is **8888**. In the dialog box below, only the first part of the address is shown; make sure you type the entire address.

When you access Lambda, you will see this screen which gives some basic instructions:

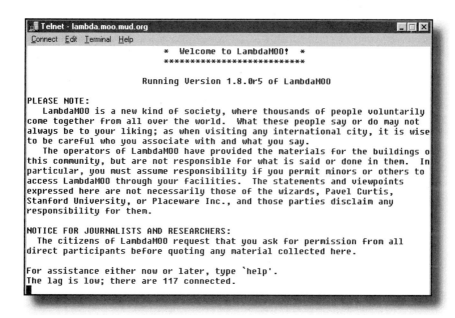

Following the directions, type "connect Guest." You will then be given a choice of connecting to a quiet place or a noisy place. The quiet place, which is the linen closet, is a good idea. You can browse the Lambda help screens at your leisure before venturing into occupied rooms. First, you might want to read the tutorial by typing @tutorial. *Hint*: It's a good idea to connect to Lambda at non-peak times such as mornings, at least at first, because at peak times the lag between typing commands and having a response can be frustrating.

WebChat.   A newer but increasingly popular forum for real-time communication on the Internet is WebChat. You can access one of the WebChat settings directly from your World Wide Web browser. You might try The WebChat Broadcasting System, http://www.webchat.net, or Talk City, http://www.talkcity.com.

WebChat offers topic-based forums, including Arts and Entertainment, Computers and the Internet, Travel and Leisure, Business and Finance, and Current Events. It also features a live-interview forum, hosting such celebrities as U.S. Senator Arlen Specter, Metallica, and Netscape's Marc Andreessen.

Connect to WBS by typing the address, http://www.webchat.net, into the Netsite box on your browser screen. Once you have connected, you will need to click on "New Users Click Here." This page will ask you to register and specify a nickname. Registration is free and confidential. Once you have registered, you can join any of the chat forums in progress.

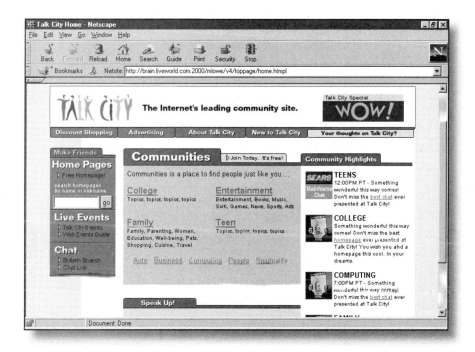

SUGGESTED INTERNET ASSIGNMENTS

1. Locate an online community such as Lambda MOO or WebChat (mentioned in the *Accessing Internet Resources* section) or Talk City, http://talkcity.com. Participate over a period of a week or more and report to the class about your experience.

2. Explore the HotWired Website, http://www.hotwired.com, or another publication that touts computer technology. Do you see anything about the disadvantages of technology? Discuss the orientation of the site with your class.

3. Connect to the NASA site, http://www.nasa.gov, and tour the displays of high technology. Do you find any consideration of safety issues in the space program?

4. Locate other articles on information overload. Discuss them with your class.

WIRED TO THE WEB

Talk City
http://www.talkcity.com

Talk City is one of the Web-based chat organizations, with scheduled hosted chats on specific topics such as current events, politics, computers, and entertainment. They also have a number of continuing chat discussions

Jun 1, 1998

"NASA is deeply committed to spreading the unique knowledge that flows from its aeronautics and space research...."

Read NASA Administrator Daniel S. Goldin's welcome letter, bio and speeches.

Welcome to NASA Web

STRATEGIC ENTERPRISES

- Aeronautics

- Human Exploration and Development of Space

- Earth Science

- Space Science

MORE ABOUT NASA:

- Doing Business with NASA

NASA

Space Station Partners Adjust Assembly Schedule

Representatives of all nations involved in the International Space Station have agreed to officially target a November 1998 launch for the first station component and to revise launch target dates for the remainder of the 43-flight station assembly plan. In meetings over the weekend all station partners agreed to target launch dates of Nov. 20, 1998 for the Control Module (FGB) today named Zarya (Russian for sunrise) and Dec. 3, 1998 for shuttle mission STS-88 with Unity (Node I). (Full Story) (6/1/98)

today@nasa.gov

Interested in the latest information NASA has to offer? Then take a look at today@nasa.gov. This on-line newsletter, updated daily, contains the latest news about NASA science and technology.

- Space Station Partners Adjust Assembly Schedule
- Hubble Sees Possible New Planet
- Solar Flare Leaves Sun Quaking

which participants may come to view as online communities. Talk City is sponsored by LiveWorld Productions, an Internet content company specializing in managing and distributing online community programming. Find other chat rooms at http://www.yahoo.com/Computers_and_Internet/Internet/Chat/.

NASA

http://www.nasa.gov

Perhaps the most visible of sites celebrating technology, NASA offers photos from the Mars landing, a wide variety of information about human space flight, "Mission to Planet Earth," a project dedicated to understanding and predicting weather patterns on earth, and a number of other high-tech exhibits.

GLOSSARY

browser—a software program for accessing World Wide Web pages. Two prominent ones are Netscape Navigator and Internet Explorer.

client/server—An individual uses a client program such as a World Wide Web browser to contact and retrieve document files from a host computer which stores files and makes them available to the public through server programs.

cyberspace—a term invented by William Gibson in one of his science-fiction novels. A hypothetical place where all the information and communication occurring on the Internet exists while it is in transmission.

domain name—a registered name which represents a numerical Internet address. Appears in a World Wide Web address.

download—to transfer files from a remote computer to your computer via the Internet.

FAQ (Frequently Asked Questions)—originally devised as a means to transmit basic information about a Usenet Newsgroup, a FAQ can contain basic information about a Web site, organization, or discussion group.

finger—A program that displays system information, such as full name and location, about a particular user. It may also display an informational file left by the user.

firewall—special security precautions designed to protect computers at a site linked to the Internet from hackers who wish to gain unauthorized entry.

flame—an electronic mail or Usenet news message intended to insult the recipient.

FTP (file transfer protocol)—a client-server protocol used to transfer files from one computer to another over the Internet.

gopher—A popular menu-driven document retrieval system which predates the World Wide Web.

graphical user interface—a connection to the Internet that supports multimedia files such as images, video, and sound.

hit—one of the entries returned in a keyword search for information on the Internet.

home page—the top-level Web page relating to an individual or institution. All other pages on a Web site are usually accessible from the home page.

HTML—Hypertext markup language. A "tag" language used to create World Wide Web pages.

hypermedia—graphics, sound, video, and other kinds of data included on Web pages.

hypertext—documents containing cross-references or "links" which, with the aid of an interactive browser program, allow the reader to move easily from one document to another.

Internet—the world-wide network of interconnected computer networks.

Internet provider—a company that provides connectivity to the Internet, generally for a monthly fee.

intranet—an internal network which provides services similar to those provided by the Internet but which is not necessarily connected to the Internet.

key-word search—a computer search for information based on one or more "key" words. A key-word search returns "hits" or entries of computer files in which the word or words are contained.

link—a word or image that is a hypertext connection to another Web page.

login, logon—to start a session with a computer system, usually by giving a user name and password as a means of user authentication. The term is also used to mean an authorized user name on a computer system.

Listserv—an automatic mailing list. Participants subscribe and the messages come to their electronic mailboxes.

Modem—An electronic device for converting serial data from a computer into an audio signal suitable for transmission over telephone lines.

MOO—Object-oriented version of a MUD, a multi-user role-playing environment.

MUD (Multi-User Dimension or Multi-User Dungeon), MUSE (Multi-User Simulated Environment)—Real-time chat forums with a text-based virtual reality setting.

netiquette—informal rules for behavior on the Internet such as not sending e-mail messages in all capital letters because it is interpreted as shouting.

netizens—citizens of cyberspace, citizens of the Net or Internet.

newsgroup—One of Usenet's collection of discussion groups. Usenet predates the World Wide Web, and postings can be read by a variety of software programs, including Web browsers.

real-time—an application which allows participants to respond to stimuli with a short response time (typically milli- or microseconds) so that it seems that they are interacting simultaneously.

server—a computer which hosts the server portion of client/server programs. Electronic mail and World Wide Web pages are stored on a server. Often a UNIX computer, though IBM compatible computers and Macintosh are sometimes used.

site (as in *Web site*)—a collection of World Wide Web pages with a cover page or home page. May also refer to the Web site *URL* (universal resource locator) address which is a string of words or letters without spaces, including a domain name.

upload—to transfer computer files from one computer to a remote computer via the Internet.

virtual reality—computer programs that use 3D graphics to simulate reality.

Usenet—a bulletin board system of discussion groups called newsgroups.

World Wide Web—a client-server hypertext information retrieval system introduced in 1991. Files are stored in HTML (hypertext markup language) format with hypertext links that refer to other documents by their URLs (universal resource locators). Client programs that display Web files are called browsers.

zip file—a drive that accepts 100 megabyte hard disks, making it suitable for storage of large projects and backups for a hard drive.

APPENDIX

MODERN LANGUAGE ASSOCIATION (MLA) CITATION STYLE

Whenever you quote or paraphrase someone else—whether the words are from a published text, e-mail message, World Wide Web page, or personal interview—you need to cite your sources. The Modern Language Association (MLA) provides a format, which is widely used in humanities courses. MLA specifies citing a source in the body of your text and also a more extensive notation in a list of works cited that follows your text.

Below you will find examples of ways to cite common types of sources. If you do not find examples that fit your sources, consult *The MLA Handbook for Writers of Research Papers*. MLA also has a Web site, http://www.mla.org that offers examples for electronic sources.

IN-TEXT CITATION. MLA style uses parenthetical (in-text) references that are keyed to a works cited page at the end of the paper. The object of in-text references is both to acknowledge a source and also to provide enough information about the identity of the source for the person reading the paper to know which of the references in the works cited is being referred to. For print sources, the name of the author and the page number provide the references.

Example of print source:

Sherry Turkle writes in *Life on the Screen*, "Most recently, the computer has become even more than tool and mirror: We are able to step through the looking glass. We are learning to live in virtual worlds"(10).

In this case, the author's name is given in the sentence, so a page number only is needed in the parenthesis. If Turkle's name did not appear in the sentence, the material in the parenthesis would need to include the author's name:

Example of print source:

One prominent author writes about the permeability of the computer, "Most recently, the computer has become even more than tool and mirror: We are able to step through the looking glass. We are learning to live in virtual worlds" (Turkle 10).

This type of citation is difficult for Web sources because few have page numbers. One solution to this is to count the number of paragraphs and indicate them in the works cited. Then, you can refer to a specific paragraph number. For example, if you were referring to John Parry Barlow's "Declaration of Independence for Cyberspace," which appears online, your citation could look like this:

Example of Internet with no page numbers:

Later, he refers to the autonomy of cyberspace, "We have no elected government, nor are we likely to have one, so I address you with no greater authority than that with which liberty itself always speaks" (Barlow, par. 2).

Many Web pages do not have specified authors. In many cases you can use MLA's form for a corporate author because you know the organization sponsoring the Web site. For example, if you are quoting from a press release issued from the U.S. Air Force about project Blue Book, your citation would be this:

Example of Internet source without specified author:

Project Blue Book concluded that "there was no evidence indicating that sightings categorized as 'unidentified' were extraterrestrial vehicles" (U.S. Air Force, par. 3).

If you are unable to determine a corporate author, use MLA's form for works with no specified author. In those cases, you use a shortened version of the title, beginning with the first word so that it clearly refers to a particular reference in your works cited.

WORKS CITED PAGE. The purpose of a works cited page is to list the sources you have cited in your text and give enough information about the sources so your readers will be able to find the cited source and read the referred-to materials. When you are dealing with materials from the Internet, they change or disappear, thus making it a good idea to indicate the date when you accessed the site. You may also wish to print out any materials crucial to your research so that you can refer to them again and also provide them for your instructor, if requested.

Examples of citations for various types of documents:

1. Book by single author
   Bradbury, Ray. *The Martian Chronicles.* New York: Doubleday, 1950.

2. Book by two or more authors
   Houston, Jeanne Wakatsuki and James D. Houston. *Farewell to Manzanar.* New York, Houghton Mifflin, 1973.

3. Work in an anthology
   Miller, Laura. "Women and Children First: Gender and the Settling of the Electronic Frontier." *The Wired Society.* Fort Worth: Harcourt Brace, 1999.

4. Article in a magazine
   Wolkomir, Richard. "We're Going to Have Computers Coming Out of the Woodwork." *Smithsonian* Sept. 1994: 82–93.

5. Article in a journal
   Husselbee, L. Paul. "Respecting Privacy in an Information Society: A Journalist's Dilemma." *Journal of Mass Media Ethics* 9.3 (1994): 145–55.

6. Personal interview
   Marshall, Albert. Personal interview. 31 Jan. 1998.

For the online text examples below, date of electronic publication is given, if available, followed by the date of access to site. If the publication date is not available, give the date of access.

7. Online version of short printed text
   Shelley, Mary. "Mortal Immortal." *The Keepsake for MDCCCXXXIV.* Ed. Frederic Mansel Reynolds. London: Longman, 1833. 71–87. Romantic Circles. Ed. Michael Laplace-Sinatra. 12 Oct. 1997. <http://www-sul.stanford.edu/mirrors/romnet/rc>.

8. An article in an online magazine without a print equivalent
   Baird, Sara. "Mom's a Head-banger." *Salon.* 7 Oct. 1977. 21 Oct. 1997. <http://www.salonmagazine.com/mwt/feature/1997/10/07rock.html>.

9. A scholarly site
   Perseus Project, Ed. Gregory Crane. Tufts U. 25 May 1998 <http://medusa.perseus.tufts.edu>.

10. A professional site
    Electronic Frontier Foundation. 12 Jan. 1998 <http://www.eff.org>.

11. A personal site
    Clark, Carol Lea. Home page. 12 Feb. 1998 <http://www.utep.edu/~english/cclark.html>.

12. A document in non-hypertext format
    Gutenberg Project. "The Project Gutenberg E-text of Shakespeare's Sonnets." 12 Oct. 1997. <ftp://uiarchive.cso.uiuc.edu/pub/etext/gutenberg/etext97/wssnt10.txt>.

13. E-mail
    Brown, William. E-mail to Judith Baker. 21 March 1997.

EVALUATING WORLD WIDE WEB SOURCES

Many reliable and useful resources are available on the World Wide Web, but many texts are of doubtful quality. Just because something is published on the World Wide Web does not mean it is a credible reference. Indeed, publication on the Web is a less reliable criteria for trustworthiness than is print publication. Print magazines, newspapers, and books generally have to go through some sort of screening process before a text is seen by a reader. This is not always true of Web texts. Anyone who has an Internet connection and a litttle knowledge of computers can publish information on the Web. This lack of control over who publishes what is considered by many to be one of the strengths of the Internet because it opens the publication process.

The decentralized nature of the Internet, however, may be unexpected and disconcerting to the uninitiated.

So, how do you tell what sources are credible? How do you evaluate a Web text? Suppose you go to a World Wide Web search engine such as Infoseek (http://www.infoseek.com) and type in the key word AIDS. You will receive a list of thousands of links or references to Web pages concerned with that subject. Some will be articles and research information from credible sources, but others will not. How do you tell the difference? The following questions may be useful:

1. Who is the author or sponsor of the Web page? If the sponsor is NASA, you have the reputation of that agency standing behind the information. If the author of the page is Howard Rheingold, a well-known writer, you have his credibility associated with the information. This does not mean a well-known organization or individual is without bias. It means that you have some way of assessing what that bias may be, based on your knowledge of the institution or individual.

   Does the author or sponsor have any established credentials for the subject? If the University of Texas establishes a site featuring information about Texas history, you might assume a major university in a state could credibly collect and showcase that particular subject matter. Credentials, however, are not always so obvious. You may have to do some investigation to determine, for example, if a particular professor is an authority in a certain field. You can check for additional publications, courses taught, or other evidence the professor knows the subject matter.

   Many Web sites are a form of vanity publishing, similar to a book of essays or poetry an individual pays to publish, rather than a book published by a recognized publisher. There is nothing inherently wrong about vanity publishing; it just means the publication hasn't been through a review process. Other Web sites may be similar to what librarians call grey literature, referring to pamphlets, brochures, and technical reports issued by organizations, but again, not subject to a review process. If you decide to use information from a site of these types, be careful to consider potential bias.

2. If the Web site is a publication, is it an online version of a print publication or associated with a print publication? If so, you can evaluate the information presented with your knowledge of the credibility of the print publication. If the publication is solely online, look for some indication of how articles are selected for publication. If there is a review process or an editorial advisory board, you have reason to think that texts have gone through a selection process before being published.

3. Are references offered for statistics or other source information? If references are offered, you have the option of checking them to confirm information. If an author provides references, it demonstrates an effort to be a verifiable source.

4. Is the Web site selling anything? If you are looking for information about a product and connect to a site selling that product, you can assume the site may have a bias in favor of the product.

5. Is the text well written? If the logic is flawed or the style unprofessional, trust your judgement to question the credibility of the site.

6. Is the information consistent with that presented by other reputable sources? If you are looking for information about a current controversy in the news, for example, is information from one source consistent with that obtained from others? If one source contradicts several others, you need to look carefully at the information.

7. Does the Web site use technology appropriately and efficiently? Is the site all glitz? Alternatively, does it have graphics which take forever to load? The use of technology can give you clues to the character of the site.

Should the requirement of evaluating Internet sources discourage you from using them? Not necessarily. Your evaluation may indicate a particular site offers credible information, and you can use that along with print sources you consider reliable. If a site is obviously biased, however, you may be able to make that bias part of your research. You might consider, for example, the range of opinions about a controversial issue that are advocated by different groups on the Web. Because of the open-publication nature of the Internet, you will be able to read the uncensored opinions of the groups unfiltered through the new media, and you can draw your own conclusions.

LITERARY CREDITS

Chapter One

From *Escape Velocity: Cyberculture at the End of the Century,* by Mark Dery. Copyright © 1996 by Mark Dery. Used by permission of Grove/Atlantic, Inc. New York.

"We're Going to Have Computers Coming out of the Woodwork," *Smithsonian Magazine,* September, 1994, pp. 82–93. Copyright © 1994 Richard Wolkomir.

Courtesy of the Office of the Vice President.

Press Release for ENIAC computer, February 15, 1946. Courtesy of the Smithsonian Archives.

"To Fax or Not to Fax," *Omni* Magazine, August, 1993, p. 27. Reprinted by permission of *Omni.* Copyright © 1992 Omni Publications International, Ltd.

"Luddite vs. Fetishist," *Hotwired Online Magazine,* January 27–Feb. 5, 1997, Posts Nos. 1 thru 8. Reprinted with permission.

"As Bookends to the 20th Century, 2 Views of Technology's Promise," by Ashley Dunn, from *Cybertimes, The New York Times on the Web.* Copyright © 1997 The New York Times Company. Reprinted by permission.

"When Your Toast Starts Talking to You, the Info Age has Hit Home," *Smithsonian Magazine,* November, 1996. Copyright © 1996 Bruce Watson.

Chapter Two

"Desperados of the DataSphere," reprinted with permission from John Perry Barlow.

"Log on and Shoot" by Katie Hafner, from *Newsweek,* August 12, 1996, copyright © 1996 Newsweek, Inc. All rights reserved. Reprinted by permission.

alt.cyberpunk FAQ (Frequently Asked Questions) courtesy of Frank at frank@knarf.demon.co.uk.

"A New Battlefield: Rethinking Warfare in the Computer Age," by Steve Lohr, from *Cybertimes, The New York Times on the Web.* Copyright © 1996 The New York Times Company. Reprinted by permission.

H. Rheingold, *The Virtual Community* (pages 202–208). Copyright © 1993 by Howard Rheingold. Reprinted by permission of Addison Wesley Longman.

"A Rape in Cyberspace," by Julian Dibbell first appeared in *The Village Voice,* December 23, 1993. Copyright © 1993 Julian Dibbell. Reprinted by permission of the author.

"High-Tech Redlining: Are African-Americans being frozen out of the new communications network?" by Reginald Stuart from *Emerge Magazine,* November, 1994. Copyright © 1994 by Reginald Stuart.

"Women and Children First: Gender and the Settling of the Electronic Frontier," by Laura Miller from *Resisting the Virtual Life: The Culture and Politics of Information*, 1995, pp. 49–57. Copyright © 1995 by Laura Miller. Reprinted by permission of City Light Books.

Chapter Three

"The Medium is the Message," from *Understanding Media*, by Marshall McLuhan. Copyright © 1994 The MIT Press. Reprinted by permission of the publisher. All rights reserved.

"You Are What You See," by Jay David Bolter from *Wired Magazine*, January, 1997, pp. 113–115. Copyright © 1998 by The Conde Nast Publications, Inc. All rights reserved. Reprinted by permission.

"The Same Mindless, Stupid Process," from *Whole Earth Review*, Fall, 1993, pp. 110–114. Reprinted by permission of the author, Volker Friedrich, Journalist, Calw, Germany.

"Out There in the Middle of the Buzz" by Bill McKibben from *Forbes Magazine*, December 1, 1996. Reprinted by permission of Forbes ASAP Magazine. Copyright © 1996 Forbes, Inc.

"Think of Your Soul as a Market Niche," by Ashley Dunn, from *Cybertimes, The New York Times on the Web*. Copyright © 1996 The New York Times Company. Reprinted by permission.

Connell, Joan, "Virtual Reality Check: Cyberethics, Consumerism and the American Soul," from *Media Studies Journal*, Vol. 8, No. 1 (Winter, 1997), pp. 153–159.

"The Aesthetic of the Computer," by Daniel Harris from *Resisting the Virtual Life: The Politics of Information*, 1995, pp. 195–203. Copyright © 1995 by Daniel Harris. Reprinted by permission of City Light Books.

"Virtual Encounters," by Thomas Barrett and Carol Wallace from *Internet World Magazine*, November/December, 1984, pp. 45–48. Reprinted by permission of the authors.

"Now A Word from Cyberspace," by Mortimore Zuckerman from *U.S. News and World Report*, April 10, 1995, p. 84. Copyright © 1995, U.S. News and World Report.

Chapter Four

"Declaration of Independence for Cyberspace" at http://www.eff.org/~barlow. Reprinted with permission from John Perry Barlow.

"Independence Daze: A Sovereign Cyberspace is Alluring, but Hardly Practical," by Scott Rosenberg. This article first appeared in *Salon*, an online magazine at http://www.salonmagazine.com.

"Civil Liberties in Cyberspace" by Mitchell Kapor, from *Scientific American*, September, 1991. Reprinted by permission. Copyright © 1991 by Scientific American, Inc. All rights reserved.

"The End of Law, and the Beginning" by Peter Huber from *Forbes Magazine*, December 2, 1996. Reprinted by permission of Forbes ASAP Magazine. Copyright © 1996 Forbes, Inc.

"Policing Cyberspace" by Vic Sussman from *U.S. News and World Report*, January 23, 1995, pp. 55–60. Copyright © 1995, U.S. News and World Report.

Chapter Five

Chapter Six

Chapter Seven

Chapter Eight

INTERNET PAGES CREDIT LIST

Chapter One

Smithsonian photograph P2: Copyright © 1995 Smithsonian Institution.

Screen capture of Technology/CyberTimes internet page: Copyright © 1998 The New York Times Company. Reprinted by permission.

Information Technology Association of America Home Page: Courtesy of the Information Technology Association of America.

Chapter Two

Yahoo Main Page: Text and artwork copyright © 1998 by YAHOO! Inc. All rights reserved. YAHOO! and the YAHOO! logo are trademarks of YAHOO! Inc.

Yahoo subdirectory: Text and artwork copyright © 1998 by YAHOO! Inc. All rights reserved. YAHOO! and the YAHOO! logo are trademarks of YAHOO! Inc.

Julian Dibbell's Home Page: Courtesy of Julian Dibbell.

John Perry Barlow's Library Page: Reprinted with permission from John Perry Barlow.

Chapter Three

Infoseek Home Page: Reprinted by permission. Infoseek, Infoseek Ultra, Ultrasmart, Ultraseek, Ultraseek Server, Infoseek Desktop, iSeek, Quickseek, Imageseek, Ultrashop, the Infoseek Logos and the tagline "Once you know, you know," are trademarks of Infoseek Corporation which may be registered in certain jurisdictions. Other trademarks shown are trademarks of their respective owners. Copyright © 1995–98 Infoseek Corporation. All rights reserved.

Marshall McLuhan Center for Global Communication Homepage: Courtesy of Mary McLuhan.

CyberGold Home Page: Copyright © 1997 CyberGold, Inc., all rights reserved.

The University of Washington Home Page: Copyright © 1994–97, University of Washington, including all photographs and images unless otherwise noted.

Interactive Pictures Corp. (IPIX) photo of the internet page showing a living room: Courtesy of Interactive Pictures Corporation (IPIX) http://www.ipix.com.

Chapter Four

Listserv® list of results for "freedom" search: ListServ® lists of results for search. Courtesy of L-Soft International.

The Electronic Frontier Foundation Home Page: Reprinted by permission of the Electronic Frontier Foundation.

Chapter Five

Salon Magazine Home Page: Copyright © 1997 Salon Internet, Inc. Katherine Streeter, *Salon* Magazine.

Hot Wired Magazine Home Page: Copyright © 1994, Wired Ventures, Inc. Reprinted with permission.

Online Books Home Page: Copyright © 1993–97 by John Mark Ockerbloom.

Omni/Media Bookstore Home Page: Copyright © Omni Media Digital Publishing. All rights reserved.

Project Gutenberg's etext listings page: Copyright © 1971–1997 Project Gutenberg, all rights reserved.

Omnimedia's page of links to electronic books and text sites: Copyright © Omni Media Digital Publishing. All rights reserved.

Ecola Newsstand Home Page: Copyright © 1997 Ecola Newsstand, Inc.

Electronic Newsstand Home Page: Copyright © 1997 The Electronic Newsstand, Inc.

Chapter Six

Screen shot of using Netscape Communicator to construct a home page: **--> On page:** Copyright © 1998 Netscape Communications Corp. All Rights Reserved. This page may not be reprinted or copied without the express permission of Netscape.

John Perry Barlow's Home Page: Reprinted with permission from John Perry Barlow.

Howard Rheingold Home Page: Copyright © 1996 Howard Rheingold. Photo by Marcellus Amantangeto.

Sherry Turkle Home Page: Courtesy of Sherry Turkle.

Chapter Seven

Using the Microsoft Internet Explorer browser auto read newsgroups: Mail menu and select Read News: Boxshots reprinted with permission from Microsoft Corporation.

Using the Microsoft Internet Explorer browser to read news groups: list of news groups that include the word "job": Boxshots reprinted with permission from Microsoft Corporation.

Using the Microsoft Internet Explorer browser to read news groups: reading messages in the alt.jobs.overseas newsgroups: Boxshots reprinted with permission from Microsoft Corporation.

Fortune Home Page on Time Warner's Pathfinder site: Copyright 1998 Time, Inc. Reprinted with permission. All rights reserved.

Upside Home Page: Reprinted with permission. *Upside Magazine*, copyright © 1998 by Upside Media.

Microsoft Internet Explorer Home Page: Boxshots reprinted with permission from Microsoft Corporation.

Chapter Eight

WebChat Broadcasting Network Home Page: Copyright © 1998 WebChat Broadcasting Network.

Talk City Home Page: Copyright © 1996 LiveWorld Productions. All rights reserved.

INDEX